GRAPE

Tim Atkin is wine correspondent of the *Observer* and the presenter of *Grape Expectations* on the Carlton Food Network. He also writes for *Wine, Decanter, The Wine Spectator* and *The London Review of Books*, and appears regularly on radio and terrestrial television. He won the Glenfiddich Drink Writer of the Year Award in 1988, 1990 and 1993 and the Wine Guild of the United Kingdom's Wine Columnist of the Year Award in 1991, 1992, 1994 and 1996. In 1994 he was the first recipient of the Wines of France Award. The following year he was co-winner of The Bunch Award, described by Auberon Waugh as the 'Booker Prize of wine writing', and winner of the Waterford Crystal Wine Correspondent of the Year Award. He has contributed to a number of books on wine, including the recently published *New World of Wine*, as well as publishing two of his own, *Chardonnay* and *Vins de Pays d'Oc*. He is a regular member of *Wine* magazine's tasting panels and has judged wines in the UK, France and Australia.

Anthony Rose joined the *Independent* as its wine correspondent in 1986 after winning the *Observer*/Peter Dominic New Wine Writer Award. He has won a number of awards, including the 1991 Qantas Wine Writer of the Year, the 1994 Glenfiddich Drink Writer of the Year and the Wine Guild of the United Kingdom's Wine Columnist of the Year Award in 1988, 1989 and 1993, as well as its trophy in 1993. He has judged wine competitions in Australia, South Africa, France, New Zealand and the United States as well as the UK, and contributes to *Decanter* and *Wine* magazines. He has appeared on television and radio and contributed to *Le Grand Atlas du Vin, The Harrods Book of Wine, Second Helpings (A Taste of the Glenfiddich)*, the *Which? Wine Guide, Webster's Wine Guide* and the *Oxford Companion to Wine*. He also gives talks on wine at Leith's School of Food & Wine.

GRAPEVINE

1998

The Definitive
Wine Buyer's Guide to
over 2000 of the Best-Quality,
Good-Value Wines

ANTHONY ROSE
& TIM ATKIN

EBURY PRESS
London

First published in 1997 by Ebury Press

1 3 5 7 9 10 8 6 4 2

Ebury Press
Random House, 20 Vauxhall Bridge Road,
London SW1V 2SA

Random House Australia (Pty) Limited
20 Alfred Street, Milsons Point, Sydney,
New South Wales 2061, Australia

Random House New Zealand Limited
18 Poland Road, Glenfield
Auckland 10, New Zealand

Random House South Africa (Pty) Limited
PO Box 337, Bergvlei, South Africa

Random House UK Limited Reg. No. 954009

A CIP catalogue record for this book is available from the British Library

ISBN 0 09 185242 0

Designed and typeset by Behram Kapadia

Printed and bound by Cox & Wyman, Reading, Berks

Contents

The *Grapevine* Guide to Cross-Channel Shopping 568

For Helen Long

Acknowledgements

Like its four predecessors, this new edition of *Grapevine* could only have been written with the help of a large number of helpful wine buyers, marketing people, independent wine merchants and PRs, who organised extensive tailor-made tastings, checked the answers to our endless flow of questions and faxes, provided samples at short notice and submitted themselves to the annual *Grapevine* inquisition.

Our thanks to the following people: at Asda: Nick Dymoke-Marr, Alistair Morrell, Russell Burgess, Alan Crompton-Batt and Illy Jaffar; at Booths: Chris Dee, Ricardo Benzo and Rosamund Hitchcock; at Budgens: Annie Todd and Tony Finnerty; at the Co-op: Master of Wine Arabella Woodrow and Paul Bastard; at Fuller's: Roger Higgs; at Greenalls Cellars: David Vaughan; at Kwik Save: Master of Wine Angela Muir and Anna Betts; at Majestic Wine Warehouses: Debbie Worton, Jeremy Palmer, Tony Mason, Chris Hardy and Emma Davis; at Marks & Spencer: Viv Jawett, and again Ricardo Benzo and Rosamund Hitchcock, Sonia Neill, Angela Johnson, Mike Jefferys and Chris Murphy; at Morrison's: Stuart Purdie; at Nicolas: Eric Gandon and Jill Campion; at Oddbins: Katie MacAulay, Karen Wise and Steve Daniel; at Safeway: Master of Wine Liz Robertson and Victoria Molyneux; at Sainsbury's: Master of Wine Claire Gordon Brown, Robin Tapper and Allan Cheesman; at Somerfield: Angela Mount and Leah Nicholls; at Spar: Liz Aked; at Tesco: Judith Candy, Ann-Marie Bostock, Helen Robinson and Nicki Walden; at Thresher, Wine Rack and Bottoms Up: Kim Tidy, Julian Twaites, Matthew Dickinson, Lucy Warner, David Howse, Helen Munday, Ralph Hayward, Tim Waters and David McDonnell; at Unwins: Bill Rolfe, Myrto Cutler, Bob Maybank and Jim Wilson; at Victoria Wine: Geraldine Jago, Richard Lowe, Nicola Harvey and Master of Wine Hugh Suter; and at Waitrose (John Lewis): Joe Wadsack and Masters of Wine Julian Brind and Dee Blackstock.

From the independent wine merchants: at Adnams: Simon Loftus, Alastair Marshall and Rob Chase; at the Australian Wine Club: Master of Wine Phil Reedman, Craig Smith and Mark Manson; at Averys: Masters of Wine Michael Peace and John Avery; at Berry Brothers & Rudd: Deborah Arnold; at Bibendum: Dan Jago and Sue Chambers; at Bordeaux Direct: Peter Greet; at Eldridge Pope: Matthew Cooper; at Justerini & Brooks: Master of Wine Hew

Blair and Richard Weetch; at Lay & Wheeler: Master of Wine Hugo Rose; at Lea & Sandeman: Charles Lea and Patrick Sandeman; and at Tanners: James Tanner.

At our publishers, Ebury Press, our thanks to Katharine Leck, who edited the book with brisk efficiency, Ros Ellis, Philippa Hayward, Mandy Greenfield and Fiona MacIntyre. Once again Fiona Wild read the manuscript, took out the laddist jokes and ensured political correctness, while Behram and Sally Kapadia carried out the design and typesetting. Back in the nether regions of south London, Lyn Parry pulled the book together in the last week. And lastly, an enormous thank you to our agent, Julian Alexander.

How to use *Grapevine*

Wines are divided into four price brackets:

Under £3
£3–5
£5–8
Over £8

We have made every effort to ensure that the wines we list are available, but some, inevitably, may be out of stock. By tasting in a concentrated two-month period, we aim to be as up-to-date as possible. For the first time this year we have also quoted the price of each wine. These were correct at the time of going to press, but may change. The same is true of the wines themselves. It's important to remember that wine develops in bottle – for better or worse.

Our scores need to be looked at in the context of their accompanying tasting note. Scores are not immutable or definitive. Every wine has its own intrinsic qualities and, by definition, our comments are subjective. If you like drinking retsina, that's your prerogative (and, quite possibly, your lookout).

With two palates to consider each wine, we hope to eliminate some of our individual prejudices. Nevertheless, just because we like something doesn't mean you have to, and vice-versa. If tastes were uniform, we might as well pour a few samples into a computer, give you the printout and take a holiday in the Bahamas...

Grapevine's scoring system and symbols
The scores and symbols used in *Grapevine* work as follows:

Quality (out of 20)
20   Nirvana
19   The suburbs of Nirvana
18   Truly outstanding
17   World-class
16   Excellent
15   Very good
14   Good everyday drinking

13	Everyday drinking
12	Drinkable (occasionally with a peg over your nose)
11	Almost drinkable
10	Almost undrinkable
9 and below	Faulty or plain disgusting

Value for money

🍷🍷🍷	Superb value
🍷🍷	Good value
🍷	Fair value
no symbol	Poor value

Unlike other guides, we score on quality as well as value for money. Hence it is perfectly possible for a wine to score 17 and 🍷 or 14 and 🍷🍷🍷. We also rate wines according to sweetness (for whites, sparkling wines and rosés) and weight (for reds and fortifieds), as well as drinkability.

Drinkability

▲	Drink now
▬	Drink now or keep
▼	Past it

Ratings for individual chains and merchants

Each of the chains in this guide is given a star rating out of five. These range from one and a half stars, represented as ☆(☆), to five stars, or ☆☆☆☆☆. We have chosen not to give star ratings to the independent wine merchants, as they are already our selection of the best specialists.

How we taste

We taste later and more thoroughly than any other guide. All the wines listed in this book were sampled between June and late-August 1997. At every outlet we ask to look at the top ten best-selling wines, as well as a representative range from the chain's main list. In every case, this includes wines under £5, as well as more expensive fare.

We also visit and interview every retailer in person. It goes without saying that we are both independent judges. We do not write for, blend wines for or accept advertising or funding from retailers. The sight of a wine writer penning the introduction to Unwins' wine list or appearing in the Tesco in-house magazine is not an edifying one. Above all else, we try to take a journalistic approach to the subject of wine.

Another special feature of *Grapevine* is that we include wines we don't like, as well as those we do. We believe that a critic's job is to criticise constructively, pointing out the bad as well as the good. Apart from providing a few laughs, this has a positive result: several wines that we trashed in last year's guide have not reappeared.

We try not to overdo it, though. Some of the poorest wines we taste are not listed. We see it as our to role to throw out some of the truly awful bottles. Where we've left them in, they tend to be popular wines, top ten best-sellers or wines with an undeservedly inflated reputation.

We aim not to go over the top in our descriptions or get caught up in the wayward tendrils of the vine. We try to give you enough information to make the wine sound interesting – or not, on occasions. But more than that, we have no desire to dictate what you should enjoy. Happy drinking!

The 1998 *Grapevine* Awards

Supermarket of the Year: Waitrose

For having the guts to challenge the current supermarket obsession with price points, and maintaining a consistently high-quality range of wines.

High-Street Chain of the Year: Oddbins

For its return to form as Britain's best high-street chain, selecting wines of flair and individuality, and for the enthusiasm and service provided by its peerless staff.

Most Improved Chain of the Year: Unwins

For displaying the flexibility and open-mindedness to improve its shops and its wine range. And for investing in the future of the local off-licence.

By-the-Case Merchant of the Year: Majestic

For combining a top-quality range and excellent customer service with a nose for one-off deals and bargains. And for proving that wine companies can be profitable, after all.

Independent Wine Merchant of the Year: Lay & Wheeler

For its copious treasure trove of well-selected wines from every corner of the viticultural globe, its friendly service, its expertise and its outstanding list.

Winemaker of the Year: Kym Milne

For his contribution to improving the basic quality of the wines we drink and for having the courage and talent to make the most of interesting local, as well as international, grape varieties in Italy, South Africa and Hungary.

Grapevine's Wines of the Year

This year we have again selected four cases of the year: red, white and sparkling from the high-street off-licences and supermarkets, and one from the independent merchants. These are 48 wines that we think represent a variety of characterful, value-for-money drinking. There are plenty of other outstanding wines in the pages that follow, but we picked these particular bottles for their combination of quality and availability. Stockists are listed after each wine.

Apart from the sparkling wines, most of our chosen wines – independent wine merchants excepted – cost under £5. Most score 16 or more for quality and 👝👝👝 for value for money. Where they score slightly less, it tends to be because they are inexpensive. A wine that scores 15 and 👝👝👝 and sits on the shelf at £2.99 is arguably as worthy of recognition as a £20 claret or red Burgundy.

White Wines of the Year Case

1996 Volcanic Hills, Leányka, Neszmély, £3.49
Your chance to try a wine made entirely from Leányka, the so-called 'little girl's grape' of Hungary. It's a lemon-zesty, perfumed white with crisp acidity and plenty of character. One for Humbert Humbert and Lolita?
Stockist: Unwins

1996 Espiga White, Vinho Regional Estremadura, £3.89
A stunningly packaged new-wave Portuguese blend of Fernão Pires, Arinto, Seara Nova and Sauvignon, with peach and apricot fruit flavours and lovely fresh acidity. An excellent seafood white.
Stockist: Booths

1996 Tesco Muscadet de Sèvre et Maine Sur Lie, £3.99
Rich, buttery, lees-influenced Muscadet with a delightful twist of spritz and acidity. One of the best Muscadets on the market at the moment. Given that frost looks to have wiped out much of the vintage in 1997, why not buy a case or two of this now?
Stockist: Tesco

1996 Safeway Australian Chardonnay/Colombard, £4.29
Attractively packaged Victorian blend of Chardonnay and Colombard, with melony flavours and superb length for a wine at this price. Pleasantly restrained but still unmistakably Australian.
Stockist: Safeway

1995 Château de Nages Réserve du Château, Costières de Nîmes, £4.49
Rich, textured, aromatic Provençal blend of Grenache and Roussanne with mealy concentration and balancing acidity. The most thrilling southern French white we've had this year – and not a Chardonnay grape in sight.
Stockist: Oddbins

1996 Sauvignon Blanc Pecile, Grave del Friuli, £4.75
Juicy, mouth-watering Sauvignon Blanc from a winery that seems to have discovered the secret of producing value-for-money whites in Friuli, one of Italy's most fashionable regions. The package looks really stylish, too.
Stockist: Fullers

1996 Domaine du Tariquet, Sauvignon Blanc, Vin de Pays des Côtes de Gascogne, Yves Grassa, £4.79

Spritzy, grapefruit and lemon-zesty Sauvignon Blanc from Gascony's Yves Grassa, which explodes out of the glass with almost New Zealand-like pungency. One of the best Gascon whites we've ever tasted.
Stockists: Bottoms Up, Thresher Wine Shops, Wine Rack

1996 Peter Lehmann Semillon, Barossa Valley, £4.99

From the Baron of the Barossa himself, this is an exuberant, lightly oaked Semillon with ice cream-soda and lemon-peel flavours. Like all good Semillon, it's lovely to drink young, but also looks set for a long life.
Stockists: Asda, Fuller's, Oddbins, Safeway

1996 Casa Leona Chardonnay Reserve, La Rosa, £4.99

From a brilliant Chilean winery, whose unoaked version is one of the best sub-£4 Chardonnays on the market, this is an elegant, toffee-fudge and lemon butter-like white with considerable verve and length.
Stockist: Marks & Spencer

1996 Villiera Chenin Blanc, Paarl, £4.99

Subtly oaked, beautifully turned-out South African Chenin Blanc from the youthful Jeff Grier, who has managed to extract a remarkable degree of flavour and peachy richness from a comparatively neutral grape.
Stockists: Bottoms Up, Thresher Wine Shops, Wine Rack

1996 Alsace Gewürztraminer, Turckheim, £5.95

Elegantly refreshing, rose-petal-scented Alsace white with spritz and acidity for balance. An excellent introduction to the (Turkish) delights of Alsace's spiciest grape variety.
Stockists: Safeway, Sainsbury's, Somerfield

1992 Piesporter Goldtröpfchen, Weingut Grans Fassian, £5.99

Mature, bottle-aged, medium dry Mosel Riesling like this is a rare delight for under £6. Crisp, petrolly and complex, with a lingering caress of honey.
Stockist: Spar

Red Wines of the Year Case

1994 La Langue, Domaine St Benoît, Vin Pays d'Oc, £3.99

A profoundly aromatic, herby, spicy blend of Syrah, Grenache and Merlot from the Languedoc-Roussillon, with undertones of thyme and pistachio and a supple fruit texture. With wines like this, the south of France is hard to beat on value for money.
Stockist: Victoria Wine

1996 Santa Ines Carmenère, £4.49

This is an unusual, deeply coloured Chilean red made from the rare Carmenère grape of Bordeaux. It's rich, stylish, silky-smooth and well balanced, with restrained blackcurrant fruit and polished tannins.
Stockist: Tesco

1994 Salice Salentino, Vallone, £4.95

Made from Puglia's Negroamaro grape (literally 'bitter black') by the elegant Vallone sisters on their estate outside the Baroque city of Lecce, this is a mature, rich, chocolatey example of the variety, with a characteristically refreshing bitter twist.
Stockists: Oddbins, Victoria Wine

1995 Château Villepreux, Bordeaux Supérieur, £4.99

Elegant, well-priced *petit château* Bordeaux red with grassy freshness and a hint of vanilla oak. With good claret under £5 increasingly hard to find, this is one of the few really good ones we've had this year.
Stockist: Waitrose

1996 Valdivieso Malbec, £4.49 to £4.99

Rich, chocolatey, sumptuously textured Chilean Malbec from the forward-looking Valdivieso Winery, with excellent blackcurrant fruit flavour and silky balance. Hugely drinkable and thoroughly enjoyable.
Stockists: Bottoms Up, Fuller's, Thresher Wine Shops, Wine Rack

1996 La Palma Reserve Cabernet/Merlot, Rapel, £4.99

Deeply coloured, Bordeaux-style blend with refreshing acidity, coffee-bean oak and succulent cherry and blackcurrant fruit flavours. No apologies for including a third Chilean red in our wines of the year, because Chile does this sort of thing better than anyone at present.
Stockists: Co-op, Oddbins, Sainsbury's

1995 Guelbenzu Jardin, Navarra, £4.99

Vibrant, structured Navarra red made entirely from unoaked Garnacha at one of the region's best, traditional wineries, showing masses of cherry and loganberry fruitiness and fine tannins.
Stockist: Majestic

1996 Beyerskloof Pinotage, Stellenbosch, £5.49

If you want to find out what South Africa's Pinotage grape tastes like, buy a bottle or three of this earthy, strawberry fruity number from Beyers Truter, one of the best exponents of the variety in the Cape.
Stockists: Oddbins, Victoria Wine

1995 Quinta do Crasto Tinto, Douro, £5.75

Stylish, modern Portuguese red with exuberant damson fruit and sweet, spicy oak made by Australian David Baverstock in Portugal's picturesque Douro Valley, from grapes that are normally used for Port. Could the table-wine revolution be coming?
Stockists: Fullers, Oddbins

1995 Cosme Palacio Rioja, £5.99

A modern, all-Tempranillo red from the Rioja Alavesa region, which combines oak and structured blackberry and cassis fruitiness in a harmonious whole. Rioja never used to taste like this, but we've seen the future – and it works.
Stockists: Berkeley Wines, Oddbins, Safeway, Waitrose, Wine Cellar

1995 Villa Pigna, Colle Lungo, £5.99

A barrique-aged, old-vine Montepulciano red with soft, plummy fruit, polished tannins and a sweet oak finish. This bold, full-bodied and stylishly packaged *rosso* is extremely well priced at under £6.
Stockist: Fuller's

1995 Rosemount Estate Shiraz, South Australia, Rosemount Estate, £5.99

From one of Australia's leading wineries, this McLaren Vale/Langhorne Creek blend is classic stuff at a good price. Rich, chocolatey and smoothly oaked, with the authentic liquoricey character of Aussie Shiraz.
Stockist: Marks & Spencer

Sparkling Wines of the Year Case

Segura Viudas Brut Reserve, £5.99
Richly coloured, sumptuously textured Spanish Champagne-method fizz from the quality-conscious Segura Viudas operation, combining ripeness and buttery fruit flavour with elegance in a luxurious mouthful.
Stockist: Oddbins

1994 Seaview Pinot Noir/Chardonnay, £8.49
Rich, toasty, full-blown Aussie vintage blend of the Champagne grapes, Pinot Noir and Chardonnay, from the giant Southcorp group. A Champagne-method fizz that delivers on flavour and value.
Stockists: Berkeley Wines, Bottoms Up, Fuller's, Majestic, Oddbins, Safeway, Sainsbury's, Somerfield, Thresher Wine Shops, Unwins, Waitrose, Wine Cellar, Wine Rack

Lindauer Special Reserve, £8.99
From New Zealand's biggest winery and fizz specialist, Montana, this is a malty Pinot blend of the Champagne grapes, Pinot Noir and Chardonnay, with a soft cushion of bubbles and rich fruit flavours. One of the best-looking, best-value New Zealand sparklers on the market.
Stockists: Bottoms Up, Oddbins, Sainsbury's, Thresher Wine Shops, Wine Rack

1992 Graham Beck Blanc de Blancs, £8.99
Partially oak-fermented Cape fizz made entirely from Chardonnay grapes, showing a distinctive, vanilla-like character that enhances the wine's varietal character. An elegant steal at this price.
Stockist: Oddbins

1993 Australian Sparkling Shiraz, Southcorp, £8.99
A comparatively brave listing for Marks & Spencer, this is an unusual but traditional Australian style of Shiraz, formerly known as sparkling Burgundy. Tastes a bit like a Kir Royale with tannin.
Stockist: Marks & Spencer

Scharffenberger Brut, £9.49
From the cool-climate Anderson Valley in Mendocino, this Pommery-owned, Pinot Noir-dominated fizz with its rich, mouth-filling mousse is one of the New World's best-value sparklers.
Stockist: Asda

1994 Green Point, £11.49

With a little more Pinot Noir than in previous releases, this Yarra Valley fizz made by Dr Tony Jordan at Moët & Chandon's Australian outpost is a mature, classy, strawberry fruity wine with beguiling elegance and depth.
Stockists: Bottoms Up, Fuller's, Majestic, Oddbins, Tesco, Thresher Wine Shops, Unwins, Victoria Wine, Wine Rack

Tesco Blanc de Blancs Champagne, Duval-Leroy, £13.99

From one of the region's best up-and-coming houses, this is an attractive, all-Chardonnay Champagne with lemony elegance, brioche and hazelnut undertones and beautiful balance.
Stockist: Tesco

Waitrose Brut Rosé Champagne, Union Auboise, £14.95

Waitrose's Champagnes are consistently among the best on supermarket shelves. This frothy, malty, complex pink fizz with super length and flavour from the Union Auboise co-operative is a good example.
Stockist: Waitrose

Grand Cru Bouzy, J.L. Malard NV, £16.99

Super aromatic, milk-chocolate characters with a creamy mousse and lots of Pinot Noir-derived intensity from one of the best villages in Champagne. A wine sourced for Bottoms Up's J.L. Malard label by buyer Julian Twaites.
Stockist: Bottoms Up

1990 Vintage St Gall Champagne, Union Champagne, £18.99

A super all-Chardonnay fizz from the excellent Union Champagne Co-operative, showing more richness, intensity of flavour and yeasty complexity than the majority of vintage fizz at this price.
Stockist: Marks & Spencer

Billecart-Salmon NV Champagne, £19.49

Elegant, stylish, Chardonnay-dominated Champagne from one of our favourite family-owned Grande Marque houses, with a delightful, biscuity note and beautiful balance. It's gone up in price recently, but it's still one of the best Grandes Marques Champagnes around.
Stockist: Oddbins

Independent Wine Merchants' Case of the Year

1995 Faugères, Les Jardins, Domaine St Antonin, £5.35

Chunky, herb-infused Faugères from the Languedoc with come-hither blackberry fruit, cigar-box spice and meaty, sinewy tannins. Still youthful, but already a very impressive wine.
Stockist: Adnams

1995 Talenti, Rosso di Montalcino, £8.50

As you'd expect from one of the top names in Montalcino, this is a stylish, savoury Sangiovese with perfectly judged tannins, youthful acidity and voluptuous liquid cherry fruit. Best drunk young.
Stockist: Bibendum

1990 Château Lestage Simon, Cru Bourgeois, Haut-Médoc, £9.95

From the best Bordeaux vintage of the last ten years, this is a perfumed, concentrated red with beautifully integrated oak, showing the richness and cassis-fruit flavours of the year. Stylishly balanced.
Stockist: The Wine Society

1996 Podere Il Vescovo, Gamay di Toscana, Fattoria di Manzano, £9.95

An Italian Gamay that is more expensive than almost anything you'd find in Beaujolais. Taste the wine and you can see why: a dark, brooding, super-concentrated red with liquid cherry fruit and a firm structure of tannin.
Stockist: Lea & Sandeman

1996 Chablis, Vieilles Vignes, Emmanuel Dampt, £9.99

Rich but youthful, lemon butter-style Chablis showing old-vine concentration and a citrusy, zippy tang. Every bit as enjoyable as the excellent 1995.
Stockist: Bordeaux Direct

1994 Geoff Weaver Chardonnay, Lenswood, £9.99

With its intense melony elegance and buttery, lees-derived flavours, this delightfully complex, barrel-fermented Chardonnay from the cool-climate Lenswood hills confirms Geoff Weaver's standing as one of Australia's best winemakers.
Stockist: The Australian Wine Club

1995 Domaine du Grand Tinel, Châteauneuf-du-Pape, £10.95
Ripe, savoury, concentrated, Grenache-based red from one of our favourite Châteauneuf producers. Powerful, but not overwhelming stuff, with plenty of oomph and alcohol for winter meditation.
Stockist: Avery's

1990 Château Plaisance, St Emilion Grand Cru, £11.10
Rich, spicy, blackberry fruity Merlot-based claret, whose aromas remind us of northern Rhône Syrah, believe it or not. Attractively mellow claret at a nice price for a 1990, one of the best vintages of the decade.
Stockist: Berry Brothers & Rudd

1993 Alsace Gewürztraminer, Clos Windsbuhl, Zind-Humbrecht, £12.99
Made by French Master of Wine, Olivier Humbrecht, this is a concentrated, but beautifully balanced Gewürztraminer with classic lychee and exotic spice-box fruit. Still surprisingly zesty and fresh for a four-year-old wine. About as good as dry Gewürz gets.
Stockist: Eldridge Pope

1994 Henschke Keyneton Estate Shiraz/Cabernet, Eden Valley, £13.95
A stunning Shiraz-dominated red from the Eden and Barossa Valleys, made by one of Australia's outstanding red-wine producers, combining intense aromas and flavours in a mulberry and blackberry fruity package. Rich but elegant, with beautifully handled tannins and definition. Wow!
Stockist: Lay & Wheeler

1994 Côte Rôtie, Cuvée du Plessy, Gilles Barge, £17.30
Gilles Barge is one of the best producers in Côte Rôtie, even though he's less well-known than the likes of Guigal and Jasmin. This superb, herb-infused Syrah comes predominantly from the Côte Blonde and shows silky tannins, refreshing acidity, mulberry and blackberry fruit and a twist of spice. Stunning wine.
Stockist: Tanners

1995 Dry River Pinot Noir, Martinborough, £17.95
Made by the eccentric, obsessive Neil McCallum, this is up there with Ata Rangi and Martinborough in the pantheon of New Zealand's leading Pinot Noirs. An intense, vanilla oaky red with flavours of cherry and wild strawberry and beautifully handled tannins, especially for the vintage.
Stockist: Justerini & Brooks

Introduction

Diversity, what diversity?

Tina Turner may not be the first person you think of as you sit down to a glass of Muscadet, Chilean Chardonnay, Bulgarian Merlot or Australian Shiraz, but the well-preserved *chanteuse*'s signature tune is strikingly appropriate. When it comes to wine, we're simply the best. We've got the best buyers, the biggest spread of wine and, believe it or not, most of the best writers on the subject. Anyone who has ever spent five minutes in a supermarket in France, Spain, South Africa or even Australia will appreciate the diversity of wine available in Britain. With only a small domestic industry to slake our collective thirst, we have always looked overseas for our wine-drinking needs. Once upon a time it was mainly to France, Germany and Portugal. These days we buy wine from everyone: Uruguay, Morocco, Israel, Macedonia and China, as well as all the more obvious choices.

Time for a bit of self-congratulation? We're not so sure. Our worry is that the diversity on which we pride ourselves is under threat. The reason is the increasing domination of the supermarkets, or multiple grocers as they're known in retail-speak. Hang on a bit, you're thinking. Supermarkets such as Tesco, Sainsbury's, Asda and Safeway have done an enormous amount to popularise wine in the last two decades, turning it from a middle-class hobby into an everyday beverage. And we'd agree with you.

The problem is that the supermarkets have been so successful that other wine retailers, whether they be high-street off-licences or independent wine merchants, are finding it very hard to compete. So what? Well, think about this for a second. If you add together the wine ranges of the top ten supermarkets (the so-called Big Four listed above, plus the Co-op, Somerfield, Budgens, Marks & Spencer, Waitrose and Morrison's), you're probably looking at a grand total of no more than a few thousand wines, leaving aside duplications of well-known brands like Lindemans' Bin 65 and Moët & Chandon Champagne. Those supermarkets account for roughly seven in every ten bottles of wine sold in this country. Still happy about the diversity of the British wine scene?

Before supermarket buyers start sticking pins in effigies of Atkin and Rose, we should make it clear that we have nothing against them *per se*. Indeed, nearly every single supermarket has significantly improved its range in the last year, sourcing better wines and working more and more closely with suppliers to improve quality and reliability. Some of them also do a very good job of selling more expensive and esoteric wines, too.

There is no doubt that we are well served by our supermarkets, extremely well served, but we need other sources, too. Otherwise we shall end up fulfilling this chilling prediction, made earlier this year by one rather blasé supermarket executive: 'The world is shrinking. There will be 50 serious buyers and 50 serious producers, with an alliance between producer and retailer, developing a healthy [sic] trade through from the producer to the consumer.'

For the time being we still have a resilient, if not exactly flourishing, high-street wine scene. The Thresher Group is still there (with its various different shops, including Thresher Wine Shops, Bottoms Up and Wine Rack), Fuller's is still there, Oddbins is still there, Unwins is still there, Victoria Wine is still there. But the number of chains is dwindling. This year it was Davisons' turn to bail out, selling its shops to Unwins. In previous editions we've lamented the loss of Peter Dominic and Augustus Barnett. Who will be next? Victoria Wine is said to be struggling to make a profit and, at the time of writing, Greenalls Cellars (the parent company of Cellar 5, Wine Cellar and Berkeley Wines) had just completed a management buy-out.

A high-street success story

Not everyone is long-faced in the high street. One chain, which not so long ago was on its knees and elbows, has had a very successful year. With a strong showing on the London Stock Exchange's Alternative Investment Market since it went public last November, and pre-tax profits of nearly £2m, Majestic has reversed a seemingly irreversible trend. This is good news for wine drinkers. By being nimble on its feet and giving its well-heeled customers what they want (good service and wines they can't find in their local supermarket), Majestic and its sundry converted cinemas and abattoirs has proved that there's still life in the high street. Let's hope so.

New World versus Old

It is no coincidence, in our view, that the country that Majestic's customers favour most has had a rather good couple of years. A few years ago France was said to be heading for the vinous scrapheap, pushed there by the fruitier, more immediate wines of the New World. France, it must be acknowledged, needed a boot up the *derrière*. Many of its most famous appellations had been coasting for years, relying on their historical reputations to see them through. Suddenly they faced a challenge. Why drink mediocre Sancerre when you could drink New Zealand Sauvignon Blanc at half the price? Ditto Mâcon Blanc and Aussie Chardonnay, or Bordeaux Rouge and Chilean Cabernet Sauvignon.

France needed to wake up fast. And, by and large, it has. There are still some shocking wines produced in France, many of which sell for shockingly high prices. But France has started to reinvent itself in the 1990s, just as it did in the 1890s after the phylloxera crisis threatened to wipe out its vineyards. From Burgundy to Bordeaux, the Loire to the Languedoc, France has caught on to the modern winemaking revolution. The result is cleaner, more expressive

Introduction

wines, whether they be from *vins de pays* or (theoretically) more exalted appellations.

Many regions of France benefited from good to very good vintages in 1995 and 1996. Burgundy came out top in 1995, the Loire in 1996, but Bordeaux had its best two back-to-back vintages since 1990, the Rhône made very good wines in both years and Champagne seems to have solved the problems it had in the late 1980s, releasing softer, bottle-aged wines at almost every price level. The Languedoc-Roussillon suffered in 1996, but is generally the most dependable French wine region of the lot for value for money. The franc's exchange rate against the pound has provided an added boost.

France's re-emergence as a wine force has been mirrored by difficulties in the New World. Partly because of worldwide demand, but also because of shortages of wine (especially red wine, of which more later), prices have gone up, steeply on occasion, in Chile, South Africa, New Zealand and California. As a result the New World no longer outscores France on value for money as a matter of course. Given the choice between a 1996 Sancerre from a producer like Vincent Pinard and a thin, over-cropped Marlborough Sauvignon Blanc at the same price, we know which one we'd rather drink.

Out of the Black Forest?

France isn't the only European country to have changed for the better. Germany, too, is trying to do something about its image. It may be too late to rescue the reputation of a once-great winemaking nation from the negative impact of sugar water like Liebfraumilch and Hock, but the Germans are trying to get us interested in new, drier, full-bodied styles of wine from warmer, southerly regions such as Baden and the Pfalz. Big money is being spent promoting these modern wines, with stockists benefiting from cash incentives from the London-based German Wine Information Service. Not all of them are worth drinking (or even opening, for that matter), and we still believe that most of the great German wines are medium dry or sweet styles from the smaller estates, but the new wines are a tentative goose-step in the right direction. We were particularly impressed by Fire Mountain and Lone Wolf, neither of which sounds or looks particularly Germanic. Perhaps that's the point.

Red wine and Dr Serge Renaud

However hard it tries, Germany is not going to be in a position to benefit from one startling trend: the move towards red wines. (There are a few good German Pinot Noirs and Dornfelders — before Germanophiles write in to point this out — but hardly enough to fill a bucket, never mind interest a supermarket buyer.) At the end of the 1980s, 70 per cent of the wine we drank in this country was white. Seven years later it's only 50 per cent, and falling.

The reason? Twofold, we think. First, the consistent good publicity given to red wine since the French epidemiologist, Professor Serge Renaud, appeared on nationwide American television arguing that moderate red-wine drinking 'prevents coronary heart disease by as much as 50 per cent'. This is the so-called French paradox, which explains why the French live longer than the Americans, despite a high-fat diet and a disinclination to jog or attend aerobics classes. Like consumers across the Atlantic, we're supplementing the benefits of exercise with the occasional glass of Sangiovese.

And second, the fact that red wine is intrinsically more interesting than white and that, as our tastes mature, we recognise the fact. Red wines reflect the climate and the soil in which the grapes were grown to a far greater degree than whites. This is because red wines, unlike most whites, are fermented with their skins, the part of the grape that contains the greatest concentration of tannins, yeast and flavour compounds.

There's something else to bear in mind here: red wines today are a lot softer than they were 20 years ago, when longevity was regarded as the primary aim of any serious winemaker. Now the emphasis is on drinkability. The good news is that, thanks to a better understanding of how wine is made, we can have our cake *and* eat it. Increasingly wines that taste good when they're young age well, too.

Argentina awakes

The problem with the red-wine boom is that it's created shortages of everything from South African Pinotage to Chianti Classico. The most famous reds, such as Château Le Pin and Penfolds' Grange, have become collectors' items (with stratospheric prices to match), but even at the lower end of the market, red wines are hard to find. So much so that British retailers and wine merchants are facing a potential dearth of drinkable *rouge, rosso*, red and *tinto* in the coming year. It's still possible to find basic, liver-bashing plonk on the open market, but if they want to secure something a little more interesting, the competition is intense.

This is where Argentina comes in. The land of tango, Evita and steaks the size of telephone directories also produces rather a lot of wine. Once upon a time all of this was consumed locally, which was just as well. But as the Argentines themselves are drinking progressively less (if generally better) wine, so producers in Mendoza have begun to look for consumers in other countries. It helps that much of what is planted in Argentina is red. The world's fifth-biggest wine producer has handy volumes of Spanish and Italian grapes to hand (Tempranillo, Sangiovese and Bonarda), as well as Malbec, Merlot and Cabernet Sauvignon, the trio of south-west French varieties.

Supply meets demand? Er, not quite. While some of the best Argentine reds from the likes of Catena, Peñaflor, Norton, Etchart, Vistalba and La Agricola are already developing a following here, the majority of the stuff produced in the

Introduction

land of Diego Maradona is still very old-fashioned: high-octane *tinto* with not much in the way of fruit or interest. Argentina may eventually prove the answer to the prayers of red-wine drinkers deprived of good glugging, but not yet.

Wine prices and Andrew Lloyd Webber

Talking of Argentina, one man who did rather well out of the red-wine shortage this year was Andrew Lloyd Webber, composer of *Evita, Jesus Christ Superstar, Cats* and all those other musicals that the chattering classes pretend to despise. Lord Lloyd Webber sold part of his cellar at Sotheby's in May and banked £3m as a result.

Some of the prices were, shall we say, a little inflated. A case of 1982 Pichon-Lalande sold for £5,000 a case – roughly £3,000 above its market value. What was the appeal? Did Sotheby's offer free tickets to *Starlight Express* with every lot? Was it the ALW moniker stamped on every case that tempted people to buy? Or was it the fact that, with a worldwide shortage of red wine, especially fine red wine, the apparently over-inflated prices may look cheap in another few years? After all, Lord Lloyd Webber was laughed at when he bought a good chunk of his wine, supposedly over the odds, at another large auction three years ago. His profit? A tidy £1m, allegedly. So whatever you do, don't cry for Andrew Lloyd Webber.

The 1996 en primeur campaign

If some of the prices at the Sotheby's sale looked pretty silly, they were a comparative bargain when set against what the top Bordeaux châteaux are asking for their 1996 reds as futures. *En primeur*, as the pre-release system is known in France, has been around for a long time, but has only really developed as a consumer phenomenon since the landmark 1982 vintage. It enables punters to reserve quantities of wine before it is bottled, providing châteaux and fine-wine merchants with useful cash flow in the process.

This year the *en primeur* market went ballistic, especially for the top 20 or so 'names' from the Right and Left Banks of the Gironde (Margaux, Haut-Brion, Latour, Lafite, Mouton-Rothschild, Cos d'Estournel, Pichon-Lalande, Léoville-Las-Cases, Montrose, Pichon-Baron, Léoville-Barton, Ducru-Beaucaillou, Pétrus, La Conseillante, L'Evangile, Vieux Château Certan, La Fleur, Le Pin, Cheval Blanc and Ausone). Worse still, tiny, little-known names such as Valandraud and La Mondotte were asking small fortunes for their wines in the hope of becoming the new Château Le Pin, the Pomerol property deified by American wine guru, Robert Parker.

Why? Was it a great vintage? The weather patterns and our tasting notes would suggest not. But this didn't stop people buying, especially in the Far East, a market that seems to be full of people with a lot more money than taste.

If 1997 is a better vintage in Bordeaux than 1996, those 1996s will look dramatically over-priced. Our feeling is that there are better buys to be had elsewhere, especially in the Rhône and Burgundy, which also had good vintages in 1996. Whatever happens, if you felt the urge to buy 1996 Bordeaux this year, you'll be able to enjoy the wines over the next decade or so. Or possibly sell them to Taiwan, Singapore or Japan.

Fizz and the millennium

There's also more than a touch of hype about the build-up to the millennium celebrations. The rumour is already circulating that stocks of Champagne might run out as the great party approaches. Time to reach for the credit card and put away a few cases of good fizz? That's what some of the shadier 'investment' companies would like you to believe. Even normally responsible retailers have been talking about misleading 'shortages'. One very dodgy company even resorted to a lie, claiming that 'within the next 12 months maximum yields for Champagne per hectare are set to be halved'. If you believe that, you'll believe that England has the best cricket team in the world.

If you want to drink the finest, limited-edition Champagne (fancy de-luxe *cuvées* and 1990 vintage bubbly from the likes of Bollinger, Krug or Roederer), you may have to buy ahead. But, for the rest of us, it'll be more than all right on the night. There are currently more than a billion bottles of Champagne in the region's cool, chalky cellars to satisfy worldwide demand of 246 million bottles per annum. Add the results of the 1996 and 1997 crops (the last two years that can legally feature in a non-vintage Champagne, come the 1999 rush) and you have an awful lot of fizz.

Whatever you've been told, there will be more than enough non-vintage Champagne come New Year's Eve 1999. Some of it may be remarkably cheap, too, thanks to increasingly sharp-clawed competition between British retailers. One chain, the normally rather undynamic Co-op, offered Moët & Chandon Brut Impérial at £5 off earlier this year, taking advantage of cheaper prices on the Continent to ship a reported 50,000 bottles to the UK and undercut the competition. As the millennium gets closer, expect a rash of similar deals.

Farewell, Quercus suber?

Whatever its price and whatever its provenance, no wine is safe from TCA. This harmless-sounding acronym is short for 2,4,6 trichloroanisole, the stuff that is responsible for the mouldy, musty nature that characterises a 'corked' wine. This taint can vary in strength – some corked wines are disgusting, while others are merely subdued – but it severely reduces your enjoyment of an affected bottle.

TCA is an enormous, four-Nurofen headache for wine producers. Some reports say that as many as one in every ten bottles of wine is corked – an estimated total of 1.4 billion bottles. This may be an exaggeration, but TCA is still horribly prevalent. Even the EC cork industry (hardly a disinterested source) admits that between 1 and 3.5 per cent of wines are blurred or rendered undrinkable by corkiness.

Where does TCA come from? Until recently it was thought that it developed during the manufacture of corks (particularly when they are bleached with chlorine), but recent research has demonstrated that TCA occurs naturally in many *Quercus suber* (cork oak) trees. Australia's biggest wine company, Southcorp, sampled 120 trees from four Portuguese forests and found a TCA taint in 58 of them.

RIP cork? Not yet. There are still more than 7,500 million corks manufactured every year and, despite the existence of reliable synthetic alternatives, some people still like the pull and pop of a genuine cork. (You get this with a plastic cork, too, but there is still a lot of resistance to anything that appears less 'natural' than traditional cork.) It is also worth bearing in mind, if you're in favour of screwcaps and alternative stoppers such as Tage, Supremecorq, Aegis and E-Cork, that cork forests are the natural habitat of many potentially threatened species of wildlife. Cut down the trees and you destroy their habitat. Around 25,000 European jobs depend on the cork industry, mainly in Spain and Portugal, both countries with high unemployment.

Our opinion is that corked wines are an unnecessary evil. There is some evidence that the more expensive the cork, the smaller the risk of TCA. So if you're spending money on a top Bordeaux, Burgundy or New World wine, there's less chance of a dud bottle. It has also been suggested that wines with plastic corks may age differently. Most wine is drunk within a day or two of purchase, however. For less expensive, everyday wines, screwcaps and plastic corks make very good sense.

For the moment retailers are treading warily, although most of the major supermarkets and high-street chains have introduced a few wines with new-style packaging. The breakthrough in public perception may come this year, though. Tesco and Marks & Spencer have both announced major initiatives with screwcaps for the autumn. Keep your eyes (and palates) on those gondola ends.

Wine buying and ethics

Should wine consumers worry about things like the environment, or the lot of workers employed in the cork industry? The broader theme of wine and politics was in the news again this year, thanks to a brave report on Radio Four's *Food Programme* by British wine journalist, Andrew Jefford, on conditions in the winelands of the South African Cape. Jefford found that not much had changed since the ANC came to power: in general, the same (white) people ran the wine farms, the same coloureds and blacks worked in the vineyards for little money and with no prospects.

The ensuing furore, which resulted in one British newspaper calling, somewhat hysterically, for a renewed consumer boycott of Cape wines, was a little unfair on the producers who have worked hard to make the winelands a more equitable place (Hamilton Russell, Thelema, Long Ridge, Stellenzicht, Clos du Ciel, Twee Jongezellen, Rustenberg, Vriesenhof and Klein Constantia). But it focused much-needed attention on the whole question of the exploitation of agricultural labour.

South Africa is not alone in paying its workers a pittance. Many Californian wineries could not survive without Mexican labour, for example. And many of the great vineyards of France use student or migrant pickers to bring in the grapes. Anyone who thinks vineyard work is about bucolic merriment should work in one for a day or two. There may be a few masochists out there who enjoy picking grapes or pruning vines, but most people do it because they desperately need the money.

Time to spend a little more money?

Is there a connection between cheap wine and cheap labour? Possibly. Buying more expensive wines may not encourage producers to pay higher wages, although it is noticeable that in South Africa many of the farms that treat their workers well are smaller operations, selling premium-priced wines. But our feeling is that producers everywhere are less likely to shave corners on a wine that retails at £4.99 than on one that is barely profitable.

We've said it before, but it is truer than ever that most countries find it difficult to produce drinkable wine under £2.99. There are a few, but not many, in the pages of this book. Spending a little more on wine is not a selfless act. The liquid in the bottle invariably tastes better, and the variety of wine styles is greater, once you climb out of the bargain basement.

Star turns of 1997

Who were the good guys in 1997? Well, as we've already said, France had a very good year, with the Loire and the Rhône especially noteworthy. If you like Sancerre, Muscadet, Crozes-Hermitage or Gigondas, now is a good time to get out your cheque book. We also tasted more enjoyable wines from Bordeaux and Beaujolais, partly as a result of better vintages, in 1997 than in previous years.

Other stars included southern Italy, which gets more exciting with every vintage, Romania (one or two drinkable reds), Hungary (for its good-value white wines) and especially Chile. Prices may have gone up from this long, thin sliver of South America, but the quality under £5 is still very good indeed. Argentina, as discussed, is improving, as is South Africa. All three New World countries are providing more intense competition than ever for Australia, the New World's leading supplier to British wine drinkers.

Introduction

Several wineries and winemakers deserve special praise this year, for making two or more wines that scored well in our tastings: La Chablisienne, Yves Grassa and Château de Nages in France; La Rosa (aka La Palma) in Chile; Tatachilla in Australia; Catena in Argentina; Neszmely in Hungary; Marqués de Griñon in Spain; and a globe-trotting trio of flying winemakers, Nick Butler, Peter Bright and our award-winner, Master of Wine Kym Milne.

Must improve

Pass that vat of manure. It's time we pelted a few under-achievers. In the stocks this year are cheap Australians (the wines, not the odd, uncharacteristic penny-pincher Down Under), Bulgarian reds and Californian wines under £6.

Australia has had to deal with small vintages and a boom in worldwide demand, but the quality of its basic wines (the stuff that sells for under £4) is frequently disgraceful. Even in the £4–5 sector, where Australia used to be so reliable, we've had too many dull or disappointing wines this year.

Bulgaria is a much more depressing prospect, dogged as it is by political and land-reform problems. Bulgaria had a head-start on the rest of Eastern Europe, thanks to outside investment in the 1970s, but its red wines seem to be getting worse. The promise of the so-called Young Vatted style pioneered by Safeway has faded somewhat, leaving lots of rather sharp, rustic reds. The whites are better than they were, but that's not saying very much.

California seems to be almost incapable of making drinkable wine under £6. If Chile can do it, why can't California? It has the grape varieties, the climate and (away from places like the Napa and Sonoma Valleys) reasonably priced vineyard land. But not, it would seem, the will. Perhaps that's why American wine drinkers are so obsessed with Chile. Like Lobster Thermidor, reasonably priced Chilean reds and whites are something they can't make at home.

Music to your ears...

And finally, as they say on *News at Ten*, we were amused to hear about a piece of research carried out this year by Leicester University. In a bizarre, in-store experiment, the pointy-heads discovered that ethnic music can affect your shopping habits. Montmartre-style French accordion music helped Gallic wine outsell German by nearly three to one. When they switched tapes and played Bavarian oompah music instead, it was Germany that came out on top. Perhaps there's hope for German wine, after all.

See you next year.

Asda ☆☆☆☆

Address: Asda House, Southbank, Great Wilson Street, Leeds LS11 5AD

Telephone/fax: 0113 243 5435; 0113 241 8146

Number of branches: 212

Opening hours: 9.00am to 8.00pm Monday and Tuesday; 9.00am to 10.00pm Wednesday to Friday; 9.00am to 8.00pm Saturday; 11.00am to 5.00pm Sunday

Credit cards accepted: Access, Switch, Visa

Discounts: £1 off any six bottles of still wine costing over £2; from Christmas, buy two bottles and save £5 on Champagne and 3-litre bag-in-box

Facilities and services: Glass loan; in-store tastings

Special offers: Regular fortnightly promotions (buy two bottles and save around £1)

Top ten best-selling wines: Asda Liebfraumilch; Asda Lambrusco Bianco; 1996 Asda Frascati Superiore; Asda Cape White ; Asda Claret, Paul Barbe; 1996 Merlot delle Venezie, Gabbia d'Oro; Asda Sicilian Rosso, Vino da Tavola; Asda Cape Red; Asda Chianti; Bulgarian Cabernet Sauvignon Reserve Oriachovitza

Range:

GOOD: Southern France, Italy, Eastern Europe, Chile

AVERAGE: White Burgundy, Loire, Bordeaux, Beaujolais, Rhône, England, Germany, Portugal, Spain, Australia, New Zealand, Argentina, South Africa, Port and Sherry, Champagne and sparkling wines

POOR: United States

UNDER-REPRESENTED: Red Burgundy, Alsace

'Asda Price Guarantee: Permanently Low Prices Now and Forever.' As you enter the portals of Asda HQ in Leeds, you'll find this expression of Asda's core values literally carved into a great big slab of stone, as if Moses himself had just come from a marketing session with Asda chairman (and now Tory Party bigwig) Archie Norman. The lower the price, the bigger the volume, and that's what drives the business at Asda. 'We're a business that thrives on volume,' says head of wine buying, Nick Dymoke-Marr. 'We'd rather sell big volumes at £2.99 than nothing at £3.49.'

And with an average bottle price of £3.18, Asda is selling big volumes. It's been a good year at Asda for wines, and not just because we gave the company the *Grapevine* Wine Merchant of the Year award last year. There may only be 370 wines in the Asda stable, making it one of the smaller supermarket ranges, but sales have grown by over 10 per cent in the past year. The result is that Asda's share of the grocers' market has reached 13 per cent according to Dymoke-Marr, putting it in third place after Tesco and Sainsbury's.

Having grafted ex-Safeway buyer Russell Burgess onto the busy wine buying team, Asda has been keener than ever to 'get its hands dirty', working where possible, that is, with Asda's major sources of supply to get the basic level sorted. 'We like to get involved with the wet stuff in the bottle,' says Dymoke-Marr. Even if the basic quality is all right, it can be tweaked to the required style by the buyer asking, for instance, for a bit of oak chip for extra richness or a bit of extra sugar to cut the acidity. 'We have to become more technically expert than before to get the quality.'

Asda buyers Dymoke-Marr, Alistair Morrell and now Russell Burgess work closely on this basis with a number of suppliers, among them Fairview Estate in the Cape, La Agricola in Argentina and San Pedro in Chile. In other areas, it commissions a small squadron of flying winemakers, including Nick Butler, Gaetane Carron, Peter Bright and John Worontschak, with Ben Riggs working in Greece and Hugh Ryman, who does a special Gyöngyös Chardonnay for Asda in Hungary. And to keep tabs on the range, a product-improvement panel, known to the lads from Leeds as PIMP, has been set up with regular tastings each week.

With the enthusiastic backing of the team, Burgess has leapt feet first into Argentina, with 13 new wines from Catena and La Agricola on-stream by the autumn of 1997. 'There are 1,500 wineries in Argentina, only ten of which currently export,' says Burgess. 'With domestic consumption going down from 94 to 46 litres, there's plenty of slack to be taken up.'

'Yes, no-one's grasped the nettle yet,' says Nick Dymoke-Marr, slavering at the bit at the prospect of getting his mitts on some of Argentina's interesting grape varieties from the reportedly excellent 1997 vintage. Along with the 13 new Argentine wines, Asda aims to bring in nine Bulgarian and three new South African wines.

The wine department has also been devoting time and energy to converting more of its generic, or regional, wines to Asda's own-label. Ownership of the brand is not so much a cost advantage as an endorsement of quality, according to Dymoke-Marr. And streamlining the range in this way attracts the full back-up of the company's various marketing services. 'There's more pride in selling your own name,' says Dymoke-Marr. By autumn 1997, seven in ten wines sold were Asda's own brand.

As a measure of the acceptance of New World wines at Asda, 20–25 per cent of sales are now from the New World, compared with less than 2 per cent five years ago. South Africa and, latterly, Argentina (with 50,000 cases of the Argentine red and 40,000 of the white sold) have worked particularly well for Asda over the past year. 'These two countries,' says Dymoke-Marr, 'represent the best value at the moment.' Chile has also been popular, although he worries that it's in danger of pricing itself too high.

This has been the problem with Australia. 'Sales of Australian wine are stable but the trend is worrying,' says Dymoke-Marr, citing Penfolds Kalimna Bin 28 as a wine that was phenomenal value at around £6 a bottle two years ago, but less so now that it's shot up to £9. Even Jacob's Creek, which was £3.79 two to three years ago, is now £4.99, 'without the value added in terms of any improvement in quality'.

In Europe, France has bounced back strongly, thanks to the quality and volume of the 1996 harvest and the strength of the pound. With assistance from Dymoke-Marr's affinity for Italy, not least its food and drink, sales of Soave, Frascati, Chianti and Valpolicella are up between 15 and 30 per cent. Bulgaria, too, has put in a good performance. The two main areas of disappointment have been Spain, which is struggling after a couple of difficult vintages, and California. California and value for money under £6 is a bit of an oxymoron, but Asda is working on a project with broker Jason Korman to flesh out the range.

Throughout the year 140 tastings were conducted for customers by Jayne Bridges, Stephen Barrett and Dennis Hare. The proceeds from the tickets, at £3 a throw, go to the Macmillan Cancer Trust, and customers get the chance to buy at a special 10 per cent discount. On the back of the success of this project, stores will now hold in-store tastings on Fridays and Saturdays, with staff themselves becoming more involved. Asda is extending its training programme with a view to creating a career path for staff, as well as stopping those who are genuinely interested in wine from drifting off to become Oddbins' managers.

By the time *Grapevine* is launched, Asda's own information guide 'Wines and Spirits Uncorked' will have been re-written and will be given a fresh airing. Dymoke-Marr himself takes to the road along with Jayne Bridges and training manager Ian Scott to launch the new tome.

Since it switched to selling wines by style, rather than country, in September 1994, the somewhat vague presentation of the wines on the shelf has been sharpened up with 'Toblerone-style' markers. The 'wines for special occasions', known as 'Wow! wines' at Asda didn't really work as a concept. 'A wine for a special occasion is any wine to many customers,' says Dymoke-Marr. So it's been replaced by wooden bays with eight reds and eight whites, as recommended by the press. To date, a trial in six stores has shown a 300 per cent increase in sales. Pity we hacks don't get a commission.

White

Under £3

ARGENTINA

1997 Asda Argentinian White, £2.99   14/20
Dry 🍾🍾🍾 |
A spicy, brilliantly priced blend of Chenin Blanc and the aromatic Torrontés grape from La Agricola, with masses of crisp, grapey fruit.

FRANCE

1996 Montagne Noire Vin de Pays de L'Aude, £2.99   14/20
Dry 🍾🍾🍾 |
Surprisingly flavoursome, crisp, southern French white with fresh, pear-like notes, made from a blend of Ugni Blanc, Maccabeu and Sauvignon Blanc grapes.

Asda Vin de Pays des Côtes de Gascogne, £2.99   14/20
Dry 🍾🍾🍾 |
Tangy, grapefruit and crisp apple-style Gascon white made from Ugni Blanc and Colombard. Very drinkable stuff.

GERMANY

Asda Liebfraumilch, £2.59   12/20
Medium sweet 🍾 |
From Germany's southerly Pfalz region, this is a clean, grapey-sweet Lieb, with less sulphur dioxide and a bit more flavour than many.

1996 Liebfraumilch Gold, £2.99   14/20
Medium dry 👜👜👜 ▯
Much more of a wine than the basic Lieb, with floral aromas, good balance, restrained sweetness and thirst-quenching acidity. A Lieb, for heaven's sake, that's actually drinkable.

GREECE

1996 Temple Ruins Greek White, £2.99   13/20
Dry 👜👜 ▯
Unusually well-made Greek white, made by giant Aussie winemaker Ben Riggs from McLaren Vale's Wirra Wirra in a joint venture with Achaia Clauss. The wine itself is not a colossus, but decent enough in a ginger spicy way.

ITALY

Asda Lambrusco Bianco, £2.49   12/20
Medium sweet 👜 ▯
Fresh, frothy, innocuous Italian fizzy white with a hint of sherbet lemon. Suck it and see. On second thoughts…

1996 Coltiva Il Bianco, Vino da Tavola, £2.69   14/20
Off-dry 👜👜👜 ▯
Made from Italy's ubiquitous Trebbiano grape by Chilean Andres Ilabaca, the winemaker at Santa Rita, this is a clean, central Italian quaffer with soft, buttery weight.

Asda Sicilian Bianco, Vino da Tavola, £2.89   14/20
Dry 👜👜👜 ▯
Made from a typically Sicilian blend of Trebbiano, Grecanico and Catarratto, this is a dry, zippy, characterful white with a dusting of nutmeg spice.

1996 Asda Frascati Superiore, £2.99   14/20
Dry 👜👜👜 ▯
A pleasantly nutty Roman white with a surprising amount of character for a sub-£3 wine.

PORTUGAL

1996 Valdoro, Tierra de Barros, Vino de la Tierra, Spanish Country White, Estremadura, £2.69   12/20
Dry 🍷 |
Clean, but rather basic western Spanish plonk, with little except its lowly price tag to get you excited.

SOUTH AFRICA

Asda Cape White, £2.99   12/20
Medium dry 🍷 |
From the Simonsig winery, this is a sweet and innocuously fruity, medium dry Cape white made from unspecified grape varieties. What you see is what you get.

£3–5

AUSTRALIA

1996 Asda South East Australia Semillon/Chardonnay, £3.49 13/20
Dry 🍷 |
Neutral, quaffing Aussie blend of Semillon and Chardonnay made to a price point.

1996 Peter Lehmann Semillon, Barossa Valley, £4.99   16/20
Dry 🍷🍷🍷 |
From the Baron of the Barossa himself, this is an exuberant, lightly oaked Semillon with ice cream-soda and lemon-peel flavours.

1996 Cranswick Oak-Aged Marsanne, Director's Reserve, £4.99
                                                                 16/20
Dry 🍷🍷🍷 |
Toasty, herbal-scented Marsanne with rich-textured, buttery, smoky bacon flavours, good length and refreshing acidity.

CHILE

1996 Rowan Brook Reserve Chardonnay, Casablanca, £4.99   15/20
Dry 🍾🍾🍾 |
Oak-aged Casablanca Chardonnay with notes of vanilla, ice cream soda and a lemony tang.

ENGLAND

Coleridge Hill English White, £3.99   13/20
Off-dry |
Bitter and a little angular, with a floral note and tart acidity. A potential albatross.

FRANCE

1996 Montagne Noire Sauvignon Blanc Vin de Pays d'Oc, £3.49
                                                              13/20
Dry 🍾 |
Soft, innocuous, southern French Sauvignon Blanc, which lacks a bit of zing and varietal character.

1996 Montagne Noire Chardonnay Vin de Pays d'Oc, £3.99   14/20
Dry 🍾 |
Decent, well-priced, southern French Chardonnay rounded out by oak fermentation.

1996, Muscadet de Sèvre et Maine Sur Lie, Domaine Gautron
£4.49   16/20
Bone dry 🍾🍾🍾 |
Creamy, concentrated, beautifully weighted Muscadet sur lie with lots of zip and flavour.

1996, Cuckoo Hill Viognier, Vin de Pays d'Oc, £4.99   15/20
Dry 🍾🍾 |
Restrained, well-made Viognier made in the south of France by Nick Butler, with elegant peachy fruit and fresh acidity.

1996 La Domèque, Tête de Cuvée Blanc, Vieilles Vignes, Vin de
Pays d'Oc, £4.99   16/20
Dry 🍾🍾🍾 |
Intensely spicy, complex blend of Roussanne, Marsanne and Muscat, with subtle aromas and crisp, tangy fruit flavours.

1996 James Herrick Chardonnay, Vin de Pays d'Oc, £4.99   14/20
Dry ☁ ▮
Clean and reliable, if slightly characterless, southern French Chardonnay from Languedoc-based Englishman James Herrick. Previous vintages have been better.

1996 Yves Grassa Barrel-Fermented Chardonnay, Vin de Pays des Côtes de Gascogne, £4.99   16/20
Dry ☁☁☁ ▮
From Gascony's leading producer, this is a brilliantly made Chardonnay with mealy complexity and citrus-fruit elegance. Stylish stuff.

GERMANY

1996 Northern Star Medium Dry White, Rheinhessen, £3.29 13/20
Medium sweet ☁ ▮
From Aussie Nick Butler, this is a fragrant, Müller-Thurgau-based, new-wave German white with honeyed sweetness. Drink it in preference to Lieb.

1996 Villa Eden Vineyards Riesling Kabinett, £4.99   14/20
Medium dry ☁ ▮
In its distinctive blue bottle, this is a fresh, clean, peachy Riesling with decent varietal character. A little pricey.

HUNGARY

1996 Hungarian Sauvignon Blanc, Private Reserve, Sopron Region, £3.29   15/20
Dry ☁☁☁ ▮
One of the best-value Sauvignon Blancs on the market. Grapefruity, assertive Hungarian white from the Neszmely co-operative, with nettley undertones and excellent length and zip.

1996 Hungarian Chardonnay, Private Reserve, Mecsekalja Region, £3.29   14/20
Dry ☁☁☁ ▮
Not quite as good as the Sauvignon, but this is still a fresh, tangy, boiled sweets-style Chardonnay with no oak, at a very good price.

1996 Gyöngyös Barrel-Fermented Chardonnay, Matraalja, £3.99
14/20

Dry 👜👜 |

A huge improvement on recent vintages, this is a full-flavoured, fudge and oak-like Chardonnay from Hungary's Matra Mountains region.

ITALY

1996 Orvieto Classico Poggio de Olmo, £3.79   14/20
Dry 👜👜 |

More expensive than Asda's sub-£3 white and not as good. Fresh and pleasant, if a little neutral.

1996 Soave Classico Superiore, Sanroseda, £3.99   13/20
Bone dry |

Bitter grape-skin flavours predominate in this rather austere Veneto white.

1996 Chardonnay Trentino La Vis, £3.99   15/20
Bone dry 👜👜👜 |

Crisp, unoaked, cool-climate north Italian Chardonnay with a green-olive-like tang.

1996 Pinot Grigio, Valdadige, La Vis, £3.99   14/20
Dry 👜👜 |

Clean, zesty, well-made Trentino Pinot Grigio, with crunchy, lemon-zesty fruit and a peachy overtone.

1996 Frascati Superiore Colli di Catone, £3.99   15/20
Dry 👜👜👜 |

Rich, flavoursome Frascati doesn't have to be a contradiction in terms, as this herbal, spicy and well-textured Roman white amply demonstrates.

1996 Due Bianchi, Pinot Bianco/Sauvignon Blanc, £4.49   14/20
Dry 👜 |

Made in north-east Italy's Friuli region by Aussie John Worontschak, this is a modern, zesty, lightly peachy blend of Pinot Blanc and Sauvignon Blanc, with a splinter or two of oak.

PORTUGAL

1996 Fiuza Estate Sauvignon Blanc, £3.99 15/20
Dry 👅👅👅 ▮
It's not easy to make a Sauvignon Blanc in the warmth of Portugal that tastes as good as this wine from Aussie Peter Bright. Fresh, grassy and crisp with a hint of grapefruit.

SOUTH AFRICA

1997 Kumala Semillon/Chardonnay, £3.49 13/20
Dry 👅 ▮
Boiled sweets-style blend of Semillon and Chardonnay from the Cape. Fruity, if simple.

1997 Van Loveren Sauvignon Blanc, Robertson, £3.69 12/20
Dry ▮
Dilute, characterless Cape white, which lacks the faintest expression of Sauvignon Blanc character. Or did we both have colds when we tasted this?

1997 Fairview Estate Dry White, £3.79 15/20
Dry 👅👅👅 ▮
Elegant, dry, well-made Cape white from iconoclastic winemaker, Charles Back, with notes of tobacco and spice and a crisp finish.

1996 Fairview Estate, Gewürztraminer, £3.99 15/20
Dry 👅👅👅 ▮
For 30 pence more than the Sauvignon Blanc, why not treat yourself to this dry, fragrant, rose-petal-infused Cape Gewürztraminer from Charles Back.

SPAIN

1996 Raimat Chardonnay, £4.99 14/20
Bone dry 👅 ▮
Decent, banana fruity, unoaked Chardonnay from west of Barcelona. A little over-priced.

UNITED STATES

1997 Arius Colombard/Chardonnay, £3.99   12/20
Dry |
Flat, heavy, charmless, West Coast blend of Colombard and Chardonnay. The package looks a lot better than the wine, which, to give it the benefit of the doubt, may have been a rather tired cask sample.

£5–8

AUSTRALIA

1995 Mount Hurtle Chardonnay, £7.99   16/20
Dry 👛👛 ➡—
A cross-regional blend made by the raucous Geoff Merrill, this is a concentrated, stylishly oaked, extremely well-balanced Chardonnay with a light caress of butterscotchy oak.

FRANCE

1996 Château de Trignon, Côtes du Rhône Blanc, £5.49   15/20
Dry 👛👛 |
Fresh, modern, slightly spicy blend of Marsanne and Roussanne, two of France's best white grapes, with full-bodied alcohol and weight.

1996 St Véran Domaine des Deux Roches, £6.49   16/20
Dry 👛👛👛 |
Lemony, intense, unoaked Mâconnais Chardonnay from the consistently outstanding Domaine des Deux Roches. Elegant but full-flavoured.

1995 Asda Chablis, Guy Mothe, £6.99   16/20
Bone dry 👛👛👛 ➡—
An Asda exclusive sourced from grower Guy Mothe, this is attractively unoaked for maximum fruit impact, with plenty of flavour and minerally personality.

1996 Sancerre Domaine de Sarry, £6.99   16/20
Dry 👛👛 |
Tinned-pea and gooseberry aromas and flavours make this concentrated Loire white a rival to New Zealand's in-yer-face style of Sauvignon Blanc. Clean and lingering.

1996 Pouilly Fumé, Les Cornets, Domaine Patrick Coulbois, £7.75

17/20

Bone dry 🍾🍾🍾 ➡

A more traditional Loire Sauvignon Blanc, with an alluring lime-juice and flint-like quality, ultra-crisp acidity and tapering flavours.

ITALY

1996 L'Arco Oak-Aged Chardonnay, £5.99 15/20

Dry 🍾🍾 ▮

Stylishly oaked Veneto Chardonnay with undertones of butter and angelica spice. Elegant stuff.

UNITED STATES

1997 Arius Old Vines Colombard, £5.99 13/20

Dry ▮

Pricey, faintly bitter Californian Colombard, which lacks fruit and excitement. Another problem with the sample perhaps?

Over £8

FRANCE

1995 Chablis Premier Cru, Fourchaumes, Domaine du Colombier, G. Mothe, £11.99 16/20

Bone dry 🍾 ▮

Rich, old-fashioned grower's Chablis with minerally depth and a note of eau-de-vie de Mirabelle (our entry for Pseuds' corner).

1995 Pouilly Fuissé, Domaine Léger-Plumet, £11.99 14/20

Dry ▮

Coarsely oaked, bitter toffee-apple-like Chardonnay from a domaine that usually makes better wines than this.

Red

Under £3

ARGENTINA

1997 Asda Argentinian Red, £2.99   14/20
Medium-bodied 👛👛👛 ▮
A justifiably popular blend of Bonarda and Malbec grapes from La Agricola, this is heady, juicy and full-flavoured with a nip of tannin.

CHILE

1996 Terra Alta Cabernet Sauvignon/Garnacha, £2.99   13/20
Full-bodied 👛👛 ▮
From Terra Alta in north-east Spain, this firm, decently priced blending of Cabernet Sauvignon and Garnacha by Nick Butler finishes dry.

FRANCE

1996 Montagne Noire Vin de Pays de L'Aude, £2.99   13/20
Medium-bodied 👛👛 ▮
A soft, vibrantly coloured blend of Merlot, Grenache and Carignan, with plum fruit and a rasp of acidity.

Asda Claret, Paul Barbe, £2.99   13/20
Medium-bodied 👛👛 ▮
Soft, grassy and very reliable drinking with a slightly dry finish, from négociant Paul Barbe.

GREECE

1996 Temple Ruins Greek Red, £2.99   12/20
Medium-bodied ▮
Tawny-coloured Greek blend with flavour of tinned tomato and dry tannins. Not worth paying to visit these ruins.

ITALY

1996 Merlot delle Venezia, Gabbio d'Oro, £2.39   12/20
Light-bodied 🍷 🍾
Soft, slightly sweetened Italian plonk with rather simple fruit flavours.

1996 Coltiva Il Rosso Vino da Tavola, £2.69   13/20
Medium-bodied 🍷🍷🍷 🍾
A collaborative effort between Chilean winemaker Andres Ilabaca and the Coltiva Winery, using the Sangiovese grape to good effect. Clean, cherry fruity and refreshing.

Asda Sicilian Rosso, Vino da Tavola, £2.89   12/20
Full-bodied 🍷 🍾
Sweetish, raisiny, Sicilian plonk with furry tannins and a hit of alcohol.

£3–5

AUSTRALIA

1996 Asda South East Australia Shiraz/Cabernet, £3.99   12/20
Medium-bodied 🍾
Eucalyptus and oak-scented Aussie blend with coarse, confected flavours, which reminded us of bath salts.

1996 Asda South East Australia Cabernet Sauvignon, £4.79   13/20
Full-bodied 🍾
Heftily oaked Aussie Cabernet Sauvignon with flavours of desiccated coconut, woodsmoke and plumskin. Rather confected.

1996 Peter Lehmann Vine Vale Grenache, Barossa Valley, £4.99
14/20
Medium-bodied 🍷 🍾
Light, raspberry and loganberry fruity Barossa Valley Grenache with a bubble gummy sweetness.

BULGARIA

1993 Oriachovitza Reserve Cabernet Sauvignon, £3.29   13/20
Medium-bodied 💰 |
Firm, chewy, old-fashioned, central Bulgarian Cabernet Sauvignon with a patina of oak.

CHILE

1996 Rowan Brook Cabernet/Malbec, £3.29   14/20
Medium-bodied 💰💰💰 |
Herby, minty, green-pepper-like Chilean blend from the Canepa Winery. Good at the price.

1997 Gato Nero Merlot, Lontue Valley, £3.99   15/20
Medium-bodied 💰💰💰 |
Soft, grassy, liquorice and blackcurrant-like Chilean Merlot from the go-ahead Viña San Pedro Winery.

FRANCE

1996 Montagne Noire Syrah/Merlot, £3.49   14/20
Medium-bodied 💰💰💰 |
From Foncalieu, this is a juicy, well-balanced red with fleshy tannins, sweet blackberry fruit and a rounded texture.

Asda Fitou, £3.49   14/20
Medium-bodied 💰💰💰 |
Aromatic, garrigue-scented Languedoc quaffer from the Mont Tauch co-operative, with robust fruit and tannins.

1996 Grenache, Vin de Pays d'Oc, Tramontane, £3.49   13/20
Full-bodied 💰 |
The modern package belies the rather traditional wine in the bottle, but this is still a decent, gluggable, raspberry fruity Grenache with a plonky nose.

1996 Syrah, Vin de Pays d'Oc, Tramontane, £3.49   13/20
Full-bodied 💰 |
From the same operation, this is a similarly plonky, hard-edged rouge with cherry and plum-skin undertones.

1996 Asda Oak-Aged Côtes du Rhône, £3.99   14/20
Medium-bodied 👝👝 ▌
Peppery, well-made, youthful Côtes du Rhône blend of Grenache and Syrah with a light strawberryish finish.

1996 Mas Segala Côtes du Roussillon Villages, £3.99   15/20
Medium-bodied 👝👝👝 ▌
A Roussillon assemblage of Grenache, Syrah and Carignan, with a vibrant colour and equally impressive, juicy, berry fruit flavours underpinned by firm, spicy tannins.

1996 Château Fonfroide, Ginestet, Bordeaux, £3.99   14/20
Medium-bodied 👝👝 ▌
A well-packaged step up from the basic Asda claret, with smoother tannins and riper fruit flavours.

1995 Domaine de Grangeneuve Coteaux du Tricastin, £4.49   15/20
Full-bodied 👝👝👝 ▌
Throat-warming blend of Grenache, Cinsaut and Syrah from the southern Rhône Valley with chunky, robust tannins and a core of sweet blackberry fruit.

1996 Beaujolais Villages, Domaine des Ronze, £4.69   14/20
Medium-bodied 👝👝 ▌
Bubble gum and strawberry jam-like Gamay with juicy fruit and surprisingly firm tannins.

1995 Château l'Eglise Vieille, Ginestet, AC Haut Médoc, £4.99
15/20
Full-bodied 👝👝 ▌
Also from Ginestet, a chunky, oak-aged claret, which needs a year or two to soften. Serious stuff at a very good price.

1996, Buzet Cuvée 44, £4.99   13/20
Full-bodied ▌
Firm, chunky, Merlot-based rouge from Buzet in south-west France. A wanna-be claret that doesn't quite get there.

1993 Château La Domèque Corbières, £4.99   15/20
Full-bodied 👝👝 ▌
A blend of Syrah, Grenache and Carignan from the Languedoc, with notes of thyme and rosemary and a kernel of sweet fruit.

1995 Cuvée Simone, James Herrick, Vin de Pays d'Oc, £4.99   15/20
Medium-bodied 🍷🍷 |
A Syrah-dominated red from Englishman James Herrick's Languedoc estate, named after his wife, Simone (as opposed to Cuvée, the winery dog). Not as thrilling as the first release in 1995, but still a good, peppery, blackberry fruity quaffer.

ITALY

1996 Asda Chianti, £3.29   14/20
Light-bodied 🍷🍷🍷 |
Light cherry fruity, albeit basic, Chianti with refreshing acidity and a clean aftertaste.

1996 Barbera del Piemonte, £3.79   14/20
Light-bodied 🍷🍷 |
Cheap for Piemonte's Barbera, this is a savoury fruity, softly textured Barbera with added oak influence.

1995 Asda Chianti Classico, £3.99   15/20
Medium-bodied 🍷🍷 |
Made mainly from Tuscany's Sangiovese grape, this is an attractive, traditional style of Chianti with black-cherry notes, elegant balance and a typically bitter flourish on the finish.

1996 Due Rossi Merlot/Refosco, £4.49   15/20
Medium-bodied 🍷🍷🍷 |
A Veneto blend of Merlot and Refosco, this is a grassy, plummily fruity rosso made by Aussie John Worontschak in a refreshingly modern style.

PORTUGAL

1996 Bright Brothers Trincadeira Preta, Estremadura, £3.99   15/20
Full-bodied 🍷🍷🍷 |
Very well priced at under £4, this is a fresh, peppery, blackberry fruity mouthful made from the native Trincadeira grape, with smooth tannins and refreshing acidity.

1995 Bright Brothers Old Vines, Estremadura, £3.99   14/20
Full-bodied 🍷🍷 |
Tobaccoey, smoky oaky red made from local grapes by Peter Bright. A little bit dusty and dry.

1996 Bright Brothers Douro, £3.99 16/20
Full-bodied 🍷🍷🍷 ▮

From the Douro's Pinhão Valley, an area better known for Port, this is a deeply coloured, vibrantly brambly tinto from Peter Bright.

SOUTH AFRICA

1997 Kumala Shiraz/Cabernet, £3.99 14/20
Medium-bodied 🍷🍷 ▮

Approachable, pleasantly fruity Cape blend of Shiraz and Cabernet Sauvignon, with sweet supple flavours and a shade of oak.

1997 Landskroon Estate Cabernet Franc, £3.99 14/20
Medium-bodied 🍷🍷 ▮

Blackberry and mulberry fruity, up-front Cape Cabernet Franc with soft tannins and a rasp of thirst-quenching acidity.

1995 Landskroon Estate Pinotage, £4.49 15/20
Full-bodied 🍷🍷🍷 ▮

Well-made, concentrated Cape Pinotage with plenty of aroma, clearly defined strawberry fruit flavours and an earthy, baked banana undertone typical of South Africa's native grape.

1996 Fairview Shiraz, £4.99 16/20
Full-bodied 🍷🍷🍷 ▬

One of Charles Back's best wines, with intense blackberry fruit, sweet oak and smooth tannins. A very harmonious Cape Shiraz.

SPAIN

1996 Rama Corta Cabernet/Tempranillo, £3.79 14/20
Medium-bodied 🍷🍷 ▮

Sweetly fruity, brambly La Mancha blend of Cabernet Sauvignon and Tempranillo with good length and lots of appeal.

1996 Terra Alta Old Bush Vines Garnacha, £3.79 12/20
Full-bodied ▮

Tiring, rather chewy Spanish plonk with gum-coating tannins and a rustic finish.

1993 Rioja Campillo Crianza, £4.99
Medium-bodied 💰💰 🍷

15/20

Mature, well-priced Rioja Crianza with pronounced American oak and a sweet strawberry fruit middle.

£5–8

AUSTRALIA

1996 Rosemount Shiraz/Cabernet, £5.99
Medium-bodied 💰 🍷

14/20

Spicy-oaky, bramble-fruity blend of Shiraz and Cabernet Sauvignon with a minty undertone. A decent wine-bar wine at an inflated price.

FRANCE

1995 Château de Parenchère, Bordeaux Supérieur, £5.25
Medium-bodied 💰💰 🍷

15/20

An Asda stalwart, still youthful and full of colour, this smooth, chocolatey, oak-matured claret should develop rather well over the next couple of years.

1994 Château Peybonhomme-Les-Tours, Cru Bourgeois, Côtes de Blaye, £5.99
Full-bodied 💰 🍷

14/20

A Merlot-based blend from the Côtes de Blaye, with mature fruit and a rather lean, gawky finish.

1996 Morgon, Michel Jambon, £5.99
Medium-bodied 💰💰 🍷

15/20

Well-priced for a Beaujolais cru (one of the top ten villages in the region), this is a concentrated, loganberry fruity Gamay with refreshing acidity and good length of flavour.

1995 La Domèque, Syrah Vieilles Vignes, Tête de Cuvée, Vin de Pays d'Oc, £6.49
Full-bodied 💰 🍷

15/20

Hefty, rather extracted, old-vine Syrah from the Languedoc, with burly tannins and an optimistic price tag.

1996 Fleurie, Clos de la Chapelle des Bois, F. Verpoix, £6.85   16/20
Medium-bodied 👝👝 ▮
A step up in intensity and character from the Asda Morgon, this is alluring,
domaine-bottled Beaujolais from the most famous cru of them all. Succulent,
fresh and full of wild-strawberry-like fruit flavours.

1994 Château Haut Plantey, Grand Cru St Emilion, £7.75   16/20
Medium-bodied 👝👝 ▬
Coffee-bean oaky, modern-style St Emilion with luscious tannins and fruit
concentration and a sturdy finish.

ITALY

1993 Barolo, Bricco Fontanile, Angelo Veglio, £7.75   15/20
Full-bodied 👝 ▮
Ageing but still authentic Nebbiolo, with mouth-puckering tannins and leathery
fruit. Needs food.

Over £8

FRANCE

1996 Châteauneuf-du-Pape, Prince de France, £8.49   16/20
Medium-bodied 👝👝 ▮
Closer to Côtes du Rhône Villages than Châteauneuf-du-Pape, this is a
pleasantly peppery Provençal rouge with sweet raspberry fruit. Very drinkable.

Rosé

£3–5

SOUTH AFRICA

1996 Fairview Estate Dry Rosé, £3.79   15/20
Dry 🍶🍶🍶 |
Day-Glo pink rosé verging on a red wine from Charles Back. Refreshing strawberry and redcurrant quaffer with a dry finish.

Sparkling

£3–5

SPAIN

Asda Cava, £4.99   14/20
Dry 🍶🍶 |
Fresh, youthful, lemony Spanish fizz with a nutty tang.

Asda Cava Rosado, £4.99   14/20
Dry 🍶🍶 |
Bronze-pink, Champagne-method Spanish sparkler with frothy strawberry and cherry fruit flavours.

£5–8

AUSTRALIA

Seaview Rosé Brut, £6.49   15/20
Off-dry 👜👜👜 ▮
Gluggable, strawberry-scented fizz from Australia's biggest and best sparkling-wine producer. A thoroughly moreish party bubbly.

Cranswick Pinot-Chardonnay, £6.99   15/20
Off-dry 👜👜 ▮
Ripe, tropically fruity Aussie fizz made from the Champagne grapes Pinot Noir and Chardonnay, with a sweet sherbety tang.

Over £8

FRANCE

Asda Champagne, £11.99   16/20
Dry 👜👜👜 ▮
Tangy, youthful non-vintage blend with a degree of yeasty complexity and nice, smooth-textured fruit.

Asda Champagne Rosé, £11.99   15/20
Dry 👜👜 ▮
Bronze-pink, youthful, big-bubbled rosé Champagne with flavours of chocolate and strawberries. Good, if a little one-dimensional.

Nicolas Feuillatte Chardonnay Blanc de Blancs Champagne, £15.99   15/20
Dry 👜 ▮
All-Chardonnay Champagne from the Nicolas Feuillatte operation, aka the Chouilly co-operative. Young, fresh and rather simple.

Nicolas Feuillatte Demi Sec Champagne, £15.99   14/20
Medium dry ▮
Sweetish, appley fizz in which sugar overwhelms the fruit flavours.

1990 Asda Vintage Champagne, £18.99   16/20
Dry 🍾🍾 ▮
Mature vintage Champagne with some toasty, brioche-like, bottle-aged characters and a nutty aftertaste.

UNITED STATES

Scharffenberger Brut, £9.49   16/20
Dry 🍾🍾🍾 ▮
From the cool-climate Anderson Valley in Mendocino, this Pommery-owned, Pinot Noir-dominated fizz with its rich, mouth-filling mousse is one of the New World's best-value sparklers.

Fortified

£3–5

SOUTH AFRICA

1997 Danie de Wet Fortified Muscat de Frontignan Blanc, £4.99
                                                           15/20
Very sweet 🍾🍾 ▮
Fortified Cape Muscat from former Grapevine Winemaker of the Year, Danie de Wet, this is grapey with honeyed sweetness and well-judged fortification. The Cape's answer to Beaumes de Venise.

SPAIN

Asda Fino Sherry, £3.79   15/20
Bone dry 🍾🍾🍾 ▮
Fresh, savoury, tangy, dry Fino at an excellent price.

Asda Amontillado, £3.79   14/20
Medium dry 🍾🍾 ▮
On the sweet side for an Amontillado, with flavours of toffee and crême brûlée.

£5–8

AUSTRALIA

Stanton & Killeen Liqueur Muscat, £5.99   17/20
Very sweet 👜👜👜 ▮
Tawny-hued, traditional Rutherglen sticky, with massively sweet, rose-petal fruit, complex notes of coffee and raisin and good balancing acidity.

PORTUGAL

Asda Ruby Port, £5.29   14/20
Full-bodied 👜 ▮
From Smith Woodhouse, this is a spirity, robustly fruity, intensely sweet fortified red from the Douro Valley.

Asda Vintage Character Port, £6.49   15/20
Full-bodied 👜👜 ▬
Also from the Symington-owned firm of Smith Woodhouse, this is a more refined, plum and peppery spice-like Port, with robust tannins and raisined sweetness.

1991 Asda LBV Port, £6.99   16/20
Full-bodied 👜👜👜 ▬
Once again from you know who, this is a mature style with palate-warming flavours of sweet blackberry fruit and robust alcohol.

Booths ☆☆☆☆

Address: 4–6 Fishergate, Preston, Lancashire PR1 3LJ

Telephone/fax: 01772 251701; 01722 255642

Number of branches: 24

Opening hours: Generally 8.00am to 8.00pm Monday to Friday; 8.00am to 7.00pm Saturday; 10.00am to 4.00pm Sunday

Credit cards accepted: Access, Delta, Switch, Visa

Discounts: 5 per cent off any six wines; 15 per cent off £150 or more spent on wine

Facilities and services: Weekly in-store tastings; free glass loan; tutored tastings for groups

Special offers: 'Lots', apparently

Top ten best-selling wines (by volume): Alta Mesa Red; José Neiva Red; Tapas Red; Gabbia d'Oro Red; Booths Côtes du Rhône; Château Lamothe-Vincent; Kumala Cinsaut/Pinotage; Clear Mountain Chenin Blanc; Booths Claret; José Neiva White

Range:

GOOD: Red Bordeaux, red and white Burgundy, regional France, Spain, Portugal, Italy, Australia, New Zealand, Chile

AVERAGE: White Bordeaux, Loire, Beaujolais, Rhône, Alsace, Germany, Eastern Europe, South Africa, United States, Champagne and sparkling wines

POOR: None

UNDER-REPRESENTED: None

It was anniversary time at Booths this year – 150 years since the company was founded in Market Street, Blackpool by the 19-year-old philanthropist Edwin Henry Booth. Bunting went up in 24 supermarkets across the counties of Lancashire, Cumbria, Cheshire and Yorkshire, an Anniversary Ale was brewed in Harrogate and special magnums of 1989 Bollinger Grande Année Champagne were commissioned from Reims. Oh, and the end-of-year financial results weren't bad, either.

Booths

Over in the wine department Chris Dee, the 28 ¾-year-old Adrian Mole of supermarket wine, was enjoying himself. Dee works alone, selecting and sourcing Booths' 550 wines, but revels in the responsibility. 'They give me the freedom and I exploit it,' he told us, coiffed in a black Ruud Gullit rasta wig. 'We stock as many wines as Waitrose and they've got five wine buyers.' They also don't have the same taste in headgear.

Waitrose and Booths are often compared (mostly, it must be said, by Booths). Booths has colonised the wealthier parts of the North-West around Preston and Lytham in the way Waitrose has targeted the smart bits of the South-East. There is also a degree of similarity between the two wine ranges. Both supermarkets can sell expensive domaine-bottled wines and curiosities, as well as less exalted fare. A good example is the 1994 Ruche di Castagnole Monferrato, an off-the-winery-wall curiosity at £11.99. The bottles on the shelf run from a 1988 La Tâche, Domaine de la Romanée-Conti at £184.99 to Tapas Red at £2.49. Dee is proud of the fact that the average bottle price at Booths is £3.75, higher than all his competitors in the north of England.

Nevertheless, there is one big difference between the two wine departments – apart from the number of staff, that is. Dee believes in changing the range at a brisk, some might say breathless pace. There are five new lines every week, which means that half of Booths' wines are replaced every year. 'It gives people something to come back for,' he explains.

Working alone means that Dee can act quickly. He reckons he can find something he likes and get it on the shelf within two weeks. 'If it doesn't sell, it's out,' he says, 'although we don't view space in the wine department the way they do in the cereals' department. As long as the whole range works, I'm happy.'

Dee has an aversion to 'project wines'. 'I am a wine selector, not a quasi winemaker. Centre forwards should score goals and winemakers should make wines.' All the same, he did come up with one concept this year, a Spanish Tempranillo called 'Scraping the Barrel'. The first sample we tasted was oxidised, so the name was all too apposite. But Dee promises us that it's a stonker.

The top ten best-sellers at Booths are evidence of customers' changing tastes. Apart from shadowing the trend towards increased red-wine consumption, they are moving away from cheap Liebfraumilch, Hock and Lambrusco and 'that sort of crap'. 'I think I've tapped a rich seam of customers whose tastes are like mine,' says Dee. 'They're fickle and I'm encouraging them to be even more so.'

Dee takes a pick-and-mix approach to his range. He asks suppliers to send 'whatever's great and new', rather than working his way systematically through, say, the Spanish range. 'There's an elasticity to what we do,' he explains. 'I don't mind listing 30 new Chilean wines if they're good enough.' The biggest alterations this year have come in the Portuguese and Italian ranges. So successful are the Portuguese additions that three of them have gate-crashed Booths' top ten.

The freedom enjoyed by Dee is extended to store managers, too. The top five Booths supermarkets take the entire wine range, but the other 19 can pick and choose. 'We don't have planograms,' says Dee dismissively. 'The managers are autonomous, although I try to give them as much information as possible.'

The arrangement works. Sales are up 17 per cent by value over the last year, with strong growth from Australia, France, Portugal and South America. And Dee has achieved this without leaving Preston. Well, almost. He was spotted in a Zermatt disco by a member of the *Grapevine* team on a Swiss wine familiarisation exercise and there are plans to visit Portugal and Bordeaux in the near future.

Closer to home, Booths extended its empire into Yorkshire this year, with a new store in Ilkley. They clearly drink a lot of wine in Geoffrey Boycott land, because it's 'already up there with our top five stores'. The locals must recognise a good wine range when they see one, because Booths remains one of the best two or three supermarkets in the country for wine lovers. It has a quirky and generally very well-selected line-up of wines, with strengths in both the New and Old Worlds and commendable individuality.

Some might regard the pace of change as a little bewildering. Even Dee points out that there's 'no point in getting rid of something that a customer really likes. You can't just add new wines willy-nilly.' If something sells, he'll keep it on the list, even if he doesn't like it. But the constant momentum of the Booths range means that he can buy small parcels of wine (as little as 10 cases in some instances), sell them and move on to something else. 'It's dynamic and exciting,' he argues. 'I believe that our wines are bold, interesting and quivering with flavour.' We'd second that.

White

£3–5

ARGENTINA

1996 Libertad Chenin Blanc, Mendoza, £3.69   13/20
Dry 😊 |
Soft, warm-climate, ripe pear-like Chenin Blanc with an alcoholic punch, from the sprawling Catena group.

CHILE

1997 Viña Tocornal, Rapel Valley, £3.29   14/20
Dry 🍾🍾 ▮
Modern, pleasantly fruity Chilean Sauvignon Blanc for summer drinking. Clean, refreshing and very well priced.

1997 Viña Tocornal Via Vigna Chardonnay, Rapel Valley £3.99 14/20
Dry 🍾🍾 ▮
From the same Chilean operation in the Rapel Valley, this is a fresh, young, appley Chardonnay with zesty acidity. Another bargain.

1997 Isla Negra Chardonnay, Viña Cono Sur, Casablanca Valley £4.49 15/20
Dry 🍾🍾🍾 ▮
Lively, grapefruity, full-flavoured, cool-climate Chardonnay from the Casablanca Valley, with attractive elegance at the price.

FRANCE

1996 Château Lamothe-Vincent, Bordeaux Sec, £3.99   15/20
Dry 🍾🍾🍾 ▮
Grassy, refined Bordeaux Sauvignon Blanc with super weight and length of flavour for less than £4. Further evidence that Bordeaux whites are on the up.

1996 Château Béranger, Picpoul de Pinet, Coteaux du Languedoc, £3.99 14/20
Dry 🍾🍾 ▮
Weighty, well turned-out Languedoc white made from the local Picpoul grape and showing a seafood-friendly tang.

1996 Vouvray, Lacheteau, £4.49   16/20
Medium dry 🍾🍾🍾 ▮
Super concentrated demi-sec Chenin Blanc from the top-notch 1996 vintage, with Cox's apple fruit and honeyed sweetness.

ITALY

1996 Verdicchio Classico, Cantine Co-op, Marche, £3.55   14/20
Dry 👜👜 🍷

Soft, nutty blend of Verdicchio with Trebbiano and Malvasia, with a characterful bitter twist. Very Italian.

PORTUGAL

José Neiva Oak-Aged, Vinho Regional Estremadura, £3.29   13/20
Dry 👜 🍷

Over-oaked, Portuguese attempt at a modern-style white made by José Neiva. We think José should dispense with some of the barrels and let the fruit speak for itself.

1996 Espiga White, Vinho Regional Estremadura, £3.89   16/20
Dry 👜👜👜 🍷

A stunningly packaged new-wave Portuguese blend of Fernão Pires, Arinto, Seara Nova and Sauvignon, with peach and apricot fruit flavours and lovely fresh acidity.

SOUTH AFRICA

1996 Western Ridge Chenin Blanc, £3.49   13/20
Dry 👜 🍷

Decent, if neutral, Cape white made from the ubiquitous Chenin Blanc, or Steen.

1996 Western Ridge Sauvignon Blanc, £3.49   14/20
Dry 👜👜 🍷

Faintly nettley Cape Sauvignon Blanc with some gooseberry and green-bean notes.

Clear Mountain Chenin Blanc, £3.59   12/20
Dry 🍷

Watery, thin and rather disappointing. You'd be better off with the Western Ridge Sauvignon Blanc or Chardonnay.

1996 Altus Sauvignon Blanc, Paarl, Boland Wynkelder, £3.99 15/20
Dry 🍾🍾🍾 ▮
There's plenty of ripe, softly fruity gooseberry flavours in this well-made, stylish white, proving that South Africa has begun to get the measure of Sauvignon Blanc.

SPAIN

1996 Santa Lucia Viura, Vino de la Tierra Manchuela, £3.29 14/20
Dry 🍾🍾🍾 ▮
From the expanse of central Spain, this is a commendable attempt to inject some character into the local Viura grape. Crisp, lightly oaked and enjoyable, with a good fresh finish.

£5–8

AUSTRALIA

1996 Deakin Estate Chardonnay, Victoria, £5.19 14/20
Dry 🍾 ▮
Lots of alcohol and charry oak balanced by a stab of zesty acidity.

1996 Clancy's White, Barossa Valley, £7.49 15/20
Dry 🍾 ▮
A flavoursome, herby blend of Chardonnay and Semillon from the ultra-reliable Peter Lehmann winery. Good, if pricey.

1995 Grant Burge Old Vine Semillon, Barossa Valley, £7.49 17/20
Dry 🍾🍾🍾 ▬
Rich, concentrated, smoky oaky essence of Barossa Valley Semillon with flavours of honey and lemon zest. Extraordinary stuff.

1996 Penfolds Organic Chardonnay/Sauvignon, Clare Valley, £7.49
17/20
Dry 🍾🍾🍾 ▮
From one of Australia's very few organic vineyards, this is a beautifully crafted, subtly oaked Clare Valley blend with real elegance and class.

1995 Grant Burge Chardonnay, Barossa Valley, £7.99 16/20
Dry 👜👜 ▮
Sumptuous, toffee fudge-scented Barossa Valley Chardonnay with well-judged oak and ripe, in-your-face flavours.

NEW ZEALAND

1995 Cat's Pee on a Gooseberry Bush, Gisborne, £6.99 15/20
Dry 👜 ▮
An extra year in bottle has intensified the flavours of this elderfloral, catty white from Coopers Creek. Does what it says on the label.

SPAIN

1996 Con Class Sauvignon, Rueda, £5.49 16/20
Dry 👜👜👜 ▮
Super-intense, citrus fruity Sauvignon Blanc from one of Spain's leading white-wine regions. Aromatic, concentrated and beautifully made. Look out, Graves.

Over £8

AUSTRALIA

1994 St Hubert's Chardonnay, Yarra Valley, £9.39 17/20
Dry 👜👜👜 ▮
Melony, cool-climate, quasi-Burgundian Yarra Valley Chardonnay with appealing cinnamon and vanilla oak characters and considerable finesse.

FRANCE

1994 Chablis Vieilles Vignes, Daniel et Etienne Defaix, £10.99 16/20
Dry 👜👜 ▮
Honeyed, unoaked, old-fashioned Chardonnay with an idiosyncratic edge. Traditionalists should slurp this up.

1990 Château Roumieu, Sauternes, £14.89 17/20
Very sweet 👜👜 ▮
Lusciously peachy, barley sugar-like Sauternes with botrytis-induced flavours, toasty oak and pleasing sweetness and concentration.

**1996 Mas de Daumas Gassac Blanc, Vin de Pays de l'Hérault,
£15.49**   14/20
Medium dry
Sweet, apricot-jam characters make this pioneering blend of Viognier, Petit
Manseng and Chardonnay a little heavy and obvious. We've enjoyed the
elegance of previous vintages a lot more.

Red

Under £3

FRANCE

1996 Booths Côtes du Rhône, £2.99   14/20
Medium-bodied
Soft, peppery, classic Côtes du Rhône with mouth-wateringly juicy flavours,
especially at this price.

ITALY

Gabbia d'Oro Rosso, Vino da Tavola, £2.79   11/20
Medium-bodied
Pale, sugary, thin Piatto d'Oro rosso. Sweet, confected and old.

MACEDONIA

Papaver red, Country Wine, £2.89   12/20
Medium-bodied
Beetrooty, faintly spicy Macedonian red with rasping acidity and an earthy
twang.

PORTUGAL

1996 Alta Mesa Red, Vinho Regional Estremadura, £2.79   13/20
Medium-bodied
Sweetish, raisiny Portuguese plonk with soft tannins and a hint of pepper.

Vinha Nova, Vinho de Mesa, £2.99 13/20
Medium-bodied 🍾🍾 ┃
Baked, decently made Iberian red with some sweetness and robust tannins and acidity.

SPAIN

Tapas Red, Vino de Mesa, £2.49 11/20
Medium-bodied ┃
Simple, sweetened-up Spanish plonk with a confected finish. Most tapas-bar owners would run the Seville marathon to get away from this.

1996 Viña Alarba Tinto Garnacha Pura, Calatayud, £2.99 12/20
Medium-bodied 🍾 ┃
Coarse, extracted Spanish Garnacha with a chewy finish.

£3–5

ARGENTINA

1996 Libertad Sangiovese/Malbec, Mendoza, £3.69 13/20
Medium-bodied 🍾 ┃
Light, strawberryish, warm-climate blend of Sangiovese and Malbec with a plonky aftertaste.

CHILE

1997 Cono Sur Pinot Noir, Rapel Valley, £4.49 14/20
Medium-bodied 🍾🍾 ┃
Juicy, raspberry and cherry fruity Chilean Pinot Noir with refreshing acidity. Pleasant stuff from a winery that makes consistently good, affordable Pinots.

FRANCE

Booths Claret, Bordeaux, £3.49 14/20
Medium-bodied 🍾🍾🍾 ┃
Characterful red Bordeaux at an excellent price, with smooth, herbaceous fruit characters and good balance. One of the best inexpensive clarets in the high street.

1995 Domaine de La Condamine L'Evêque Mourvèdre, Vin de Pays des Côtes de Thongues, £3.69
14/20
Medium-bodied 👜👜 ▮
Fresh, spicy, bitters and liquorice-like Mourvèdre with a dry finish.

1994 Moncenay Pinot Noir, Vin de Pays de la Côte d'Or, £3.89
12/20
Light-bodied ▮
Cheap red Burgundy is almost an oxymoron. This wishy-washy Pinot Noir shows you why.

1995 Côtes du Rhône Villages, St Maurice, Cuvée Réservée, £4.69
14/20
Full-bodied 👜 ▮
Attractively peppery aromas give way to rather firm and chewy, traditional-style flavours on this basic Côtes du Rhône Villages red.

1995 Booths Oak-Aged Claret, Bordeaux Supérieur, £4.99   14/20
Medium-bodied 👜 ▮
Coarsely oaked, but the underlying fruit is good. Still, we'd rather drink the cheaper Booths Claret.

PORTUGAL

1996 José Neiva Red, Vinho Regional Estremadura, £3.29   13/20
Medium-bodied 👜👜 ▮
Light, smoky bacon-like Portuguese red with raspberry sweetness and cinnamon spice.

1996 Quinta das Setencostas, Alenquer, £3.99   15/20
Medium-bodied 👜👜👜 ▮
A southern Portuguese blend of Periquita, Camarate and Tinta Miúda, with peppery, Rhône-like characters, well-judged oak and undertones of clove and pepper.

SOUTH AFRICA

1995 Western Ridge Ruby Cabernet, £3.49   14/20
Medium-bodied 👜👜 ▮
Full-coloured, grassy, pleasantly herbaceous Cape quaffer with chocolatey tannins.

1996 Western Ridge Cabernet/Shiraz, £3.69   13/20
Full-bodied 👜 ▌

Oaky, acetone-scented Cape blend of Cabernet and Shiraz with a rustic green edge.

SPAIN

1996 Iuvene Tinto, Rioja, £4.99   15/20
Medium-bodied 👜👜 ▌

Bubble gum and strawberry fruity, unoaked Rioja with the accent on youth and approachability.

£5–8

AUSTRALIA

1994 Wakefield Estate Cabernet Sauvignon, Clare Valley, £6.75
             14/20

Full-bodied ▌

Minty, rather unbalanced Clare Valley Cabernet Sauvignon with lots of oak and alcohol and a tart, acidified finish.

CHILE

1996 Viña Linderos, Cabernet Sauvignon, Maipo Valley, £5.89   14/20
Medium-bodied 👜 ▌

Soft, easy drinking Chilean Cabernet Sauvignon with an earthy under-belly. Ought to be £1 cheaper.

1995 Viña Carmen Grande Vidure/Cabernet, Maipo Valley, £6.99
             17/20

Full-bodied 👜👜👜 ▬

Made by the talented Alvaro Espinoza, this is one of Chile's best red wines, showing texture, sweet blackberry fruit and fine-grained tannins balanced by classy vanilla oak.

FRANCE

1995 Faugères, Gilbert Alquier, £6.99   16/20
Medium-bodied 👜👜 ▬
Rich, heady, powerful Languedoc red, which packs a punch of fruit, peppery spice and tannin. Needs time in bottle to soften.

SPAIN

1991 Mont Marçal Cabernet Sauvignon Reserva, Penedès, £5.49
15/20

Medium-bodied 👜👜 ▮
Mature, elegant, well-made Cabernet Sauvignon from Catalonia's Penedès region, showing blackcurrant sweetness and attractive vanilla oak.

1994 Conde de Valdemar Crianza, Rioja, £5.49   16/20
Medium-bodied 👜👜👜 ▮
Well-made, concentrated Rioja with just the right balance of oak and fruit, from one of the best producers in the region.

Over £8

AUSTRALIA

1994 Grant Burge Old Vine Shiraz, Barossa Valley, £9.39   17/20
Full-bodied 👜👜👜 ▮
Polished, smoothly oaked, full-throttle Barossa Valley Shiraz, with smoky American oak and mint and blackberry-fruit sweetness.

FRANCE

1995 Domaine de l'Hortus Grande Cuvée, Pic St Loup, Coteaux du Languedoc, £9.99   16/20
Full-bodied 👜👜 ▬
From one of the best domaines in the south of France, Jean Orliac's top cuvée red is a superb, Syrah-based, oak-matured red from fashionable Pic St Loup.

Mature Margaux, £10.49   15/20
Medium-bodied 👜 |

Great name; pretty good wine. Beginning to dry a little on the palate perhaps, but this is an appealingly leafy, old-fashioned Margaux (1977 Château Brane-Cantenac, apparently) at a decent price. One for traditionalists.

ITALY

1994 Chianti Classico Querciabella, £9.75   17/20
Medium-bodied 👜👜👜 ▬

Chocolatey, spicy, well-endowed Chianti Classico, with sinewy tannins, assertive oak and masses of fruit concentration.

1994 Ruche di Castagnole Monferrato, Casa Brina, £11.99   16/20
Medium-bodied 👜👜 |

Grapey, aromatic, almost Gewürztraminer-like aromas make Ruche an idiosyncratic Piedmontese red grape. A soft, Turkish delight of a red wine in flagrante delicto.

1991 Amarone Classico, Brigaldara, £13.99   16/20
Full-bodied 👜👜 |

Rustic, liquoricey, old-fashioned Amarone, with a touch of volatility adding complexity to this powerful, full-bodied Veneto rosso.

Sparkling

£3–5

FRANCE

1993 Cray Brut Rosé, Crémant de Loire, £4.99   15/20
Dry 👜👜👜 |

Grassy, green-pepper-like Loire fizz with creamy softness and rounded maturity. Excellent value.

Fortified

£3–5

SPAIN

Booths Manzanilla, Hidalgo, £4.69   16/20
Bone dry 🍶🍶🍶 ▮
Salty, tangy, ultra-fresh Manzanilla with dry, nutty, savoury flavours, from the traditional Hidalgo bodega.

Over £8

PORTUGAL

Churchill's Dry White Port, £8.99   16/20
Sweet 🍶🍶 ▮
The sort of wine normally drunk only in Portugal, this is an intense tawny Port-meets-Madeira-style fortified white with loads of character. Dry, however, it is not.

Booths Crusted Port, Martinez Gassiot, £9.99   15/20
Full-bodied 🍶 ▮
Traditional, full-blooded Crusted Port with lots of peppery flavours and a spirity note.

SPAIN

San Emilio, Pedro Ximenez, Lustau, £11.69   16/20
Very sweet 🍶🍶 ▮
Luscious, unctuous, brown-treacle-like Sherry with flavours of sticky toffee pudding and raisins. One of the few wines that is good with chocolate. Pour it over vanilla ice cream.

Budgens ☆(☆)

Address: 9 Stonefield Way, Ruislip, Middlesex HA4 OJR

Telephone/fax: 0181 422 9511; 0181 422 1596

Number of branches: 114 (including 8 Fresh Save stores and 6 petrol forecourt stores)

Opening hours: Varies according to location, but generally 8.00am to 9.00pm, Monday to Saturday; 10.00am to 4.00pm Sunday

Credit cards accepted: Delta, Electron, MasterCard, Switch, Visa

Discounts: 5 per cent off single cases

Facilities and services: By-the-case sales; in-store tastings; glass loan and home delivery on trial at a small number of stores

Special offers: Discounts on at least two wines at all times, changing every two weeks

Top ten best-selling wines (by volume): Bordeaux Blanc Sec; Rioja Tinto Don Marino IV; Blanc de Blancs Special Cuvée; Budgen's Claret; Clear Mountain Cape Red; Chardonnay du Lac, Vin de Pays; Frascati; Côtes du Rhône Villages; Diego de Almagro Crianza, Valdepeñas

Range:

GOOD: None

AVERAGE: White Burgundy, Bordeaux, Loire, regional France, Alsace, Eastern Europe, England, Italy, South Africa, Australia, California, Chile, Champagne and sparkling wines, Sherry

POOR: Red Burgundy, Spain, Germany, New Zealand

UNDER-REPRESENTED: Argentina

'Basically, I'm it,' says Tony Finnerty, the high street's eternal Lone Ranger. Finnerty is still responsible for sourcing, selecting and fine-tuning Budgens' wine range, even if this year he's taken on an assistant buyer, Esme Banks, a 'Tonto-ess' in his words, to help out with admin.

No wonder he looks a little saddle-sore. He rarely gets time to venture into

Budgens

central London, never mind visit Australia, South Africa or South America. The poor guy's got so much work to do that he can't afford to visit a wine region unless he can get back to the office within a few days.

Finnerty has had an even heavier workload than usual in 1997, having launched a new in-store look for the wine department in its higher-profile sites, known as Metro stores. The small Ruislip-based supermarket chain now has five different 'trading formats', as they're known in marketing lingo, in the east and south-east of England: Metro, Primary, Village, Fresh Save and Convenience/Forecourt. Most of Budgens' 114 stores are Village sites, but the upmarket Metro branches are where most of the attention is focusing just now.

The first Metro opened in Kensington in May, complete with a didgeridoo player and free Champagne. At the time of writing in late summer it had already been pronounced a tub-thumping success. Sales in the new, half-barrels-and-wooden-flooring-style wine department were up by 76 per cent and now account for 13.5 per cent of the store's turnover, compared with 10 per cent in an average Budgens. Not surprisingly, the idea is to convert more stores, with a further 17 designated for refitting by the end of 1997.

The Metro wine department certainly looks the part, with a new layout, an eye-catching colour scheme and plenty of space for people to browse. There are even a few fine wines distributed among the wooden barrels. To fill the expanded space (and to keep Budgens' customers interested), Finnerty has beefed up the general range to 450 wines (of which Primary stores get 350, Village 300, Fresh Save 75 and Forecourt 40).

'In Kensington, we've doubled the range and brought in new wines across the spectrum,' says Finnerty. Kensington is the model that other Metro stores will follow, with an expanded line-up of clarets, Burgundies, Tuscan reds and top-end New World wines as well as cheaper fare, such as French vins de pays. The new format, according to Finnerty, gives more space to 'centres of excellence' and is intended to, er, showcase Budgens' range. It also helps to sell high-priced wines, such as 1993 La Fleur Pétrus at £39.99 a pop.

Finnerty is pleased with the way things are heading in general. The average bottle price at Budgens has risen to £3.54 ('way up for us') and sales are up by 18 per cent by volume and 9 per cent by value. The Lone Ranger has also just finished a Consumers' User's Guide, an 'informative booklet that will be in or around every wine department', in an attempt to boost sales even further. 'The book answers the 30 basic questions that customers often ask before they buy a bottle of wine.' The idea is to help them to home in on 30 or 40 wines out of the full range and feel comfortable with their choice.

Finnerty's ambitions for the Metro format don't stop there, however. He's looking at wholesaling, or 'outselling', to restaurants and businesses, and he plans to have a wine adviser (without the didgeridoo) in every Metro store.

He also believes that the limited number of top stores will enable him to buy small, bespoke parcels and offer them to Budgens' customers, 'something which Tesco and Sainsbury's can't do'.

The Metros are only a small part of the Budgens story, however. Most stores are small, local and considerably less ritzy. Still, Finnerty is confident that wine sales are moving ahead of the market, thanks to the chain's 'Greater Local Value' (GLV for short) promotions and cut-price specials. The first targets the catchment area around a particular store; the second reduces prices on specific wines by a pound or so for a limited period to encourage people to try something new. Budgens' biggest growth area is between £3.50 and £4.50.

This is all very encouraging for Budgens and the health of the wine market in general. Nevertheless, we still have strong reservations about some of the wines that wind up on Budgens' shelves. Many of the lower-priced bottles (including some of the top ten best-sellers) verge on the undrinkable and would not be given house room at Safeway, Asda or Sainsbury's. These are offset, to a degree, by innovative listings from places like Switzerland, Bulgaria and Greece, but the range remains something of a dog's breakfast, with no real coherence or sense of direction. Our advice is to tread extremely warily and follow our recommendations. We've tasted things like the Blanc de Blancs Special Cuvée so that you don't have to.

Finnerty and Budgens have done a lot to change the wine department's image this year. The Metro format looks good and some decent new wines have been introduced across the various types of store. But for the time being, the stuff in the bottle (and let's face it, that's what counts) is too unreliable for our liking.

White

Under £3

BULGARIA

1995 Preslav Chardonnay/Sauvignon Blanc, Vinex Preslav, £2.99
14/20

Dry 🍾🍾🍾 |

One of a number of commendable whites we've seen from the Preslav winery this year, this Chardonnay/Sauvignon Blanc blend combines freshness and spritz with a buttery texture.

FRANCE

Blanc de Blancs Special Cuvée, Jean Montbray, £2.49   10/20
Off-dry ▮
Stewed, tart, sulphurous French plonk made from unspecified grapes. No surprises there or here.

1996 Bordeaux Blanc Sec, Bovey et Fils, £2.69   13/20
Off-dry 👛👛 ▮
Clean, slightly sweetened white Bordeaux with crisp apple fruit.

1996 Domaine Baroque, Vin de Pays des Côtes de Gascogne, Peter Hawkins, £2.99   14/20
Dry 👛👛👛 ▮
Made by expat Peter Hawkins, this is a tangy, grapefruity Gascon blend of Ugni Blanc and Colombard for summer drinking.

1996 Chardonnay, Vin de Pays de l'Île de Beauté, François Dulac, £2.99   13/20
Dry 👛👛 ▮
Boiled sweets-style Corsican Chardonnay made to a price on the island's flat east coast.

£3–5

ARGENTINA

1996 Flichman Chardonnay Mendoza, £4.99   14/20
Dry 👛 ▮
A fresh, lemon-zesty Chardonnay made from one of Mendoza's best red-wine producers, here turning its hand and cool fermentation equipment to whites. Ought to be a little cheaper.

AUSTRALIA

1996 Norman's Lone Gum Chenin Blanc, £4.99   13/20
Off-dry ▮
Sweetish, slightly confected Aussie Chenin Blanc, which ought to be £1 cheaper. Dullness is a lone gum, as John Lennon might have put it.

FRANCE

1996 Domaine Villeroy-Castellas Sauvignon Blanc, Vin de Pays des Sables du Golfe du Lion, £3.99   12/20
Dry
Heavy, baked southern French Sauvignon Blanc with minimal varietal character, from the sandpit vineyards of Listel.

1996 Mâcon Igé, Les Vignerons d'Igé, £4.99   14/20
Dry
Well-priced, full-flavoured co-operative Mâcon with some of the buttery notes of the Chardonnay unhindered by oak.

1996 Bourgogne Blanc, Charles Viénot, £4.99   14/20
Dry
Spritzy, crisp, cleanly defined white Burgundy in an appealing package, with citrus-fruit notes and a rounded texture.

1995 Laroche Grande Cuvée, Vin de Pays d'Oc, £4.99   15/20
Dry
Oaky, modern-style Chardonnay made by the Chablis house of Laroche on holiday down in the Midi. Smoky, nutty and nicely balanced.

1996 James Herrick Chardonnay, Vin de Pays d'Oc, £4.99   14/20
Dry
Clean, if slightly characterless, Chardonnay from Languedoc-based Englishman, James Herrick. Nothing like as good as earlier vintages of the same brand.

Sans Souci Premières Côtes de Bordeaux, Borie Manoux, £4.99
                                                     10/20
Sweet
Sans souci? We think the producers of this gluey, actively nasty sticky ought to be seriously worried.

GREECE

1995 Vin de Crète White, Kourtaki, £3.49   14/20
Dry
Baked Mediterranean white with a herbal undertone and hints of resin and lime. Unusual, but not unpleasant.

ITALY

1996 Frascati Superiore Casale del Grillo, £4.49 15/20
Dry 🍯🍯🍯 ▮
Pleasant, nutty, spicy Roman white made from a blend of Malvasia, Greco and Trebbiano, with character and a tangy bite.

ROMANIA

1995 Tarnava Valley Chardonnay, Jidvei, £4.49 11/20
Medium dry ▮
From the Jidvei winery in Romania, this is a sweet, old-fashioned, unreconstructed Chardonnay with a cloying aftertaste.

SOUTH AFRICA

1996 Helderberg Sauvignon Blanc, Vinfruco, £4.75 12/20
Off-dry ▮
Soft, mawkish and dilute Cape white apparently made from the Sauvignon Blanc grape.

SWITZERLAND

1996 Chasselas Romand, Vin de Pays de Romandie, Martigny, £3.99 13/20
Dry 🍯 ▮
Screw-capped Swiss Chasselas at a fair price for the land of gnomes and cuckoo clocks. An après-ski thirst-quencher with neutral flavours. Downhill all the way from here.

£5–8

AUSTRALIA

1996 Rymill Botrytis Gewürztraminer, half-bottle, £5.99 16/20
Very sweet 🍯 ▮
A rich, peachy, botrytised Coonawarra sticky, made from the rare (for Australia) Gewürztraminer grape, showing flavours of honey and lychee balanced by fresh acidity.

NEW ZEALAND

1996 Nobilo Full Harvest Sauvignon Blanc, £6.99   15/20
Off-dry 🍾 ▮
Soft, squashy, gooseberry and apple flavours in a silly, over-designed bottle
(including a label that manages to imitate two Californian wineries at once).
Over-priced, even for New Zealand.

Over £8

FRANCE

1992 Rully Blanc, Raoul Clercet, £14.99   13/20
Dry ▮
Not the best example of what the excellent 1992 white Burgundy vintage has
to offer, especially at £14.99. Gluey, over-oaked and fading.

Red

Under £3

BULGARIA

1994 Stara Zagora Merlot/Cabernet, £2.29   13/20
Medium-bodied 🍾🍾🍾 ▮
Basic, chewy Bulgarian Merlot/Cabernet Sauvignon at a very cheap price. It
lacks a bit of fruit, but what do you expect?

£3–5

CYPRUS

Keo Othello, £3.99   12/20
Full-bodied ▮
One of the few Cypriot reds to have escaped from the island, this is a baked,
old-fashioned Rhône-style red with soupy fruit flavours. Unlikely to make
anyone jealous if they see you with a bottle in hand.

FRANCE

Budgens Claret, Marcel Theron, £3.45　　　　　　　13/20
Light-bodied 🌶🍷
Grassy, refreshing, decently priced red Bordeaux from négociant Marcel
Theron.

1996 Côtes du Rhône Gargantua, £3.59　　　　　　14/20
Medium-bodied 🌶🌶🍷
Light, peppery, co-operative Côtes du Rhône made in an easy-quaffing
Beaujolais style with some attractively spicy notes.

1995 Corbières Château St Louis, Pasquier Meunier, £3.69　13/20
Full-bodied 🌶🍷
Chewy, four-square Languedoc red with a rustic, dry finish.

**1996 Côtes du Rhône Villages Cuvée Réserve, Celliers des
Dauphins, £3.99**　　　　　　　　　　　　　　15/20
Medium-bodied 🌶🌶🌶🍷
Showing more stuffing and oomph than the basic Côtes du Rhône, this is a
robustly peppery Rhône red showing the red fruit characters of the Grenache
grape.

1995 Cahors Marquis Rocadour, Cheval Quancard, £4.49　13/20
Full-bodied 🍷
Firm, savoury, south-west French blend with Malbec clearly in the ascendant. A
bit hard on the palate.

1994 L'Esprit de Teyssier Bordeaux Supérieur, £4.99　　15/20
Medium-bodied 🌶🌶🍷
Supple, Merlot-dominated second label of Château Teyssier in St Emilion, with
attractive flavours of chocolate and fruit cake.

GREECE

1995 Vin de Crète Red, Kourtaki, £3.49　　　　　　11/20
Full-bodied 🍷
A blend of Cotsifali, Liatiko and Mandilaria (just so that you know), with chewy,
dry tannins and coarse flavours. Minotaur's blood.

ROMANIA

1995 Pietroasa Young Vatted Cabernet Sauvignon, £3.49   13/20
Medium-bodied 👜👜 ▯
Made by Australian Graham Dixon with Romanian Razvan Macici, this is a juicy, sweetened Cabernet Sauvignon with a core of blackcurrant fruit.

SOUTH AFRICA

Clear Mountain Cape Red, £3.39   12/20
Medium-bodied ▯
Basic, slightly confected South African plonk made from we've no idea what.

1996 Helderberg Shiraz, Vinfruco, £4.99   15/20
Medium-bodied 👜👜 ▯
A fruity, well-made, red fruit and bramble-like number with smoky oak and a firm nip of tannin.

SPAIN

1993 Diego de Almagro Crianza, Valdepeñas, Felix Solis, £3.39
14/20

Medium-bodied 👜👜 ▯
Modern, chewy oaky blend of Cencibel and Tempranillo, with plenty of fruit and vanilla sweetness at this price.

Rioja Tinto Don Marino IV, £3.99   12/20
Medium-bodied ▯
Coarse, jammy, confected non-vintage Rioja. We've no idea who Don Marino IV is and we really don't care.

1991 Marqués de Caro Tinto Reserva, Cherubino Valsangiacomo, £3.99
10/20
Full-bodied ▯
Cooked, raisiny, extracted Valencian tinto. The only redeeming feature is the copper wire around the bottle.

1994 Palacio de la Vega Crianza Cabernet/Tempranillo, £4.99
16/20

Medium-bodied 👜👜👜 ▬
From one of our favourite Spanish wineries, this is a supple, skilfully oaked Navarra blend of Cabernet Sauvignon and Tempranillo, with style, balance and blackcurrant sweetness.

UNITED STATES

1994 Sutter Home Zinfandel, £4.29   14/20
Medium-bodied 🌢 ▮
Medicinal, camphor-like Californian Zin from a company better known for its blush wines. Decent enough, if a little sweet and simple.

1994 Glen Ellen Cabernet Sauvignon, £4.99   13/20
Medium-bodied ▮
Sweet, jammy, confected, planed-down Cabernet Sauvignon. One for the cola drinker.

£5–8

FRANCE

1995 Bourgogne Rouge, Charles Viénot, £5.99   12/20
Medium-bodied ▮
Jammy, hollow, over-chaptalised (too much sugar added to increase the alcohol content) red Burgundy that is hardly worthy of the appellation. Where's the fruit, Monsieur Viénot?

1995 Gigondas, Domaine de La Murielle, Producteurs Associés Vacqueyras, £6.99   16/20
Full-bodied 🌢🌢🌢 ▬
Rich, heady, Provençal rouge from the leading southern Rhône appellation of Gigondas, with a punch of tannin, pepper and sweet fruit.

ITALY

1994 Nexus Grave del Friuli San Simeone, Gino Brisotto, £7.99
    16/20

Medium-bodied 🌢🌢 ▬
Mocha-scented, north-eastern Italian Cabernet Sauvignon made in an elegant, Margaux-like style and packaged in a heavy-duty designer bottle.

Over £8

AUSTRALIA

1994 Penfolds Bin 389 Cabernet/Shiraz, £10.99   17/20
Full-bodied 🍶🍶🍶 ⬤—
Dark, brooding, sweetly aromatic, oak-aged blend of Cabernet Sauvignon and Shiraz from Australia's biggest wine group. Rich, concentrated, spicy and full of charry, blackberry-fruit flavours. Essence of Australia.

ITALY

1993 Vino Nobile di Montepulciano, Avignonesi, £9.99   17/20
Full-bodied 🍶🍶🍶 ❘
From one of the best estates in Tuscany, this is a concentrated, demanding red blend of Prugnolo (aka Sangiovese), Canaiolo and Mammolo, with savoury, aniseedy characters, a touch of raisin and robust tannins.

1992 Barolo Villademonte, Fratelli Martini, £9.99   14/20
Medium-bodied ❘
In a silly, sloping-shouldered bottle, this is a basic, chewy, but rather insubstantial Nebbiolo at a ludicrous price.

Sparkling

£5–8

AUSTRALIA

Seppelt Great Western Brut, £5.49   14/20
Off-dry 🍶🍶🍶 ❘
Frothy, easy-drinking, softly gluggable Aussie sparkler from the Seppelt winery. Good for parties and Buck's fizz.

FRANCE

Blanquette de Limoux, Blanc de Blancs, Divinaude, £7.99   13/20
Off-dry ▮
From France's oldest sparkling-wine region, this is a simple, big-bubbled fizz
with aggressive acidity and lumpen fruit.

NEW ZEALAND

Lindauer, Montana, £7.49   15/20
Dry 👓👓 ▮
Deeply coloured, well-made New Zealand tank-method sparkler from
Montana, showing sherbety flavours and a citrus-fruit tang.

Over £8

FRANCE

Henri Germain Brut Reserve, £12.49   15/20
Dry 👓👓 ▮
An equal blend of the three Champagne grapes, Pinot Noir, Pinot Meunier and
Chardonnay, with attractive reserve wine characters and a veneer of fresh,
lively fruit. Decent quaffing fizz.

Champagne Pierre Callot Grand Cru, Blanc de Blancs, £16.99
                                                                     16/20
Dry 👓👓👓 ▮
An all-Chardonnay Champagne from the Grand Cru village of Avize on the
Côte des Blancs. Aromatic and elegant, with a honeysuckle note.

Fortified

Under £3

SPAIN

Moscatel de Valencia Vittore, Cherubino Valsangiacomo, £2.99
11/20

Very sweet ▮
Old-fashioned, high-octane Moscatel with marmalade and candied-fruit characters and a cloying, syrupy sweetness.

£3–5

SPAIN

Budgens Amontillado Sherry, Bodegas Manuel Gil, £3.99   14/20
Medium dry 🍷🍷 ▮
Almondy, inexpensive Amontillado with more sweetness than other, more traditional styles and caramel and toffee-like flavours.

La Guita Manzanilla, Perez Marin, £4.99   15/20
Dry 🍷🍷 ▮
Well-priced, well-packaged, Marmitey Manzanilla from the port of Sanlúcar de Barrameda. Elegantly dry with a nutty tang.

Co-op ☆☆(☆)

Address: National Buying, Marketing and Distribution Group, PO Box 53, New Century House, Manchester M60 4ES

Telephone/fax: 0161 834 1212; 0161 827 5117

Number of branches: 2,500 licensed stores

Opening hours: Varies from store to store

Credit cards accepted: All major credit cards

Discounts: Occasionally on large orders

Facilities and services: Glass loan and in-store tastings in selected superstores; home delivery arranged at local level

Special offers: To Co-op members; monthly promotions

Top ten best-selling wines: Co-op Lambrusco Bianco; Co-op Liebfraumilch; Co-op Hock; Co-op Cava; Co-op Cape Red; Co-op Corbières Rouge; Co-op Australian Red; Co-op Chianti; Co-op Tempranillo Oak-Aged; Co-op California Red

Range:

GOOD: Portugal, Australia, Chile, South Africa

AVERAGE: Bordeaux, Beaujolais, Burgundy, regional France, Eastern Europe, Italy, Spain, Germany, England, United States, Argentina, New Zealand, Champagne and sparkling wines

POOR: Too many of the wines UK-bottled in Irlam

UNDER-REPRESENTED: None

A British institution came under attack this year, and we're not talking about the House of Lords. The Co-operative Wholesale Society, with its pharmacies, farms and funeral parlours, was the object of stock-market speculation in the spring. CWS and its fraternal rival, Co-operative Retail Services, moved jointly to deny the rumours of a sale and to repel boarders. Andrew Regan and his Lanica Trust did not get their hands on the Co-op. And that was that.

Or was it? With hindsight, the attentions of a City wheeler-dealer might have done the Co-operative movement a lot of good. 'Even though no bid was mounted,' says wine development manager, Dr Arabella Woodrow, 'it pushed us into the public eye. We were headline news in the business press and there was an outcry from people who didn't want the Co-op to be taken over by asset-strippers. It focused attention on the benefits of the Co-op.'

It also focused attention on the continuing stand-off between CWS and CRS. There has been talk of a merger between these two sizeable chunks of the Co-operative movement for some time, but as yet no real progress. When will it happen? You tell us. We've been asking the same question for four years now, every time, in fact, that we try to get our brains round the sprawling structure of the Co-op. According to CWS's chief executive, Graham Melmoth, much quoted at takeover speculation time, 'It will happen, the question is just when. I have a sense that the pace will quicken over the next year or so.'

Let's hope so. When it does happen, we won't have to explain how the Co-op works. For the time being, things are as complicated as ever. As we explained last year, and the year before that, the Co-op is an umbrella organisation for 51 different co-operative societies, with a geographical spread from Anglia to the Channel Islands and from the Midlands to the Borders. The biggest of these societies is CWS, which is strong everywhere but Wales, south-west England and central Manchester.

Still with us? Right. Dr Arabella Woodrow and Paul Bastard, group product manager, buy the wines for CWS Retail and an extended body of independent co-ops, known as the Co-operative Retail Trading Group (CRTG) and formed in 1993, but do not necessarily buy for other parts of the co-operative movement. CRS is a rival organisation, whose fascias used to include Leo's, Lo-cost and Pioneer, but have now been simplified under a single, ultra-catchy name, Co-operative. This combines 'the Society's 180-strong food superstore proposition', as well as its 270 convenience stores.

So independent is CRS, in fact, that it has its own dynamic new wine buyer, Angus Clark, and a rapidly improving wine list. (We were particularly intrigued by a Spanish sticky billed in a press release as Don Cortex Sweet White.) So much so that we aim to give Pioneer its own entry next year, if no rapprochement has taken place by then.

How do you know who bought the wine range in your local co-op? By default, effectively. CWS buys for 1,300 of the overall 2,500 stores, but doesn't really advertise the fact. Co-operative Pioneer, on the other hand, is forcefully branded. Unfortunately, things are never quite as clear-cut as they seem at the Co-op. CRS buys wines from CWS, you see, but not vice-versa. 'We're three times as big as they are. They wouldn't have the same buying power without us,' says Paul Bastard. This is true, especially for Co-op own-label wines. But guess what? CRS is in the process of introducing its own Co-operative-branded wines to replace them.

Good, now we've got that out of the way, we can get on with telling you about the wine range. But not before we ask what exactly are the 'benefits' of which Arabella Woodrow speaks. Paul Bastard is proud to answer the question: 'We're not a collection of superstores in profitable areas; we try to be all things to all men. If the Co-op disappeared, a lot of small shops in small communities would go. People would be left with absolutely nothing.'

This is all very admirable, but the size, shape and structure of the Co-op are decidedly old-fashioned. A bit of rationalisation, not to mention someone to knock a few stubborn heads together, might not be a bad thing. Even Bastard acknowledges that the Co-op has dawdled in the dynamism stakes. 'In the 1950s we had 25 per cent of the grocery business. Now it's down to 7 per cent. We didn't re-invent ourselves. There's been a certain unwillingness to change and break with our traditions.' The other problem is that, as Woodrow puts it: 'The Co-op is not really a national company. It's fragmented. The movement is national, but local co-ops have their own identity. That's how the Co-op was born.'

Now the Co-op has been pricked into action. 'We've got to attack as never before,' says Bastard. Naturally, that attack includes wine, which accounts for roughly 6 per cent of the Co-operative movement's turnover. Refurbishments are under way in the best sites, and beers, wines and spirits (as well as newspapers) have an increased role to play in this brave new co-operative world. 'We're going down the convenience route,' says Woodrow.

Part of the plan is to steer customers away from the Co-op's rather boring top ten best-sellers. 'We're going to offer a wider selection, even in our smaller stores,' adds Woodrow. 'There'll be a decent Chardonnay, a claret and a Champagne as well as the top ten.' The problem facing Woodrow and Bastard is not unique: how do you fit a 560-strong range of wines into one square metre of shelf space? The answer is that you don't, unless you smash the bottles with a hammer first.

The new convenience range, as it's known, should run to 115 wines. This means that one of our criticisms – that the best bits of the range didn't filter down to the smaller neighbourhood stores – is being addressed, slowly. 'People get frightened if you change too radically,' says Woodrow. 'You need through-put to whiz the wines through.'

As it stands, the Co-op wine range is a rather strange animal. There are enough interesting and well-sourced wines to interest the most committed imbiber. We were impressed by brave and pretty idiosyncratic listings, such as Neethlingshof Gewürztraminer from the Cape, an unoaked Madeleine

Angevine from Sharpham Vineyard in England, Cooper's Creek Oak-Aged Semillon from New Zealand, a Romanian Merlot and Segada Branco, a Portuguese white from the Ribatejo.

So, no complaints on that score. The area that does concern us, however, is the Co-op's own-labels, the stuff that accounts for 50 per cent of sales. Woodrow rightly points out that 'Four years ago we had a basic range with no frills. We've changed that, but there's still a maintenance job to be done on own-label.' Our own feeling is that an overhaul would be closer to what's required.

The problem, in our view, can be put down to poor UK bottling. Of the Co-op's 170 own-label wines, 50 or so are bottled in Irlam, on the outskirts of Manchester, by contract bottlers with whom the Co-op has a supplier agreement until 1999. Not all the Irlam wines taste dull and fruitless, but too many seem to suffer from an industrial approach to bottling.

Some of the better own-label wines are a tribute to Woodrow's love of puns and word-play: Bad Tempered Cyril, Fair Martina, Rougir Syrah and Hungaroo all sound like clues to a cryptic crossword. They're also very good wines, which, significantly in our view, are not bottled here.

If it could sort out the bottom end of the range, the Co-op would be in a strong position. The buyers have added 100 new wines in the last year, concentrating on Chile, Argentina, new-wave Germany, France and Italy. Paul Bastard is particularly excited about the renaissance of the Old World. 'The Old World gives you better length of flavour at the same price as the New World. It's developed away from austere, fruitless wines.' The Old World still dominates sales, with 28 per cent from France, 16 per cent from Germany and more than 10 per cent from both Italy and Spain.

The Co-op has also shown that it's not afraid to court controversy. Earlier this year it got hold of a large parcel (60,000 cases, allegedly) of Moët & Chandon Champagne from the Continent and sold it at the knock-down, but perfectly legal price of £14.99, £5 cheaper than in the rest of the high street. Sales (and the accompanying publicity) were so good that the Co-op went back for a second helping.

The ensuing brouhaha forced Moët to drop its UK price by £1 to £18.99, which can only be good news for the consumer. Moët wasn't happy, but wine drinkers were. Somehow the move seemed true to the updated spirit of the Rochdale pioneers who founded the Co-operative movement 150 years ago. A drop of Champagne socialism at the Co-op? We reckon it's rather appropriate in Tony Blair's New Labour Britain.

White

Under £3

BULGARIA

1996 Preslav Chardonnay/Sauvignon Blanc, £2.99   14/20
Dry 🍬🍬🍬 🍾
Modern, well-made, refreshingly lemony Bulgarian blend of Sauvignon Blanc and Chardonnay, the world's two most popular varieties.

GERMANY

Co-op Hock Deutscher Tafelwein, £2.69   11/20
Medium sweet 🍾
Musty, sulphurous and sweet. Probably worse than the slightly more expensive Lieb below.

Co-op Liebfraumilch, Rheinhessen, £2.85   12/20
Medium sweet 🍬 🍾
A confected German mish-mash of a wine, with a bit of grapey fruit and tart acidity.

ITALY

Co-op Lambrusco Bianco, £1.99   12/20
Sweet 🍬 🍾
Baked and sweet. A fizzy Italian alco-pop, which falls a bit flat on the finish.

£3–5

ARGENTINA

1996 La Rural Chardonnay, £4.49   14/20
Off-dry 🍬 🍾
Sweetish, well-made Argentine Chardonnay from the Catena Group. A bit pricey, given that the same operation also makes the superior Alamos Ridge Chardonnay for £4.99.

AUSTRALIA

Angove's Butterfly Sauvignon/Chenin Blanc, £3.89   14/20
Dry 🍷🍷 ▮
A ripe, tropical fruity quaffer from the reliable Angove's winery in the Riverland. Plenty of flavour and good balance, especially at this price from Australia.

CHILE

1996 Long Slim Chardonnay/Semillon, £3.49   14/20
Dry 🍷🍷 ▮
A smartly packaged, unoaked Chilean blend with fresh acidity and peachy fruit. Nicely balanced.

ENGLAND

Summerhill Dry, £4.49   14/20
Dry 🍷 ▮
From David Cowderoy, one of England's star winemakers (not hard, mind you), this is a light, refreshing, aptly named quaffing white with hedgerow-fruit character and crispness. It's 50 pence cheaper at Victoria Wine.

1996 Co-op Dart Valley, £4.99   15/20
Dry 🍷🍷 ▮
An unusual, oak-aged Madeleine Angevine from the Sharpham Vineyard, showing fresh, lemony fruit and spicy complexity.

FRANCE

Chardonnay/Viognier, Vin de Pays de Vaucluse, £3.49   15/20
Dry 🍷🍷🍷 ▮
A full, fruity southern Rhône blend with apricoty fruit and a tangy aftertaste, made from France's two trendiest grapes. It's good to see French co-operatives making wines like this.

Co-op Bordeaux Sauvignon Blanc, £3.49   12/20
Dry ▮
Nettley, high-acid Bordeaux white. Bog-standard stuff.

1996 Château Pierrousselle Blanc, Entre-Deux-Mers, £3.99   14/20
Dry 👜👜 🍶
For 50 pence more, you can buy a bottle of this grassy, herbal blend of Semillon and Sauvignon Blanc. No contest, squire.

1994 Monbazillac, Domaine du Haut-Rauly, half-bottle, £3.99
15/20
Sweet 👜👜👜 🍶
Attractively priced, south-west French sticky in a mini-Sauternes mould (as it were), with honey and apricot richness and a touch of noble botrytis.

1996 Fleur du Moulin Chardonnay, Vin de Pays d'Oc, £4.29   14/20
Dry 👜👜 🍶
Well-made, if formulaic, Languedoc Chardonnay with buttery fruit, fresh acidity and a hint of oak, from Domaines Virginie in Béziers.

GERMANY

1996 Lone Wolf Vineyards, £4.99   15/20
Dry 👜👜 🍶
One of a growing number of drier, new-wave German whites and also one of the best. A fruit-salad Baden blend made by Aussie Nick Butler. Should make you howl with pleasure.

HUNGARY

1995 Hungaroo Sauvignon Blanc, £3.89   15/20
Dry 👜👜👜 🍶
Grapefruity, ultra-modern Hungarian Sauvignon Blanc from the Neszmely winery, with zesty acidity, good balance and freshness. Hard to beat under £4.

ITALY

1996 Co-op Frascati Superiore, £3.69   14/20
Dry 👜👜 🍶
Gassy, nutty, buttery Frascati with an almondy twist.

NEW ZEALAND

1996 Terrace View Sauvignon Blanc, Kemblefield, £3.99 14/20
Bone dry 👜👜 ❘
Assertive, green-bean-like New Zealand Sauvignon Blanc from Hawkes Bay, with nettley fruit and crisp acidity. Well priced for a Kiwi white.

PORTUGAL

1996 Segada Branco, Vinho Regional Ribatejo, £3.99 16/20
Dry 👜👜👜 ❘
A Ribatejo blend of Fernão Pires and Tallia grapes, this is a really interesting new-wave white from winemaker José Neiva, with a tangy, citrus-peel fruitiness and mouth-filling weight and flavour.

1995 Fiuza Chardonnay, Vinho Regional Ribatejo, £4.99 15/20
Dry 👜👜👜 ❘
Rich, butterscotchy, southern Portuguese Chardonnay made by Aussie Peter Bright, with toasty oak complexity and warming alcohol.

SOUTH AFRICA

1996 Long Mountain Semillon/Chardonnay, £3.99 13/20
Dry 👜 ❘
Made in South Africa by Orlando's winemaker, Robin Day, this is a soft, buttery, unoaked blend with rather neutral flavours.

£5–8

CHILE

1995 Viña Casablanca Chardonnay/Sauvignon Blanc, £5.99 16/20
Dry 👜👜👜 ❘
From the cool-climate Casablanca Valley close to the Pacific Ocean, this is a richly oaked, pineapple and tropical citrus-fruit white with lots of flavour and zing.

GERMANY

1994 Bernkasteler Badstube Riesling Kabinett, Von Kesselstatt, £6.99   16/20
Medium dry 🍾🍾🍾 |
A featherweight Mosel Riesling from one of the region's most dynamic producers. Crisply refreshing and juicy, with a touch of honeyed bottle development.

NEW ZEALAND

1996 Cooper's Creek Oak-Aged Semillon, Gisborne, £5.99   15/20
Dry 🍾🍾 |
Zippy, herbaceous New Zealand Semillon, which could easily be mistaken for Sauvignon Blanc, showing well-handled oak and good, gooseberry fruit definition.

SOUTH AFRICA

1996 Neetlingshof Gewürztraminer, £5.99   16/20
Dry 🍾🍾🍾 |
If you thought all South African whites were baked and full-flavoured, try this elegantly spicy, almost delicate Cape Gewürz, with fresh acidity and restrained lychee fruitiness.

SPAIN

1996 Albacora Verdejo/Chardonnay, £5.49   16/20
Dry 🍾🍾🍾 |
A barrel-fermented blend of Spain's Verdejo with the globe-trotting Chardonnay, this is a spicy, modern, ripe pear-like white with plenty of concentration and subtle oak.

UNITED STATES

1995 Hedges Fumé/Chardonnay, £6.59   14/20
Dry 🍾 |
A Washington State medley of mainly Sauvignon Blanc with 30 per cent Chardonnay, this is a weighty Columbia Valley white with an apple-core note.

Red

Under £3

ARGENTINA

Mission Peak Red, La Agricola, £2.99   14/20
Medium-bodied 🍶🍶🍶 |
A juicy, well-priced Argentine blend of Bonarda, Sangiovese and Malbec from the modern La Agricola winery. Robustly fruity stuff.

BULGARIA

1996 Plovdiv Cabernet Sauvignon/Rubin, £2.99   14/20
Medium-bodied 🍶🍶🍶 |
An unusual, grassy Bulgarian blend made in an approachable style for early drinking.

ITALY

Co-op Vino da Tavola Rosso, £2.99   13/20
Medium-bodied 🍶🍶 |
Heady, southern Italian quaffer with herbal undertones and raisiny fruit flavours. Decent plonk.

SOUTH AFRICA

Co-op Cape Red, £2.99   13/20
Light-bodied 🍶🍶 |
Soft, light, thirst-quenching, redcurranty Cape red at a good price. A decent barbie, or rather braai, red.

SPAIN

1994 Marqués de la Sierra Garnacha, Calatayud, £2.99   13/20
Full-bodied 🍶🍶 |
Chewy, traditional Garnacha with a pruney note. Needs a leg of lamb and possibly a side of beef, too.

£3–5

ARGENTINA

1996 Balbi Vineyards Malbec, £3.99 14/20
Full-bodied 👜👜 🍷
Robustly savoury, full-bodied Argentine Malbec with smoky oak character and juicy liquorice and blackcurrant flavours.

AUSTRALIA

Co-op Australian Red, £3.29 13/20
Medium-bodied 👜👜 🍷
Simple, juicy, well-priced Aussie red with squashy raspberry fruit and a splinter or two of oak character.

1995 Hunters Cellars Night Harvest, £4.99 13/20
Medium-bodied 🍷
Sweetly confected, strawberry jam and ginger-spicy red with a minty undertone. Why did they pick at night, we wonder?

CHILE

1994 Long Slim Cabernet/Merlot, £3.49 14/20
Medium-bodied 👜👜 🍷
Soft, easy-drinking Chilean blend bottled in the UK to keep the price down. Great name and label.

1996 Viña Gracia Merlot, £3.49 15/20
Medium-bodied 👜👜👜 🍷
Supple, juicy, vibrantly blackcurranty red made for uncomplicated glugging.

1995 Four Rivers Cabernet Sauvignon, £3.99 14/20
Medium-bodied 👜 🍷
Slightly coarser, blackcurrant pastille-like Cabernet Sauvignon with chunky, dry tannins.

1996 La Palma Cabernet/Merlot Reserve, £4.99 16/20
Medium-bodied 👜👜👜 🍷
From the excellent La Rosa winery, this is a smoky oaky, vanilla-like, Bordeaux-style blend with attractive, almost Old World fruit flavours.

FRANCE

Co-op Corbières Rouge, £3.09 13/20
Medium-bodied 🍷🍷 🍾
Supple, lightly peppery southern French red with surprisingly high acidity. Built for robust foods.

Co-op Vin de Pays d'Oc Merlot/Cabernet, £3.59 12/20
Medium-bodied 🍾
Basic, chewy Languedoc blend, which leaves you groping for your toothbrush.

Co-op Oak-Aged Côtes du Rhône, £3.99 14/20
Medium-bodied 🍷 🍾
Soft, modern, easy-drinking Côtes du Rhône from Gabriel Meffre, which falls a little short on the palate.

1996 Château Pierrousselle Rouge, £4.59 15/20
Medium-bodied 🍷🍷 🍾
An attractively priced, pencilly Bordeaux with green-pepper flavours and firmish tannins. As good as its white counterpart.

GREECE

1996 Epsilon St George Cabernet Sauvignon, £4.49 12/20
Full-bodied 🍾
Great label; great name; baked wine. Beta minus.

HUNGARY

1994 Chapel Hill Cabernet Sauvignon, Balatonboglar, £3.49 13/20
Light-bodied 🍷 🍾
Not to be confused with Pam Dunsford's Aussie winery of the same name, this is a typically light, pleasantly peppery Cabernet Sauvignon with tart acidity.

ITALY

1995 Piccini Sangiovese di Toscana, £3.49 14/20
Medium-bodied 🍷🍷 🍾
A thirst-quenching Tuscan rosso made from Chianti's Sangiovese grape, with cherry fruitiness and rustic tannins.

1995 Co-op Montepulciano d'Abruzzo, £3.49   14/20
Full-bodied 👜👜 🍷

A robust, tobaccoey, thickly fruity Montepulciano red from the Girelli winery. Well made.

1995 Co-op Chianti, £3.99   14/20
Medium-bodied 👜👜 🍷

Pleasant, savoury, cherryish Chianti. A good pasta quaffer.

NEW ZEALAND

1995 Terrace View Cabernet Sauvignon/Merlot, £3.99   15/20
Light-bodied 👜👜👜 🍷

The second label of Hawkes Bay winery, Kemblefield, this is a light, well-priced, strawberry fruity blend with nice elegance.

PORTUGAL

1995 Portada Tinto, Vinho Regional Estremadura, £3.99   14/20
Medium-bodied 👜👜 🍷

From well-travelled winemaker José Neiva, this is a lightish, heftily oaked, southern Portuguese red with spicy, berry fruit and cinnamon notes.

1994 Star Mountain Oak-Aged, Vinho Regional Beiras, £4.49 15/20
Full-bodied 👜👜 ➡

A blend of Touriga Nacional and Tinta Roriz, two of the main Port grapes, this is a burly, broad-shouldered red, which takes no prisoners. Needs time to soften.

ROMANIA

1994 Sahateni Barrel-Matured Merlot, £4.49   15/20
Medium-bodied 👜👜👜 🍷

Stylishly packaged in a designer bottle and made by Aussie Graham Dixon, this is easily the best Romanian red we've tasted, with sweet vanilla oak, plenty of blackcurrant fruit and succulent tannins. Shows the potential is there.

SOUTH AFRICA

1996 Cape Indaba Merlot, £4.49   14/20
Medium-bodied 👜👜 🍷

Sweet, supple, if slightly confected, plummy Cape red, which tastes more like Pinotage than Merlot.

1995 De Leuwen Jagt Shiraz, £4.49   15/20
Medium-bodied 💰💰💰 🍾
Oaky, but concentrated Cape Shiraz with great blackberry fruit, firm tannins and a lengthy finish.

1996 Jacana Cabernet Sauvignon, £4.99   15/20
Medium-bodied 💰💰 🍾
Made by Englishman Hugh Ryman, this is an ambitious, oak-saturated Cape Cabernet with enough cassis and plum fruitiness for balance. Impressive stuff.

SPAIN

Co-op Tempranillo Oak-Aged, Utiel Requena, £3.29   13/20
Medium-bodied 💰 🍾
From the Spanish Levante, this is a coconut and strawberry confection, which reminds us of Don Darias and other Dons of that ilk.

1995 Marco Real Merlot/Syrah, £3.99   14/20
Medium-bodied 💰💰 🍾
A refreshing, well-balanced Navarra red with attractive black-cherry fruit.

UNITED STATES

Co-op California Red, £3.39   14/20
Medium-bodied 💰💰 🍾
Deeply coloured, softly fruity Californian red from the pressure cooker of the San Joaquin Valley, with some pleasant fruit flavours. One of the best West Coast cheapies.

£5–8

FRANCE

1994 Morgon Les Charmes, Domaine Brisson, £6.99   16/20
Medium-bodied 💰💰 🍾
From Gérard Brisson's excellent Morgon domaine, this is a spicy, cherryish, oak-matured Gamay made in a refreshing, but traditional style.

SOUTH AFRICA

1996 Fairview Pinotage, £5.99 15/20
Full-bodied 💰💰 🍷
If you've never tasted South Africa's most characterful local grape, buy a bottle of this chocolatey, nicely oaked example with a typically wild edge.

UNITED STATES

1994 Fetzer Eagle Peak Merlot, £6.99 15/20
Full-bodied 🍷 🍷
From Mendocino County's Fetzer winery, this is a rich, tobaccoey Merlot with lots of sweet, spicy oak and marked acidity.

Over £8

NEW ZEALAND

1995 Babich Mara Syrah, £8.99 15/20
Medium-bodied 🍷 🍷
One of New Zealand's few Syrahs, this is an oaky, deeply coloured Hawkes Bay red, which doesn't quite go the distance.

Rosé

£3–5

FRANCE

Rougir Syrah, Vin de Pays d'Oc, £3.49 14/20
Dry 🍷🍷🍷 🍷
Rougir is French for blush (geddit?), but this clean, fresh, raspberry fruity Syrah rosé has no need to.

Sparkling

£3–5

SPAIN

Co-op Cava Brut, £4.99   13/20
Bone dry 🥂 ▯
Very youthful, crisp-apple Spanish sparkler with a lean streak of acidity and a
very dry finish.

Over £8

AUSTRALIA

Brown Brothers Pinot Noir/Chardonnay, £9.99   16/20
Dry 🥂🥂🥂 ▯
From Victoria's King Valley, this is an elegant, creamy, well-made fizz with the
complexity of bottle-aged maturity and good fruit quality.

FRANCE

De Bracieux Champagne, £11.99   15/20
Dry 🥂🥂 ▯
Sweetish, big-bubbled Champagne with rich, malty flavours and a lively tang of
acidity. Very commercial.

Fuller's ☆☆☆☆(☆)

Address: Griffin Brewery, Chiswick Lane South, London W4 2QB

Telephone/fax: 0181 996 2000; 0181 996 2087

Number of branches: 72

Opening hours: 10.00am to 10.00pm Monday to Saturday; 11.00am to 10.00pm Sunday

Credit cards accepted: Access, Switch, Visa

Discounts: One free bottle with every unmixed case; 10 per cent off a case at the Brewery Store

Facilities and services: Glass loan with 50 pence deposit per glass; free home delivery locally and nationally from the Brewery Store on case orders (tel. 0181 996 2085); in-store Saturday tastings

Special Offers: See discounts

Top ten best-selling wines: Tocornal Chardonnay; Bright Brothers Argentine Red; Nottage Hill Chardonnay; Brossault Brut Non Vintage Champagne; 1996 Winter Hill White; 1996 Winter Hill Red; Bright Brothers Argentine White; Errázuriz Sauvignon Blanc; Jacob's Creek Semillon/Chardonnay; Fat Bastard Chardonnay

Range:

GOOD: Bordeaux, Rhône, Burgundy, Loire, regional France, Spain, New Zealand, Australia, Chile, Champagne and sparkling wines

AVERAGE: Bordeaux, Beaujolais, Portugal, Italy, Eastern Europe, United States, Argentina, South Africa

POOR: None

UNDER-REPRESENTED: Alsace, Germany

It's been three years since Roger 'Higgsy' Higgs rollerbladed into the Griffin Brewery, Fuller's hop-scented riverside HQ, bringing the enthusiasm and buying nous that you'd expect from a former Oddbins employee to a well-run, if traditional, family-owned company. They must still wonder what's hit them down in Chiswick.

Higgs' first move was to taste his way through the existing Fuller's wines and carry out a few summary executions (farewell to a group of Greek wines), but by his own admission it has taken time to create a range that fully reflects his own tastes. 'You can't change these things overnight, even if you'd like to. You've got to consider your customers, your staff and the availability of the wines you'd like to buy.'

Nowadays, the 600-strong wine range is 'pretty much where I want it to be', even if Higgs, like everyone else, is finding it harder and harder to source good wine in the face of competition from America, Scandinavia and the Far East. 'The Americans have discovered Australia and they're buying shed-loads from Chile, too. The Far East has gone crazy over the 1996 Bordeaux crus classés. And the Scandinavians are buying from Australia, Chile, Argentina and South Africa and they don't seem to be too fussy about how much they pay, either.'

It's a seller's market out there. Yet Higgs has still managed to chivvy, cajole and charm hundreds of winemakers into supplying Fuller's with one of the best ranges in Britain, a competitively priced line-up of goodies from the New and Old Worlds, with particular strengths in France, Australia, Chile and Spain. At first, people mentioned the resemblance to Oddbins – a number of wines popped up in both chains – but not any longer. 'We've got similar customers and target markets, but there's no point in being a me-too Oddbins,' says Higgs.

Higgs' three years in Chiswick have coincided with – some might say been instrumental in – an upturn in the fortunes of Fuller's wine shops. The chain has won awards, changed its appearance, increased its profits and acquired prominent high-street sites in the swisher bits of west and central London. It's also opened the Brewery Store as a wine showcase.

This has happened against a background of declining high-street sales. Higgs was saddened by the demise of Davisons, a former member with Unwins and Fuller's of the amusingly named Leonard Tong buying group, but says that 'You've got to invest in your shops and they didn't.' There appears to be no such problem at Fuller's. In the last year it has opened new stores in Dorking, Wimbledon, Cornhill and Parson's Green and closed four smaller 'corner offies' in less salubrious locations.

The old distinction between Gold, Silver and Bronze stores has gone too, to be replaced by London Stores (30 per cent of the estate), Wine Stores (50 per cent) and Community Stores (20 per cent), depending on location and, to a certain degree, demography. If you live near a Community Store, you might not have access to the full range. 'Managers can buy what they want,' says Higgs, 'but customer profile and turnover do come into it. Community Stores tend to sell cheaper wines.'

Higgs believes that 'The convenience off-licence is dead, because supermarkets are just as convenient', but feels that a chain like Fuller's can still compete. 'There are certain things the supermarkets can't do, like special purchases and personal service. But we've got to offer customers more than the classic off-licence range. Why should anyone make a special trip to Fuller's to buy a bottle of Jacob's Creek?'

Fuller's certainly doesn't have a problem selling higher-priced wines than the supermarkets. In its best branches, such as Old Brompton Road, Fulham Road and South Kensington, the average spend on wine is over £6 a bottle. Even in its least profitable store, dubbed 'Fort Apache' by Higgs, the comparable figure is £3.88. 'There are a lot of people out there who want something more than £2.99 wines reduced to £2.49 in a wine fair. Cheap wines encourage people to buy a bottle, not to drink wine.'

This is not to say that Higgs has eschewed £2.99 wines. In fact, he's got some very tasty numbers from Argentina at the lower end of the price spectrum. Still, if you look at the best-selling wines at Fuller's, cheapness does not appear to be customers' primary concern when they buy Fat Bastard Chardonnay or Errázuriz Sauvignon Blanc.

What else do Fuller's customers drink? The answer is mainly French, Australian and South American wines, the parts of the world that seem to interest Higgs most of all. France, in particular, has made a come-back this year, thanks to the hugely improved exchange rate and some good to very good vintages in 1995 and 1996. 'The new exchange rate,' according to Higgs, 'makes the difference between a wine selling at £5.49 and £4.99.' It's also significant that regional France accounts for at least half of Gallic wine sales.

Higgs is still the big noise around the Griffin Brewery, but this year he's taken on a buying assistant, Louis Finan, from the marketing department. This has enabled him to travel to South America and France. He's also found time to compose 'Higgsy's Hints' in Griffin, the quarterly in-house magazine: 'sharper than a hedgehog's pointy bits and as kind to your wallet as a slow buff with a soft cloth,' apparently.

He may need to take on someone else if the business continues to expand towards its target of 100 stores. The shops are bringing in good money – 23 per cent of Fuller's turnover and 10 per cent of its profit – with sales up 13 per cent in the last year, according to Higgs. The other good news is that a selection of 40 Fuller's wines is also available in the company's 200 pubs. Higgs has 'total control' here and makes sure that the wines are Vacu-Vin'ed between servings.

What does the youthful Higgs have in store for us next? More specialisation is the answer. 'We want to become more and more niche,' he says, 'offering parcels as well as a good core range.' Concha y Toro's excellent Pinot Noir-Explorer was one such 500-case parcel snapped up by Higgs on a trip to South America. There will also, in due course, be 1995 clarets bought en primeur and offered, Oddbins-style, on the shelf.

Fuller's may still be better known as a brewer (access to a pint of London Pride is one of the boons of living in the capital), but the wine side of the business is catching up fast. And on rollerblades.

White

Under £3

ARGENTINA

1997 Bright Brothers Argentine White, Mendoza, £2.99   14/20
Dry 👜👜👜 |
A full, spicy, honeyed blend of Chenin Blanc and Torrontés made by the Aussie Peter Bright at the Peñaflor winery

FRANCE

1996 Winter Hill White, Vin de Pays de l'Aude, £2.99   13/20
Dry 👜👜 |
Clean, appley, uncomplicated white made by flying winemakers in the south of France. It's about time they dropped the 'French Wine Made by Australians' tag. After all, there's nothing much to be proud of.

HUNGARY

1996 Eagle Mountain Irsai Oliver, £2.99   15/20
Dry 👜👜👜 |
Perfumed, floral, crisply fruity, rose-petal-style white from Hungary's go-ahead Neszmely co-operative. Hard to do much better than this at £2.99.

£3–5

ARGENTINA

1996 La Rural Pinot Blanc, £3.99   15/20
Dry 👜👜👜 |
Soft, peachy, well-balanced Argentine white from the Catena group. A good alternative to Chardonnay from an impressive, well-funded operation.

1995 Alamos Ridge Chardonnay, £4.99   16/20
Dry 🍷🍷🍷 ▮
Modern, pineappley Argentine Chardonnay with a shade of toasty oak.
Another attractive wine from the Catena group. A great restaurant wine.

AUSTRALIA

1995 Lonsdale Ridge Colombard, £3.99   15/20
Dry 🍷🍷🍷 ▮
Lemon- and lime-like Victorian Colombard with fresh acidity and lots of flavour.
One of the few Aussie whites that's worth seeking out under £4.

1996 Jackdaw Ridge Semillon/Chardonnay, £3.99   14/20
Dry 🍷🍷 ▮
Clean, refreshing, if slightly neutral Aussie blend of Semillon and Chardonnay
with a grapefruity twist. Decent, honest drinking.

1995 Nottage Hill Riesling, £4.99   15/20
Dry 🍷🍷 ▮
Toffee-apple and petrol-scented Riesling, which is starting to develop some
interesting bottle-aged characters. More interesting than the Chardonnay but
much harder to sell, apparently.

CHILE

1996 La Palma Chardonnay, £3.99   15/20
Dry 🍷🍷🍷 ▮
Buttery, citrus fruity Chilean Chardonnay from the La Rosa winery. One of the
best Chardonnays in the world at this price.

1996 Concha y Toro Gewürztraminer, £3.99   14/20
Dry 🍷🍷 ▮
There aren't many Gewürztraminers made in Chile, but this dry, spicy, well-
defined wine is a highly enjoyable example of the ultra-floral, tart's window-box
grape of Alsace.

1996 Valdivieso Chardonnay, £4.49   15/20
Dry 🍷🍷🍷 ▮
Broad, toffeeish Chilean Chardonnay with ripe melon and vanilla oak flavours,
from a winery that knows how to provide value for money.

1996 Errázuriz Sauvignon Blanc, £4.99   16/20
Dry 👜👜👜 ▪

Fresh, grapefruity Chilean Sauvignon Blanc from the cool-climate Casablanca Valley, midway in style between the crispness of the Loire Valley and the pungency of Marlborough in New Zealand.

FRANCE

1996 La Parterre Sauvignon, Vin de Pays du Jardin de la France, £3.49   15/20
Dry 👜👜👜 ▪

A fresh, nettley, deeply flavoursome Loire Sauvignon Blanc, made by an Australian flying winemaker. Crisp and stylish. The wine, that is.

1996 Berticot Sauvignon, Côtes de Duras, £3.99   15/20
Dry 👜👜👜 ▪

Citrus fruity, spritzy, south-west French Sauvignon Blanc with good length of flavour. One to worry the New Zealanders?

1996 Domaine des Martin Terret/Sauvignon Blanc, Vin de Pays d'Oc, £3.99   14/20
Dry 👜👜 ▪

A soft, juicy Languedoc blend of the local Terret (better known as the grape behind vermouth) and Sauvignon Blanc, from the well-travelled Jacques Lurton. Pleasant, if one-dimensional.

1996 Château Haut-Grelot, Bordeaux, Premières Côtes de Blaye, £4.99   16/20
Dry 👜👜👜 ▪

An excellent follow-up to last year's *Grapevine* award winner. A zingy, grapefruity Bordeaux white with an attractively mealy texture.

1996 Bourgogne Chardonnay, Joseph Bertrand, £4.99   15/20
Dry 👜👜 ▪

Clean, well-made Burgundian Chardonnay with citrusy acidity and good zip. At long last Burgundian winemakers seem to be waking up to the challenge of the New World.

1996 Château Lacroix, Bordeaux Blanc, £4.99   15/20
Dry 👜👜 ▪

Toasty, stylish, barrel-fermented Bordeaux white dominated by the Semillon grape. Soft, peachy and well made. Another impressive Bordeaux Blanc.

ITALY

1996 Sauvignon Blanc Pecile, Grave del Friuli, £4.75   16/20
Dry 🍾🍾🍾 ▮

Juicy, mouth-watering Sauvignon Blanc from the Grave del Friuli winery at a
wonderful price. The package looks really stylish, too.

1996 Pinot Grigio Pecile, Grave del Friuli, £4.79   15/20
Dry 🍾🍾🍾 ▮

Friuli in north-east Italy makes some of the country's best and priciest white
wines, which makes this apple- and pear-like Pinot Grigio another steal at
under £5.

SOUTH AFRICA

1997 First Cape Chenin Blanc, £3.49   14/20
Dry 🍾🍾 ▮

Pear-drop and angelica spice-scented Cape Chenin made for early drinking by
Aussie Master of Wine and Air Miles specialist, Kym Milne.

1996 Jacana Old Bush Vine Chenin, £4.99   15/20
Dry 🍾🍾 ▮

Textured, mealy, old-vine Cape Chenin with sweet, toasty oak from Englishman
Hugh Ryman. Almost Chardonnay-like, which may or may not be a good thing.

SPAIN

1996 Castillo de Montblanc Chardonnay, £3.99   14/20
Dry 🍾🍾 ▮

Light, cool-climate Spanish Chardonnay with added oak character from Hugh
'Grant' Ryman, the thinking woman's flying winemaker.

1996 Nekeas Barrel Fermented Chardonnay, £4.99   16/20
Dry 🍾🍾🍾 ▬

From one of Navarra's most exciting modern wineries, this is a smoky, stylishly
oaked Chardonnay with elegant melon and citrus-fruit notes.

£5–8

ARGENTINA

1995 Catena Chardonnay Agrelo Vineyard, £7.99   17/20
Dry 👜👜👜 ▮

Rich, tropical, mouth-filling Argentine Chardonnay with oak, fruit and acidity in lovely balance. Among the best whites from South America.

AUSTRALIA

1996 Katnook Sauvignon, Coonawarra, £7.99   17/20
Dry 👜👜👜 ➡

One of Australia's best Sauvignons (admittedly a pretty small field), this is a zingy, ripe gooseberry-flavoured white with generous length on the palate.

CHILE

1995 Valdivieso Reserve Chardonnay, £5.99   15/20
Dry 👜 ▮

Sweetish, toffee and vanilla fudge-like Chilean Chardonnay from the Valdivieso winery. A bit of a one-glass wine.

FRANCE

1995 Mâcon Davayé, Domaine des Deux Roches, £5.99   16/20
Dry 👜👜👜 ➡

From an excellent vintage for white Burgundy, this fresh, elegant, unoaked Chardonnay confirms this domaine's position as a top-notch producer of stylish Mâconnais.

1996 Fat Bastard Chardonnay, Vin de Pays d'Oc, £5.99   16/20
Dry 👜👜 ▮

A promising follow-up to last year's successful launch (bastard being a pun on Burgundy's Bâtard-Montrachet). Skilfully executed, barrel-fermented stuff with considerable flavour and elegance for a southern French Chardonnay.

GERMANY

1995 Serrig Herrenberg Riesling Kabinett, Bert Simon, £5.99
16/20

Medium dry 🍬🍬🍬 ▬

Juicy, peachy Mosel Riesling with a crisp tang of citrus acidity and a little bit of sweetness. Great value from Germany.

ITALY

1996 Carato Chardonnay Barrique Bidoli, £5.49   16/20
Dry 🍬🍬🍬 ▮

Elegant, toasty, green-olive-like Italian white fermented in oak barrels for extra complexity. Lovely stuff.

SOUTH AFRICA

1996 Fairview Chardonnay, £5.99   14/20
Dry 🍬 ▮

Pleasant, if over-oaked, Cape Chardonnay from wine and cheese specialist Charles Back, which lacks flavour on the finish.

1996 Neil Ellis Sauvignon Blanc, £6.99   16/20
Dry 🍬🍬🍬 ▮

Restrained, Sancerre-like Cape Sauvignon Blanc from the talented Neil Ellis, showing grassy undertones and plenty of class. Confirms the promise of the cool-climate Elgin region.

1996 Neil Ellis Chardonnay, £7.99   17/20
Dry 🍬🍬🍬 ▬

Another stylish white from Elgin, an area better known for apples than grapes, this is a fresh, lively Chardonnay with miles more elegance and flavour than most South African whites. Perfectly poised.

Over £8

AUSTRALIA

1995 Scotchman's Hill Chardonnay, Geelong, £9.99   16/20
Dry 👜👜 ▯
Oaky, developed, densely flavoured Victorian Chardonnay with crisp acidity, toffee-fudge characters and cool-climate elegance. Exciting stuff.

FRANCE

1995 Bourgogne Chardonnay, Ultra 35, £8.99   17/20
Bone dry 👜👜👜 ▬
Modern, stylishly packaged white Burgundy from Denis Philibert, with intense citrus-fruit flavours and sophisticated oak. Amazingly good for a Bourgogne Blanc.

1996 Coteaux du Layon Chaume, Domaine des Forges, £8.99
                                                            17/20

Sweet 👜👜👜 ▬
Sweet apple and honey-like Chenin Blanc with refreshing balancing acidity and good concentration. A heavenly, palate-coating sticky.

1996 Sancerre Cuvée Flores, Vincent Pinard, £9.49   18/20
Bone dry 👜👜👜 ▬
From the amusingly named Monsieur Pinard (French for plonk), this is a refreshing, richly flavoured Sauvignon Blanc with undertones of nettle and fruit. One of the best dry white Loires we've tasted in ages.

NEW ZEALAND

1996 Te Awa Farm Hawkes Bay Chardonnay, £8.95   16/20
Dry 👜👜 ▯
Toasty, elegant, well-made Hawkes Bay Chardonnay with butterscotch and citrus-fruit characters. Highly drinkable in a sub-Burgundian mould.

1996 Hunter's Sauvignon Blanc, Marlborough, £9.49   16/20
Dry 👜👜 ▬
Fresh, nettley, concentrated Marlborough Sauvignon Blanc from the charming Jane Hunter, OBE. A lot subtler than most in-your-face New Zealand whites.

1996 Sacred Hills Barrel Ferment Chardonnay, £9.99   17/20
Dry 🍶🍶🍶 ▬–

Stylish, buttery, nutmeg-scented Hawkes Bay Chardonnay from the eccentric Mason brothers. One of New Zealand's best Chardonnays, with none of the sweet-and-sour character that mars too many Kiwi examples of the world's most famous grape.

SOUTH AFRICA

1995 Bouchard Finlayson Kaimansgaat Chardonnay, £8.99   17/20
Dry 🍶🍶🍶 ▬–

A Franco-South African collaboration between Paul Bouchard of Bouchard Aîné and Peter Finlayson, this is one of South Africa's most exciting Chardonnays, showing texture, refreshing acidity and delicacy of flavour. And £4 cheaper at Fuller's than it is at Greenalls' Wine Cellar.

UNITED STATES

1995 Schug Carneros Chardonnay, £12.99   16/20
Dry 🍶 ▮

Buttery, appley California Chardonnay, which doesn't quite pull it off at nearly £13. At that sort of price Chardonnay has to be really exceptional to be good value.

Red

Under £3

ARGENTINA

1997 Bright Brothers Argentine Red, £2.99   13/20
Light-bodied 🍶 ▮

Light, strawberryish Argentine red blend from Aussie Peter Bright, working in the shadow of the Andes.

FRANCE

1996 Winter Hill Red, Vin de Pays de l'Aude, £2.99   14/20
Medium-bodied 👜👜👜 ❙
Supple, plummy, easy-drinking southern French red made in a Beaujolais mould.

£3–5

ARGENTINA

1996 Lurton Malbec, £3.99   14/20
Medium-bodied 👜 ❙
Youthful, rustic Mendoza Malbec made by Frenchman Jacques Lurton at the tongue-twisting Escorihuela winery. The tannins are a little raw at the moment.

AUSTRALIA

1996 Jackdaw Ridge Shiraz/Cabernet, £3.99   12/20
Medium-bodied ❙
Confected, smoky bacon-like Aussie red blend with a bitter medicinal finish. Australia could lose a lot of friends with wines like this.

1996 Peter Lehmann Grenache, Barossa Valley, £4.49   15/20
Full-bodied 👜👜 ❙
Sweetish, loganberry fruity Aussie Grenache with fresh acidity and plenty of warming alcohol. A good introduction to the throaty delights of the Barossa Valley.

CHILE

1996 La Palma Merlot, Rapel Valley, £3.99   15/20
Medium-bodied 👜👜👜 ❙
Juicy, green-pepper-like Chilean Merlot with supple tannins and good length of flavour. Very drinkable.

1996 Valdivieso Malbec, £4.49   16/20
Medium-bodied 👜👜👜 ❙
Savoury, chocolatey Chilean red with lots of colour, flavour and sweet mulberry fruit and a nice nip of tobaccoey tannins.

1996 La Palma Reserve Cabernet/Merlot, £4.99   15/20
Medium-bodied 👜👜👜 ⏤

Deeply coloured, plummy Bordeaux-style blend with refreshing acidity, coffee-bean oak and succulent tannins. Chile does this sort of thing better than anyone at present.

FRANCE

1996 Roq Dur Unfiltered Syrah, Vin de Pays d'Oc, £3.49   13/20
Full-bodied 👜 🍷

Rustic, blackberry fruity Languedoc Syrah with a plonky finish. Marginally better than queuing outside the Hard Rock Café.

1996 Château de Lancyre, Coteaux du Languedoc, £3.99   13/20
Full-bodied 👜 🍷

Basic, chewy, southern French rouge, which is a little disappointing for an appellation wine, especially from an up-and-coming region like the Languedoc.

1996 Touraine Gamay, Paul Buisse, £4.99   15/20
Medium-bodied 👜👜 🍷

Skittle-bottled Loire Gamay with summery, thirst-quenching acidity and more flavour than most Beaujolais at this price.

1996 Château Cazeneuve Terres Rouges, Pic St Loup, £4.99   14/20
Full-bodied 👜 🍷

Charry, faintly rustic Languedoc red, which needs time to open out.

ITALY

1995 Montepulciano d'Abruzzo Barrique La Luna Nuova
Casalbordino, £3.99   15/20
Medium-bodied 👜👜 🍷

Savoury, chocolatey, refreshing Abruzzo red made by Georgio Dalla Cia of South Africa's Meerlust estate. Characterful stuff.

SOUTH AFRICA

1996 First Cape Cinsault, £3.99   13/20
Full-bodied 👜 🍷

Lightly coloured, raisiny Cape plonk with an alcoholic punch.

SPAIN

1993 Viña Caliza Oak Aged Tempranillo, Valdepeñas, £3.99   14/20
Medium-bodied 🍷🍷 ▮

Perfumed, coconutty Valdepeñas red with attractive strawberry fruit and a dry, oaky finish. Poor man's Rioja Crianza.

1995 Berberana Oak Aged Tempranillo Rioja, £4.49   14/20
Medium-bodied 🍷 ▮

More tannic than in previous vintages, this is a chewy, wet woody Tempranillo with a sturdy finish.

1995 Enate Cabernet/Merlot, Somontano, £4.99   15/20
Medium-bodied 🍷🍷 ▮

The computer-loving Jesús Altajona has produced a spicy, refreshing, oak-aged Bordeaux-style blend, which promises a little more than it delivers.

1995 Marqués de Griñon Merlot, £4.99   14/20
Medium-bodied 🍷 ▮

Dry and oaky with a core of sweet cherry fruit and a faintly green, unripe edge.

£5–8

ARGENTINA

1995 Gran Lurton Cabernet Sauvignon, £6.99   15/20
Medium-bodied 🍷 ▮

Coarsely oaked Mendoza Cabernet Sauvignon from Jacques Lurton, where plummy, chocolatey fruit is overwhelmed by splinters.

AUSTRALIA

1995 Four Sisters Grenache, McLaren Vale, £5.99   15/20
Full-bodied 🍷🍷 ▮

Soft, peppery, fleshy McLaren Vale Grenache from Trevor Mast of Mount Langhi Giran. A good warm-climate glugger.

1993 Rouge Homme Coonawarra Shiraz/Cabernet, £5.99   16/20
Medium-bodied 🍷🍷 ▬

Stylish, cinnamon spicy Coonawarra blend with well-defined tannins and a green-pepper bite. Good value from Australia's leading red-wine region.

Fuller's

1996 Best's Victoria Shiraz, £6.99

16/20

Medium-bodied 👛👛 ➖

Elegant, minty, coolish-climate Victorian Shiraz with fine-grained tannins and attractive blackberry fruit richness.

1994 Rouge Homme Richardson's Red Block Coonawarra, £7.49

17/20

Medium-bodied 👛👛👛 ➖

A rich, aromatic blend of Cabernet Sauvignon, Merlot, Malbec and Cabernet Franc, with coffee-bean oak and refreshing cassis fruitiness.

CHILE

1995 Valdivieso Reserve Pinot Noir, £5.99

14/20

Medium-bodied ▮

Bitter, over-oaked Chilean Pinot, which has lost some of its fruit. You'd be better off buying the Merlot, Cabernet Franc (see below) or Malbec from the same winery.

1995 Casa Lapostolle Merlot, £5.99

16/20

Medium-bodied 👛👛👛 ➖

Sweetly perfumed, deeply hued Chilean Merlot made by Pomerol's Michel Rolland, with soft cassis fruit and medium-weight tannins.

1995 Valdivieso Reserve Cabernet Franc, £7.99

16/20

Medium-bodied 👛👛 ➖

Classy, well-oaked Chilean red made from the comparatively rare (well, west of the Andes, anyway) Cabernet Franc grape. Chile's answer to a good St Emilion.

FRANCE

1995 Château Les Pins, Côtes du Roussillon Villages, £5.99

16/20

Medium-bodied 👛👛 👛

Chocolatey, chewy, richly concentrated Roussillon red made in a modern, new oaky style in a region whose wines are improving by the vintage.

1996 Valréas Côtes du Rhône Villages, Domaine de la Grande Bellane, £5.99

15/20

Medium-bodied 👛 ▮

An organic southern Rhône blend of 75 per cent Syrah with 25 per cent Grenache, this is a lightish, spicy, peppery red with refreshing acidity.

1995 Château Ste Agnès, Pic St Loup, £6.99   16/20
Full-bodied 👜👜 ➡

Not quite as good as the stunning 1994, but this oaky, thickly tannic Languedoc red with its heady bouquet and alluring spice is still an exciting introduction to the delights of Pic St Loup.

1995 Château Lancyre, Grande Cuvée, Pic St Loup, £7.99   17/20
Full-bodied 👜👜👜 ➡

Another Pic St Loup throat-warmer, this time showing more aromatic Syrah character, blackberry fruit, chunky tannins and style. Concentrated essence of the Midi.

ITALY

1995 Villa Pigna, Colle Lungo, £5.99   16/20
Full-bodied 👜👜👜 ➡

A barrique-aged, old-vine Montepulciano with soft, plummy fruit, polished tannins and a sweet oak finish.

1995 Briccolo Cabernet del Friuli, S. Daniele, £5.99   15/20
Medium-bodied 👜👜 ▮

Grassy, elegant, cool-climate Cabernet from north-east Italy with an assertively oaky finish.

1994 La Luna E I Falò, Barbera d'Asti, £6.49   14/20
Full-bodied ▮

Chewy, rather extracted Italian red smothered by hefty, charry oak. Not as good as the book of the same name by Cesare Pavese.

PORTUGAL

1995 Quinta do Crasto Tinto, Douro, £5.75   16/20
Medium-bodied 👜👜👜 ➡

Stylish, modern Portuguese red with exuberant damson fruit and sweet, spicy oak, made by Australian David Baverstock from grapes that are normally used for Port.

SOUTH AFRICA

1995 Fairview Cabernet Franc/Merlot, £5.99   13/20
Full-bodied

Bitter, raisiny Cape Bordeaux-style blend with a hot-climate finish. An untypical lapse from Charles Back.

1995 Jacana Merlot, £6.99   16/20
Full-bodied 🍷🍷 ━

Rich, faintly Porty South African Merlot with sweet, charry oak, supple tannins and a core of blackcurrant fruit. One of a number of impressive wines under the Jacana label.

1995 Clos Malverne Auret Cabernet/Pinotage, £7.95   16/20
Full-bodied 🍷🍷 ━

A sagey, herbal-scented blend of Cabernet Sauvignon and Pinotage from one of the Cape's leading wineries, with wild strawberry fruit and attractive oak.

Over £8

AUSTRALIA

1992 Moyston Chalambar Shiraz, Seppelts, £8.49   15/20
Medium-bodied 🍷

Drying a little on the palate, but with enough blackberry fruit and sweet American oak to be worth a punt.

1995 Grant Burge Old Vine Shiraz, £8.99   17/20
Full-bodied 🍷🍷🍷 ━

Rich, spicy, smoky Barossa Valley Shiraz with a lovely core of sweet plum and blackberry fruitiness, from the experienced Grant Burge. The age of the vines is apparent in the wine's concentration.

1995 Scotchman's Hill Pinot Noir, Geelong, £9.99   15/20
Medium-bodied 🍷

Light, leafy, elegant, raspberry fruity Victorian Pinot Noir, which is slightly overshadowed by oak.

1990 Stonewell Shiraz, Peter Lehmann, £14.99   15/20
Full-bodied

Hefty, muscular Barossa Valley Shiraz with chunky, extracted tannins and masses of new oak. A bit four-square.

CHILE

Valdivieso Caballo Loco Number One, £9.99   16/20
Medium-bodied 👛👛 ▬

Powerful, oaky, broad-shouldered Chilean super-blend from one of South America's most impressive wineries. Needs at least another two years in bottle.

FRANCE

1994 Château Haut Bages Monpelou, Pauillac, £8.99   14/20
Medium-bodied ▮

Grassy, greenish, cru bourgeois claret from an overrated Bordeaux vintage.

1994 Château Grand Renouil, Canon Fronsac, £11.99   16/20
Medium-bodied 👛👛 ▬

From the same vintage, this is a green, malty, heftily oaked Right Bank claret with stylish fruit and a firm, dry finish. Should develop rather nicely over the next few years.

NEW ZEALAND

1995 Sacred Hill Basket Press Cabernet, £8.99   17/20
Medium-bodied 👛👛👛 ▬

An elegant, delicately minty Hawkes Bay Cabernet Sauvignon with finely judged tannins and subtle oak shading. Another winner from the Mason brothers.

1993 Enate Cabernet Sauvignon Reserva, Somontano, £9.99
                                                              16/20
Medium-bodied 👛👛 ▮

Firm, well-structured, stylishly labelled Spanish Cabernet Sauvignon from Somontano's Enate winery in the green foothills of the Pyrenees. Drink up.

SPAIN

1994 Marqués de Griñon Valdepusa Syrah, £8.99   16/20
Medium-bodied 👛👛 ▬

A little less polished than last year's spectacular effort, but this is still a brooding, chocolatey red with good richness and depth. It's also one of the few Syrahs made in Spain.

Rosé

£3–5

FRANCE

1996 Château Lacroix Merlot Rosé, Bordeaux, £4.99   15/20
Dry 🍷🍷 🍸
Made by an English winemaker at Château Teyssier, this Merlot-based rosé is a refreshing, summer-pudding-like number with plenty of flavour.

1996 Château de Lancyre, Pic St Loup, £4.99   15/20
Dry 🍷🍷 ▬
Pale-pink Languedoc rosé from the fashionable Pic St Loup appellation, with fresh acidity and restrained strawberry fruitiness.

Sparkling

Over £8

FRANCE

Brossault Brut, Non Vintage, £11.99   16/20
Dry 🍷🍷 🍸
Youthful, malty, big-bubbled fizz at a price.

Château de Boursault Brut, Non Vintage, £14.99   16/20
Dry 🍷🍷 🍸
Lemony, elegant Champagne with a rich, mouth-filling mousse and good length of flavour. The only Champagne house we know of that calls itself a château.

Joseph Perrier Brut, Non Vintage, £15.99   17/20
Dry 🍷🍷🍷 🍸
An equal blend of the Champagne grapes, Chardonnay, Pinot Noir and Pinot Meunier, made in a classy, malty-flavoured style by one of our favourite Champagne houses.

Fortified

£5–8

AUSTRALIA

Stanton & Killeen Muscat, £5.99 per half-bottle　　　16/20
Very sweet 🌢🌢🌢 |
Sweet, raisiny, silky, aromatic, rose-petal-scented fortified white – midway between a Tawny Port and a Muscat de Beaumes de Venise. Deliciously drinkable.

Greenalls Cellars

Including:

Wine Cellar ☆☆☆(☆)
Berkeley Wines ☆☆(☆)
Cellar 5 ☆(☆)

Address: PO Box 476, Loushers Lane, Warrington WA4 6RR

Telephone/fax: 01925 444555; 01925 415474

Number of branches: 27 Wine Cellar, 72 Berkeley Wines, 267 Cellar 5, 75 Greenalls Food Stores, 22 Night Vision Video

Opening hours: Generally 10.00am to 10.00pm Monday to Saturday; 12.00am to 2.00pm and 7.00pm to 10.00pm Sunday; food stores normally open 7.30am to 10.30pm

Credit cards accepted: Access, American Express, Visa

Discounts: Normally 10 per cent per case of 12 (not including special offers and promotions)

Facilities and services: Local delivery for case quantities (Wine Cellar and Berkeley Wines); mail order via the Internet (Wine Cellar); glass loan (Wine Cellar, Berkeley Wines, Cellar 5 with purchase); tastings (Wine Cellar)

Special offers: Monthly promotions in all stores; specific wine region/country promotions – 'buy any six bottles and get 15 per cent off' – in Wine Cellar and Berkeley Wines

Top ten best-selling wines (by volume):

Wine Cellar:

Grafton Chenin Blanc; Kumala Ruby Cabernet/Merlot; Hardy's Bordeaux Red; Philippe de Baudin Sauvignon Blanc; Lindemans Bin 65 Chardonnay; La Baume Grenache/Shiraz; Gemini Vin de Pays d'Oc Merlot; Koonunga Hill Chardonnay; Jacob's Creek Semillon/Chardonnay; Nottage Hill Shiraz/Cabernet

Berkeley Wines:

Liebfraumilch; Grafton Chenin Blanc; Lambrusco Bianco; Bulgarian Cabernet Sauvignon; Jacob's Creek Semillon/Chardonnay; Kumala Chenin Blanc/Chardonnay; Hardy's Stamp Semillon/Chardonnay; La Baume Grenache/Shiraz; Cuvée Australe; Jacob's Creek Shiraz/Cabernet

Cellar 5:

Liebfraumilch; Lambrusco Bianco; Grafton Chenin Blanc; Santa Maria Medium; Bulgarian Cabernet Sauvignon; Jacob's Creek Semillon/Chardonnay; Santa Maria Dry; Hardy's Stamp Semillon/Chardonnay; Hock; Romanian Merlot

Range:

GOOD: Regional France, Spain, Bordeaux, Australia, New Zealand, Argentina, Chile, United States, Champagne and sparkling wines

AVERAGE: Burgundy, Rhône, Loire, Alsace, Beaujolais, Italy, Portugal, England, Eastern Europe, South Africa, Germany

POOR: None

UNDER-REPRESENTED: None

Only Wine Cellar stocks the full range. All wines listed below are stocked by Wine Cellar (WC), Berkeley Wines (BW) and Cellar 5 (C5), unless otherwise indicated.

We're going to miss Nader Haghighi, Greenalls Cellars' very own Mr Publicity. A press conference waiting to happen, Haghighi loved the limelight, however dim the bulbs. No photo-call was too tacky (he once appeared in a Santa Claus suit flanked by two of the Warriors), no trade event too minor. Coverage was what mattered. Ask him a question, wave a tape recorder under his nose and the reply could, and usually did, go on, and on, and on.

It's also farewell to Haghighi-speak, with its 'segmentation', 'flexible branding', 'propositions' and 'repositioning'. It was perfectly possible to listen to whole sentences of this bizarre amalgam of Iranian, English and an American marketing handbook and barely understand a word. No matter. When Haghighi was around, you knew you were going to enjoy yourself – and not always at his expense. The man, as the newsroom saying goes, was good copy.

Haghighi has moved to another part of the business, as marketing and commercial director of Greenalls' 800 pubs and restaurants, to be replaced at the helm of Greenalls Cellars (the wine-retailing bit of the empire) by former finance director, John Brearley. Mr Brearley has some act to live up to. Or does he? Some people believe that while Haghighi talked a good 'retail proposition', the shop-floor reality was something else altogether. There are even those who argue that Haghighi moved on before fan and faeces collided.

There was certainly no lack of activity during Haghighi's reign at Greenalls Cellars. Where once there was only Cellar 5 and Berkeley Wines, now, thanks to Haghighi, we have Wine Cellar, Greenalls Food Stores and Night Vision, too. We nearly, at one point, had Hugglers as well, until Haghighi was forced to abandon the name by a baby-nappy company, which had bagged it first.

What does the legacy add up to? It's probably too early to say whether Haghighi revolutionised British retailing, as he would like you to believe, or just wasted millions of pounds refitting shops for the sake of it. What is beyond doubt is that Haghighi was, and is, a man with ideas. The coffee-shop-and-croissant format that he introduced in certain branches of Wine Cellar and the idea of selling wine off the shelf for people to have with their lunch are both valid attempts to reverse the decline of the traditional high-street off-licence.

Haghighi wasn't the only person to leave Greenalls Cellars during the last 12 months. Of equal significance was the departure of Kevin Wilson, one half of the company's wine-buying team and an extremely astute trader. David Vaughan, Wilson's partner in wine, is still there in Warrington, but the loss of Wilson to Compass Catering is a considerable one. At the time of writing, Greenalls was interviewing for a replacement. Meanwhile, Mr Vaughan is buying everything for the off-licences, as well as the pubs and restaurants. If Vaughan looks a little tired at the moment, who can blame him?

Vaughan and Wilson did a lot to improve the image of Greenalls Wine Cellars' list, shipping in vast numbers of new wines from every corner of the viticultural globe. There was some genuine innovation here – the boys took an early interest in the Languedoc-Roussillon, Washington State and Oregon and recognised the potential of Argentina before anyone else. By the time Wilson left, the range, at Wine Cellar at least, had become one of the most interesting (if not always the cheapest) in the high street.

The current range reflects their joint enthusiasms. 'We've put a lot of work into finding good wines from Chile, Argentina and southern France this year,' says Vaughan. 'Our emphasis was to find as many good-quality wines as possible to replace Australian reds, which are creeping up in price.'

Of these three areas, Chile has been the sales star. 'We've gone from 7,500 cases to 30,000 in 12 months,' he adds. Despite the price increases, Australia also continues to grow, albeit at a less spectacular rate than Chile. Vaughan reports a boom in vins de pays and 'single property wines from Fitou and Corbières' at the expense of more traditional French areas, which are showing a 'slow decline'.

He is also encouraged by the chain's ability to sell more expensive red wines, although presumably this applies to upmarket Wine Cellars rather than to the considerably less opulent Cellar 5s and Night Visions. With this in mind,

Greenalls bought a bunch of 1995 en primeur clarets, as it did with the 1994s, and will be offering them on the shelf before too long.

Now that Vaughan is home alone, on what will he focus? The answer is Portugal, Argentina and Australia. He is particularly excited about Argentina. 'There's some really good stuff being made there and it will fill that vital gap between £4.49 and £4.99.' By Christmas Vaughan says he should have as many as 20 Argentine wines on his list. British wine drinkers have either forgotten or forgiven Diego Maradona's Hand of God.

The full Greenalls' range currently stands at around 700 wines, a match for almost anyone in size. The problem is that not all the shops get all the wines, for reasons of space or demography. If you are fortunate enough to live near a Wine Cellar, you should have access to the lot, but Berkeley Wines (450 wines), Night Vision (200), Cellar 5 (150–350) and Food Stores (150–350) are less likely to stock the more esoteric lines. What do you mean you don't want to take home a bottle of Château Latour with your copy of Independence Day?

With so many different brand propositions – sorry, shops – it is always going to be difficult to generalise about Greenalls Wine Cellars. Stroll into a Wine Cellar in Epsom or Ascot and you're in one of the best-appointed off-licences in the country. Wander, or possibly stagger, into one of the rougher Cellar 5s and you might find it hard to believe that it belongs to the same company.

The emphasis, as far as the buying department is concerned, is on Wine Cellar. Wine Cellar produces a stylish, full-colour list; Wine Cellar has its own site on the Internet; and Wine Cellar is where journalists are taken for tastings and, not so long ago, for Naderisation sessions. The problem here is that there are only 27 Wine Cellars out of a total estate of 463 off-licences. To be fair, more openings are due in the coming months, building towards a 'critical mass of 50', according to Vaughan. But that still leaves a lot of C5s.

In his first 'Welcome to Wine Cellar' piece in the well-designed new list, managing director John Brearley makes a good deal of noise about Greenalls' £8m investment in Wine Cellar. 'The sales in Wine Cellar justify that investment,' says Vaughan. This may well be true, although you need to sell a lot of wine to recoup £8m. What about the rest of the estate? The latest figures are surprisingly good, given the general decline of high-street offies, with profits up 30 per cent in the six months to the end of March 1997.

'Greenalls is taking a long-term view of its off-licences,' says Vaughan. 'The performance has been pretty good, even if it's small in overall group terms.' A quarter of Greenalls' turnover comes from the off-licences, but rather less of its profit. It is surely significant that Greenalls is planning to invest £200m (£192m more than it's spending on Wine Cellar) in its pubs.

Where next for Greenalls Wine Cellars? As in previous years, we are not quite sure. Things were further complicated by the fact that, on August 29,

Greenalls Cellars was the object of a management buyout for £56 million by CVC Capital Partners and NatWest Ventures. With guess whom at the helm? Welcome back, Mr Haghighi.

White

Under £3

FRANCE

Port Neuf White, £2.99   13/20
Dry 🍷🍷 |
Crisp, clean Gascon-style white with a green-apple bite.

SOUTH AFRICA

Grafton Chenin Blanc, £2.99   13/20
Dry 🍷🍷 |
Soft, faintly honeyed Cape Chenin Blanc with a warming alcoholic caress.

£3–5

ARGENTINA

1996 Viejo Surco Torrontés/Chenin, £3.89   14/20
Dry 🍷🍷 |
Made at one of Argentina's most forward-thinking wineries, La Agricola, this is a spicy, aromatic blend of Chenin Blanc and the native Torrontés. Grapey and refreshing.

AUSTRALIA

1996 Hardy's Stamp Riesling/Traminer, £4.49   15/20
Medium dry 👜👜 |
Australia's answer to Alsace's Edelzwicker, blending Riesling and Traminer (aka Gewürztraminer), this is a fragrantly fruity, lychee and lime-like aperitif white.

1996 Lindemans Unoaked Cawarra Chardonnay, £4.69 (WC/BW only)   15/20
Dry 👜👜 |
It says unoaked on the label, but we reckon there's the faintest smidgeon of toasty oak here. If so, it's no bad thing, as it adds to the wine's clean, buttery flavours.

CHILE

1996 Errázuriz Sauvignon Blanc, £4.99   16/20
Dry 👜👜👜 |
Fresh, grapefruity Chilean Sauvignon Blanc from the cool-climate Casablanca Valley, midway in style between the crispness of the Loire Valley and the pungency of Marlborough in New Zealand.

FRANCE

1996 Chardonnay, Vin de Pays du Jardin de la France, Donatien Bahuaud, £3.99   15/20
Dry 👜👜👜 |
Light, spritzy, unoaked Loire Valley Chardonnay with mouth-watering acidity.

1996 Coeur de Cray, Sauvignon de Touraine, £4.99 (WC/BW only)   16/20
Dry 👜👜👜 |
Specially selected by Mancunian wine merchant, Paul Boutinot, this is a crisp, nettley, well-made Loire Sauvignon Blanc in a stylish bottle.

ITALY

1996 Puglian White, Cantele, Kym Milne, £3.69   15/20
Dry 👜👜👜 |
An intriguing Puglian blend of Chardonnay, Verdeca and Garganega made by Australian Kym Milne. Flavoursome, spicy stuff with a herbal tang.

NEW ZEALAND

1996 New Zealand Dry White, £4.49   14/20
Dry 🍶 🍷

A zesty, faintly tropical Kiwi white, made in the Gisborne region from unspecified 'premium' grapes.

SOUTH AFRICA

1996 Kumala Chenin/Chardonnay, £3.79   12/20
Dry 🍷

A green and rather hollow Western Cape white. Not the best advertisement for the Rainbow Nation.

SPAIN

1996 Enate Macabeo/Chardonnay, £4.99 (WC/BW only)   16/20
Dry 🍶🍶🍶 🍷

From the trendy northern Spanish region of Somontano, this is an appealingly packaged, unoaked blend of Macabeo and Chardonnay, with plenty of fruit and a zingy twist of acidity.

1996 Viñas del Vero Chardonnay, £4.99 (WC/BW only)   16/20
Dry 🍶🍶🍶 🍷

From Somontano's other mould-breaking winery, Vitano, this is an appealingly packaged, unoaked blend of Macabeo and Chardonnay, with plenty of fruit and a zingy twist of acidity.

1996 Marqués de Griñon Durius Blanco, £4.99 (WC/BW only) 15/20
Dry 🍶🍶 🍷

The Marqués in question is Carlos Falco, the man behind a very well-made range of reds and whites. This is a soft, alluring white blend with pear and grapefruit notes.

UNITED STATES

1994 Columbia Crest Semillon/Chardonnay, £4.99 (WC/BW only)
16/20

Dry 🍶🍶🍶 🍷

A Washington State interpretation of a successful Australian formula, this Semillon/Chardonnay blend is a rich, toasty, concentrated white with lemon-curd and hazelnut characters.

126

£5–8

AUSTRALIA

1994 Leasingham Domaine Chardonnay, £7.99 (WC only)   16/20
Dry 👜👜 |
Leasingham's wines are no longer the bargain they once were, but the quality produced at this Clare Valley winery is still extremely good. A rich, melony, oak-tinged Chardonnay with masses of smoky flavour. Still youthful for a 1994.

FRANCE

1996 Fat Bastard Chardonnay, Vin de Pays d'Oc, £5.99 (WC/BW only)   16/20
Dry 👜👜 |
A promising follow-up to last year's successful launch ('bastard' being a pun on Burgundy's Bâtard-Montrachet). Skilfully executed, barrel-fermented stuff with considerable flavour and elegance for a southern French Chardonnay.

1996 Pouilly-Fumé Les Logères, Guy Saget, £7.99   17/20
Bone dry 👜👜👜 ▬
Intense, minerally Loire Sauvignon Blanc with flinty, nettley flavours, crisp acidity and excellent length of flavour. Should develop further in bottle.

1995 Louis Jadot Bourgogne Chardonnay, £7.99 (WC/BW only)
                                                                14/20
Dry |
Good, if basic, white Burgundy at an optimistic price – you'd be better off buying a Chardonnay from New Zealand or Chile.

GERMANY

1995 Hochheimer Hölle Riesling Kabinett, Domdechant Werner, £7.99 (WC/BW only)   16/20
Medium dry 👜👜 ▬
A crisp and assertive Rheingau Riesling with less than 10 per cent alcohol. Tangy, citrus-fresh and elegant.

ITALY

**1996 Casal di Serra, Verdicchio di Castelli di Jesi Classico
Superiore, Umani Ronchi, £5.99** (WC/BW only)   16/20
Dry 🍷🍷🍷 ▮
A rich, beautifully made single-vineyard bianco with the buttery, hazelnutty
flavours of the Verdicchio grape balanced by spritz and zippy acidity.

NEW ZEALAND

1996 Kim Crawford Sauvignon Blanc, £6.99 (WC/BW only)   16/20
Dry 🍷🍷 ▮
Assertive, green-bean and asparagus-scented Marlborough Sauvignon Blanc
from one of New Zealand's most sought-after winemakers. Crisp and well
made.

1996 Esk Valley Sauvignon Blanc, Hawkes Bay, £6.99 (WC only)
                                                            16/20
Dry 🍷🍷 ▮
Esk Valley specialises in red wines, but this rich, minerally, almost grapefruity
Sauvignon Blanc shows that its whites aren't bad, either.

SOUTH AFRICA

1996 Stellenzicht Chardonnay, £7.99 (WC only)   17/20
Dry 🍷🍷🍷 ▮
Stylish, complex Stellenbosch white, which has made good use of barrel-
fermentation to produce an elegant but full-flavoured Chardonnay with
undertones of toffee fudge.

UNITED STATES

1995 Château Ste Michelle Riesling, £5.79 (WC/BW only)   15/20
Off-dry 🍷 ▮
Aromatic, lemon- and lime-like Washington State Riesling, which is beginning to
develop some age-derived, petrolly complexity.

1994 Château Ste Michelle Chardonnay, £6.99 (WC/BW only) 16/20
Dry 🍷🍷 ▮
Attractively mature West Coast Chardonnay with ripe flavours of nut, toffee
and buttered popcorn and nicely integrated oak.

Over £8

AUSTRALIA

1995 Château Reynella Chardonnay, £9.99 (WC only) 14/20
Dry ▮
Deeply coloured McLaren Vale Chardonnay from the Hardy's Group, with too much oak for the amount of flavour. An over-priced Hardy Chardy.

FRANCE

1995 Chassagne-Montrachet, Domaine Pillot, £14.99 (WC only)
14/20
Dry ▮
Gluey, faintly bitter white Burgundy. We expect a bit more from a famous white-wine village like Chassagne-Montrachet.

NEW ZEALAND

1994 Hunter's Chardonnay, £10.99 (WC only) 15/20
Dry ▮
A wine in which the fruit is rapidly being overtaken by the acidity, giving it a sweet-and-sour character. Well made, if over-priced.

SOUTH AFRICA

1995 Bouchard Finlayson Chardonnay, Kaaimansggat, £12.99 (WC only) 16/20
Dry 🍇🍇 ▮
A Franco-South African collaboration between Paul Bouchard of Bouchard Aîné and Peter Finlayson, this is one of South Africa's best Chardonnays, showing texture, refreshing acidity and delicacy of flavour.

UNITED STATES

1994 Benziger Chardonnay, Carneros, £8.99 (WC only) 16/20
Dry 🍇🍇 ▮
Rich, oaky, flavoursome Carneros Chardonnay from the Benziger winery. Barrel-fermentation has produced a toasty, no-holds-barred white with a supple butterscotch note.

Red

Under £3

FRANCE

Port Neuf Rouge, £2.99   14/20
Medium-bodied 🍾🍾🍾 ▮
A minty, green-pepper-like vin de table, which is extremely drinkable at the price. Better than most basic claret and a lot cheaper.

£3–5

ARGENTINA

Balbi Vineyards Red, £3.69   14/20
Full-bodied 🍾🍾 ▮
Robust, full-bodied Argentine tinto with smoky oak character and juicy liquorice and blackcurrant flavours.

AUSTRALIA

1995 Penfolds Bin 35, Rawson's Retreat, Shiraz/Cabernet/Ruby Cabernet, £4.99 (WC/BW only)   14/20
Full-bodied 🍾 ▮
Thyme- and mint-scented Aussie blend, which finishes a little chewy and extracted. Needs a hearty stew, but then don't we all.

CHILE

1995 Villa Montes, Domaine Apalta Cabernet Sauvignon, £4.99 (WC/BW only)   14/20
Full-bodied 🍾 ▮
Dry, oaky, almost geranium-like Chilean Cabernet Sauvignon, which is a bit too coarse and chewy for our ultra-refined palates.

1994 Casa Lapostolle Cabernet Sauvignon, £4.99 (WC/BW only)

16/20

Medium-bodied 🍷🍷🍷 ➤

Made by Pomerol's Michel Rolland, this is stylish, aromatic, beautifully turned-out Cabernet Sauvignon, which manages to combine exuberant blackcurrant fruit with minerally complexity.

FRANCE

1996 Costières de Nîmes, Maurel Vedeau, £4.49 (WC/BW only)

15/20

Full-bodied 🍷🍷 ▮

A sage and blackberry-perfumed Provençal blend with robust tannins and a core of sweet fruit.

1995 Bush Vine Grenache, Coteaux du Languedoc, Galet Vineyards, £4.49 (WC/BW only)

14/20

Full-bodied 🍷 ▮

Well-made, modern Grenache from the Coteaux du Languedoc, with muscular tannins and a drying finish. Lacks fruit.

1996 Fitou Domaine de Gardie, Mont Tauch, £4.99 (WC/BW only)

14/20

Full-bodied 🍷 ▮

Spicy, four-square Fitou with chunky tannins and some nice Mediterranean herbiness.

1995 Château Haute Roque, Faugères, £4.99 (WC/BW only) 15/20

Full-bodied 🍷🍷 ➤

Fresh, pungent Languedoc red redolent of the Syrah and Grenache grapes. Cinnamon and blackberry fruit underpinned by slightly chunky tannins.

1996 Coeur de Cray Pinot Noir, Vin de Pays du Jardin de la France, £4.99 (WC/BW only)

13/20

Light-bodied ▮

Light, fruity Loire Pinot Noir with rasping acidity. A bit hollow, but then Pinot Noir under a fiver usually is.

SOUTH AFRICA

1996 Kumala Ruby Cabernet/Merlot, £3.99   12/20
Full-bodied ▮
Youthful, rather undistinguished Western Cape red with a vinegary edge and chewy, warm-climate tannins.

1995 First River, Stellenbosch Dry Red, £4.49 (WC/BW only)
15/20

Medium-bodied 💰💰 ▮
We're not sure what the grapes are in this supple, grassy red, but Cabernet Sauvignon must be among them. A good claret alternative.

SPAIN

1995 Enate Cabernet/Merlot, £4.99 (WC/BW only)   15/20
Medium-bodied 💰💰 ▮
The computer-loving Jesús Artajona has produced a spicy, refreshing, oak-aged Bordeaux-style blend, which promises a little more than it delivers.

1994 Viñas del Vero Cabernet Sauvignon, £4.99 (WC/BW only)
16/20

Medium-bodied 💰💰💰 ▬
Big bottle, big wine. At under £5, this is one of the best Cabernet Sauvignons we've tasted from Spain. Rich, structured and oaky with a kernel of cassis fruitiness.

UNITED STATES

1995 Saddle Mountain Grenache, Columbia Valley, £3.99   15/20
Full-bodied 💰💰💰 ▮
Juicy-fruity, brambly Washington State Grenache with pure, sweet succulence and soft tannins. Much better than most basic Côtes du Rhône.

£5–8

AUSTRALIA

1995 Peter Lehmann Black Label Shiraz, Barossa, £6.49 (WC/BW only)   17/20
Full-bodied 🍶🍶🍶 ▬

As characterful as the man who made it, this is a massively oaked Barossa Shiraz with enough blackberry fruit and stuffing to stand up to the barrel staves. Concentrated stuff.

1995 Hardy's Bankside Shiraz, £6.49 (WC/BW only)   16/20
Full-bodied 🍶🍶 ▬

A blend of Padthaway and Clare Valley grapes has produced one of the best inexpensive Aussie Shirazes on the market. Robust at the moment, but give it time.

1994 Leasingham Cabernet/Malbec, £7.99 (WC only)   16/20
Full-bodied 🍶 ▬

A dense, inky Clare Valley blend, which combines power, fruit and oakiness in a sweet minty red. Very drinkable, if a little over-priced.

CHILE

1995 Carmen Grande Vidure/Cabernet Reserve, £6.99 (WC only)   17/20

Full-bodied 🍶🍶🍶 ▬

Made by the talented Alvaro Espinoza, this is one of Chile's best red wines, showing texture, sweet blackberry fruit and fine-grained tannins balanced by classy vanilla oak.

1994 Errázuriz Reserva Cabernet Sauvignon, £7.49 (WC only)   15/20

Medium-bodied 🍶 |

Overtly minty Aconcagua Valley Cabernet Sauvignon with fine tannins, well-integrated oak and a green edge.

FRANCE

1996 Fleurie, Mommessin, £7.49 (WC/BW only)   15/20
Medium-bodied 🍷 ▐
Expensive, faintly soupy cru Beaujolais with structured cherry fruitiness and a
nip of tannin.

1994 Louis Jadot Bourgogne Pinot Noir, £7.99 (WC/BW only) 13/20
Medium-bodied ▐
Leafy, drying red Burgundy with a trace, but only a trace, of Pinot Noir
character.

1994 Château de Gironville, Haut-Médoc, £7.99 (WC only)   15/20
Medium-bodied 🍷 ▬▬
Coffee-bean-scented cru bourgeois claret with lashings of oak and sweet,
fleshy fruitiness.

ITALY

1994 Jorio, Montepulciano d'Abruzzo, Umani Ronchi, £6.99
(WC only)   16/20
Full-bodied 🍷🍷🍷 ▬▬
Oak-aged single-vineyard Montepulciano with masses of plummy
concentration and tannin. A super Abruzzo, if that's not a contradiction in
terms.

PORTUGAL

1995 Quinta de Pancas Cabernet Sauvignon, £5.99 (WC only)
                                               15/20

Full-bodied 🍷 ▬▬
Oaky, modern Portuguese Cabernet Sauvignon with dry tannins (which may
soften with age) and some attractive cassis fruitiness.

SOUTH AFRICA

1995 First River Cabernet Sauvignon, £5.49 (WC/BW only)   15/20
Medium-bodied 🍷🍷 ▐
Pleasant, if faintly baked, Cape Cabernet Sauvignon with good concentration
and an earthy undertone.

1994 Stellenzicht Shiraz, £7.99 (WC only)   15/20
Full-bodied 🍷 ▬
Australian-style Cape Shiraz (right down to the Aussie spelling of the Syrah grape) with far too much coconutty oak and extraction. May soften with age, but don't put your shavings – sorry, savings – on it.

SPAIN

1995 Cosme Palacio Rioja, £5.99 (WC/BW only)   17/20
Medium-bodied 🍷🍷🍷 ▬
A modern, all-Tempranillo red from the Rioja Alavesa region, which combines oak and structured blackberry and cassis fruitiness in a harmonious whole. Rioja never used to taste like this, but we've seen the future – and it works.

UNITED STATES

1993 Columbia Crest Cabernet Sauvignon, £5.99 (WC/BW only)
                                                          15/20
Medium-bodied 🍷 ▮
Oaky, green-pepper Cabernet Sauvignon from Washington State's Columbia Valley, which is starting to dry out on the palate.

1994 Hedges Cabernet/Merlot, £6.99 (WC/BW only)   14/20
Medium-bodied ▮
Another Columbia Valley red, this time showing chocolatey oak and rather chewy, hard tannins.

Over £8

AUSTRALIA

1994 Mount Langi Ghiran Shiraz, £12.99 (WC only)   17/20
Medium-bodied 🍷🍷🍷 ▬
Intense, densely coloured, black-pepper-like Victorian Shiraz with sweet, spicy fruit flavours, masses of concentration and finely judged tannins.

CHILE

1992 Montes Alpha Cabernet Sauvignon, £8.99 (WC only)   15/20
Medium-bodied 🍷 |
A French oak-aged Cabernet Sauvignon from winemaker Aurelio Montes.
Time to move on to a more recent vintage, we feel.

NEW ZEALAND

**1994 Esk Valley Merlot/Cabernet Sauvignon/Cabernet Franc,
£8.99** (WC only)   16/20
Medium-bodied 🍷🍷 |
Forward, elegant, easy drinking Hawkes Bay blend with supple, chocolatey fruit
flavours and medium-weight tannins. The Southern Hemisphere's answer to a
Margaux claret.

UNITED STATES

1992 Benziger Sonoma Cabernet Sauvignon, £8.99 (WC only)
                                                 15/20
Medium-bodied 🍷 |
Solid, sweetly oaked Sonoma Cabernet Sauvignon with good flavour and fruit
but a dryish finish.

1993 Château Ste Michelle Merlot, £9.99 (WC only)   16/20
Medium-bodied 🍷🍷 ➤
Chocolatey, flavoursome Washington State Merlot with fleshy fruit and robust
tannins. Should improve.

Rosé

£3–5

ARGENTINA

1996 Balbi Syrah Rosé, £3.99 (WC/BW only)   15/20
Off-dry 🜪🜪🜪 ▮
Deep -hued, redcurranty Argentine rosé with thirst-quenching fruit and acidity. Halfway to a Beaujolais in style.

FRANCE

**1996 Côtes du Ventoux Rosé, Vignerons de Beaumes de Venise,
£3.99** (WC/BW only)   15/20
Dry 🜪🜪🜪 ▮
A well-made, food-friendly rosé from a southern Rhône village better known for its sweet, fortified Muscats. Rosehip and raspberry are the dominant flavours here.

Sparkling

Over £8

UNITED STATES

Shadow Creek Blanc de Noirs NV, £9.99   15/20
Dry 🜪🜪 ▮
Made at Moët & Chandon's Napa Valley base, this is a Pinot Noir-dominated fizz with a pinkish tinge, a fine mousse and soft, warm-climate fruit flavours.

Kwik Save ☆(☆)

Address: Warren Drive, Prestatyn, Clwyd LL19 7HU

Telephone/fax: 01745 887111; 01745 882504

Number of branches: 900

Opening hours: Varies across the country. Most shops keep the following hours: 9.00am to 5.00pm Monday and Tuesday; 9.00am to 6.00pm Wednesday; 9.00am to 8.00pm Thursday and Friday; 9.00am to 5.30pm Saturday; 10.00am to 4.00pm Sunday in selected stores

Credit cards accepted: Delta, Switch. Certain shops are carrying out experiments to see whether it is worth while accepting all credit cards (as part of their grand restructuring project), but as yet credit cards are not officially accepted

Discounts: None

Facilities and services: None

Special offers: On selected promotional products; there is always some sort of promotion on

Top ten best-selling wines: These are actually the top-selling brands (so they include the various white dry/medium, red and rosé styles under that brand name): Les Oliviers Vin de Table Français; Liebfraumilch; Hock; Lambrusco; Macedonian Country Red; Gabbia d'Oro Italian table wine; Lovico Suhindol Bulgarian red; Pelican Bay Australian Wine; Flamenco Spanish wine; Soave DOC

Range:

GOOD: Regional France

AVERAGE: Bordeaux, Spain, Portugal, Italy, England, Greece, Bulgaria, Hungary, Romania, Australia, South Africa

POOR: Germany, Champagne and sparkling wines

UNDER-REPRESENTED: Burgundy, United States, Chile, Argentina

If the best things in life are free, then shopping at Kwik Save, where margins are pared to the bone on life's barest essentials, isn't far behind. Okay, so the no-frills envelopes won't always stick down and the shopping may not match Harrods or Fortnum & Mason for glamour. And yes, you may have to stand in line at the off-licence counter like a Job Centre applicant, if you're really desperate for that British Sherry — sorry, British Fortified Wine (believe it or not, Kwik Save shifts 5,000 cases of the stuff each week).

And yet, while hedonistic seekers of radicchio and sun-dried tomatoes shop elsewhere, Kwik Save is taking one aspect of the good life increasingly seriously. And that's wine. Until five years ago, wine at Kwik Save was a dull affair indeed, consisting of little more than bog-standard Lieb, Hock, British Sherry (as it then was) and various other alcoholic staples of working-class culture. The company's lack of a wine focus was reflected in the fact that it didn't even have the sort of fixtures and fittings that supermarkets acknowledge help customers browse and choose.

Until, that is, some bright spark had the idea of taking Angela Muir, Master of Wine, on board. With her buying skills and considerable clout in the wine world (she is widely credited with taming the heat of La Mancha in Spain with temperature-controlled stainless-steel fermentation), Muir has transformed Kwik Save with a range of no-nonsense, good-value wines, mostly at under £3. For every 200 bottles of wine sold in the UK, anoraks please note, Kwik Save's proportion has now risen from one bottle five years ago to six. That's still way behind the likes of Sainsbury's and Tesco, but according to Kwik Save's head buyer David Graves, they are now a nose ahead of Somerfield in the take-home wine stakes.

It's still not enough for Graves, though. Finding itself squeezed between the established supermarkets and the discounters, Kwik Save brought in consultants, who identified wine as an exciting growth area (we could have told them that, mind you, and our fees are very reasonable). Among various changes recommended, new stores will do away with overhead storage and change their entrances to make them more consumer-friendly. Three to four hundred Kwik Save shops still have over-the-counter sales, and these will all be replaced by free-flow aisles for wine, a process that is expected to take three to four years.

Modernising the shops and making them more customer-friendly should have a major impact, not just on wine sales, but on polishing the Kwik Save image too. That isn't to suggest that Kwik Save will abandon its traditional customers overnight in favour of the Burgundy and Champagne-drinking classes. Let's face it, with a name like Kwik Save, it is hardly likely to. The aim is to attract more adventurous customers prepared to splash out a little bit extra on a bottle of wine.

Kwik Save

Up to a point, the process is already under way. Whereas in 1996 four out of five bottles of wine sold were under £3, today it is only just over three in every five. 'Liebfraumilch, Hock and Lambrusco are in huge decline,' says Muir with a mischievous grin. 'Customers are voting with their feet and turning to Chile, Argentina and South Africa.' Glory be, there's even an Aussie wine in Kwik Save's top ten best-sellers at last.

Muir has taken on half a dozen new South Africa wines, including four from Aussie winemaker Kym Milne. She is also trying out a handful of more expensive products, such as Lindemans Bin 65 Chardonnay from Australia's Penfolds and a Sonoma Zinfandel from California's Gallo. She hopes in due course to have 16 over-£4 wines on the shelves of 30 of Kwik Save's bigger stores.

If the 'specially selected' wines do well, they will become part of the range, which now extends to 140 wines. 'We have the confidence to believe that people will buy the more expensive wines in the £4–6 range,' says Muir. Her optimism is borne out by figures that show sales of red wines up 40 per cent, a sign that Kwik Save customers are becoming more discerning in their tastes.

Muir insists that value for money – Kwik Save's stock-in-trade – will not be sacrificed as a result of the supermarket's ambition to move upmarket. To this end, she and the buying team will continue to expend energy on telling suppliers what is required. 'We want to keep the people we've got,' says Muir, talking of her suppliers. 'Where we've beaten them up on quality and price, we're getting the results we want in the bottle. The Bulgarians, for example, have responded to being talked to nicely. Where we're able to focus on what we want, we've had good results, even on wine costing £1.87.'

As another sign of its commitment to making wine more interesting, Kwik Save has expanded its buying team to three. Angela Muir will remain as consultant, sourcing and recommending wines, while the rest of the team will be responsible for negotiating prices as well as stock and quality control. Kwik Save is getting there, but don't expect to find the full range of 140 wines on every Kwik Save shelf in the country. A basic range of 20 wines goes into all 900-odd licensed stores; 800 stores have 50 of the range; 700 stores take 80 wines; and 500 stores take 110 wines, with the full monty on the shelves of the biggest 300 Kwik Saves.

White

Under £3

AUSTRALIA

Pelican Bay Dry White, South East Australia, McWilliams, £2.99

14/20

Dry 🍶🍶🍶 ▮

Tropical fruity Colombard/Semillon blend rounded out with a hint of oak flavour. One of the best cheap Aussie whites on the market.

Pelican Bay Medium Dry, South East Australia, McWilliams, £2.99

13/20

Medium dry 🍶🍶 ▮

Aromatic, gluggable blend of Fruity Gordo, sultana and the kitchen sink, made with the cross-dressing Lieb-drinker in mind.

BULGARIA

Khan Krum Riesling/Dimiat, Bulgarian Country Wine, £2.69

12/20

Off-dry 🍶 ▮

Floral, grapey blend from Bulgaria's best white wine area. Decent, if marred by a faintly bitter aftertaste.

1996 Preslav Chardonnay Sauvignon, £2.89   14/20

Dry 🍶🍶🍶 ▮

Affordable Bulgarian blend of the two most popular white grapes, Chardonnay and Sauvignon Blanc, made in a modern, lightly oaked style. Crisp, fresh and fruity.

CHILE

1996 White Pacific, Sauvignon Blanc/Chardonnay, Rancagua, £2.99

13/20

Dry 🍶🍶 ▮

Decent, soft, well-made quaffable Chilean white conceived and executed in an international style.

ENGLAND

1995 Denbies, English Table Wine, £2.99   14/20
Medium dry 🛍🛍🛍 ▮
A well-made blend of Müller-Thurgau, Reichensteiner and Bacchus, brimming with English character, if a little tart on the finish. Still a good buy at under £3.

FRANCE

Les Oliviers, Vin de Table Français, Bessière, £1.97   12/20
Dry 🛍 ▮
Sharp, slightly resinous French white plonk with a green-apple bite. Still, what can you expect for under £2? Not a lot.

1996 Muscadet, Donatien Bahuaud, £2.79   14/20
Dry 🛍🛍🛍 ▮
Reflecting the general high quality of the 1996 vintage, this is a refreshingly fruity, full-flavoured Muscadet, if that's not a contradiction in terms.

Cuvée VE, Bordeaux Sauvignon, £2.95   14/20
Dry 🛍🛍🛍 ▮
Fresh, zesty, grapefruity Bordeaux white, which consistently delivers at the price. VE is not, in case you were wondering, a cross between a medal and a sexually transmitted disease, but stands for Vite Epargne – literally Quick Save.

1996 Graves Blanc, Dulong, £2.99   11/20
Dry ▮
Unbalanced, clumsily oaked Bordeaux white. Not even Kwik Save can source drinkable white Graves at under £3.

1996 Sauvignon de Touraine, £2.99   14/20
Dry 🛍🛍🛍 ▮
Classically grassy Loire Sauvignon from one of the region's best co-operatives, Oisly et Thésée, with bags of flavour at the price.

1996 Skylark Hill Very Special White, Vin de Pays d'Oc, Jean et Luc Viennet, £2.99   12/20
Off-dry 🛍 ▮
Sweetish, baked and undistinguished. Not Very Special at all.

**1996 Vin de Pays des Côtes de Gascogne, Domaine de la Hitaire,
Dulong, £2.99**   14/20
Dry 🍷🍷🍷 ▯

Zesty, crisp Gascon dry white with an appley tang and lovely fruitiness. A
bargain.

GERMANY

Linden Hock, K. Linden, £2.39   9/20
Sweet ▯

Bitter, over-sulphured, apple-core Hock, a name that is totally debased by wines
like this.

Linden Liebfraumilch, K. Linden, £2.59   11/20
Sweet ▯

Marginally better, but still suffering from an overzealous use of sulphur.

**1996 Niersteiner Spiegelberg Kabinett, Rheinhessen, St Ursula,
£2.89**   12/20
Medium sweet 🍷 ▯

Floral grapiness flattened by too much sulphur. The packaging looks better than
the wine tastes.

1996 Piesporter Michelsberg, Mosel-Saar-Ruwer, K. Linden, £2.97
                                                                  13/20
Sweet 🍷🍷 ▯

Fresh, young, appley Mosel white, which proves that Germany can make
drinkable wine under £3.

1996 St Laurens, Pfalz, Kendermann, £2.99   11/20
Medium sweet ▯

Sulphurous, old-fashioned German wine. Not even the clear Bordeaux bottle
can disguise the fact that this is a thin and sugary white.

GREECE

Retsina Kourtaki, £2.89   14/20
Dry 🍷🍷🍷 ▯

Ah! The authentic whiff of stem ginger and linseed oil to remind you of your
Greek island idyll.

HUNGARY

Hungarian Chardonnay, £2.99   13/20
Dry 💰💰 ▮
From Hungary's go-ahead Neszmely co-operative, this is a pleasant, unoaked Chardonnay with citrus-fruit notes and clean acidity.

ITALY

Lambrusco Bianco '4', £1.55   10/20
Sweet ▮
Nasty, confected, sherbety Italian bianco. At 4 per cent alcohol, this is barely a wine.

Gabbia d'Oro, Vino da Tavola Bianco, £2.39   13/20
Dry 💰💰 ▮
Baked, southern-influenced white with a lime-like twist in sub-Frascati mould.

Venier, Soave DOC, £2.67   14/20
Dry 💰💰💰 ▮
Clean, fresh, faintly pear-droppy white from the Veneto's largest producer.

Silvano Bianco, DOC Alcano, Casa Vinicola Firriato, £2.79   13/20
Dry 💰💰 ▮
Soft, aromatic Sicilian quaffer from Aussie Kym Milne, showing a bit too much oak character for the weight of fruit. Still, at £2.79...

SOUTH AFRICA

1996 Jade Peaks Chenin Blanc, Coastal Region, £2.79   13/20
Dry 💰💰 ▮
Grassy, almost Sauvignon Blanc-like Chenin Blanc made to a price in the Cape by flying Aussie winemaker, Kym Milne.

Impala Cape White, Goue Vallei Winery, Cape Province, £2.99
12/20
Dry 💰 ▮
Same country, different flying winemaker, in this case England's own golden boy, Hugh Ryman. The wine is floral, but bitter on the finish.

SPAIN

Flamenco, DO Valencia, Vicente Gandia, Medium Dry White, £2.59
12/20
Medium dry 👜 ▮
Sweet, bland Levante plonk from the giant Gandia operation.

Flamenco, DO Valencia, Vicente Gandia, Sweet White, £2.59 11/20
Very sweet ▮
Same again, but yuckily sweet. Sick-bag time.

UNITED STATES

California Cellars White, Canandaigua Winery, £2.99
11/20
Off-dry ▮
Thin, confected California white made for the undiscerning from indiscernible grape varieties grown somewhere in the vast Central Valley region.

£3–5

AUSTRALIA

1996 Colombard/Chardonnay, South East Australia, £3.39
14/20
Dry 👜👜 ▮
Peachy, nicely oaked Aussie white with good weight and texture.

Pelican Bay Chardonnay, South East Australia Southcorp, £3.59
13/20
Off-dry 👜 ▮
Oaky, flavoursome, buttery Aussie Chardonnay made for Kwik Save by Southcorp, aka Penfolds. A faintly musty edge put us off here.

FRANCE

1996 Skylark Hill Chardonnay, Vin de Pays d'Oc, Jean et Luc Viennet, £3.39
13/20
Dry 👜 ▮
Pleasantly appley, southern French Chardonnay with a hole in the middle where the flavour should be.

GERMANY

1993 Riesling Auslese, Bereich Mittelhardt, St Ursula, £3.89   13/20
Sweet 🍬 ▮
Faintly honeyed, sweet-and-sour German Auslese with some, but not much, aged Riesling character here.

SOUTH AFRICA

1996 Impala Cape Chenin/Chardonnay, Goue Vallei Winery, £3.49
12/20
Off-dry ▮
Pear-drop and paint-stripper aromas and little redeeming fruit on the palate.

SPAIN

Con Class, DO Rueda, £3.49   15/20
Dry 🍬🍬🍬 ▮
Made in north-eastern Spain from the local Verdejo grape, this is a fresh, floral and crisply defined Rueda white with plenty of oomph.

UNITED STATES

Paul Masson Carafe White, California, £3.49   13/20
Off-dry 🍬 ▮
If you're as ancient as we are, you may remember the all-purpose Paul Masson carafe. Well, it's back, though not necessarily by popular demand. A decent grapefruity white with a candy store finish.

Red

Under £3

AUSTRALIA

Pelican Bay Red, South East Australia, McWilliams, £2.99   12/20
Medium-bodied ▮
Fading, sweetish, tomato-skin plonk from the irrigated vineyards in the back of
Australia's behind.

BULGARIA

Cabernet Sauvignon/Merlot, Lovico Suhindol, £2.69   12/20
Medium-bodied 💰 ▮
A rustic, affordable Bulgarian blend with faintly chewy tannins.

1995 Merlot/Cabernet, Liubimetz, £2.79   13/20
Medium-bodied 💰💰 ▮
Full-flavoured, chocolatey Bulgarian blend with well-handled oak character and
dry tannins.

1993 Reserve Gamza, Lovico Suhindol, £2.89   13/20
Medium-bodied 💰💰 ▮
Coconutty red with soft, mature, cherryish fruit made from Bulgaria's native
Gamza grape.

1995 Cabernet Sauvignon, Straldja, £2.99   12/20
Medium-bodied ▮
Dry, leafy, old-fashioned Bulgarian plonk posing with its flashy label as
something more modern.

FRANCE

Les Oliviers Vin de Table Français, Bessière, £1.97   10/20
Medium-bodied ▮
Coarse, tart rot-gut rouge. Even French routiers would balk at this one.

1996 Les Forges, Vin de Pays de l'Aude, £2.39   11/20
Medium-bodied
Pongy, sulphurous, southern French rouge, which lacks balance on the palate.

Selection Cuvée VE, Rouge de France, Vin de Table Français, Domaines Virginie, £2.59   12/20
Medium-bodied
Decent, basic southern plonk from the sprawling Virginie operation.

1996 Cabernet Sauvignon, Vin de Pays d'Oc, Dulong, £2.79   14/20
Medium-bodied
Overtly grassy, soft, claret-style red from the south of France, with more character than most Bordeaux rouge at the price.

1995 Corbières, Domaines Virginie, £2.79   12/20
Full-bodied
Deeply coloured, coarsely oak-chipped red, which has sacrificed any southern French character it may once have had.

1996 Cuvée VE Claret, Calvet, £2.95   14/20
Medium-bodied
Supple, quaffable claret at a very reasonable price.

1996 Côtes du Rhône, François Dubessy, £2.99   14/20
Medium-bodied
Juicy, lightly peppery, carbonic maceration-style Rhône red from a good recent vintage.

1996 Skylark Hill Very Special Red, Vin de Pays d'Oc, Jean & Luc Viennet, £2.99   12/20
Light-bodied
Light, quaffable Beaujolais-meets-Languedoc red.

1996 Skylark Hill Merlot, Vin de Pays d'Oc, Calvet, £2.99   12/20
Medium-bodied
Chunky, chewy, rather one-dimensional southern French Merlot from Bordeaux négociant Calvet.

1996 Skylark Hill Shiraz, Vin de Pays d'Oc, Calvet, £2.99   11/20
Medium-bodied
Did someone say Shiraz? We can't find any trace of Shiraz, or even Syrah for that matter, in this basic, jammy, high-acid red.

1996 Merlot/Cabernet, Vin de Pays d'Oc, Jean & Luc Viennet, £2.99   14/20
Light-bodied 👛👛👛 🍷
Light, elegantly grassy southern French blend made by Aussie Nick Butler.

1996 La Roseraie, Saint Chinian, £2.99   13/20
Medium-bodied 👛👛 🍷
Soft, fruity, well-made Languedoc rouge with hints of spice and pepper.

ITALY

Lambrusco Rosso '4', £1.55   13/20
Medium-bodied 👛👛 🍷
The most interesting of Kwik Save's Lambrusco selection, this is a fizzy, low-in-alcohol red with a sweet balance of fruit and tannins. Try it with strawberries.

Gabbia d'Oro, Vino da Tavola Rosso, £2.39   11/20
Light-bodied 🍷
Pale, sugary, thin Piatto d'Oro red.

1996 Silvano Rosso, Casa Vinicola Firriato, Sicilian Red, £2.79
      13/20
Medium-bodied 👛👛 🍷
Spicy, youthful Sicilian red from Aussie Kym Milne, showing a hint of bitters character softened by oak chip.

Venier, Valpolicella DOC, GIV, £2.97   14/20
Light-bodied 👛👛👛 🍷
Light, pretty, raspberry-fruity Valpol, with some genuine Veneto character.

Venier, Montepulciano d'Abruzzo, GIV, £2.99   14/20
Medium-bodied 👛👛👛 🍷
Attractive, plummy, easy-drinking Central Italian red for those trattoria moments.

ROMANIA

1996 Val Duna Merlot, DOC Recas, £2.79   13/20
Medium-bodied 👛👛 🍷
Far cleaner and fruitier than most Romanian reds, this is a modern, faintly chewy Merlot with a dry finish.

SPAIN

Tempranillo/Cabernet Sauvignon, Cariñena, San José Co-op, £2.99 `   14/20
Medium-bodied 👝👝👝 🍾
Soft, plum and blackcurrant-fruity Spanish red from the little-known Cariñena region in Aragon.

1989 Hoya de Cadenas Reserva, Vicente Gandia, £2.99   14/20
Medium-bodied 👝👝👝 🍾
Mature, traditional, gamey, sweetly oaked Rioja taste-alike from Valencia's Vicente Gandia. Great at the price.

UNITED STATES

California Cellars Red, Canandaigua Winery, £2.99   13/20
Medium-bodied 👝👝 🍾
Young, strawberry-fruity California glugger with soft tannins and a sweetish finish.

£3–5

ARGENTINA

1995 Malbec/Syrah, Balbi Vineyards, £3.29   14/20
Medium-bodied 👝👝 🍾
Typical of the good value emerging from Argentina, this is a soft, spicy blend of Argentina's staple red grape, Malbec, with some Syrah.

AUSTRALIA

Pelican Bay Shiraz/Cabernet Sauvignon, Southcorp Wines, £3.59
                                                              14/20

Medium-bodied 👝👝 🍾
Juicy, spicy, sweetly oaked Aussie red at a very appealing price.

BULGARIA

1993 Reserve Merlot, Liubimetz, £3.09   14/20
Medium-bodied 👜👜👜 |
Modern, sweetly oaked Bulgarian Merlot with good balance and lingering blackberry fruitiness.

FRANCE

1996 Beaujolais, François Dubessy, £3.49   14/20
Light-bodied 👜👜👜 |
Young thirst-quenching Gamay. If only all cheap Beaujolais tasted as good as this.

1995 Côtes de la Malepère, Domaine des Bruyères, Domaines Virginie, £3.49   13/20
Medium-bodied 👜👜 |
Midi-meets-Bordeaux blend of Cabernet Sauvignon and Merlot, Grenache and Cinsault. Lightly oak-chipped for added interest.

ITALY

1996 Chianti DOCG, Cecchi, £3.49   14/20
Medium-bodied 👜👜👜 |
Thirst-quenching, youthful, pasta-bashing Chianti with vibrant black-cherry fruitiness. One of the best basic Chiantis around.

UNITED STATES

Paul Masson Carafes, California, £3.49   12/20
Medium-bodied |
Confected, lightly peppery, Ribena-like California red from the Monterey-based Paul Masson Winery.

Rosé

Under £3

FRANCE

Selection Cuvée VE, Rosé de France, Domaines Virginie, £2.59

12/20

Off-dry 🝊 ▮
Sweet and mawkish southern French rosé, which reminded us of an American blush wine.

ITALY

Lambrusco Rosé '4', £1.55   12/20
Sweet 🝊 ▮
Cherryade for grown-ups.

PORTUGAL

Portuguese Rosé de Cambriz, Vinho de Mesa, £2.39   13/20
Off-dry 🝊🝊 ▮
Bronze-pink, spritzy Mateus rosé clone with some sweetness and an authentically earthy Portuguese bite.

Sparkling

Over £8

FRANCE

Louis Raymond Champagne, F. Bonnet, £8.99   12/20
Dry ▮
Youthful, sweetened-up bargain-basement fizz. You would be far better off buying New World fizz at this price.

Bonnet Brut Heritage Champagne, F. Bonnet, £12.99   13/20
Dry 🥂 ▮
More authentic and more flavoursome, but still rather thin and undistinguished
for Champagne.

Fortified

Under £3

SPAIN

Castillo de Liria, Moscatel de Valencia, £2.99   12/20
Very sweet 🥂 ▮
Ultra-sweet, marmaladey confection. Strictly for trifles.

£3–5

GREECE

Mavrodaphne of Patras, £3.69   14/20
Full-bodied 🥂🥂 ▮
Sweet, raisiny, well-made fortified red with appealing blackberry-fruit flavours
and deceptively strong alcohol. Greece's answer to the Roussillon's Banyuls —
only cheaper.

Majestic ☆☆☆☆(☆)

Address: Odhams Trading Estate, St Albans Road, Watford, Herts WD2 5RE

Telephone/fax: 01923 816999; 01923 819105

Number of branches: 65

Opening hours: Generally 10.00am to 8.00pm Monday to Saturday; 10.00am to 6.00pm Sunday and bank holidays

Credit cards accepted: American Express, Delta, Diners, MasterCard, Switch, Visa

Discounts: Six-bottle, case and five-case discounts, plus discounts on Champagne and sparkling wine, as well as promotional offers. Seven promotional periods a year, with multi-buy and bottle discounts

Facilities and services: Parking at all stores (except Mayfair); free delivery within 30 miles; mail-order service (tel. 01727 847935); glass loan with deposit; in-store tastings; en primeur, Port and fine German wine offers

Special offers: See discounts

Top ten best-selling wines (by volume): Pinot Grigio del Veneto, Pasqua; Blanc de Blancs, Henri Lambert; Côtes du Rhône, Lys d'Or; Bourgogne Chardonnay, Trapet; Domaine Le Puts Blanc; Chardonnay, Jean de Balmont; Fortant Grenache; Lindemans Cawarra Semillon/Chardonnay; Mâcon Lugny, Louis Latour; De Telmont Reserve Brut Champagne

Range:

GOOD: Bordeaux, Burgundy, Beaujolais, Loire, Rhône, regional France, Alsace, Germany, Spain, New Zealand, Champagne and sparkling wines

AVERAGE: Italy, Portugal, Australia, United States, Chile, South Africa, Port, Sherry and fortified wines

POOR: Eastern Europe

UNDER-REPRESENTED: Hungary, Argentina, Australian estate wines

A Majestic in Mayfair? To those of us who remember the chain's stack-it-high origins (not to mention some of the dodgier moments in its history), the idea might sound, shall we say, a little incongruous. But the blue-rinsed residents of South Audley Street and their younger, Porsche-driving counterparts have welcomed the new store with open chequebooks since its launch in November 1996. The average spend is around £200, with a huge amount of delivered business. Who wants to go shopping when a little man will drop the bubbly round in a van?

The opening of a store in London's W1 completes the transition of Majestic Wine Warehouses from a business with very little future to one of the wine trade's most prominent success stories. And all that in just over six years. As buyer Jeremy Palmer comments, 'In 1991, we all had to take a pay cut to keep the company afloat. Nowadays we're in a very healthy position.'

This year's milestones, W1 aside, include a well-received placing on the Alternative Investment Market of the London Stock Exchange, a more than acceptable set of annual financial results (a biggest-ever profit of nearly £2 million) and (just as significant) the opening of Majestic's first store north of the border in Glasgow in July, bringing the chain's total number of branches to 65 – and still expanding.

The AIM placing in November 1996 stopped short of a full-scale flotation, which would have been a more expensive exercise, according to street-wise trading director, Tony Mason. But it was still a welcome vote of confidence in the business. The aims, so to speak, were fivefold: to raise capital, to create a market for the company's shares, and especially the share options of Majestic's staff, to increase the profile of the business and to drum up finance for further property acquisition.

The £2 million raised from selling 21 per cent of the company's equity to brokers and financial institutions has done very nicely, thank you (the remainder belongs to chairman, John Apthorp, and his family, Majestic staff and private investors). Majestic has more than returned the favour. Shares opened at £1.60 and, at the time of writing, were trading at around £2.60.

Sweden was the setting for another successful Majestic coup. Having bought 40,000 cases of wine in 1996, Tony Mason, the British wine trade's arch wheeler and dealer, went back to Stockholm to plunder the cellars of the former wine and spirits monopoly, Vin & Sprit, in March 1997. This time, the haul was even bigger, at nearly 90,000 cases of cut-price claret. 'It's a huge parcel,' says Mason with the glee of a born trader, 'a mixture of around 25 per cent blue-chip fine wine and Swedish-bottled claret at the cheaper end.'

How did he do it? The monopoly over-bought and was left, in the wake of French nuclear testing in the South Pacific, with a lot of stock on its books. 'The wholesalers have now been privatised in Sweden,' adds Mason, 'but not the retailers. There's an anarchic situation over there and we've taken advantage.

Majestic

Not many British retailers could be confident of shifting 90,000 cases of claret, but this is Majestic, where France still accounts for 55 per cent of sales and customers are very keen on the wines of the Gironde. 'There's been a genuine revival of interest in the appellations of France,' says buyer Chris Hardy.

Why? It's partly a reaction to the stronger exchange rate, which has brought prices down, and partly a stylistic thing. French wines, especially those from the Midi, are much fruitier (and therefore better armed to compete with the New World) than before. The fact that France has enjoyed good vintages in 1995 and 1996 has also helped.

Majestic is certainly at its most confident when buying in France. 'We're more like tradesmen than wine merchants,' says Tony Mason, 'and it's easier to do what we do well in France than in the New World. We can go to a trade fair, pick up a few wines and be back at work two days later. With the exception of South America and Australia, we've seen a shift by our customers from the New World to France.'

Their Francophilia notwithstanding, Majestic's punters are also pretty keen on Australia, the country that occupies second place in sales. There is nevertheless a rather timid buying policy in Australia, and to a lesser extent California, where Majestic seems loath to buy wines from smaller estates, preferring the safer options offered by the likes of Mondavi and Penfolds. Things are a little better in New Zealand and Chile, but the New World is not really Majestic's forte.

One area where Majestic's customers are happy to take a risk of sorts is by buying en primeur. (There's no guarantee, after all, that the wines will increase in price on release.) Having dallied with the 1995 Bordeaux vintage, Majestic showed greater commitment in 1996. 'We bought 1,000 cases,' says Jeremy Palmer. 'There's a definite buzz in Bordeaux, a mood. And we're seeing plenty of demand.'

Majestic also got more deeply involved with Germany this year, hoovering up a large range of estate-bottled goodies from the likes of Richter, Loosen, Von Bühl, Von Kesselstatt, Studert-Prüm and Bürklin-Wolf. The gamble has paid off, with 700 cases of estate wine sold in a matter of weeks over the summer. 'People are beginning to understand that German wines are fantastic value,' says marketing director, Debbie Worton. 'This is the third year we've supported estate wines like these and our bullish stand has paid off.'

If Germany is doing well, alongside France, Chile and sparkling wines, Italy, Portugal and Eastern Europe continue to under-perform. Bulgaria is something Majestic can do without, given its customers' expensive tastes (the average bottle price is still one of the highest in the country at £4.75, excluding Champagne and sparkling wines). But it could do much better in Italy.

All the same, the 800-strong range is pretty good overall. The same goes for the business as a whole. With its Stock Exchange placing behind it, Majestic is keen to expand further. There are plans to open another 35 stores by the turn of the century, provided Majestic and Kwik Fit's former agents can come up with the right sites.

Against all the odds, the wine warehouse formula has survived and prospered. How have the Majestic boys and girls done it? 'We look at the supermarkets as our main competition,' says Tony Mason, 'and concentrate on the things they can't do – range, depth of stock, delivery, tastings and knowledgeable staff. Selling by the case means that you can cut out the guy who just wants a can of beer or a packet of fags and concentrate on customer service.' No doubt the residents of South Audley Street approve.

White

Under £3

FRANCE

1996 Chardonnay Jean de Balmont, Vin de Pays du Jardin de la France, £2.99   13/20
Dry 🍾🍾 ▮
Appley, fresh, unoaked Chardonnay from one of France's most extensive vin de pays areas. Has the acidity you would expect from the northerly Loire Valley.

1996 Semillon, Vin de Pays Agenais, £2.99   14/20
Dry 🍾🍾🍾 ▮
From a famous rugby-playing region in la France profonde, this is a soft, herby thirst-quencher at a good price.

£3–5

AUSTRALIA

1996 Lindemans Cawarra Semillon/Chardonnay, £4.49   14/20
Dry 🍾 ▮
Vanilla and ice cream-soda-scented white with citrus fruit zing and a hint of spicy oak.

1995 Rothbury Trident, £4.79 15/20
Dry 🍷🍷 ▮

An unusual blend of Sauvignon Blanc, Semillon and Chardonnay from one of the Hunter Valley's best wineries. Grassy Semillon is the dominant prong of this fresh, youthful white.

CHILE

1996 Carta Vieja Antigua Chardonnay, Maule, £4.99 15/20
Dry 🍷🍷 ▮

Rich, buttery, sweetly oaked Chilean Chardonnay with notes of toffee and caramel fudge. A crisp finish prevents the wine from cloying.

FRANCE

1996 Sauvignon Lot 279, £3.49 14/20
Dry 🍷🍷 ▮

Not quite as thrilling as it was on first release, but this remains a well-made, grassy Bordeaux Sauvignon Blanc from the négociant firm of Calvet.

1996 Domaine Le Puts, Vin de Pays des Côtes de Gascogne, Hugh Ryman, £3.69 14/20
Bone dry 🍷🍷 ▮

Made to the classic Hugh Ryman formula, this is a modern bone-dry Gascon white with a grapefruity twist.

1996 Domaine de Saint Lannes, Vin de Pays Côtes de Gascogne, £3.69 15/20
Dry 🍷🍷🍷 ▮

A step up in intensity and depth of flavour, this French-made Gascon white has attractive notes of guava and mango underpinned by fresh acidity.

1996 Chardonnay Cuvée Australienne, Vin de Pays du Jardin de la France, £3.99 13/20
Dry 🍷 ▮

What would French traditionalists make of a vin de pays called Cuvée Australienne? Our guess is pas beaucoup. A decent, if somewhat unexciting, unoaked Loire Chardonnay.

1996 Cheverny Blanc, Oisly et Thésée, £3.99   15/20
Bone dry 💰💰💰 ▮

A nettley, pungent blend of Chenin Blanc, Sauvignon Blanc and Chardonnay, made at one of the Loire's stellar co-operatives. Crisp, steely and ideal with white fish.

1995 Bourgogne Chardonnay Meilleurs Climats, Emile Trapet, £4.49   13/20
Dry ▮

Old-fashioned, wet-wool aromas and tart green acidity make this an unexciting white Burgundy.

1996 Big Frank's Viognier, Vin de Pays d'Oc, £4.99   16/20
Dry 💰💰💰 ▮

Aromatic, understated Viognier from Polish American painter-turned-vigneron, Big Frank Chludinski. It's hard to find Viognier as good as this apricoty example at under £5.

GERMANY

1991 Graacher Himmelreich Riesling, Friedrich Wilhelm Gymnasium, £3.99   12/20
Medium sweet ▮

Fading, faintly bitter-sweet Mosel Riesling, which has seen plenty of better days. Clapped-out.

ITALY

1996 Chardonnay delle Colline Pescaresi, Borgo Reale, £3.49
   13/20
Dry 💰 ▮

Fresh, if neutral, Abruzzo Chardonnay made to a cool-fermented, stainless-steel formula. Might just as well be a Trebbiano.

1996 Verdicchio dei Castelli di Jesi Classico, Borgo Reale, £3.89
   15/20
Bone dry 💰💰💰 ▮

A step up from the same producer's Chardonnay, this is a superior dry white with some of the nutty character of the Verdicchio grape and a refreshing, bitter zing.

1996 Pinot Grigio del Veneto, Vino da Tavola, Pasqua, £3.99   12/20
Dry
Thin, pear-droppy Italian white, which trades on the Pinot Grigio name. Best poured over the side of your gondola.

PORTUGAL

1995 Dry Muscat, João Pires, £4.49   8/20
Dry
Medicinal, bitter Portuguese white, which reminded us of horseradish. Not exactly what you're looking for in a Muscat, even with your roast beef.

SPAIN

1993 Misela de Murrieta, Rioja Blanco, £4.99   15/20
Bone dry
An oak-aged blend of Viura and Malvasia made in an uncompromisingly traditional style – bone dry and almost Fino Sherry-like. Drink with salted almonds and olives.

£5–8

AUSTRALIA

1996 Ironstone Semillon/Chardonnay, Margaret River, £5.99   16/20
Dry
From the consistently excellent Cape Mentelle winery in Western Australia, this is a highly drinkable blend in which the herbal, grapefruity characters of the Semillon are nicely rounded out by 25 per cent Chardonnay.

1995 Preece Chardonnay, Mitchelton, £6.99   15/20
Dry
Clothed in smoky, coconutty oak, this is a Victorian Chardonnay that doesn't quite gell. Good enough, but a little over-priced.

1995 Yalumba Family Reserve Chardonnay, £7.49   17/20
Dry
A big, rich, leesy Aussie Chardonnay made in a Meursault mould, with plenty of alcohol and flavour, subtle oak and acidity.

FRANCE

1996 Mâcon Fuissé, Domaine Giroux, Cuvée Prestige, £5.49   14/20
Bone dry
Clean but rather tart Chardonnay from the best part of the Mâconnais region.
Finishes lean and mean.

1994 Pinot Blanc, Haegelin, £5.49   13/20
Off-dry
Soft, easy-drinking Pinot Blanc, which pulls up short of breath some way from
the finishing line.

1996 Pouilly Fumé Le Chant des Vignes, Joseph Mellot, £5.99
16/20
Bone dry
Reflecting the high quality of the 1996 vintage in the Loire, this is a very pure,
well-priced (for Pouilly Fumé) Sauvignon Blanc with well-defined, nettley
crispness.

1995 Mâcon-Lugny, Louis Latour, £6.29   16/20
Dry
From Beaune négociant Louis Latour, this is a flavoursome white in a good-
looking bottle, which manages to be authentically Burgundian and well-priced
at the same time.

1995 Riesling Bollenberg, Haegelin, £6.49   16/20
Bone dry
Fresh, well-crafted Alsace Riesling from the Bollenberg vineyard site, showing
attractive lime-zesty fruitiness and a lot of character.

1996 Pouilly Vinzelles 1996, Château de Laye, £7.99   14/20
Dry
Confected, baked banana and bubble-gum-like Chardonnay, which should be
more authentic at the price.

1996 Chablis, Vocoret, £7.99   16/20
Bone dry
Traditional, chalky Chablis with steely acidity and a taut profile. One for purists.

1995 Saint Romain Blanc, Thévenin, £7.99   17/20
Dry 🍯🍯🍯 ▬

Elegant, modern, appealingly oaked Chardonnay from the hillside Côte de Beaune village of Saint Romain. Flavoursome, minerally white Burgundy, which sings on the palate.

1995 Saumur Blanc Vieilles Vignes, Domaine Langlois, £7.99 17/20
Bone dry 🍯🍯🍯 ▬

A barrel-fermented Loire valley curiosity, made entirely from old-vine Chenin Blanc. Fruit concentration, clean acidity and well-judged oak make this an interesting alternative to white Burgundy.

GERMANY

1996 Deidesheimer Leinhöhle Riesling Kabinett Halbtrocken, Von Bühl, £5.99   16/20
Off-dry 🍯🍯🍯 ▬

From the traditional Von Bühl estate in the Palatinate, this is a peachy, youthful Riesling with the richness you would expect to find in a Pfalz Riesling, allied to spritz and style.

1995 Ruppertsberger Gaisböhl Riesling Kabinett, Bürklin-Wolf, Pfalz, £5.99   16/20
Medium dry 🍯🍯🍯 ▬

Spicy, modern, elegant Riesling from the excellent Bürklin-Wolf estate in the Pfalz. Fresh, zesty, grapefruity and highly drinkable.

1993 Oppenheimer Kreuz Riesling Auslese, Louis Guntrum, Rheinhessen, £6.49   15/20
Sweet 🍯 |

Mature, honeyed Riesling, which is well-made but a touch over-priced and old-fashioned.

1995 Wehlener Sonnenuhr Riesling Kabinett, Studert-Prüm, Mosel, £6.99   17/20
Medium dry 🍯🍯🍯 ▬

Super-fresh, mouth-watering Mosel Riesling with featherweight alcohol and lingering fruit flavours. Like biting into a Cox's apple.

ITALY

1996 Castello di Tassarolo, Gavi, Piedmont, £7.49   14/20
Dry

Gavi is an ultra-trendy wine, which disappoints more often than not. This gluey example is a case in point. A wine for fashion victims.

NEW ZEALAND

1996 Delegats Chardonnay, Hawkes Bay, £5.99   14/20
Off-dry

Sweetish, heftily oaked Hawkes Bay Chardonnay, which starts soft but finishes lean.

1996 Oyster Bay Sauvignon, Marlborough, £6.99   15/20
Dry

From the same winery, this is an aromatic, tinned pea-like Sauvignon Blanc, which has been better in previous vintages.

1995 Church Road Chardonnay, Montana, Hawkes Bay, £7.99
    17/20

Dry

Made by the talented Tony Prichard at Montana's Hawkes Bay base, this is a beautifully-crafted, pineappley North Island Chardonnay, which proves that the 1995 vintage wasn't all bad.

SOUTH AFRICA

1996 Neil Ellis Chardonnay, £7.99   17/20
Dry

From the cool-climate Elgin district, better known for apples than grapes, this is a fresh, lively Chardonnay with miles more elegance and flavour than most South African whites. Perfectly poised.

UNITED STATES

1994 Kautz-Ironstone Chardonnay, Sierra Foothills, £5.49   14/20
Dry

Sweet, one-dimensional Californian Chardonnay with clumsy oak and a hollow centre.

1995 Seghesio Sonoma Sauvignon Blanc, £5.99   15/20
Dry 🥂 ▮
A well-made, Fumé Blanc-style Sauvignon with a dash of Semillon, partly barrel-fermented for roundness and complexity.

Over £8

AUSTRALIA

1996 Cape Mentelle Semillon/Sauvignon, Margaret River, £8.99
16/20
Dry 🥂🥂 ▮
Passion fruity, Western Australian blend from French-owned Cape Mentelle, with notes of toasty oak and grapefruit zest.

FRANCE

1994 Gewürztraminer Les Princes Abbés, Schlumberger, £8.49
17/20
Dry 🥂🥂🥂 ▬
If you want to know what top-class Alsace Gewürztraminer tastes like, we suggest you buy a bottle of this finely crafted, rose-petal-scented white, with its exotic lychee and peach fruit flavours.

1996 Sancerre Les Roches, Vacheron, £8.99   16/20
Dry 🥂🥂 ▮
From one of the most consistent producers in the Sancerre appellation, this is a well-made, minerally Sancerre with good length and concentration. Fuller and fruitier than the more restrained 1995, but just as good.

1996 Pouilly Fuissé, Drouin, £9.99   15/20
Dry 🥂 ▮
A rather expensive white Burgundy trading on the Pouilly Fuissé name. Decent, but lacks excitement.

1994 Chablis Grand Cru Blanchots, Vocoret, £14.99   17/20
Bone dry 🥂🥂🥂 ▬
Fiercely traditional, oak-aged Chablis from one of the best Grand Cru sites in the appellation, showing super concentration and richness and enough acidity for a long life.

1994 Pinot Gris Grand Cru Kitterlé, Schlumberger, £16.99   16/20
Off-dry 👜👜 ━
From the same producer as the Gewürztraminer, this is a super-rich, late picked
Pinot Gris with a hint of botrytis and a whopping 14 per cent alcohol.

GERMANY

1990 Ockfener Bockstein Riesling Auslese, Dr Fischer, Saar, £8.99
                                                                17/20
Sweet 👜👜👜 |
Mature, petrolly Saar Riesling with masses of flavour and concentration. The
overt sweetness is beautifully balanced by acidity and juicy richness.

NEW ZEALAND

1996 Dashwood Marlborough Sauvignon Blanc, Vavasour, £8.49
                                                                16/20
Dry 👜 |
Tinned-pea, cool-climate Sauvignon Blanc from Marlborough's Awatere Valley,
showing tropical fruit flavours and good concentration. Slightly over-priced.

1996 Sacred Hill Reserve Chardonnay, £9.99   16/20
Dry 👜👜 ━
Toasty, stylishly oaked Hawkes Bay Chardonnay from the Mason brothers (no
relation to Majestic's Tony). Elegant and well-made, with toffee fudge and citrus-
fruit notes.

Red

£3–5

ARGENTINA

1996 La Rural Malbec, Mendoza, £3.99   14/20
Medium-bodied 👜👜 |
Typical of the good value emerging from Argentina, this is a soft, plummy,
glugging red made from Mendoza's most widely planted variety.

AUSTRALIA

1995 Cranswick Shiraz/Cabernet Sauvignon, £3.99   13/20
Medium-bodied |

Lighter, less intense Aussie red than the Angove's Classic below, with simple and rather dilute fruit flavours and charry oak.

1995 Angove's Classic Reserve Cabernet Sauvignon, £4.99   15/20
Full-bodied 👜👜 |

Ripe, spicy, sweetly oaked Aussie Cabernet from the giant Angove's operation, with supple tannins and straightforward blackcurrant fruit.

CHILE

1995 Santa Rita Reserva Merlot, £4.99   16/20
Medium-bodied 👜👜👜 ━

Minty, densely coloured Chilean Merlot with textured tannins and well-judged oak. Lashings of flavour for under £5. Can Bordeaux compete?

1994 Carta Vieja, Antigua Selección Cabernet, £4.99   16/20
Medium-bodied |

Dry and over-oaked Chilean Cabernet Sauvignon with sweet, if hollow, plum fruit flavours.

FRANCE

1996 Côtes du Rhône, Les Chevaliers aux Lys d'Or, £3.29   13/20
Medium-bodied 👜 |

Lightly peppery, Beaujolais style southern Rhône red with drying tannins and hefty alcohol.

1996 Fortant de France Grenache, Vin de Pays d'Oc, £3.79   13/20
Medium-bodied 👜 |

Confected, bubble-gummy southern French Grenache from pasta magnate Robert Skalli's négociant operation in the port of Sète.

1995 Claret Lot 278, Bordeaux, Calvet, £3.89   14/20
Medium-bodied 👜👜 |

Fresh, grassy, youthful claret. Good affordable stuff from négociant Calvet.

1990 Château de Brussac, Bordeaux, £3.99

15/20

Medium-bodied 👜👜👜 🍷

Supple, attractively drinkable, Merlot-dominated claret at a knock-down Swedish, ex-monopoly price.

Pinot Noir, Oisly et Thésée, £3.99

14/20

Light-bodied 👜👜 🍷

Bright, strawberry fruity Loire Pinot Noir from the Oisly et Thésée co-op, with soft tannins and some genuine varietal character.

1990 Château Héroult, Bordeaux Supérieur, £3.99

14/20

Medium-bodied 👜👜 🍷

Another spoil from the Swedish monopoly treasure chest, this is a gamey, chunky red, which needs drinking up.

1989 Château La Roque, Bandol, £3.99

15/20

Full-bodied 👜👜👜 🍷

A stupendous bargain at under £4, this is an opportunity to taste mature, leathery Mourvèdre, the leading grape of Bandol. Drink up.

1989 Château Vieux Vantenac, Bordeaux Supérieur, Côtes des Francs, £3.99

15/20

Medium-bodied 👜👜👜 🍷

The pick of Majestic's Swedish bargain basement, this sub-£4 claret is still very much alive and thrashing, with an attractive core of sweet fruit and lush tannins.

1995 Château de Luc, Corbières, £4.99

15/20

Full-bodied 👜👜 ⌐

Densely coloured, youthfully robust, oak-aged Corbières, bursting with Mediterranean spice and blackberry fruit flavours. A modern take on a classic style.

1995 Bourgogne Pinot Noir, Edouard Delauney, £4.99

14/20

Medium-bodied 👜 🍷

Surprisingly drinkable for a cheap Bourgogne rouge, this is a lightish, raspberry fruity Pinot Noir with no oak intervention.

1990 Château Noriou Lalibarde, Côtes de Bourg, £4.99

15/20

Medium-bodied 👜👜 🍷

Farmyardy, Merlot-based claret with an attractive core of mature, sweet fruit. Another Stockholm special.

1990 Château St Germain, Premières Côtes de Blaye, £4.99 14/20
Medium-bodied 🍷 ❚
Rustic, traditional, Right Bank claret with a malty, chocolatey overtone. Decent value at under £5.

ITALY

Squinzano, Mottura, £3.69 14/20
Full-bodied 🍷🍷 ❚
A typical Puglian blend of Negroamaro and Malvasia Nera, showing ripe, tobacco and raisin characters and a dry finish.

PORTUGAL

1994 Pedras do Monte, Vinho Regional Terras do Sado, £3.29 13/20
Full-bodied 🍷 ❚
From a Portuguese namesake, Antonio Rosa, this is an all Perequita red with strawberry-jam fruit and a nip of volatility.

SPAIN

Navajas, Rioja, £3.99 12/20
Light-bodied ❚
Over-oaky, over-smoky Rioja red, which lacks fruit and class. A raspberry lollipop in a bottle.

1995 Guelbenzu Jardin, Navarra, £4.99 16/20
Medium-bodied 🍷🍷🍷 ▬
Vibrant, structured Navarra red made entirely from unoaked Grenache at one of the region's best traditional wineries, showing masses of cherry and loganberry fruitiness and fine tannins.

£5–8

AUSTRALIA

1994 Ironstone Cabernet/Shiraz, £5.99 15/20
Medium-bodied 🍷🍷 ▬
Flavoursome, attractively minty red made at Western Australia's Cape Mentelle winery, with sweet American oak flavours and punchy tannins.

CHILE

1994 Felipe Edwards Cabernet Sauvignon Reserva, Colchagua Valley, £5.99   15/20
Medium-bodied 🏺🏺 🍾
Ripe, cassis fruity Chilean Cabernet Sauvignon with a veneer of sweet oak and plenty of colour.

FRANCE

1995 Château Calissanne, Cuvée du Château, Côteaux d'Aix, £5.49   15/20
Full-bodied 🏺 ▬
Firm, chunky Provençal red, which needs time to soften in bottle. A dryish blend of Carignan, Cabernet Sauvignon and Syrah.

1996 Chinon Les Garous, Couly-Dutheil, £5.99   16/20
Medium-bodied 🏺🏺🏺 🍾
Classic, perfumed Loire Cabernet Franc from merchants Couly-Dutheil, with fresh, grassy, unoaked fruit and fine tannins. Eminently quaffable, especially chilled.

1994 La Cuvée Mythique, Vin de Pays d'Oc, £5.99   16/20
Full-bodied 🏺🏺🏺 ▬
One of the best reds in the voluminous Val d'Orbieu range, this successfully combines Mediterranean and Bordeaux grapes in a flavoursome, spicy oaky whole. Still a bargain at under £6.

1996 Domaine de la Janasse, Vin de Pays de la Principauté d'Orange, £5.99   17/20
Full-bodied 🏺🏺🏺 ▬
The youthful Christophe Sabon is among the most innovative winemakers in the southern Rhône, as this unusual blend of Syrah and Merlot demonstrates. Very fruity, intensely flavoured stuff.

1996 Brouilly, Duboeuf £6.99   15/20
Light-bodied 🏺🏺 🍾
From the King of the Beaujolais, Georges Duboeuf, this is a good expression of the Gamay grape, with the concentration of a cru wine, showing sweet raspberry fruit and good vinosity.

1989 Château Graves de By, Médoc, £6.99

13/20

Medium-bodied |

Close your eyes and this ageing, dried-out claret could almost be Bulgarian.

1994 Mas de Bressades Cabernet/Syrah, Vin de Pays du Gard, £6.99

17/20

Full-bodied 🍶🍶🍶 ▬

An exciting blend of Cabernet Sauvignon and Syrah from southern Provence, with spicy new oak and sumptuous blackberry and cassis fruit lushness underpinned by tannic structure.

1989 Château de Lisse, St-Emilion, £7.99

16/20

Medium-bodied 🍶🍶🍶 |

Venerable, sweetly fruity, Merlot-based claret from the vaunted bicentenary vintage. An ideal red for Christmas lunch.

ITALY

1994 San Crispino Sangiovese di Romagna, Ronco, £5.99

14/20

Medium-bodied |

Basic, rather boring Bolognese-bashing Sangiovese with a dry finish.

1995 Pater Sangiovese, Frescobaldi, £5.99

15/20

Medium-bodied 🍶 |

Ripe, morello-cherry and plum fruitiness, slightly marred by clumsy oak handling.

NEW ZEALAND

1996 Delegat's Cabernet Sauvignon/Merlot, Hawkes Bay, £5.99

14/20

Medium-bodied |

Light, herbaceous and a bit pricey. A typical example of the struggle for ripeness in 1996 in Hawkes Bay.

PORTUGAL

1994 Duas Quintas Tinto, Ramos-Pinto, £5.49

15/20

Full-bodied 🍶🍶 ▬

From the Port house of Ramos-Pinto, this is a modern Douro red made from Tinta Roriz and Touriga Nacional grapes. Rich, spicy and concentrated.

SOUTH AFRICA

1995 Drostdy-Hof Merlot, £5.49   13/20
Full-bodied |
Baked, leafy, old-style Cape Merlot from the under-performing Bergkelder group.

1993 La Motte Millennium, £7.99   16/20
Full-bodied 👜👜 ▬
From the state-of-the-art La Motte estate, this is a classy, elegant, Bordeaux-style blend with finely judged cassis fruit, oak and tannins.

SPAIN

1994 Guelbenzu, Navarra, £5.99   15/20
Medium-bodied 👜👜 |
An oaky blend of mainly Cabernet Sauvignon and Tempranillo with a dash of Merlot, from Navarra's Guelbenzu winery. This is pretty good in a dryish modern idiom, but we prefer the unoaked red, Jardín.

UNITED STATES

1995 Kautz-Ironstone Cabernet Franc, £5.99   15/20
Medium-bodied 👜👜 |
On the developed side for a 1995 red, this is a lightish, but perfectly pleasant, rhubarb and raspberry-like red with elegant acidity.

1994 Seghesio Sonoma Zinfandel, £6.99   16/20
Medium-bodied 👜👜👜 ▬
Pure, bright, modern-style Zinfandel with the emphasis on blackberry fruit rather than tannin and oak. Well-balanced stuff.

Marietta Old Vine Lot 18, £7.49   16/20
Full-bodied 👜👜 ▬
A Zinfandel and Petite Sirah-based Sonoma red with spicy, cigar-box tannins and good warm-climate fruit richness and concentration.

Over £8

AUSTRALIA

1993 Cape Mentelle Cabernet/ Merlot, Margaret River, £8.99
16/20

Medium-bodied 👜👜 ━
A classy Bordeaux blend from one of Western Australia's best estates, showing cool-climate elegance allied to chocolatey richness, structure and sweet oak.

1991 Lindemans Shiraz Reserve Bin 8200, Hunter River, £9.99
14/20

Medium-bodied ▮
Pricey, eucalyptus-scented Hunter Shiraz, which lacks oomph and concentration. A botched attempt to re-create a Hunter style of yesteryear.

1993 Morris Rutherglen Durif, £9.99
15/20
Full-bodied 👜 ▮
From the pressure cooker of Rutherglen, better known for its fortified stickies, this is a dry, oven-baked red that lacks subtlety. Slightly porty and alcoholic.

1993 Penfolds Old Vine Shiraz/Grenache/Mourvèdre, £9.99   17/20
Full-bodied 👜👜👜 ━
Concentrated, old-vine Barossa red from Australia's biggest wine group, successfully combining three warm-climate grapes in a spicy, sweet, chocolatey whole with understated oak.

FRANCE

1995 Saint Amour, Domaine des Pierres, Trichard, £8.49   16/20
Medium-bodied 👜👜 ━
An excellent cru Beaujolais from a good vintage, with a surprising degree of concentration for a Saint Amour. Should develop in a Pinot Noirish direction over the next year or two.

1989 Château Le Fournas Bernadotte, Haut-Médoc, Cru Bourgeois, £8.99
15/20
Medium-bodied 👜 ▮
Pleasant, minty, mature Left Bank claret, which doesn't quite live up to the reputation of the vintage.

1995 Organic Crozes-Hermitage, Jacques Frelin, £8.99   16/20
Full-bodied 🍷🍷 ➡
Chocolatey, sumptuously oaked organic Crozes-Hermitage with classic, spicy
Syrah flavours and ripe tannins.

1993 Bourgogne Rouge, Leroy, £9.99   14/20
Medium-bodied ▮
Great vintage; famous name; disappointing wine.

1995 Gevrey-Chambertin, Jaffelin, £11.99   15/20
Medium-bodied ▮
Closer to a cru Beaujolais than a Gevrey-Chambertin. Supple, youthful,
cherried Pinot Noir with an injection of oak. Lacks the expected class of what
is supposed to be one of Burgundy's best wine villages.

SOUTH AFRICA

1994 Neil Ellis Cabernet Sauvignon, Stellenbosch, £8.99   17/20
Medium-bodied 🍷🍷🍷 ➡
Four pounds cheaper than the Kanonkop below and a good deal more
drinkable, this is a minty, juicy, well-crafted Stellenbosch Cabernet Sauvignon
from one of the Cape's most thoughtful producers.

1992 Kanonkop Cabernet Sauvignon, £12.99   15/20
Full-bodied 🍷 ➡
From an estate better known for its Pinotage, this warm, chewy Cabernet is a
slight disappointment.

SPAIN

1993 Guelbenzu Evo, Navarra, £9.99   17/20
Medium-bodied 🍷🍷🍷 ▮
A Cabernet Sauvignon-dominated Navarran blend (with Tempranillo and
Merlot for good measure), showing rich, gamey fruit, a sweet middle and a
lingering finish. Classy stuff.

UNITED STATES

1994 Seghesio Sonoma Sangiovese, £9.99   16/20
Medium-bodied 🍷🍷 ▯
Confusingly Tuscan in name and appearance, this is a Californian Sangiovese
with a hefty whack of sweet oak and tasty Sangiovese fruit. Sonoma Valley
meets Chianti Classico.

1993 Calera Pinot Noir, Central Coast, £10.99   15/20
Medium-bodied 🍷 ▯
Sweet, jammy and a little over-alcoholic, but this retains enough authentic Pinot
Noir character and fruit to interest Burgundophiles.

Rosé

£3–5

FRANCE

1996 Château Méaume Rosé, Bordeaux, £4.49   15/20
Dry 🍷🍷 ▯
Made from the Merlot grape at a property owned by a former Majestic
director, this is a good, summery, thirst-quenching rosé with soft, green-pepper
notes and an elegant dry finish.

£5–8

FRANCE

1996 Château de Sours Rosé, Bordeaux, £5.99   15/20
Dry 🍷 ▯
Another property, another ex-Majestic director. This is consistently Esme
Johnstone's best wine, showing rosehip and redcurrant juiciness and a hint of
sweetness. Optimistically priced.

Sparkling

£5–8

AUSTRALIA

Seaview Rosé NV, £5.99　　　　　　　　　　　　　　15/20
Off-dry 🍾🍾🍾 ▮
Gluggable, strawberry-scented fizz from Australia's biggest and best sparkling wine producer. An enjoyable party bubbly.

Over £8

FRANCE

Langlois Crémant de Loire NV, £8.49　　　　　　　　　　16/20
Dry 🍾🍾🍾 ▮
A well-made Chenin Blanc fizz whose natural acidity lends a refreshing zing to this appley, full-flavoured wine. A superior party fizz.

De Telmont Grande Réserve NV, £13.99　　　　　　　　15/20
Dry 🍾 ▮
Majestic's ultra-reliable house Champagne, showing attractive strawberry fruit characters and a degree of maturity.

Oeil de Perdrix NV, £14.99　　　　　　　　　　　　16/20
Off-dry 🍾🍾 ▮
Deeper-hued than in previous years, this is an attractive, raspberry-fruity rosé Champagne from the Aube district. Very drinkable.

Ayala Brut NV, £15.99　　　　　　　　　　　　　14/20
Dry ▮
Young, big-bubbled Champagne with rather coarse fruit flavours and little in the way of bottle development.

UNITED STATES

Gloria Ferrer Blanc de Noirs NV, £9.99   15/20
Dry 👜👜 ▮
Youthful, red fruit-scented California fizz with a clean, dry finish. Good value at under £10.

Shadow Creek Blanc de Noirs NV, £9.99   15/20
Dry 👜👜 ▮
Made at Moët & Chandon's Napa Valley base, this is a Pinot Noir-dominated fizz with a pinkish tinge, a fine mousse and soft, warm-climate fruit flavours.

Marks & Spencer ☆☆☆(☆)

Address: Michael House, Baker Street, London W1A 1DN

Telephone/fax: 0171 935 4422; 0171 268 2674

Number of branches: 286

Opening hours: Variable

Credit cards accepted: Delta, M&S Chargecard, Switch

Discounts: 12 bottles for the price of 11

Facilities and services: Mail-order service available through Marks & Spencer Wine Cellar, offering a mixed selection of wines delivered to the customer's home (for details call 0345 565 566); in store tastings at selected stores

Special offers: Wines of the month – a red and a white; price reductions

Top ten best-selling wines (by volume): Oudinot Champagne; Mandeville Chardonnay; Young Valencia Red; Vin de Pays de Gers; Cava; Italian Red; Italian White; Pinot Grigio; Domaine St Pierre; Casa Leona Chardonnay

Range:

GOOD: White Burgundy, Chile, Australia, Champagne and sparkling wines

AVERAGE: Loire, Bordeaux, regional France, Italy, Spain, Portugal, Germany, Israel, England, Uruguay, Argentina, New Zealand, South Africa, Sherry and Port

POOR: United States

UNDER-REPRESENTED: Rhône, red Burgundy, Eastern Europe

Marks & Spencer is no ordinary supermarket; nor, for better or worse, does its wine range conform to your common-or-garden supermarket stereotype. The most glaring differences are in size and presentation. At 200-odd wines, M&S has one of the smallest (and most perfectly formed, it would claim) ranges going. Even then, the full range is found only in the top 50 stores, scaling down to 80 products in 40–50 of the smaller stores. And all, bar the fine wines, are St Michael brand.

Why does this work for M&S and its relatively well-heeled customers when the likes of Tesco have a heady mix of getting on for 800 wines? Marks & Spencer is the largest retailer in the country, but not the largest food-and-wine retailer. As a specialist food outlet, it's weak on traditional groceries and strong on the ready-prepared side. Altogether, food and wine accounts for 40 per cent of its turnover, or around £3 billion, giving M&S between 5 and 6 per cent of the take-home market.

If the bigger supermarkets offer 30,000 food products, M&S runs closer to 3,000. Of these, it aims to change about one-third throughout the year by developing or improving them. The same goes for wine. Size isn't everything, M&S seem to be saying. 'Our aim is to be comprehensive without giving multi-choice,' says Mike Jefferys, who heads the commercial side of the wine department. 'We're not restricted in our offers, but we're happy that in the available space we can offer a continuing stream of newness.' Got that?

M&S is fortunate to have the kind of customer who's looking for novelty. So renewal, or 'product development' in M&S speak, is the key to the range. 'M&S customers are used to seeing and trying new things,' says Jefferys. So even though it's limited in size, the range, according to him, offers 'real choice and variety rather than variations on a theme'.

There's no wine buying team as such, but a head of new product development, Chris Murphy; a head of quality control, Master of Wine Jane Kay; and a commercial side run by Mike Jefferys. How does it all work? 'On a procurement-based system,' says Murphy, with sphinx-like clarity. What this means essentially is working with suppliers rather than buying off the shelf. Murphy emphasises the importance of travelling and building up relationships with suppliers in order to get the desired product right.

Does this approach make M&S a little over-reliant on a limited number of suppliers in key areas? The M&S view is that it doesn't matter if that supplier can deliver 'the quality, value, choice and interest the customer is looking for'. True enough, and we have no quibble with, among others, Montana in New Zealand, Rosemount in Australia, Viña La Rosa and Carmen in Chile. The problem is that links with the likes of Girelli in Italy, Trapiche in Argentina and Domaines Virginie in the south of France can tie M&S and its customers down to too much of an identikit house style.

Another key feature of the M&S range is exclusivity. It doesn't like to call its wines own-label, but exclusive-label. Lindemans Bin 65 is the obvious exception, but according to Murphy, M&S sells more Lindemans Bin 65 than anyone else in the world. Emblazoned with the all-important M&S brand, St Michael is one of the few labels you can serve with confidence, even if it's the boss and her husband who are coming to dinner. And the labels themselves are among the best in the high street – colourful, stylish and eye-catching.

Over the past year, the surge of red-wine consumption, in line with the general trend, has taken the split between white and red at M&S to close on

50:50. After a cautious start, M&S's rather conservative customers have taken the New World on board in a big way. 'We've had a clear-out and we're concentrating on the New World for the autumn,' says Murphy, 'particularly because that's when the new vintage whites come on-stream.' As in the previous year, overall sales have increased by 'more than 10 per cent'.

Australia tops the New World charts, with Chile nudging it and South Africa nibbling away. The autumn expansion will bring in eight new wines from Australia, six from South Africa and 11 from South America (of which six are from Argentina and five from Chile). California, Murphy concedes, continues to be a difficult area, but having just returned with Jefferys from the West Coast, he seems confident that Marks will deliver on California by the spring of 1998.

Despite the continuing growth in the New World, M&S's great strength still lies in France, which accounts for two in every five bottles sold. Italy is 'an area of strength and growth', and M&S is also starting to get better results with Spain, now that the basic quality of Spanish whites is improving.

Germany, however, remains a problem. Customers are moving away from Germanic styles and lower-alcohol wines, according to Murphy, and into value-for-money wines such as the fruity Vin de Pays du Gers and Spanish white. It has tried to stop the rot by employing a Kiwi winemaker from Montana, Jamie Marfell, to make a fresher, modern style of Liebfraumilch. And love Lieb or hate the stuff, M&S has done a rather good job.

There are a dozen or so wines at £2.99 in the range, but M&S's strength is in the middle range. The average bottle price is £4.25, which is higher than all the other supermarkets with the exception of Waitrose. The continuing case offer of 12 for the price of 11 is highly successful, along with the regular red and white of the month, both reduced for the duration. Increasingly M&S is looking into how it can support food promotions with wine, after the success of a promotion highlighting Italian foods and wines over a period of six weeks.

Customer evenings are a welcome new initiative. An evening of wine tasting in the summer organised in conjunction with the *Yorkshire Post* sold out, so M&S is now looking at a programme of customer evenings, in addition to its regular in-store tastings. And Wine Cellar, the mail-order service available to Chargecard customers, is 'modest but worthwhile', says Murphy.

As you'd expect from a company that prides itself on its technical *savoir faire*, M&S was one of the first to pioneer the new plastic cork as a way of getting rid of the perennial problem of cork taint. Until now, only litres of plonk have gone into screwcap bottles, but in an attempt to reverse the downmarket image, M&S is putting a Pinot Grigio and a Montepulciano into screwcap bottles in the autumn, promoting this as a quality improvement. 'We're of the view that we should go to screwcap, but it's a collective job to persuade customers that this is right for them,' says Murphy. With its exacting technical standards, M&S is well placed to get the message across.

White

Under £3

FRANCE

1996 Vin de Pays du Gers, £2.99   13/20
Dry 🍶🍶 |
A crisp, inexpensive, lemony blend of Ugni Blanc and Colombard made at the enormous Plaimont operation.

GERMANY

1996 Liebfraumilch, Qualitätswein, Klosterhof, £2.99   14/20
Medium sweet 🍶🍶🍶 |
A Rheinhessen blend of Müller-Thurgau, Faber and Bacchus in a Burgundy bottle made by visiting Kiwi winemaker, Jamie Marfell. Fresh, fruity and pleasantly grapey, this is easily the best Liebfraumilch on the market. In fact, it's actually drinkable.

SPAIN

1996 Las Falleras DO Utiel-Requena, Schenk, £2.99   13/20
Dry 🍶🍶 |
Crisp, light, cool-fermented Viura from Schenk in Utiel-Requena. Clean and well-made.

£3–5

ARGENTINA

1996 Tupungato Chenin Blanc, Trapiche, £3.49   13/20
Dry 🍶🍶 |
From the cool-climate Tupungato district in the foothills of the Andes, this is a peardroppy white with a refreshing bitter twist.

AUSTRALIA

1997 Australian Medium Dry, South East Australia, Southcorp wines, £3.99 15/20
Off-dry 👜👜👜 ▮
A fragrant blend of two-thirds Riesling and one-third Traminer from the giant Southcorp operation, with floral spice, elegant honeyed fruit and tangy acidity. Very good for a cheap Aussie.

1996 South East Australian Chardonnay, Cellarmasters, £4.99
15/20
Dry 👜👜 ▮
Elegant new-wave Australian Chardonnay with really well-judged oak and buttery flavours underpinned by zesty acidity.

CHILE

1997 Lontue Valley Sauvignon Blanc, Viña San Pedro, £3.99 15/20
Dry 👜👜👜 ▮
Nettley, ultra-fresh Chilean Sauvignon Blnac from the Maipo Valley's Lontue district, with plenty of grapefruit zest and flavour.

1997 Casa Leona Chardonnay, La Rosa, £3.99 15/20
Dry 👜👜👜 ▮
Stylish, full-flavoured, unoaked Chilean Chardonnay from Viña La Rosa, which runs circles round most New- and Old-World Chardonnay at under £4.

1996 Casa Leona Chardonnay Reserve, La Rosa, £4.99 16/20
Dry 👜👜👜 ▮
From the same peerless source, this is a toffee-fudge and lemon butter-like Chardonnay with considerable verve and length.

ENGLAND

1995 Leefords Vineyard, 1995, £4.99 15/20
Dry 👜👜 ▮
From one of the best vineyards in England, the Battle Wine Estate, this unusual blend of Kerner, Seyval Blanc, Huxelrebe and goodness knows what else is made in a fresh, dry, nettley style reminiscent of Loire Valley Sauvignon Blanc. Its aim is true.

FRANCE

1996 Gold Label Chardonnay, Vin de Pays d'Oc, Domaines Virginie, £4.49 13/20
Dry
Oak-dominated, lightly buttered, southern French Chardonnay with a hollow middle from Domaines Virginie. Needs more fruit.

1996 Viognier Domaine de Mandeville, Vin de Pays d'Oc, Olivier de Mandeville, £4.99 14/20
Dry
Lighter and less exciting than previous vintages, but this pioneering Languedoc Viognier is still pleasantly drinkable and faintly apricoty.

1996 Vouvray AC, Domaine de La Pouvraie, Gilbert Vincendeau, £4.99 15/20
Medium dry
Honeysuckle-scented Loire Chenin with relatively restrained sweetness and clean, appley fruit flavours.

ITALY

Italian White, Girelli, 1 litre, £3.99 13/20
Dry
Clean, decent, faintly nutty, if neutral, Italian party *bianco*. One of a number of M&S Italians sourced from Trentino-based wine merchant, Stefano Girelli.

1996 Orvieto Classico DOC, Schenk, £3.99 14/20
Dry
Aromatic, lightly spicy Orvieto blend of Trebbiano Toscano, Verdello and Grechetto with a delicate freshness and fair concentration.

NEW ZEALAND

1996 Kaituna Hills Gisborne Chardonnay, Averill Estate, £4.99
16/20

Dry
Extremely well priced for New Zealand, this peachy, intensely fruity, stylish Gisborne Chardonnay is made for M&S by Montana.

SOUTH AFRICA

1997 Cape Country Colombard, Breede River Valley, KWV, £3.79
13/20
Dry 🍷 ▮
Pleasantly fragrant and fresh, guava-like Cape Colombard from the modernising KWV operation.

1997 Cape Country Chenin Blanc, Coastal Region, KWV, £3.79
14/20
Dry 🍷🍷 ▮
From the winningly named Kobus de Kock, this is a more substantial, tropical fruity, unoaked Chenin Blanc with guava and melon notes.

1997 McGregor Chenin Blanc, Breede River Valley, KWV, £3.99
13/20
Off-dry 🍷 ▮
Confected, banana and peardrop-style, cool-fermented Chenin Blanc, which lacks a bit of soul.

SPAIN

1996 Rioja Roseral, AGE, £3.99
14/20
Dry 🍷🍷 ▮
Fresh, modern, unoaked Rioja Alta white, which manages to squeeze a little bit of character and lemony flavour out of the normally anodyne Viura grape.

URUGUAY

1997 Sauvignon/Gewürztraminer, Juanicó, £3.99
15/20
Dry 🍷🍷🍷 ▮
Unusual blend of the two aromatic grapes Sauvignon Blanc and Gewürztraminer, this is a fragrantly spicy Uruguayan *blanco* made by vociferous Aussie, Peter Bright. Crisp and refreshing.

£5–8

AUSTRALIA

1997 Honey Tree Semillon/Chardonnay, South East Australia, Rosemount Estate, £5.50 15/20
Dry 🍾🍾 |
Rich, pineappley, flavoursome, cross-regional Aussie blend of Semillon and Chardonnay, with delicate fudge-like oak flavours and soft-textured fruit.

1995 Hunter Valley Chardonnay, Rosemount Estate, £7.50 16/20
Dry 🍾🍾 |
A classic Hunter Valley Chardonnay in the Rosemount style, with lots of sweet oak, buttery texture and well-worked citrus-fruit flavours.

1996 Haan Chardonnay, Barossa Valley, Cellarmasters, £7.99 15/20
Dry |
Would-be elegant Barossa Valley Chardonnay, which lacks a little mid-palate weight. Not one to crow about at £7.99, but still a pleasantly modern Aussie white.

FRANCE

1996 Vigne Antique, Chardonnay Barrel-Fermented, Domaines Virginie, £5.99 16/20
Dry 🍾🍾🍾 |
Citrus fruity, concentrated Languedoc Chardonnay from high-altitude, cool-climate vineyards, with good oak-influenced complexity.

1996 Petit Chablis, La Chablisienne, £6.99 16/20
Bone dry 🍾🍾 |
Chalky, crisp, citrus fruity, unoaked Chardonnay from the impressive La Chablisienne co-operative, with a light, delicate finish.

1995 Chablis, La Chablisienne, £7.99 14/20
Bone dry |
Less impressive, surprisingly, than its Petit Chablis nephew, this is a tiring, faintly almondy Chablis with more weight, but freshness and zing are a bit lacking.

NEW ZEALAND

1996 Kaituna Hills Marlborough Sauvignon Blanc, Averill Estate, £5.50   16/20
Dry 🍶🍶🍶 |
Textbook Marlborough Sauvignon Blanc from Montana, showing capsicum and gooseberry intensity, with refreshing acidity, super length and flavour.

1995 Saints Gisborne Chardonnay, Montana, £7.99   16/20
Dry 🍶🍶 |
Rich, almost golden-hued Gisborne Chardonnay from New Zealand's biggest winery, Montana, showing lots of vanilla oak and buttery winemaking complexity, especially for the much-criticised 1995 vintage.

UNITED STATES

1996 Canyon Road Chardonnay, Geyser Peak, £5.99   15/20
Dry 🍶🍶 |
Californian blend of Chardonnay with Chenin Blanc and Colombard for padding, made in a lightly oaked style. Clean and refreshing with some buttery, leesy notes.

Over £8

AUSTRALIA

1996 Vine Vale Chardonnay, Barossa Valley, Cellarmasters, £8.99
                                                                 17/20
Dry 🍶🍶🍶 ━
A Barossa Valley Chardonnay that smells rather like Semillon to us. No matter. It's a very good wine with rich, toasty concentration and ice-cream-soda characters.

CHILE

1996 Carmen, Winemaker's Reserve Chardonnay, £8.99   17/20
Dry 🍶🍶🍶 ━
Produced in Chile's cool-climate Casablanca Valley and made by Carmen's talented winemaker, Alvaro Espinoza, this is a tightly focused melon fruit-flavoured, top-of-the-range Chardonnay with stylish oak.

FRANCE

1981 Chablis Premier Cru, Grande Cuvée, La Chablisienne,
£12.99   17/20
Bone dry 👛👛 ➰
Mature, toasty, barrel-fermented Chablis but still surprisingly youthful, with a
backbone of assertive acidity and minerally citrus-fruit flavours.

Red

Under £3

SPAIN

1996 Las Falleras, Utiel-Requena, Schenk, £2.99   13/20
Medium-bodied 👛👛 ❘
A blend of Bobal and Tempranillo grapes, this has a light, fruity, pleasantly
peppery style.

£3–5

ARGENTINA

1997 Tupungato Merlot/Malbec, Trapiche, £3.99   14/20
Medium-bodied 👛👛 ❘
A juicy, soft, strawberryish, easy-drinking blend of Merlot and Malbec from
Mendoza. Looks good too.

AUSTRALIA

1995 South East Australian Shiraz, Cellarmasters, £4.99   13/20
Full-bodied ❘
Coarsely oaked, rather obvious Aussie Shiraz with more splinters than fruit and
a dry finish.

CHILE

1996 Casa Leona Merlot, La Rosa, £3.99   15/20
Medium-bodied 🍷🍷🍷 ▮
Exuberantly berry fruity, unoaked Chilean Merlot from Viña La Rosa, with supple tannins and lovely fruit concentration.

1995 Casa Leona Cabernet Sauvignon, La Rosa, £3.99   15/20
Medium-bodied 🍷🍷🍷 ▮
Soft, easy-drinking, well-made Chilean Cabernet Sauvignon with smooth tannins and luscious blackcurrant fruit.

1996 Alta Mira Cabernet Sauvignon, Viña San Pedro, Lontue Valley, £3.99   14/20
Medium-bodied 🍷🍷 ▮
Chunky, aromatic, densely fruity Lontue Valley Cabernet Sauvignon made by Frenchman Jacques Lurton and Kiwi Brett Jackson, with an upright backbone of tannin.

1995 Casa Leona Merlot Reserve, La Rosa, £4.99   16/20
Medium-bodied 🍷🍷🍷 ▮
Stylish, French oak-matured Chilean stunner from the failsafe La Rosa winery. Tight and oaky at the moment, but this will develop into something rather special.

1995 Casa Leona Cabernet Sauvignon Reserve, La Rosa, £4.99
                                                              16/20
Medium-bodied 🍷🍷🍷 ▮
Chewier, more tannic Cabernet Sauvignon, which needs a year or two in bottle. Once more the fruit quality is superb, showing concentrated cassis characters and spicy oak.

FRANCE

1995 Gold Label Cabernet Sauvignon, Vin de Pays d'Oc, Domaines Virginie, £3.99   13/20
Medium-bodied 🍷 ▮
Decent, if one-dimensional, sweetish Languedoc Cabernet Sauvignon from Domaines Virginie in Béziers.

1995 Domaine Jeune Counoise Vin de Pays du Gard, Paul Jeune, £4.49 15/20
Full-bodied 🍾🍾🍾 |
Made from Châteauneuf's rare Counoise grape in the nearby Gard department, this is an aromatic, robustly peppery red in a really good package. Very drinkable.

French Full Red, Côtes du Roussillon Villages, Vignerons Catalans, 1 litre, £4.99 14/20
Medium-bodied 🍾🍾 |
Chunky, spicy, Roussillon red made from a blend of Syrah, Grenache and the workhorse Carignan grape. Peppery, pleasantly fruity stuff in a screwtop bottle.

1996 Classic Claret, La Guyennoise, £4.99 14/20
Medium-bodied 🍾 |
Basic blend of Merlot, Cabernet Franc and Cabernet Sauvignon with green-pepper notes and firm tannins. We'd rather drink Chilean at this price.

1996 Bois de Vigne, Côtes-du-Rhône, Français Père-et-Fils, £4.99 13/20
Full-bodied |
Bog-standard, southern Rhône red with rustic tannins and a dry aftertaste.

1996 Le Vallon des Oliviers, Côtes du Ventoux, Château Pesquié, £4.99 15/20
Full-bodied 🍾🍾 |
Aromatic, Syrah-dominated Rhône blend from the slopes of Mont Ventoux, with youthful, chunky blackberry fruit and a slightly green finish.

1996 La Tour du Prévôt, Côtes du Ventoux, Perrin Vin & Domaines, £4.99 15/20
Full-bodied 🍾🍾 |
Grenache-dominated Côtes du Ventoux made from old vines and blended at Château de Beaucastel in Châteauneuf-du-Pape. Sweet cherry and raspberry fruit with a liquoricey note.

ITALY

1996 Castel del Monte DOC, Torre Vento Estate, £3.99 13/20
Full-bodied 🍾 |
Rather dry, fruitless blend of the local Uva di Troia and Montepulciano grapes in Puglia, with pruney fruit flavours. Pretty label, shame about the dull wine.

SPAIN

1990 Penedès Cabernet Sauvignon, Pere Ventura, £4.49   15/20
Medium-bodied 🍷🍷🍷 ▮

Sweetly oaked, well-made Cabernet Sauvignon from the Penedès region, with smooth tannins from barrel- and bottle-aged maturity. Leafy and vanilla-like in a Rioja mould.

1994 Tempranillo Rioja DOC, Bodegas AGE, £4.99   12/20
Medium-bodied ▮

Chewy, American oak-chippy Rioja made entirely from the Tempranillo grape but smothered by bitter oak.

1994 Roseral, Rioja Crianza, Bodegas AGE, £4.99   15/20
Medium-bodied 🍷🍷 ▮

For the same price and from the same producer, why not try a bottle of this attractively spicy, strawberry fruity blend of Tempranillo and Mazuelo, with well-judged vanilla oak.

URUGUAY

1996 Tannat Matured in Oak, Juanicó, £4.99   14/20
Full-bodied 🍷 ▮

Robust, coffee-bean-scented Tannat from a place called Cánelones. Tastes older than it should.

£5–8

AUSTRALIA

1996 Honeytree Shiraz/Cabernet South East Australia, Rosemount Estate, £5.50   14/20
Medium-bodied ▮

With a trendy, minimalist, American-influenced label, this is a soft, juicy, commercial Shiraz with sweetish berry fruit and mint, typical of the Rosemount style. A bit pricey.

1995 Rosemount Estate Shiraz, South Australia, Rosemount Estate, £5.99

16/20

Full-bodied 🍷🍷🍷 🍾

From the same Hunter Valley winery, this McLaren Vale/Langhorne Creek blend is much more like it. Rich, chocolatey and smoothly oaked, with the authentic liquoricey character of Aussie Shiraz.

1996 Cabernet Sauvignon, Cellarmasters, £5.99

15/20

Full-bodied 🍷🍷 🍾

Full, spicy, liquoricey Aussie Cabernet Sauvignon with nicely judged vanilla oak sweetness and a minty undertone.

FRANCE

1994 Moueix Merlot, Bordeaux, J.P. Moueix, £5.99

13/20

Full-bodied 🍾

From Christian Moueix of Château Pétrus celebrity, this is a rustic, rather dry and extracted Merlot at an ambitious price.

1995 Cabernet/Merlot, Vigne Antique, £5.99

15/20

Medium-bodied 🍷🍷 🍾

Well balanced, with sweet fruit concentration and integrated oak influence. A bit dry on the aftertaste, however.

1995 Vigne Antique (Barrique-Aged), Vin de Pays d'Oc, Charles Blagden, £6.99

14/20

Full-bodied 🍾

A rather expensive shot at a Languedoc super-red, this is a decent, chocolatey, blackberry fruity style of southern French Syrah with chewy tannins and obvious oak.

ITALY

1995 Chianti Classico DOCG, Basilica Cafaggio, £6.99

16/20

Medium-bodied 🍷🍷 ▬

Sourced by M&S supplier Girelli from the Cafaggio estate in Greve, this is a medium-weight, savoury Chianti with attractive cherry fruitinesss and refreshing acidity.

SOUTH AFRICA

1996 Bellevue Estate, KWV, £6.99   15/20
Medium-bodied 🝑 ▬
Coffee-bean oaky, cassis fruity Cape Bordeaux blend from KWV, with a good middle palate undermined by rather rustic dry tannins.

Over £8

AUSTRALIA

1995 The Ridge Coonawarra Cabernet Sauvignon, Cellarmasters, £8.99   15/20
Medium-bodied 🍾
Piercing blackcurrant fruit, spicy oak and minty undertones make this a vibrant, if rather obvious, Coonawarra Cabernet with an astringent finish.

1995 Coonawarra Winegrowers Shiraz, Cellarmasters, £8.99
                                                             15/20
Full-bodied 🍾
Coarse, powerfully oaked, chewy Coonawarra Shiraz at an optimistic price. We'd like to see a bit more subtlety coming from coolish-climate Coonawarra, normally one of Australia's best regions for premium wines.

1994 McLean's Farm Shiraz, St Halletts, £8.99   16/20
Full-bodied 🝑🝑 🍾
Good, honest Barossa Valley Shiraz from Bob 'Sir Lunch-a-Lot' McLean, showing the classic St Hallett hallmarks of smooth fruit, mint and American oak sweetness.

FRANCE

1993 Margaux, Lucien Lurton, £8.99   16/20
Medium-bodied 🝑🝑 🍾
Elegant, nicely balanced, mature Cabernet Sauvignon-dominated Margaux from Château Brane-Cantenac, with smooth oak maturity. Classic Margaux at a good price.

1990 Les Hauts de Smith, Pessac-Léognan, £12.99   15/20
Medium-bodied ▮
Second wine of Château Smith-Haut-Lafitte, a property that has improved enormously over the last two or three years. Too late for this vintage, though, which is a little light and green-tinged.

Les Plantes du Mayne, 1989, £13.99   16/20
Medium-bodied 🛍 ▮
Rich, chocolate and coffee aromas with a sweet core of mature, Merlot-based fruit and a grassy finish.

1992 Château Beausejour-Bécot, St Emilion, £14.99   17/20
Medium-bodied 🛍🛍 ▮
From a property reclassified in 1996 as a Premier Grand Cru Classé, this is surprisingly concentrated for 1992, with smooth oak, rich green pepper and blackcurrant fruit and a hint of herbaceousness.

ITALY

1994 Canfera VDT di Toscana, Cafaggio, £8.99   15/20
Medium-bodied 🛍 ▮
Stylishly packaged, designer-bottled super-Tuscan, with medium-weight Sangiovese fruit and sweet oak, which lacks a third dimension. A follower of fashion.

Rosé

Under £3

SPAIN

1996 Las Falleras DO Utiel-Requena, Schenk, £2.99   14/20
Dry 🛍🛍🛍 ▮
Pleasantly fresh, dry, redcurranty Levante *rosado* made from the local Bobal grape. Well priced.

£3–5

FRANCE

1996 Gold Label Rosé de Syrah, Vin de Pays d'Oc, Domaines Virginie, £3.99   14/20
Dry 👜👜 ▮
A fruity, youthful, raspberryish Languedoc rosé, this is a wine for summery execution.

Sparkling

£5–8

AUSTRALIA

1994 Australian Blanc de Blancs, Bottle-Fermented, Southcorp Wines, £7.99   16/20
Dry 👜👜👜 ▮
Yeasty, well-made, all-Chardonnay fizz from coolish-climate regions in South Australia and Victoria, with a crisp, elegant mousse.

NEW ZEALAND

Bluff Hill Traditional Method Sparkling Wine, Montana, £6.99
    15/20
Dry 👜👜 ▮
Copper-tinged sparkling blend of Chardonnay and Pinot Noir from Montana with a youthful, tangy bite, made from Marlborough and Gisborne grapes.

SOUTH AFRICA

Charles Beck Brut, Madeba, £6.99   15/20
Dry 👜👜 ▮
A youthful Robertson blend of three-quarters Pinot Noir and one-quarter Chardonnay, this a well-made and delicately textured Cape fizz.

Over £8

AUSTRALIA

1993 Australian Sparkling Shiraz, Southcorp, £8.99   16/20
Dry 🍾🍾🍾 ▌
A comparatively brave listing for Marks & Spencer, this is an unusual but traditional Australian style of Shiraz, formerly known as sparkling Burgundy. A bit like a Kir Royale with tannin.

FRANCE

Chevalier de Melline Champagne, Blanc de Blancs, NV, Union Champagne, £15.99   16/20
Dry 🍾🍾 ▌
Elegant, delicately toasty, all-Chardonnay fizz from the Côte des Blancs south of Epernay, with good length of flavour and youthful bubbles.

1990 Vintage St Gall Champagne, Union Champagne, £18.99
17/20
Dry 🍾🍾🍾 ▌
Another all-Chardonnay fizz also from Union Champagne, showing more richness and intensity of flavour and yeasty complexity.

1985 Orpale Champagne, Union Champagne, £22.50   17/20
Dry 🍾🍾🍾 ▌
Biscuity, mature, rich, Côte des Blancs Chardonnay from top vineyard sites owned by the Union Champagne co-operative. Still remarkably fresh for a 12-year-old vintage Champagne.

Morrison's ☆☆(☆)

Address: Junction 41 Industrial Estate, Carr Gate, Wakefield, West Yorkshire WF2 0XF

Telephone/fax: 01924 870000; 01924 875120

Number of branches: 86

Opening hours: Majority 8.30am to 8.00pm weekdays; 8.00am to 6.00pm Saturdays; 10.00am to 4.00pm Sundays

Credit cards accepted: Access, Delta, Switch, Visa

Discounts: Up to 10 per cent off six bottles of specific wines

Facilities and services: Occasional in-store tastings; free glass loan

Special offers: Regular bin-ends and other themed promotions

Top ten best-selling wines: Minervois, Cellier La Chouf; Gabbia d'Oro, Vino Rosso; Morrison's Hock; Morrison's Liebfraumilch; Morrison's Lambrusco Bianco; Gabbia d'Oro, Vino Bianco; Vin de Pays de l'Hérault, Marquis de l'Estouval; Rioja Navajas; Vin de Pays de l'Hérault Escoudou; Liebfraumilch St Hubertus

Range:

GOOD: Regional France, Germany, Champagne and sparkling wines

AVERAGE: Loire, Bordeaux, Spain, Portugal, Bulgaria, Chile, South Africa, Australia

POOR: Romania, Hungary, Italy, Greece

UNDER-REPRESENTED: Burgundy, England, Argentina, United States, New Zealand

Morrison's jovial wine buyer Stuart Purdie is not by nature the stay-at-home kind. But as the lone wine-department buyer, the opportunities for globetrotting much further south than the Watford Gap have been few and far between. Until this year, that is. From being chained to the spittoon at company HQ in Wakefield, Purdie now has two good reasons for getting out and about.

Morrison's

Morrison's is on the move. In addition to three new store openings in its northern heartland, this family-led chain has dipped a toe further south to open new branches in Letchworth, Northampton and Erith. The other reason why Stuart Purdie is going about with a broad grin is because the wine department has at last taken on an extra nose and a new pair of hands in the shape of Fiona Smith, a second wine buyer.

For anyone unfamiliar with Morrison's supermarkets, they are attractive places to browse and spend time, not to mention money. Based on a traditional, street-market approach to shopping (an irony, as we mentioned last year, that won't have escaped the small shopkeeper squeezed from the high street by supermarket competition), Morrison's boasts competitive prices across the board amid aggressive promotions that bark louder than its chairman, Yorkshire entrepreneur, Ken Morrison.

Purdie slots in like Cinderella in a glass slipper. He's proud of his ability to do deals and pick up the odd bargain. 'From our size of operation, we're good at snaffling up bin-ends,' says Purdie. Last year, for instance, he cashed in on the Swedish drinks monopoly Vin & Sprit's bargain-basement sale. This year, Purdie has taken himself not just south of the Watford Gap but, in his new role as hunter-gatherer, to the exotic southern hemisphere itself.

Trips to the vineyards of Chile and South Africa gave him a first-hand look at what's going on there and a chance to snap up a few bin-ends. 'In South Africa, we found one or two experiments in a couple of major wine cellars and said we'd take the wine. Danie de Wet blended a Chardonnay to our requirements. I went to one of the smaller KWV co-operatives and found 30 barrels sitting in the warehouses. They'd been mucking around with a Shiraz and I said I'd take the lot, 1000 cases.'

Morrison's customers have developed a taste for the New World, with Chile now the fastest-growing wine country. Purdie was stimulated by his visit there into buying six new wines for the range. Argentina too is up-and-coming. New Zealand hardly gets a look-in because 'it doesn't have a bottom rung of the ladder'. But Australia, despite price increases, remains good business, even though Morrison's will lose the Wyndham range – apart from the popular TR2 – because Orlando, which owns the brand, needs the wine for its ever-expanding Jacob's Creek brand.

Purdie insists he's not expanding the New World for the sake of it, and in fact a helpful exchange rate and better prices have brought France back into focus. The non-traditional south is doing best, although Purdie reports a revival of interest in Bordeaux, thanks to an improvement in the 1995 and 1996 vintages. Elsewhere, Morrison's is aiming to improve its regional blends such as Côtes du Rhône, Chianti and Valpolicella.

Against a downward trend in the UK, Liebfraumilch and Hock are holding their own at Morrison's. Growing interest in new-wave, slightly drier styles, such as St Ursula's Devil's Rock and the Riesling and Silvaner from Zimmermann-Graeff, suggest encouragingly that price isn't everything.

According to Purdie, prices have remained consistent, with as many wines going down as up. 'Exchange rates have helped enormously,' he concedes, but the £2.99 price tag is still a ceiling for many Morrison's shoppers. 'I was in store with a badge saying Stuart Purdie, wine buyer,' he recalls, 'when a customer approached me with a bottle of Piesporter and asked me if it would go with chicken. I said yes, but buy two bottles of Rawson's Retreat at £4-odd and you save £1. She said she hadn't spent that on the chicken. Customers still think of the food as the important part of the meal. Wine is more of an afterthought.'

Given the incentive, though, people are prepared to spend more, says Purdie, and when they do, they come back for more. So Morrison's is increasingly promoting wines with the help of suppliers such as Val d'Orbieu's Chais Cuxac and Sutter Home in California. When he reduced the Chais Cuxac Chardonnay and Cabernet, first from £4.19 to £3.99, then down to £2.99, sales increased fifteen-hundredfold. 'Once customers have tried it, they're beginning to realise there is a benefit, unlike Blue Nun for instance, which goes back to its original sales.' Purdie also credits Morrison's with putting Sutter Home on the map after it was reduced at Christmas from £4.49 to £3.49.

Wine sales, estimated by Purdie to be on a par with those of Waitrose, continue to grow. 'This year we're flying,' says Purdie, 'thanks to much better promotional activity and new merchandising ideas.' What's merchandising? Basically, it's the way wines are sold. Morrison's aptly named Wine Seller, for instance, is a shoulder-height cube with 16 squares, each one holding a different wine. Buy any two wines from the Wine Seller and you save £1. Along with 10 other wines on promotion, this means that Morrison's regularly has 26 wines being promoted. The upshot is that a wine like the popular Minervois, La Chouf, sells over eight cases per store per day. An accompanying leaflet gives a rundown on the 16 wines, with a description of each. On the back there's a typical description of each grape variety – Cabernet Sauvignon, the classic grape of Bordeaux, for example – and how it varies in style and taste from one country to another. Drink Pink, offering a discount on the whole range of rosés, was another promotion for the lazy days of summer. Now that the arrival of Fiona Smith, fresh from frozen foods, as it were, has untied Purdie's hands, the wine department is poised for new finds. 'In the past we were largely operating on what was available,' says Purdie. 'Now we can actually go out and find things. Long-term, we're going to try to create more opportunities, rather than wait for them to come and land in our lap. We're growing, but we can still make snap decisions.' Music, no doubt, to the ears of Chairman Ken.

White

Under £3

FRANCE

1996 Vin de Pays de L'Hérault Escoudou, Caves Saint Arnould, £2.29   12/20
Dry 🍷 ▮
Baked, faintly appley Midi white for the price-conscious.

Morrison's Côtes du Roussillon, £2.95   14/20
Dry 🍷🍷🍷 ▮
An extra 66 pence goes a long way in the south of France, as this fresher, crisper, pleasantly peachy white demonstrates.

1996 Bordeaux Sauvignon Blanc, Cascades, Yves Pagès, £2.99
                                                                13/20
Dry 🍷🍷 ▮
Crisp, grassy, peardroppy Bordeaux Sauvignon in a good-looking package.

GERMANY

Morrison's Hock, £2.65   11/20
Medium sweet ▮
Flat, soupy, old-fashioned Hock, which lacks fruit and aroma.

1995 Morrison's Liebfraumilch, Pfalz, Zimmermann-Graeff, £2.69
                                                                12/20
Medium sweet 🍷 ▮
Marginally better than the Hock.

ITALY

Gabbia d'Oro Bianco, £2.45   14/20
Dry 🍷🍷🍷 ▮
Well-priced, pleasantly fruity Italian table wine with the faintest of nutty tangs. Surprisingly good value.

Morrison's Lambrusco Bianco, £2.49   13/20
Sweet 🍾 ▮
Spicy, ultra-fresh Lambrusco with sweet fizz and a lively zip.

1996 Morrison's Frascati Superiore, £2.99   14/20
Bone dry 🍾🍾🍾 ▮
Spritzy, well-defined Roman white with real zing and citrus fruity flavours.

£3–5

AUSTRALIA

1995 Wyndham Estate TR2 Medium Dry White Wine, £3.99   13/20
Sweet 🍾 ▮
A floral, aromatic, if rather obvious boudoir of a wine, with a hint of orange-peel zest and plenty of sweetness.

1995 Hanwood Estates Chardonnay, McWilliams, £4.79   15/20
Dry 🍾🍾 ▮
Relatively restrained, oak-influenced Aussie Chardonnay with attractively ripe melon and peach characters.

AUSTRIA

1995 Lenz Moser Grüner Veltliner, £3.49   14/20
Dry 🍾🍾 ▮
An unusual white-pepper-like Austrian white made from the native Grüner Veltliner grape. Fresh and honeyed with cleansing acidity.

BULGARIA

1993 The Bulgarian Vintners' Reserve Chardonnay 'Rousse', Aged in Oak, £3.69   15/20
Dry 🍾🍾🍾 ▮
Commendably fresh and youthful for a four-year-old wine, this new-wave white, aged in American oak, is a smoky, flavoursome bargain.

CHILE

**1996 Gato Blanco Sauvignon Blanc, Lontue Valley, San Pedro,
£3.49**   14/20
Dry 👜👜👜 🍸
Soft, grapefruity Chilean Sauvignon Blanc from Viña San Pedro, with good
varietal grassiness. An excellent drink at the price.

1996 Castillo de Molina Sauvignon Blanc, San Pedro, £3.95   15/20
Dry 👜👜👜 🍸
From the same Chilean winery, this is a more intense, fuller-flavoured example
of the Sauvignon Blanc grape, with fresh gooseberry fruit, crispness and length
of flavour.

**1996 Castillo de Molina Chardonnay Reserve, Lontue Valley, San
Pedro, £4.95**   16/20
Dry 👜👜👜 🍸
Characterful Chilean Chardonnay from Viña San Pedro in which toasty oak,
clean acidity and melon fruit flavours harmoniously intermingle.

ENGLAND

1995 Three Choirs Estate Premium, Medium Dry, £3.99   13/20
Medium dry 👜 🍸
A tad disappointing, given that 1995 was one of Britain's best ever vintages. But
this is still a fresh, pleasantly fruity introduction to the hedgerow delights of
English wine.

FRANCE

**1996 Sauvignon de Saint-Bris, Les Héritiers du Marquis de
Bieville, £3.99**   15/20
Bone dry 👜👜👜 🍸
Aromatic, minerally Sauvignon Blanc from the tiny Saint-Bris appellation in
northern Burgundy. Well chosen at under £4.

**1996 Chais Cuxac Chardonnay, Vin de Pays d'Oc, Aged in Oak, Val
d'Orbieu, £3.99**   13/20
Dry 👜 🍸
Simple, over-wooded Languedoc Chardonnay with banana-like fruit flavours. A
botched attempt at a New World style.

1994 Pinot Blanc Tradition, Preiss-Zimmer, £4.19 15/20
Dry 👜👜 🍷
A weighty Alsace with some bottle-aged kerosene characters and good fresh acidity.

1994 Château Saint Gallier, Graves, £4.75 13/20
Dry 🍷
Unusual, fennel-scented, oak-aged white Graves which, believe it or not, smells better than it tastes. No better than it was a year ago, however.

ITALY

1996 Pinot Grigio Delle Venezie, Vigneti del Sole, £3.19 14/20
Dry 👜👜 🍷
Fresh, spritzy, seafood-friendly Veneto white from the giant Pasqua winery.

Eclisse White, Puglia, £3.29 14/20
Dry 👜👜 🍷
Soft, spicy, attractively packaged Puglian white from the heel of Italy, with the fruity New World thumbprint of Australian winemaker Kym Milne.

1995 Orvieto Classico, Uggiano, £3.49 14/20
Dry 👜👜 🍷
Nutty, spicy, medium-bodied Umbrian white, with refreshing acidity and the distinctive character of the local Grechetto grape.

SOUTH AFRICA

Morrison's South African White, Paarl, £3.25 14/20
Dry 👜👜 🍷
A pleasant, well-made Chenin Blanc/Riesling blend combining grapey aromas and softness of texture.

UNITED STATES

Morrison's Californian White, £3.49 10/20
Medium dry 🍷
Suck a wine gum in preference to this sweet, flat and confected stuff from the Golden State.

1995 Sutter Home California Chardonnay, £4.79   15/20
Off-dry 👜👜 ▮

Rather like the 1994, this is ripe, sweet and buttery with undertones of toffee fudge and spicy oak.

£5–8

GERMANY

1993 Ürziger Würzgarten Riesling Auslese, Ewald Pfeiffer, Mosel, £6.99   17/20
Sweet 👜👜👜 ▮

Juicy, maturing Mosel Riesling, which manages to achieve the right balance of fruit sweetness and refreshing acidity. An excellent Indian summer white.

NEW ZEALAND

1996 Montana Marlborough Barrique Fermented Reserve Chardonnay, £7.49   17/20
Dry 👜👜👜 ▮

Stylish, barrel-fermented Marlborough Chardonnay, which is a welcome addition to the excellent Montana range. Packed with flavours of butterscotch, citrus fruit and elegantly toasty oak.

Red

Under £3

FRANCE

1996 Marquis de l'Estouval, Vin de Pays de l'Hérault, £2.19   12/20
Medium-bodied 👜 ▮

Basic, beetrooty plonk, which is only a vat away from being tipped into the wine lake.

Minervois, Cellier La Chouf, £2.75
Medium-bodied 🍷🍷🍷 ▌

14/20

Spicy, chunky, bitters and blackberry-flavoured Languedoc rouge at a ridiculously good price. Not surprising it's among Morrison's top ten best-sellers.

Morrisons Côtes du Roussillon Red, Foncalieu, £2.99
Medium-bodied 🍷🍷🍷 ▌

15/20

Robustly spicy, deeply coloured Roussillon red with more flavour than you're entitled to at under £3.

ITALY

Gabbia d'Oro, Vino Rosso, £2.45
Light-bodied ▌

11/20

Pale, sugary, thin Piatto d'Oro rosso.

ROMANIA

1994 Classic Pinot Noir, Dealul Mare, £2.99
Light-bodied ▌

11/20

Dry, beetrooty, charmless Pinot Noir with a tomato-skin character. One for the firing squad, Nicolae.

£3–5

BULGARIA

1991 The Bulgarian Vintners' Reserve Stambolovo Merlot, Haskovo, £3.69
Medium-bodied 🍷 ▌

14/20

An ageing if well-made Merlot, which is starting to dry out. Catch it while you can.

CHILE

1995 Castillo de Molina Cabernet Sauvignon, San Pedro, £3.95
15/20

Medium-bodied 👜👜👜 ▯
Fresh, well-priced Chilean Cabernet Sauvignon with pure blackcurrant fruit enhanced by spicy oak character.

FRANCE

Morrisons Côtes du Rhône, £3.19
13/20
Full-bodied ▯
Faintly peppery, bog-standard southern Rhône red with dry tannins.

Morrisons Claret, £3.35
14/20
Medium-bodied 👜👜 ▯
Firm, fresh, grassy red Bordeaux with juicy fruit flavours and restrained tannins.

1995 Côtes de Saint Mont, Bastz d'Autan, £3.69
13/20
Medium-bodied ▯
Rustic, oak-aged Gascon rouge with a vinegary edge. D'Artagnan would put this, or its maker, to the sword.

1995 Chais Cuxac, Cabernet Sauvignon, Vin de Pays d'Oc, Val d'Orbieu, £3.99
14/20
Medium-bodied 👜👜 ▯
Young, attractive, oak-aged Languedoc Cabernet Sauvignon with firm tannins, from Serge Dubois of the Cuxac co-operative.

ITALY

1994 Morrison's Chianti, £4.69
14/20
Medium-bodied 👜👜 ▯
Cocktail-cherry and new oak flavours make this Chianti from Uggiano in the Florentine hills very drinkable, if atypical.

MOROCCO

Cabernet/Syrah Berkane, Casablanca, £3.39
13/20
Full-bodied 👜 ▯
Pruney, rather baked Moroccan rouge, which passes the magic-carpet test. We like the tongue-in-cheek label. Play it again, Stuart…

SOUTH AFRICA

Morrison's South African Red, Paarl, £3.25   10/20
Medium-bodied
Soapy, confected Cape plonk, which reminded us of bath salts.

1995 Bovlei Merlot, Wellington, £3.99   13/20
Medium-bodied
Dry, sawdusty Cape Merlot, which tastes more like something from Bulgaria than Wellington.

SPAIN

1994 Remonte Cabernet Sauvignon, Navarra, Crianza, £3.89 15/20
Medium-bodied
Peppery, well-priced Navarra Crianza made in a modern style with charry American oak flavours and plenty of fruit.

UNITED STATES

Morrison's Californian Red, £3.49   11/20
Medium-bodied
Green, chewy, sweetened-up California red, which we found actively unpleasant. Wish they all could be Californian? No, actually, we don't.

1995 Nathanson Creek Merlot, California, Sebastiani, £4.99 14/20
Medium-bodied
Minty, juicy California Merlot from the price-conscious Sebastiani winery, with a bit of sweetness. Don't be fooled by the Château Lafite-like engraving on the label.

URUGUAY

1994 Castel Pujol Tannat, £3.99   15/20
Medium-bodied
Made from Uruguay's best red grape, the Tannat of south-west France, this is a fresh, tobaccoey red with nicely balanced tannins.

£5–8

AUSTRALIA

1995 Wyndham Estate Shiraz, Bin 555, £5.25   15/20
Medium-bodied 👜👜 ▮
Classic, blackcurrant and spicy-oaky Aussie Shiraz made to a consistently winning formula. A little sweet but very drinkable.

ITALY

1993 Barbera d'Alba, Feyles, £5.39   16/20
Medium-bodied 👜👜👜 ▬
Authentic Piedmontese Barbera in the local Albese bottle at a very reasonable price, this is a meaty, cherry-spicy rosso, which needs food – white truffles will do nicely, thank you – to show at its best.

SPAIN

1990 Navajas Reserva Rioja, £5.99   14/20
Medium-bodied ▮
Sawdusty Rioja Reserva, which is dominated by desiccated-coconut oak characters. Mutiny on the Bounty time.

UNITED STATES

1994 Willamette Valley Vineyards Pinot Noir, £7.99   16/20
Medium-bodied 👜👜👜 ▮
Well-made, raspberry-fruity Pinot Noir from a good vintage in Oregon, with subtle oak intervention. A vast improvement on the 1993.

Over £8

FRANCE

1993 Château Teyssier Saint Emilion Grand Cru, £9.29   15/20
Medium-bodied 👜 ▮
From an average Bordeaux vintage, this medium-bodied claret is still youthful, with Merlot aromas and sweetness and a lean streak of acidity.

Rosé

£3–5

FRANCE

1996 La Source, Vin de Pays d'Oc, Syrah Rosé, £3.35   14/20
Dry 👜👜 ❙
Soft, strawberry fruity Syrah rosé from the Languedoc, which is almost a red wine.

UNITED STATES

1996 Sebastiani White Zinfandel, £3.99   13/20
Medium sweet 👜 ❙
Sweet, pink and fizzy – for the sweet, pink and dizzy. California's answer to Lambrusco.

Sparkling

£3–5

ITALY

Gianni d'Asti, £4.85   15/20
Sweet 👜👜 ❙
Grapey, sherbety Italian fizz for the dolce of tooth.

£5–8

SPAIN

1993 Morrison's Vintage Cava, £5.29　　　　　　　　16/20
Dry 🍾🍾🍾 ▯
Mature, bottle-aged Champagne-method fizz with yeasty complexity, a fine rich mousse and good tangy length of flavour.

Over £8

FRANCE

Paul Hérard Blanc de Noirs Demi-Sec, £11.39　　　　16/20
Medium sweet 🍾🍾 ▯
Sweetish, old-fashioned Champagne showing bags of malty, strawberry fruity Pinot Noir character. Drink with – or instead of – summer pudding.

Fortified

£3–5

GREECE

Mavrodaphne of Patras, £3.75　　　　　　　　　　14/20
Full-bodied 🍾🍾 ▯
Sweet, raisiny, well-made fortified red with appealing blackberry-fruit flavours and deceptively strong alcohol. Greece's answer to the Roussillon's Banyuls – only cheaper.

Nicolas ☆☆☆(☆)

Address: 157 Great Portland Street, London WIN 5PH

Telephone/fax: 0171 436 9338; 0171 637 1691

Number of branches: 14, all in the London area

Opening hours: Normally 10am to 10pm Monday to Friday; 11am to 9pm Sunday, but slight variations from shop to shop

Credit cards accepted: Access, American Express, Switch, Visa

Discounts: Each month, 10–20 per cent off selected wines and Champagnes (can be by the bottle); twice a year 'four-for-the-price-of-three' offer on selected Bordeaux and 15–20 per cent discount on 40-odd brands of Champagne (no minimum purchase); occasional regional promotion with 15 per cent discount per case

Facilities and services: Glass loan; home delivery free in central London; 48-hour countrywide delivery service; in-store tastings; free gift wrapping; 'butler service'

Special offers: See discounts

Top ten best-selling wines: 1996 Petite Récolte, Vin de Pays des Côtes de Thau; 1996 Petite Récolte, Vin de Pays de la Principauté d'Orange; 1996 Petite Récolte, Vin de Pays des Coteaux du Pont du Gard; 1996 Colombelle Plaimont, Vin de Pays des Côtes de Gascogne; 1995 Réserve de la Maison Nicolas, Bordeaux; 1994 Château Lagrave-Bechade; 1996 Jurançon Sec Grain Sauvage; 1995 Domaine de la Berthète; 1995 Château Lacaussade St Martin; Champagne Veuve Galien Brut

Range:

GOOD: Bordeaux, Burgundy, Loire, Rhône, Beaujolais, Alsace, Savoie, south-west France, Champagne and sparkling wines

AVERAGE: Provence, Languedoc-Roussillon, Jura

POOR: Australia, Spain

UNDER-REPRESENTED: Just about everywhere else

Nicolas

There we were tasting a cross-section of the Nicolas range for *Grapevine* 1998 when in walked a customer looking for a bottle of Seppelt's Great Western Sparkling Brut. The French manager politely explained they didn't stock the popular Aussie fizz and pointed her in the direction of an off-licence that did. Two hundred of its voluminous, 1,300-strong range may come from outside France, but Nicolas is barely worth le détour if you are looking for an interesting New World wine.

Nicolas's strong suit is France. That's not surprising really. Ooh-là- là Nicolas is, after all, a French chain, and French wines account for 90 per cent of its vinous turnover. After taking over the chain from Rémy Martin in 1988, Castel Frères chose London as Nicolas's UK showcase. For the first four years of business it battled to survive the recession and poor exchange rates. By the fifth year, the strategy had started to pay off.

1996 was a record year for Nicolas, with 1997 looking even more promising. 'The market in England is developing,' says general manager Eric Gandon. 'We are more established and have become better known, especially for things like our Petites Récoltes range, our Champagne offers and exclusive malt whiskies.'

In 1997 Nicolas opened new premises in Primrose Hill and Muswell Hill and at the time of going to press there were plans for three more shops in prime locations: Marylebone High Street, Fleet Street and Maida Vale, bringing the total in the UK to 14. Nicolas sticks to London because the capital suits the upmarket French image and the style of its business. It is also practical to concentrate resources in one area. Long-term, the aim is to set up between 20 and 30 shops in the London area.

Across the Channel in France Nicolas has developed 70 new shops, bringing the total to 370, plus 40 franchises. Average turnover is considerably lower there, though, because French supermarkets dominate the market with cut-throat margins. The London shops, although a relatively small proportion of the Nicolas empire, account for as much as 5 per cent of the company's overall turnover. Belgium has been less successful than England, but Castel are pinning hopes on a new shop in Germany.

The overwhelmingly Gallic range is, as Jean-Paul Sartre might have said, Nicolas's raison d'être. The wines are bought in France by Alain Favereau, Nicolas's self-styled 'architect, selector and range-builder'. Every three weeks a different area of France, such as Beaujolais, the Loire or the Languedoc, is targeted and promoted. The range is freshened up with new products that do well during the regional promotions.

The value-for-money Petites Récoltes range, all vins de pays, represents one in five bottles sold in France. This year Nicolas has added to the line-up to bring the total to 20. It is currently developing a new French varietal range and plans to change the Nicolas Reserve house label – the Bordeaux Reserve alone sells a million bottles – to give it a younger, more appealing look.

Eric Gandon claims that Nicolas's success in England's 'dynamic and aggressive marketplace' is due to the fact that Nicolas deliberately sets out to be different from its high-street rivals. The product is certainly different and the service attentive. Nicolas's well-appointed shops look stylish and inviting, and customers are clearly reassured by the if-it's-French-it-must-be-good image. 'We consciously try not to double up on wines available in other shops and supermarkets,' says Gandon. 'Like Marks & Spencer, we're strong on exclusivity.'

Just as well, really. When we looked at the prices of one or two wines available elsewhere, Nicolas's prices were markedly higher. Eric Gandon insists that the company does what it can to be competitive, but says, 'We're not here to break the market or be seen as a discounter. The customer isn't always looking for the best deal in town. The cachet of a French label is important, along with convenience, a good selection and the enjoyment of browsing, too. We did a survey on what made people shop at Nicolas and price was quite low down.'

The calibre of the staff is a major asset at Nicolas. They are subjected to the Le Maître Caviste Nicolas course, a gruelling four-year apprenticeship, with plenty of exams to keep them on their toes. Until recently it was Nicolas's policy that all staff should be French. But after introducing a few Englishmen and -women, one of them a manager, blending English and French personnel in an entente cordiale looks a likely way forward. Look out for Franglais parlé signs.

White

£3–5

FRANCE

1996 Petite Récolte Nicolas, Vin de Pays des Côtes de Thau, Union des Coopératives du Vignoble de Thau, £3.95   14/20
Dry 🗑 ▮
Fresh, apple-fruity blend of mainly Colombard with a dollop of Ugni Blanc and Listan, from the sprawling Plaimont co-operative.

1996 Petite Récolte Nicolas, Vin de Pays des Terroirs Landais, Coteaux de Chalosse Cave Les Gruchottes à Sallèles d'Aude, £3.95   14/20

Bone dry 👛👛 ▮

Sourced from vineyards near the oyster beds of Bouzigue in the Languedoc, this is a raspingly fresh, shellfish-friendly white based on the local Terret grape.

1996 Colombelle Plaimont, Vin de Pays des Côtes de Gascogne, Union de Producteurs Plaimont, £4.90   15/20

Dry 👛👛 ▮

Three south-west French co-operatives have combined to produce this aromatic, spicy blend of Ugni Blanc, Colombard, Gros Manseng and the ornamental Baroque grape. Characterful stuff.

1995 Réserve de la Maison Nicolas Bordeaux, Bordeaux Contrôlée, £4.95   15/20

Dry 👛 ▮

Blended specially for Nicolas's popular house-wine range, this is a good, softly textured dry white Bordeaux with lightly grassy fruit flavours.

£5–8

AUSTRALIA

1994 Marienberg, McLaren Vale Chardonnay, South Australia, £7.99   14/20

Dry ▮

One of the few New World wines on Nicolas's shelves, this old-style, yellow-gold McLaren Vale Chardonnay is clumsily over-oaked, with a rather bitter aftertaste. Stick to La France, les mecs!

FRANCE

1996 Château Haut-Rian, Entre Deux Mers, Michel Dietrich, £5.99   16/20

Dry 👛👛👛 ▮

A blend of 70 per cent Semillon with 30 per cent Sauvignon Blanc produced in the Entre-Deux-Mers region by growers Isabelle and Michel Dietrich, this is a modern, fragrant, full-flavoured white Bordeaux.

1996 Jurançon Sec Grain Sauvage, Jurançon Sec, Cave des Producteurs de Jurançon, £6.75   16/20
Dry 👜👜👜 |

From the dominant Jurançon co-operative in the verdant foothills of the Pyrenees, this is a distinctive, grapefruity dry white made exclusively from the assertively characterful local Gros Manseng grape.

1995 Jean-Victor Senner Pinot Blanc, Alsace, £6.95   16/20
Dry 👜👜 |

Unusually fresh and characterful for the frequently neutral Pinot Blanc grape, this is a weighty, ripe, pear-like white with a delectably refreshing spritz.

1995 Reuilly Le Croz, Claude Lafond, £7.50   15/20
Bone dry 👜 |

A minerally, old-fashioned Loire Valley Sauvignon Blanc, which will appeal to lovers of similarly traditional styles in Sancerre and Pouilly Fumé. It needs food to help strim the herbaceous borders.

1996 Quincy, Pierre Duret, £7.50   17/20
Bone dry 👜👜👜 —

Zippy, pungent, almost New Zealand-style Sauvignon Blanc from one of the Loire's most under-rated appellations close to Sancerre. A stylish wine with the backbone to age for another year or two at least.

1995 Muscat Lieu-dit Dorfburg, Vin d'Alsace, André Senner, £7.60   16/20
Dry 👜👜 |

A blend of Muscat Ottonel and Muscat d'Alsace made at Ingersheim, this is typically spicy and aromatic with a crisp, dry flourish.

Over £8

FRANCE

1995 Domaine du Coteau de la Biche, Vouvray, £8.50   17/20
Bone dry 👜👜👜 —

Christophe Pichot has fermented the Chenin Blanc grape of Vouvray in used oak barrels to produce a white with the classic flavours of apple and honey, nicely juxtaposed by racy acidity.

1995 Château Brondelle, Graves, Vignobles Belloc Rochet, £8.70
16/20

Dry 🍴🍴 ⬦

A soft, peachy, concentrated dry white Graves made at a 10-hectare estate in one of the most southerly districts of Bordeaux, from a combination of old Semillon and Sauvignon Blanc vines.

1995 Petit Chablis, Les Vaux Sereins, Petit Chablis, £8.99   16/20
Dry 🍴🍴 ⬦

Petit Chablis frequently lives down to its modest name, which makes this rich but steely example an interesting exception to the rule. It's as good as grown-up Chablis.

1996 Menetou Salon Domaine de Chatenoy, Menetou Salon, B. Clément et Fils, £9.99
17/20

Dry 🍴🍴🍴 ⬦

Assertive, aromatic, ultra-modern Sauvignon Blanc from growers Bernard and Pierre Clément, with notes of passionfruit and grapefruit typical of the outstanding 1996 vintage in the Loire Valley.

1994 Château de La Guiche, Montagny, A. Goichot, £11.50   16/20
Dry 🍴🍴 ⬦

Stylishly oaked Côte Chalonnaise Chardonnay from grower André Goichot, showing richness and buttery flavours and the sort of balance we would normally associate with a good village Meursault.

1989 Château de la Mulonnière, Coteaux du Layon Beaulieu, B. Marchal, £11.50
16/20

Sweet 🍴🍴 ⬦

Mature, almondy, almost marzipan-like Loire sweet wine from one of the Loire's best vineyard sites. The acidity of the Chenin Blanc grape here keeps the wine fresh and extremely appealing.

1993 Rully L'Hermitage, Domaine Chanzy, Rully, £13.90   15/20
Bone dry 🍴 ▬

Nothing to do with Hermitage in the Rhône Valley, this is a domaine-bottled Côte Chalonnaise Chardonnay from the austere (for white Burgundy) 1993 vintage. It's stylish enough, if on the lean and tart side.

1990 Château de Cérons, Cérons, J. Perromat, £18.90   17/20
Sweet 🍷🍷🍷 ➡

Super-rich oak and botrytis characters dominate the nose and palate on this honeyed, beautifully rich, but balanced Bordeaux sticky. From one of the best vintages for sweet Bordeaux in recent years, this blend of mainly Semillon with a touch of Sauvignon Blanc would make a delectably luscious alternative to Sauternes.

1995 Meursault Clos de la Baronne, Meursault, R Manuel, £19.90
                                                                 16/20
Dry 🍷🍷 ➡

A little pricey at nearly £20, but this is a well-made village Meursault with well-integrated oak and citrus-fruit flavours. It's still young and would benefit from a couple of years' ageing in the bottle.

1989 Gewürztraminer Vendange Tardive, Alsace, Domaine Schlumberger, £19.90   18/20
Sweet 🍷🍷🍷 ┃

Unctuous attar of rose-scented white from one of Alsace's best producers, with sensuous, alluring sweet spicy fruit and superb class and balance. For once, the expense is justified by the astonishing concentration of fruit.

Red

£3–5

FRANCE

1996, Petite Récolte Nicolas, Vin de Pays de la Principauté d'Orange, Cave Les Gruchottes à Sallèles d'Aude, £3.95   14/20
Medium-bodied 🍷🍷 ┃

Fresh, juicy, strawberry-soft Rhône blend of Carignan, Grenache, Cinsault and Syrah with a hint of pepper. Good, highly quaffable rouge.

1995 Domaine des Tuileries d'Affiac Merlot, Vin de Pays d'Oc, £4.99   15/20
Medium-bodied 🍷🍷 ┃

Modern, intensely grassy, unoaked Merlot from the Languedoc, with plenty of colour and enough flavour to frighten the Bordelais.

£5–8

FRANCE

1995 Le Masoulier, Vin de Pays de l'Hérault, Sélection Moulin de Gassac, £5.69
15/20
Full-bodied 🍷 ▮
A meaty, Mediterranean red selected by Aimé Guibert of Mas de Daumas Gassac. A robust and spicy quaffer, which should really be under £5.

1996 Domaine Banchereau, Anjou, Saint-Aubin de Luigné, £5.90
16/20

Medium-bodied 🍷🍷🍷 ▬
From one of the best post-war Loire vintages, this is a vibrantly coloured Cabernet Franc-based domaine red, with grassy flavour and well-structured tannins. Could do with a few months in the bottle to soften down.

1994 Château LaGrave Bechade, Côtes de Duras Contrôlée, £5.99
15/20
Medium-bodied 🍷🍷 ▮
Mature, pleasantly herbaceous Bordeaux-style red from south-west France, with soft, tobacco-ish tannins and a firm finish.

1995 Domaine de la Berthète, Côtes du Rhône Villages, P. Maillet, £6.90
17/20
Full-bodied 🍷🍷🍷 ▬
Robust, thrillingly spicy, youthful Côtes du Rhône Villages red with blackberry fruit and angostura spice. Concentrated, rich and full-bodied.

1995 Château Bellevue La Forêt, Côtes du Frontonnais, £6.90
15/20

Medium-bodied 🍷🍷 ▮
Made predominantly from the local Negrette grape, this south-western French blend is rather unusual. The soft, juicy red-fruit character is halfway in style between an easy-drinking Beaujolais and a more serious red Burgundy.

1993 Séguret, Domaine de L'Amandine, Côtes du Rhône Villages, J. Verdeau, £6.99
16/20
Full-bodied 🍷🍷 ▮
Leathery, chunky, old-fashioned southern Rhône red with attractively robust fruit sweetness. This oak-aged Syrah/Grenache blend needs a good, hearty stew or casserole to accompany it.

1993 Clos La Coutale, Cahors, V. Bernède et Fils, £7.39   14/20
Full-bodied 👜 ▯
Dry, rustic Cahors blend of mainly Cot, or Malbec, with Merlot and Tannat.
Hard to imagine this softening before the fruit dries out.

1995 Reuilly, Les Landries, Reuilly, Claude Lafond, £7.50   16/20
Light-bodied 👜👜👜 ▯
Super-value, unoaked Loire Valley Pinot Noir with rosehip and wild strawberry
aromas and masses of varietal character. It's unusual to find Pinot Noir this full
of flavour in the Loire.

**1995 Château Lacaussade St Martin, Premières Côtes de Blaye,
Jacques Chardat, £7.50**   15/20
Medium-bodied 👜 ▯
Youthful, modern red Bordeaux from Jacques Chardat in the Blaye hills, with
succulent, Merlot-based fruitiness and a dusting of oak. A little light on the
finish.

Over £8

FRANCE

**1996 Chiroubles Domaine des Gatilles, Chiroubles, Terroirs
Beaujolais, £8.50**   16/20
Medium-bodied 👜👜 ▯
Peppery, cherryish Gamay from the fashionable Chiroubles appellation in
northern Beaujolais. A charmer.

**1993 Bourgogne Epineuil, Domaine de L'Abbaye Royale Saint-
Pierre, Bourgogne Epineuil, Dominique Gruhier, £8.70**   15/20
Light-bodied 👜 ▯
A delicate, raspberry-fruity northern red Burgundy with a core of gracefully
maturing, sweet oak and fruit from an ancient Cistercian domaine. Could
become habit-forming.

**1993 Château de Chambert, Cahors, SCA Château de
Chambert, £8.99**   16/20
Full-bodied 👜👜 ▭
From the same appellation as the cheaper Clos La Coutale, this is a similar
blend dominated by the Malbec grape but a much more enticing wine.
Modern, sweetly oaked with well-structured tannins and good length of flavour.

1989 Château Clos L'Eglise, Pomerol, £9.90

16/20

Medium-bodied 🍷🍷 ▮

Savoury, supple Castillon claret with enjoyable, luscious Merlot texture and sweet oak. A good-value Saint Emilion alternative at under £10.

1994 Château Bel Air, Lussac St Emilion, EARL Château Bel Air, £9.95

16/20

Medium-bodied 🍷🍷 ▬

From one of Saint Emilion's satellite appellations in the surrounding hills, this is a savoury, attractively textured claret, perfect for Christmas lunch.

1993 Château Fourcas-Hosten, Listrac, Société Civile du Château Fourcas-Hosten, £10.99

15/20

Medium-bodied 🍷 ▮

Typical of the Listrac appellation in the Médoc, this is a firm, chewy, old-style claret from a decent if unspectacular Bordeaux vintage. Needs a shoulder of lamb to lean on.

1995 Mercurey, Domaine de la Croix Jacquelet, Mercurey, J. Faiveley, £11.30

14/20

Medium-bodied ▮

Youthful, oaky Côte Chalonnaise Pinot Noir with lots of colour and spice, slightly marred by excessively rustic tannins and a green edge.

1993 Prieuré de St Jean de Bébian, Coteaux du Languedoc, Le Brun-Lecouty, £12.50

16/20

Full-bodied 🍷🍷 ▬

Complex, mature Languedoc blend of Grenache, Syrah and Mourvèdre from one of the region's best-known estates. Peppery and intense in a Châteauneuf-du-Pape mould. The tannins are a little on the dry side.

1993 Château de Marsannay, Marsannay, P. Chandivin, £13.50 16/20

Medium-bodied 🍷🍷 ▬

Old-fashioned, faintly farmyardy Côte de Nuits red from an excellent vintage, on which the oak and strawberry fruitiness are nicely integrated.

1990 Psaume, Pomerol, Christian Moueix, £18.90

17/20

Medium-bodied 🍷🍷🍷 ▮

Psaume is the second wine of Christian Moueix's property, La Grave Trigant de Boisset, and is made almost entirely from the Merlot grape. Lovely savoury, supple, complex wine from an outstanding vintage, with vanilla oakiness adding an extra dimension. Likely to lead you into temptation.

1989 Clos des Lambrays, Grand Cru, F. & L. Saier, £35 18/20
Medium-bodied 🍾🍾🍾 ⍩
Mature, stylishly poised Grand Cru Burgundy from Morey Saint Denis in the Côte de Nuits, with the authentic concentration and character of first-class Pinot Noir. Sweet, gamey and dangerously drinkable.

Rosé

£3–5

FRANCE

1996 Petite Récolte Nicolas, Vin de Pays des Coteaux du Pont du Gard, Cave Les Gruchottes à Sallèles d'Aude, £3.95 13/20
Dry 🍾 ⍩
Basic rhubarby Rhône rosé made from Grenache and Cinsault with the price-conscious consumer in mind.

£5–8

FRANCE

1996 Domaine de la Berthete, Côtes du Rhône, P. Maillet, £6.32
15/20
Dry 🍾 ⍩
Ripe, dry, redcurranty Rhône rosé with plenty of flavour and elegance. A wine that needs food.

1996 Les Clos de Paulilles, Collioure, Baie de Paulilles, £7.70 16/20
Dry 🍾🍾 ⍩
Deeply coloured, thirst-quenching Roussillon rosé from Bernard Dauré of the Château de Jau. This is a well-structured, cherry-fruity Syrah-Grenache blend designed with food in mind.

Over £8

FRANCE

1995 Château de Marsannay, Marsannay, P. Chandivin, £9.90   16/20
Dry ♨♨ ▮
A Burgundian rosé with almost enough colour, flavour and character to qualify as a red wine. Rosé for grown-ups.

1995 Domaine du Prieuré Allauzen, Tavel, £9.95   14/20
Dry ▮
Heavy and rather alcoholic southern French rosé made from a kitchen sink of grape varieties including, to name just a few, Grenache, Cinsault, Clairette, Mourvèdre, Carignan and Syrah.

Sparkling

Over £8

FRANCE

René Muré, Crémant d'Alsace Cuvée Prestige, R. Muré, £9.50
16/20

Dry ♨♨ ▮
Alsace is not the first place you would look for good sparkling wine, but this is a yeasty, crisp, full-flavoured and extremely well-made fizz. Good value at under £10.

Champagne Veuve Galien Brut, Georges Goulet, £15.99   15/20
Dry ♨ ▮
At the cheap end of Nicolas's extensive Champagne range, this Chardonnay/ Pinot Noir blend from Georges Goulet is soft and pleasant without being exciting.

Fortified

Over £8

ITALY

Grand Marsala Hors d'Age, Nicolas-Charenton-Seine, £19.95

17/20

Very sweet 🍷🍷🍷 ▬

Mature, alluringly complex Sicilian fortified wine with notes of burnt caramel, coffee and raisins. One to drink rather than cook with.

Oddbins ☆☆☆☆(☆)
Oddbins Fine Wine ☆☆☆☆☆

Address: 31–3 Weir Road, London SW19 8UG

Telephone/fax: 0181 944 4400; 0181 944 4411

Number of branches: 234 (seven of which contain Oddbins Fine Wine stores)

Opening hours: Generally 10.00am to 9.00pm Monday to Saturday; Sunday opening times vary – please ask your local branch for details

Credit cards accepted: Access, American Express, Switch, Visa

Discounts: 10 per cent off mixed cases during weekly tastings; 5 per cent off mixed cases at any time; seven bottles for the price of six on Champagne and sparkling wines

Facilities and services: Regular in-store tastings; free home delivery within the locality of the shop (minimum one case); glass loan (with deposit); ice; staff on hand to advise; sale or return on bulk purchases

Special offers: Regular promotions on Champagne and sparkling wines, malt whisky and beer

Top ten best-selling wines: Heidsieck Dry Monopole Champagne; Mumm Cuvée Napa Brut; Glenloth Dry White; Glenloth Shiraz/Cabernet; Lindemans Cawarra Colombard/Chardonnay; Oddbins White; Montana Sauvignon Blanc; Perrier Jouët Champagne; Lindemans Bin 65 Chardonnay; Santa Carolina Sauvignon Blanc

Range:

GOOD: White Burgundy, Bordeaux, Loire, Alsace, Spain, Germany, Australia, California, Chile, South Africa, Champagne and sparkling wines

AVERAGE: Red Burgundy, Rhône, regional France, Italy, England, Eastern Europe, New Zealand, Argentina

POOR: None

UNDER-REPRESENTED: Portugal

If you're a European wine producer, it's not just your sense of humour that's in danger of being challenged by Ralph Steadman's wickedly inventive portraits in the latest Oddbins list. You may even be able to handle California winemaker Randall Grahm's wacky surrealism. But, like the owners of Château Châtlac in the television ad, what will have you reaching desperately for the Kronenbourg is the sheer extent to which the New World now dominates the list.

With seven of its top ten wines (and two of the remaining three, Champagnes) coming from the New World, it's pretty clear that what Oddbins' customers want is the next best thing to having fun without your clothes on: that is, wines with a maximum of fruit and flavour and a minimum of the farmyard. And the end is not in sight. Not for the New World, anyway.

Having already frightened the culottes off most French producers, Oddbins is now focusing its attention on Argentina's 'mind-boggling Barberas, stunning "new-wave" Tempranillos and Chianti-frightening Sangioveses'. 'It's still early days, but it will work,' says head buyer Steve Daniel, who's more bullish than most about Argentina's prospects. 'Argentina is becoming more open-minded, seeing the opportunities, investing in vineyards and wineries. Chile is more New World, Argentina has a lot of funkiness and warm, sweet fruit. You won't see the full impact until the 1997 reds come on-stream. They're looking impressive.'

The importance of the New World to Oddbins and its customers cannot be overstated. Oddbins is the only major retailer we know of whose sales of Australian wines outstrip France. 'Australia is still the top seller and I can't see that changing,' says Daniel. 'Penfolds have taken big price increases, but their reds are the best they've ever made and they'll keep selling. What's much harder is finding good stuff under a fiver, although the price of white wines will soften.'

Chile and South Africa are catching up fast. 'Australia was the first choice for value for money, and people are still incredibly loyal', says Daniel, 'but a lot of people are actually coming in and saying they want a Chilean wine. For a decent red or white, Chile should be the first port of call'. Thanks to brilliant-value wines from the likes of Viña La Rosa (La Palma), Concha y Toro, Errázuriz and Casa Lapostolle, Oddbins easily outperforms the market with Chilean sales at 15 per cent and growing. 'We haven't found it harder to get Chilean wines', says Steve Daniel. 'We've been at it longer than anyone else, so we're first in the queue'.

Oddbins' relatively belated discovery of South Africa, meanwhile, is dismissed in typically aggressive style. 'Oddbins entered the South African scene later than most, which led certain people, who should have known better [not us, surely?] to suggest that we'd missed a trick and were lagging behind the rest for a change.' Perish the thought. What's certainly true is that Oddbins has benefited from the quantum leap in quality in South African Chardonnay and

Sauvignon Blanc and much more flavour and better balance in its reds. Dovetailing with Australia and Chile, where Big is Beautiful, the focus on the Cape's smaller, quality-conscious estates and better co-ops suits the Oddbins style and its search for personality.

The Fat Diva hasn't started singing quite yet for France or the rest of Europe, however. 1997 produced a shorter-than-expected crop in much of the southern hemisphere. A quality 1996 vintage and a strong pound have also handed some of the initiative back to Europe. 'With reasonable prices and a good vintage, we're seeing better quality in the Loire than in New Zealand,' says Daniel. 'We've seen things like Sancerre start to motor. Burgundy is good, whites especially, because the quality's been there. And the biggest percentage increase is in Alsace.'

A summer mailing of 10,000 cases of Bordeaux 1995 En Primeur On the Shelf went out to customers, with more of the 1996 vintage to follow. The south of France, however, remains a little under-explored at Oddbins. 'It isn't yet up there with the best of the New World,' Daniel comments. 'You don't yet get the similar feeling of reassurance, but hopefully the time will come when the south of France will get their act together en masse.' Or when Oddbins' travel budget shrinks?

German wine sales are small beer at only 1–2 per cent, but the estate Mosel and Pfalzes sell because Oddbins' customers appreciate new finds, like the discovery of Huxelrebe specialists, Weingut Wittman in Rheinhessen. Italian sales come in at about 10 per cent, but Italy is still a problem because of 'huge resistance to top-end Italian, not many of which represent good value for money. We want our Italian wines to be Italian,' says Daniel. Which is why Oddbins have gone to the south and the islands of Sicily and Sardinia in search of value for money and local interest.

After last year's unseemly spectacle of Oddbins' parent company Seagram trying to ditch its offspring while leaving its embattled staff to deny the rumours, there's a more settled feeling this year at Oddbins' HQ. To reach the 300-mark, new Oddbins shops are opening at the rate of roughly 15 a year. A new superstore and Fine Wine shop opened in Battersea in August. With an extra 400–500 wines and a lowest price of £5.99 a bottle, Oddbins Fine Wine shops increased sales by 40 per cent over the past year. And, not before time, Oddbins is finally getting Epos, the costly electronic system that allows companies to keep up-to-the-minute track of sales.

Like the buyers themselves, the range is constantly in transit. The managers have the full list of 1,200 wines and it's up to them to decide what to stock. An average Oddbins, if there is such a thing, stocks around 800 wines. Unbelievably, it seems that nearly one-third of all Oddbins' sales are of fizz, partly explained by the constant 'seven for the price of six' offers, and even (on selected lines) '15 for the price of 12'. Adding fizz to the equation, wine accounts for three-quarters of Oddbins' sales and the company claims to be the biggest seller of sparkling wine in the country, with about 23 per cent – nearly one in four bottles – of the total Champagne market

With an average bottle price of £5.09, Oddbins has become the first high-street retailer – supermarkets and wine warehouses included – to crack the £5 barrier. 'It's still a tough, tough market out there,' says Daniel. 'At this rate, there will be very few players left,' he warns, in a gloomy end-game scenario. 'The ones who are struggling are those without a point of difference from the supermarkets, which will always be more convenient. It's up to us to have a point of difference and create an enjoyable shopping environment with service.'

If availability is sometimes sacrificed, the size and quality of Oddbins' range does give customers the exciting feeling that they're always discovering new things. Add to that the atmosphere generated by its enthusiastic staff, plus incentives like bin-ends, discounts and special purchases, and you can see why Oddbins attracts such a loyal following. Above all, there's no neat formula or planogram. Oddbins is as Oddbins does. That's the point.

Wines marked 'OFW only' are available only at Oddbins Fine Wine stores.

White

Under £3

AUSTRALIA

Killawarra Dry White, South East Australia, £2.99   14/20
Off-dry 👜👜👜 |
Soft, sweetish, fruit salad-like Aussie white with a lime-like tang. Excellent at the price.

FRANCE

1996 Le Secret Blanc, Vin de Pays de Vaucluse, £2.99   14/20
Dry 👜👜👜 |
A banana-fruity blend of Ugni Blanc and Clairette made by Gaetane Carron. Pleasantly fresh and crisp.

SOUTH AFRICA

Collingbourne Cape White, Western Cape, £2.69　　　13/20
Dry 🍾🍾🍾 ▮
Cheapie Cape blend of Chenin Blanc, Semillon and Clairette, with a lemony tang.

£3–5

AUSTRALIA

1996 W.W. Chardonnay, McLaren Vale, £4.99　　　13/20
Dry ▮
Light, soft and rather plodding McLaren Vale Chardonnay with a bitter oak aftertaste.

1996 W.W. Semillon, McLaren Vale, £4.99　　　15/20
Dry 🍾🍾 ▮
From the same winery, this is a much better-defined white with fair length of flavour.

1996 Ballingal Estate Chardonnay, South East Australia, £4.99
14/20
Dry 🍾 ▮
Ripe butter and tropical fruit-style Chardonnay with lots of alcohol and oak. A bit obvious and in yer face.

CHILE

1996 La Palma Chardonnay, Rapel, £3.99　　　15/20
Dry 🍾🍾🍾 ▮
Unoaked, stainless-steel-fermented Chilean Chardonnay from the La Rosa Winery, with fresh melon and pineapple fruit flavours.

FRANCE

1996 Cuvée de Grignon Blanc, Vin de Pays de l'Aude, £3.19　　12/20
Bone dry ▮
No relation to Spain's Marqués de Griñon, this is a tart, appley southern French plonk.

226

1996 Domaine Garras, Vin de Pays des Côtes de Gascogne, £3.69

14/20

Dry 👜👜 🍾

Attractively grassy, zingy Gascon white for summer drinking, made from Colombard and Gros Manseng grapes by Roland Gessler.

1996 Oddbins White, Vin de Pays des Côtes de Gascogne, £3.99

15/20

Dry 👜👜👜 🍾

Same blend of grapes, same producer, but with a bit more weight, zest and character.

1995 Château de Nages Réserve du Château, Costières de Nîmes, £4.49   16/20

Dry 👜👜👜 🍾

Rich, textured, aromatic Provençal blend of Grenache and Roussanne, with mealy concentration and balancing acidity.

GERMANY

1996 Kendermann Dry Riesling, Pfalz, £3.99   14/20

Off-dry 👜👜 🍾

One of the better new-wave drier German whites, with full, peachy fruit and tangy acidity.

1996 K. Vineyards Riesling, Kendermann, Rheingau, £4.99   15/20

Medium dry 👜 🍾

Sweeter, cleanly made Rheingau Riesling from the giant Kendermann operation. A little pricey.

1996 Müller Thurgau, Messmer, Pfalz, £4.99   15/20

Off-dry 👜👜 🍾

Floral, grapey, concentrated Pfalz white with beguiling spritz and sweetness. If there were a campaign to promote the humble Müller-Thurgau grape, this would be a front-runner.

HUNGARY

1996 Nagyrede Pinot Gris Reserve, £3.59   14/20

Dry 👜👜 🍾

Rich, ripe and delicately spicy, with lots of colour, oak and flavour from Aussie Kym Milne. A good-value alternative to Alsace.

SOUTH AFRICA

1996 Stellenzicht Pinot Gris, Stellenbosch, £4.99   15/20
Dry 👜👜 🍾
Crisp, zippy Cape interpretation of Alsace's best white grape variety, with excellent peachy concentration.

SPAIN

1996 Santara Chardonnay, £3.99   13/20
Dry 👜 🍾
Confected oak and pineapple-chunk Spanish Chardonnay from Hugh 'the guru' Ryman.

1996 Albacora Sauvignon Blanc, Duero, £4.99   16/20
Dry 👜👜👜 🍾
Ultra-fresh, startlingly grapefruity Duero white, which shows how far Spain has come with its white wines in recent years.

£5–8

AUSTRALIA

1996 Normans Bin C207 Chardonnay, South Australia, £5.99 14/20
Off-dry 🍾
Sweet, oaky, alcoholic and rather ordinary for a wine at nearly £6. One to be consigned to Norman's bin.

1996 Deakin Estate Alfred Chardonnay, Victoria, £5.99   16/20
Dry 👜👜👜 🍾
Intense, richly oaked Chardonnay made in a modern style, showing flavours of citrus fruit and a buttery texture.

1996 Penfolds Old Vine Semillon, Barossa, £6.99   16/20
Dry 👜👜 🍾
Light, creamy, subtly oaked Barossa Valley Semillon with refreshing acidity. Drink it now or keep for a year or two and watch it gain in complexity as it ages.

CHILE

1995 Villard Casablanca Vineyard Chardonnay, Aconcagua, £5.99
15/20

Dry 🍾🍾 |
Ultra-ripe, concentrated Chilean Chardonnay from Frenchman Thierry Villard, with peachy intensity and sweet vanilla oakiness.

1996 Villard Reserve Barrel-Fermented Chardonnay, Casablanca Valley, £7.49
16/20

Dry 🍾🍾 |
Golden-hued, toasty, full-blown Chilean Chardonnay with masses of oak, butterscotch, toffee fudge and tropical fruitiness. Makes up in whopping flavours for what it lacks in subtlety.

FRANCE

1996 Pinot Blanc Auxerrois, Albert Mann, Alsace, £6.25   16/20
Dry 🍾🍾🍾 |
Belying the Pinot Blanc grape's normally justified reputation for neutrality, this is a well-made, floral, pear-like white with a twist of acidity and excellent fruit definition.

1996 Menetou-Salon Clos de Ratier, Henry Pellé, £6.99   16/20
Dry 🍾🍾🍾 |
Gooseberryish, abundantly aromatic, almost New Zealand-style Sauvignon Blanc from an excellent vintage. A good alternative to Sancerre.

1996 Château de la Genaiserie Coteaux du Layon, Yves Soulez, £6.99
14/20

Sweet |
Simple, baked-apple and honey-style sticky with overbearing alcohol.

1996 Vouvray Les Chairs Salées, Domaine des Aubuisières (Sec), £6.99
17/20

Off-dry 🍾🍾🍾 ━
Another stunning 1996 Loire Valley white, showing the Chenin Blanc's ripe pear and apple flavours and a fleck of honey, with refreshing acidity for balance.

1996 Vouvray Les Girardières, Domaine des Aubuisières (Demi Sec), £6.99
17/20

Medium sweet 🍷🍷🍷 ▬–

From the same top-notch domaine, this is similar in style but with extra fruit concentration and richness.

1995 Bourgogne Blanc, Domaine Jean Pascal, £6.99 (OFW only)
13/20

Dry ▮

Gluey, old-fashioned white Burgundy with poorly defined fruit flavours.

1996 Menetou Salon Clos des Blanchais, Henry Pellé, £7.49 (OFW only)
17/20

Dry 🍷🍷🍷 ▮

Fresh, concentrated, zingy Loire Valley white with gooseberry and passion-fruit intensity.

1996 Sancerre, Domaine de la Rossignole, £7.99
17/20

Dry 🍷🍷🍷 ▬–

Made by grower Pierre Cherrier, this is a juicy, intensely flavoured, grapefruity Sancerre with super length and complexity.

1996 Pouilly Fumé 'Comte de Berge', Jean Claude Dagueneau, £7.99
17/20

Dry 🍷🍷🍷 ▬–

Refreshing, super-crisp Sauvignon Blanc with a flinty streak and steely acidity. Further evidence of a great Loire vintage in 1996.

GERMANY

1996 Bechtheimer Hasensprung Huxelrebe Spätlese, Wittman, Rheinhessen, £5.99
16/20

Medium sweet 🍷🍷🍷 ▮

Peppery, unusually stylish Rheinhessen white made from the comparatively unknown Huxelrebe grape. If only England could make better use of the same variety.

1996 Ockfener Bockstein Riesling, Kesselstatt, Mosel-Saar-Ruwer, £5.99
15/20

Medium sweet 🍷🍷 ▮

Restrained, refreshingly tangy, featherweight Mosel Riesling with a floral note.

1996 Burrweiler Schlossgarten Riesling Kabinett Halbtrocken, Messmer, £6.49   15/20
Off-dry 👜📶
Well-made, grapefruity Pfalz Riesling with mouth-watering acidity and lightweight alcohol.

1996 Monzinger Riesling, Emrich Schönleber, Nahe, £6.49   16/20
Off-dry 👜👜 ➡
Juicy, elegant, full-flavoured Nahe Riesling with delightful zest and crisp, citrus-fruit characters.

1996 Ruppertsberger Riesling, von Bühl, Pfalz, £6.79   17/20
Off-dry 👜👜👜 ➡
Concentrated, fennel-scented Pfalz Riesling from an estate that has finally started to live up to its past reputation.

1996 Graacher Himmelreich Riesling Kabinett, Kesselstatt, Mosel-Saar-Ruwer, £6.99   16/20
Medium dry 👜👜👜 ➡
Sweet apple flavours and a spicy fragrance make this a very approachable Mosel Riesling.

1996 Josephshofer Riesling Kabinett, Kesselstatt, Mosel-Saar-Ruwer, £6.99   15/20
Medium dry 👜📶
From the same, normally reliable producer, this is spritzy and tangy but a little sulphurous. Stick to the Graacher Himmelreich.

1996 Von Bühl Riesling Kabinett Trocken, von Bühl, Pfalz, £6.99
                                                               16/20
Dry 👜👜📶
Weighty, almost tropical, citrus fruity Pfalz Riesling from the rapidly improving von Bühl, made in a dry, food-friendly style.

1996 Armand Riesling Kabinett, von Bühl, Pfalz, £7.49   15/20
Medium dry 👜 ➡
Pricey for a Kabinett, this is a concept Riesling with rather earthy flavours and a sharp bite of green-apple acidity.

1996 Westhofener Rotenstein Huxelrebe Auslese, Wittman, Rheinhessen, £7.99   18/20
Sweet 👜👜👜 ➡
From Huxelrebe specialist Weingut Wittman, this is an intense, grapefruit-zesty white with super concentration and honeyed richness.

ITALY

**1996 Falanghina, Feudi Di San Gregorio Sannio Beneventano,
£5.99**   16/20
Bone dry 🍇🍇🍇 ❘
Stylishly packaged southern Italian white made from the rare Falanghina grape.
It's weighty, nutty and intense, with a crisp, lingering finish.

1996 Maculan Vespaiolo, Breganze, £6.99   15/20
Dry 🍇 ❘
Nutty, dry, north Italian white made from the local Vespaiolo grape, with a waxy
note and an incisive nip of acidity.

1996 Maculan Dindarello Moscato, Veneto, £6.99   13/20
Very sweet ❘
Over-priced, grapey Veneto Muscat with a sickly, confected finish.

NEW ZEALAND

**1996 Montana Reserve Barrique-Fermented Chardonnay,
Marlborough, £7.49**   16/20
Dry 🍇🍇 ▬−
Full-throttle, Burgundy-style Chardonnay with plenty of sweet, coconutty oak
and citrus-fruit intensity.

**1996 Montana Reserve Vineyard Select Sauvignon Blanc,
Marlborough, £7.49**   16/20
Dry 🍇🍇 ▬−
Classic tinned-pea and green-bean characters and impressive weight make this
a good introduction to the finer points of Marlborough Sauvignon Blanc.

SOUTH AFRICA

1996 Stellenzicht Gewürztraminer, Stellenbosch, £5.49   15/20
Dry 🍇🍇 ❘
Turkish delight-scented Cape example of Alsace's abundantly fragrant
Gewürztraminer grape. Well balanced and reassuringly, refreshingly dry.

1996 Louisvale Chavant Chardonnay, Stellenbosch, £5.99   16/20
Dry 🍇🍇🍇 ❘
Buttered nut-style, barrel-fermented Cape Chardonnay with lots of flavour and
character at this price.

1995 Scholtzenhof Ken Forrester Blanc Fumé, Stellenbosch, £5.99 (OFW only)   15/20
Dry 🍷 |

Expansively oaked Cape Sauvignon Blanc, whose fruit is somewhat obscured by the splinters.

1996 Sentinel Chardonnay, Stellenbosch, £5.99   16/20
Dry 🍷🍷🍷 |

Toasty, attractive, would-be Meursault, with nutty, fudge-like flavours at a very good price.

1996 Fairview Chardonnay, Paarl, £6.49   15/20
Dry 🍷 |

Sweetly oaked, attractively restrained Paarl Chardonnay from Charles Back, with a touch of sweetness and an alcoholic kick.

1996 Stellenzicht Chardonnay, Stellenbosch, £6.49   16/20
Dry 🍷🍷🍷 ➥

From winemaker Andre van Rensberg, this is a stylish, barrel-fermented Chardonnay with excellent textured, mealy characters and fresh acidity.

1996 Jacana Chardonnay, Stellenbosch, £6.99   15/20
Dry 🍷 |

This Cape Chardonnay from flying winemaker Hugh Ryman is full-flavoured but a little clumsy and heavy. We prefer the Englishman's Jacana Chenin Blanc.

1996 Eikendal Chardonnay, Stellenbosch, £7.49   17/20
Dry 🍷🍷🍷 ➥

Delicate, extremely complex Cape Chardonnay with subtle oak influence and lingering lemony fruit flavours.

SPAIN

1996 Vega Sindoa Chardonnay, Navarra (Bodegas Nekeas), £5.49   16/20
Dry 🍷🍷🍷 |

From one of Navarra's most exciting modern wineries, this is a smoky, stylishly oaked Chardonnay with elegant melon and citrus-fruit notes.

1996 Burgans Albariño, £5.99   15/20
Dry 🫙 ▮
On the light side for Rias Baixas, this Galician white is pleasantly fresh and
seafood-friendly.

1995 Viñas del Vero Barrel-Fermented Chardonnay, Somontano, £5.99   16/20
Dry 🫙🫙🫙 ▮
From the up-and-coming Somontano region, this is a toasty, refreshing, coolish-
climate Chardonnay with good lemony concentration.

UNITED STATES

1995 Sterling Chardonnay, Napa Valley, £6.99   14/20
Off-dry ▮
Hefty, rancid butter-like Napa Valley Chardonnay from the Seagram-owned
Sterling Winery. Sweet and obvious. Time to change the currency.

Over £8

AUSTRALIA

1995 Sandalford Barrel Chardonnay, Mount Barker/Margaret River, £8.49   17/20
Dry 🫙🫙🫙 ▮
Nutty, extremely stylish, richly textured Western Australian Chardonnay, with
considerable complexity for a wine under £10.

1996 Lenswood Vineyards Sauvignon Blanc, South Australia, £8.99
16/20
Dry 🫙🫙 ▮
From Tim Knappstein's cool-climate vineyard in the hills north of Adelaide, this
is a ripe, grapefruit and passion-fruit-style Sauvignon Blanc with power and
intensity.

1996 Yarra Valley Hills Chardonnay, Victoria, £9.99   14/20
Dry ▮
Over-priced Victorian Chardonnay, which suffers from clumsy oak ageing.

1996 Penfolds Trial Bin, Adelaide Hills Chardonnay, Victoria, £11.99   17/20
Dry 👜👜 ▮

It may sound a bit like a municipal dustbin scheme, but you wouldn't want to trash this superbly crafted, toasty, cool-climate Chardonnay.

1996 Coldstream Hills Reserve Chardonnay, Yarra Valley, £14.99   16/20

Dry 👜 ▬—

Well-made Yarra Valley Chardonnay from the Penfolds-owned Coldstream Hills winery, but we couldn't help feeling that for a wine at this price it lacks a bit of passion and identity.

CHILE

1995 Casa Lapostolle Cuvée Alexandre Chardonnay, Casablanca, £8.49   17/20
Dry 👜👜 ▮

Intense, ripe peach and apricot-style Chardonnay made by Bordeaux's Michel Rolland, with creamy oak and tons of flavour.

1996 Viña Casablanca Barrel-Fermented Chardonnay, Casablanca, £8.49   15/20
Dry 👜 ▮

Oaky, alcoholic and over-complicated Chardonnay from Ignacio Recabarren, in which the whole doesn't quite add up to the sum of its parts.

1996 Errázuriz Wild Ferment Chardonnay, £8.99   16/20
Dry 👜👜 ▮

Fermented with indigenous wild yeasts for extra flavour and complexity, this is a balanced, creamy, nicely oaked Chardonnay made by the talented Kiwi winemaker, Brian Bicknell.

FRANCE

1995 Montagny Premier Cru Les Coères, Domaine Maurice Bertrand, £8.99   14/20
Dry ▮

Old-fashioned, toffee-apple-like Côtes Chalonnaise Chardonnay with a bitter finish.

1996 Tokay Pinot Gris Vieilles Vignes, Albert Mann, £9.99   17/20
Off-dry 🍷🍷🍷 ●—

Pinot Gris from A. Mann? If you think that sounds a bit grey, think again. We felt the straight Pinot Blanc was good, but this is a spicy, concentrated, sumptuous Alsace Pinot Blanc with terrific length and intensity.

1995 Gewürztraminer Harth 'Cuvée Caroline', Domaine Schoffit, £9.99   17/20
Off-dry 🍷🍷🍷 ●—

Fragrant, nettley and rose-petal-scented Gewürztraminer from Schoffit, whose low yields make this small domaine one of the best producers in Alsace

1995 Pouilly Fuissé Clos de France, Roger Lassarat, £12.99   17/20
Dry 🍷🍷🍷 ●—

Stylish, barrel-fermented Pouilly Fuissé from the dynamic Roger Lassarat. Crisp and elegant for a Mâconnais Chardonnay.

1994 Pouilly Fuissé 'Tête de Cru', Ferret, £18.99   16/20
Dry 🍷 ●—

Super-ripe, idiosyncratic Mâconnais Chardonnay verging on the indecent. Love it or hate it, but don't put it in your trousers.

1994 Pouilly Fuissé 'Hors Classe', Ferret, £19.99   16/20
Dry 🍷 ●—

Fresh, well-made Chardonnay from the same unusual Burgundian domaine, if still a little over-priced at nearly £20. Apparently the Ferrets have a following, though.

1996 Condrieu Les Chaillets, Yves Cuilleron, £19.99   18/20
Off-dry 🍷🍷🍷 |

From the youthful Yves Cuilleron, this is essence of Condrieu, with rich, apricoty, barrel-matured characters and spicy, old-vine concentration.

GERMANY

1996 Forster Jesuitengarten Riesling Spätlese, von Bühl, £9.49
         17/20

Medium sweet 🍷🍷🍷 ●—

Sweet and spicy, lusciously complex Pfalz Riesling with exotic citrus-fruit characters and harmonious sweetness.

ITALY

1995 Maculan Torcolato, Breganze, Veneto, £18.99   17/20
Sweet 👛👛 ▬
Malt whisky-scented, barrel-fermented Veneto sticky from Fausto Maculan, with rich crême brûlée notes and stylish oak sweetness. Beautifully fresh and well balanced, this is an Italian classic.

NEW ZEALAND

1996 Vavasour Awatere Sauvignon Blanc, Marlborough, £10.99
                                                                    16/20
Dry 👛 🍶
A little pricey, especially when you consider the quality of what the Loire produced in 1996, but this is still an intense, well-crafted Marlborough Sauvignon Blanc with cool-climate gooseberry and green-bean characters.

1995 McDonald Church Road Reserve Chardonnay, Hawkes Bay, £10.99   16/20
Dry 👛 🍶
Oaky, barley sugar-rich, Hawkes Bay Chardonnay from Montana's excellent McDonald Winery. Also on the expensive side.

UNITED STATES

1995 Landmark Overlook Chardonnay, Sonoma, £11.99   17/20
Dry 👛👛 🍶
Full-blown, Burgundian-style Chardonnay from a little-known Sonoma County winery, with stylish vanilla-fudge flavours and fresh acidity.

Red

£3–5

ARGENTINA

1996 Valle de Vistalba Barbera, Mendoza, £4.49   15/20
Medium-bodied 👜👜👜 ▮
Tarry, juicy, unoaked Mendoza Barbera from Casa Vinicola Nieto y Senetiner,
made in a thirst-quenching style.

1996 Valle de Vistalba Syrah, Mendoza, £4.69   15/20
Medium-bodied 👜👜👜 ▮
Matured for six months in French oak, this is an aromatic, blackberry fruity,
supple-textured Syrah with a twist and grind of the pepper mill.

1995 Valle de Vistalba Cabernet Sauvignon, Mendoza, £4.99   16/20
Medium-bodied 👜👜👜 ▮
From the same source, a deeper-hued, blackcurranty, easy-drinking red with
chunky, tobaccoey tannins and ripe flavours.

AUSTRALIA

1996 Peter Lehmann Vine Vale Grenache, Barossa, £4.69   14/20
Medium-bodied 👜 ▮
Light, raspberry and loganberry fruity Barossa Valley Grenache with a bubble
gummy sweetness.

CHILE

**1996 Luis Felipe Edwards Pupilla Cabernet Sauvignon,
Colchagua, £3.99**   14/20
Medium-bodied 👜👜 ▮
Herbaceous, inexpensive Chilean Cabernet Sauvignon with a blackcurrant-
pastille note.

1996 La Palma Merlot, Rapel, £3.99   15/20
Medium-bodied 👜👜👜 ▮
Juicy, green-pepper-like Chilean Merlot from Viña La Rosa, with supple tannins
and good length of flavour. Moreishly drinkable.

1996 La Palma Cabernet, Rapel, £3.99

15/20

Medium-bodied 👜👜👜 ▌
Soft, refreshing, supremely gluggable Chilean Cabernet Sauvignon with smooth
tannins and supple fruit.

1993 Una Fuera Cabernet Sauvignon, £4.99, Bin End

16/20

Medium-bodied 👜👜👜 ▌
Mint and liquorice-scented Cabernet Sauvignon from Domaine Paul Bruno on
the outskirts of Santiago, with fine-grained tannins and rounded, bottle-aged
characters.

1994 Una Fuera Cabernet Sauvignon, £4.99, Bin End

16/20

Medium-bodied 👜👜👜 ▬
Intensely sagey Chilean Cabernet Sauvignon from the same cut-price source,
with mint and cassis-fruit opulence and a firm grip of tannin.

1996 Casa Porta Cabernet Sauvignon, Cachapoal, £4.99

15/20

Medium-bodied 👜👜 ▌
Smooth, smoky-oaky Chilean Cabernet Sauvignon, with plum and blackcurrant
fruit character and chocolatey sweetness.

1996 Concha y Toro Explorer Bouschet, Maule, £4.99

15/20

Full-bodied 👜👜👜 ▬
Inky, ruby-purple red made from a version of France's colouring grape, the
Alicante. It's gutsy and chocolatey and rather dominated by American-oak
charriness.

1996 Concha y Toro Explorer Cabernet/Syrah, Maipo, £4.99

15/20

Full-bodied 👜👜👜 ▬
Another densely coloured, youthful red from Concha y Toro, again showing
masses of oak and sweet fruit.

1996 La Palma Reserve Cabernet Merlot, Rapel, £4.99

16/20

Medium-bodied 👜👜👜 ▬
Deeply coloured, Bordeaux-style blend with refreshing acidity, coffee-bean oak
and succulent cherry and blackcurrant fruit flavours. Chile does this sort of
thing better than anyone at present.

FRANCE

1996 Cuvée de Grignon Rouge, Vin de Pays de l'Aude, £3.19 13/20
Medium-bodied 🍷 |
Basic, faintly herbaceous, southern French plonk made to a price by Foncalieu.

1996 Château de Nages Réserve du Château, Costières de Nîmes, £4.49 15/20
Full-bodied 🍷🍷🍷 ━
Well-priced, Syrah-dominated Provençal red with delightful blackberry fruit and sweetness sprinkled with spice.

1995 Mas St Vincent, Coteaux du Languedoc, £4.99 15/20
Full-bodied 🍷🍷 |
Densely aromatic, nutmeg and cinnamon-spicy red with gutsy fruit and robust tannins. Takes no prisoners.

ITALY

1994 Duca di Castelmonte 'Cent'are', Rosso di Sicilia, £4.99 14/20
Full-bodied 🍷 |
A Sicilian blend of Nero d'Avola and Frappato, this is a cherry-fruity rosso that is subdued by a dry oak aftertaste.

SOUTH AFRICA

1996 Genus Shiraz, Coastal Region, £4.69 15/20
Full-bodied 🍷🍷 |
From the Simonsvlei co-operative, this is a ripe, fruity, full-flavoured Shiraz with raspberry-jam notes and well-integrated oak.

1996 Sentinel Cabernet Sauvignon, Stellenbosch, £4.99 15/20
Medium-bodied 🍷🍷 |
Elegant, grassy, mini-Médoc-style Cabernet Sauvignon from négociant Slayley Cellars, with a splinter or two of oak and luscious red-fruit flavours.

SPAIN

1994 Palacio de la Vega Crianza, Navarra, £4.99 13/20
Medium-bodied |
Sawdusty and chewy, although the underlying fruit is good. We've had much better from Palacio de la Vega.

£5–8

AUSTRALIA

1995 Normans Bin C106 Cabernet Sauvignon, South Australia, £5.99   13/20
Full-bodied
Oak and eucalyptus-scented Aussie Cabernet Sauvignon with rather coarse green tannins. We know where Norman's bin, but we're not quite sure where he's going with this one.

1995 d'Arenberg d'Arry's Original, McLaren Vale, £6.49   16/20
Full-bodied
Strapping liquorice and blackberry fruity McLaren Vale blend of Shiraz and Grenache with a porty muscularity.

1995 d'Arenberg The Custodian Grenache, McLaren Vale, £7.99
16/20
Full-bodied
Powerful, sweet-and-savoury McLaren Vale Grenache showing flavours of raspberry and plum topped by oak and warming alcohol.

CHILE

1995 Cono Sur Selection Reserve Cabernet Sauvignon, £5.99
16/20
Medium-bodied
Supple, elegant, attractively balanced Chilean Cabernet Sauvignon from Concha y Toro offshoot, Cono Sur, showing vanilla oak and black cherry fruit.

1995 Viña Porta Merlot, £6.49   15/20
Full-bodied
A blend of 85 per cent Merlot and 15 per cent Cabernet Sauvignon, showing sweet oak and chewy tannins.

1996 La Palma Reserve Merlot, Rapel, £6.99   16/20
Medium-bodied
Smooth, coffee-bean oaky red from Viña La Rosa, with attractive fruit but a few too many barrel staves.

1995 Viña Casablanca El Bosque Estate Cabernet Sauvignon, Maipo, £6.99
15/20

Full-bodied 🝖 ⸙
Spearminty, blackcurrant-pastille red with rugged dry tannins, from the Maipo Valley.

1996 Cono Sur Selection Reserve Pinot Noir, Chimbarongo, £6.99
15/20
Medium-bodied 🝖🝖 ⸙
A Pinot Noir that is a little subdued by oak influence on the nose, but the cherry fruit quality comes through nicely on the palate. The Reserve has been better.

1996 Viña Casablanca Santa Isabel Estate Merlot, Casablanca, £7.99
17/20
Medium-bodied 🝖🝖🝖 ⸚
Mocha and green-pepper-scented Merlot with intense cassis-like concentration, showing that Chile's cool Casablanca Valley can deliver on reds as well as whites.

1996 Viña Casablanca Santa Isabel Estate Cabernet Sauvignon, Casablanca, £7.99
16/20
Full-bodied 🝖🝖 ⸚
Made, like the Merlot, by Chile's star winemaker, Ignacio Recabarren, this is tighter and a little chewier. Perhaps he should have blended the two together.

FRANCE

1996 Château de Mousquet, Bordeaux Supérieur, £5.49
15/20
Medium-bodied 🝖 ⸙
Modern-style, youthful red Bordeaux with light, thirst-quenching redcurrant fruitiness and medium-weight tannins.

1995 Côtes du Rhône Parallèle '45', Paul Jaboulet Aîné, £5.99
15/20
Full-bodied 🝖 ⸙
Smooth, peppery, rustic Côtes du Rhône from Gérard Jaboulet, the late master of Hermitage La Chapelle, with a core of Grenache fruit sweetness.

1996 Chinon Domaine de la Perrière, £6.79
16/20

Medium-bodied 🍾🍾 ▬–

Intense, blackcurrant-fruity essence of Loire Cabernet Franc, with notes of green pepper and lead pencil. Needs time to develop.

ITALY

1990 Taurino Notarpanaro, Rosso del Salento, £5.49
14/20

Full-bodied ▮

Sun-warmed, ultra-traditional Puglian rosso with baked, raisiny fruit and hefty alcohol and tannins.

1995 Torre Vento, Torre del Falco, Murgia Rosso, £5.49
16/20

Medium-bodied 🍾🍾🍾 ▮

Refreshing, stylish, southern Italian blend with well-rounded oak and blackcurrant fruit intensity.

1995 Rubrato, Feudi di San Gregorio, £5.99
14/20

Medium-bodied ▮

Awkwardly oaked, over-spiced Italian red that lacks fruit. You'd be better off sticking to the white from the same property.

PORTUGAL

1995 Quinta do Crasto, Douro, £5.99
16/20

Full-bodied 🍾🍾🍾 ▬–

Stylish, modern Portuguese red with vibrant damson fruit and sweet, spicy oak, made by Australian David Baverstock from grapes that are normally used for Port.

SOUTH AFRICA

1996 Clos Malverne Devonet Cabernet Sauvignon & Merlot, Stellenbosch, £5.49
13/20

Full-bodied ▮

Inky, warm-climate blend with cooked, jammy flavours and a rasping bite of acidity. A disappointment, considering the high quality normally associated with Clos Malverne.

1996 Beyerskloof Pinotage, Stellenbosch, £5.49   16/20
Full-bodied 🍷🍷🍷 ▬

If you want to find out what South Africa's Pinotage grape tastes like, buy a bottle or three of this earthy, strawberry fruity number from Beyers Truter, one of the best exponents of the variety in the Cape.

1995 Stellenzicht Merlot Cabernet Franc, Stellenbosch, £5.99
    14/20

Medium-bodied ▮

Dusty, ginger-spicy Cape blend of the St Emilion grapes Merlot and Cabernet Franc, with sweet oak and a green edge.

1996 Louisvale LV Cabernet Sauvignon, Stellenbosch, £5.99   15/20
Medium-bodied 🍷 ▮

Supple, smoothly oaked Cape Cabernet Sauvignon, which is surprisingly evolved and drinkable for such a young wine.

1996 Jacana Cabernet Shiraz Merlot, Stellenbosch, £5.99   16/20
Full-bodied 🍷🍷 ▬

From winemakers Hugh Ryman and Peter Flewellyn, this is a richly oaked, berry fruity bush-vine blend of Cabernet Sauvignon, Shiraz and Merlot, showing well-handled vanilla-oak sweetness and good concentration.

1995 Jacana Pinotage, Stellenbosch, £5.99   15/20
Full-bodied 🍷 ▮

Modern, American oak-infused Pinotage from the same winemaking duo, with chocolate and mulberry fruit flavours and rather imposing dry tannins.

1995 Stellenzicht Cabernet Sauvignon, Stellenbosch, £6.49   16/20
Medium-bodied 🍷🍷 ▮

Ripe, flavoursome, well-made Cabernet Sauvignon with elegant tannins, finely judged oak and refreshing acidity. Stylish stuff from Andre van Rensberg.

1996 Clos Malverne Pinotage, Stellenbosch, £6.49   17/20
Full-bodied 🍷🍷🍷 ▬

A powerful, modern Cape Pinotage from one of South Africa's best exponents of this weird crossing of Pinot Noir and Cinsaut. This is supple and richly oaked with intense black-fruit flavours.

1995 Fairview Tower Red, Paarl, £6.99   14/20
Medium-bodied
An oak-aged blend of Merlot, Cabernet Sauvignon and Malbec with a touch of
chocolate, but unyielding acidity and tannins.

1996 Glen Carlou Pinot Noir, Paarl, £6.99 (OFW only)   15/20
Medium-bodied
Loganberry fruity, warm-climate Cape Pinot Noir with sweet oak and an
alcoholic afterburn.

1996 Wildekrans Pinotage, Walker Bay, £7.49   15/20
Medium-bodied
Strawberry fruity Walker Bay Pinotage with prominent oak and lightish alcohol.
It aims for elegance but just misses.

SPAIN

1992 Palacio de la Vega Cabernet Sauvignon, Navarra, £7.99 16/20
Medium-bodied
Mature, concentrated, chocolatey Spanish Cabernet Sauvignon from one of
Navarra's best bodegas.

UNITED STATES

1995 Redwood Trail Pinot Noir, California, £5.49   13/20
Light-bodied
Soupy, sweet California Pinot Noir, which pays lip service to négociant red
Burgundy.

1994 Sterling Vineyards Cabernet Sauvignon, Napa, £6.99   15/20
Medium-bodied
Minty-sweet Napa Valley Cabernet Sauvignon with well-judged spicy oak,
plenty of flavour and nicely balanced tannins. Decently priced (for Napa Valley).

Marrieta Old Vine Red Lot 19, Geyserville, £7.49   16/20
Full-bodied
Hot-climate, Sonoma County non-vintage blend of mainly Zinfandel with a
touch of Petite Sirah, Carignan and Gamay, this is robustly fruity with a
liquoricey bite.

Over £8

AUSTRALIA

1994 Sandalford Shiraz, Margaret River/Mount Barker, £8.49 17/20
Full-bodied 🍷🍷🍷 ➡–
Spicy, peppery, intensely fruity Western Australian Shiraz from a rapidly improving winery.

1995 Tatachilla Foundation Shiraz, McLaren Vale, £9.49 (OFW only) 18/20
Full-bodied 🍷🍷🍷 ➡–
Pure, unadulterated essence of Australia Shiraz, with cleverly judged oak and well-defined, sweet blackberry fruit. Impressive stuff from an increasingly impressive winery.

1996 Coldstream Hills Pinot Noir, Yarra Valley, £9.99, Bin End 14/20

Medium-bodied 🍷
Simple, faintly herbaceous, cherry fruity Yarra Valley Pinot Noir with a façade of oak, from the Penfolds-owned Coldstream Hills Winery.

1995 d'Arenberg Ironstone Pressings, McLaren Vale, £9.99 16/20
Full-bodied 🍷🍷 ➡–
Dense, dark and brooding, and that's just the export manager! This chewily uncompromising Grenache-based red from McLaren Vale has a bucketful of alcohol and muscular tannins.

1994 Château Reynella Basket-Pressed Cabernet Merlot, McLaren Vale, £9.99 16/20
Full-bodied 🍷🍷 ➡–
Coffee-bean oaky, sweetly fruity Bordeaux-style blend with all the rich, blackcurrant-fruit lushness you'd expect from McLaren Vale. Our only quibble is with the accelerating price.

1994 Château Reynella Basket-Pressed Shiraz, McLaren Vale, £9.99 16/20
Full-bodied 🍷🍷 ➡–
Minty, concentrated, prominently oaked McLaren Vale mouthful of lush blackberry fruit and flavour. Unsubtle, but enjoyable.

1995 Normans Chais Clarendon Shiraz, McLaren Vale, £9.99   17/20
Full-bodied 🝷🝷🝷 ⬤━

Coconutty, powerfully oaked, smooth, concentrated essence of blackberryish McLaren Vale Shiraz. A stormin' Norman.

1995 Normans Chais Clarendon Cabernet Sauvignon, McLaren Vale, £9.99   16/20
Full-bodied 🝷🝷 ⬤━

Youthful, profoundly oaked, chocolatey Cabernet Sauvignon, which is good but just lacks the vibrancy of the Shiraz.

1996 Yarra Valley Hills Pinot Noir, Victoria, £11.99   16/20
Medium-bodied 🝷🝷 ▮

Rich, textured Yarra Valley Pinot Noir with plenty of red-fruit stuffing and varietal character.

1996 Coldstream Hills Reserve Pinot Noir, Yarra Valley, £14.99
                                                  17/20

Medium-bodied 🝷🝷 ▮

Considerably more interesting than the straight Yarra Valley Pinot Noir, this is a well-made, strawberry spicy red with supple tannins and attractive oak.

1994 Leasingham Classic Clare Shiraz, Clare, £15.99   17/20
Full-bodied 🝷🝷 ⬤━

Inky, come-hither Clare Valley Shiraz with super-spicy concentration and structure underpinned by sweet mint and vanilla-oak flavours.

1994 Leasingham Classic Clare Cabernet Sauvignon, Clare, £15.99   16/20
Full-bodied 🝷 ━

Liquorice and tobacco-scented, powerfully concentrated, oaky stuff. No longer the bargain it used to be, though.

CHILE

1995 Casa Lapostolle Cuvée Alexandre Merlot, Rapel, £8.99   17/20
Medium-bodied 🝷🝷🝷 ⬤━

Made by Bordeaux superstar, Michel Rolland, this is one of Chile's best reds – vibrant, full of berry fruit flavours and stylishly oaked.

FRANCE

1995 Château Paloumey Cru Bourgeois, Haut-Médoc, £8.49   17/20
Medium-bodied 👛👛👛 ▬
From a much-praised vintage, this is a juicy, supple claret with well-judged oak, for relatively early drinking.

1995 St Joseph Cuvée Prestige, Cuilleron, £9.99 (OFW only)   16/20
Medium-bodied 👛👛 ▬
Fragrant, peppery St Joseph Syrah from Condrieu-based Yves Cuilleron, with typically elegant, finely textured fruit.

1995 Crozes Hermitage Domaine de Thalabert, Paul Jaboulet Aîné, £10.49   16/20
Full-bodied 👛👛 ▬
Serious northern Rhône Syrah from the respected Rhône firm of Jaboulet, showing robust, rich and smoky blackberry fruitiness.

**1995 Pommard 'Les Tavannes', Maison Fery-Meunier, £13.99
(OFW only)**   17/20
Medium-bodied 👛👛👛 ▬
Well-priced, chocolatey, modern-style Pinot Noir from one of the Côte de Beaune's best red-wine communes.

1995 Hermitage La Chapelle, Paul Jaboulet Aîné, £27.99   18/20
Full-bodied 👛👛👛 ▬
One of the Rhône Valley's very best wines from a very good vintage, this is a deep-hued, powerfully aromatic, spicy, super-concentrated Syrah, which combines intensity of flavour with elegant structure.

SOUTH AFRICA

1994 Veenwouden Classic, Coastal Region, £12.99   17/20
Full-bodied 👛👛👛 ▬
A blend of Cabernet Sauvignon and Merlot, this is ripe and well made, with good concentration of cassis fruit embellished by stylish oak maturation.

1994 Veenwouden Merlot, Coastal Region, £12.99   14/20
Medium-bodied ▮
Porty, sweet, hot-climate Merlot with lashings of oak and alcohol. Rather clumsy and wooden.

UNITED STATES

1995 Sterling Vineyards Winery Lake Pinot Noir, Carneros, £9.99
17/20
Medium-bodied 🍾🍾🍾 |
From one of the best Pinot Noir vineyards in the Carneros district of the Napa
Valley, this is a rich, wild-strawberry fruity Pinot Noir, with finely judged oak
maturation and excellent concentration.

1994 Viader, Napa Valley, £18.99 (OFW only)
17/20
Full-bodied 🍾🍾 ➡-
A Cabernet Sauvignon/Cabernet Franc blend in a broad-shouldered bottle,
with stunning cassis-fruit concentration and a hint of mint and smooth oak.

Sparkling

£5–8

AUSTRALIA

1996 Deakin Estate Brut, £6.49
15/20
Dry 🍾🍾 |
Big-bubbled, tropical fruity Aussie sparkler, with notes of pineapple and lime
zest and a broad, sherbety mousse.

SPAIN

Segura Viudas Brut Reserve, £5.99
16/20
Dry 🍾🍾🍾 |
Richly coloured, richly textured Spanish fizz from the quality-conscious Segura
Viudas operation, combining ripeness and buttery fruit flavour with elegance in
a luxurious mouthful.

Over £8

FRANCE

Henri Harlin NV Champagne, £12.49   14/20
Dry 🜊 ▮
Basic, price-fighting Champagne with a green edge and a lemony bite.

1989 Henri Harlin Champagne, £16.49   14/20
Dry 🜊 ▮
Slightly richer than the non-vintage, but this should be considerably better from a year like 1989. At least it's cheap.

Billecart-Salmon NV Champagne, £19.49   17/20
Dry 🜊🜊🜊 ▮
Elegant, stylish, Chardonnay-dominated Champagne from one of our favourite family-owned Grande Marque houses, with a delightful, biscuity note and beautiful balance.

1989 Billecart-Salmon Champagne, Cuvée Nicolas François Billecart, £29.99   18/20
Dry 🜊🜊🜊 ▮
From the same house, this is one of the wines we'll be drinking come the millennium. Rich, toasty and still developing, with flavours that play and linger on the palate.

SOUTH AFRICA

1991 Graham Beck Blanc de Blancs, £8.99   17/20
Dry 🜊🜊🜊 ▮
Partially oak-fermented Cape fizz made entirely from Chardonnay grapes, showing a distinctive, vanilla-like character, which enhances the wine's varietal character. A steal at this price.

Safeway ☆☆☆☆

Address: Safeway House, 6 Millington Road, Hayes, Middlesex UB3 4AY

Telephone/fax: 01622 712987

Number of branches: 410

Opening hours: 8.00/8.30am to 8.00pm Monday to Saturday (or 10.00pm in selected stores); 10.00 am to 4.00pm Sunday

Credit cards accepted: Access, Delta, Switch, Visa

Discounts: Various wine fairs during the year including the May Wine Fair and New World October Wine Fair; regular price promotions; 5 per cent off a case of any six wines over £2.99 per bottle

Facilities and services: occasional in-store tastings; free glass loan with a selection of glasses in selected stores

Special Offers: See discounts

Top ten best-selling wines: 1996 Safeway Liebfraumilch; Safeway Lambrusco; 1996 Safeway Chenin Blanc ; 1996 Safeway Muscadet; 1996 Safeway Vin de Pays de l'Ardèche Blanc; 1996 Safeway Côtes du Rhône; 1996 Safeway Sicilian Red; 1996 Safeway Chilean Cabernet Sauvignon, Lontue; Safeway Claret NV; 1992 Safeway Barrel-Matured Cabernet Sauvignon, Svischtov

Range:

GOOD: Regional France, Eastern Europe, Australia, South Africa, organic wines, Champagne and sparkling wines

AVERAGE: Burgundy, Bordeaux, Loire, Alsace, Rhône, Portugal, Italy, Germany, England, New Zealand, Chile, Argentina

POOR: United States

UNDER-REPRESENTED: None

With fewer branches and a smaller range of wines than the Big Two, Tesco and Sainsbury's, Safeway has earned a reputation for ploughing a more adventurous furrow than either of its rivals. The very name is an ironic misnomer. Not-so-safe Safeway was instrumental in ushering in the New World era and was one of the first to bring Eastern Europe in from the cold. It sponsored the first

Safeway

Organic Wine Challenge and championed English wines when customers could no more tell English from British than Stork from butter.

Little did they know it, but Safeway's wine-department customers were booking a ticket on a roller-coaster. Today, as the global wine village contracts, the frantic pace of exploration has slowed somewhat. After the buzz of discovery, the talk in the wine department is of a wine's 'career path' and of a 'maturing range'. Now that the bold and sometimes even risky decisions of yesteryear have been tested in the cold light of commercial reality, the Safeway range is growing up.

The wine range does not expand ad infinitum to meet the egotistical whims of a prima-donna wine buyer. It's more a case of: never mind the width, feel the quality. 'The advantage of a smaller range is that you can keep on top of it and keep it moving,' says Safeway's quality and wine affairs controller, Liz Robertson. It stays at a trim 400 wines, roughly one-third of which are regularly pruned for a variety of reasons, whether it's lack of availability or the vintage producing something better or cheaper. Some changes, admits Robertson, are simply to do with performance – or rather lack of it. 'We're getting less tolerant,' she admits.

Typical of the new phase of development is the fact that as each new country is tamed, those wines that perform are harnessed to Safeway's own-label range. Last year it was Australia, this year it's been South Africa and South America and a similar process is going on in Eastern Europe. 'They were mostly producer labels,' says Robertson, 'but now the range has matured, the decision has been made about what needs to come in-house.'

The purpose is threefold. Apart from giving the range a more familiar, lived-in feel, it enables Safeway to keep prices down, to dress up the wines with more eye-catching labels and to promote them regularly to bring in new customers. About 50 per cent of the range is now own-label. You might not know it unless you know what to look for, though. Basically the label has the magic words 'Selected by Safeway' in a discreet band at the bottom, along with the standard back-label format.

The taming of the range helps it dovetail with the bold new quality and style guides introduced just as we went to press last year. By categorising all wines in the range with a bronze, silver or gold band and by giving each a brief descriptive note, the scheme is designed to prevent the need for costly in-store advisers, with which other supermarkets are toying. 'It's just Scotch mist to pretend that there are enough advisers to be had,' says Robertson.

'What supermarkets need to concentrate on is helping customers to help themselves. People are in a hurry and they want help without long, tedious conversations.' So how does the scheme work? 'Bronzes are for everyday drinking, silvers for special occasions and gold quite simply the best,' she explains. Around 50 per cent of the range is bronze, 30 per cent silver and 20 per cent gold. White wines are described as either 'dry and crisp', 'dry and smooth', 'dry and full', 'medium', or 'sweet/dessert'; while reds are 'light and soft', 'smooth and mellow', 'dry and firm' or 'rich and mature'.

We confessed to being somewhat bemused by the two different shades of bronze, one of which (on the Liebfraumilch, what else?) looked suspiciously like the gold band adorning the Safeway Vintage Champagne. 'We were hoping it would be self-explanatory, but not everyone understands it,' admits Robertson candidly. On the plus side, she says that there has been a huge drop in the basic Aussie red and white (bronzes), while the silver range, at a typical £4.99, has taken off, particularly in red, underlining the general trend towards red wine drinking. 'The big push for silver, particularly in the New World, is evidence of a more informed, more affluent customer.' It was noticeable that when the range had to be replenished with a clutch of higher-priced reds at Easter, the lion's share came from Australia, Chile and South Africa.

Despite the 'maturing' of the range, the New World is big at Safeway, and getting bigger. In fact, astonishingly for a supermarket, sales are virtually neck and neck with Europe, Safeway claims. Now that Australasia (New Zealand apart) has found its level at between 50 pence and £1 a bottle dearer than the rest of the southern hemisphere, Chile and South Africa are the boom countries. 'South Africa wasn't ready for the vacuum suck from the northern countries,' says Robertson, 'but in 18 months it has caught up and now it's neck and neck with Chile. In Argentina, there are fewer suppliers with the right attitude or the understanding of what's required.'

France is still enormously strong, thanks to a combination of good recent vintages, a strong pound and the gradual transformation of the south of France from an ocean of plonk to lagoons of quality. 'Everything is in the south of France's favour,' says Robertson. 'It's going to be an area we'll all continue to shop in because it has the sunshine, the value and a variety of styles. There are better grape varieties too, and they now have the technology and the brains to use them.'

From generic red Bordeaux to the posher châteaux, Bordeaux is doing well at Safeway, partly, claims Robertson, because it has an established reputation. White Bordeaux too, 'after a terrible stretch of years', is making a comeback. Difficulties in the Loire have been mitigated by good vintages in 1995 and 1996, giving producers the necessary breathing space to work out how to tackle the New World.

Eastern Europe, where Safeway was among the early pioneers, remains an important part of the wine range. And despite the emergence of quality-minded co-operatives such as Hungary's Neszmely, Safeway continues to invest considerable time, energy and belief in flying winemakers. Improved technology allows them to make better wines, but there are problems, as Robertson explains. 'They are still held back by politics and the problem of vineyard ownership, particularly in Bulgaria.'

Safeway

Success with some of its more innovative projects has been mixed. English wines, for instance, are now down to a single brand, Stanlake. 'The last adventure into lots of English wines was quite difficult,' Robertson admits. Organic wines hover at around ten in number, without really taking off in any significant way, and the Organic Wine Challenge has lapsed.

Young Vatted wines, based on the New World-led trend towards youthful freshness and primary fruit flavours, are a welcome innovation. There's now a Young Vatted Merlot from Bulgaria, a Young Vatted Tempranillo from Spain, a Young Vatted Teroldego from Italy, a Young Vatted Syrah from the south of France, even a Young Vatted Claret (or should that be Trojan Horse?) from that bastion of the old world, Bordeaux itself.

The born quality controller in Liz Robertson insists that the Safeway vintage guarantee remains the cornerstone of the range. While it's not a legal requirement, every wine at Safeway has to declare its vintage on the label, unless there's some very good reason not to. Robertson claims that it gives more power to her elbow in exerting control over suppliers. 'The very fact that Safeway requires a vintage is a big incentive for wineries to conform,' she says. 'It means their books have to reflect it, so it's a lot simpler for them to give in and comply. Our wines are younger and fresher for it,' she insists.

Cork, too, is another quality issue that exercises the Robertson quality-control standard. Safeway is kicking out the dreaded agglomerate cork, which causes so many problems of mustiness. By Christmas it aims to be free of them. 'Cork for common wine has had its day,' says Robertson. Plastic corks are a growing business, with more and more suppliers knocking at the Safeway door. Screwtops are another possibility under consideration. Basically, 'The challenge will be to make the stopper so attractive that it's acceptable to consumers.'

Robertson is optimistic that wine prices will remain stable for a while yet. 'Western Europe is cheaper for us this year because of the rate of exchange and because it's fighting for its market.' This means that the £2.99 price tag is still there, although, according to Robertson, it isn't really viable. 'The real price of basic wine at a proper margin is £3.19–£3.29. It shows how artificial the £1.99 was.' Safeway's average bottle price sale is over £3.50, with customers increasingly prepared to pay more for quality.

With sales continuing to grow, Safeway now has a 10 per cent share of the market, putting it at number three behind Tesco and Sainsbury's. The wine department has expanded correspondingly. No fewer than three new wine buyers came on board during the year: ex-Waitrose Master of Wine, Neil Sommerfelt, Pam Collington and Justin Howard-Sneyd. They joined the buying team of Sarah Kynoch and Julie Marshall, with Lynda Clarkson, the buying controller, in overall charge. A fresh bunch, for sure, but – not unlike the Safeway range – a rapidly maturing one, with career paths mapped out.

White

Under £3

GERMANY

1996 Safeway Liebfraumilch, £2.85　　　　　　　10/20
Medium sweet 🍾

Hard, gluey, soupy German white, which assaults rather than caresses the palate.

ITALY

Safeway Lambrusco, £2.49　　　　　　　　　　　12/20
Sweet 🍾

A Lambrusco that smells like Retsina. A wine without freshness or much else in the way of redeeming character.

SOUTH AFRICA

1997 Safeway South African Chenin Blanc Early Release, Stellenbosch, £2.79　　　　　　　　　　　　14/20
Dry 🍾🍾🍾 🍾

Fresh, peardrop and banana-like Cape White made for early consumption.

£3–5

AUSTRALIA

1996 Safeway Australian Oaked Colombard, £3.99　　14/20
Dry 🍾🍾 🍾

Soft-textured, super-ripe, tropically fruity Colombard with prominent oak. Obvious but very commercial.

1996 Safeway Semillon/Chardonnay, South East Australia, £3.99
14/20

Dry 🍷🍷 ▮

Muted, tropical fruit flavours unencumbered by oak make this a decent Aussie quaffer from the giant Southcorp operation.

1996 Safeway Australian Chardonnay/Colombard, £4.29
16/20

Dry 🍷🍷🍷 ▮

Attractively packaged Victorian blend of Chardonnay and Colombard, with melony flavours and superb length for a wine at this price.

1996 Oxford Landing Sauvignon Blanc, South East Australia, £4.99
14/20

Dry 🍷 ▮

Soft, faintly gooseberryish wine-bar white from the Yalumba winery. Lacks a bit of the flavour intensity of previous vintages.

1996 Peter Lehmann Semillon, Barossa Valley, £4.99
16/20

Dry 🍷🍷🍷 ▮

From the Baron of the Barossa himself, this is an exuberant, lightly oaked Semillon with ice-cream-soda and lemon-peel flavours.

1996 Hardy's Nottage Hill Chardonnay, £4.99
16/20

Off-dry 🍷🍷 ▮

Lots of oak and lots of sweet tropical fruit. A flavoursome Aussie Chardonnay with undertones of vanilla fudge.

1996 Safeway Australian Oaked Chardonnay, £4.99
15/20

Dry 🍷🍷 ▮

More restrained than the Nottage Hill, this is a well-crafted, drier, oaked Chardonnay from the same stable. More of a food wine.

BULGARIA

1996 Bulgarian Chardonnay, Rousse, £3.49
13/20

Off-dry 🍷 ▮

Sweetish, Muscat grape and pear-drop-like white, which bears little resemblance to Chardonnay as we know and like it.

CHILE

1996 Safeway Chilean Sauvignon Blanc, Lontue, £3.99   15/20
Dry 👜👜👜 ❘
A tangy, grapefruity Chilean Sauvignon Blanc made by Frenchman Jacques Lurton at the San Pedro winery.

1996 Safeway Chilean Chardonnay, Central Valley, £3.99   14/20
Dry 👜👜 ❘
Solid, sweetish, well-made Chilean Chardonnay from Concha y Toro, unoaked for optimum fruit impact.

1996 Caliterra Chardonnay, Central Valley, £4.49   15/20
Dry 👜👜👜 ❘
From Curicó in Chile's warm Central Valley, this is an attractive, unoaked Chardonnay with melon and grapefruit characters.

FRANCE

1996 Safeway Muscadet, £3.29   14/20
Bone dry 👜👜 ❘
Clean, fresh, zesty Muscadet from the excellent 1996 vintage, justifiably among Safeway's top ten best-sellers.

1996 Safeway Chenin Blanc, Vin de Pays du Jardin de la France, £3.29   14/20
Bone dry 👜👜 ❘
Crisp, appley, well-made Loire Valley Chenin Blanc with zip and flavour and none of the variety's bitter tendency.

1996 Safeway Vin de Pays de l'Ardèche Blanc, £3.29   13/20
Off-dry 👜 ❘
Sweetish, basic southern French blanc, or should that be plonk?

1996 Safeway Sauvignon, Vin de Pays du Jardin de la France, £3.29   14/20
Dry 👜👜 ❘
Ultra-fresh, nettley Loire Sauvignon Blanc with a citrus fruity tang.

1996 Safeway Chardonnay, Vin de Pays du Jardin de la France, £3.49 | 14/20

Dry 🍾🍾🍾 |

Fresh, unoaked, well-made Loire Chardonnay, made in a mini-Chablis mould.

1996 Domaine du Rey, Vin de Pays des Côtes de Gascogne, £3.89
16/20

Dry 🍾🍾🍾 |

Suitable for vegetarians and vegans because no animal products have been used in the winemaking, this is an exciting, aromatic, grapefruity white from Gascon grower, Guy Arrouy.

1996 Safeway Bordeaux Blanc, Aged in Oak, £3.99 | 14/20
Dry 🍾🍾 |

Assertively oaked Bordeaux blend of Semillon and Sauvignon with some attractive lemony flavours.

1996 Château du Plantier, Entre Deux Mers, £3.99 | 15/20
Dry 🍾🍾 |

Flavoursome, well-made co-operative white Bordeaux with herby undertones and crisp fruit.

1996 Safeway Vin de Pays d'Oc, £3.99 | 13/20
Dry |

Confected, baked banana-style, southern French Chardonnay, which is thin on fruit and short of stuffing.

1996 James Herrick Chardonnay, Vin de Pays d'Oc, £4.99 | 14/20
Dry 🍾 |

Clean, if slightly characterless, southern French Chardonnay from Languedoc-based Englishman James Herrick. Nothing like as good as earlier vintages.

HUNGARY

Safeway Hungarian Chardonnay, 3-litre wine box, £12.99 (= £3.25 per bottle) | 13/20
Dry 🍾 |

Light, nettley, if rather dilute Hungarian Chardonnay with a tart finish.

1996 Safeway Matra Mountain Chardonnay, Nagyrede, £3.49 | 14/20
Dry 🍾🍾 |

Pleasant, oak-influenced, overtly pineapple-chunky Hungarian Chardonnay made by Aussie Master of Wine Kym Milne.

1996 Riverview Chardonnay/Pinot Gris, Neszmely, £3.99　　　14/20
Off-dry 🍷 ▮
Produced at the model Neszmely co-operative, this is an enjoyable, if somewhat sweet-and-sour Hungarian blend.

ITALY

1996 Safeway Soave, £3.49　　　　　　　　　　　　　　　14/20
Dry 🍷🍷 ▮
Soft textures and fresh pear flavours make this Veneto white a good buy at under £3.50.

1996 Safeway Casa di Giovanni Grillo, Vino da Tavola di Sicilia, £3.99　　　　　　　　　　　　　　　　　　　　　　　　15/20
Dry 🍷🍷🍷 ▮
Made entirely from Grillo, the Sicilian grape that crops up in Marsala, this is a spicy white with flavours of nut and butter.

1996 Bianco di Custoza, Cantine Giacomo Montresor, £4.49　15/20
Dry 🍷🍷 ▮
Single-vineyard, Lake Garda white showing excellent concentration, with butter and green-olive flavours and a welcome bitter twist.

NEW ZEALAND

1996 Taurau Valley, Gisborne, £3.99　　　　　　　　　　14/20
Off-dry 🍷🍷 ▮
A fruity, easy-drinking introduction to New Zealand whites from North Island's Gisborne region.

SOUTH AFRICA

1996 Umfiki Sauvignon Blanc, Breede River Valley, £3.99　　12/20
Dry ▮
Dusty, bitter and rather fruitless Sauvignon Blanc from the Cape's hot Breede River Valley region.

1996 Long Mountain Chardonnay, Western Cape, £4.29　　14/20
Dry 🍷🍷 ▮
Made by Orlando, the makers of Jacob's Creek, this is an unoaked Cape Chardonnay with melon and apple fruitiness and a clean aftertaste.

SPAIN

1995 Agramont Viura/Chardonnay, Navarra, £4.79   15/20
Dry 👛👛 🍾
A stylish, modern, oak-aged blend of the local Viura grape with Chardonnay, showing ripe flavours of peach and toffee.

£5–8

FRANCE

1996 Safeway White Burgundy, £5.49   15/20
Dry 👛👛 🍾
A lemony, intense white Burgundy from the Buxy Co-operative in the Côte Chalonnaise, with a fresh, elegant texture. Needs food.

1995 Safeway Montagny Premier Cru, £6.99   17/20
Dry 👛👛👛 ▬
From the unfancied Côte Chalonnaise, this is a crisp, concentrated White Burgundy from the reliable Buxy Co-operative. Characterful stuff.

1995 Château de Mercey, Hautes Côtes de Beaune, £7.99   16/20
Dry 👛👛 ▬
From a first-rate white Burgundy vintage, this is a full-flavoured, buttery, oaky Chardonnay with fresh balancing acidity.

ITALY

1996 Chardonnay del Salento 'Caramia', Barrique-Aged, £5.99
16/20
Dry 👛👛 🍾
Rich, stylish, southern Italian, textured white with Burgundian-style characters and considerable winemaking complexity. If only more Italian whites were like this.

NEW ZEALAND

1996 Millton Vineyard Semillon/Chardonnay, Gisborne, £5.99
15/20

Dry 👜👜 ▮

Nettley, idiosyncratic Kiwi blend of Semillon and Chardonnay from James Millton's organic bug-farm at Gisborne. Unusual stuff for New Zealand.

1996 Villa Maria Private Bin Sauvignon Blanc, Marlborough, £6.49
16/20

Dry 👜👜👜 ▮

Classic asparagus and green-bean-style Sauvignon Blanc from the impressive Villa Maria operation. Flavoursome stuff.

1995 Millton Vineyard Chardonnay, Barrel-Fermented, Gisborne, £7.99
16/20

Dry 👜👜 ▮

Deeply coloured, heavily oaked organic white, which is exceptionally rich, buttery and full-flavoured for such a modest New Zealand vintage.

SOUTH AFRICA

1995 Vergelegen Chardonnay, Stellenbosch, £6.49
15/20

Dry 👜 ▮

Too much oak for the weight of fruit. Clean and fresh, if rather overpriced.

Over £8

AUSTRALIA

1994 Geoff Merrill Chardonnay, South East Australia, £9.99   16/20
Dry 👜👜 ▬

Nutty, evolved Aussie Chardonnay with a core of sweet, melony fruit and a powerful, mule-like kick of alcohol.

FRANCE

1995 Chablis Premier Cru Les Lys, Ancien Domaine Auffray, £9.99   17/20
Bone dry 🍷🍷🍷 ⏵
Intense, characterful premier cru Chablis from William Fèvre, combining oak, fruit and steely acidity in a complex Chardonnay of considerable finesse.

1995 Puligny Montrachet 'Les Charmes', Domaine Gérard Chavy et Fils, £14.99   16/20
Dry 🍷 ⏵
Good rather than great, this is a fresh Côtes de Beaune Chardonnay with chalky acidity and citrus-fruit crispness.

UNITED STATES

1995 Fetzer Barrel Select Chardonnay, Mendocino, £8.99   15/20
Off-dry ▌
Sweet, toasty and rather obvious, overwrought Chardonnay from Mendocino County's Fetzer winery.

1995 Fetzer Chardonnay Reserve, Sangiacomo Vineyard, Sonoma-Carneros, £12.99   17/20
Dry 🍷🍷 ⏵
The quality of the vineyard shines through on this super-concentrated, Burgundian-style California Chardonnay, with rich, leesy flavours, toasty oak and toffee fudge.

Red

Under £3

BULGARIA

1996 Safeway Young Vatted Cabernet Sauvignon, Sliven, £2.99
14/20
Medium-bodied 🍷🍷🍷 ▌
Not quite as juicy and approachable as some of the previous Young Vatted Cab Sauvs, this is still modern for Bulgaria, with sweet cassis fruit unhindered by oak.

FRANCE

Safeway Vin de Pays de Vaucluse, £2.99 13/20
Medium-bodied 💰💰 🍷
Fruity, lightly peppery southern Rhône quaffer made to a price by Aussie Nick Butler.

ITALY

1996 Safeway Rosso Veronese, £2.99 13/20
Light-bodied 💰 🍷
Sweet, simple, lightly fruity Veronese red with a nip of refreshing acidity.

£3–5

AUSTRALIA

1996 Safeway Shiraz, South East Australia, £4.69 15/20
Medium-bodied 💰💰 🍷
Lightly oaked Aussie Shiraz with hints of pepper and nutmeg spiciness from the reliable Griffith-based McWilliams winery.

1995 Hardy's Nottage Hill Cabernet Sauvignon/Shiraz, South East Australia, £4.99 14/20
Medium-bodied 💰 🍷
Charry and rather obvious, but this best-selling Aussie blend has plenty of flavour and what the Aussies like to refer to as 'grunt'.

BULGARIA

1992 Safeway Barrel-Matured Cabernet Sauvignon, Svischtov, £3.29 13/20
Medium-bodied 💰 🍷
Browning, chewy, old-fashioned Bulgarian red with residual fruit sweetness and a lead-pencil character.

1991 Safeway Cabernet Sauvignon Reserve, Sliven, £3.29 10/20
Full-bodied 🍷
Gluey, pruney, over-oaked Bulgarian red, which should have been buried under the rubble of the Berlin Wall.

1996 Bulgarian Vintners' Aged in Oak Merlot, Rousse, £3.79 13/20
Full-bodied 🍷 ▮

Chewy, robust Bulgarian Merlot with a little too much tannin and oak for the weight of fruit.

CHILE

Alpaca Plain Cabernet Sauvignon, Curico, 3-litre bag-in-box, £12.49 (= £3.12 per bottle) 14/20
Medium-bodied 🍷🍷 ▮

Lavender and mint-scented Cabernet Sauvignon with blackcurrant-pastille flavours, refreshing acidity and balancing sweet ripe fruit and tannins.

1996 Safeway Chilean Cabernet/Malbec, Central Valley £3.99
14/20

Medium-bodied 🍷🍷 ▮

Soft, juicy, luscious quaffing Chilean blend of Cabernet Sauvignon and Malbec from Chile's biggest winery, Concha y Toro.

1996 Safeway Chilean Cabernet Sauvignon, Lontue, £3.99 15/20
Medium-bodied 🍷🍷🍷 ▮

Approachable, succulent claret alternative from Chile's San Pedro winery. Not surprising that this very juicy and highly drinkable red is in Safeway's top ten.

FRANCE

1996 Safeway Vin de Pays de l'Ardèche, £3.29 14/20
Medium-bodied 🍷🍷🍷 ▮

Deeply coloured, aromatic Rhône rouge with sweet plum and chocolatey fruit flavours and a spicy note on the aftertaste.

1996 Safeway Côtes du Rhône, £3.69 14/20
Medium-bodied 🍷🍷 ▮

A top ten best-seller at Safeway, this is an ultra-modern, juicy Côtes du Rhône. The content belies the rather old-fashioned label.

Safeway Claret NV, £3.75 13/20
Medium-bodied 🍷 ▮

Pricey for a basic red Bordeaux, this is a chewy and rather green claret, slightly softened by some oak maturation.

1996 Château du Ragon, Bordeaux, £3.99 14/20
Medium-bodied 👝👝 ▮
For a few pence more than the Safeway basic Bordeaux, this is an attractive, youthfully fruity petit château red with a faintly rustic edge.

1996 Safeway Merlot, Vin de Pays d'Oc, £3.99 14/20
Medium-bodied 👝👝 ▮
Soft, fleshy, grassy southern French Merlot with succulent tannins. Everything basic claret should be, but rarely is.

1995 Safeway Cabernet Sauvignon, Vin de Pays d'Oc, £3.99 14/20
Medium-bodied 👝👝 ▮
Easy-drinking southern French Cabernet Sauvignon with a grassy undertone and attractive blackberry fruitiness.

1996 Safeway Syrah, Vin de Pays d'Oc, £3.99 14/20
Medium-bodied 👝👝 ▮
Spicy, blackberry fruity quaffer from southern France.

1996 Safeway Domaine Vieux Manoir de Maransan, Côtes du Rhône, £4.49 15/20
Medium-bodied 👝👝 ▮
Forward, quaffing Côtes du Rhône with youthful colour, soft tannins and voluptuously juicy blackberry fruit.

1995 Les Chevaliers Bourgueil, £4.99 15/20
Medium-bodied 👝👝 ▮
Pleasant, grassy Bourgueil showing the typical aromatic, refreshing character of the Cabernet Franc grape in its Loire Valley heartland.

ITALY

1996 Safeway Sicilian Red, £3.29 14/20
Medium-bodied 👝👝 ▮
A blend of the local Nero d'Avola with Sangiovese, showing ripe, raisin and damson fruit and a nip of dry tannin. Italy's answer to Côtes du Rhône.

1996 Zagara Nero d'Avola, Vino da Tavola di Sicilia, £3.99 15/20
Medium-bodied 👝👝👝 ▮
Distinctive Sicilian rosso made by Aussie Kym Milne from the Nero d'Avola grape. Lively cherry fruit and lashings of oak make this an ultra-modern (for Sicily) red.

ROMANIA

Safeway Romanian Cabernet Sauvignon, 3-litre bag-in-box, £12.49 (= £3.12 per bottle) 14/20
Medium-bodied 👜👜 ▮
Decently made and pleasantly mature, with enough fruit sweetness to make a satisfying party red.

SOUTH AFRICA

1996 Safeway Quagga Cinsaut/Cabernet, Western Cape, £3.69 14/20

Medium-bodied 👜👜 ▮
Light coloured, prematurely ageing, old-fashioned Cape red, but still showing a kernel of sweet, wild strawberry fruitiness.

1996 Rosenview Cinsaut, Stellenbosch, £3.79 15/20
Medium-bodied 👜👜👜 ▮
Smoky-oaky, vibrantly fruity Cape red made from the Cinsaut grape. With its distinctive flavour of red fruit, it tastes not unlike the native Pinotage.

1996 Simonsvlei Shiraz Reserve, Paarl, £4.99 15/20
Full-bodied 👜👜 ▮
Sweetly oaked, brambly Cape Shiraz with rich flavours and undertones of chocolate and coffee bean.

SPAIN

1996 Viña Albali Tempranillo, Valdepeñas, £3.19 14/20
Medium-bodied 👜👜 ▮
Young, plum and cherry fruity unoaked Tempranillo showing the modern face of one of Spain's best red grape varieties.

1996 Safeway Young Vatted Tempranillo, La Mancha, £3.49 15/20
Medium-bodied 👜👜👜 ▮
Made from the same red grape, but a little more robust, with more marked acidity and chewy tannins as well as a tad more oomph.

1995 Berberana Tempranillo (Oak-Aged) Rioja, £4.99 15/20
Medium-bodied 👜👜 ▮
Tempranillo again, cropping up this time in a modern, oaky, well-made Rioja, with flavours of vanilla and cassis and gentle, appealing tannins.

£5–8

AUSTRALIA

1996 Safeway Australian Oaked Shiraz, £5.29 16/20
Full-bodied 💰💰💰 ➖
From the giant BRL-Hardy operation, this is a succulently minty, extremely well-judged Shiraz with a long, lingering aftertaste.

1995 Rosemount Estate Shiraz, South Australia, £7.49 16/20
Full-bodied 💰💰 ➖
Thick, oaky, concentrated Aussie Shiraz with masses of oak and spicy fruit and smooth tannins. Stylish stuff.

1994 Mount Hurtle Shiraz, Geoff Merrill, £7.99 17/20
Full-bodied 💰💰💰 ➖
Densely coloured blend of McLaren Vale and Goulburn Valley Shiraz, with lovely, voluptuous licorice and blackberry fruit and deftly handled oak maturation, from the moustachioed Geoff Merrill.

FRANCE

1996 Regnié, Duboeuf, £5.99 15/20
Medium-bodied 💰 🍾
From the king of the Beaujolais, Georges Duboeuf, this is a brightly hued, raspberry fruity Gamay with a not unpleasant hint of bubblegum.

1993 Safeway Margaux, £7.99 16/20
Medium-bodied 💰💰 🍾
Mature, extremely drinkable Margaux from an average vintage in Bordeaux, with supple tannins and some of the class of Château Durfort-Vivens, of which this is the second label.

ITALY

1996 Tenuta San Vito Chianti Putto, £5.99 15/20
Medium-bodied 💰💰 🍾
Muscular, organic Chianti, which really needs food to show at its best.

SPAIN

1995 Cosme Palacio y Hermanos Rioja, £5.99   17/20
Medium-bodied 🛍️🛍️🛍️ ▬

A modern, all-Tempranillo red from the Rioja Alavesa region, which combines oak and structured blackberry and cassis fruitiness in a harmonious whole. Still in its infancy.

UNITED STATES

1994 Fetzer Santa Barbara Pinot Noir, £6.99   16/20
Medium-bodied 🛍️🛍️🛍️ ▮

Succulent, sweetly oaked Central Coast Pinot Noir, with luscious loganberry fruit and a soft finish. Brilliant value.

Over £8

CHILE

1995 Cono Sur Pinot Noir, 20 Barrels, Rapel Valley, £9.99   17/20
Medium-bodied 🛍️🛍️🛍️ ▬

The best Pinot Noir we've tasted from Chile, this is concentrated and complex, with restrained but stylish oak treatment and good ageing potential.

FRANCE

1995 Safeway Beaune, £8.99   15/20
Medium-bodied 🛍️ ▮

Young, rustic village Pinot Noir with robust acidity and tannins and some attractive Pinot Noir fruit flavours.

1995 Safeway Châteauneuf-du-Pape, £8.99   16/20
Full-bodied 🛍️🛍️ ▮

Heady, aromatic, Grenache-based southern Rhône red, with classic brown-sugar character and a hint of pepper.

Rosé

£3–5

ARGENTINA

1996 Balbi Syrah Rosé, £3.99   15/20
Off-dry 🍾🍾🍾 |
Deep-hued, redcurranty Argentine rosé with thirst-quenching fruit and acidity.
Halfway to a Beaujolais in style.

AUSTRALIA

1996 Breakaway Grenache, South Australia, £4.49   15/20
Off-dry 🍾🍾🍾 |
Ultra-fresh, rosehip and strawberry-scented, stylish Day-Glo Aussie rosé from
Merv Hughes look-alike, Geoff Merrill, with appealing raspberry fruitiness and
full flavour.

FRANCE

1996 Safeway Rosé d'Anjou, £3.49   14/20
Medium dry 🍾🍾 |
Sweet, green-pepper-like Loire rosé with a thirst-quenching tang.

Sparkling

£5–8

ITALY

Safeway Asti, £5.49   15/20
Sweet 🍾🍾 |
Good grapey, sherbety, sweet north-west Italian fizz with a welcome tang of
acidity.

SPAIN

Safeway Cava Brut, £5.29   14/20
Dry 👍👍 🍾
Youthful, well-made Spanish fizz with a lemony tang of acidity.

Freixenet Cordon Negro Brut, £6.99   12/20
Dry 🍾
As dull as Spanish ditchwater, and unredeemed by the frosted black bottle.

Over £8

FRANCE

Safeway Albert Etienne Champagne Rosé, £13.99   15/20
Dry 👍👍 🍾
Mature, bronze-pink fizz with plenty of Pinot Noir flavour. Much more enjoyable than the advanced colour would suggest.

1990 Safeway Albert Etienne Vintage Brut, £14.99   16/20
Dry 👍👍👍 🍾
Rich, Pinot-dominated vintage Champagne at a very tasty price. Consistently enjoyable and consistently good value.

Chartogne-Taillet Champagne Brut, Cuvée Ste Anne, £15.99
                                                          15/20
Dry 👍👍 🍾
Youthful, malty, grower's Champagne with tart acidity and a hint of balancing sweetness.

Veuve Clicquot Yellow Label Brut, £22.99   17/20
Dry 👍👍 🍾
Well-made, ultra-reliable, non-vintage Champagne with elegant, tapering fruit flavours and fine poise.

Fortified

£3–5

FRANCE

1996 Dom Brial Muscat de Rivesaltes, 37.5 cl., £3.99   14/20
Very sweet 🍷 |
Youthful, grapey, orange-peel-scented fortified Muscat de Rivesaltes with a
faintly spirity afterburn.

Sainsbury's ☆☆☆☆

Address: Stamford House, Stamford Street, London SE1 9LL

Telephone/fax: 0171 695 6000; 0171 695 7925; or freephone: 0800 636262

Number of branches: 396 (including 13 Savacentres), plus J. Sainsbury Vins, Bières et Spiritueux in Calais

Opening hours: Branch-specific; regular late night opening

Credit cards accepted: Access, American Express, Switch, Visa

Discounts: 5 per cent off six bottles of wine (which can be mixed), plus multi-buy offers, special offers and special purchases

Facilities and services: Home delivery through Sainsbury's The Magazine (0800 716129); glass loan; in-store tastings on an ad hoc basis

Special offers: See discounts, plus offers to Reward Card holders

Top ten best-selling wines (by volume): Sainsbury's Liebfraumilch; Sainsbury's Lambrusco Bianco; Sainsbury's Bordeaux Sauvignon Blanc; Sainsbury's South African Chenin Blanc; Sainsbury's Vin Rouge de France (1.5 litre); Sainsbury's Claret; Bulgarian Reserve Cabernet Sauvignon; Sangiovese di Toscana, Cecchi; Sainsbury's Tempranillo/Cabernet Sauvignon, La Mancha; Sainsbury's Cava

Range:

GOOD: Bordeaux, Loire, Languedoc-Roussillon, Beaujolais, Burgundy, Italy, Australia, Chile, South Africa, Champagne and sparkling wine

AVERAGE: Rhône, Alsace, England, Portugal, Spain, Germany, Hungary, Romania, Bulgaria, New Zealand, Argentina

POOR: California

UNDER-REPRESENTED: None

'Fresh Food, Fresh Ideas' read the large posters that started to appear on advertising hoardings all over the country this summer. After 1996, when the talk was of humble rather than pork pies, when stale ideas were the order of the day, and when Sainsbury's reported its first fall in underlying profits in over two decades, 1997 has been a much more positive year for the company.

Allan Cheesman, the wine department's director, reflects the new mood of optimism in Stamford Street. 'When the company wasn't doing well, it permeated through,' the fitness-mad retailer told us, straight from a three-mile jog on a treadmill. 'Now we're on a high, there's a real buzz about the place.' Such up-beat talk is more than mere bravado. In the space of six months, Sainsbury's share price rose from a nadir of £3.08 to £4.35. New chief executive Dino Adriano, who took over in March, has clearly made an impact.

Cheesman is remarkably bullish about his department's performance at the moment. 'This is the best wine buying team we've ever had and I've just told them so,' he informed us during our annual interview. Cheesman was especially pleased that Rebecca Hull, his buyer for the Americas, New Zealand and Australia, had just been awarded the prestigious Master of Wine qualification, bringing the MW tally to two. (Marketing manager Claire Gordon-Brown is the other one.) The rest of the team is: senior manager Robin Tapper, category manager Andy Adcock, who replaced Mark Kermode, and buyers Gerard Barnes, Joanne Convert, Lindsay Talas and Kirstie Owen. Nicolas Thiriot runs the Calais store (discussed in our cross-Channel section).

The other bit of good news, as far as Cheesman is concerned, is that Sainsbury's is gaining ground on Tesco, the country's number-one wine retailer. 'Tesco was 3 per cent ahead of us at one time, but now we've cut the gap to 1 per cent and they've got 300 more stores than we have.' Sainsbury's is ahead of its rival in sales from every country except Germany and France, apparently.

Booming wines sales have been further inflated by the strong pound, according to Cheesman. 'I can't remember a time in my career when the pound has been worth 253 pesetas, 3,000 lire and 10.5 francs. It's made it easier to offer value for money at £2.99. French prices have come down for things like claret, Muscadet, Bergerac Blanc and Vin de Pays d'Oc.'

Cheesman used to be opposed to the £2.99 bottle – laudably in our view – unless it could really deliver on flavour and value. With the shifting exchange rate, he's softened his views a little, although he says that the real growth as far as Sainsbury's is concerned is in the £3.50–£6 sector. There is even, he adds, a limited demand for fine wines over £10. Cheesman is proud that, at £3.69, Sainsbury's average bottle price is '40 pence ahead of the competition'. He appears to have forgotten about Waitrose, but it's certainly true of Tesco.

Cheesman is a big fan of French wines, which increased their market share from 22 to 25 per cent at Sainsbury's in the last year. 'I think France is finding its niche,' he says. 'The way I see France is as six different countries which need to be treated separately. The Languedoc-Roussillon alone is the fourth-biggest wine producing area in the world.'

He also recognises the importance of the New World, which now accounts for an impressive 25 per cent of sales. Australia alone takes a 15 per cent slice of the tart, making Sainsbury's the biggest retailer of Aussie wine in the country, according to Cheesman. He concedes that prices have gone up steeply Down Under, putting pressure on £3.99 Aussie reds and whites, but says that the big Australian companies are being realistic. 'They realise that they'll have a lot of wine to sell in two years' time when the new plantings come on-stream.'

It could be argued that, in planting Chardonnay, Australia picked the wrong grape, or to be more precise the wrong colour of grape. In line with most high-street and supermarket chains, Sainsbury's has seen big increases in red-wine sales over the last year. 'In 1990, the split was 70:30 in favour of whites,' says Cheesman. 'Now it's 50:50.'

If Australia can't deliver red wines in sufficient volumes at reasonable prices, who can? Argentina is a possibility. Cheesman feels that Argentine wines 'don't quite deliver', but says that the likes of Trapiche are 'trying very hard to bring some sense to the South American psyche', an indication that he's less than chuffed about price hikes from Chile. 'The wines are very exciting and the investment is staggering, but there's a lot of pressure on prices because of demand from the United States.'

The Sainsbury's approach, in Chile as elsewhere, is to work with 'partnership suppliers'. 'You have to work with people to get the volumes,' says Cheesman. Within reason Sainsbury's likes to have as many suppliers as possible. In Chile alone, it buys wine from Canepa, Valdivieso, Viña Casablanca, Santa Rita, San Pedro and the Curicó co-op. 'If you only deal with one supplier', adds Cheesman, 'you end up cutting off your nose to spite your face'.

Despite the comparative diversity of suppliers, Sainsbury's has taken the decision to reduce its range in the last year, from 600 to 500 wines, an example of what Claire Gordon-Brown calls 'streamlining'. Cheesman calls it 'defining choice'. After talking to its customers, Sainsbury's took a long, hard stare at its wine range and removed what it saw as areas of duplication. 'Do we need four Lambruscos in four colours?' asks Cheesman. 'Do we need a third Bulgarian Cabernet Sauvignon?'

This does not mean that the range is being dumbed down, according to Cheesman. There will continue to be a 'tail of 50 fine wines at £10 to £20', as much for the sake of perception as profit. (In fact, after a few years' absence, a specific Fine Wine area has been reintroduced in 75 out of 396 stores. After the demise of Vintage Selection in 1994, the clarets and Burgundies were simply dotted around the shelves.) Our view is that Sainsbury's is taking a slightly safe option by focusing on the wines that sell best. This makes hard-nosed retailing sense, but it reflects our view that Sainsbury's is taking fewer risks than its closest competitors.

'Fresh ideas applies to wine as well as food,' Robin Tapper told us. But it's hard to see any real evidence on the shelves. What does come across, however, is an extremely well-chosen core selection, with very few obvious weaknesses. Sainsbury's may not be as innovative as Asda, Tesco or Safeway, but it's often a better place to buy things like basic claret, Champagne, Sherry, Port, Côtes du Rhône and Beaujolais.

Tapper rejects the idea of innovation for innovation's sake. 'What we're looking to do', he says, 'is offer a clear, uncluttered range with definition and quality at all tiers. We want to make wine simple and remove the gobbledegook. Customers don't want a geography lesson. They want to know what it's made from, what colour it is and what food to eat it with.' Tapper sees this as a way of 'communicating directly with our customers' and bypassing journalists, if necessary. If he's right about what wine drinkers really want, we'll see you at the Job Opportunities' Centre.

Wines marked 'FW only' are available only at stores with Fine Wine areas.

White

Under £3

GERMANY

Sainsbury's Liebfraumilch, £2.85   13/20
Medium sweet 🍾🍾 ▮
Decent, basic, floral Lieb. Cleanly made and grapey.

ITALY

Sainsbury's Lambrusco Bianco, £2.39   12/20
Medium sweet 🍾🍾 ▮
A light, frothy confection with lemonade-like sweetness and fizz.

MACEDONIA

1996 Macedonian Chardonnay, £2.85   13/20
Dry 🍾🍾 ▮
Buttery, faintly honeyed, unoaked Balkan Chardonnay made to a good price.

SPAIN

Sainsbury's Spanish Sweet White, £2.99   13/20
Sweet 👛👛 🍸
Peachy, pineappley Spanish white from La Mancha, with restrained sweetness
and a soft finish.

£3–5

AUSTRALIA

**1996 Hardy's Banrock Station Chenin/Semillon/Chardonnay,
£3.99**   13/20
Dry 👛 🍸
Oak-chippy, warm-climate Aussie quaffer made from a trio of premium grapes.
Faintly smoky, if rather bland.

1996 Koonunga Hill Semillon/Sauvignon, Penfolds, £4.99   15/20
Dry 👛👛 🍸
Refreshing, melon and grapefruit-zesty Aussie blend with a herbal, Semillon-
derived tang, from the country's biggest wine group.

FRANCE

Sainsbury's Bordeaux Sauvignon Blanc, £3.49   13/20
Dry 👛👛 🍸
Soft, grapefruity, basic white Bordeaux with decent Sauvignon Blanc zing.

**1996 Chenin Blanc, Vin de Pays du Jardin de la France, Lurton,
£3.89**   14/20
Dry 👛👛 🍸
A grapey, nettley Loire Chenin Blanc, which could almost be a Sauvignon Blanc.
Crisp, clean and zingy.

**1996 Sauvignon Blanc, Vin de Pays du Jardin de la France, Lurton,
£3.99**   13/20
Off-dry 👛 🍸
Soft, sweetish Sauvignon Blanc from the same stable. One of a bewildering
number of Sauvignon Blancs at Sainsbury's.

1996 Réserve St Marc Sauvignon Blanc, Vin de Pays d'Oc, £3.99
15/20

Bone dry 👜👜👜 ▮

Rich, unoaked, lemon butter and asparagus-style Sauvignon Blanc with assertive acidity, from southern France.

1996 Muscadet de Sèvre et Maine, Lurton, £3.99   14/20
Bone dry 👜👜 ▮

Crisp, sharpish Loire white made by Jacques Lurton at the Ackermann winery. We've had better 1996 Muscadets.

1996 Chardonnay, Vin de Pays d'Oc, Maurel Vedeau, £4.45   14/20
Dry 👜👜 ▮

A little too cinnamon oaky for our taste, but this peachy, full-flavoured southern French Chardonnay is a pleasant enough drink.

1996 Muscadet de Sèvre et Maine Sur Lie, La Goëlette, £4.49
15/20

Bone dry 👜👜👜 ▮

For 50 pence more than the Jacques Lurton Muscadet, you get a lot of genuine sur lie character for your money. A creamy, stylish white.

1995 Château Les Bouhets, Bordeaux Blanc, £4.49   15/20
Dry 👜👜 ▮

From winemaker Christophe Olivier, this is a rich, pleasantly flavoursome Sauvignon Blanc with a gooseberry tang.

1996 Vouvray, La Couronne des Plantagenets, Demi-Sec, £4.59
15/20

Medium dry 👜👜 ▮

Floral, honeysuckle-scented Vouvray with juicy, appley fruit and well-balanced acidity and sweetness.

1996 Sainsbury's Classic Selection Muscadet de Sèvre et Maine, £4.99
15/20

Bone dry 👜👜 ▮

A chunky bottle, but a far from chunky wine. Fine and elegant, with a bone-dry tang and good sur lie richness.

GERMANY

1995 Mainzer St Alban Kabinett, £3.49   14/20
Medium dry 👛👛 ▮
A step up from the bog-standard Lieb, this is a light-bodied, tangy blend from
the Rheinhessen, with restrained sweetness.

1996 Fire Mountain Riesling, Pfalz, £3.99   15/20
Dry 👛👛👛 ▮
One of the best new-wave, drier-style German whites, which combines
Australian technology with cool-climate lime and peach Riesling flavours.

ITALY

1996 Sainsbury's Soave Superiore, Pagus di Montecchia, £3.99
                                                          15/20
Bone dry 👛👛👛 ▮
Intense, nutty, well-made Soave from Carlo Corino, with good length and fresh
acidity.

Sainsbury's Pinot Grigio, Atesino, £3.99   15/20
Dry 👛👛👛 ▮
Fresh, abundantly fruity, nutty Pinot Grigio from the GIV winery, with ripe-pear
notes and zesty acidity.

**1995 Sainsbury's Verdicchio Classico dei Castelli di Jesi, Umani
Ronchi, £3.99**   15/20
Dry 👛👛👛 ▮
Delicately nutty, lime-fresh Adriatic white with juicy acidity and excellent
definition of flavour.

1996 Sainsbury's Frascati Secco Superiore, £4.49   14/20
Bone dry 👛👛 ▮
Soft, pleasant, well-made Roman glugger from the Colli Albani. A little pricey
for Frascati.

1996 Pinot Grigio Cortegiara, £4.95   15/20
Dry 👛👛 ▮
Well-made, concentrated, intensely textured, crisp white with a hazelnutty
undertone.

SOUTH AFRICA

Sainsbury's South African Chenin Blanc, £3.39   13/20
Dry 🍷🍷 ▮
From the Swartland co-operative, this is a simple, fruity Cape Chenin for glugging rather than pondering over.

1996 Springfield Estate Sauvignon Blanc, £4.99   16/20
Dry 🍷🍷🍷 ▮
Elegant, gooseberryish Cape Sauvignon Blanc, which is strong competition for the Loire and New Zealand at this price.

1996 Sainsbury's South African Chardonnay, Reserve Selection, £4.99   14/20
Off-dry 🍷 ▮
Overtly oaked, almost coconutty Cape Chardonnay with rather obvious tropical fruit flavours.

£5–8

AUSTRALIA

1996 Denman Estate Chardonnay, Mildara Blass, £5.45   14/20
Off-dry 🍷 ▮
Golden-hued, old-fashioned, honey and tinned pineapple-style Chardonnay with powerful alcohol. A bit of a one-glass wonder.

1995 Sainsbury's New Classic Selection Australian Chardonnay, £5.99   15/20
Off-dry 🍷🍷 ▮
Ripe, full-flavoured Chardonnay from BRL-Hardy, with toasty vanilla oak and toffee-fudge richness. Very drinkable.

CHILE

1996 Santa Carolina Chardonnay Reserva, Maipo, £5.75   16/20
Dry 🍷🍷🍷 ▮
A broad, buttery, well-made Chilean Chardonnay from Pilar González, with added barrel-fermented complexity and lees-derived richness and texture.

FRANCE

1996 Quincy, Clos des Victoires, £5.95   15/20
Dry 👜👜 ❚
Blended by Sancerre grower, Henri Bourgeois, this is a good-value Loire Sauvignon Blanc with good varietal character and medium length.

1996 Sainsbury's Gewürztraminer, Cave de Turckheim, £5.95
                                             16/20
Dry 👜👜👜 ❚
Spicy, full-flavoured, textbook Alsace Gewürz from the Turckheim co-operative, with plenty of body, lychee fruit and fresh acidity.

1995 Quatre Terroirs Chardonnay, Vin de Pays d'Oc, £5.95   12/20
Dry ❚
Rather tired, baked-apple Chardonnay from the Limoux area, showing a tart green edge.

1996 Bergerac Sec, Domaine de Grandchamp, Sauvignon Blanc, £5.95   16/20
Dry 👜👜👜 ❚
From Hugh Ryman's family estate in the Bergerac, Château la Jaubertie, this is a ripe, unoaked, gooseberry fruity Sauvignon Blanc, which runs a lot of Sancerre close in quality.

1995 Pacherenc du Vic Bilh, Moelleux Autumnal, 37.5 cl., £5.95
(FW only)   16/20
Very sweet 👜👜👜 ❚
A blend of Petit Manseng and Courbu grapes with rich oak, pineapple and honey notes and refreshing acidity, from the foothills of the French Pyrenees.

1996 Sainsbury's Classic Selection Pouilly-Fumé, Fouassier, £6.95
                                             16/20
Bone dry 👜👜👜 ❚
Intense, minerally, crisply flavoured Sauvignon Blanc with good richness and Pouilly-Fumé flintiness.

1996 Sainsbury's Classic Selection Sancerre, Fouassier, £6.95
                                             15/20
Bone dry 👜👜 ❚
From the same producer, this is a pleasant, grapefruity Sancerre with a nettley bite.

1995 Mâcon Chardonnay, Domaine Les Ecuyers, £6.95   16/20
Dry 👜👜👜 ▐
Full, ripe, spicy Mâcon Chardonnay with attractive, honeyed intensity from the village of Chardonnay in Burgundy, which may have given its name to the world's most popular grape.

1995 Sainsbury's Classic Selection Chablis, Domaine Ste Céline, Brocard, £7.45   16/20
Bone dry 👜👜👜 ▐
Good benchmark Chablis, unoaked for maximum lemon and mineral fruit impact.

1995 Château Carsin, Cadillac, 50cl, £7.95 (FW only)   16/20
Very sweet 👜👜 ▐
Made by Aussie Mandy Jones, this is a stylish, elegant, botrytis and new oak-dominated sweet Bordeaux white made entirely from Semillon grapes. Lusciously drinkable.

ITALY

1996 Lugana San Benedetto, Zenato, £5.29   15/20
Dry 👜👜 ▐
Rich, soft, juicy, white peach-flavoured Lake Garda quaffer in a Burgundy bottle.

1996 Pinot Grigio Collio, Enofriulia, £6.75   16/20
Dry 👜👜 ▐
Spritzy, refreshing, food-friendly, north-east Italian Pinot Grigio with lingering acidity, from négociant, Puiatti.

NEW ZEALAND

1996 Sanctuary Sauvignon Blanc, Marlborough, £6.45   15/20
Dry 👜 ▐
Fresh, green-bean and gooseberry fruity Marlborough Sauvignon Blanc from Grove Mill, with lively acidity and good balance. Well priced for Marlborough Sauvignon Blanc.

1996 Sanctuary Chardonnay, Marlborough, £6.45   15/20
Dry 👜👜 ▐
Elegant, well-made New Zealand Chardonnay from the same source, with subtle notes of vanilla and butter and a citrus-fruit core.

SOUTH AFRICA

1996 Danie de Wet Grey Label Chardonnay, Robertson, £5.45
15/20

Dry 🍶🍶 ▮
Fresh, youthful, subtly oaked Robertson Chardonnay, which could do with a little more stuffing. Trying to be too elegant, perhaps.

Over £8

FRANCE

1994 Château Rabaud-Promis, Sauternes, 37.5 cl., £9.95 (FW only)
17/20

Very sweet 🍶🍶🍶 ▬
Oak-aged, botrytis-affected Bordeaux sticky made mainly from Semillon grapes and showing excellent intensity of flavour and acidity.

1990 Château de Cérons, Cérons, 37.5 cl., £9.95 16/20
Very sweet 🍶🍶 ▮
Sweet, coconutty, honeyed Cérons sweet white, which has been gently softened by bottle age.

Red

Under £3

FRANCE

Sainsbury's Bordeaux Rouge, Ginestet, £2.95 14/20
Medium-bodied 🍶🍶🍶 ▮
Attractively juicy, modern claret with none of the hard edges so often associated with cheap Bordeaux.

1996 Sainsbury's Cabernet Sauvignon, Vin de Pays d'Oc, £2.99
14/20

Medium-bodied 🍷🍷🍷 |
From the Roussillon-based Vignerons Catalans operation, this is a well-made, cassis fruity quaffer with ripe tannins and grip.

Sainsbury's Vin de Pays des Bouches du Rhône, £2.99   14/20
Medium-bodied 🍷🍷🍷 |
Pepper and brown-sugar-like Provençal glugger made for supple, easy drinking.

MACEDONIA

1996 Macedonian Country Red, Povardarski, £2.69   12/20
Medium-bodied |
Cheap, oak-chippy Macedonian red made, apparently, from the local Vranac grape. Grapes, like life, are cheap in this part of the world.

1996 Macedonian Cabernet Sauvignon, Povardarski, £2.85   13/20
Medium-bodied 🍷 |
Marginally better, but still rather oak-chippy and coarse.

SPAIN

Sainsbury's Spanish Red Wine, La Mancha, £2.99   12/20
Medium-bodied 🍷 |
Basic, chewy, central Spanish plonko, apparently made from Garnacha grapes.

£3–5

AUSTRALIA

1996 Hardy's Banrock Station Mataro/Grenache/Shiraz, £3.99
14/20

Full-bodied 🍷🍷 |
Better than the companion white, this is a spicy, chocolatey oaky red with smooth tannins and vibrant blackcurrant fruit. One of the better cheap Aussies on the market.

Sainsbury's Australian Cabernet Sauvignon, £4.85   14/20
Full-bodied 🍷 ▮
Rapidly maturing, but quite complex Aussie Cabernet Sauvignon, with lots of oak and smooth tannins.

1995 Sainsbury's Australian Shiraz, Barossa Valley, £4.85   15/20
Full-bodied 🍷🍷 ▮
Vibrant, spicy, blackberry fruity Shiraz from the enormous Southcorp group, with well-judged oak and balance. Super value at under a fiver.

BULGARIA

1991 Reserve Cabernet Sauvignon, Iambol, Domaine Boyar, £3.79
14/20

Medium-bodied 🍷🍷 ▮
Smoky, chocolatey, mature Bulgarian Cabernet Sauvignon with firm tannins. Good value at under £4.

CHILE

1996 La Palma Reserve Cabernet Sauvignon/Merlot, £4.99   16/20
Medium-bodied 🍷🍷🍷 ▮
Silky, beautifully oaked Chilean blend of Cabernet Sauvignon and Merlot with sumptuous blackcurrant fruit and vanilla spice. One of a series of excellent wines we've had from La Palma/La Rosa this year.

FRANCE

Sainsbury's Côtes du Rhône, £3.25   14/20
Medium-bodied 🍷🍷🍷 ▮
Flavoursome, superbly priced Côtes du Rhône with cherry and plum notes and a spicy finish.

Sainsbury's Cabernet Sauvignon/Syrah, Vin de Pays d'Oc, £3.45
15/20

Full-bodied 🍷🍷🍷 ▮
Vibrantly fruity, blackberryish Languedoc blend of Cabernet Sauvignon and Syrah from Foncalieu. Great value.

Sainsbury's Syrah/Mourvèdre, Vin de Pays d'Oc, £3.45   14/20
Full-bodied 👜👜👜 |

A herby, spicy, well-chosen southern French blend of Syrah and Mourvèdre with firm tannins and a dry finish.

1995 Costières de Nîmes, Les Garrigues, £3.75   15/20
Medium-bodied 👜👜👜 |

Robust, traditional, blackberry fruity southern French blend in a good package.

Sainsbury's Claret, £3.75   14/20
Medium-bodied 👜👜 |

Modern, juicy, easy-drinking claret, which expresses its origin with pride.

Sainsbury's Merlot/Cabernet Sauvignon, Vin de Pays d'Oc, £3.79
13/20
Medium-bodied 👜 |

Refreshing, thirst-quenching Bordeaux-style blend from Foncalieu, with a slight rasp of acidity.

1996 Réserve St Marc Shiraz, £3.99   14/20
Full-bodied 👜👜 |

Inky, New World-influenced, southern French Syrah (sorry, Shiraz), which lacks a bit of finesse.

1996 Merlot, Vin de Pays de la Cité de Carcassonne, CIRA, £3.99
15/20
Medium-bodied 👜👜👜 |

Refreshing, blackcurranty Merlot with medium-weight tannins, good depth of flavour and a flourish of acidity.

1996 Cabernet Sauvignon, Vin de Pays d'Oc, Caroline de Beaulieu, £3.99   14/20
Medium-bodied 👜👜 |

Good, modern, blackcurranty southern French Cabernet Sauvignon with a succulent texture. Well made at the price.

Sainsbury's Beaujolais, £3.99   15/20
Light-bodied 👜👜👜 |

A refreshing, juicy Beaujolais with classic, softly fruity Gamay flavours. What Beaujolais used to taste like before it got ideas above its humble station.

Sainsbury's Vin Rouge de France, 1.5 litres, £4.99   13/20
Medium-bodied 🍷🍷🍷 ▐
Smooth, southern French plonk in a plastic bottle with simple, but robust berry fruit flavours.

Sainsbury's Cuvée Prestige Claret, £4.99   15/20
Medium-bodied 🍷🍷 ▐
Made by Bordeaux-based Australian, Mandy Jones, this is an upfront, lightly oaked, blackcurranty red with supple tannins. The sort of thing that might give cheap Bordeaux a good name.

1994 Fitou, Château de Ségure, Mont Tauch, £4.99   16/20
Full-bodied 🍷🍷🍷 ▐
Cinnamon and rosemary-scented Languedoc stunner at a very good price, from Fitou's impressive Mont Tauch co-operative.

ITALY

1996 Sangiovese di Toscana, Cecchi, £3.79   15/20
Medium-bodied 🍷🍷🍷 ▐
Savoury, chocolatey Tuscan Sangiovese with juicy plum-skin notes and fleshy tannins.

1996 Sainsbury's Valpolicella Classico, £3.99   14/20
Medium-bodied 🍷🍷 ▐
Made by Carlo Corino, this is a concentrated, cherry and plum-like Valpolicella with good balance and acidity.

1994 Sainsbury's Copertino Riserva, £4.29   16/20
Full-bodied 🍷🍷🍷 ▐
A Puglian blend of Negroamaro and 5 per cent Malvasia Nera, with flavours of raisin, ginger spice and a dash of coffee. A gloriously modern interpretation of a traditional style.

ROMANIA

1996 Idle Rock Romanian Pinot Noir, £3.75   14/20
Medium-bodied 🍷🍷 ▐
Bubble gum and red-fruit-like Pinot Noir, which shows that Romania is moving in the right direction.

1996 Idle Rock Romanian Merlot, £3.75   14/20
Medium-bodied 🍾🍾 ⬩

From the same region, Dealul Mare, this is a solid, chocolatey Merlot with well-judged tannins. Another promising Romanian red.

SOUTH AFRICA

1995 Sainsbury's South African Cabernet Sauvignon/Merlot Reserve Selection, £4.99   15/20
Full-bodied 🍾🍾 ⬩

Exuberant, blackcurrant fruity, full-flavoured Cabernet/Merlot blend with throat-warming tannins.

1996 Swartland Merlot Reserve, £4.99   16/20
Medium-bodied 🍾🍾🍾 ⬩

Elegant, characterful, green-pepper-scented Cape Merlot with sweet vanilla oak and a smooth texture. Proof that sub-£5 South African reds can compete with Chile and Australia on equal terms.

SPAIN

1995 Sainsbury's La Mancha Tempranillo/Cabernet Sauvignon, £3.49   14/20
Medium-bodied 🍾🍾🍾 ⬩

Considerably better than Sainsbury's basic, sub-£3 red, this is a nice, thirst-quenching tinto made in a juicy, mulberry fruity style.

1994 Dama de Toro, Bodegas Fariña, £4.25   14/20
Full-bodied 🍾 ⬩

Juicy, vibrant, if slightly oaky, Spanish red from the isolated Toro region. A wee bit rustic.

£5–8

FRANCE

1995 Château de la Tour, Bordeaux Rouge, £5.45   15/20
Medium-bodied 🍾🍾 ⬩

Not to be confused with Château Latour, this is a chunky, Cabernet Sauvignon-based new-wave claret with good presence and flavour.

1993 Château La Voulte-Gasparets, Corbières, £5.45   16/20
Full-bodied 👝👝👝 ▮
Leathery, mature, bitters-infused Corbières from a Sainsbury's stalwart. Traditional stuff.

1996 Côtes du Rhône Villages, Domaine de la Grande Bellane, Valréas, £5.95   15/20
Medium-bodied 👝 ▮
An organic southern Rhône blend of 75 per cent Syrah with 25 per cent Grenache, this is a lightish, spicy, peppery red with refreshing acidity and a sweet core of fruit.

1994 Crozes-Hermitage, Cave de Tain l'Hermitage, £5.95   15/20
Medium-bodied 👝👝 ▮
Made at the respectable local co-op, this is a robust, but authentic Syrah with more character than length of flavour.

1993 Vacqueyras, Brotte, £6.45   12/20
Full-bodied ▮
Stewed, pruney village Rhône red with a chewy finish. Lacks fruit.

1995 Château Segonzac, Premières Côtes de Blaye, £6.95   16/20
Medium-bodied 👝👝👝 ▬
Lots of colour, lots of oak and masses of sweet, inky, concentrated cassis fruit with spicy undertones.

1995 Chorey-lès-Beaune, Paul Dugenais, £6.95   16/20
Medium-bodied 👝👝👝 ▮
Superbly priced Côte d'Or red Burgundy from Labouré-Roi (aka Paul Dugenais), with youthful, raspberry and mulberry flavours and a hint of oak. Very good value.

1995 Châteauneuf-du-Pape, Les Galets Blancs, £7.95   14/20
Full-bodied ▮
Greenish and suspiciously cheap for a Châteauneuf, with a dry, rustic aftertaste.

SOUTH AFRICA

1995 Sainsbury's South African Pinotage, Reserve Selection, £5.45
15/20

Full-bodied 👜👜 ▮
Chunky, densely fruity Pinotage with pleasant oak-matured complexity. A good example of South Africa's native grape.

1995 Bellingham Merlot, £5.95
15/20
Full-bodied 👜👜 ▮
Sweet and rather chunky Cape Merlot with ripe, almost Australian-style blackcurrant fruit concentration.

SPAIN

1991 Conde de Siruela Crianza, Ribera del Duero, £6.95
14/20
Medium-bodied 👜 ▮
A weird combination of horseradish and green pepper on the nose. Equally idiosyncratic on the palate. Needs roast beef.

Over £8

FRANCE

1994 Château de Rully Rouge, £9.95
17/20
Medium-bodied 👜👜👜 ▮
Gamey, chocolatey, well-oaked Côte Chalonnaise Pinot Noir from Antonin Rodet, with a core of sweet strawberry fruit.

1994 Château Belgrave, Haut-Médoc, £13.95
17/20
Medium-bodied 👜👜👜 ▬
Stylish, coffee-bean oaky, fifth-growth claret, which is still in short trousers but should soften over the next five years. Classic stuff.

Rosé

£3–5

FRANCE

1996 Cabernet Rosé de la Loire, Vin de Pays du Jardin de la Loire, £3.99   14/20
Dry 👓👓 ❘
Refreshing, capsicum-like Loire rosé from Jacques Lurton, with an appealingly dry finish.

1996 Domaine de la Tuilerie Rosé, Hugh Ryman, Vin de Pays d'Oc, £3.99   14/20
Off-dry 👓👓 ❘
Bronze-pink, Merlot rosé from Hugh Ryman, which looks a little older than it should do. Soft, fruity and raspberry sweet.

1996 Domaine de Sours Rosé, Bordeaux, £4.99   15/20
Dry 👓👓 ❘
The second label of rosé specialist, Château de Sours in the Entre Deux Mers, this is a supple, delicately grassy, rosehip-flavoured quaffer.

SPAIN

1996 Sainsbury's Navarra Cabernet Sauvignon Rosado, £3.99
14/20
Off-dry 👓👓 ❘
Full-flavoured, bronze-hued rosado with a powerful kick of alcohol, from the Principe de Viana winery.

Sparkling

£3–5

SPAIN

Sainsbury's Cava Rosado, £4.99   15/20
Dry 🍷🍷🍷 ▌
Bright, bronze-pink fizz with elegant strawberry fruit and soft texture. A very
good companion to Sainsbury's enjoyable straight Cava.

£5–8

AUSTRALIA

Sainsbury's Australian Sparkling Wine, £5.49   13/20
Dry 🍷 ▌
Simple, aggressive, tropical fruit-style fizz from Seppelts Great Western, the
home of Aussie fizz.

FRANCE

1992 Sainsbury's Crémant de Loire Brut, £5.99   15/20
Dry 🍷🍷🍷 ▌
Mature, honeyed, blended Loire fizz with a creamy mousse and a crisp, dry
finish. Very quaffable.

SOUTH AFRICA

Graham Beck Brut, Robertson, £6.99   16/20
Dry 🍷🍷🍷 ▌
Creamy, fine, elegant Cape sparkler made from Chardonnay and Pinot Noir
grapes and showing subtle, toasty flavours and good length.

SPAIN

Sainsbury's Cava, £5.25   15/20
Dry 🍾🍾🍾 ▮
A refreshing, mouth-filling Cava with nutty bottle age and clean acidity. One of
the best cheap sparklers on the market.

Over £8

AUSTRALIA

1994 Seaview Pinot Noir/Chardonnay, £8.49   16/20
Dry 🍾🍾🍾 ▮
Rich, toasty, full-blown Aussie blend of the Champagne grapes, Pinot Noir and
Chardonnay. A fizz that delivers on flavour and value.

FRANCE

Sainsbury's Champagne, Blanc de Noirs Brut, £11.99   14/20
Dry 🍾 ▮
Youthful, Pinot Noir-based co-operative fizz with a tart finish. Has been better
in previous years.

Sainsbury's Champagne Extra Dry, Duval Leroy, £12.95   15/20
Dry 🍾🍾 ▮
Fresh, creamy, attractively textured Champagne with the accent on lemon
elegance. A good basic supermarket bubbly.

Fortified

£3–5

FRANCE

Sainsbury's Muscat de St Jean de Minervois, 37.5 cl., £3.49   15/20
Very sweet 👜👜 ▐
Exotic, fortified Muscat with grape and melon sweetness. So well made you hardly notice the 15 per cent alcohol.

SPAIN

Sainsbury's Aged Amontillado, Hidalgo, 37.5 cl., £3.29   16/20
Dry 👜👜👜 ▐
Burnt toffee and crème brûlée-like Amontillado with a classically dry finish and masses of flavour. Super stuff.

Sainsbury's Palo Cortado, Lustau, 37.5 cl., £3.49   16/20
Medium dry 👜👜👜 ▐
A sweeter style, thanks to the addition of Pedro Ximenez grapes, showing stylish flavours of dates and almonds.

Sainsbury's Old Oloroso, Croft, £3.49   17/20
Bone dry 👜👜👜 ▬
Completing an excellent range of Sherries, this is a powerful, liquoricey, dry Oloroso with commendable complexity and a nutty, tobaccoey tang.

Pedro Ximenez, Cream of Cream, £3.95   14/20
Very sweet 👜👜 ▐
Super-concentrated, raisin and licorice-like Montilla made from PX grapes. Poor man's Sherry, best poured over vanilla ice cream.

Sainsbury's Fino, Croft, £4.69   15/20
Bone dry 👜👜 ▐
Ultra-fresh, tangy, salted almond-like Fino with a yeasty, nutty, dry aftertaste. Best sipped after a Spanish holiday.

£5–8

PORTUGAL

1990 Sainsbury's Late Bottled Vintage, £7.99   16/20
Full-bodied 👜👜👜 ▮
Spicy, complex, concentrated LBV, with lots of guts and fire power and sturdy tannins.

Over £8

PORTUGAL

Sainsbury's Ten-Year-Old Tawny, Quinta do Noval, £9.99   15/20
Full-bodied 👜 ▮
Faintly spicy, aged Tawny from the English-run Quinta do Noval. Too much fiery alcohol for the fruit here.

1985 Sainsbury's Vintage Port, Quinta Dona Matilde, £14.95   17/20
Full-bodied 👜👜👜 ▮
Minty, chocolatey, rich, fruitcake and almond-style vintage Port, which is drinking perfectly.

Somerfield
(including **Gateway**) ☆☆(☆)

Address: Somerfield House, Whitchurch Lane, Bristol BS14 OTJ

Telephone/fax: 01179 359359; 01179 780629

Number of branches: Just over 600, of which 80 per cent are Somerfield; the remaining 20 per cent are Gateway stores, which are being converted

Opening hours: 8.30am to 8.00pm Monday to Friday; 8.30am to 6.00pm Saturday; 10.00am to 4.00pm Sunday; opening hours vary slightly from store to store, depending on location and size

Credit cards accepted: all major credit cards

Discounts: Buy 11 bottles (mixed) and get a twelfth free; seven bottles for the price of six on Champagne

Facilities and services: Monthly in-store tastings in top 100 stores; glass loan and home/office shopping on trial in a small number of stores

Special offers: Regular fortnightly Price Check promotion; four-weekly promotions including price promotions, multi-buys and Premier Points, the Somerfield loyalty scheme

Top ten best-selling wines: Somerfield Claret; Somerfield Hock; Somerfield Liebfraumilch, Rheinberg; 1996 Somerfield Vin de Pays de l'Ardèche, UVICA; 1996 Somerfield Vin de Pays des Côtes de Gascogne; Somerfield Lambrusco Light; Somerfield Castillo Imperial Tinto; Somerfield Bulgarian Country Red; 1997 Somerfield South African Dry White; 1996 Somerfield Chilean Cabernet Sauvignon, La Rosa

Range:

GOOD: French country wines, Rhône, Italy

AVERAGE: Bordeaux, Portugal, Spain, Germany, Eastern Europe, Australia, New Zealand, Chile, sparkling wines

POOR: Champagne

UNDER-REPRESENTED: Burgundy, California

Somerfield (including Gateway)

Somerfield's trading manager, Angela Mount, doesn't have the luxury of a big buying team à la Tesco, Safeway or Sainsbury's. Until last year she needed more arms than the goddess Kali to handle press releases, leaflets on food and wine suggestions, plus a column for the in-store magazine, not to mention travelling overseas and selecting all the wines. You get the strong impression that Mount likes running the show, but even for such a practised juggler there are only so many balls that the impressively energetic Mount can keep in the air at any one time.

At last, with the arrival of ex-soft-drinks buyer Mark Jarman, solitary days at the tasting bench are becoming a thing of the past. It wasn't just Mount's isolation that needed treating. As she herself acknowledges, Somerfield needed a new buyer to address some of the weaknesses in the range. So Jarman's current job is to select wines from Germany, Eastern Europe and fortified wines, with Iberia as the consolation prize. The new duo have assistants Niki Anthony and Leah Nicholls to help out, but, compared to the Big Four, Somerfield is still short on personnel for the size of the operation: over 600 stores and a range of 380 wines.

Ex-Smirnoff brand manager Angela Mount is still strongly influenced by her marketing background. It's not surprising then that her conversation is littered with arcane references to 'sectors' and 'premiumising'. This latter bit of supermarket mumbo-jumbo is at the heart of the new Somerfield philosophy. Essentially it's all about going upmarket, mirroring the long-term process of transforming itself from an ugly Gateway duckling into a wannabe swan called Somerfield.

We'd actually thought after last year's tasting that the conversion of Gateway to Somerfield would have been completed by this year. Around one-fifth of the stores still display the old Gateway moniker, although Mount says confidently that the conversion should be completed by next spring. The group has certainly come a long way in five years. In 1992 it was losing 10 per cent year-on-year. David Simons' arrival as chief executive in February 1993 steadied the storm-tossed ship. When Somerfield was floated as a public company in 1996, the share price was £1.45. By the summer of 1997 it had climbed to £1.95.

In the bad old Gateway days, Mount says that she was finding great wines but didn't have the support or back-up of the stores to sell them. 'Things are much better now, with stores getting behind the product,' she says. 'The old Gateway was more downmarket. We've seen a move to younger, more aspirational customers and more families.' Overall, sales were up last year by 12 per cent in value, placing Somerfield fifth in the supermarket league table, behind Tesco, Sainsbury's, Asda and Safeway. Much-improved sales of sparkling wines, which have chronically underperformed at Somerfield, reflect the upwardly mobile trend.

With a strong focus on the high street, Somerfield tends to have a larger than average number of smaller stores. None has the breadth of range of the Big Four, a handicap that limits the range in an average store to 200–250 wines. 'The smaller the store, the harder my job,' says Mount, among whose tasks it is to work out how to fit a quart into a pint pot. 'I have to assume that anyone going into one of the smaller stores wants to buy a claret or a Beaujolais, which means I can't afford to let the bread-and-butter wines slip.' The quality of the Somerfield top ten is a lot better than last year, thanks in part to the appearance for the first time of two New World wines, but there's still room for improvement.

Somerfield has around 175 own-label wines and the number is growing. To create an own-label brand costs money, but it gives the supermarket greater flexibility with pricing and promotions, and customers like the feeling of reassurance. The trend with own-label is upmarket. 'We sell a hell of a lot of Côtes du Rhône, so the strategy is to bring in a higher-priced Côtes du Rhône. It's premiumising own-brand,' says Mount, letting the ex-Smirnoff mask slip. She is looking at doing the same for South America and South Africa. In Chile, for instance, there's a basic range of red and white, and at a higher level a Sauvignon Blanc, a Chardonnay and a Cabernet Sauvignon. The next step is to bring in a higher-quality reserve wine.

But 'Not all customers want an own-brand wine all the time,' says Mount. So the policy is to have a mix of own-label and other products. There's been a strong increase in sales of wines over £4, particularly in the New World. 'People are going in for a Gigondas or a Châteauneuf-du-Pape, ' she points out. 'We really want to encourage that.' Of course she does. With an average bottle price similar to Asda's, but well below Sainsbury's, at around £3.25 (without taking Price Check promotions into account), the more Somerfield can sell its higher-priced wines, the better it is in the long run, not just for profits, but for image and the ability to bring in customers who can't see beyond the £1.99 Price Check tag.

To the obvious distaste of competitors, one of whom once memorably called Mount 'the scum of the earth', Somerfield is still offering the £1.99 bottle in its successful fortnightly Price Check promotions. 'I would accept criticism for dragging the market down,' says Mount, 'if we were simply buying up cheap parcels of wine and flogging them off. But we're not. It's almost always our own wines we're promoting.' Last year Somerfield dropped its Argentine wine from £2.99 to £1.99, for instance. 'The idea is to encourage customers to try them.'

Price Check sells 'a significant amount of wine', she admits, but the strategy has changed a little from the pile-it-high, flog-it-cheap attitude of yesteryear. Now Somerfield is developing Price Check at a higher price. When Australia was promoted down from £3.49 to £2.49, it went well, says Mount. 'You have to offer a significant reduction to make it worthwhile.' One of the most successful Price Check promotions has been the reduction on Chilean Cabernet Sauvignon from £3.99 to £2.99. It's brought this deliciously juicy Cabernet from Viña La Rosa into Somerfield's top ten best-selling wines, ahead of the cheaper Chilean red at £3.49 and even a number of £2.99 wines.

New World wines account for over 20 per cent of sales, of which Australia comprises 9 per cent, followed by Chile and South Africa. South America is growing at the fastest rate. So Mount's most recent focus has been on South America, and not just the nightlife in Rio and Copacabana. At the time of the *Grapevine* tasting she was planning to bring in a new range of Chilean and Argentine wines for the autumn. She is particularly excited by Argentina, where Aussie Peter Bright has made some wines for Somerfield at Peñaflor. 'We launched an own-brand Argentine red and white and will launch higher-priced wines at the varietal level.'

'The quality reputation that Australia once had has now been extended to cover all New World wines,' according to Mount. Admitting that the New World range needed addressing, she has also been on a buying trip to Australia ' to secure stocks'. This must be a good thing, because, although Australia does well, the range is limited to little beyond the likes of own-label Chardonnay and safe, introduction-to-Oz brands such as Jacob's Creek and Lindemans Bin 65. 'We're catching up, but now have the confidence to develop the repertoire.' In store layouts, too, the New World now achieves pride of place on shelves.

Italy has long been a favourite area for Mount and, as a result, Italian wines are much more focused at Somerfield than those of Spain or Portugal. She is working in the south and also in Sicily on a couple of projects with Peter Bright and Kym Milne. Reviewing Burgundy and California is her next priority. Mark Jarman, after finding a couple of new Riojas (the 1987 Vina Caña Reserva at £5.99 is particularly good), will be focusing on Eastern Europe next, where (confession time again), 'there's still a lot of work to be done', and then the rest of Spain and Portugal.

Charged with the somewhat thankless task of trying to arrest the terminal decline in sales of the traditional German wines, Liebfraumilch and Hock, Jarman is looking at new-wave German whites. 'You have to have a degree of cynicism,' says Mount, with a degree of cynicism. 'It will take an almighty miracle to turn people back to quality German wines, and a lot of quality German wine is expensively priced.' It's certainly a challenge. But just one of the many challenges that the new Somerfield team will be addressing in tandem over the coming year.

White

Under £3

ARGENTINA

Somerfield Argentinian White, £2.99   13/20
Off-dry 👜👜 ▮
Sweetish, banana ice-lolly-style Argentine blend of Pedro Ximenez, Torrontés and Chenin Blanc, made by Australian Peter Bright at Peñaflor.

BULGARIA

Somerfield Bulgarian Aligoté/Chardonnay, Suhindol, £2.85   13/20
Medium dry 👜👜 ▮
A fruity Bulgarian blend of Chardonnay with Aligoté, which is sweetened up for British palates. Clean and pleasant enough.

FRANCE

1996 Sauvignon, Vin de Pays du Jardin de la France, Vinival £2.99
12/20

Off-dry 👜 ▮
Nettley, tart Loire Valley white with a faintly confected note.

GERMANY

Somerfield Hock, R. Müller, £2.59   13/20
Medium sweet 👜👜👜 ▮
Decent, floral Lieb with a hint of spritz and spice for interest and freshness.

Mosel Riesling Halbtrocken, £2.85   12/20
Medium sweet 👜 ▮
Sulphurous, gluey, faintly appley Riesling with a sharp finish. Not the best advertisement for one of Germany's best wine regions.

£3–5

AUSTRALIA

1997 Somerfield Australian Dry White, Penfolds, £3.49   13/20
Medium dry 🐚 ▮
From Australia's irrigated Riverland region, this is an aromatic, tutti-frutti Aussie Riesling with a zesty tang and pronounced sweetness.

1996 Penfolds Bin 21 Rawson's Retreat White, £4.49   15/20
Dry 🐚🐚🐚 ▮
A tangy, herbal blend of Semillon, Chardonnay and Colombard from the sprawling Southcorp group, with commendable freshness, zip and flavour.

1997 Somerfield Australian Chardonnay, Southcorp, £4.65   15/20
Dry 🐚🐚🐚 ▮
Made by Philip John, the man behind Lindemans' popular Bin 65, this is a fresh, citrus fruity Chardonnay with the faintest echo of oak treatment.

1996 Lindemans Cawarra Unoaked Chardonnay, £4.69   15/20
Dry 🐚🐚🐚 ▮
Nice, elegant, butter and citrus-fruit-like Chardonnay from the same stable as the Bin 65 below. Pleasantly refreshing stuff.

1996 Jacob's Creek Chardonnay, £4.99   15/20
Off-dry 🐚🐚 ▮
An Aussie best-seller from Orlando, which is deservedly popular, showing restrained peach and pineapple fruitiness and a touch of clove and cinnamon oak spice.

1997 Lindemans Bin 65 Chardonnay, £4.99   15/20
Off-dry 🐚🐚 ▮
Another big Aussie Chardonnay, this time from the giant Southcorp operation. Sweetish tropical fruit flavours and a hint of oak make this classic brand a winning formula.

1996 Nottage Hill Chardonnay, £4.99   16/20
Dry 🐚🐚🐚 ▮
Yet another Australian best-seller, this time from BRL-Hardy, with notes of tropical fruit, toffee fudge and caramel. Drier and with a bit more length of flavour than the competition.

1995 Lindemans Coonawarra Botrytis Riesling, half-bottle, £4.99
17/20

Very sweet 🍷🍷🍷 ▬

Intense, candied orange and lemon-peel-style, botrytis-infected Riesling from the coolish-climate Coonawarra region. Unlike many Aussie stickies, this isn't at all cloying.

BULGARIA

1996 Somerfield Bulgarian Chardonnay £3.35　　　　14/20
Dry 🍷🍷🍷 ▮

Clean, fresh, unoaked Bulgarian Chardonnay from the Suhindol region, made in a crisp modern style.

CHILE

1997 Somerfield Chilean White, £3.49　　　　　　12/20
Off-dry ▮

A peculiar Chilean blend of Chenin Blanc and Muscat made to a price. Unlike the country itself, this is rather dull and flat.

1997 Somerfield Chilean Sauvignon Blanc, Canepa, £3.99　15/20
Dry 🍷🍷🍷 ▮

Attractive, grapefruit zesty Chilean Sauvignon Blanc from the ultra-reliable Canepa winery. New Zealand Sauvignon can't compete at this price.

1996 Somerfield Chilean Chardonnay, £3.99　　　　14/20
Dry 🍷🍷 ▮

Rich, buttery, attractively oaked Chardonnay from the La Rosa winery. This scores at a price where Aussie Chardonnay has hung up its boots.

FRANCE

1996 Chardonnay Vin de Pays du Jardin de la France, Vinival, £3.49　　　　　　　　　　　　　　　15/20
Dry 🍷🍷🍷 ▮

Ripe, peachy, unoaked Loire Valley Chardonnay with crisp balancing acidity at a knock-down price.

1996 Domaine Bordeneuve, Vin de Pays des Côtes de Gascogne, £3.65   14/20
Off-dry 👝👝 ▮
Grapefruit and guava-like Gascon white from the eccentric, but highly talented, Yves Grassa.

1996 Muscadet de Sèvre et Maine Sur Lie, Vinival, £3.99   14/20
Dry 👝👝 ▮
Soft, easy-drinking sur lie Muscadet with a faint prickle of lees-derived spritz.

1996 Somerfield Chardonnay Vin de Pays d'Oc, James Herrick, £3.99   13/20
Dry 👝 ▮
Basic, over-oaky southern French Chardonnay made for Somerfield by an ex-pat Brit living in the Languedoc.

1996 Alsace Pinot Blanc, Turckheim, £4.59   15/20
Dry 👝👝👝 ▮
Spritz-fresh, lively Alsace Pinot Blanc from the Turckheim co-operative, with ripe pear notes and a seafood-friendly tang.

1995 Domaine de Rivoyre Chardonnay, Vin de Pays d'Oc, £4.99   15/20
Dry 👝👝 ▮
Pineapple, attractively oaked southern French Chardonnay from Hugh 'Grant' Ryman. Perfect for your four weddings.

1996 James Herrick Chardonnay, Vin de Pays d'Oc, £4.99   14/20
Dry 👝 ▮
Clean and reliable, if slightly characterless southern French Chardonnay from Languedoc-based Englishman James Herrick. Previous vintages have been better.

1996 Viognier Chais Cuxac, Val d'Orbieu, £4.99   15/20
Dry 👝👝 ▮
Ripe, apricoty, if faintly blowsy southern French white with good varietal richness, made from the Viognier grape at the Cuxac co-operative.

GERMANY

1995 Somerfield Rheinhessen Auslese, £4.29   11/20
Sweet
Almondy, gluey, old-fashioned German sticky at an inflated price. We'd rather drink Liebfraumilch.

HUNGARY

1996 Castle Ridge Sauvignon Blanc, £3.49   15/20
Bone dry
Crisp, nettley, attractively youthful Sauvignon Blanc from the Neszmely co-operative, with sweet-and-sour notes and more than a hint of green bean and elderflower.

ITALY

1996 Somerfield Soave, GIV, £3.39   13/20
Dry
Basic, faintly nutty, bog-standard Soave from Italy's biggest producer in the Veneto region. This is a top ten best-seller at Somerfield, so it must be doing something right.

1996 Le Trulle Chardonnay del Salento, Cantèle, £4.39   15/20
Dry
Well-made, smoky-oaky Puglian Chardonnay with excellent texture, balance and refreshing acidity, made by Kym Milne working in the heel of Italy.

1996 Salice Salentino Bianco, £4.99   16/20
Dry
Elegant, very well-made, unoaked Chardonnay from Australian Kym Milne, with ripe, yeasty complexity and a citrus fruity tang.

MOLDOVA

1996 Kirkwood Chardonnay, £3.55   14/20
Dry
Better than it has been in previous vintages, this is a tangy, lightly oaked Chardonnay from itinerant English winemaker Hugh Ryman, with a hint of vanilla fudge.

SPAIN

1995 Somerfield Rioja Almenar Bianco, £3.99   15/20
Dry 🍷🍷🍷 🍶
Traditional oak-influenced white Rioja made from Viura grapes, with notes of toast, coffee and citrus fruit and plenty of body.

£5–8

AUSTRALIA

1996 Penfolds The Valleys Chardonnay, £6.95   15/20
Dry 🍷 🍶
A South Australian blend from the Clare and Eden Valleys with attractive flavours of melon and oak. Should be £1 cheaper.

1996 Rosemount Hunter Valley Chardonnay, £6.99   15/20
Dry 🍷 🍶
In-yer-face New South Wales Chardonnay, with toffee fudge and sweet oak flavours allied to plentiful alcohol and lemony fruit.

FRANCE

1996 Alsace Gewürztraminer, Turckheim, £5.95   16/20
Dry 🍷🍷🍷 🍶
Elegantly refreshing, rose-petal-scented Alsace white with spritz and acidity for balance. An excellent introduction to the (Turkish) delights of Alsace's spiciest grape variety.

NEW ZEALAND

1996 Coopers Creek Chardonnay, Gisborne, £7.15   16/20
Dry 🍷🍷 🍶
Made by Kim Crawford, this is a fruit-steered North Island Chardonnay with subtle oak influence and lingering intensity.

1996 Coopers Creek Sauvignon Blanc, Marlborough, £7.49   15/20
Dry 🍷 🍶
Elderflower and gooseberry fruity Marlborough Sauvignon Blanc with good weight and depth and clean, refreshing, tangy acidity. On the pricey side, though.

Over £8

AUSTRALIA

1990 St Hilary Padthaway Chardonnay, £8.99   16/20
Dry 👜👜 ⚱
Full-flavoured Padthaway Chardonnay from the giant Wyndham-Orlando group, with flavours of pineapple chunks and spicy, nutty oak. A sizeable step up from Jacob's Creek in quality and character, not to mention price.

Red

Under £3

ARGENTINA

1996 Somerfield Argentine Red, San Juan, Peñaflor, £2.99   13/20
Medium-bodied 👜👜 ⚱
Soft, strawberryish, easy-drinking Sangiovese from Australian Peter Bright working at Peñaflor.

BULGARIA

1996 Somerfield Iambol Bulgarian Cabernet Sauvignon, £2.85
                                                                13/20

Medium-bodied 👜👜 ⚱
Blackcurrant-fruity, modern (for Bulgaria) Cabernet Sauvignon with plenty of colour, alcohol and tannin.

1996 Somerfield Bulgarian Country Red, £2.89   12/20
Medium-bodied 👜 ⚱
A curious blend of Burgundy's Pinot Noir and Bordeaux's Merlot grapes, this ends up as a beetrooty red with rather raw tannins.

1996 Iambol Merlot, Domaine Boyar, £2.99   13/20
Medium-bodied 👜👜 ⚱
Similar to the Cabernet Sauvignon, but with rather more accessible tannins and fruit concentration.

PORTUGAL

1996 Alta Mesa, Estremadura, £2.99   13/20
Medium-bodied 👜👜 ❘
Well-priced pepper and raisin-like quaffer made partially from Portuguese grapes by José Neiva. An impression of sweetness on the aftertaste makes this an approachable blend.

SPAIN

Somerfield Castillo Tinto Imperial, £2.99   10/20
Medium-bodied ❘
Plonky La Mancha blend apparently made from Bobal, Tempranillo and Garnacha, none of which distinguishes itself here.

£3–5

AUSTRALIA

Somerfield Australian Dry Red, Penfolds, £3.49   13/20
Medium-bodied 👜 ❘
Decent, upfront fruity, inexpensive Aussie blend of Grenache, Cinsaut and Shiraz, with drying oak characters.

BULGARIA

1992 Oriachovitza Cabernet Sauvignon Reserve, Sahatoris, £3.99
                                                          14/20

Medium-bodied 👜👜 ❘
Mature, almost Rioja-like Bulgarian red with sweet vanilla oak, good concentration and smooth tannins.

CHILE

1996 Somerfield Chilean Cabernet Sauvignon, Viña La Rosa, £4.29
                                                          15/20
Medium-bodied 👜👜👜 ❘
Attractively juicy, green-pepper-like Chilean Cabernet Sauvignon with well-judged oak adding length, balance and flavour.

FRANCE

1996 Somerfield Vin de Pays de l'Ardèche, UVICA, £3.25   14/20
Medium-bodied 👜👜👜 |
Bubble gummy Rhône rouge made in a soft Beaujolais style. A very acceptable, raspberry fruity thirst-quencher.

Somerfield Corbières, Val d'Orbieu, £3.35   14/20
Full-bodied 👜👜 |
Spicy, garrigue-scented southern French red from the giant Val d'Orbieu operation, with typically robust tannins.

1996 Somerfield Merlot Vin de Pays d'Oc, Jeanjean, £3.35   14/20
Medium-bodied 👜👜 |
Juicy, well-made, green peppery Languedoc Merlot from wine giants Jeanjean, with fruit character and flavour to the fore.

Somerfield Claret, Eschenauer, £3.39   13/20
Medium-bodied 👜 |
Softly grassy, Merlot-based claret, which finishes with a dry rasp of tannin.

1996 Côtes du Rhône Villages, Domaine de Prébaya, Selles, £3.99
14/20

Medium bodied 👜👜 |
For a bit more than the basic Somerfield Côtes du Rhône, you can buy this well-made, domaine-bottled, unoaked blend of Grenache and Syrah. Well worth the extra 70-odd pence.

1995 Château Valoussière, Coteaux du Languedoc, Jeanjean, £4.49
15/20

Full-bodied 👜👜 |
On the oaky side, but this juicy, concentrated, thyme-infused rouge, made by merchants Jeanjean with a high percentage of Syrah, is still a good Languedoc quaffer.

1995 Buzet Cuvée 44, £4.99   13/20
Full-bodied |
Firm, chunky, Merlot-based rouge from the Buzet co-operative. A wanna-be claret that doesn't quite make it.

Somerfield Médoc, Peter Sichel, £4.99   14/20
Medium-bodied 👜 ▌
More gutsy than the basic Somerfield claret, this is a traditional, Cabernet Sauvignon-based red Bordeaux with robust blackcurrant fruitiness and firm tannins.

1995 Beaumes de Venise, Côtes du Rhône-Villages, £4.99   14/20
Full-bodied 👜 ▌
From a southern Rhône village better known for its sweet fortified Muscats, this is a supple, palate-warming red with brambly sweetness, a hint of pepper and lots of alcohol.

1996 Vacqueyras, La Soleiade, Selles, £4.99   15/20
Full-bodied 👜👜 ▌
Made from the same grape varieties as the Beaumes de Venise, this is an attractively spicy, robustly fruity, southern Rhône blend with juicy blackberry fruit sweetness.

ITALY

1996 Somerfield Tuscan Red, GIV, £3.49   14/20
Light-bodied 👜👜 ▌
Light, savoury, partially oaked Tuscan Sangiovese at a very good price.

1996 Squinzano, Mottura, £3.69   13/20
Full-bodied 👜 ▌
Coarse, raisiny Puglian blend of Negroamaro and Malvasia Nera, with too much alcohol and dry tannin.

1996 Le Trulle, Primitivo del Salento, Cantèle, £4.49   15/20
Medium-bodied 👜👜👜 ▌
Raspberry fruity Puglian red made by Kym Milne from the Primitivo grape, which may be related to California's Zinfandel. With sweet plummy fruitiness and tobaccoey tannins. Very drinkable stuff.

1995 Riparosso Illuminati, £4.99   15/20
Full-bodied 👜👜 ▌
From the mountainous Abruzzi region in central Italy, this is a refreshing, concentrated, raspberry and cherry fruity Montepulciano.

PORTUGAL

1995 Bright Brothers, Atlantic Vines, Baga, Vinho Regional Beiras, £3.99   14/20
Full-bodied 👛👛 🍾
Pruney, robust, Portuguese winter warmer made from Bairrada's Baga grape by itinerant Australian winemaker, Peter Bright.

ROMANIA

1995 Romanian Young Vatted Cabernet, Pietroasa, £4.49   14/20
Full-bodied 👛👛 🍾
Made by Australian Graham Dixon, this is a decent, if pricey, Romanian Cabernet Sauvignon, with oak-matured blackcurrant fruit flavours and dryish tannins.

1994 Romanian Barrel-Matured Merlot, £4.49   16/20
Medium-bodied 👛👛👛 🍾
Also made by Graham Dixon, this is the best Romanian wine we've ever tasted, with sweet oak vanilla, black cherry fruit flavours and good length. If we were American, we'd probably call it the Château Pétrus of Romania.

SOUTH AFRICA

1996 Rawson's South African Ruby Cabernet/Merlot, £3.99   14/20
Full-bodied 👛👛 🍾
No relation to Penfolds' Rawson's Retreat, as far as we're aware, this is a soft, grassy, warm-climate blend of Ruby Cabernet and Merlot.

SPAIN

1996 Señorio de Val, Valdepeñas, £3.59   12/20
Medium-bodied 🍾
Simple, plonky, central Spanish tinto made from the Cencibel grape.

Somerfield Rioja Almaraz, £3.99   12/20
Medium-bodied 🍾
Dry, old-fashioned, over-oaked and rather jammy Rioja.

1996 Navarra Garnacha, Las Campanas, £3.99   15/20
Medium-bodied 👜👜👜 ▯
Sweet and juicy, bubble gummy, northern Spanish Garnacha made by the carbonic maceration method, with more oomph and flavour than most Beaujolais, which uses the same fermentation technique.

£5–8

CHILE

1995 Canepa Private Reserve Merlot, San Fernando, £5.49   15/20
Medium-bodied 👜👜 ▬
Still-youthful, lightly minty Merlot with refreshing acidity and a brushstroke of oak.

FRANCE

1996 Gigondas, Château St André, Selles, £5.99   16/20
Full-bodied 👜👜👜 ▬
Intense, peppery, well-made southern Rhône red with surprising elegance for a Gigondas and a lift of balancing acidity.

SPAIN

1987 Somerfield Rioja Viña Caña Reserva, Beronia, £5.99   16/20
Medium-bodied 👜👜👜 ▬
Well-priced, venerable 10-year old Rioja Reserva with juicy, savoury fruit, smoky American oak and super concentration.

UNITED STATES

1994 Fetzer Zinfandel, £5.99   15/20
Full-bodied 👜👜 ▯
Supple, tobaccoey, almost Rioja-like American Zinfandel with lashings of coconutty American oak and mulberry fruit.

Over £8

FRANCE

1995 Châteauneuf-du-Pape, Domaine de la Solitude, GAEC Lanson, £9.49   17/20
Full-bodied 💰💰💰 ➖
Broad, spicy, powerfully fruity, Grenache-based Côtes du Rhône made in a reassuringly traditional style with good concentration and intensity.

ITALY

1993 Piccini Chianti Classico Riserva, £8.49   16/20
Full-bodied 💰💰 ❘
A little pricey perhaps, but this is still a good, mature Tuscan Sangiovese with sinewy tannins, quality fruit and a pleasing bitter tang.

UNITED STATES

1992 Fetzer Barrel-Select North Coast Cabernet Sauvignon, £9.99   15/20
Full-bodied 💰 ❘
Chocolatey, intensely oaky, West Coast Cabernet Sauvignon, which is a little heavy on acid and tannins and a bit raw.

Rosé

£3–5

FRANCE

1996 Bordeaux Clairet, £3.99   14/20
Dry 💰💰 ❘
Light, green-pepper and liquorice-like Bordeaux rosé with bracing acidity.

Sparkling

£5–8

NEW ZEALAND

Lindauer Brut £7.49   15/20
Dry 💧💧💧 ▮
A zesty, faintly biscuity New Zealand fizz, which gets better with every vintage, showing good weight and flavour and a lemony lift for elegant balance.

SPAIN

Somerfield Cava Brut, Blanc de Blancs, Castell de Villaman, £5.29
                                                           14/20

Dry 💧💧 ▮
Youthful, tangy, decently made Catalan fizz with a rather pointless blanc de blancs tag. All Cava is made from white grapes. Well, in theory anyway.

Somerfield Rosé Cava, Castell de Villaman, £5.29   13/20
Dry 💧 ▮
Aggressive, big-bubbled pink Cava with some coarse red-wine tannins.

Over £8

AUSTRALIA

1994 Seaview Pinot Noir/Chardonnay, £8.49   16/20
Dry 💧💧💧 ▮
Rich, toasty, full-blown Aussie blend of the Champagne grapes, Pinot Noir and Chardonnay. A fizz that delivers on flavour and value.

FRANCE

Prince William Champagne, Palmer, £11.99   12/20
Dry |
Coarse, basic, jumped-up Champagne with angular acidity and aggressively youthful bubbles. The Queen should revoke the royal seal.

Prince William Blanc de Blancs, Michel Gonet, £15.29   12/20
Dry |
Weird, vinegary, all-Chardonnay Champagne with swingeing acidity. Send it to the Tower.

Fortified

£3–5

SPAIN

Los Acros Amontillado, Lustau, half-bottle, £3.69   16/20
Bone dry 🜚🜚🜚 |
Traditional burnt toffee and almond-style Amontillado from one of the best houses in Jerez. Less is more.

Capataz Andres Cream Sherry, Lustau, half-bottle, £3.69   16/20
Very sweet 🜚🜚🜚 |
Sweet-style Sherry blended with Pedro Ximenez for added weight and coffee and chocolate richness.

Somerfield Fino Sherry, Caballero, £4.39   14/20
Bone dry 🜚 |
Light, tangy, salty, refreshing Fino from Puerto Santa Maria near Jerez.

313

Spar ☆☆(☆)

Address: 32–40 Headstone Drive, Harrow, Middlesex HA3 5QT

Telephone/fax: 0181 863 5511; 0181 863 0603

Number of branches: 2,500, of which 2,031 are licensed

Opening hours: Varies, but an average of 98 hours a week per store; Spar Express stores open for at least 112 hours a week

Credit cards accepted: At individual retailer's discretion

Discounts: At individual retailer's discretion

Facilities and services: Glass loan and in-store tastings in some branches; 450 retailers belong to the Spar Wine Club

Special offers: Promotions of two bottles for £5

Top ten best-selling wines: Spar Liebfraumilch; Spar Lambrusco (4 per cent); Spar Valencia Red; Spar Bulgarian Country Red; Spar Soave; Spar French Country Red; Spar Bulgarian Country White; Spar French Country White; Spar Vin de Pays de l'Aude Red; Campo Rojo Cariñena

Range:

GOOD: Czech Republic, Hungary, South Africa, Chile

AVERAGE: Bordeaux, white Burgundy, regional France, Germany, Italy, Spain, Portugal, Bulgaria, Australia, fortified and sparkling wines

POOR: United States

UNDER-REPRESENTED: Red Burgundy, Alsace

Not many people know this, as the immortal Michael Caine once told us in a clipped cockney accent, but Spar is the world's biggest chain of grocery stores, with over 22,000 branches in 27 countries. It was set up in Holland in 1932 and has since gone on to colonise the world with those little green fir trees. While we're talking figures, here are a few more you might not be aware of: Spar celebrated its 40th anniversary as a British off-licence retailer in 1997, selling wines, beers and spirits in over 2,000 different locations.

Wine, as you can imagine, is an important product at Spar, although buyer Liz Aked admits that 'We don't have the clout of a Tesco or a Sainsbury's. We're a nice size for producers to deal with, a regular purchaser rather than a chain that requires mega-volumes.' A good example of a happy producer is the Madeba winery in South Africa's Robertson district, which supplies Spar with 25,000 cases of pretty good Cape red and white. Aked has a similarly close relationship with Canepa in Chile, Normans in Australia and Val d'Orbieu in the south of France.

She has spent much of the last year ensuring that 'we maintain supply and quality, especially from the New World'. Like most wine buyers, she has found it hard to get hold of well-priced red wines. 'It's a seller's market, no doubt about it,' she says. 'Worldwide demand for reds is amazing. I'm already looking a year ahead to secure the volumes we need.'

All this means more foreign travel for Aked and her assistant, Jo Power, selecting and blending the wines they want. The team is back to two buyers after a more or less amicable divorce from the wine department of Spar Landmark, the cash-and-carry arm of the business. A year ago Stuart Croucher moved into the Spar offices as a third wine buyer. But 'We recognised that the end users of Spar and Spar Landmark were very different,' says Aked, diplomatically.

Aked and Power are doing very well on their own, thank you. Spar doesn't have the biggest range of wines in the high street, at 200-odd lines, but the average quality is high, certainly when set against competitors such as Budgens and the Co-op. Of those 200 wines, 125 are Spar own-labels and it's here that the Harrow-based store is at its most impressive, with the exception of two rather dodgy Californians, for this is where the partnerships come in: 'To get good wines, you have to work with people much more than you used to,' according to Aked.

The New World isn't the only focus at Spar. France has come roaring back, thanks to better winemaking and a couple of decent vintages. 'There's been a big change since 1995,' Aked reckons. 'The French have had a good look at what they've got planted and how they make their wines. There's still some very good value for money to be found in France.' This is true enough, although we feel that Spar relies a little too heavily on Val d'Orbieu as a supplier from the Languedoc-Roussillon. Still, Aked promises us that she's got a new project on the starting grid with the impressive Morel-Vedeau operation.

Not all of Spar's 200 wines find their way into every store. The estate is 'segmented' (oh, how we love that word) into Neighbourhood (local), Express (urban areas) and Supermarket-size stores, with size determining the wine range. The supermarkets get all 200 wines, but even in the smaller Express and Neighbourhood stores, at least 100 Spar wines will be on the shelves.

Spar

Actually, we say that you'll be confronted by Aked's wines when you walk into a Spar, but this isn't strictly true. Like the Co-op, Spar leaves its managers the freedom to buy wines from elsewhere if they choose. 'All our stores are independent,' says Aked, 'so the formats are up to them.' Around 80 per cent of the average range is sourced by the Spar wine department, but Aked doesn't have absolute control. 'The smaller stores are not as committed to listing good wines and tend to be stuck in Lieb, Lambrusco and Perry territory.' The Welsh Valleys, just in case you're planning a holiday there, are a vinous twilight zone, apparently.

Such delights are on the slide, however. Liebfraumilch sales are down by 30 per cent, those of Lambrusco by 25 per cent. The demise of these wines has helped to push Spar's average bottle price up to £3.35. And it hasn't harmed sales, which are up by 25 per cent in value. 'Lieb has got another 10 per cent to fall,' says Aked, 'but we've got to cater for people who want sweet sugar water. It's a cash cow.' It sure is. Germany still accounts for 17 per cent of sales, behind France (25 per cent), but ahead of Italy (15 per cent) and Australia (10 per cent).

Aked still thinks the range can be improved. She's working with La Agricola, one of Argentina's most go-ahead wineries, and wants to concentrate elsewhere on wines that provide good value between £3.99 and £4.99. She also concedes that she's not 'entirely happy' with her Californian wines. Otherwise, things are fine and dandy.

Spar is a very reliable place to buy wine, stocking a limited but very well-selected , value-for-money range of everything from Czech whites to Chilean Malbecs. The franchised formula is clearly a success, provided people don't stray too far from the Aked-sourced wines. Those 2,031 licensed store managers have good reason to feel satisfied, give or take the odd maverick in the Welsh Valleys.

White

Under £3

BULGARIA

Spar Bulgarian Country White, Muskat/Ugni Blanc, £2.99   14/20
Off-dry 🍬🍬🍬 🍸
Fresh, grapey, well-made blend of Muskat and Ugni Blanc, with a lemon sherbet aftertaste.

GERMANY

Spar Liebfraumilch, £2.99 13/20
Medium sweet 👜👜 🍷
Decent, floral, drinkable Lieb. Less sugary and dull than many.

ITALY

Spar Lambrusco Bianco 4 per cent, £1.99 12/20
Sweet 👜👜 🍷
Light, refreshing, simple-drinking Italian Emilia Romagna fizz with only 4 per cent alcohol. Means you can drink plenty before falling over.

£3–5

AUSTRALIA

1996 Lindemans Cawarra Colombard/Chardonnay, £4.15 14/20
Off-dry 👜👜 🍷
Soft, peachy, tropical fruity blend with a smidgeon of oak character.

CHILE

1996 Chilean Sauvignon Blanc, Canepa, £4.49 15/20
Dry 👜👜👜 🍷
Tangy, modern, assertively grapefruity Chilean Sauvignon Blanc from the excellent Canepa winery.

1996 Chilean Chardonnay, Canepa, £4.49 15/20
Dry 👜👜👜 🍷
From the same first-rate source, this is a refreshing, fruit-driven, crisply turned-out Chardonnay.

CZECH REPUBLIC

Spar Czech Country White, £3.35 14/20
Dry 👜👜👜 🍷
A blend of Olaszrizling and Müller-Thurgau, with lightly peppery, fragrant aromas, fresh acidity and good weight.

FRANCE

Spar French Country White, £3.99   12/20
Dry ▮
Baked-appley, southern French plonk in a litre bottle. Strictly for student parties.

Spar Oaked Chardonnay, Vin de Pays d'Oc, £4.35   14/20
Off-dry �△�△ ▮
Decent, modern-style Midi Chardonnay from Val d'Orbieu, with sweetish fruit flavours and charry oak.

1996 Vouvray, Donatien Bahuaud, £4.35   13/20
Medium sweet ▮
Sweet, old-fashioned and rather coarse Chenin Blanc from Donatien Bahuaud.

1996 James Herrick Chardonnay, £4.99   14/20
Dry �△ ▮
Clean, if slightly characterless Chardonnay from Languedoc-based Englishman, James Herrick. Nothing like as good as earlier vintages.

HUNGARY

Spar Misty Mountain Chardonnay, £3.49   14/20
Dry �△☆☆ ▮
Zippy, lemony, well-made, unoaked Chardonnay from the Neszmely co-operative, one of Hungary's best white-wine operations.

ITALY

Spar Sicilian Vino da Tavola, £3.39   13/20
Dry ☆☆ ▮
Full, tart, spicy Sicilian blend with lively acidity and appealing crispness of flavour.

Spar Soave, £3.39   15/20
Dry ☆☆☆ ▮
Excellent value from the Soave co-operative, with zesty acidity, good weight and a nutty tang.

1996 Spar Trebbiano d'Abruzzo, £3.49   14/20
Dry 👜👜👜 🍶
A blend of Trebbiano with a little Cococciola (not to be confused with the Real Thing), this is a decent, lightly spicy Abruzzo white.

Spar Rondolle Bianco, Bombino/Chardonnay, £3.99   13/20
Dry 👜 🍶
A rich, golden-hued blend of Bombino and Chardonnay, which finishes a little flat and bitter.

PORTUGAL

Spar Doña Elena, Vinho de Mesa, £3.35   14/20
Bone dry 👜 🍶
Fresh, ginger-spicy Portuguese branco from the Ribatejo region. Distinctively crisp and dry.

SOUTH AFRICA

1996 Table Mountain Chenin Blanc, £3.49   13/20
Dry 👜👜 🍶
Light, peardrop and banana-like Cape white with a citrusy bite.

South African Classic White, £3.99   15/20
Dry 👜👜👜 🍶
A softly textured Colombard/Chenin Blanc blend from Robertson's Madeba winery, with ripe pear notes and crisp acidity. Very refreshing.

SPAIN

Campo Verde, Cariñena, £3.25   12/20
Dry 🍶
Gluey, resinous, old-fashioned Spanish white from Zaragoza. Time to rewrite the manuscript.

UNITED STATES

Fir Tree Ridge White, £3.99   12/20
Medium dry 🍶
Confected, rather mawkish Central Valley white for the sweet of tooth.

£5–8

FRANCE

1994 Chablis, La Chablisienne, £7.99   16/20
Dry 🍾🍾 |
Rich, honeyed, minerally, unoaked Chablis with a chalky, dry note of acidity.

GERMANY

1992 Piesporter Goldtröpfchen, Weingut Grans Fassian, £5.99
17/20

Medium dry 🍾🍾🍾 ━
Mature, bottle-aged Mosel Riesling like this is a rare delight under £6. Crisp, petrolly and complex.

Red

Under £3

BULGARIA

Spar Bulgarian Country Red, £2.99   13/20
Medium-bodied 🍾🍾 |
A blend of Cabernet Sauvignon and Cinsaut from Russe, with lightish raspberry fruit flavours and peppery tannins.

FRANCE

Spar Vin de Pays de l'Aude, Val d'Orbieu, £2.99   13/20
Medium-bodied 🍾🍾 |
Bright, fruity, Beaujolais-style Languedoc quaffer with a rustic edge.

SPAIN

Spar Valencia Red, Vicente Gandia, £2.99   12/20
Medium-bodied 🍶 ▮

Softish, slightly sweetened Levante red from Vicente Gandia. Decent plonk.

£3–5

AUSTRALIA

Australian Four Winds, £4.15   14/20
Medium-bodied 🍶🍶 ▮

One of the better supermarket own-label Aussies, this is a charry, liquoricey, minty red with a soft finish.

1996 Lindemans Cawarra Shiraz/Cabernet, £4.39   15/20
Medium-bodied 🍶🍶🍶 ▮

Soft, smooth, juicy Shiraz/Cabernet Sauvignon blend with nicely ripe blackberry and plum fruitiness.

BULGARIA

1993 Bulgarian Merlot/Gamay, £3.35   13/20
Medium-bodied 🍶🍶 ▮

Cherryish, lightly oaked Russe blend of Merlot and Gamay with a dry aftertaste.

1995 Chilean Cabernet Sauvignon, Canepa, £4.49   14/20
Medium-bodied 🍶🍶 ▮

Soft, smooth, juicy, deeply coloured Cabernet Sauvignon with blackcurrant-pastille fruit.

1996 Chilean Merlot, Canepa, £4.49   13/20
Medium-bodied ▮

Chewy, rasping Chilean Merlot from the same winery, which needs more flesh and fruit. Don't we all.

1996 La Fortuna Malbec, £4.99   15/2(

Medium-bodied 👜👜 |

Sagey, savoury, unoaked Malbec from Chile's Lontue Valley, with smooth tannin:
and a chocolatey finish.

CZECH REPUBLIC

Spar Czech Country Red, £3.55   13/2(

Light-bodied 👜 |

A light, thirst-quenching Czech red blend of Frankovka and Vavrinecke grapes.

FRANCE

1996 Spar Vin de Pays de la Cité de Carcassonne, £3.35   14/20

Medium-bodied 👜👜 |

Juicy, well-balanced, southern French quaffer made from Grenache, Mourvèdre
Carignan and Cinsaut.

1995 Spar Côtes du Ventoux, Le Rossignol, £3.49   14/20

Medium-bodied 👜👜 |

From the slopes of Mont Ventoux, this is a good, Grenache-based Côtes du
Rhône substitute, with pleasant, sweet spiciness.

Spar Coteaux du Languedoc, Val d'Orbieu, £3.55   14/20

Full-bodied 👜👜 |

Robust, spicy, extremely drinkable Languedoc red with aromatic, blackberry
fruit characters.

1996 Spar Claret, Rolland et Cie, £3.75   14/20

Medium-bodied 👜👜 |

Pleasant, grassy, slurping claret with softly focused fruit.

1995 Château Bories-Azeau, Corbières, Val d'Orbieu, £3.75   14/20

Full-bodied 👜👜 |

Aromatic, chunky, thyme-scented Corbières with classic Mediterranean
flavours and a hot aftertaste.

Spar Corsican Pinot Noir, Cuvée San Michele, Vignerons des Piève, £3.99   14/20

Full-bodied 👜👜 |

Authentic, if chewy, Corsican Pinot Noir with a nice core of raspberry fruit
sweetness and a firm finish.

1994 Côtes de St Mont, Tuilerie du Bosc, £3.99   15/20
Medium-bodied 🌡🌡🌡 ▮
An oak-aged blend of Tannat and Cabernet Sauvignon from the Plaimont winery. Light, elegant and sweetly oaked.

1995 Gemini Merlot, Vin de Pays d'Oc, Yves Pagès, £3.99   14/20
Medium-bodied 🌡🌡 ▮
Approachable, partially oak-aged Languedoc Merlot in a strikingly modern bottle.

Spar French Country Red, Val d'Orbieu, £3.99   13/20
Medium-bodied 🌡 ▮
Light, quaffable but rather basic Midi rouge from Val d'Orbieu.

1995 Spar Oaked Merlot, Vin de Pays d'Oc, Rolland et Cie, £4.35
14/20

Medium-bodied 🌡 ▮
A wee bit pricey perhaps, but this is still a juicy, sweetly oaked Midi Merlot with decent tannins.

HUNGARY

Spar Misty Mountain Merlot, Villány, £3.49   13/20
Light-bodied 🌡 ▮
From Hungary's southern frontier, this is a light, slightly austere dry red with a cherried finish.

ITALY

Spar Sicilian Vino da Tavola, £3.39   14/20
Medium-bodied 🌡🌡 ▮
Savoury, damsony, Sicilian rosso with sweet plum fruitiness and a bitter twist.

Spar Ariento Sangiovese del Rubicone, £3.49   13/20
Light-bodied 🌡 ▮
Sweet, morello cherry-like Sangiovese from Romagna. Finishes a little chewy.

1995 Spar Montepulciano d'Abruzzo, Cantina Tollo, £3.75   14/20
Medium-bodied 🌡🌡 ▮
Attractively labelled, refreshingly fruity Montepulciano with crisp definition and acidity.

Spar Rondolle Rosso, Vino da Tavola di Puglia, £3.99   14/20
Full-bodied 👜👜 ▮
Chunky, robust Puglian blend of the local Negroamaro with Cabernet Sauvignon, made by Aussie Kym Milne.

1995 Spar Chianti, £4.45   15/20
Medium-bodied 👜👜 ▮
Moreish, highly drinkable Chianti with cherry and almond flavours and a pleasing nip of tannin.

PORTUGAL

Spar Doña Elena, Vinho de Mesa, £3.35   13/20
Medium-bodied 👜👜 ▮
From the Benfica co-operative, this is a mature, sweetish, leather and aniseed-like red, which is pretty good for the price.

SOUTH AFRICA

Table Mountain Pinot Noir, £3.99   11/20
Light-bodied ▮
Stewed, coarse Cape Pinot, which should have been left on the cable car on the way up to the summit.

South African Classic Red, £3.99   15/20
Medium-bodied 👜👜👜 ▮
Attractively robust, blackberry spicy Robertson blend from Madeba, with well-judged oak and smooth tannins.

SPAIN

Campo Rojo, Cariñena, £3.25   14/20
Medium-bodied 👜👜 ▮
Better than the corresponding white, this is a smooth, decently fruity red for hispanophiles on a budget.

1996 Albor Rioja, £3.99   14/20
Medium-bodied 👜👜 ▮
Lighter and more expensive than the Campo Rojo, but with attractive, compensating elegance.

UNITED STATES

Fir Tree Ridge Red, £3.99 12/20
Light-bodied |
Sweet, faintly pongy West Coast blend. Pretty pointless.

£5–8

AUSTRALIA

1995 Lussac-St Emilion, Dulong, £5.45 15/20
Medium-bodied 👜👜 |
Good, honest, Right Bank Merlot-based claret at an attractive price.

1995 Hardy's Bankside Shiraz, £6.49 16/20
Full-bodied 👜👜 |
A blend of Padthaway and Clare Valley grapes has produced one of the best inexpensive Aussie Shirazes on the market. Robust at the moment, but give it time.

PORTUGAL

1993 Vinha do Monte, Alentejo, Sogrape, £5.99 15/20
Full-bodied 👜👜 |
Traditional southern Portuguese red with lots of personality. Beginning to dry on the finish, but still interesting, in a raisiny sort of way.

Rosé

£3–5

FRANCE

1996 Spar Rosé de Syrah, Val d'Orbieu, £3.49 14/20
Dry 👜👜 |
Colourful, dry, well-made saignée rosé with attractive, cherry fruity notes.

Sparkling

Over £8

FRANCE

Spar Champagne, Marquis de Prevel, £12.75   13/20
Dry 🍷
Youthful, slightly coarse, big-bubbled fizz with a rather tart, green-apple finish.

Fortified

£3–5

FRANCE

Spar Muscat de St Jean de Minervois, Val d'Orbieu, £3.15   15/20
Very sweet 🍷🍷🍷
Sweet, soft, nicely balanced Muscat with grapey fruit, alcohol sweetness and acidity in harmony.

£5–8

PORTUGAL

1990 Spar Old Cellar LBV Port, Smith Woodhouse, £7.79   16/20
Full-bodied 🍷🍷🍷
Cinnamon and nutmeg-spicy Late Bottled Vintage Port with lots of peppery, warm-climate fruitiness and smooth elegance.

Tesco ☆☆☆☆

Address: Old Tesco House, Delamare Road, Cheshunt, Herts EN8 9SL

Telephone/fax: 01992 632222; 01992 658225

Number of branches: 580, plus Tesco Vin Plus in Calais

Credit cards accepted: Access, Switch, Visa

Opening hours: 8.30am to 8.00pm Monday to Thursday; 8.30am to 9.00pm Friday; 8.00am to 8.00pm Saturday; 10.00am to 4.00pm Sunday

Discounts: 5 per cent off any six bottles

Facilities and services: Tesco Clubcard; Tesco Direct; in-store tastings; glass loan; tutored tastings; Tesco Recipe Collection Magazine

Special offers: Wines of the month; Wine Festival promotion in April, May and June

Top ten best-selling wines: Tesco Hock; Tesco Romanian Country Red; Tesco Claret; Tesco Chilean Cabernet Sauvignon; Tesco Cape Chenin Blanc; Tesco French White; Tesco Liebfraumilch; Tesco French Red, Vin de Pays de l'Aude; Tesco Valpolicella; Tesco Cava

Range:

GOOD: Bordeaux, Spain, Italy, Australia, Argentina, Chile, South Africa, Champagne and sparkling wines

AVERAGE: Rhône, Beaujolais, Burgundy, Loire, regional France, Germany, Portugal, Austria, Eastern Europe, New Zealand

POOR: United States

UNDER-REPRESENTED: Alsace

Fancy a glass of Canadian red? What about a Welsh Seyval Blanc, a Uruguayan Chardonnay/Sauvignon or an Argentine Bonarda? If you're bored with the same old countries and wine regions, Tesco is the place to park your shopping trolley. With an enormous, some might say sprawling, wine range of over 800 different wines, Tesco lists far more bottles than its three biggest supermarket rivals, Asda, Safeway and Sainsbury's.

Tesco

Does more mean better? There is a conflict here between genuine consumer choice and innovation for innovation's sake. Wines from Brazil, Cyprus and the Gobi Desert (okay, we made the last one up, but it's only a slight exaggeration) are all very well, but do they justify their niche on the shelves? Buying controller Judith Candy defends the diversity of Tesco's range: 'Our approach is to try new things all the time. We don't want to be so focused that we don't take risks. We make mistakes occasionally, and we have to go back and change them, but a lot of what we put in is great. Wines from countries like Peru, Uruguay and Brazil are fun for our customers, though not always for our technologists.' Or the winemakers, one suspects.

Some of Tesco's competitors accuse the chain of duplication, of leaving the customer to make a choice that is the wine buyers' responsibility. Once again, Candy rejects the charge. 'We've never had research saying that our customers see duplication in the range. Customers praise the size of the range, especially in the New World.'

Our feeling is that, while there are areas of the Tesco line-up that could do with a prune (Italian whites, for example), the overall range is impressive. And at a time when supermarkets are 'refocusing' their wine departments (i.e. chucking out anything that isn't profitable), it's good to see someone willing to list unusual wines. Consumers cannot live by Liebfraumilch, Hock, Frascati, Muscadet, Côtes du Rhône and Australian Chardonnay alone.

Tesco's willingness to try new things has been strongly in evidence over the last year. In the spring it launched a trio of wines called simply 'Great with...' Originally there were four of these – Great with chicken/steak/pasta/fish – but fish is being hauled in. ('People don't eat as much fish as they used to,' explains Candy.) Still, the other three – a Vin de Pays d'Oc Chardonnay, a French Merlot and a Montepulciano d'Abruzzo – have been a huge success with Tesco's customers. 'We've been struggling with wine and food for years,' says Candy. 'There's a group of customers out there who find the whole thing confusing. These wines are light, friendly and sell at under £3.50. The idea is to bring a bit of humour to the subject and leave people a little less mystified.'

The other area of innovation – and this could have sizeable consequences for the wine business in Britain – is Tesco's decision to get behind screwcaps. Where most other supermarkets have only tinkered with alternatives to cork, accepting the fact that as many as one in ten bottles of wine will be tainted by 'corkiness', Tesco has put its money where its palate is.

In October and November 1997 the chain aims to sell as many as 500,000 bottles of screwcap wine. And we're not talking sugary Lambrusco here. This is decent stuff: St Hallett's Poacher's Blend from Australia, a Barrel-Fermented Chenin Blanc from South Africa, Laperouse Red and White from the south of France and a South African Shiraz/Cabernet Sauvignon. These are all £4–5 wines. 'The approach we've taken is to make a big splash,' says Candy. 'Big promotion, premium wines, gondola ends.'

Tesco is taking a risk here, but it's risk that benefits the consumer. If the promotion helps to raise consumers' awareness of corked wines and of the synthetic alternatives to traditional (and depressingly fallible) cork, then it will have done us all an enormous favour. 'The situation with corks is outrageous,' says Candy. 'We estimate that one in 12 wines is corked. And we reckon that hardly any wines are brought back to store because of a cork taint.' In other words, people think it's the fault of the wine.

It is significant that of the five wines in the screwcap promotion, three are from the New World. This is the part of Tesco's business that continues to grow apace. While wines from Chile, Australia, South Africa, Argentina and the United States are flying off the shelves, those from Italy and Germany are gathering a light film of dust. Sweeter styles are generally in decline. It's not all bad news for the Old World, however. France has fought back this year, with southern *vins de pays* leading the charge, Spain is holding steady, and drier, new-style German whites are starting to develop a small following.

France is still the largest part of Tesco's business, with 30 per cent of sales and 125 wines on the list. But Australia is catching up. A range of 121 Aussie wines makes Tesco one of the biggest retailers of wines from Down Under. The significant point here is that sales aren't all down to own-label Chardonnay and Cabernet/Shiraz. Tesco shifts genuinely largely amounts of premium Oz wine (or 'Swine) from the likes of Chapel Hill, Tim Adams, Lindemans, Maglieri, St Hallett, Shaw & Smith and Mountadam.

Will you find all these vinous goodies at your local Tesco? Not necessarily, squire: 31 stores carry the full 800-strong range, but the smallest stores (known, somewhat confusingly, as A and B stores) are restricted to 200 wines. Nevertheless, nearly 100 stores stock most of Tesco's list.

That list is divided between own-labels (frequently made by flying winemakers, such as John Worontschak, Peter Bright, Kym Milne and Nick Butler), brands and smaller quantities of *domaine* and estate-bottled wines. The most popular wines, as the chain's top ten illustrates, tend to be the cheaper ones (Tesco's average bottle spend is still only £3.25), but it's encouraging to see two New World wines among the best-sellers. It may or may not be significant that the Tesco range known as 'Les Domaines' is being dropped. 'The concept of *domaine* wines and smaller parcels will remain,' says buyer Helen Robinson, 'but they won't be labelled in the same way. They looked too similar and we decided it wasn't the right communication with the customer.'

One 'communication' that Tesco's customers clearly appreciate is the spring Wine Festival from mid-April to mid-June. For four successive fortnights within the promotion, Tesco sliced 10 per cent off the price of its Australian, Chilean,

Tesco

sparkling and South African ranges. Sales in those areas doubled, according to Judith Candy. 'People bought more expensive wines and experimented with new flavours, which is just what we wanted.' The special parcels bought for the festival were an impressive haul, with some genuinely good deals. 'The special-purchase idea worked really well,' adds Candy. 'Customers accepted the fact that the wines were one-off parcels.'

Another area of Tesco's business that is forging ahead is its cross-Channel store in Calais, Tesco Vin Plus. Tesco claims that sales have more than doubled in the last year, thanks to an improved exchange rate (if you're a Brit) and the number of tourists sloshing through Calais. Sales in Britain are not quite as strong, but they've still increased by 20 per cent in the last year, keeping Tesco ahead of its supermarket competitors as the biggest wine retailer in the country.

To make sure it remains there, Tesco has undergone some internal restructuring after Jaguar-driving Stephen Clarke's promotion to another part of the business. Ann-Marie Bostock now heads the team of mainly female buyers, but she is not, strictly speaking, a replacement for Clarke. Her title is category manager and her responsibilities are slightly different. Under her there are two buying controllers, Judith Candy and Sara Marsay, one buyer, Helen Robinson, and one trainee buyer, Charles Clowes, the department's honorary male. Lucky chap.

From October there will be a slight change of emphasis within the department. Instead of each buyer specialising in a given area, be it South Africa or Italy, they will be collectively responsible for the whole range. There will be specific roles within three loosely defined areas, however: selecting the product, buying it and selling it to the customer. 'It'll make us more effective as a team,' Candy assures us.

More effective? The prospect is a frightening one for Tesco's competitors. The Cheshunt-based chain is already better at selling wine than anyone else. But watch out Sainsbury's, Safeway and Asda. Candy feels there's plenty of scope for expansion and improvement. 'The way we see it is that consumption is still only 18 litres per head. Wine is an acceptable, everyday beverage. But we're just on the edge of making it a mass-market drink.'

White

Under £3

FRANCE

Tesco French White, £2.79   11/20
Off-dry ▮
Musty, sweetened-up French plonk. Very basic stuff.

Tesco Muscadet, £2.95   13/20
Bone dry 🌢🌢 ▮
Clean, fruity, well-made Muscadet with bracing acidity.

GERMANY

Tesco Hock, £2.39   11/20
Medium sweet ▮
Sugary, sweet grape-water. Yawn...

Tesco Liebfraumilch, £2.85   12/20
Medium sweet 🌢 ▮
Marginally better, but don't beat down the doors of your local Tesco to secure
a bottle.

£3–5

ARGENTINA

Picajuan Peak Chardonnay, £3.99   15/20
Dry 🌢🌢🌢 ▮
From Argentina's La Agricola winery, this is a peachy, rich, full-flavoured,
unoaked Mendoza Chardonnay at an excellent price.

AUSTRALIA

Tesco Clare Valley Riesling, £4.99   16/20
Off-dry 👝👝👝 ❘
Soft, lime zest-like Clare Valley Riesling from the Watervale district. The kind of thing that ought to give Riesling a good (or much better) name.

CHILE

1996 Santa Ines Sauvignon Blanc, £3.99   15/20
Dry 👝👝👝 ❘
Commercial, grapefruity, softly textured Chilean Sauvignon Blanc with aromatic intensity and a crisp aftertaste.

Luis Felipe Edwards Chardonnay, £4.99   15/20
Dry 👝👝 ❘
Citrusy, nicely packaged, unoaked Chilean Chardonnay with good mid-palate fruit ripeness and zing.

FRANCE

1996 Marsanne, Domaine de Montauberon, Vin de Pays des Côtes de Thongue, £3.99   14/20
Dry 👝👝 ❘
Mealy, flavoursome Languedoc Marsanne with a herbal, high-acid tang.

1995 Tesco Domaine Saubagnère, Vin de Pays des Côtes de Gascogne, £3.99   15/20
Dry 👝👝👝 ❘
Oak-influenced, *domaine*-bottled Gascon white from Yves Grassa, the leather-jacketed King of Armagnac country. Ripe, concentrated and characterful with appealing spritz.

1996 Tesco Muscadet de Sèvre et Maine Sur Lie, £3.99   15/20
Dry 👝👝👝 ❘
Rich, buttery, lees-influenced Muscadet with a delightful twist of spritz and acidity. One of the best Muscadets on the market at the moment.

Tesco Alsace Pinot Blanc, £4.49   13/20
Dry ❘
Light and a little on the earthy side. A neutral wine from a neutral grape.

1995 Tesco White Burgundy, Viré, £4.59   13/20
Dry
From the Viré co-operative in the Mâconnais, this is a bog-standard white Burgundy with a gluey undertone.

1996 Gaston Dorléans Vouvray Demi-Sec, £4.99   15/20
Medium dry
From an excellent vintage in the Loire, this is an easy-going introduction to the Chenin Blanc grape, with flavours of ripe pear and honey underpinned by fresh acidity.

1996 Greenwich Meridian 2000 White, £4.99   14/20
Dry
Silly name, given that this wine probably won't last until New Year's Eve 1999. But this is a clean, modern, pleasantly crisp and grassy Bordeaux Sauvignon Blanc all the same.

1995 Tesco Oak-Aged White Burgundy, £4.99   15/20
Dry
Smoky oaky, well-priced white Burgundy from a very good vintage, with concentrated citrus-fruit flavours.

1996 Tesco Viognier, £4.99   16/20
Dry
Aromatic, full-flavoured, apricoty southern French white with tropical fruit intensity and a genuine glimpse of Condrieu's Viognier grape.

GERMANY

1994 Wiltinger Scharzberg Riesling Kabinett, £3.49   12/20
Medium dry
Eggy, sulphurous, almondy Riesling Kabinett whose quality reflects its humble price rather too accurately.

1995 Riesling Pfalzer Landwein, £3.79   11/20
Dry
Tiring and rather confected dry Pfalz Riesling made by Notting Hill-based Aussie John Worontschak.

1996 Fire Mountain Riesling, £3.99
Off-dry 🍾🍾🍾 ▌
15/20

Made by another Australian, Linley Schultz, this is a lemon and lime-like New World-style Riesling from the southerly Pfalz region, with attractive balancing sweetness.

1995 Grans Fassian Riesling Trocken, £4.99
Bone dry 🍾🍾 ▌
15/20

Dry and full-bodied for a Mosel Riesling, this *domaine*-bottled white needs food to show at its best.

HUNGARY

1996 Tesco Reka Valley Sauvignon Blanc, Neszmely, £3.49
Dry 🍾🍾🍾 ▌
15/20

Zingy, aromatic, refreshingly gooseberryish Sauvignon Blanc with crunchy acidity and excellent length. A steal at this price.

NEW ZEALAND

1996 Tesco New Zealand Sauvignon Blanc, £4.49
Dry 🍾🍾 ▌
14/20

Fuller, green-bean-like North Island Sauvignon Blanc with a tropical undertone, from the warmish Gisborne region.

PERU

Tesco Peru White, £3.49
Dry ▌
12/20

The most interesting thing about this wine is where it comes from. Unfortunately, this sweet-and-sour Lima number is not as exotic as its source.

SOUTH AFRICA

Tesco Cape Chenin Blanc, £3.49
Dry 🍾🍾 ▌
13/20

Appley, well-made, ripely textured Cape Chenin Blanc with juicy fruit flavours unencumbered by oak.

1996 Rylands Grove Chenin/Colombard, £3.49   14/20
Dry 🍯🍯🍯 |
Ripe, melon and guava-like Cape blend from Kym Milne. Good at the price.

Tesco Franschhoek Semillon, £3.79   14/20
Dry 🍯🍯 |
Creamy, herbal, cool-climate, unoaked Semillon from the Cape's Franschhoek Valley with an assertive, lemony tang.

1996 Fairview Sauvignon Blanc/Chenin, £3.99   14/20
Dry 🍯🍯 |
A soft, approachable Cape blend of Sauvignon Blanc and Chenin Blanc, with ripe pear flavours and lively acidity.

1996 Long Mountain Dry Riesling, £3.99   13/20
Dry |
Innocuous, faintly tart Cape Riesling made by the Australian Orlando operation.

1996 Rylands Barrel-Fermented Chenin Blanc, Kym Milne, £3.99
15/20
Dry 🍯🍯🍯 |
Rich, toasty, barrel-fermented Cape Chenin with tons of honey and citrus-fruit flavours seductively balanced by oak.

1997 Goiya Kgeisje Chardonnay/Sauvignon Blanc, £3.99   13/20
Off-dry 🍯 |
Banana and pear-drop fruity Cape Nouveau in a great package. Gluggable, if simple.

1996 Tesco Robertson Chardonnay, Danie de Wet, £3.99   14/20
Dry 🍯🍯 |
From Chardonnay specialist, Danie de Wet, this is an extremely well-priced, unoaked Chardonnay with tangy, tropical citrus-fruit flavours.

Tesco South African Chardonnay/Colombard, John Worontschak, £3.99
14/20
Off-dry 🍯🍯 |
Ultra-fresh, melon and pineapple fruity South African blend with plenty of flavour at the price.

1996 Van Loveren Special Late Harvest Gewürztraminer, £3.99
13/20

Very sweet 🍷 ▮
Sweet and rather soulless, rose-petal-scented Cape Gewürz with gooey, confected fruit flavours. Not very 'special' at all.

1996 Rylands Grove Sauvignon Blanc, £4.99   15/20
Dry 🍷🍷 ▮
Catty, capsicum fruity Cape Sauvignon Blanc with soft, grapefruity characters and good length. Watch out New Zealand?

1996 Tesco Reserve Chardonnay, £4.99   12/20
Dry ▮
Tart, rather lean Chardonnay from the warm-climate Robertson region. Finishes with a green edge.

URUGUAY

Tesco Pacific Peak Chardonnay/Sauvignon, £3.99   13/20
Dry 🍷 ▮
Flattish, neutral Uruguayan blend from Bodegas Castillo Viejo. The interest lies almost entirely in the wine's origin.

£5–8

AUSTRALIA

1996 Tesco McLaren Vale Chardonnay, £5.99   15/20
Dry 🍷🍷 ▮
Classic, full-flavoured Aussie Chardonnay with lots of colour, oak and tropical fruit intensity. Rich, pineappley and very drinkable.

1996 Normans Unwooded Chardonnay, £5.99   15/20
Off-dry 🍷🍷 ▮
Sweetish, melony, unoaked Chardonnay with good texture and ripe, almost honeyed fruit flavours.

CHILE

1994 Errázuriz Chardonnay Reserva, £7.49   17/20
Dry 🍶🍶🍶 ❘
Rich, complex, nutty, well-worked Curicó Chardonnay, with toasty oak, buttery intensity and an elegant, tapering finish.

FRANCE

1995 Domaine St James Viognier, Vin de Pays d'Oc, £5.29   13/20
Dry ❘
Bitter, apple-core Viognier from southern France. We expect better things from Viognier specialist Henri Gualco.

1995 Château Roquefort, Bordeaux, £5.99   16/20
Dry 🍶🍶🍶 ❘
Weighty, concentrated, Graves-like Bordeaux with elegant, toasty oak, made from Semillon and Sauvignon Blanc grapes.

1995 Tesco Alsace Gewürztraminer, £5.99   15/20
Dry 🍶🍶 ❘
Ginger spicy, well-made Alsace Gewürz from Ammerschwihr, with floral intensity and good length of flavour.

1995 Alsace Heinberger Riesling Graffenreben, £6.99   15/20
Bone dry 🍶 ❘
Fresh, minerally Alsace Riesling from the Bellingham co-operative with zesty, lime-like undertones. Should show a bit more complexity at this price.

1996 Pouilly-Fumé, Cuvée Jules, Fouassier, £6.99   16/20
Bone dry 🍶🍶🍶 ❘
Lively, piercingly fruity Pouilly-Fumé with crisp, gooseberry and capsicum notes from a super vintage. Very good value.

1995 Tesco Chablis, Labouré-Roi, £6.99   14/20
Dry ❘
Basic, quaffing, unoaked Chablis made by Nuits St Georges négociant, Labouré-Roi.

GERMANY

Tesco Steinweiler Kloster Liebfrauenberg Auslese, £5.29   15/20
Sweet 👜👜 ▮
Rich, peachy, lusciously sticky German white with refreshing acidity. A very drinkable Auslese at a very affordable price.

SOUTH AFRICA

1996 Vergelegen Sauvignon Blanc, £5.99   15/20
Dry 👜👜 ▮
Nettley, concentrated, well-made Cape Sauvignon Blanc from Martin Meinert, with good gooseberry fruit characters typical of the grape variety.

Over £8

AUSTRALIA

1995 Tim Adams Semillon, £8.99   17/20
Dry 👜👜👜 ━
From Tim Adams, this is an intense, creamy, lemon-meringue-like, barrel-fermented Semillon with zesty acidity and delightful balance. The wine has developed considerably in the last year.

Red

Under £3

FRANCE

Tesco French Red Wine, Vin de Pays de l'Aude, £2.79   12/20
Medium-bodied 👜 ▮
More interesting than the basic French white, this is a robust, faintly raisiny Languedoc quaffer with a rasp of acidity.

Tesco Claret, £2.99   12/20
Medium-bodied 🌡 🍾
Decent, blackcurrant fruity claret from négociant Yvon Mau. Pretty basic, but what do you expect for under £3?

Tesco French Cabernet Sauvignon, Vin de Pays de la Haute Vallée de l'Aude, £2.99   13/20
Medium-bodied 🌡🌡 🍾
Chunky, robustly fruity, southern French Cabernet Sauvignon from the Limoux co-operative in the hills of the Aude. Honest quaffing.

Les Vieux Cépages Carignan, Vin de Pays de l'Hérault, £2.99   13/20
Full-bodied 🌡🌡 🍾
Juicy, concentrated, well-priced, southern French *rouge* made from the workhorse Carignan grape. A good winter warmer.

ITALY

Tesco Valpolicella, £2.97   13/20
Light-bodied 🌡🌡 🍾
Light, quaffable, cherry and raspberry fruity Valpol with soft tannins.

ROMANIA

Tesco Romanian Country Red, £2.79   11/20
Light-bodied 🍾
Beetrooty, slightly sweetened, old-fashioned Romanian red from the Black Sea coast. You pays your money...

Tesco Reka Valley Pinot Noir, £2.99   11/20
Medium-bodied 🍾
Old-fashioned, beetrooty Romanian Pinot Noir with a faintly baked, tomato-skin character. Sweet, cheap and not very nice. Who drinks this stuff?

£3–5

ARGENTINA

Picajuan Peak Bonarda, Mendoza, £3.29   14/20
Medium-bodied 🍾🍾🍾 |
Full-flavoured, spicy, plummy Mendoza *tinto* made from Italy's Bonarda grape
and showing attractive warmth and sweetness.

Picajuan Peak Sangiovese, £3.49   14/20
Medium-bodied 🍾🍾🍾 |
Lovers of Chianti may find this rather different from the Sangiovese they're
used to, but we really like it. A chocolatey, gutsy, bitters spicy Argentine red
from La Agricola.

CHILE

Tesco Chilean Cabernet Sauvignon, £3.99   15/20
Medium-bodied 🍾🍾🍾 |
Richly coloured, youthful Chilean Cabernet Sauvignon with ripe blackcurrant
fruit, smooth tannins and considerable elegance.

1996 Santa Ines Carmenère, £4.49   15/20
Medium-bodied 🍾🍾🍾 |
Unusual, deeply coloured red made from the rare Carmenère grape of
Bordeaux. Rich, stylish and well balanced, with restrained blackcurrant fruit and
polished tannins.

FRANCE

1995 Moulin de la Doline, Fitou, £3.99   14/20
Full-bodied 🍾🍾 |
Robust, herby spicy Mediterranean red with dryish tannins and a firm, fruity
aftertaste.

Tesco Claret Reserve, Bordeaux Supérieur, £3.99   14/20
Medium-bodied 🍾🍾 |
Soft, supple, flavoursome claret from Yvon Mau made for immediate drinking.
Delivers the goods at the price.

1996 Buzet, Cuvée 44, £4.99   13/20
Full-bodied |
Firm and rather chewy, wanna-be claret from France's south-west. Expensive for what it is, given what you can get from Chile at this price.

1996 Greenwich Meridian 2000 Red, Bordeaux, £4.99   14/20
Medium-bodied 👜 |
Specially selected by Yvon Mau for the millennium celebrations, this is a good basic claret, which should be drunk now rather than saved for Greenwich in the year 2000.

1995 Tesco Vintage Claret, Bordeaux Supérieur, £4.99   15/20
Medium-bodied 👜👜 |
Spicy, oak-aged, well-selected claret from one of the better vintages of the 1990s. Good depth of flavour.

ITALY

1993 Villa Pigna Rosso Piceno Superiore, £3.49   14/20
Medium-bodied 👜👜👜 |
Aromatic, well-made red from the Italian Marches, with juicy, savoury fruit flavours rounded out by oak.

PORTUGAL

1995 Campo dos Frades Cabernet Sauvignon, Vinho Regional Ribatejo, £3.99   14/20
Full-bodied 👜👜 |
Chunky, plummy, robust Ribatejo Cabernet Sauvignon from Australian Peter Bright, with a nice core of sweet, leafy fruit.

SOUTH AFRICA

Tesco Cape Cinsaut, £3.49   12/20
Full-bodied 👜 |
Rustic, plonky Cape red with all the charm of a Bruderbond convention.

1996 Swartland Cabernet Sauvignon/Shiraz, £4.49   15/20
Medium-bodied 👜👜👜 |
Sweet, juicy, coffee-scented Cape blend from one of the country's best co-operatives, with well-judged oak and silky tannins.

Tesco Beyers Truter Pinotage, £4.99   16/20
Full-bodied 👜👜👜 ▮
From the king of Cape Pinotage, Beyers Truter, this is a classic, oak-matured red with flavours of mulberry and blackberry. Concentrated essence of Pinotage.

Tesco South African Reserve Cabernet, £4.99   15/20
Medium-bodied 👜👜 ▮
Elegant, harmonious, oak-aged Cabernet Sauvignon with well-integrated fruit and tannins and some bottle-aged maturity.

Tesco South African Shiraz/Cabernet Sauvignon, John Worontschak, £4.99   15/20
Medium-bodied 👜👜 ▮
Bounty Bar, oaky Cape blend in a revolutionary screwcap bottle, made by Aussie John Worontschak. Lots of blackberry fruit and vanilla characters here.

SPAIN

1996 Tesco Viña Mara, Rioja Alavesa, £4.29   15/20
Medium-bodied 👜👜👜 ▮
Modern, Tempranillo-based Rioja with the emphasis on fruit and freshness rather than on oak and age. Juicy, sumptuous stuff.

URUGUAY

Tesco Pacific Peak Tannat/Merlot, £3.49   14/20
Medium-bodied 👜👜👜 ▮
Tesco have been a little free and easy with their geography on this unusual Uruguayan blend of Tannat and Merlot, but the wine itself is youthful, plummy and well made. Much better than the companion white.

£5–8

AUSTRALIA

1995 Tesco Coonawarra Cabernet Sauvignon, Rymill Winery, £6.99   16/20
Medium-bodied 👜👜👜 ▮
Fresh, oak-aged Cabernet Sauvignon with elegant, green-pepper fruit and spicy undertones.

1994 Tesco McLaren Vale Shiraz, Maglieri, £6.99   16/20
Full-bodied 🍷🍷🍷 ●—

Powerful, concentrated, cinnamon spicy McLaren Vale Shiraz from the outstanding Maglieri winery, with prominent, charry oak and an essence of sweet blackberry fruit.

1994 Maglieri Shiraz, McLaren Vale, £7.49   17/20
Full-bodied 🍷🍷🍷 ●—

Ripe, heady McLaren Vale Shiraz with oodles of aromatic blackberry fruit and sweet vanilla oak. Exactly what Australian Shiraz should taste like at this price.

1995 Old Penola Estate Cabernet Sauvignon, Coonawarra, £7.99
17/20

Medium-bodied 🍷🍷🍷 ●—

From Australia's best cool-climate red-wine region, this is an elegant, cassis-like Cabernet Sauvignon with refreshing acidity and well-integrated oak.

CHILE

1993 Don Maximiano Cabernet Sauvignon, Errázuriz, £7.49   17/20
Medium-bodied 🍷🍷🍷 ●—

Assertively minty, French oak-aged Cabernet Sauvignon from one of Chile's top wineries, with elegant tannins and fruit and refreshing acidity. Built to last.

FRANCE

1994 Domaine de Lanestousse, Madiran, £5.49   15/20
Full-bodied 🍷🍷 ●—

Firm, serious Madiran with the inky, densely textured flavours of the Tannat grape and a sheen of new oak. Strapping stuff.

1993 Château Côte Montpezat, Côtes de Castillon, £6.99   16/20
Medium-bodied 🍷🍷🍷 ●—

Soft, supple, lush, vanilla oaky Merlot (with 20 per cent Cabernet Franc), made by superstar winemaker Michel Rolland from an underrated Right Bank vintage.

1996 Tesco Châteauneuf-du-Pape, £6.99   15/20
Full-bodied 🍷 🍶

Lightly coloured, savoury, spicy Grenache-based red with a peppery undertone. A commercial-style Châteauneuf-du-Pape.

1993 Château Lapelletrie, St Emilion Grand Cru, £7.99   15/20
Medium-bodied 👜👜👜 ▬

A less good example of the 1993 vintage, with chewy, slightly old-fashioned tannins that are starting to dry out.

ITALY

1995 Villa Pigna, Cabernasco, £5.99   16/20
Medium-bodied 👜👜👜 ▬

In a tall, elegant, broad-shouldered bottle, this is a judiciously oaked Bordeaux-style red from the Italian Marches. Super value and a good wine to impress your friends with.

1995 Rosso di Montalcino, Cantina Leonardo da Vinci, £6.99   16/20
Medium-bodied 👜👜👜 ▮

Vibrant, juicy, mini-Brunello made from the Sangiovese grape with the accent squarely on cherry fruit. Would put a smile on the face of La Gioconda.

SOUTH AFRICA

1995 Schoone Gevel Merlot Reserve, £5.99   16/20
Medium-bodied 👜👜👜 ▮

Coconutty oaky, cool-climate Merlot from the Franschhoek Valley, or Vallei if you're an Afrikaner, with smooth, chocolatey flavours and tannins.

1996 Diemersdal Merlot, £5.99   16/20
Medium-bodied 👜👜👜 ▬

Youthful, fleshy Cape Merlot with chunky concentration, sweet oak succulence and good balance.

1996 Diemersdal Syrah, £5.99   16/20
Medium-bodied 👜👜👜 ▬

A little oakier than the Merlot, but this has the same degree of concentrated sweet fruit, balanced by restrained tannins and oak treatment.

1995 Clos Malverne Auret Cabernet Sauvignon/Pinotage, £7.99
18/20

Full-bodied 👜👜👜 ▬

A super concentrated blend of Cabernet Sauvignon and Pinotage from one of the Cape's top wineries, showing smooth, savoury oak and sweet, layered fruit flavours. A stunner.

SPAIN

1990 Tesco Viña Mara Rioja Reserva, £5.49   16/20
Medium-bodied 👜👜👜 ▮
From the respected Berberana winery, this is a mature, but still fruity Rioja
Reserva with succulence, sweet oak and youth on its side.

Over £8

FRANCE

1994 Château Le Sartre, Pessac-Léognan, £8.99   16/20
Medium-bodied 👜👜 ▮
Oaky, modern-style Pessac-Léognan red with lashings of vanilla toastiness and
appealing fruit sweetness. One to be drunk *in camera*, we presume.

1992 Chevalier de Gruaud, St Julien, £9.99   15/20
Medium-bodied 👜 ▮
A subsidiary label of Château Gruaud-Larose, which is a little light on fruit –
hardly surprising, given the vintage.

**1993 Château Cantemerle, Grand Cru Classé, Haut-Médoc,
£10.99**   17/20
Medium-bodied 👜👜👜 ▬▬
Modern, sweetly oaked, fifth-growth claret at a good price, showing coffee-
bean and rich blackcurrant notes and a degree of polished elegance.

1993 Lacoste-Borie, Pauillac, £11.99   17/20
Medium-bodied 👜👜👜 ▬▬
Youthful second wine of the Château Grand-Puy-Lacoste, with vibrant fruit and
a surprising degree of concentration for the vintage.

1993 Château Pedesclaux, Grand Cru Classé, Pauillac, £12.99
                                                             16/20
Medium-bodied 👜 ▬▬
Well-made, chunky, firmly tannic Pauillac fifth growth, with plenty of flavour and
sweet oak. A little four-square.

1993 Château St Georges, St Georges St Emilion, £13.99   17/20
Medium-bodied 👜👜 ▮
Very drinkable, voluptuous, Merlot-based claret from the St Georges satellite
of St Emilion.

1989 Château Trimoulet, St Emilion Grand Cru, £14.99   18/20
Medium-bodied 🍾🍾🍾 ▮
Lusciously fruity Merlot with sumptuous flavours of fruitcake and spice and sweet, leathery maturity.

1993 Beaune Premier Cru, Louis Jadot, £14.99   17/20
Medium-bodied 🍾🍾🍾 ▬
From one of the best recent red Burgundy vintages, this is a still-youthful, nicely balanced Côte de Beaune Pinot Noir with sweet oak, wild strawberry fruit and commendable richness of flavour.

SOUTH AFRICA

1994 Plaisir de Merle Cabernet Sauvignon, £9.99   17/20
Medium-bodied 🍾🍾🍾 ▬
Made at Nederberg's top estate in Paarl, this is a stylishly packaged, richly concentrated, chocolatey oaky Cabernet Sauvignon, which should age well.

Rosé

£3–5

FRANCE

Tesco Cabernet de Saumur, Cave des Vignerons de Saumur, £3.79
14/20

Off-dry 🍾🍾 ▮
Light, grassy, slightly sweet Cabernet Franc-based rosé with an attractive, fennel note.

ITALY

Tesco Rosé del Umbria, £3.49   15/20
Dry 🍾🍾🍾 ▮
Deeply coloured, thirst-quenching Umbrian *rosato* with cherry and strawberry fruit flavours. Very drinkable.

SOUTH AFRICA

1997 Van Loveren Blanc de Noirs Muscadel, £3.49   14/20
Medium sweet 👛👛 |
Copper-tinged Cape rosé made from the red Muscadel grape, with pronounced sweetness and grapey, Muscat-like characters.

Sparkling

£3–5

SOUTH AFRICA

1996 Tesco South African Sparkling Sauvignon Blanc, £4.99   15/20
Dry 👛👛 |
An unusual, gooseberry fruity fizz made from a grape that rarely ends up in sparkling form. An intriguing curiosity to fool your friends with.

SPAIN

Tesco Cava, £4.99   13/20
Dry 👛 |
Earthy, traditional Cava with big bubbles and little in the way of finesse.

£5–8

AUSTRALIA

1993 Tesco Australian Sparkling Chardonnay, £6.99   14/20
Off-dry 👛 |
Simple, fruity, decently made Aussie fizz with buttery, peachy undertones. Looks better than it tastes.

SOUTH AFRICA

Tesco South African Sparkling, John Worontschak, £6.99   15/20
Dry 👃👃 ❙
Made in Robertson by itinerant Aussie, John Worontschak, this is a yeasty, savoury Cape fizz with nutty complexity and a soft mousse.

Over £8

FRANCE

Tesco Blanc de Noirs Champagne, £11.99   16/20
Dry 👃👃👃 ❙
Made entirely from black grapes, this is a firm, well-structured, red fruit-like fizz with a savoury tang.

Tesco Champagne Brut, £12.95   16/20
Dry 👃👃👃 ❙
Clean, refreshing, well-made, own-label Champagne with lively acidity, lots of flavour and bottle-matured complexity.

Tesco Blanc de Blancs Champagne, Duval-Leroy, £13.99   17/20
Dry 👃👃👃 ❙
Attractive, all-Chardonnay Champagne with lemony elegance, brioche and hazelnut undertones and beautiful balance.

Tesco Millennium Champagne, £19.99   14/20
Dry ❙
Old-fashioned, tiring vintage Champagne, which has less chance of making it to the millennium than Peter Mandelson.

1990 Tesco Vintage Champagne, £19.99   17/20
Dry 👃👃👃 ▬
Much more exciting than the Millennium Champagne, this is a fresh, Pinot-dominated vintage fizz with rich, creamy and still remarkably youthful balance and texture.

SOUTH AFRICA

1993 Simonsig Kaapse Vonkel, £8.95   16/20
Dry 👃👃👃 ❙
Complex Cape fizz made from Pinot Noir and Chardonnay grapes, with notes of chocolate and wild strawberry and an appealing bottle-aged texture.

The Thresher Group

Including:

Thresher Wine Shops ☆☆☆(☆)
Wine Rack ☆☆☆☆
Bottoms Up ☆☆☆☆(☆)
Drinks Cabin ☆☆
Huttons ☆☆

Address: Sefton House, 42 Church Road, Welwyn Garden City, Herts AL8 6PJ

Telephone/fax: 01707 328244; 01707 371398

Number of branches: 813 Wine Shop, 361 Drinks Cabin, 116 Wine Rack, 87 Bottoms Up, 120 Huttons, 26 joint-venture franchises

Opening hours: Minimum trading hours 10.00am to 10.30pm Monday to Saturday; 10.00am to 10.00pm, Sunday; Huttons open from 8.00am

Credit cards accepted: Access, American Express, Switch, Visa

Discounts: On cases of table wine (including sparkling wine) under £120: 10 per cent at Bottoms Up, 5 per cent at Wine Rack and Thresher Wine Shops; on cases of table wine (including sparkling wine) over £120: 10 per cent at all three; on mixed cases of Champagne: 15 per cent (10 per cent off six, if under £120) at Bottoms Up, seven bottles for the price of six at Wine Rack, and 10 per cent off cases over £120 at Thresher Wine Shops; also special discounts for club members

Facilities and services: Glass loan; free local delivery; in-store tastings every Friday and Saturday at Wine Rack, occasionally at Thresher Wine Shops; clubs: Cellar Key (Wine Rack), Imbibers (Bottoms Up), Wine with Food Club (Thresher Wine Shops)

Special offers: Wine Buyer's Guarantee in Thresher Wine Shops (take a wine back if you don't like it and replace it with something else, or get your money back); Drinks Direct Gifting Service (any bottle delivered within mainland UK for £9.99 plus store price, or £5.99 within two days) – for orders ring 0800 23 22 21; Bottoms Up 'Try before you Buy' and Bottoms

The Thresher Group

Up price guarantee (buy any wine cheaper by the case within seven days of purchase, and the difference will be refunded and a free bottle of wine thrown in)

Top ten best-selling wines:

Thresher Wine Shops

Jacob's Creek Semillon/Chardonnay; Bulgarian Country Medium, Muscat/Ugni Blanc; Jacob's Creek Shiraz/Cabernet; Bulgarian Iambol Vintage Première Cabernet Sauvignon; Tollana Dry White; Penfolds Bin 21 Semillon/Chardonnay/Colombard; Albor Rioja Tinto Tempranillo; Gallo White Grenache; Bulgarian Russe Red, Cabernet Sauvignon/Cinsault; Tollana Medium Dry White

Wine Rack

Jacob's Creek Semillon/Chardonnay; Domaine du Tariquet, Vin de Pays des Côtes de Gascogne; Tollana Dry White; Lindauer Brut; Penfolds Bin 21 Semillon/Chardonnay/Colombard; Jacob's Creek Shiraz/Cabernet; Pinot Grigio, Fiordaliso; Albor Rioja Tinto, Tempranillo; Bulgarian Iambol, Vintage Première Cabernet Sauvignon; Bulgarian Country Medium, Muscat/Ugni Blanc

Bottoms Up

Jacob's Creek Semillon/Chardonnay; Jacob's Creek Shiraz/Cabernet; Domaine du Tariquet, Vin de Pays des Côtes de Gascogne; Pinot Grigio Fiordaliso; Penfolds Bin 21 Semillon/Chardonnay/Colombard; Tollana Dry White; Albor Rioja Tinto, Tempranillo; Oxford Landing Cabernet Sauvignon/Shiraz; Tollana Medium Dry; Vin de Pays du Gers, Au Loubet

Range:

GOOD: Alsace, Bordeaux, Burgundy, regional France, Spain, Germany, Portugal, England, South Africa, Australia, New Zealand, Chile, Champagne and sparkling wines

AVERAGE: Beaujolais, Loire, Italy, Eastern Europe, California, Rhône

POOR: None

UNDER-REPRESENTED: None

'It's been a year of few surprises,' according to Ralph Hayward, Thresher's broad-shouldered managing director. By the standards of recent times, when Thresher has seemingly 'segmented' everything, from its delivery vans to the boardroom carpet, the last 12 months have been comparatively quiet up in Welwyn Garden City. No new 'retail brands' (shops to you and us), no takeovers, just lots of hard work at the high-street coal face.

After a number of changes of image and name, Thresher has finally stopped shuffling the pack. For readers who are unfamiliar with the various Thresher playing cards, they are as follows: Huttons (which used to be called Food and Drinks Stores from Thresher) and Drinks Cabin at the cheaper end, Thresher Wine Shops in the middle and Bottoms Up and Wine Rack at the top. There are also a couple of one-offs – Home Run (a video and convenience store) and Booze Barn (a wine warehouse-style operation in Staples Corner, North London).

Of these, Booze Barn is the most recent creation, having opened its doors in October 1996. Tim Waters, director of retail brands marketing (we don't understand the title, either), says that Booze Barn is much more than a 'me too Majestic'. He points to the fact that it sells by the bottle as well as by the case, unlike its stack-it-high rival. Booze Barn can certainly compete in terms of range, as it takes the full Thresher line-up of 875 wines, but first indications are that it hasn't quite fulfilled its potential, partly as a result of its retail-park location. 'It's still on test,' says Waters. 'It's a learning process in its current format.' One thing Waters is pleased about is the number of women who come to Booze Barn, attracted by crèche facilities and what he calls 'the service offering'.

Nevertheless, we sensed a tinge of disappointment when we spoke to the Thresher management. There might be more Booze Barns, and there might not. 'We won't segment for segmentation's sake,' says Hayward. 'But if we can get Booze Barn to work, we'll put 30 of them on the street.' So if you live near a retail park, keep your eyes open for men in suits from Thresher HQ truffling around the site.

The other part of the Thresher empire which is under-performing is Drinks Cabin. Hayward admits that the traditional high-street offie is losing out to the supermarkets. On the other hand, Huttons, the convenience store that appears to have been named after the editor of The Observer, is 'buoyant'. So, according to Hayward, are Thresher Wine Shops, Bottoms Up and Wine Rack, the real focus of the business. 'We're moving increasingly towards specialism,' he adds. 'Our strategic emphasis is behind drink.'

Hayward points to strong sales growth over the last year: 'We've out-performed the supermarkets on beer and are in line with the market on wine. Our wine sales are up 7.3 per cent.' This is considerably more impressive than Thresher's great high-street rival, Victoria Wine, which has suffered from personnel changes and poor sales during the last year. Unsurprisingly, the best wine stores are nearly all Wine Racks and Bottoms Ups, where vino can account for as much as 45 per cent of the sales mix.

The Thresher Group

If the segmentation process appears to have come to a halt, there has been movement elsewhere at Thresher. Matthew Dickinson, a bright young buyer from Sainsbury's, has replaced John 'goatee' Woodriffe and now handles South America, Italy, Burgundy and Germany, as well as the delights of wine cans and bag-in-box. Otherwise, the team, like the old Led Zeppelin album, remains the same. Kim Tidy is overall wine-buying supremo, with Julian Twaites, David McDonnell and Lucy Warner completing the team. It's a successful unit. As well as enjoying themselves, they buy some very good wines, especially in Spain, France and the New World.

Another man who enjoys himself, and still gets a full salary, is David Howse, Thresher's increasingly eccentric PR man. Not content with putting amusingly captioned photographs on the front of the list mailed to journalists, Howse writes strange, rambling letters, dispenses wine advice on the radio and sends cassettes about Argentina to thousands of Thresher employees. As he himself puts it, 'On them I unleash the full awfulness of the un-fettered Howse…Poor inunciation [sic], mixed metaphors, meaningless references…the lot.' The fellow is priceless, and well done Thresher for indulging his whimsy.

There is nothing indulgent about the Thresher wine range, of course, although some might argue that the South African spread (63 wines and counting in Wine Rack, 35 in Bottoms Up and 22 in Thresher Wine Shops) is a mite over-generous. The rugby-loving Lucy Warner, whose trips to the Cape have a habit of coinciding with major internationals, is unrepentant: 'South Africa is very buoyant for the fourth year running. The 1997 vintage is very good and the quality from the top estates is superb.' She's certainly teamed up with some excellent producers, notably Villiera, Fairview, Kym Milne and Warwick, but the range could still do with more focus, in our view.

Thresher's customers may take a different view. Cape wines now account for 6 per cent of sales, up from 4 per cent a year ago. This is smaller than France (20 per cent), Italy (11 per cent), Germany (8 per cent) and Australasia (an enormous 21 per cent), but it's still big and growing very fast. Thresher's New World sales, thanks to South Africa, Chile, California, Australia and New Zealand, now comprise 40 per cent of the business. Australia alone accounts for one in every five bottles sold.

The next big New World thing is Argentina, which Thresher has been working at for over a year now. The new Corazón range has been developed with some of Argentina's most forward-thinking wineries, such as Catena, Peñaflor, Jacques Lurton, La Agricola and Balbi. There are also some very good wines from Etchart, making Thresher's Argentine line-up one of the best in the high street, alongside Oddbins and Tesco.

Kim Tidy is excited about Argentina. 'There's been a switch in the market towards red wines and that's where Argentina is strong,' he says. 'With the right investment, it could be very successful. The Argentines aren't as malleable as, say, the Australians, but then neither are the South Africans and look what we've achieved there.'

Australia, despite the flexibility of its producers, is proving a headache for Tidy. Finding good red wines under £5 from Down Under over the last year has been a 'nightmare', apparently. 'We've only managed to find one thing, Tatachilla Shiraz/Grenache, which is worth the money. We've also had to de-list a lot of top-end wines, which have become too expensive.' Tidy thinks the situation won't remedy itself until 1999, when new plantings of red grapes come on-stream. But he's still managed to get hold of good stocks of wines from super estates like Chapel Hill, Mountadam, Heritage, The Willows and Tim Adams.

California is another difficult area. 'It isn't really offering value for money,' says the amusingly dressed Julian Twaites. 'Washington State is more interesting for us than California.' Twaites points to the wines produced by Columbia Crest to justify his point. Fair enough, but the new West Coast list looks like an admission of defeat to us, with four of the six red wines coming from the world's biggest producer, Gallo. It can't be right that Portugal is worth twice as many listings as California, surely?

Maybe Thresher are just taking a more hard-nosed approach to wine retailing. The old enthusiasms for Alsace and New Zealand are still there, but they're a little more restrained than in the past. The same is true of Italy, the northern Rhône and the south of France, all regions or countries where Thresher's range is not as exciting as it once was, despite innovations such as Original Zin and Original Sin from Puglia.

Apart from South Africa and booming millennium-driven Champagne and sparkling-wine sales, the other growth areas are Chile, the Loire, New Zealand and (surprisingly, given the rather limited range) California. The currency fluctuations of the last year have been a 'big boost' for French producers, in general, according to Kim Tidy. This has helped Thresher to do some very good deals in Bordeaux and Champagne.

What of the shops? Well, the three main brands (this marketing speak is contagious) work well on the whole, although the quality and knowledge of the staff varies considerably. Bottoms Up has developed a youthful, friendly feel and sells lot of wine by the case in places like Greenwich and Fulham. Wine Rack feels a little older and more traditional, although it takes the full South African range, too. And Thresher Wine Shops are good local wine shops. Bottoms Up is still the flagship, with 860 wines, compared to Wine Rack's 600 and Thresher Wine Shops' 450. It's also our favourite of the three.

If Thresher is going to expand further, it will be with Wine Rack and Bottoms Up rather than, say, Drinks Cabin. Both could eventually number as many as 200 stores, according to Ralph Hayward. But after last year's heady negotiations, when Thresher was said to be on the verge of buying Oddbins, 1997 has been a lot less frenetic. 'We're not actively talking to anyone at this minute,' adds Hayward. 'But a minute is a long time in retailing.'

All wines are available in Thresher Wine Shops (TWS), Wine Rack (WR), Bottoms Up (BU,) Drinks Cabin and Huttons, unless otherwise indicated.

White

Under £3

FRANCE

1996 Elm Grove, Vin de Pays de l'Aude, Val d'Orbieu, £2.99
(TWS/WR/BU only)   13/20
Dry 👛👛 ▯
Clean, fruity, appley Languedoc white blended for Thresher by Master of Wine, Angela Muir. Looks good at the price.

£3–5

ARGENTINA

1996 Corazón Chardonnay/Chenin, Peter Bright, £3.79
(TWS/WR/BU only)   13/20
Dry 👛 ▯
From Aussie Peter Bright at Argentina's biggest winery, Peñaflor, this is a refreshingly crisp blend of Chardonnay and Chenin Blanc, with neutral fruit flavours.

1996 La Rural Pinot Blanc/Chardonnay, £3.99 (TWS/WR/BU only)
                                                                             14/20
Dry 👛👛 ▯
A cool fermented blend of 75 per cent Pinot Blanc and 25 per cent Chardonnay, from Nicolas Catena's La Rural winery. Soft, fragrant and peachy.

1996 Etchart Torrontes, Cafayate, £3.99 (TWS/WR/BU only)   15/20
Dry 🍷🍷🍷 ▮
A textbook Torrontes from the isolated Cafayate region, showing exuberant floral fragrance and a crisp lime and grapefruity tang. Like eating fresh grapes.

1996 Corazón Chenin, Jacques Lurton, £4.99 (TWS/WR/BU only)
15/20
Dry 🍷🍷 ▮
Full, perfumed, lime-zesty Argentine white made by Jacques Lurton at the tongue-twisting Escorihuela winery in downtown Mendoza.

AUSTRALIA

Red Cliffs Riesling/Gewürztraminer, £3.99 (TWS/WR/BU only) 14/20
Off-dry 🍷🍷 ▮
Lemon-peel-scented Victorian blend of the aromatic grapes, Gewürztraminer and Riesling, showing crisp acidity and good fruit.

1996 Tollana Unoaked Chardonnay, £4.69 (TWS/WR/BU only)   15/20
Dry 🍷🍷 ▮
From Lindemans Bin 65 meister, Philip John, this is an elegant, unoaked style of Aussie Chardonnay with restrained peach and melon fruit flavours.

1995 Red Cliffs Chardonnay, £4.99 (TWS/WR/BU only)   14/20
Off-dry 🍷 ▮
Ageing rapidly, but this rather obvious oak and tropical fruit-salad-style Chardonnay is still perfectly enjoyable. Still, we'd advise you to buy the 1996 instead.

BULGARIA

1994 Domaine Boyar Khan Krum Chardonnay Reserve, Preslav, £3.79 (TWS/WR/BU only)   14/20
Dry 🍷🍷 ▮
Still youthful for a three-year-old Chardonnay, this modern, subtly oaked, citrus fruity Chardonnay is encouraging stuff from a country we'd almost given up on.

CHILE

1996 Las Colinas Chardonnay, Jacques Lurton, £3.99
(TWS/WR/BU only) 14/20
Dry 🍷🍷 ▮
From Lontue's San Pedro winery, this has all the Jacques Lurton hallmarks of clean, buttery fruit and drinkability.

FRANCE

1996 Vin de Pays du Gers, Au Loubet, Plaimont, £3.39 13/20
Off-dry 🍷 ▮
Basic, sweet-and-sour apple-style white from Gascony's giant Plaimont co-operative. Made to a price.

1996 Domaine du Tariquet, Vin de Pays des Côtes de Gascogne, Yves Grassa, £3.99 15/20
Dry 🍷🍷🍷 ▮
A blend of Ugni Blanc with the superior Colombard grape from Yves Grassa. You get a lot more character, zip and grapefruit zest for an extra 60 pence.

1996 Southlands Sauvignon Blanc, Vin de Pays d'Oc, Nigel Sneyd, BRL-Hardy, £4.49 (TWS/WR/BU only) 14/20
Dry 🍷 ▮
Produced at BRL-Hardy by Aussie Nigel Sneyd, this is a soft, gooseberry fruity Sauvignon Blanc with attractive aromas and crisp varietal character.

1996 Domaine du Tariquet, Sauvignon Blanc, Vin de Pays des Côtes de Gascogne, Yves Grassa, £4.79 (TWS/WR/BU only) 16/20
Dry 🍷🍷🍷 ▮
Spritzy, grapefruit and lemon zesty Sauvignon Blanc from Gascony's Yves Grassa, which explodes out of the glass with almost New Zealand-like pungency. One of the best Gascon whites we've ever tasted.

1996 Château Haut-Genestras, Entre Deux Mers, £4.79
(TWS/WR/BU only) 15/20
Dry 🍷🍷 ▮
Herbal, modern-style, Semillon-dominated Bordeaux white with a full texture and good Sauvignon Blanc-derived acidity and length. Zingy stuff.

1996 Southlands Chardonnay, Vin de Pays d'Oc, Meffre, £4.99
(TWS/WR/BU only)　　　　　　　　　　　　　　　　　　15/20
Dry 🍾🍾 ▮
Made specially for Thresher by Thierry Boudinaud of Gabriel Meffre, this is a
buttery, New World-style Chardonnay with lots of flavour and pure fruit
characters.

1996 Sparks Chardonnay, Vin de Pays d'Oc, Meffre, £5.00 (TWS
only)　　　　　　　　　　　　　　　　　　　　　　　15/20
Dry 🍾🍾 ▮
Modern, toasty, partially barrel-fermented, new-wave Chardonnay. Your chance
to give £1 to the children's charity, Sparks.

GERMANY

Solus, QbA, Langenbach, £3.99 (TWS/WR/BU only)　　　13/20
Medium sweet 🍾 ▮
Repackaged in a peculiarly shaped blue bottle – they had to do something to
make it interesting – this is Thresher's 'super' Liebfraumilch, showing sweet
grapey fruit and less sulphur than most cheap (well, cheapish) German whites.

HUNGARY

Butlers Blend White, Neszmely, Mor Region, £3.39　　　14/20
Dry 🍾🍾 ▮
An unpronounceable blend of the two local grapes, Leányka and Ezerfürtú,
made by Aussie Nick Butler. Pleasantly dry and lightly spicy with a crisp finish.

1995 Gyöngyös Chardonnay, Hugh Ryman, £3.69 (TWS/WR/BU
only)　　　　　　　　　　　　　　　　　　　　　　14/20
Dry 🍾🍾 ▮
Fresher and better made than it has been in recent vintages, this lemony, lightly
oaked Hugh Ryman Chardonnay is back on form.

1995 Gyöngyös Sauvignon Blanc, Hugh Ryman, £3.69
(TWS/WR/BU only)　　　　　　　　　　　　　　　　13/20
Dry 🍾 ▮
Less good than the Chardonnay, this is a tart, rather fruitless white, which lacks
varietal character and excitement.

ITALY

1996 Pinot Grigio, Fiordaliso, GIV, £4.49 (TWS/WR/BU only)   14/20
Dry 🜂 ▯
From the enormous GIV winery in Verona, this is a clean, if neutral, Pinot Grigio at an ambitious price.

1996 The Original Sin, Puglia, Kym Milne, £4.99 (TWS/WR/BU only)
                                          15/20

Dry 🜂🜂 ▯
Puglia might not be everyone's idea of the Garden of Eden, but this smoky, richly textured, ripely fruity Italian Chardonnay in a trendy blue bottle is almost as good as an evening under a tree with Eve (or Adam, if you prefer).

SOUTH AFRICA

1996 Arniston Bay, Chenin Blanc/Chardonnay, Western Cape, £3.99 (TWS only)   14/20
Dry 🜂🜂 ▯
Attractively packaged Cape blend of mainly Chenin Blanc and 25 per cent Chardonnay, with soft, ripe pear notes and good flavour at the price.

1997 Winelands Sauvignon, Kym Milne, Stellenbosch, £4.49 (TWS/WR/BU only)   15/20
Dry 🜂🜂🜂 ▯
Soft, full, nettley Sauvignon Blanc from Kym Milne, with masses of flavour and personality and undertones of elderflower and gooseberry.

1996 Winelands Bush Vine Chenin Blanc, Stellenbosch, Kym Milne, £4.49 (TWS/WR/BU only)   15/20
Dry 🜂🜂🜂 ▯
Buttery, concentrated, almost Chardonnay-like, old-vine Chenin Blanc from Master of Wine Kym Milne, with extra weight derived from lees contact after fermentation.

1997 Winelands Chardonnay, Worcester, Kym Milne, £4.79 (TWS/WR/BU only)   15/20
Dry 🜂🜂 ▯
Ultra-fresh, lemony Chardonnay with the accent on fruit flavour, rather than oak or winemaking tricks.

From Halves To Hogsheads, Chapter Two NV, Fairview, Paarl, £4.99 (BU only)
15/20
Dry 👛👛 ▮
Characterful, full-flavoured, smokily oaked blend of Sauvignon Blanc, Chenin Blanc and a bit of Chardonnay from the talented Charles Back. An off-the-wall idea that works rather well.

From Halves To Hogsheads, Chapter Three, Madeba, Robertson, £4.99 (BU only)
16/20
Dry 👛👛👛 ▮
Same name, different source, different grape. From the warm-climate Robertson district, this is a lemon butter and toasty oak-style Chardonnay from the Madeba winery. Alluringly refreshing.

1996 Sinnya White, Robertson Valley, £4.99 (TWS/WR/BU only)
14/20
Off-dry 👛 ▮
A pleasantly aromatic blend of Riesling and Gewürztraminer, which finishes a little sweet and obvious. About £1 over-priced.

1996 Villiera Chenin Blanc, Paarl, £4.99 (TWS/WR/BU only)
16/20
Dry 👛👛👛 ▮
Subtly oaked, beautifully turned-out South African Chenin Blanc from the brilliant Jeff Grier, who has managed to extract a remarkable degree of flavour and peachy richness from a comparatively neutral grape.

SPAIN

1996 Santara Viura/Chardonnay, Conca de Barbera, Hugh Ryman, £3.49 (TWS/WR/BU only)
13/20
Dry 👛 ▮
Light, easy drinking, faintly oaky Spanish blend of Viura and Chardonnay from Hugh Ryman. Basic stuff, which is unlikely to set your castanets clicking.

1996 Santara Chardonnay, Conca de Barbera, Hugh Ryman, £3.99 (TWS/WR/BU only)
15/20
Dry 👛👛👛 ▮
From the same Spanish hacienda, this is a richer and more appealing white, with a creamy texture, peachy fruit and balancing freshness.

£5–8

AUSTRALIA

1995 Samuel's Bay Chardonnay, Adam Wynn, £6.99
(TWS/WR/BU only)   16/20
Dry 🍂🍂 ▮
Made by the wisecracking Adam Wynn of Mountadam in South Australia, this is a rich, deliberately unoaked style of Chardonnay with excellent concentration. Great with fish dishes.

1996 Primo Estate, Colombard, £6.99 (WR/BU only)   16/20
Dry 🍂🍂 ▮
From the expanses of the Adelaide Plains, this is a zippy, grapefruity Colombard from the sportscar-driving Joe Grilli, unoaked for maximum fruit impact. Worth trying with Oriental food.

1994 Riddoch Chardonnay, Coonawarra, £6.99 (TWS/WR/BU only)
16/20

Dry 🍂🍂 ▮
Intensely buttery, toffee-fudge and vanilla-scented Coonawarra Chardonnay with masses of flavour and intensity. The French would hate this, but perhaps that's no bad thing.

1996 Samuel's Bay Riesling, Eden Valley, Adam Wynn, £6.99
(TWS/WR/BU only)   16/20
Dry 🍂🍂 ▮
Fragrant, lime and greengage-like Riesling from the cool-climate Eden Valley, showing fresh fruit flavours and crisp, lingering acidity.

CHILE

1996 Trio Chardonnay, Concha y Toro, £5.49 (TWS/WR/BU only)
16/20

Dry 🍂🍂🍂 ▮
A brilliant follow-up to last year's stunning debut from Ignacio Recabarren. The price has crept up a little, but even so, this crisply etched, lightly oaked, lemony Chardonnay is well worth its £5.49 – and then some. We just wish they'd do something about the awful label.

1995 Santa Carolina Cinco Estrellas Chardonnay, £7.59
(TWS/WR/BU only)   16/20
Dry 👜👜 ❘
The top-of-the-range Chardonnay from Santiago's Santa Carolina winery, made by Ignacio Recabarren and Pilar González. Rich and tropical, with a massive whack of oak and flavours of buttered popcorn.

FRANCE

1996 Muscadet, Côtes de Grandlieu Sur Lie, Clos de La Fine, £5.49 (TWS/WR/BU only)   16/20
Bone dry 👜👜👜 ❘
Still one of the best sur lie Muscadets on the market, showing crisp, nettley, green-apple flavours and lees-derived spritz.

1996 Château Bonnet Unoaked, Entre-Deux-Mers, Lurton, £5.80
16/20
Dry 👜👜👜 ❘
A modern, grapefruit and guava-fruity white Bordeaux blend of Sauvignon Blanc, Semillon and Muscadelle from the godfather of the Entre-Deux-Mers region, André Lurton. Refreshing, tangy stuff with excellent length of flavour.

1996 Turckheim Gewürztraminer Reserve, £5.99
(TWS/WR/BU only)   16/20
Dry 👜👜👜 ❘
From the impressive Turckheim co-op, this is a classic, well-priced Gewürz with notes of rose petal and ginger spice and a lift of fresh acidity.

WR/001/96 Chardonnay, Vin de Pays d'Oc, James Herrick, £6.99
(WR only)   16/20
Dry 👜👜 ❘
A superior Chardonnay cuvée from James Herrick's Narbonne-based winery, with fresh, minerally complexity and subtle oak characters. A well-crafted Languedoc Chardonnay.

1995 Château Bonnet Oaked, Lurton, £7.49   16/20
Dry 👜👜 ❘
From André Lurton's property in the Entre-Deux-Mers, this is toastier and more Graves-like than the unoaked version also stocked by Thresher. More texture than assertive fruit flavours, but still excellent.

1996 Sancerre, La Cresle de Laporte, £7.99 (TWS/WR/BU only)

15/20

Dry 🍶 ▮

Well made, if a little short of excitement, given the excellent vintage in the appellation.

1996 Pouilly-Fumé, Les Duchesses, Laporte, £7.99
(TWS/WR/BU only)

16/20

Dry 🍶🍶 ▮

Nettley, minerally, concentrated Loire Sauvignon Blanc, with a flinty undertone. Better than the Sancerre and no more expensive.

ITALY

1996 Caramia, Chardonnay del Salento, Puglia, Kym Milne, Cantele, £5.99 (WR/BU only)

16/20

Dry 🍶🍶🍶 ▮

Rich, stylish, southern Italian Chardonnay with textured, Burgundian-style characters and considerable minerally complexity. If only more Italian whites were like this.

NEW ZEALAND

1996 Villa Maria Private Bin Sauvignon Blanc, £6.49
(TWS/WR/BU only)

15/20

Dry 🍶🍶 ▮

Villa Maria's bottom-of-the-range Sauvignon Blanc is still one of the best-value whites in New Zealand. A thoroughly modern, grapefruit and gooseberry-like Marlborough Sauvignon Blanc with plenty of flavour and oomph.

SOUTH AFRICA

1996 Hartenberg Weisser Riesling, Stellenbosch, £5.69 (WR only)

15/20

Off-dry 🍶 ▮

Aromatic, sweetish, lime-zesty Cape Riesling in a Burgundy bottle. A little pricey.

1996 Villiera, Blanc Fumé, Paarl, £6.29 (WR/BU only)   16/20
Dry 👜👜 🍾
Restrained, smoky, pleasantly textured Cape Sauvignon Blanc from Jeff Grier,
designed with food in mind.

SPAIN

1995 Albariño Condes del Alberei, Rias Baixas, £5.99   16/20
Dry 👜👜 🍾
From Galicia's Rias Baixas region, this is a peachy, apricoty, well-crafted example
of Spain's most interesting white grape.

UNITED STATES

1994 Colombia Crest Chardonnay, Washington State, £5.99   15/20
Dry 👜 🍾
Vanilla fudge and coffee-bean-like West Coast Chardonnay with pronounced
sweetness and a crème brûlée note.

Over £8

AUSTRALIA

1995 Amberley Semillon, Western Australia, £9.99 (WR/BU only)
18/20
Dry 👜👜👜 ▬
From Western Australia's Margaret River region, this is a beautifully made,
ageworthy Semillon with subtle oak and fresh, herbal fruit characters. An
excellent food wine.

1996 Amberley Sauvignon, Western Australia, £9.99 (WR/BU only)
18/20
Dry 👜👜👜 🍾
From the same winery, this is an elegant, superbly crafted Western Australian
Sauvignon Blanc, which is as close to top-notch white Graves as you'll get in
the New World.

FRANCE

1995 St Véran, Domaine des Deux Roches, Les Terres Noires, £8.99 (TWS/WR/BU only)   17/20
Dry 🍾🍾🍾 |
One of the oakier wines from the outstanding Domaine des Deux Roches, this superb Mâconnais Chardonnay still retains the finesse and flavour that characterise the winery's output.

1994 Zind Humbrecht, Riesling Gueberschwihr, £10.49 (WR only)
17/20
Bone dry 🍾🍾 |
Blue paraffin-scented, bracingly austere Alsace Riesling from Master of Wine Olivier Humbrecht. Complex, minerally, intense Riesling from a very good site.

NEW ZEALAND

1996 Dashwood Sauvignon Blanc Marlborough, £8.49 (WR/BU only)   16/20
Dry 🍾🍾 |
Crisp, green-bean and asparagus-like Sauvignon Blanc from the Vavasour winery, showing good concentration and zip. Needs food, we reckon.

1995 Wairau River Sauvignon Blanc Marlborough, £8.49 (TWS/WR/BU only)   14/20
Dry |
From a rain-saturated harvest, this is a decent, if dilute, Sauvignon Blanc, which typifies the problems experienced by Marlborough in 1995.

1995 Montana 'P' Patutahi Gewürztraminer, Gisborne, £8.99 (WR only)   15/20
Off-dry 🍾 |
Heavy, mid-golden, ultra-ripe Turkish delight of a wine. One for the harem.

1996 Palliser Sauvignon Blanc Martinborough, £9.99 (TWS/WR/BU only)   16/20
Dry 🍾🍾 |
From one of New Zealand's most consistent wineries, this is a delightful, faintly tropical, passionfruity New Zealand Sauvignon Blanc, with less acidity than the wines produced on the other side of the Marlborough Sound.

1994 Montana 'O' Ormond Estate Chardonnnay Gisborne, £10.99
(WR/BU only)   17/20
Dry 🍾🍾🍾 ▬

Buttery, hazelnutty Gisborne Chardonnay from one of Montana's top vineyards, showing considerable complexity and zing. Close your eyes and you could almost be in Puligny-Montrachet.

Red

Under £3

BULGARIA

1996 Domaine Boyar Iambol Cabernet Sauvignon, £2.99
(TWS/WR/BU only)   14/20
Medium-bodied 🍾🍾🍾 |

Plummy, youthful Cabernet Sauvignon, made in an upfront, young vatted style with a nip of acidity. The modern visage of Bulgaria.

1996 Domaine Boyar Iambol Merlot, £2.99 (TWS/WR/BU only)
     14/20

Medium-bodied 🍾🍾🍾 |

In a similar vein, but with a bit more juicy blackcurrant fruit.

FRANCE

1996 Elm Grove Vin de Pays de l'Aude, £2.99 (TWS/WR/BU only)
     13/20

Light-bodied 🍾🍾 |

Easy quaffing, red-fruit-style rouge from southern France. Light and pleasant, especially at £2.99.

SPAIN

Valencia Red, Vicente Gandia, £2.79 (TWS/WR/BU only)   13/20
Medium-bodied 🍾🍾 |

From one of the Levante's biggest wine exporters, this is a mellow, cherryish red at an attractive price, made from the Cencibel grape.

Casa Rural Cencibel, Martinez Bujanda, £2.99 (TWS/WR/BU only)

14/20

Medium-bodied 👜👜👜 ▮

Same grape variety, different region. A luscious, sweetly fruity Spanish tinto with a bit of bottle age.

£3–5

ARGENTINA

1996 Libertad Sangiovese/Malbec, £3.49 (TWS/WR/BU only)

13/20

Medium-bodied 👜 ▮

Raisiny, faintly plonky Argentine red blend with a soft finish. Not easy to spot the Sangiovese or Malbec character here, however.

1996 Corazón Bonarda, Jacques Lurton, £3.79 (TWS/WR/BU only)

13/20

Medium-bodied 👜👜 ▮

Made from Italy's – and now Argentina's – Bonarda grape, this is South America's answer to Beaujolais, even if it's a bit chunkier than Gamay. A spicy, chocolatey glugger.

1996 Corazón Tempranilla, La Agricola, £3.99 (TWS/WR/BU only)

14/20

Medium-bodied 👜👜 ▮

From the promising La Agricola winery, this is a ripe, strawberry fruity red made from Tempranilla (aka Tempranillo), Spain's – if not necessarily Argentina's – best grape variety (sic). Mouth-filling stuff.

1996 La Rural Malbec, £3.99 (TWS/WR/BU only)   14/20

Medium-bodied 👜👜👜 ▮

A savoury, spicy, well-packaged example of Argentina's signature red grape, from one of the Catena group's many wineries.

AUSTRALIA

1996 Nanya Estate Malbec/Ruby Cabernet, South Australia, £3.99
(TWS/WR/BU only)   14/20
Full-bodied 👜👜 |
With its distinctive ganja label, this is a smoky, full-flavoured red with tobaccoey tannins and plummy fruit.

1996 Tatachilla Grenache/Mataro, South Australia, £4.79
(TWS/WR/BU only)   15/20
Medium-bodied 👜👜 |
Lightly coloured, spearminty Aussie blend of two warm-climate varieties, with pleasant loganberry fruit, sweet oak and a dryish finish.

1995 Red Cliffs Cabernet Sauvignon, Coonawarra, £4.99
(TWS/WR/BU only)   15/20
Medium-bodied 👜👜 |
Supple, grassy, green-pepper-like Cabernet Sauvignon from the cool-climate Coonawarra region. Well priced at under £5, particularly for Australia.

CHILE

1995 Las Colinas Merlot /Cabernet, £3.99 (TWS/WR/BU only)
13/20

Medium-bodied 👜 |
Herby, slightly old-fashioned, blackcurrant-pastille-like Chilean red from Pilar González at the Santa Carolina winery. Finishes rather dry and chewy.

1996 Valdivieso Merlot, £4.99 (TWS/WR/BU only)   15/20
Medium-bodied 👜👜 |
Abundantly aromatic, lusciously fruity Chilean Merlot with a nip of thirst-quenching acidity. A good summer quaffer.

1996 Valdivieso Malbec, £4.99 (TWS/WR/BU only)   16/20
Medium-bodied 👜👜 |
Rich, chocolatey, sumptuously textured Chilean Malbec from the same winery, with excellent flavour and balance. Hugely drinkable.

FRANCE

1995 Côtes du Ventoux, La Mission, £3.49 (TWS/R/BU only)   13/20
Full-bodied 👜 |
Peppery, Grenache-based would-be Côtes du Rhône from Franco-Chilean winemaker Gaetane Carron. A little bit plonky. La Mission, but not Haut-Brion.

Claret Regional Classics NV, P. Sichel, £3.99   14/20
Medium-bodied 👜👜 |
A blend of the 1995 vintage with 25 per cent from 1994, using Merlot to good effect in a well-priced improvement on last year's earthy, disappointing effort.

1995 Corbières, Domaine Les Colombies, £4.39
(WR/BU and selected TWS only)   15/20
Medium-bodied 👜👜👜 |
A typical blend of Carignan, Grenache and Syrah, showing thyme and lavender notes, with spicy concentration and a sweet middle.

1995 Château de Laurens, Faugères, £4.49 (TWS/WR/BU only) 15/20
Full-bodied 👜👜👜 |
A pungent, inky, oak-aged blend of Grenache, Syrah and Cinsaut, which doesn't take any prisoners. Chunky, concentrated stuff with a core of sweet blackberry fruit.

1995 Coteaux du Tricastin, Domaine de Montine, £4.49
(WR/BU and selected TWS only)   14/20
Full-bodied 👜 |
Traditional, perfumed southern Rhône plonk with a rustic finish. We've enjoyed this more in previous vintages.

1996 Southlands Merlot, Vin de Pays d'Oc, Meffre, £4.49
(TWS/WR/BU only)   14/20
Full-bodied 👜 |
Solid, well made, if a little four-square. A chunky, blackberry fruity Merlot from Thierry Boudinaud.

1996 Southlands Shiraz, Vin de Pays d'Oc, Meffre, £4.49
(TWS/WR/BU only)   14/20
Full-bodied 👜 |
Pleasant, faintly bubble gummy Languedoc Syrah (sorry, Shiraz), with pronounced acidity and robust tannins.

1995 Southlands Cabernet Sauvignon, Vin de Pays d'Oc, BRL-Hardy, £4.99 (TWS/WR/BU only) 14/20
Medium-bodied 🌡 🍾
BRL-Hardy's Nigel Sneyd has come up with a decent, if light, berry-fruity red. A bit anonymous.

1995 Côtes du Rhône, Domaine des Moulins, Georges Duboeuf, £4.99 (WR/BU and selected TWS only) 15/20
Medium-bodied 🌡🌡 🍾
A fresh, peppery, youthful Côtes du Rhône, which, unsurprisingly – given the man who made it – tastes a little like a Beaujolais Villages.

1995 Les Hauts de Goëlane, Oak-Aged Claret, £4.99 15/20
Medium-bodied 🌡🌡 🍾
Modern, nicely oaked, well-balanced blend of Cabernet Sauvignon, Cabernet Franc and Merlot ,with a touch of extra oomph and backbone compared to the basic claret.

1995 Le Merlot de J. et F. Lurton, £4.99
(WR/BU and selected TWS only) 15/20
Medium-bodied 🌡🌡 🍾
Unusual to find a pure Merlot wine from Bordeaux, but this is an aromatic, well-priced claret with stylish oak and green-pepper notes. Finishes a little dry.

1996 Sparks Merlot, Vin de Pays d'Oc, Meffre, £5.00 (TWS only) 14/20
Medium-bodied 🌡 🍾
A sweet, juicy, well-made Midi Merlot from Thierry Boudinaud, which ought to retail at £3.99. Mind you, £1 per bottle goes to charity, so perhaps we shouldn't be too critical.

HUNGARY

Butlers Blend Red, Villany Region, £3.29 (TWS/WR/BU only) 13/20
Light-bodied 🌡 🍾
A light, rhubarby blend from southern Hungary of the local Kekfrankos and the more international Merlot. Lacks a bit of stuffing and fruit.

ITALY

1996 The Original Zin, Kym Milne/Augusto Cantèle, £4.99
(TWS/WR/BU only)   15/20
Full-bodied 👜👜 🍷

In a revolutionary crown-capped blue bottle, this is a rich, pleasantly pruney Zin (well, Primitivo actually, which may or may not be the same grape), with robust tannins and plenty of southern Italian character.

PORTUGAL

1995 Douro Red Bright Bros, Peter Bright, £4.99
(TWS/WR/BU only)   14/20
Full-bodied 👜 ➖

Peter Bright makes wine in so many countries these days that it's easy to forget that he made his name in Portugal. This robust Douro blend, with its leathery, spicy notes and punchy tannins, is a wine for a winter evening by the fire.

1996 Trincadeira Preta, Peter Bright, £4.99
(BU/WR and selected TWS only)   15/20
Full-bodied 👜👜 🍷

Same winemaker, different grape variety, this time from the Estremadura region. Refreshing acidity and sweet raspberry fruit make this an enjoyable and distinctive indigenous red.

1995 Fiuza Cabernet Sauvignon, £4.99 (TWS/WR/BU only)   16/20
Medium-bodied 👜👜👜 ➖

Elegant, vanilla oak and green-pepper-like red from Peter Bright, showing luscious tannins and a sweet middle palate, combined with typical Cabernet Sauvignon varietal character.

ROMANIA

1996 River Route Limited Edition Cabernet Sauvignon, £4.49
(WR/BU only)   14/20
Medium-bodied 👜👜 🍷

One of a number of improved reds we've had this year from Romania, this is a plummy, softly textured Cabernet Sauvignon in a winning package.

1996 River Route Limited Edition Merlot, £4.49 (WR/BU only) 13/20
Medium-bodied 👜 🍷

Oakier and more astringent, without the charm of the Cabernet Sauvignon.

SOUTH AFRICA

1996 Paarl Heights Red, Boland Co-op, £3.69 (TWS/WR/BU only)
10/20

Medium-bodied |
Cooked, rubbery and rather nasty. As a British wine importer once said of another Cape red, this is like the aftermath of an explosion in a Liquorice Allsorts factory. Paarl Depths.

1996 Winelands Cinsaut/Tinta Barocca, Kym Milne, £3.99
(TWS/WR/BU only)   14/20
Medium-bodied 👜👜 |
A sweetly juicy blend of southern France's Cinsaut and the Portuguese Tinta Barocca from Kym Milne, showing mulberry fruit and a Demerara sugar note.

From Halves To Hogsheads Zinfandel/Cabernet, Hartenberg,
£4.99 (BU only)   13/20
Medium-bodied |
Light, smoky and faintly sour blend of Zinfandel and Cabernet Sauvignon. We like the package more than the wine.

SPAIN

1996 Santara Tempranillo, Conca de Barbera, Hugh Ryman, £3.49
13/20

Medium-bodied 👜 |
From the cool-climate Conca de Barbera region, this is a decent, if slightly bitter Tempranillo from Hugh Ryman.

Copa Real Plata, Martinez Bujanda, £3.89 (TWS/WR/BU only) 15/20
Medium-bodied 👜👜👜 |
Lashings of sweet coconutty oak and soft, spicy, strawberry jam fruitiness. A bargain from Martinez Bujanda.

1991 Viña Albali Reserva Valdepeñas, Bodegas Felix Solis, £3.99
(TWS/WR/BU only)   14/20
Medium-bodied 👜👜 |
A Rioja taste-alike from Valdepeñas on the edge of the central Spanish plain, with vanilla oak characters and richly mature fruit.

1996 Viña Marcos Tempranillo, Chivite, £3.99 (TWS/WR/BU only)
14/20

Medium-bodied 💰💰 🍷
From Navarra's largest family-owned winery, this is a modern, plummy, unoaked Tempranillo with no frills but decent flavours.

1996 Albor Rioja, £3.99   15/20
Medium-bodied 💰💰💰 🍷
A modern-style, unoaked Rioja made using the carbonic maceration technique, allowing the strawberry fruit of the Tempranillo grape to express itself.

1995 Hermanos Lurton Tempranillo, £4.59   15/20
Medium-bodied 💰💰 🍷
From flying winemaker Jacques Lurton, this is an interesting interpretation of the same grape, with sweet savoury oak and spicy fruit flavours.

1996 Valdemar Rioja Tinto, Martinez Bujanda, £4.69
(TWS/WR/BU only)   14/20
Medium-bodied 💰 🍷
Youthful, exuberantly fruity Tempranillo from the go-ahead Martinez Bujanda winery, showing a trace of the farmyard when we tasted it.

1995 Marqués de Griñon Rioja, £4.99   14/20
Medium-bodied 💰 🍷
We've had a number of faulty bottles of this wine during our tastings, which is a shame given how good it was last year. Hard to judge objectively, but untainted bottles should be a treat.

UNITED STATES

1995 Columbia Crest Côte de Columbia Grenache, £4.99   12/20
Medium-bodied 🍷
A malty, tutti-frutti Washington State blend of Grenache, Lemberger and Cabernet Sauvignon, exhibiting weird characters of ginger and bath salts. Tastes like a wine made from hybrid grapes.

£5–8

AUSTRALIA

1996 Rosemount Grenache/Shiraz, South East Australia, £6.49
(WR/BU only)   15/20
Medium-bodied 🍾 ▯
Commercial, well-made, sweetly fruity Grenache/Shiraz from Philip Shaw of
Rosemount, with notes of liquorice and cinnamon.

1994 The Franc, Cabernet Franc, Clare Valley, Tim Knappstein, £6.99 (WR/BU only)   14/20
Medium-bodied 🍾 ▯
Sagey, South Australian Cabernet Franc, which might surprise lovers of Loire
reds. Oaky and a bit obvious.

1996 Samuel's Bay Malbec, Padthaway, Adam Wynn, £7.49
(TWS/WR/BU only)   17/20
Full-bodied 🍾🍾🍾 ▯
Herby, aromatic, sagey, richly concentrated Malbec from the warm-climate
Padthaway region, with lovely smooth tannins and unoaked, chocolatey fruit.

1996 Samuel's Bay Pinot Noir, Eden Valley, Adam Wynn, £7.99
(WR/BU only)   16/20
Medium-bodied 🍾🍾 ▯
One of a number of enjoyable Samuel's Bay wines from Adam Wynn, this is a
leafy, full-flavoured Pinot Noir with some elegance and red-fruits varietal
character.

1996 Samuel's Bay Grenache, Barossa Valley, Adam Wynn, £7.99
(TWS/WR/BU only)   15/20
Full-bodied 🍾 ▯
Brown-sugar-scented, richly proportioned Grenache from Adam Wynn, with
lots of sweet, powerfully alcoholic fruit. A little overbearing at 15 per cent
alcohol, unless you're a heavy-metal freak.

1994 Leasingham Cabernet/Malbec, Clare Valley, £7.99
(WR/BU only)   15/20
Full-bodied 🍾 ▯
Splintery, over-oaked Clare Valley blend of Cabernet Sauvignon and Malbec
with a charry, chewy finish. A shame, because there's some good fruit
underneath there somewhere.

1994 St Hallett Barossa Shiraz, £7.99 (TWS/WR/BU only)   15/20
Medium-bodied 💰 🍷
Liquorice and blackberry fruity Barossa Valley Shiraz from the home of Old Block. Oaky and surprisingly light for a St Hallett wine.

CHILE

1996 Trio Merlot, £5.49 (TWS/WR/BU only)   15/20
Medium-bodied 💰💰 🍷
Made by Ignacio Recabarren, a former *Grapevine* award winery, at the Concha y Toro winery, this is a fresh, modern, lightly oaked Merlot with grassy undertones.

1995 Trio Cabernet, £5.49 (TWS/WR/BU only)   14/20
Medium-bodied 💰 🍷
From the same winery and winemaker, this is dry and a bit chunky on the palate.

1995 Valdivieso Reserve Cabernet Franc, £7.99 (WR/BU only) 15/20
Full-bodied 💰 🍷
Powerful, fleshy, densely oaked Valdivieso Cabernet Franc with plenty of blackcurrant fruit and a charry, smoky bacon note.

FRANCE

1995 Château de Violet, Minervois, £5.49 (BU/WR only)   16/20
Full-bodied 💰💰💰 ●━
Violets and bitters-scented, attractively modern Minervois blend of Syrah and Grenache. Chunky, but concentrated and extremely well made.

1995 Côtes du Rhône, Château St Estève d'Uchaux, Tradition, £5.69 (WR/BU and selected TWS only)   16/20
Medium-bodied 💰💰💰 🍷
As the name suggests, this is a traditional, gutsy Côtes du Rhône with plenty of pepper, tannin and oomph. It's worth trading up to something like this from basic Rhône reds.

1994 Château Sauvage, Premières Côtes de Bordeaux, £5.99 15/20
Medium-bodied 💰 🍷
An unoaked blend of mainly Merlot and Cabernet Sauvignon with a touch of Cabernet Franc, made in a light, fruity style underpinned by rustic tannins.

1994 Côtes du Rhône, Château du Grand Prébois, £5.99
(WR/BU and selected TWS only)   14/20
Full-bodied |
Traditional, Grenache-based Côtes du Rhône, which is a little dry and cooked
on the finish. We prefer the Château St Estève.

1995 Château Puy Bardens, Unoaked, Premières Côtes de Bordeaux, £6.29   16/20
Medium-bodied 🍷🍷 ●─
Attractive, Merlot-based Premières Côtes claret, which shows you what a
difference a decent vintage can make. Vibrantly youthful and luscious.

1994 Château Bonnet Oaked Red, £6.99   14/20
Medium-bodied |
Oaky, modern-style Bordeaux, which just about crawls out from underneath
the barrel staves. A little hollow.

1993 Château Coucheroy, Graves, £6.99   15/20
Medium-bodied 🍷🍷 |
A coffee-bean oaky Graves blend of Cabernet Sauvignon and Merlot with six
months in barrel for added complexity. The fruit is a little herbaceous and dry,
as you'd expect for a 1993.

1995 Château Suau Oaked, Premières Côtes de Bordeaux, £6.99
                                                          16/20
Medium-bodied 🍷🍷 ●─
Flavoursome Bordeaux hillside blend with plenty of oak, tannin and fruit. Needs
a year or two in bottle, but looks very promising.

1995 Château Langoiran, Cuvée Prestige, Premières Côtes de Bordeaux, £7.70   15/20
Medium-bodied 🍷 |
Robust, chewy Premières Côtes Bordeaux, which should be a little softer and
riper given the presence of 85 per cent Merlot in the blend.

ITALY

1994 Primitivo del Salento Barrique Aged, £5.99 (WR/BU only)
                                                          14/20
Full-bodied |
Baked, raisiny Primitivo from Kym Milne, working in Puglia alongside négociant,
Cantèle. Oaky, dry and rustic. One of the very few undistinguished wines we've
had from Kym Milne this year.

SOUTH AFRICA

1995 Bellingham Pinotage, Franschhoek, £5.29 (TWS/WR/BU only)
15/20

Medium-bodied 👝👝 |
Commercial, strawberry fruity Pinotage with a hint of liquorice and pleasant oak.

1996 Winelands Shiraz/Cabernet, Kym Milne, £5.99 (WR/BU only)
16/20

Full-bodied 👝👝👝 ➖
An outstanding Cape blend from Kym Milne: a rich, chocolatey spicy Shiraz/Cabernet with sweet vanilla oak and nice succulence.

1994 Villiera Merlot, Paarl, £7.79 (TWS/WR/BU only)   15/20
Medium-bodied 👝 |
Elegant, sweetly oaked Cape Merlot with enjoyable green-pepper flavours and an astringent edge.

SPAIN

1994 Conde de Valdemar Rioja Crianza, Martinez Bujanda, £5.99
16/20

Medium-bodied 👝👝👝 |
Ample, modern, American oaky blend of Tempranillo with 15 per cent of the comparatively rare Mazuelo grape. Spicy and nicely balanced.

1994 Valduera Reserva Ribera del Duero, £6.99 (BU/WR only) 16/20
Full-bodied 👝👝 ➖
From one of Spain's best red-wine regions, this is a stylish Tempranillo red, showing youthful tannins and a firm backbone of fruit and American oak.

1996 Regalia de Ansuero, Ribera del Duero, £6.99   14/20
Full-bodied ➖
Inky, faintly pongy Ribera red, which is still in short trousers. Ought to be £2 cheaper, but that's Ribera for you.

1992 Conde de Valdemar Rioja Reserva, Martinez Bujanda, £7.69
15/20

Medium-bodied 👝 |
Made from Tempranillo and a smidgen of Mazuelo, this is older than the 1994 Reserva (we're amazing mathematicians, aren't we?), but not necessarily any wiser. Traditional in flavour, with a leathery note.

1990 Marqués de Griñon Reserva, £7.99 (BU/WR only)   16/20
Medium-bodied 👜👜 ━
A smartly oaked, nicely mature Rioja Reserva, which was aged for two years in a mixture of French and American oak. Very modern, with the Tempranillo grape to the fore. Highly enjoyable.

Over £8

AUSTRALIA

1996 St Hallett Grenache, Barossa, £8.99 (TWS/WR/BU only)   14/20
Full-bodied 🍶
Pungent, minty, lavender-scented Barossa Grenache with masses of Porty alcohol and a dry, raisiny bite.

1995 Tim Adams, The Fergus, Clare Valley, £8.99 (WR/BU only)
                                                              17/20

Full-bodied 👜👜👜 ━
Made by Tim 'Bonecrusher' Adams, this brooding, brambly, sweetly oaked Clare Valley Grenache is a big, broad-shouldered, mint and blackberry fruity number with heart-warming alcohol.

1995 Chapel Hill Shiraz, McLaren Vale, £8.99 (WR/BU only)   16/20
Full-bodied 👜👜 ━
Typically impressive, concentrated McLaren Vale Shiraz from Pam Dunsford, in which the oak is subtler than it used to be and the fruit better defined.

1996 Apex Grenache/Mourvèdre/Shiraz, Barossa Valley, £9.99
(WR/BU only)   17/20
Full-bodied 👜👜👜 ━
Rich, spicy, densely textured, southern Rhône-style Aussie blend of Grenache, Mourvèdre and Shiraz, which highlights the vibrant fruit sweetness of the best Barossa reds.

1994 St Hallett Blackwell Shiraz, Barossa Valley, £9.99
(TWS/WR/BU only)   15/20
Full-bodied 👜 🍶
Named after St Hallett's winemaker, Stuart Blackwell, this is a smooth, substantially oaked Aussie Shiraz with liquorice and blackberry flavours and puckering acidity.

1993 Chapel Hill Cabernet Sauvignon, £9.99 (WR/BU only)   16/20
Medium-bodied 🍷🍷 ▮
Minty, chocolatey blend of McLaren Vale and Coonawarra Cabernets, showing green-pepper elegance and fine-grained tannins.

FRANCE

1994 St Joseph, Pierre Coursodon, £9.99 (BU/selected WR only)
16/20

Full-bodied 🍷🍷 ▬–
Chunky, robust, northern Rhône Syrah from the sprawling St Joseph appellation. Needs another year or two in bottle, but the fruit quality is already apparent.

1994 Chorey-Lès-Beaune, Domaine Tollot-Beaut, £11.49
(TWS/WR/BU only)   16/20
Medium-bodied 🍷🍷 ▮
Light, elegant, smoothly fruity, vanilla oak-influenced Pinot Noir from the reliable Tollot-Beaut stable.

1994 Châteauneuf-du-Pape, Domaine Font de Michelle, £11.99
(WR/BU and selected TWS only)   16/20
Full-bodied 🍷🍷 ▬–
From the Gonnet brothers of Châteauneuf-du-Pape, this is a sweet, heady Grenache-based red with well-integrated oak and plenty of alcohol, fruit and spice.

1993 Château Yon Figeac, Grand Cru St Emilion, £13.99   16/20
Medium-bodied 🍷🍷 ▮
From a vintage that was better on Bordeaux's Right Bank than on its Left, this Merlot-dominated St Emilion is a fleshy, oaky, textured claret with attractive vanilla and coffee-bean notes and supple fruit.

SOUTH AFRICA

1994 Hartenberg Zinfandel, Stellenbosch, £8.49 (WR only)   15/20
Full-bodied 🍷 ▬–
Juicy, plummy, well-made Stellenbosch Zin at an optimistic price, showing good concentration and lashings of sweet oak.

1995 Warwick Pinotage, Stellenbosch, £9.99 (WR/BU only)   18/20
Full-bodied 👝👝👝 ➾
From Canadian Norma Ratcliffe, this is one of South Africa's best Pinotages, showing elegant oak, fine-grained tannins, firm backbone and a core of sweet savoury fruit. Delicious.

1993 Hartenberg Pontac, Stellenbosch, £14.99 (WR only)   18/20
Full-bodied 👝👝👝 ➾
Not a car but a grape, apparently, Pontac is one of the rare grape varieties with red juice and skin. This is a superb, mulberry fruity number with beautifully integrated sweet oak. An off-the-wall stunner.

SPAIN

1995 Marqués de Griñon Valdepusa Syrah, Vino de Mesa Toledo, £8.99 (BU only)   16/20
Medium-bodied 👝👝 ➾
A little less polished than last year's spectacular effort, but this is still a brooding, chocolatey red with good richness and depth.

1994 Pago de Carraovejas, Ribera del Duero, £9.99 (BU/WR only)
17/20
Medium-bodied 👝👝👝 ➾
A blend of 75 per cent Tempranillo with 25 per cent Cabernet Sauvignon, this shows you what Ribera del Duero is capable of at its best. A concentrated, chocolatey blend with lots of fruit texture and balancing acidity complemented by oak.

1989 Martinez Bujanda Reserva, £12.99 (BU only)   16/20
Medium-bodied 👝👝 ▮
Browning, coconutty Reserva Rioja from Martinez Bujanda, which is still hanging on in there, with leathery maturity and sweet fruit. One for traditionalists.

Rosé

£3–5

FRANCE

1996 La Liaison Rosé, Cabernet Sauvignon, Domaines Virginie, £3.99 (TWS/WR/BU only) 13/20
Off-dry 🅑 ▮
Sweetish, simple, redcurranty rosé from Domaines Virginie, with prominent acidity. Pretty basic.

Sparkling

Over £8

AUSTRALIA

1994 Green Point, £11.49 (TWS/WR/BU only) 17/20
Dry 🅑🅑🅑 ▮
With a little more Pinot Noir than in previous releases, this Yarra Valley fizz from Moët & Chandon's Australian outpost is a mature, classy, strawberry fruit sparkler with beguiling elegance and depth.

1994 Croser Brut, £11.99 (WR/BU only) 17/20
Dry 🅑🅑🅑 ▮
From Brian Croser, one of Australia's most gifted winemakers, this is a distinctively savoury, malty Piccadilly Valley fizz with 90 per cent Pinot Noir and considerable finesse.

1993 Green Point Rosé, £12.99 (WR/BU only) 17/20
Dry 🅑🅑🅑 ▮
A Pinot Noir-dominated, bronze-pink rosé from sparkling-wine wizard, Dr Tony Jordan. Stylish, aromatic and packed with red-fruit fragrance and flavour.

FRANCE

Montoy NV, Boisel, £11.99   15/20
Dry 🍾 ▮

Youthful, basic, big-bubbled Champagne, which lacks a bit of finesse. At this price, the New World has more to offer.

Jean de Praisac NV, F. Bonnet, £12.99   16/20
Dry 🍾🍾 ▮

A step up in quality and fruit intensity, this is a fresh, flavoursome, well-made fizz with some attractive, strawberryish Pinot Noir character and some bottle development.

Grand Cru Bouzy, J.L. Malard NV, £16.99 (BU only)   17/20
Dry 🍾🍾🍾 ▮

Super aromatic, milk-chocolate characters with a creamy mousse and lots of Pinot Noir-derived intensity from one of the best villages in Champagne.

Grand Cru Ambonnay, J.L. Malard NV, £16.99 (BU only)   15/20
Dry 🍾 ▮

A lighter, nuttier, Chardonnay-dominated style of Champagne, with bigger, coarser bubbles and an appley edge. Booze the Bouzy instead.

Ruinart NV, £19.99 (BU/WR only)   15/20
Dry ▮

By the standard of recent releases, this is a youthful and distinctly underwhelming fizz at an overwhelming price.

1990 Ruinart, £25.99 (BU/WR only)   15/20
Dry ▮

Toasty, faintly bitter vintage Champagne, which should be better given the reputation of the house and the year.

NEW ZEALAND

Lindauer Special Reserve, £8.99 (TWS/WR/BU only)   16/20
Dry 🍾🍾🍾 ▮

From New Zealand's biggest winery and fizz specialist, Montana, this is a malty Pinot Noir/Chardonnay blend with a soft cushion of bubbles and rich fruit flavours. One of the best-value New Zealand sparklers on the market.

UNITED STATES

Mumm Cuvée Napa Blanc de Blancs, £11.99 (TWS/WR/BU only)

15/20

Off-dry 🍷 ▮

A special cuvée from the Seagram-owned Mumm winery in the Napa Valley. Fresh, sherbety, tangy Chardonnay with a sweetish finish.

Unwins ☆☆☆

Address: Birchwood House, Victoria Road, Dartford, Kent DA1 5AJ

Telephone/fax: 01322 272711; 01322 294469

Number of branches: 385

Opening hours: 9.00am to 10.00pm Monday to Saturday; 12.00pm to 3.00pm and 7.00pm to 10.00pm Sunday

Credit cards accepted: Access, American Express, Delta, Diners, MasterCard, Switch, Transax, Visa

Discounts: 5 per cent off 6 bottles of table and sparkling wines (may be mixed); 10 per cent off 12 bottles of table and sparkling wines (may be mixed); 12.5 per cent off 12 bottles of Champagne; 12.5 per cent off all other orders over £200

Facilities and services: Free glass loan; in-store tastings; mail order; gift vouchers; monthly accounts; home delivery (most branches)

Special offers: See discounts

Top ten best-selling wines (by volume): Encanto Red; Encanto Dry White; Liebfraumilch; Hock; Jacob's Creek Semillon/Chardonnay; Lambrusco Bianco; Frascati Superiore; French Country White; Vin de Pays des Côtes de Gascogne Rouge; French Country Red

Range:

GOOD: Red Bordeaux, New Zealand, Australia, Vintage Port

AVERAGE: White Bordeaux, Burgundy, Loire, Rhône, Beaujolais, regional France, Alsace, Italy, Spain, Portugal, Austria, Bulgaria, United States, Chile, South Africa, Champagne and sparkling wines

POOR: Germany, Hungary

UNDER-REPRESENTED: Argentina, southern Italy

Something is stirring at Unwins. What was once a dozy suburban chain with a long history but not much in the way of a future has woken up. At a time of closures, shaky bottom lines and long faces in the traditional off-licence sector, Unwins continues to expand and, apparently, prosper.

Unwins

Last year we reported that Unwins had taken on ten new shops from the Cooks chain and opened stores in Calne and Petersfield. This year the boys in Dartford have gone into overdrive, acquiring Davisons' 72 stores in the South-East for an undisclosed (to us, anyway) sum. This was the single biggest transaction in the company's 154-year history.

It made a lot of sense. The two companies are both family-owned and have worked together for 20 years through a buying consortium, known, for some reason, as Leonard Tong. They also sell to similar customers in the leafier fringes of the capital. 'We made a decision within ten days,' according to retail director Philip Wetz, the grandson of Unwins' founder. 'Davisons dove-tailed into our business. There wasn't a single Davisons shop which was in direct competition with an Unwins.'

Davisons kept most of its fine wines (and has since set up a new mail-order operation), but otherwise any residual stock was included in the deal. Most of the staff moved across and the Davisons façades were all converted by July. No bad thing, this. Davisons' dung-brown, mock Tudor-style frontages badly needed a new look.

The new owners are already seeing positive results. 'A lot of the shops have already doubled their turnover,' says buyer and part-time star of the Jazz FM wine slot, Bill Rolfe. 'We've got a different range of wines and beers, longer opening hours and better supply. The managers are getting what they want to sell.'

Unwins now runs to 385 shops, making it the fourth-largest off-licence chain in the country behind the Thresher Group, Victoria Wine and Greenalls Cellars. Unlike much of its high-street competition, however, it is still independent and still, for better or worse, in family hands. As Wetz puts it, 'We're proud of this company and we want it to continue. People enjoy working for us.'

This is true enough. Unwins' shop managers are a self-evidently loyal lot. They are also pretty motivated. The company runs a series of in-house training courses under the auspices of the Wine & Spirit Education Trust, and staff are happy to jump through the various hoops en route to the Master of Wine qualification.

In the past such expertise was wasted on the lacklustre Unwins' wine range – a mixture of the convenient, the uninspired and the traditional – but things have improved dramatically of late. Unwins has added 150 new wines in the last 12 months, bringing the total to more than 700. The emphasis has been on Australia, Chile, Portugal and New Zealand, yielding some good new wines from the likes of Sandalford, Domaine Oriental, Palha-Canas and Villa Maria. Bill Rolfe acknowledges that the South African range needs a face-lift, but is otherwise pleased with the nips and tucks of recent years.

The buying department has also been restructured. Whereas, not so long ago, all of the wines appeared to be sourced by Gerald Duff, now Unwins has no fewer than six different buyers: Bill Rolfe, Richard Vaughan, Ian Dobson, Jim Wilson, Bob Maybank and Duff himself. We may bemoan the fact that these appointments have been made from within (the company still needs a few fresh ideas), but at least Unwins is trying to come to terms with the variety and complications of the modern wine world. One buyer would have trouble keeping up with what is going on in France, let alone the rest of the world these days.

Unwins is not yet in a position to compete with the likes of Oddbins, Bottoms Up and Fuller's, but its wine range is definitely improving. Prices have come down, even if they remain high on some lines, and Unwins is a lot more competitive than it was. There is also marginally less reliance on one-stop shopping, where Unwins takes a whole raft of wines from single producers – Yvon Mau in Bordeaux, Southcorp in Australia, Loron in Beaujolais, Bichot in Burgundy and the KWV in South Africa, to name but five examples – even if we would still like to see more diversity in the range.

The wine list looks brighter and more interesting than it did, too. There are no full-page adverts for suppliers and the wines are a lot easier to understand. There are occasional mistakes – the Roussillon is subsumed by the 'Vin de Pays d'Oc' region, not separated from it – but there are enough signs of a modern and more commercial approach to convince us that Unwins is finally on the move.

Apart from the acquisition of Davisons, the opening of a new, enlarged Unwins superstore in Sawbridgeworth, Hertfordshire, offering enticing case-purchase discounts and in-store tastings for customers, is further proof of a change in outlook. The Wetz family appears to have decided to invest in the business rather than bank the dividends. It is no longer illogical for Philip Wetz to talk of 'keeping our staff and our shareholders happy'.

Unwins isn't exactly flourishing, but it is 'out-performing a negative trend in the high street', according to Jim Wilson. 'The multiple specialists are down 5 per cent and we're down 0.25 per cent on still wines.' The important thing to remember is that wine accounts for less than one-third of their business and that other items, such as soft drinks, snacks, spirits and confectionery, have more than made up for the vinous shortfall. Overall, turnover rose by 9 per cent last year.

Unwins doesn't lack self-confidence at the moment. 'We're very strong in ourselves,' says Philip Wetz. 'We'll still be going strong in another ten years.' Does this mean more acquisitions? Victoria Wine, for example? 'No,' he told us with a smile. 'Not before Christmas anyway.' If it does happen in due course (and it's not beyond the realms of imagination) we're not sure that we, or Unwins' staff, could cope with the excitement.

White

Under £3

GERMANY

1996 Hock, Müller, £2.99   13/20
Medium sweet 🍶🍶 🍷
Clean, floral, grapey German cheapie for the sweet of tooth.

1995 Liebfraumilch, Müller, £2.99   12/20
Medium sweet 🍶 🍷
Hard and rather angular Lieb with a tart finish. Buy the Hock instead, if you like this kind of thing.

ITALY

Lambrusco Bianco, 4 per cent, £1.99   12/20
Sweet 🍶 🍷
Basic, fizzy, lemonade-like Italian quaffer with low alcohol and not enough flavour.

SPAIN

La Mancha White, £2.99   13/20
Dry 🍶🍶 🍷
Made exclusively from Spain's ubiquitous Airén grape variety, this is a decent party white with pear-and-apple fruitiness.

£3–5

AUSTRALIA

1996 Jacob's Creek Semillon/Chardonnay, £4.59   14/20
Off-dry 🍶 🍷
Fresh, lemon-curd-like Aussie blend with a consciously refreshing tang and a zesty finish. A little over-priced.

Stockman's Bridge Semillon/Chardonnay, £4.99   14/20
Dry 🝰 ▌
Well-made, tropical fruity white from Australia's biggest wine producer, Southcorp, showing a pleasant brushstroke of oak character.

FRANCE

French Country White, Vin de Pays de l'Hérault, £2.99   12/20
Dry 🝰 ▌
Basic, southern French plonk with not much going for it – apart from its price tag.

1996 Bergerac, Comtesse Catherine, Yvon Mau, £3.49   13/20
Dry 🝰 ▌
A blend of Sauvignon Blanc and Semillon with a dash of Muscadelle, produced in a fresh, modern style by Bordeaux's Yvon Mau. The result is clean, if a little characterless. We're not sure who Comtesse Catherine is, or was. Answers on a carte postale...

1996 Muscadet de Sèvre et Maine Sur Lie, Domaine du Plessis-Glain, £4.99   15/20
Bone dry 🝰🝰 ▌
One of several good Muscadets we have had this year, thanks to the quality of the 1996 vintage in the Loire, this is a weighty, well-made white, which spends a while on the grape lees to give it a classically tangy, bone-dry finish.

GERMANY

1995 Johannisberger Erntebringer Riesling Kabinett, Müller, £4.99
15/20
Medium dry 🝰🝰 ▌
Aromatic, peachy Mosel Riesling at a good price. A crisp, light summer thirst-quencher.

1995 Niersteiner Spiegelberg Riesling Spätlese, Müller, £4.99
15/20
Medium sweet 🝰🝰 ▬
Concentrated, fruity Riesling with more weight than the Johannisberger Erntebringer and a touch more sweetness. Impressive value for money.

HUNGARY

1996 Volcanic Hills, Leányka, Neszmely, £3.49   15/20
Dry 🍾🍾🍾 ▮
Your chance to try a wine made entirely from Leányka, the so-called 'little girl's grape' of Hungary. It's a lemon-zesty, perfumed white with crisp acidity and plenty of character. One for Humbert Humbert and Lolita?

1996 Volcanic Hills Sauvignon Blanc, Neszmely, £3.99   15/20
Dry 🍾🍾🍾 ▮
From the same go-ahead co-operative, this is a wine that ought to scare the socks and boots off producers in the Loire and New Zealand. Dry, crisp, grassy Sauvignon Blanc with a tapering finish.

ITALY

1995 Frascati Superiore, Tullio, San Marco, £4.49   14/20
Dry 🍾🍾 ▮
Good, typical Frascati with crisp acidity and a nutty note, made mainly from the Trebbiano grape with a drop of Malvasia di Candia.

1996 Verdicchio dei Castelli di Jesi Classico, Monte Schiavo, £4.49
13/20
Dry ▮
Bitter, apple-core-like central Italian white made from the Verdicchio grape. Not the best example of the style.

PORTUGAL

1996 Palha-Canas, Vinho Regional Estremadura, £4.99   16/20
Bone dry 🍾🍾🍾 ▮
A modern, highly unusual Portuguese white from the Atlantic coast, made from the local Arinto, Fernão Pires and Vital grapes, blended with a dash of Chardonnay. Weighty and fresh with a spritzy undertone. Great with grilled fish.

ROMANIA

1995 Idlerock Oaked Chardonnay, Murfatlur Region, £3.59   13/20
Dry 🍾 ▮
An oaky, Australian-influenced Chardonnay from Romania's Murfatlur region. A welcome attempt to bring Romanian winemaking into the twentieth century – while there's still time.

UNITED STATES

1995 Fetzer Echo Ridge Fumé Blanc, Mendocino, £4.99 13/20
Dry
What is it about Californian Sauvignon Blanc? West Coast winemakers seem to be frightened of the grape's intrinsic personality. The result is a drinkable, if rather bland, white, which might as well be made from Ugni Blanc.

£5–8

AUSTRALIA

1996 Ironstone Semillon/Chardonnay, £5.99 16/20
Dry
From the consistently excellent Cape Mentelle winery in Western Australia, this is a highly drinkable blend in which the herbal, grapefruity characters of the Semillon are nicely rounded out by 25 per cent Chardonnay.

CHILE

1995 Undurraga Chardonnay Reserve, £6.99 16/20
Dry
A charry, French oak-fermented Chilean white from the vastly improved Undurraga winery, showing good weight and flavour and an elegant dry finish.

FRANCE

1994 Domaine du Tariquet, Cuvée Bois, Vin de Pays des Côtes de Gascogne, £5.99 15/20
Dry
Honeyed, super-ripe Gascon white from Yves Grassa, with an overlay of splintery oak and fresh acidity. Pricey for a Gascon white.

1996 Chablis, Olivier Tricon, £6.99 15/20
Bone dry
Classic, steely Chablis with the freshness of youth unhindered by oak. Finishes a little tart.

1995 Côtes du Rhône, Guigal, £6.99   16/20
Dry 👜👜 ▮

From one of the Rhône Valley's star names, this is a soft, weighty and pleasantly characterful French white with rich, mealy fruit flavours and excellent balance.

1995 Tokay Pinot Gris, Kuentz-Bas, £7.99   10/20
Dry ▮

A wine that smells of mushroom soup. Mmm...

ITALY

1996 Frascati Superiore, Selezione San Marco, £5.99   16/20
Dry 👜👜👜 ▮

Stylishly packaged Frascati with 40 per cent of the superior Malvasia di Candia grape adding extra concentration and peachy richness. A really enjoyable Roman white.

1996 Gavi, Antario, £5.99   15/20
Dry 👜 ▮

A fresh, light-fingered Piedmontese white made solely from the local Cortese grape. Pleasant, if a little insubstantial, especially given the heavy-duty designer bottle.

NEW ZEALAND

1996 Villa Maria Private Bin, Sauvignon Blanc, £6.49   15/20
Dry 👜👜 ▮

Villa Maria's bottom-of-the-range Sauvignon Blanc is still one of the best-value whites in New Zealand. A thoroughly modern, grapefruit and gooseberry-like Marlborough white with plenty of flavour and oomph.

1995 Highfield Chardonnay, Marlborough, £7.49   14/20
Dry ▮

A buttery-textured Marlborough Chardonnay, which almost defies the vagaries of the 1995 vintage. The coolness and wetness of the year poke through on the finish.

PORTUGAL

**1995 Chardonnay Casa Santos Lima, Vinho Regional
Estremadura, £5.99**   13/20
Dry |
A rather pointless wine, given the array of local Portuguese grapes on offer.
Appley and faintly bitter.

SOUTH AFRICA

1996 Boschendal Sauvignon Blanc, £6.49   15/20
Dry 👜👜 |
Shy on the nose, but more interesting on the palate, with crisp, refreshing
acidity and a minerally, almost Sancerre-like edge.

UNITED STATES

1995 Golden State Vintners Reserve Chardonnay, £5.99 15/20
Off-dry 👜👜 |
Ripe, sweetish Central Valley Chardonnay with toasty oak and butterscotch
and caramel-fudge flavours. A little coarse.

Over £8

AUSTRALIA

1995 Sandalford Chardonnay, £9.99   17/20
Dry 👜👜👜 ▬–
Produced by one of Western Australia's largest wineries, from grapes grown in
Mount Barker, Margaret River and Pemberton, this is a rich, mealy, well-crafted
Chardonnay in a Burgundian mould. Beautifully balanced.

FRANCE

1994 Vouvray, Marc Brédif, £8.99   16/20
Off-dry 👜👜 ▬–
Classic, characterful Loire Chenin Blanc from one of Vouvray's best producers.
Lightly honeyed, appley stuff underpinned by elegant acidity.

1995 Sancerre, Les Roches, Vacheron, £9.49   16/20
Bone dry 👜👜 ▬
From one of the most consistent producers in the appellation, this is a well-made, minerally Sancerre with good length and concentration. Should continue to improve.

1994 Montagny Premier Cru, Les Bonnevaux, Arnoux Père et Fils, £10.69   14/20
Dry ▮
Oaky, faintly austere Côte Chalonnaise Chardonnay. Pricey, given the quality and origin of the wine.

1995 Riesling Grand Cru Pfersigberg, Kuentz-Bas, £12.15   17/20
Dry 👜👜👜 ▬
Intense, petrolly Alsace Riesling from one of the region's élite vineyard sites, or Grands Crus. A wine to tuck away under the stairs for two to three years or to enjoy now.

1995 Bonnezeaux, Château Perray-Jouannet, £14.99   17/20
Sweet 👜👜👜 ▬
Sweet, tangerine and vanilla-like Chenin Blanc from an excellent Loire Valley vintage. A pure, finely balanced sticky.

GERMANY

1995 Bernkasteler Doktor Riesling Kabinett, Dr H. Thanisch Müller-Burggraef, £15.99   18/20
Medium dry 👜👜👜 ▬
Super-concentrated Mosel Riesling from the legendary Doktor vineyard overlooking Bernkastel. Peachy, rich and finely balanced, with a clean, tantalising spritz.

NEW ZEALAND

1996 Coopers Creek Oak Aged Semillon, £8.79   13/20
Dry ▮
Overtly herbaceous Semillon with lean, green flavours and a veneer of oak. Disappointing for a winery of Coopers Creek's class.

1996 Villa Maria Reserve Sauvignon Blanc, Wairau Valley, £9.49
17/20

Dry 🍷🍷🍷 ⏐

Pungent, beautifully aromatic Sauvignon Blanc made, surprisingly, from young vines in the Wairau Valley. Low yields have produced a wine with remarkable concentration and a citrus-fruit saladbowl of flavours.

SOUTH AFRICA

1995 Boschendal Chardonnay Reserve, £8.99   16/20
Dry 🍷🍷 ⏐

On the light side for a Reserve Chardonnay, but this is still a well-made, lemony, mostly barrel-fermented white with good length on the palate.

Red

Under £3

SPAIN

La Mancha Red, £2.29   13/20
Light-bodied 🍷🍷 ⏐

A soft, raspberry fruity Spanish blend of Monastrel, Carignan and Tempranillo. A decent quaffing tinto.

£3–5

AUSTRALIA

Stockman's Bridge Shiraz/Cabernet, £4.99   14/20
Medium-bodied 🍷 ⏐

A minty, faintly medicinal Aussie blend with soft, juicy fruity flavours. A bit pricey, given what you can find under £5 in Chile and the Languedoc-Roussillon.

393

AUSTRIA

1996 Blauer Zweigelt, Weinviertel, Winzerhaus, £3.99　　14/20
Light-bodied 👜👜 ▮
Made at one of Austria's best co-operatives, this is a peppery, cherryish red with soft tannins produced from the unusual Blauer Zweigelt grape.

BULGARIA

1991 Mavrud Reserve Assenovgrad, Domaine Boyar, £3.49　12/20
Medium-bodied ▮
Rooty, old-fashioned Bulgarian red. Best left under somebody else's bed.

CHILE

1996 Domaine Oriental Merlot, Maule Valley, £4.49　　15/20
Medium-bodied 👜👜 ▮
Decent, deeply coloured Merlot made at the Domaine Oriental winery in Talca. Soft, juicy and full of blackcurrant fruit.

FRANCE

1995 Bergerac, Comtesse Catherine, £3.69　　14/20
Medium-bodied 👜👜 ▮
Green-pepper-scented south-west French red. A cross between a claret and a Bourgueil at an affordable price.

1995 Costières de Nîmes, Les Caves des Apôtres, £3.99　　12/20
Full-bodied ▮
A chunky, Grenache-based Provençal rouge, which pulls up some way from the finishing line.

Vin de Pays des Côtes de Gascogne, Michel de l'Enclos, £3.99
　　12/20
Medium-bodied ▮
Basic, chewy red with rasping acidity from Armagnac country.

1994 Fitou, Les Producteurs du Mont Tauch, £3.99　　14/20
Full-bodied 👜👜 ▮
From the model Fitou co-operative in the Languedoc hills, this is a spicy, well-made blend of Carignan and Grenache with plenty of flavour at under £4.

French Country Wine, Vin de Pays du Gard, £3.99, 1 litre   12/20
Medium-bodied

Sweetish southern French plonk. Not much better than Piat d'Or, but at least it's cheaper.

1995 Château du Pin, St Martial, Borie-Manoux, £4.99   12/20
Medium-bodied

A fruitless, underwhelming claret from négociants Borie-Manoux. Dry and unexciting.

1995 Cuvée Simone, James Herrick, Vin de Pays d'Oc, £4.99 15/20
Medium-bodied

A Syrah-dominated red from Englishman James Herrick's Languedoc estate and named after his wife, Simone (as opposed to Cuvée, the winery dog). Not as thrilling as the first release in 1995, but still a good, peppery, blackberry-fruity quaffer.

1995 Vacqueyras, Domaine de la Soleïade, £4.99   14/20
Full-bodied

Traditional, Grenache-based southern Rhône red, which starts well but finishes a tad dry and mouth-puckering.

HUNGARY

1996 Volcanic Hills Cabernet Franc, £3.99   13/20
Light-bodied

A blend of 90 per cent Cabernet Franc and Cabernet Sauvignon from Hungary's warm (well, warmish) south, this is a light, herbaceous red for summer glugging.

ITALY

1994 Canaletto Veduta, Casa Girelli, £3.49   13/20
Medium-bodied

The name and the picture of Venice might indicate otherwise, but this soft, raspberry sweet Puglian plonk wouldn't make the National Gallery.

MEXICO

1994 Petite Sirah, L.A. Cetto, £4.89   15/20
Full-bodied 🍷🍷 |
Rich, mature, tobacco-ish red from northern Mexico, which needs a slab of red meat in order to show at its best.

PORTUGAL

1995 Portada, Vinho Regional Estremadura, £3.99   15/20
Medium-bodied 🍷🍷🍷 |
Modern, barrique-matured Portuguese red with elegant berry fruit flavours and a spicy, wild-strawberry sweetness. Amazing value.

UNITED STATES

1995 Pepperwood Grove Zinfandel, Sonoma Valley, £4.99   15/20
Medium-bodied 🍷🍷 |
Soft, juicy, cedarwood (rather than pepperwood)-scented Californian Zinfandel made in a supple, highly commercial style.

£5–8

AUSTRALIA

1995 Ironstone Cabernet/Shiraz, £5.99   15/20
Medium-bodied 🍷🍷 ▬
Flavoursome, minty red made at Western Australia's Cape Mentelle winery, showing sweet American oak flavours and punchy tannins.

1995 Caversham Cabernet/Shiraz, Sandalford, £7.49   14/20
Full-bodied |
Made by the winningly named Bill Crapsley at the Sandalford winery, this is too coarse and dry for its own good.

1994 Maglieri Shiraz, McLaren Vale, £7.99   16/20
Full-bodied 🍷🍷🍷 |
Classic McLaren Vale Shiraz with oodles of sweet spice and peppery, berry fruitiness topped with smoky vanilla oak and luscious tannins.

FRANCE

1996 Chinon, Les Gravières, Couly-Dutheil, £5.95   16/20
Medium-bodied 🍾🍾🍾 ▬
Fresh, lead-pencil-scented Loire red from one of the region's leading producers, showing excellent concentration and green-pepper intensity. Still in short trousers.

1990 Cahors, Château Cayrou-Monpezat, Comte de Monpezat, £5.99   15/20
Full-bodied 🍾🍾 ▮
Mature, tarry Cahors red in which the firm, tannic character of the Malbec grape shines through. Needs food.

1993 Château La Croix du Breuil, Médoc, Roger Jean, £6.49   13/20
Medium-bodied ▮
From an average Bordeaux vintage, this Cabernet Sauvignon-dominated blend is rather short on fruit and accessibility.

1994 Bourgogne Pinot Noir, Château de Dracy, Baron de Charette, £6.49   14/20
Medium-bodied 🍾 ▮
Rustic, chewy Bourgogne rouge with some genuine strawberryish Pinot Noir character. A bit cooked.

1994 Côtes du Rhône, Guigal, £6.99   15/20
Full-bodied 🍾 ▮
Attractive, Grenache-based quaffer from flat-cap-sporting Marcel Guigal. Not the bargain it used to be when it was under £5.

1990 Château d'Arsac, Haut-Médoc, £7.99   16/20
Medium-bodied 🍾🍾🍾 ▮
Mature liquoricey claret from one of the finest post-war vintages. Perfect for drinking now, with a beautifully succulent middle palate.

ITALY

1995 Chianti Classico, Casina del Giglio, Baroncini, £5.99   15/20
Medium-bodied 🍾🍾 ▮
Cherry-spicy Chianti Classico with pleasantly quaffable fruit and refreshing acidity.

NEW ZEALAND

1994 Kemblefield Merlot, Hawkes Bay, £6.99   14/20
Medium-bodied ▮
Weedy, tomato-skin-like red from New Zealand's North Island. Rather spineless.

PORTUGAL

1996 Palha-Canas, Vinho Regional Estremadura, £5.49   15/20
Medium-bodied 🥤🥤 ▬
An interesting blend of local Portuguese varieties, in which the plummy fruit is slightly overshadowed by sweet oak. Needs time to settle.

SOUTH AFRICA

1996 Diemersdal Cabernet Sauvignon, £5.99   13/20
Medium-bodied ▮
A soft, faintly vinegary Cape Cabernet, which is unlikely to improve.

SPAIN

1993 Gran Sangre de Toro Reserva, Torres, £5.99   13/20
Medium-bodied ▮
Stewed, old-fashioned Spanish tinto from the under-achieving Penedès-based house of Torres. Time for a rethink.

UNITED STATES

1994 Fetzer Eagle Peak Merlot, Mendocino, £6.99   14/20
Full-bodied ▮
Charry, sweet oak is the dominant flavour on this Mendocino County Merlot from organic lifestyle specialists, Fetzer. Barely sustainable at £6.99.

Over £8

AUSTRALIA

1995 Sandalford Shiraz, £9.99   17/20
Full-bodied 🍷🍷🍷 ▬
Peppery, cool-climate (for Down Under) Shiraz, with lashings of oak balanced
by ripe, blackberry-fruit sweetness. Super stuff from Western Australia.

FRANCE

1996 Fleurie, Domaine des Carrières, £8.49   15/20
Medium-bodied 🍷 🍶
Like most Fleurie, this is somewhat over-priced, but it's got enough juicy Gamay
fruit concentration to remind us how genuine cru Beaujolais is supposed to
taste.

1990 Château La Tour de By, Médoc, £9.79   15/20
Medium-bodied 🍷 🍶
Mature, chocolatey claret, which is drying a little on the finish.

1981 Mazoyères-Chambertin, Grand Cru, Camus Père et Fils, £19.50   13/20
Medium-bodied 🍶
Soupy, old-style, tomatoey Burgundy for fogeyish Spectator readers and
Auberon Waugh. Not our kind of wine.

1990 Mazoyères-Chambertin, Grand Cru, Camus Père et Fils, £19.50   11/20
Medium-bodied 🍶
Browning, shagged-out Chambertin with no trace of the concentration and
quality we associate with the 1990 vintage. A disgrace at nearly £20 a bottle.

1989 Chambolle-Musigny, Premier Cru, Les Baudes, Domaine de la Tassée, £21.50   15/20
Medium-bodied 🍷 🍶
Much better, if still some way short of premier cru class. Leafy, ripe and decently
made.

ITALY

1992 Amarone Recioto della Valpolicella Classico, Rocca Sveva, £9.99   16/20
Full-bodied 🍾🍾 ▮
Classic, powerful, plum and damson-skin aromas and rich, dry, concentrated fruit flavours make this an enjoyable example of a classic Veneto style.

SPAIN

1983 Castillo Fuenmayor, Rioja, Gran Reserva, Bodegas AGE, £8.49   15/20
Medium-bodied 🍾 ▮
Mature, if drying, Gran Reserva from the enormous AGE operation. Ageing gracefully, as it were.

Sparkling

£5–8

AUSTRALIA

Seaview Rosé Brut, £6.49   15/20
Off-dry 🍾🍾🍾 ▮
Gluggable, strawberry-scented fizz from Australia's biggest and best sparkling-wine producer. Enjoyable party bubbly.

Over £8

FRANCE

Nicolas Feuillatte, Brut Premier Cru, £15.99   14/20
Dry 🍾 ▮
Young, appley, Chouilly co-operative-sourced fizz, which needs time to settle down and develop in bottle.

Fortified

£5–8

SOUTH AFRICA

1979 White Jerepigo, Cavendish Cape, £6.99   16/20
Very sweet 👜👜👜 ▬▬
A wine that never seems to grow old, this is like a cross between a Madeira and an Oloroso Sherry, with overtones of coffee, almond and caramel. A bargain.

Over £8

Madeira, 10 Year Old Malmsey, Henriques & Henriques, £14.99
16/20
Sweet 👜👜 ▬▬
Burnt-toffee and crème brûlée characters and a dry, lingering aftertaste make this an excellent introduction to traditional Madeira.

Victoria Wine Company

Including:

Victoria Wine Cellars ☆☆☆☆
Victoria Wine (destination wine shops) ☆☆☆
Victoria Wine (neighbourhood drinks stores) ☆☆
Haddows ☆☆

Head-office address: Duke's Court, Duke Street, Woking, Surrey GU21 5XL

Tel/fax: 01483 715066; 01483 755234

Number of branches: 1,540 shops, as follows: Victoria Wine Cellars: 68 (100 by the end of 1997) plus Cité de l'Europe, Calais; Victoria Wine (destination wine shops): 823; Victoria Wine (neighbourhood drinks stores): 461; Haddows (Scotland): 184; Firkin off-licences (Islington, Canterbury, Harborne-Birmingham, Sheffield and Cheltenham); plus three joint-venture shops in the Czech Republic

Opening hours: Varies according to location, but generally 10.00am to 10.00pm seven days a week

Credit cards accepted: Access, American Express, Visa

Discounts: 5 per cent off up to six wines, 10 per cent off more than six; seven bottles for the price of six on sparkling wines over £5.99; 10 per cent off a case of beer; bulk discounts/case discounts

Facilities and services: Post Haste, a nationwide drinks gift delivery service; gift vouchers and incentive vouchers; full exchange guarantee: Victoria Wine will exchange any product or offer a full refund if a customer is not satisfied with the quality of any item purchased; glass loan; delivery service; sale or return; corporate accounts/charge account service; VWC has a Chilla machine (which chills a bottle of wine in 4 minutes); Cellar Special Reserve Club: customers receive a copy of Cellar notes and invitations to exclusive tastings; Cellars Direct, a prototype mail-order service

Special offers: Monthly programme of promotional offers; two bottles for £5 and three for £10

Top ten best-selling wines (by volume): Pavlikeni Cabernet Sauvignon/Merlot; Bordeaux Blanc; Gallo White Grenache; Victoria Wine Liebfraumilch; Hardy's Stamps of Australia Cabernet Sauvignon; Liubimetz Bulgarian Merlot; Marquis de la Tour Brut; Sansovino Lambrusco Bianco; Clearsprings Cape Red; Ed's Red, La Mancha

Range:

GOOD: Regional France, Bordeaux, Chile, Australia, New Zealand, South Africa, sparkling wine, Sherry and Port

AVERAGE: Burgundy, Rhône, Beaujolais, Loire, Alsace, Germany, Portugal, Spain, Italy, England, Eastern Europe, Argentina, United States, Champagne

POOR: None

UNDER-REPRESENTED: None

The skies over California's Collins Ranch, Mohr-Fry Ranch and Lee Jones Ranch are clear and blue. What look like someone's holiday snaps turn out, on closer inspection, to be tasteful photos of rotary fermenters, machine harvesters, barrels and tanks, all adorning the Victoria Wine tasting room. The arsenal of winemaking ephemera are technical manager Hugh Suter's souvenirs of his various winemaking escapades. He has also made wine at the Domaine de la Roulerie in Muscadet country in the Loire.

Having been given carte blanche by his bosses to make a ten-gallon hatful of wines, the tall, self-effacing Suter seemed to be enjoying his reincarnation as Vicky Wine's very own flying winemaker. Deservedly, the Mohr-Fry Sauvignon Blanc has done well, the Lee Jones Ranch Zinfandel is a tasty number and the Muscadet, partially fermented in oak, a triumph. Victoria Wine never made quite enough of their modest Master of Wine. And now it's too late, as Suter has left to join Bibendum.

California – partly no doubt due to the Suter effect – has put on weight at Victoria Wine by a seismic 40 per cent to reach the same level as Bulgaria, both now hovering at 7 per cent of sales. The New World has made the biggest quantum leap, however, and while it hasn't yet engulfed Western Europe, it now comprises over one-third of wine sales. With no fewer than 75 wines to choose from, it's not surprising that Australia remains top of the New World pops at Victoria Wine. But the times, as Mr Dylan once put it, are a-changing. Oz is beginning to stagnate because 'the cheap stuff is pretty ropey', says senior buyer Thomas Woolrych, another late summer departure, this time to Bordeaux Direct.

The effect of Australia losing its competitive edge in the £3–£5 price bracket has brought in South Africa and South America. South Africa, with 42 wines in the list, now accounts for a useful 7.5 per cent of wine sales. The most successful area for Victoria Wine over the past year, though, has been South America, and in particular Chile. 'It's incredible,' says Woolrych breathlessly. South America still only represents 3–4 per cent of sales but is growing like cacti in the Atacama Desert, with quality and value from Carmen, Cono Sur, Canepa, Errázuriz, Valdivieso and Concha y Toro.

In Western Europe, France remains Victoria Wine's biggest-selling country, although, at less than one in four bottles sold, its share is still smaller than at most retailers. Burgundy and Bordeaux are increasing at the top end, but represent a very small section of sales, says Woolrych. France is clinging on largely due to the value for money of vins de pays from the south of France, which now account for three in five French wines sold. Italy is up by 27 per cent to 12 per cent of sales, Spain is steady at 10 per cent, while Germany is down to just over 8 per cent, but still outperforming the market at Victoria Wine. It's mainly down to that, er, yummy Lieb, although – more encouragingly – the new-wave dry white, Slate Valley, is slipping down nicely.

In line with the general attrition rate in the high street, Victoria Wine opened 30 shops and closed 40 during the past year, but it remains the biggest high-street chain, numerically just ahead of Thresher. Many of Vicky Wine's more traditional, beer-and-fag-centred off-licences are affectionately known as 'war-zone' shops and sometimes it must seem to Woking HQ as though the whole chain is under siege. They may not yet have gone the way of the butcher, the baker and the candlestick maker, but though wine and beer sales are still perky, spirits (both literally and metaphorically) are down. Mainly due to falling spirits and tobacco sales, Victoria Wine's latest figures as we went to press showed a £5m slump. 'There's long-term pressure on the small-scale high-street retailer,' concedes Richard Lowe, buying and marketing director. 'Every owner of an off-licence would sell it like a shot if he could.'

'Most loyal customers do most of their wine shopping elsewhere. Typically 65 per cent of their requirements are from the likes of Sainsbury's and Tesco, using Victoria Wine as a top-up,' Lowe explains. So one of the big issues exercising the boffins' minds at Victoria Wine is whether to go down the convenience route or continue to specialise in drinks. According to Lowe, 'We've concentrated more on being a specialist drinks retailer.'

With its parent company, Allied Domecq (whose 4,000 pubs are 15 times the size of the high-street chain) behind it, Victoria Wine has put loadsamoney into developing the specialist drinks side of the business chain in a variety of ways. For one thing, it is committed to expanding its Victoria Wine Cellars, which stock the full monty of 550 wines. A re-fit can cost anything between £50,000 and £90,000, and, at the time of writing, we were told that 100

Victoria Wine Cellars were on-stream for the end of the year. This is a positive move, because the more icing, the more palatable the cake.

When Victoria Wine hitched up with Augustus Barnett, it took a calculated decision to chuck poor Augustus in favour of Victoria Wine, because, according to its research, the Victoria Wine name was strong in the public mind. Unlike its rivals Thresher and, up to a point, Greenalls, it has long resisted doing away with the Victoria Wine name for something less familiar. So the fact that the latest developments involve using not one but two different names for its new stores amounts to something of a revolution.

Firkin, for instance, a name pinched from the successful Firkin pubs owned by Allied Domecq Leisure, is aimed at a younger audience. Launched in October 1996, there are seven new Firkin off-licences. The style, as in the Firkin pubs, is informal, down to timber floors, a long bar-style counter and staff kitted out in T-shirts and jeans. Currently there are Firkins in Sheffield, Cheltenham, Harborne-Birmingham, Islington, and Canterbury, with Bristol and Edinburgh coming on-stream. Early indications suggest that fancy beer and New World wine sales are good at Firkin, although sales of draught beer are disappointing. If the Firkins work, there could be a lot of them about, with numbers rising to 100.

If Firkin is a radical departure from Victoria Wine's reliance on its own moniker, so too is the new prototype superstore in Barnet. No relation to Joe Heitz's California wine of the same name, Martha's Vineyard is a 5,000-square-foot drinks superstore, which loosely follows the wine warehouse concept pioneered by Majestic. 'We can improve on certain things that Majestic does,' says Richard Lowe. 'Customers will be able to buy by the bottle.' The location on a suburban main road could be a problem, but the next move is more likely to be to a retail-park location. If it's successful, another half dozen or so Martha's Vineyards could be sprouting branches over the next year.

In an apparent frenzy of activity, Victoria Wine has also launched a pilot scheme in the Midlands for a mail-order service, using newspaper adverts and a large mail-drop to get the home-delivery show on the road. Mail order, as Waitrose, Marks & Spencer and a number of the supermarkets are discovering, is a potentially lucrative customer service. The Victoria Wine service, Cellars Direct, will be the first mail-order scheme run by a high-street chain.

After an uncertain start and a blip with the Channel Tunnel closure, the Calais operation in the Cité de l'Europe shopping mall is doing well with, according to Lowe, the biggest turnover of any store. Costs are high and the strength of the pound works against the New World, but it doesn't seem to deter cross-Channel traffic. For Victoria Wine, simply having a presence and good throughput is worth the hassle. Much the same is true of the Czech shops, where Victoria Wine is a partner in a joint venture with a Czech drinks company. Don't expect to find the Victoria Wine range in Prague, though. It's just a name, so who knows what thirsty Czechs will make of Victoria Wine when they visit the UK?

Given that the busiest time at Victoria Wine is between 6pm and 8pm, it admits to a fairly 'hard-nosed policy' about running promotions such as two bottles for £5, two for £10 (on a £6 bottle) and three bottles for £10 (on a £4 bottle). 'Someone comes in for one bottle and might leave with a bagload,' says Woolrych. 'It's better than 15 per cent off, or buy two and save £1.' The average bottle price at Victoria Wine is around £3.80, about 60 pence higher than the supermarkets.

You might think that a name such as Cat's Pee on a Gooseberry Bush would be more the province of an Oddbins or Bottoms Up, but with strikingly modern names like this, and labels to match, Victoria Wine has made a successful effort to be more inventive in presenting its wines on the shelf. The New Zealand Sauvignon Blanc was an early success. Now the wacky names are coming from the traditional countries: Fat Bastard Chardonnay, Wild Pig Red and Big Frank's Seriously Sticky from France; Ed's Red and White from Spain; and Ravioli Red from Italy. What next?

All wines listed below are stocked by Victoria Wine Cellars (VWC), neighbourhood drinks stores (NDS), destination wine shops (DWS) and Haddows shops (Haddows), unless otherwise indicated. All the company's shops are called Victoria Wine – neighbourhood drinks stores and destination wine shops are merely terms indicating the size and range of the stock, rather than actual shop names.

White

Under £3

FRANCE

1996 Bordeaux Blanc, £2.99   13/20
Dry 👓👓 ▌
Crisp, grassy, well-priced blend of Semillon and Sauvignon with assertive acidity.

GERMANY

1996 Victoria Wine Liebfraumilch, £2.99   13/20
Medium sweet 🍯🍯 ▐
As ever, this is one of the better Liebs around. Fresh, grapey and not too cloying. Gott sei dank, it's almost drinkable.

HUNGARY

Domaine Boyar Chardonnay/Aligoté, Pavlikeni, Country Wine, £2.99 🍯🍯 ▐   13/20
Off-dry 🍯🍯 ▐
Fresh, floral, boiled-sweets Bulgarian blend of Burgundy's two white grapes, Chardonnay and Aligoté. White Burgundy it isn't.

ITALY

Sansovino Bianco Lambrusco, £2.99   13/20
Sweet 🍯🍯 ▐
Clean, sherbety, tangy white with fizzy, appley fruit flavours and relatively restrained sweetness. Italian Babycham.

£3–5

AUSTRALIA

Brokenback Ridge Dry White, £3.99   14/20
Off-dry 🍯🍯 ▐
A fruity, perfumed, well-made Aussie white blend from the giant Southcorp operation, with fresh, citrus-peel fruit characters.

CHILE

1996 Casillero del Diablo Chardonnay, £4.99 (VWC/DWS only)
                                                              16/20
Dry 🍯🍯🍯 ▐
Attractive, pineappley Chilean Chardonnay from the enormous Concha y Toro, with refreshing acidity and toasty oak complexity. Super value.

1996 Cono Sur Gewürztraminer, £4.49 (VWC/DWS only)   15/20
Dry 🍷🍷🍷 ▯
Aromatic, rose-petal-scented Chilean Gewürztraminer with crisp, spicy
definition and a hint of lychee. Better than most cheap Alsace Gewürz.

ENGLAND

Summerhill Dry, Chapel Down, £3.99   14/20
Dry 🍷🍷 ▯
From David Cowderoy, one of England's star winemakers (not hard, mind), this
is a light, refreshing, aptly named quaffing white with hedgerow-fruit character
and crispness.

FRANCE

**1996 Colombard/Chardonnay, Vin de Pays des Côtes de
Gascogne, £3.29** (VWC/DWS only)   14/20
Dry 🍷🍷 ▯
A superior Côtes de Gascogne blend showing flavours of ripe pear and
grapefruit and commendable concentration for a wine at this relatively lowly
price.

1996 Chardonnay, Vin de Pays du Jardin de la France, £3.49
(VWC/DWS only)   15/20
Dry 🍷🍷🍷 ▯
Another Hugh Suter production, this time from the Loire Valley's catch-all
market-garden vin de pays. It's crisp, buttery and unoaked in a mini-Chablis
mould. An excellent party white.

1996 Sauvignon de Bordeaux Calvet, £3.75 (VWC only)   15/20
Dry 🍷🍷🍷 ▯
Grassy, grapefruity Sauvignon Blanc from négociant Calvet. With a few more
wines like this, Bordeaux whites should be back in business.

**1996 Domaine de la Roulerie, Muscadet de Sèvre et Maine Sur
Lie, £4.49** (VWC/DWS only)   16/20
Dry 🍷🍷🍷 ▯
Complex, lightly oaked super Muscadet made by Victoria Wine's very own
flying winemaker, Hugh Suter, with excellent sur lie crispness and character.

1996 La Langue, Oak-Fermented Chardonnay, Domaine Ste Madeleine, Vin de Pays d'Oc, £4.99 (VWC only)   15/20
Dry 🎒🎒 ▯
Modern, nicely buttery Languedoc Chardonnay, with barrel-fermentation adding an extra degree of complexity. It speaks your language.

GERMANY

1995 Slate Valley Dry Riesling, Moselland, £3.99 (VWC/DWS only)
      14/20
Dry 🎒🎒 ▯
One of Germany's new-wave dry whites, packaged in a Bordeaux bottle for anonymity/saleability. It's clean, grapey and well made. A chance to wipe the slate clean?

1986 Erdener Treppchen Riesling, Kabinett, £4.99 (VWC/DWS only)
      16/20
Medium dry 🎒🎒🎒 ▯
For anyone who wants a taste of mature Mosel at a giveaway price, this is your chance. Petrolly, honeyed and still remarkably fresh for a 12-year-old.

HUNGARY

1996 Sauvignon Blanc, Hidden Rock Reserve, £3.95 (VWC/DWS only)   15/20
Dry 🎒🎒🎒 ▯
Super-crisp, nettley Hungarian Sauvignon Blanc from the Neszmely co-operative, which out-Loires the Loire at this price. Watch out Sauvignon de Touraine, the Magyars are coming!

1996 Gewürztraminer, Mór, £3.95 (VWC/DWS only)   15/20
Dry 🎒🎒🎒 ▯
Made at the same outstanding co-operative (we should know, we gave it our Winemaker of the Year gong last year), this is a spicy, gingery Gewürztraminer that goes well with Oriental food.

ITALY

Chardonnay/Pinot Grigio, Atesino, £4.49 (VWC only)   15/20
Dry 🍷🍷 🍾
A spritzy north-east Italian blend of Chardonnay and Pinot Grigio, in which the citrus-fruit character is allowed to speak for itself. A good summery white for quaffing in the back of a gondola.

1996 Soave Classico Superiore, Sole del Garde, Zenato, £4.49
(VWC/DWS only)   14/20
Dry 🍷🍷 🍾
From the giant Zenato winery, this is a pleasant Veneto quaffer with some rounded, peachy fruit flavours.

NEW ZEALAND

1996 Cook's Chardonnay Gisborne, £4.99 (VWC/DWS only)
                                                           15/20

Dry 🍷🍷 🍾
Rich, tropical fruit-flavoured North Island Chardonnay, which is rather dominated by charry oak characters at the moment.

SOUTH AFRICA

1997 Table Bay Early Release, Chenin Blanc, £3.69 (VWC/DWS
only)   13/20
Off-dry 🍷 🍾
Light, confected, boiled-sweets-style Cape Chenin Blanc made to a price and a summer release date. Makes a change from Beaujolais Nouveau, at least.

SPAIN

1996 Ed's White, Penedès, £3.49   13/20
Dry 🍷 🍾
A crisp, neutral, white-peppery blend of the local Parellada and Xarello, better known as the Cava grapes, from Emili Esteve and Master of Wine Ed Adams.

UNITED STATES

1996 Mohr-Fry Ranch Sauvignon Blanc, £4.69 (VWC/DWS only)
15/20
Dry 🍷🍷 ▮
Made by Victoria Wine's wandering Master of Wine, Hugh Suter, this is a rich,
surprisingly alcoholic California Sauvignon Blanc with full-blown tropical fruit
flavours.

£5–8

AUSTRALIA

1995 Basedow Semillon, Oscar's Trail, Barossa, £6.49 (VWC/DWS
only)
16/20
Dry 🍷🍷🍷 ▮
Smoky, spicy, richly textured Aussie Semillon with a cream-soda and lemon-
meringue flavour. Great, but not remotely traditional.

FRANCE

1996 Fat Bastard Chardonnay, Vin de Pays d'Oc, £5.99 (VWC and
Firkin only)
16/20
Dry 🍷🍷 ▮
A promising follow-up to last year's successful launch (the bastard in question
is a pun on Burgundy's fabled Bâtard-Montrachet). Skilfully executed, barrel-
fermented stuff with considerable flavour and elegance for a southern French
Chardonnay.

1996 Château Laribotte, Barrel-Fermented, Ginestet, £5.99 (VWC
only)
15/20
Dry 🍷🍷 ▮
Ripe, concentrated white Bordeaux with plenty of flavour and oak-matured
complexity.

1995 Vouvray Demi-Sec, Les Girardières, £6.99 (VWC only)   16/20
Medium dry 🍷🍷 ▬
From a brilliant sweet white wine vintage in the Loire, this is an ultra-modern,
appley Vouvray from the youthful Bernard Fouquet of Domaine des
Aubuisières, with beautifully balanced sweetness and acidity.

NEW ZEALAND

1996 Cat's Pee on a Gooseberry Bush, Gisborne, £5.99
(VWC/DWS only)   14/20
Dry 🍷 ▮
Made at the Coopers Creek Winery, this is an asparagus and artichoke-like
white, which doesn't quite live up to its brilliant label (cat's pee here is a
tongue-in-cheek reference to the catty, aromatic properties of the Sauvignon
Blanc grape). We prefer the 1995 version.

SPAIN

1994 Dominio de Montalvo Rioja, £5.99 (VWC/DWS only)   15/20
Bone dry 🍷🍷 ▮
Austere, traditionally oaky white Rioja from Campo Viejo, with a nutty, Sherry-
like dry tang. An uncompromising flavour you'll either love or hate.

1996 Lagar de Cervera, Albariño, £6.99 (VWC only)   17/20
Dry 🍷🍷🍷 ▬
From Galicia's Rias Baixas region close to the Atlantic, this is a stunning example
of Albariño, Spain's best white grape variety, showing full, rich, spicy, unoaked
flavours and considerable freshness and vibrancy.

Over £8

FRANCE

**1994 Pouilly Fuissé, Vieilles Vignes, Domaine de la Soufrandise,
Melin, £14.99** (VWC only)   14/20
Dry ▮
Gluey, flattish Mâconnais Chardonnay made in an old-fashioned style from
ultra-ripe grapes. Pricey for what it is.

**1994 Puligny Montrachet, Premier Cru, Clos de la Mouchère,
Boillot, £23.99** (VWC only)   18/20
Dry 🍷🍷🍷 ▮
Modern, oaky, beautifully structured premier cru Puligny Montrachet, with a
backbone of fresh acidity and subtle flavours of nut, butter and lemon.

Red

Under £3

BULGARIA

Pavlikeni Cabernet Sauvignon/Merlot NV, Domaine Boyar, £2.99
13/20

Medium-bodied 👛👛 ⚱
Plummy, slightly chewy Bulgarian blend with a robust finish.

1996 Domaine Boyar Liubimetz Merlot, Domaine Boyar, £2.99
14/20

Medium-bodied 👛👛 ⚱
Lively, liquoricey, well-balanced Bulgarian red made in a modern, approachable, fruity style.

£3–5

ARGENTINA

1996 Balbi Vineyards, Malbec, £3.99 (VWC/DWS only)
14/20
Medium-bodied 👛👛 ⚱
Deeply coloured, ripely fruity Argentine red with a savoury note and a nip of acidity. Decent, if a little raw.

1996 Balbi Vineyards, Cabernet Sauvignon, £4.99 (VWC/DWS only)
15/20

Medium-bodied 👛👛 ⚱
Abundantly aromatic, blackcurrant-fruity Argentine Cabernet Sauvignon, with supple tannins and rich, concentrated fruit flavours.

AUSTRALIA

1996 Hardy's Stamps of Australia Shiraz/Cabernet, £4.49
14/20
Medium-bodied 👛 ⚱
Light, minty, quaffing blend of Shiraz and Cabernet Sauvignon, which lacks a bit of stuffing.

1996 Deakin Estate, Victoria Shiraz, £4.99 (VWC/DWS only)   15/20
Medium-bodied 🍾🍾 🍾
Ah! Essence of Oz. Masses of colour, abundant blackberry, tar and liquorice aromas and a minty, sweetly oaked finish.

1996 Salisbury Estate Grenache, £4.99 (VWC/DWS only)   13/20
Medium-bodied 🍾
Hollow, rather confected Grenache from the irrigated heartland of Australia.

BULGARIA

1996 Cabernet Sauvignon/Rubin, £3.29 (VWC/DWS only)   13/20
Medium-bodied 🍾 🍾
Anyone know where, who or what Rubin is? This is a young, unoaked, chewy blend of Cabernet Sauvignon and Rubin with marked acidity. Rubin, we have to presume, is a Bulgarian grape variety.

1996 Rocky Valley Merlot, Russe, £3.49 (VWC/DWS only)   14/20
Medium-bodied 🍾🍾 🍾
An almost claret-like Russe Merlot with some sweet blackcurrant-fruit succulence and robust tannins.

CHILE

1996 Valdivieso, Cabernet Sauvignon, £3.99 (VWC/DWS only)
                                                              14/20

Medium-bodied 🍾🍾 🍾
Blackcurrant-pastille-scented Chilean Cabernet Sauvignon with a slightly underripe, green pepper-like edge. We prefer the other reds from Valdivieso, such as the Merlot and Malbec.

1996 Cono Sur Merlot, £4.49 (VWC/DWS only)   15/20
Medium-bodied 🍾🍾🍾 🍾
Juicy, deeply coloured Chilean Merlot with supple tannins and oodles of luscious plum and blackcurrant fruit. Moreish stuff.

1996 La Fortuna Malbec, Lontue, £4.99 (VWC only)   15/20
Medium-bodied 🍾🍾 🍾
Tarry, well-made Chilean Malbec with concentrated, structured raisin and chocolate fruit character. Needs food.

FRANCE

1996 Merlot/Cabernet Sauvignon, Vin de Pays d'Oc, £3.29
(VWC/DWS only)   13/20
Medium-bodied 👜👜 |
Light, fresh, basic Bordeaux-style rouge from the Languedoc-Roussillon. An
easy-drinking glugger.

1996 Wild Pig Red, Vin de Pays des Cévennes, Meffre, £3.39
(VWC/DWS only)   14/20
Medium-bodied 👜👜👜 |
A typical southern French blend of Carignan, Syrah and Grenache from the
Gabriel Meffre operation, with soft, brambly fruit. A good Côtes du Rhône
alternative at a price that won't, er, boar you.

1996 Gamay de Touraine, £3.49 (VWC/DWS only)   14/20
Medium-bodied 👜👜👜 |
Youthful, juicy Loire Valley Gamay, which ought to embarrass many a producer
of basic Beaujolais.

1994 La Langue, Domaine St Benoît, Vin Pays d'Oc, £3.99
(VWC/DWS only)   15/20
Medium-bodied 👜👜👜 |
A profoundly aromatic, herby, spicy blend of Syrah, Grenache and Merlot with
undertones of thyme and pistachio and a supple fruit texture.

1995 Côtes du Ventoux, Jaboulet, £4.99 (VWC/DWS only)   14/20
Full-bodied 👜 |
Peppery, southern Rhône red from Tour de France territory around Mont
Ventoux. Finishes a little dry – and without the yellow jersey.

1995 La Chasse du Pape Reserve, Côtes du Rhône, Gabriel
Meffre, £4.99 (VWC/DWS only)   15/20
Full-bodied 👜👜 |
Grenache-based red in a mini-Châteauneuf-du-Pape mould from Gabriel
Meffre, this is a rich and spicy, heart-warming red.

1995 Lost Valley Vineyards, Montpeyroux, Coteaux du Languedoc,
£4.99 (VWC only)   15/20
Medium-bodied 👜👜 |
Rich, chocolatey, spicy Languedoc red with firm tannins, plenty of perfume and
red-fruit characters. A good find.

1994 Domaine de Fontbertière, Cuvée Franck Edward, Minervois, £4.99 (VWC only)   15/20
Full-bodied 👜👜 ▮
Oak-aged Minervois made by Polish-American painter, 'Big Frank' Chludinski, with a robustly chewy finish.

ITALY

1996 Montepulciano d'Abruzzo, Cortenova, £3.75 (VWC/DWS only)   14/20
Medium-bodied 👜👜 ▮
Light, quaffing Montepulciano from the Adriatic, showing raspberry fruit sweetness and dryish tannins.

Ravioli Red, Giordano, £3.99 (VWC/DWS only)   14/20
Medium-bodied 👜👜 ▮
Great with pasta? This is a cherry-fruity rosso in a jolly bottle from Italian merchants Giordano, with damsony acidity and flavour. No need to confine this to ravioli.

1996 Barbera d'Asti, Icardi, Cav. Pierino, £4.75 (VWC only)   15/20
Medium-bodied 👜👜 ▮
Well-made, distinctively packaged Barbera with chocolate and black-cherry fruit and a hint of oak for extra softness and complexity.

1996 Dolcetto d'Alba, Gigi Rosso, £4.95 (VWC only)   14/20
Medium-bodied 👜 ▮
Robust and rather chewy. We normally expect a little more charm from the Dolcetto grape of Piedmont.

1994 Salice Salentino, Vallone, £4.95 (VWC/DWS only)   16/20
Medium-bodied 👜👜👜 ▮
Made from Puglia's Negroamaro grape (literally 'bitter black') by the elegant Vallone sisters, this is a mature, rich, chocolatey example of the variety, with a characteristically refreshing bitter twist.

SPAIN

1996 Ed's Red, Tempranillo, La Mancha, £3.49   13/20
Medium-bodied 👜 ▮
Basic, four-square and rather chewy La Mancha tinto made from Spain's best red grape variety. One for Sancho Panza and his mule.

1996 Marqués de Aragón Garnacha, Calatayud, £3.75   12/20
Medium-bodied |
Strange, plum-skin-scented red, with raspberry aromas and a vinegary edge.

Don Frutos Tempranillo/Cabernet Sauvignon, £3.99 (VWC/DWS only)   13/20
Medium-bodied 👜 |
A chewy, faintly farmyardy Spanish blend with robust tannins.

1995 Dominio de Montalvo Rioja, £4.99 (VWC/DWS only)   14/20
Medium-bodied 👜 |
Coconut-oaky Rioja from Campo Viejo, with surprisingly assertive acidity, ending a little dry and old-fashioned.

SOUTH AFRICA

Clearsprings Cape Red, £3.29   14/20
Medium-bodied 👜👜👜 |
Well-made strawberry fruity Cape red at a good price. Less rustic than many, which is presumably why this agreeable quaffer features in Vicky Wine's top ten.

1996 Cape View Cinsault/Shiraz, £3.99 (VWC/DWS only)   15/20
Medium-bodied 👜👜👜 |
Minty, aromatic, overtly oaked Cape blend from Kym Milne, with supple loganberry fruit and good juicy length and flavour.

1995 Simonsvlei Pinotage Reserve, £4.49 (VWC/DWS only)   15/20
Full-bodied 👜👜 |
Brambly, perfumed, modern-style Cape Pinotage from one of South Africa's best co-operatives, with sweet, mulberry fruit and pronounced oak.

UNITED STATES

1996 Old Vine Grenache, Collins Ranch , £4.49 (VWC/DWS only)   14/20
Full-bodied 👜 |
Another Hugh Suter wine from California – lightly coloured, warm-climate Grenache with plentiful alcohol and a hint of raspberry fruit. A West Coast Côtes du Rhône.

1996 Lee Jones Ranch Zinfandel, California, £4.99 (VWC/DWS only)   15/20
Full-bodied 👜👜 ▯
Another ranch, another red, from king of the wild frontier, Hugh Suter. The result this time is a lot more satisfactory, with raspberry ripple flavours, soft tannins and a sweet, supple middle.

£5–8

AUSTRALIA

1996 Saltram Classic Shiraz, £5.99 (VWC only)   16/20
Full-bodied 👜👜👜 ▬
Liquorice and spearmint-perfumed Aussie Shiraz with supple tannins, black cherry fruit and lively acidity.

1995 Basedow Shiraz, £7.99 (VWC/DWS only)   15/20
Full-bodied 👜 ▬
More extracted Barossa Valley style with charry American oak, muscular tannins and chewy, smoky fruit.

CHILE

1995 Marqués de Casa Concha Cabernet Sauvignon, £5.99 (VWC only)   15/20
Medium-bodied 👜👜 ▯
Youthful, well-made Maipo Valley Cabernet Sauvignon from Concha y Toro, with grassy, cassis fruitiness and slightly dry tannins.

FRANCE

1995 Big Frank's Best Red, Shiraz, £5.99 (VWC only)   15/20
Full-bodied 👜 ▬
Considerably richer than the man who made it, according to his humorous back-label, this is a dense, oaky Languedoc Syrah, with plenty of flavour for the price, albeit a little four-square.

1996 Château de l'Abbaye de Saint Ferme, Bordeaux Supérieur, £6.99 (VWC/DWS only)   15/20
Medium-bodied 🥂 ▮

Grassy, youthful, well-made Bordeaux 'soup', with a smooth oak dimension and vibrant, blackcurrant fruitiness.

1993 Château La Claverie, Côtes de Francs, £7.49 (VWC only)
16/20

Medium-bodied 🥂🥂 ▮

Brown-sugar-scented Merlot-based Bordeaux with attractive vanilla oak and supple tannins. The perfect Christmas claret.

1993 Domaine de Peyremorin, Haut Médoc, £7.99 (VWC only)
16/20

Medium-bodied 🥂🥂 ▮

From the other side of the Garonne, this is a firmer, more structured, classic red Bordeaux with stylish oak and maturing fruit.

1995 Crozes Hermitage, La Petite Ruche, £7.99 (VWC only)
16/20

Full-bodied 🥂🥂 ▬

From biodynamic promotional specialists, the Chapoutier brothers, this is an aromatic, orange-peel-scented Syrah, which is a little tight and tannic at the moment. Comes complete with a politically correct braille label for the visually challenged.

ITALY

1994 Costera, Cannonau di Sardegna, £5.95 (VWC only)   16/20
Full-bodied 🥂🥂🥂 ▮

A heady Sardinian red made from the Grenache, aka Cannonau, grape with sweet vanilla oak. A super-ripe chocolate and raisin-style number with masses of flavour and texture.

1995 Chianti Classico DOCG Fonterutoli, £6.75 (VWC/DWS only)
16/20

Full-bodied 🥂🥂🥂 ▬

From a leading Chianti Classico estate, this is a well-priced (believe it or not) Tuscan red, with super colour, cherry fruit concentration and flavour and oak influence.

SOUTH AFRICA

1995 Delheim Shiraz, £5.99 (VWC only)   14/20
Full-bodied ▮
Old-fashioned-style Cape red with baked raisiny fruit and a chewy finish.

1995 Cru Monro Villiera, £7.99 (VWC only)   17/20
Medium-bodied 🍾🍾🍾 ━
Villiera is a winery whose youthful winemaker, Jeff Grier, appears incapable of
making a bad wine. This is a stylish, oaked Bordeaux-style blend, with a core of
sumptuous, tobaccoey fruit and excellent balance.

Over £8

FRANCE

1995 Rully Rouge, Les Villeranges, Faiveley, £8.99 (VWC only)
                                                            15/20

Medium-bodied 🍾 ▮
A firm, chewy Côte Chalonnaise red from a good vintage, showing
raspberryish Pinot Noir perfume and typical rusticity for the region.

1993 Baron de Brane, Bordeaux, £9.99 (VWC only)   16/20
Medium-bodied 🍾🍾 ▮
Second label of the classified Château Brane Cantenac, this is a stylish, modern,
coffee-bean-oaky claret with succulent tannins.

1993 Château de Villegeorge, Haut Médoc, £10.99 (VWC only)
                                                            16/20

Medium-bodied 🍾🍾 ▮
Considering the quality of the less than exceptional 1993 vintage in Bordeaux,
this is a very tasty, well-balanced cru bourgeois claret, which isn't overloaded
with oak. Nicely balanced stuff.

1993 Clos des Papes, Paul Avril, Châteauneuf-du-Pape, £14.99
(VWC only)   16/20
Full-bodied 🍾🍾 ━
Clos des Papes is one of the leading estates in Châteauneuf-du-Pape. This
concentrated, angostura-bitters, spicy red is rich and firmly structured with lots
of fruit sweetness and flavour.

1995 Hermitage, Pied de la Côte, Jaboulet, £19.99 (VWC only)
16/20

Medium-bodied 💰 |
Pepper and incense-like Syrah from the company that also makes the appellation's most famous red, La Chapelle. Good, if a little rustic for Hermitage.

1994 Chambolle Musigny Premier Cru Les Cras, Barthod, £24.99
(VWC only)   16/20
Medium-bodied 💰 |
Aromatic, slightly farmyardy premier cru red Burgundy from a decent vintage. The genuine article, but this needs drinking sooner rather than later.

ITALY

1992 Brunello di Montalcino DOCG, Casanova di Neri, £15.99
(VWC only)   16/20
Full-bodied 💰 ➡
Modern-style, oak-aged Sangiovese from one of southern Tuscany's star appellations. Spicy, tarry and a little green on the finish.

SPAIN

1989 Campo Viejo Rioja, Gran Reserva, £8.99 (VWC only)   15/20
Medium-bodied 💰 |
Charry, American oak-influenced Rioja Gran Reserva, which is starting to dry out.

1994 Pago de Carraovejas, Ribera del Duero, £9.75 (VWC only)
17/20

Medium-bodied 💰💰💰 ➡
A blend of 75 per cent Tempranillo with 25 per cent Cabernet Sauvignon, this super Ribera red shows what the region is capable of at its best. Concentrated, chocolatey blend with lots of fruit, texture and balanced acidity complemented by oak.

Rosé

£3–5

AUSTRALIA

1996 Hardy's Rosé Shiraz/Grenache, £4.49 (VWC/DWS only)

14/20

Off-dry 🥂🥂 |
Sweet strawberry fruity Aussie blend from one of the country's biggest wineries. A light picnic quaffer.

FRANCE

1996 Syrah Rosé, Fortant de France, Vin de Pays d'Oc, £3.99
(VWC/DWS only)   14/20
Dry 🥂🥂 |
Attractive, if dilute Languedoc rosé from varietal specialists Fortant de France.

UNITED STATES

Gallo White Grenache, £4.39   13/20
Medium sweet |
Mawkishly sweet and soupy California blush – as it should do. A triumph of advertising over content.

Sparkling

£3–5

FRANCE

Marquis de la Tour Brut, £3.99   12/20
Dry |
Very basic, sulphur-ridden sparkling wine made from heaven knows what. Its virtue is that it's cheap.

ITALY

Asti Perlino, £4.99 (DWS/NDS/Haddows only)   15/20
Medium sweet 🍾🍾 ▮
Sweet, sherbety, grown-up Asti with a cushion of grapey bubbles.

£5–8

SPAIN

1991 Freixenet Vintage Brut, £7.99 (VWC only)   13/20
Off-dry ▮
From the home of the frosted black bottle, this is a coarse, big-bubbled Spanish fizz, which is ludicrously overpriced.

Over £8

FRANCE

Millennium Cuvée Grand Cru Brut, £21.99 (VWC only)   15/20
Dry 🍾 ▮
If you're going to celebrate the millennium (and who isn't) in style, we suggest that there are better options than this decent, if overpriced, fizz, which may not survive the millennium anyway.

Taittinger Brut NV, £22.99 (VWC only)   14/20
Dry ▮
For a Grande Marque Champagne, this is a serious disappointment. Youthful, tart and simple, bolstered by compensating sweetness.

Fortified

£5–8

FRANCE

Big Frank's Seriously Sticky, 50 cl., £5.99 (VWC only)　　　15/20
Full-bodied 🗑 ┇
Authentic, fortified Maury from the Roussillon hills bottled by Big Frank Chludinski, with a raisiny, crème brûlée richness and a spirity afterburn.

Over £8

PORTUGAL

1991 Dow's Crusted, £12.49 (VWC/optional DWS only)　　　16/20
Full-bodied 🗑🗑 ➡
A good, cheaper alternative to vintage Port, this is a sweet, fruitcake-style sticky with nuts and raisins aplenty.

1984 Warre's Traditional LBV, £13.99 (VWC/optional DWS only)
　　　　　　　　　　　　　　　　　　　　　　　　　　　15/20
Full-bodied 🗑 ┇
A mature, powerfully alcoholic, violet-perfumed Port, with sweet damsony fruit and a rasp of spirit.

1986 Taylor's Quinta de Terra Feita, £16.99 (VWC/optional DWS
only)　　　　　　　　　　　　　　　　　　　　　　　17/20
Full-bodied 🗑🗑🗑 ➡
A sweet, peppery, single-quinta (vineyard) Port with lots of structure and tannin. Not ready for drinking yet, but worth sticking away for the millennium.

1984 Graham's Malvedos, £19.99 (VWC/optional DWS only)
　　　　　　　　　　　　　　　　　　　　　　　　　　　16/20
Full-bodied 🗑🗑 ┇
Spicy, evolved single-quinta Port, with peppery fig and nutmeg fruit and a donkey-kick of alcohol.

Waitrose ☆☆☆☆(☆)

Address: Doncastle Road, Southern Industrial Area, Bracknell, Berkshire RG12 8YA

Telephone/fax: 01344 424680; 01344 860428

Number of branches: 117 (by the end of 1997)

Opening hours: 8.30am to 6.00pm Monday and Tuesday; 8.30am to 8.00pm Wednesday and Thursday; 8.30am to 9.00pm Friday; 8.30am to 6.00pm Saturday; selected branches open 10.00am to 4.00pm Sunday

Credit cards accepted: Access, Delta, MasterCard, Switch, Visa, Waitrose and John Lewis account cards

Discounts: Wines-of-the-month discount of 12 bottles for the price of 11 (without 5 per cent discount) or 5 per cent discount on a mixed case of six wines, including Champagne and fortified wines

Facilities and services: Free glass loan against returnable deposit of £5; home delivery through Waitrose Direct (Freephone 0800 413331); occasional in-store tastings

Special offers: En primeur and special case offers through Waitrose Direct

Top ten best-selling wines: 1996 Le Pujalet Vin de Pays du Gers; 1996 Winter Hill Red Vin de Pays de l'Aude; 1996 Trois Couronnes, Vin de Pays de l'Hérault; 1996 Bergerac Blanc; 1996 Marche Trebbiano Moncaro; 1996 Winter Hill White, Vin de Pays de l'Aude; 1996 Pinot Grigio, Fiordaliso; Good Ordinary Claret, Bordeaux; 1996 Domaine de Rose Merlot/Syrah, Vin de Pays d'Oc; 1996 Waitrose Bordeaux Sauvignon

Range:

GOOD: Bordeaux, Burgundy, regional France, Germany, Eastern Europe, Chile, Australia, South Africa, Champagne and sparkling wines, Sherry and Port

AVERAGE: Rhône, Beaujolais, Loire, England, Italy, Spain, Argentina, New Zealand

POOR: Alsace

UNDER-REPRESENTED: United States, Portugal

Waitrose

Fancy a job as a wine buyer? Just one small snag. Masters of Wine only need apply. As the only retail outfit in the country that insists that its wine buyers are Masters of Wine, Waitrose has recently tied at least one hand behind its derrière. With no fewer than five of this rarefied breed at the end of 1995, it was down to two a year later when the dynamic David Gill left. For a while, capo di capi Julian Brind himself was forced from his executive armchair and back on the buying trail. The team is now in the process of rebuilding, with new arrivals in the shape of Masters of Wine Simon Thorpe and Susan McCraith joining Dee Blackstock. Meanwhile, a vacancy remains.

If it's tough nut for budding wine buyers to crack, Waitrose is still the closest thing to a wine lover's paradise among supermarkets. With its 117 stores all based in the South-East, the affluence of its customers creates a demand not just for value but for pure quality too. People are prepared to pay more for wine at Waitrose. The average selling price of a bottle is over £4.50, easily the highest of the supermarkets and virtually on a par with the likes of Majestic Wine Warehouses and Oddbins. This gives the wine department, such as it is, scope to include in the range wines that rival supermarkets can only dream about.

Navigating against the general supermarket tide, for instance, of ditching 'shop-window' fine wines, Waitrose introduced its Inner Cellar in December 1996. 'It's where wines are absolutely fabulous,' says Dee Blackstock, with a hint of the Joanna Lumleys, 'but limited in quantity.' In what other supermarket could you possibly hope to pick up such scrumptious stuff as Thelema Sauvignon Blanc, Chave's Hermitage, Chapoutier's Cornas or a bottle of Huet's sensational 1990 Le Haut Lieu Moelleux at £28 a throw? By the end of 1997 the plan is for the inner sanctum to be extended to 10 stores.

Waitrose is also the only supermarket offering fancy Bordeaux en primeur. Drawing on the experience of former Findlater, Mackie Todd director, Christopher Rowe, it was able to offer pre-release 1996 Clarets and Sauternes, mixing much-fancied châteaux such as Ducru Beaucaillou and Clinet with a raft of more sensibly priced properties, among them Pontet-Canet, Poujeaux, Maucaillou and Beaumont. Even on promotions – an increasing activity at Waitrose – it can afford to put interesting wines out on the shop floor. The aromatic Villa Maria Sauvignon Private Bin Blanc did well when it was showcased at £5.99, as did the sweet grapey fizz, Clairette de Die, at £6.45, when it was married with Christmas cake.

Waitrose can be innovative. It was first, for instance, with Fitou, Cook's New Zealand Chardonnay and, perhaps less worthy of praise, it supported South African wines during the dark days of apartheid. It was quick to spot the trend away from Liebfraumilch and Hock, too, bringing in David Gill to develop – successfully – a range of value-for-money Eastern European wines. It was also the first to put wines on the shelf by style, a concept currently under review.

Waitrose

On the whole, though, Waitrose doesn't feel pressurised into renewing the 500-strong range every minute of the day. 'We're happy to do new and exciting things, but there are fewer new and exciting things to do,' says Brind, with a disproportionate share of the world's troubles apparently squatting on his shoulders. 'I'm fighting for the continuation of a balanced assortment, rather than an intense cultivation of one particular area. We're always sifting and selecting the best-value wines in an ongoing programme, rather than chasing after the new gimmick or latest trend.'

As Julian's Brind's very public rating in the informative John Lewis Partnership in-house Gazette (price 2 pence) bears out, wine is still a growing market at Waitrose. Brind came a creditable third in the food- and drink-buying league, with a 5 per cent increase for the first half of 1997. The overall annual increase for wines was 6 per cent in volume (12 per cent in value).

Waitrose Direct, the mail-order side, was relaunched in February 1997. The new look, complete with packaged tasting notes and art-house black-and-white photos of buyers Dee Blackstock, Susan McCraith and Julian Brind, helped achieve a 39 per cent increase in the first three months. Regular mixed-case offers include a New World case, French Classics, an Italian selection, French Country Wines and cases featuring individual grape varieties. Getting to the parts Waitrose can't reach, the mailing reaches out to John Lewis account-card customers and the original Findlater, Mackie Todd list, as well as Waitrose account-card customers.

Thanks to its customers' traditional leanings, France remains number one by a long chalk, even if French wines have dropped back from a whopping four in every ten bottles sold to just under that. Australia is still the biggest New World country, accounting for more than one in every ten bottles sold. Not surprisingly, however, with a host of excellent-value wines in the £3.99–£5.99 price band, South America and South Africa are catching up fast. The long-awaited revamp of Spain and Portugal has been on partial hold due to staff shortages, but interesting new wines include Falcoaria from Portugal, and Enate and Solana from Spain show that even Iberia is not at a total standstill.

Germany continues to plummet. 'We've weaned people off Lieb and Hock,' says Brind, 'but still there's an older generation looking out for characterful estate wines. Waitrose has some good German estate wines, which 'do well but not as well as they deserve'. In a curious bid to reverse the downward spiral, Brind was set to reintroduce Blue Nun when we saw him in the summer, 'to see if it injects more interest'. It sounded more like a retrograde (goose-) step to us.

Regular in-store tastings now extend to 80 branches. In addition, as a form of reward, Waitrose hosts evening tastings for something like 150 customers by invitation. While it's good for the image, Waitrose's investment in shop-floor tastings is considerable. By getting its own staff to run these tastings, it will help to cut down on the financial burden of contracting them out to an external consultant.

The man charged with working out a staff training programme, in conjunction with the Wine & Spirit Education Trust, is the ebullient Joe Wadsack. The course consists of basic principles such as how to taste wine and food and wine matching. 'In the long run,' says Wadsack, 'we're aiming to induce an ongoing Oddbins-style wine culture among staff.' At this rate, Wadsack may even produce a badly needed Master of Wine from among Waitrose's own ranks.

White

Under £3

FRANCE

1996 Bergerac Blanc, Marquis de Beausoleil, £2.99   14/20
Dry 👜👜👜 ▪
Clean, nettley, well-priced alternative to white Bordeaux from south-west France. A Waitrose best-seller.

HUNGARY

1996 Matra Springs Pinot Gris/Muscat, Gyöngyös, £2.79   15/20
Dry 👜👜👜 ▪
Soft and grapey Hungarian blend of Pinot Gris with the aromatic Muscat grape, with refreshing acidity and plenty of flavour for your forint.

1996 Chapel Hill Irsai Oliver, Balatonboglar, £2.99   14/20
Dry 👜👜👜 ▪
Ginger and lychee-scented white made from the local Irsai Oliver grape, Hungary's good-value answer to Alsace's Gewürztraminer.

ITALY

1996 Marche Trebbiano Moncaro, £2.99   14/20
Dry 👜👜👜 ▪
Extremely flavoursome for the normally bland Trebbiano, with flavours of apple and ripe pear and a zing of acidity.

£3–5

AUSTRALIA

1996 Ridgewood Trebbiano, South East Australia, £3.59   14/20
Dry 🍾🍾 ▮

Sweetish, faintly tropical, fruity Aussie Trebbiano from the Riverina. A good party white.

1997 Currawong Creek Chardonnay, £3.99   14/20
Dry 🍾🍾 ▮

Lightly oaked Aussie Chardonnay with fresh, lemony fruit flavours and a tropical overtone.

1996 Wynn's Coonawarra Riesling, £4.49   15/20
Off-dry 🍾🍾🍾 ▮

Full, honeyed, lemon and lime-like Coonawarra Riesling from Peter Douglas, balanced by fresh acidity and a delicate petrolly note. About time we latched onto the delights of Aussie Riesling.

Tatachilla Growers' Chenin/Semillon/Sauvignon, £4.99   16/20
Dry 🍾🍾🍾 ▮

Tropical grapefruit zest and lemon-peel McLaren Vale white with superb length and lingering flavours. Another winner from the much-improved Tatachilla set-up.

CHILE

1996 Valdivieso Chardonnay, £4.99   15/20
Dry 🍾🍾 ▮

Broad, toffeeish Chilean Chardonnay with ripe melon and vanilla oak flavours, from a winery that knows how to provide value for money.

ENGLAND

1993 Chiltern Valley Medium Dry, South Oxfordshire, £4.99   15/20
Off-dry 🍾🍾 ▮

Ripe, nettley, hedgerow fruits-scented English white with sweetness and acidity working in tandem. 'Daisy, daisy…'

FRANCE

1996 Le Pujalet Vin de Pays du Gers, £3.15
Off-dry 👝👝 ⚱
13/20

Soft, appley, faintly sweet Gascon blend with bracing acidity.

1996 Winter Hill White, Vin de Pays de l'Aude, £3.29
Dry 👝 ⚱
13/20

Clean, appley, uncomplicated white made by flying winemakers in the south of France. It's about time they dropped the 'French Wine Made by Australians' tag. After all, there's not that much to be proud of.

1996 Waitrose Bordeaux Sauvignon, £3.49
Dry 👝👝👝 ⚱
15/20

Grassy, grapefruity Sauvignon Blanc from négociant Calvet. With a few more wines like this, Bordeaux whites could be back in business.

1996 Colombard / Sauvignon Blanc, Vin de Pays du Comté Tolosan, £3.49
Off-dry 👝 ⚱
13/20

Appley sweet-and-sour white made to a price by the Plaisance co-operative.

1996 Domaine de Planterieu, Vin de Pays des Côtes de Gascogne, £3.65
Dry 👝👝👝 ⚱
15/20

Refreshing, spritzy, full-flavoured Gascon white with grassy undertones and a grapefruity tang. Surprisingly characterful for Ugni Blanc.

1996 Sauvignon de Touraine, BRL-Hardy, £3.99
Dry 👝👝👝 ⚱
15/20

Modern, lemon-zesty Sauvignon Blanc made by the Australian BRL-Hardy group in the Loire Valley. The softness and full flavour of the wine reflect the Aussie influence.

1996 Calvet Sauvignon Blanc, Bordeaux, £3.99
Dry 👝👝 ⚱
14/20

Not quite as exciting as the Waitrose Bordeaux Blanc from Calvet, this is a grassy Bordeaux blend made in a modern style.

1996 Roussanne, Vin de Pays d'Oc, Hugh Ryman, £4.75
Dry 👝👝👝 ⚱
16/20

Oaky, butterscotch-flavoured Languedoc white, fermented in oak barrels by Englishman Hugh Ryman for added complexity. Super value.

1996 Alsace Pinot Blanc, Paul Blanck, £4.75   14/20
Dry 🍷 |
Old-fashioned, slightly vegetal Pinot Blanc de Blanck.

1996 Cuckoo Hill Viognier, Vin de Pays d'Oc, £4.99   14/20
Dry 🍷 |
Not quite as good as last year, but this is still an interesting, well-made example of the rare Viognier grape made in the south of France. It could do with a bit more fatness.

1995 White Burgundy, Bourgogne Blanc, J.-C. Boisset, £4.99   14/20
Dry 🍷 |
Clean, fresh, barrel-aged Bourgogne Blanc from Jean-Claude Boisset. Pleasant enough, if a little hollow.

GERMANY

1995 Devil's Rock Riesling, St Ursula, Pfalz, £3.75   14/20
Off-dry 🍷🍷 |
A grapey, new-style German Riesling from the giant St Ursula winery, made with the francophile consumer in mind.

ITALY

1996 Pinot Grigio delle Venezie, Fiordaliso, £3.99   14/20
Dry 🍷🍷 |
From Italy's biggest winery, GIV, this is a lively, peachy, Veneto white made from the Pinot Grigio grape.

NEW ZEALAND

1996 Cook's Chardonnay, Gisborne, £4.99   15/20
Dry 🍷🍷 |
From a very good New Zealand vintage, this is a nutty, well-made, faintly tropical North Island Chardonnay at a more than decent price.

SOUTH AFRICA

1997 Diamond Hills Chenin Blanc/Chardonnay, Western Cape, £3.89
14/20
Dry 👜👜 ❚
Ultra-fresh, peardroppy Cape blend of Chenin Blanc and the popular Chardonnay grape, with nice appley flavours and balance.

1997 Culemborg Unwooded Chardonnay, £3.95
15/20
Dry 👜👜👜 ❚
Buttery, full-flavoured, unoaked Chardonnay with tapering fruit flavours and a refreshing tang.

1996 KWV Chardonnay, £4.75
15/20
Dry 👜👜 ❚
Partially barrel-fermented Cape Chardonnay from the sprawling KWV co-operative, showing fresh citrus-fruit and vanilla characters. A welcome improvement from an old-fashioned organisation that is belatedly turning itself into a private company.

1996 Springfield Estate Chardonnay, £4.99
14/20
Dry 👜 ❚
Young, sweetish, rounded Cape Chardonnay from Robertson, with a touch of oak. A little bland.

SPAIN

Cueva Solana, £3.99
15/20
Dry 👜👜👜 ❚
An intriguing Spanish blend of Torrontés and Treixadura made in the Val de Miño by Aussie Don Lewis and Francisco Díaz Yubero, with a white pepper and crisp, greengage-fruit character.

£5–8

AUSTRALIA

1994 Penfolds Barrel-Fermented Semillon, £5.99
16/20
Dry 👜👜 ❚
Toasty, nicely maturing, barley-sugared white with a lemon-meringue filling. Should continue to age well.

1994 Houghton Gold Reserve Verdelho, Western Australia, £6.95
15/20

Off-dry 👜 ⚬

No longer quite the bargain it once was at under £5, this sweetish, full-flavoured curiosity from Western Australia is still a distinctive-tasting Aussie white.

1995 Brown Bros Late Harvest Riesling, Milawa, half-bottle, £6.99
16/20

Sweet 👜👜 ⚬

Ripe, sweet, abundantly aromatic Victorian Riesling with a floral character and orange-peel notes.

1996 Brown's of Padthaway Unoaked Chardonnay, £7.49   17/20
Dry 👜👜👜 ⚬

Concentrated, full-bodied, super-ripe Padthaway Chardonnay with flavours of lemon and butter. An unwooded style that works.

1996 Penfolds Chardonnay Sauvignon Blanc, Organic, Clare Valley, £7.49   17/20
Dry 👜👜👜 ⚬

From one of Australia's very few organic vineyards, this is a beautifully crafted, subtly oaked Clare Valley blend with real elegance and class.

FRANCE

1995 Château Terres Douces, Bordeaux, Cuvée Prestige, £5.49
14/20

Dry 👜 ⚬

Made by Bordeaux négociant Ginestet, this is a fresh, lemony, oak-matured white, which lacks the third dimension of the previous vintage.

1996 Top 40 Chardonnay, Vin de Pays d'Oc, £5.49   16/20
Dry 👜👜👜 ⚬

A Franco-Australian collaboration has resulted in a fresh, concentrated, cleverly oaked southern French Chardonnay with lots of flavour and complexity. As the name implies, this is a limited edition of 40 barrels.

1996 Tokay Pinot Gris d'Alsace, Cave de Beblenheim, £5.75   14/20
Off-dry 👜 ⚬

Pleasant, lightly spicy, off-dry Alsace Pinot Gris that lacks a bit of definition, from the Beblenheim co-operative.

1995 Waitrose Gewürztraminer, Cave de Beblenheim, £5.99 14/20
Off-dry 👜 🍾
An aromatic, slightly hollow Gewürztraminer, which falls a little flat.

1996 Mâcon Solutré, Auvigue, £6.95 17/20
Dry 👜👜👜 🍾
Delicately oaked Mâcon Chardonnay with crisp, citrus-fruit characters and real concentration. Highly enjoyable.

1996 Sancerre 'Hautes Rives' Pierre Guery, £6.99 16/20
Bone dry 👜👜👜 ━
Nettley, if faintly austere, Sancerre with juicy, elderfloral fruit and good concentration.

1996 Domaine de la Baume Chardonnay/Viognier, Vin de Pays d'Oc, £6.99 16/20
Dry 👜👜👜 🍾
From the Australian-owned La Baume winery, this is a sweetly oaked, peachy white with elegant fruit flavours and intensity.

1996 Pouilly Fumé, Masson-Blondelet, £7.49 17/20
Bone dry 👜👜👜 ━
Tighter, better and more structured than the Sancerre, this is a classically flinty Pouilly Fumé with poise and delightful length of flavour.

GERMANY

1996 Ockfener Bockstein Riesling QbA, Dr Wagner, Saar, £5.45
16/20

Medium dry 👜👜👜 ━
Crisp, racy, attractive Mosel Riesling with featherweight alcohol and a citrusy tang.

1989 Geisenheimer Mäuerchen Riesling Spätlese, Schönborn, £5.95 16/20
Medium sweet 👜👜👜 🍾
Petrolly, honeyed, appealingly mature Rheingau Riesling with a sumptuous texture and steely acidity. Terrific value.

NEW ZEALAND

1996 Millton Organic Barrel-Fermented Chenin Blanc, Gisborne, £7.99   16/20
Bone dry 👜👜 ▬
Off-the-wall New Zealand Chenin Blanc from biodynamic exponent, James Millton. There's more than a hint of honeyed Vouvray about this idiosyncratic wine.

SOUTH AFRICA

1996 Avontuur Chardonnay Le Chardon, Stellenbosch, £5.49 16/20
Dry 👜👜👜 ▮
Well-made, complex, butterscotchy South African Chardonnay at an excellent price.

1996 Springfield Special Cuvée Sauvignon Blanc, Robertson, £6.75   16/20
Dry 👜👜👜 ▮
Tangy, grapefruity, intensely flavoured Robertson Sauvignon Blanc, which shows what the Cape is capable of in the Sancerre stakes.

UNITED STATES

1995 Bonterra Organic Chardonnay, Fetzer, California, £7.49
                                                                16/20
Dry 👜👜 ▮
Full, oaky, leesy, organic Chardonnay from Fetzer's Mendocino Garden of Eden. Rich, buttery and full-flavoured.

Over £8

AUSTRALIA

1996 Cape Mentelle Sauvignon Blanc Semillon, Western Australia, £8.99   17/20
Dry 👜👜👜 ▮
Passion-fruit and guava-like Western Australian blend from the brilliant, Veuve Clicquot-owned Cape Mentelle winery. Consistently one of Australia's finest aromatic whites.

1993 De Bortoli Rare Dry Botrytis Semillon, South East Australia, £8.99   16/20
Dry 👛👛 ▮

A highly unusual wine, which smells sweet but tastes dry, rich and honeyed with a lemony twist.

1995 Henschke Sauvignon/Semillon, South Australia, £9.55   17/20
Dry 👛👛👛 ▬

From the cool-climate Eden Valley, this is a subtle, mealy, Graves-style white from one of Australia's most outstanding wineries.

FRANCE

1994 Château de la Chartreuse, Sauternes, half-bottle, £9.75
16/20

Very sweet 👛👛 ▬

Oaky, well-made Sauternes with flavours of peach, vanilla and acacia honey and a degree of botrytis-induced complexity.

1990 Vouvray 'Le Haut Lieu' Moelleux, Huet, £28.50   20/20
Very sweet 👛👛👛 ▬

Amazing, botrytis-rich Loire Valley sticky from biodynamic exponent Noel Pingay. Stunningly concentrated and richly honeyed Chenin Blanc, which would outlive us if it got the chance.

ITALY

1993 Le Grance, Vino da Tavola, Tenuta Caparzo, £11.75   17/20
Dry 👛👛 ▮

A Tuscan blend of Chardonnay, Sauvignon Blanc and Traminer with rich, skilfully executed, oaky fruit flavours and a twist of ripe pear and vanilla.

Red

Under £3

FRANCE

1996 Les Trois Couronnes, Vin de Pays de l'Hérault, £2.79   13/20
Light-bodied 🍶🍶 ▮
Clean, fresh, cherry fruity Languedoc rouge for picnicking.

1996 Domaine de Rose Merlot/Syrah, Vin de Pays d'Oc, £2.99
14/20
Medium-bodied 🍶🍶🍶 ▮
Graciously named after one of the *Grapevine* authors, we presume (no royalties received, mind), this is a run-of-the-mill Languedoc rouge at an attractive price.

ROMANIA

1996 Willow Ridge Merlot, £2.89   14/20
Medium-bodied 🍶🍶🍶 ▮
Pleasant, peppery Romanian Merlot for easy-drinking.

£3–5

ARGENTINA

1996 La Bamba Pinot Noir Syrah, Mendoza, £3.99   14/20
Medium-bodied 🍶🍶 ▮
Charry, full-flavoured Argentine blend from Peñaflor, with a modicum of strawberry fruit.

AUSTRALIA

Bushman's Crossing Dry Red, South East Australia, £3.59   13/20
Light-bodied 🍶 ▮
Light, fruity, if oaky-chippy Aussie red made with the barbie – or saddlebag – in mind.

Ridgewood Mataro Grenache, South East Australia, £3.69   14/20
Medium-bodied 👜👜 🍾

A blend of Mataro, aka Mourvèdre, and Grenache, with spicy oak, strawberry and plum fruit and simple tannins.

1996 Hardy's Southern Creek Shiraz/Cabernet, £3.99   15/20
Medium-bodied 👜👜 🍾

For an extra 30 pence you can get hold of this richly coloured, spicy Shiraz and Cabernet Sauvignon blend, with sweetly ripe berry flavours and pleasant tannins.

CHILE

1996 La Palma Merlot, Rapel Valley, £3.99   15/20
Medium-bodied 👜👜👜 🍾

Juicy, green-pepper-like Chilean Merlot with supple tannins and good length of flavour. Very drinkable.

1995 Isla Negra Cabernet Sauvignon, Rapel, £4.35   15/20
Medium-bodied 👜👜👜 🍾

Youthful, deeply coloured Chilean Cabernet Sauvignon with oaky, chocolatey sweet fruit and a green edge on the aftertaste.

FRANCE

1996 Winter Hill Red, Vin de Pays de l'Aude, £3.29   14/20
Medium-bodied 👜👜 🍾

Supple, plummy, easy-drinking southern French red made in a Beaujolais mould.

Good Ordinary Claret, Bordeaux, £3.65   14/20
Medium-bodied 👜👜 🍾

Aptly named Bordeaux rouge from Bordeaux négociant Ginestet. A good luncheon claret, as they used to say, and probably still do in Pall Mall.

1995 Waitrose Côtes du Rhône, Louis Mousset, £3.65   14/20
Medium-bodied 👜👜 🍾

Simple, peppery, faintly rustic Côtes du Rhône at an affordable price.

1996 Trinity Ridge , Vin de Pays d'Oc, £3.75   13/20
Medium-bodied 👜 🍾

Firm, grassy blend of Cabernet Sauvignon, Merlot and Syrah with a rather chewy dry finish. An unholy trinity.

1996 Winter Hill Pinot Noir/Merlot, £3.89   14/20
Medium-bodied 👜👜 ⌇

An unusual blend for the Languedoc of Burgundy's Pinot Noir grape with the Merlot of Bordeaux, producing an attractive, if faintly dry, cherryish red, from Foncalieu.

1996 Domaine de Sérame Syrah, Vin de Pays d'Oc, Jacques Lurton, £3.99   14/20
Medium-bodied 👜👜 ⌇

Robust, aromatic Mediterranean Syrah with blackberry fruit and rather rasping acidity.

1995 Red Burgundy, J.-C. Boisset, £4.99   15/20
Medium-bodied 👜👜 ⌇

Basic, but attractive, cherry fruity red Burgundy from a good vintage.

1995 Château Villepreux, Bordeaux Supérieur, £4.99   16/20
Medium-bodied 👜👜👜 ⌇

Elegant, well-priced petit château claret with grassy freshness and a hint of vanilla oak.

ITALY

1996 Laste Merlot Atesino, IGT, Concilio, £3.99   14/20
Medium-bodied 👜👜 ⌇

Soft, grassy, Cabernet Franc-like north Italian Merlot made by Australian Kym Milne.

1995 Montepulciano d'Abruzzo, Umani Ronchi, £3.99   15/20
Medium-bodied 👜👜👜 ⌇

Plum and bitters-scented Italian rosso with chocolatey flavours and a herby twist of acidity.

1996 Teroldego Rotaliano, Ca' Vit, £4.45   15/20
Light-bodied 👜👜 ⌇

Juicy, bubble gummy north Italian red made from the Teroldego grape in the sub-Alpine Trentino region.

SOUTH AFRICA

1996 Diamond Hills Pinotage/Cabernet Sauvignon, £3.99   15/20
Medium-bodied 🍷🍷🍷 ▮
Softly aromatic, flavoursome Cape blend with hints of blackberry, baked banana and spice. Very drinkable at under £4.

1996 Culemborg Unwooded Pinotage, £4.29   15/20
Medium-bodied 🍷🍷🍷 ▮
Classic Pinotage flavours of wild strawberry and raspberry jam with an earthy undertone.

1996 Du Toitskloof Cabernet Sauvignon/Shiraz, £4.49   15/20
Medium-bodied 🍷🍷 ▮
Light, perfumed, ultra-minty Cape blend with pure cassis-fruit flavours.

1995 Long Mountain Shiraz Western Cape, £4.49   14/20
Full-bodied 🍷 ▮
Made by Robin Day (not Sir Robin, that is, but the chief winemaker at Australia's Orlando) to an attempted Jacob's Creek-style formula, this is a chunky, blackberry fruity Shiraz with robust tannins.

1996 Benguela Current Savanha Merlot, Western Cape, £4.75
15/20

Medium-bodied 🍷🍷 ▮
Grassy, pleasantly fruity Cape Merlot with rounded tannins and a sweet middle. We're not sure if the Benguela Current is a kind of tide or dried grape. Answers on a postage stamp…

SPAIN

1994 Rioja Crianza, Berberana, £4.45   15/20
Medium-bodied 🍷🍷 ▮
Subtle, smoky, sweetly oaked Rioja Crianza from the respected Berberana group.

1994 Agramont Tinto Crianza, DO Navarra, £4.75   15/20
Medium-bodied 🍷🍷 ▮
Liquorice and tobacco-scented, oaky Navarra blend of Tempranillo and Cabernet Sauvignon from the modern Principe de Viana winery.

1995 Enate Tinto, DO Somontano, £4.95 15/20
Medium-bodied 👜👜 ❚
From the computer whizz-kid Jesús Altajona, this is a spicily refreshing, oak-aged blend, which promises a little more than it delivers.

£5–8

AUSTRALIA

1997 Yaldara Old Vine Grenache, Barossa Valley, £5.75 16/20
Full-bodied 👜👜👜 ━
Succulent old-vine Grenache from the traditional Barossa Valley north of Adelaide, with soft tannins and a sweet core of raspberry and rhubarb fruitiness.

1995 Tatachilla Cabernet Sauvignon, McLaren Vale, £7.45 16/20
Full-bodied 👜👜 ━
Coffee-bean oaky, chocolatey McLaren Vale Cabernet Sauvignon with ripe fruit flavours and fine tannins.

1996 De Bortoli Windy Peak Pinot Noir, Victoria, £7.95 16/20
Light-bodied 👜👜👜 ❚
Subtle, elegant rhubarb and cherry fruity Victorian Pinot Noir with a touch of oak. One of Australia's best-value Pinot Noirs.

1995 Brown's of Padthaway Cabernet Sauvignon/Malbec, £7.99
17/20
Medium-bodied 👜👜👜 ━
Chocolatey, rich, concentrated Padthaway blend of Cabernet Sauvignon and Malbec, with supple tannins and masses of flavour.

FRANCE

1995 Hautes Côtes de Beaune, Tête de Cuvée, £6.99 15/20
Medium-bodied 👜👜 ❚
Scented, attractively textured Pinot Noir with a typical touch of Hautes Côtes rusticity planed smooth by gentle oak maturation.

1995 Château des Combes Canon, Canon-Fronsac, £7.95   16/20
Medium-bodied 🎒🎒 ▬
Modern, mocha-scented Right Bank claret with lots of colour, smooth tannins and flavour.

ITALY

1991 'Poggio a' Frati' Chianti Riserva DOCG, Rocca di Castagnoli, £7.99   16/20
Medium-bodied 🎒🎒🎒 ▬
Leafy, savoury, mature, liquid cherry fruit and a pleasantly bitter tang make this an attractive, well-priced Chianti Riserva.

SOUTH AFRICA

1996 Clos Malverne Pinotage, Stellenbosch, £6.49   17/20
Full-bodied 🎒🎒🎒 ▬
Essence of Pinotage from one of South Africa's best exponents of this weird crossing of Pinot Noir and Cinsaut. This is supple and richly oaked with intense black fruit flavours.

1995 Fairview Cabernet Franc Merlot, Paarl, £6.75   16/20
Medium-bodied 🎒🎒 ▮
Light, elegant green-bean-style Cape blend from cheese and wine goatman, Charles Back. A wanna-be St Emilion.

1993 Warwick Estate Cabernet Franc, Stellenbosch, £7.99   17/20
Medium-bodied 🎒🎒🎒 ▮
Stylish, grassy, refreshing Cape Cabernet Franc with real style and finesse from red wine specialist, Norma Ratcliffe.

SPAIN

1995 Cosme Palacio y Hermanos Rioja, £5.75   17/20
Medium-bodied 🎒🎒🎒 ▬
A modern, all-Tempranillo red from the Rioja Alavesa region, which combines oak and structured blackberry and cassis fruitiness in a harmonious whole. Still in its infancy.

UNITED STATES

1994 Fetzer Valley Oaks Cabernet Sauvignon, California, £6.49

15/20

Medium-bodied 🍷 ▮

From the eco-warriors of the West Coast, this is a red in which the sweet blackcurrant fruit is marred by chewy tannins and hefty oak on the aftertaste.

Over £8

CHILE

Valdivieso Caballo Loco, Numero Uno, £9.95   16/20
Medium-bodied 🍷🍷 ▬

Powerful, oaky, broad-shouldered Chilean super-blend from one of South America's most impressive wineries. This distinctively Chilean-style red needs at least another two years in bottle.

FRANCE

1993 Château Sénéjac, Haut Médoc, Cru Bourgeois, £8.45   16/20
Medium-bodied 🍷🍷 ▮

Made by Kiwi Jenny Dobson before she decamped to Sacred Hill in Hawkes Bay, this is a classy, finely crafted claret from a light, curate's egg of a vintage.

1995 Clos St Michel, Châteauneuf-du-Pape, Guy Mousset, £9.95

17/20

Full-bodied 🍷🍷🍷 ▬

A headily aromatic, well-balanced blend of Grenache, Syrah and Mourvèdre, with lovely spice and pepper characters in abundance.

1994 Château Malescasse, Haut-Médoc, £11.45   17/20
Medium-bodied 🍷🍷🍷 ▬

A well-proportioned cru bourgeois claret with plenty of oak and cassis fruitiness. Needs time to soften.

ITALY

1993 Vino Nobile di Montepulciano DOCG, Avignonesi, £8.75

16/20

Full-bodied 🍷🍷 ━

Dense, chewy Sangiovese from one of the best producers in Montepulciano. Classically Italian, and so, it goes without saying, needs food.

NEW ZEALAND

1995 Esk Valley Merlot Cabernet Sauvignon, Hawkes Bay, £8.95

17/20

Medium-bodied 🍷🍷🍷 🍴

From red-wine specialist Gordon Russell of Esk Valley, this is a subtly oaked, voluptuously juicy New Zealand blend with fine tannins, showing that when they're good, Hawkes Bay reds can compete on the world stage.

SPAIN

1989 Marqués de Murrieta Reserva Especial, Rioja, £10.95   14/20

Medium-bodied 🍴

Pruney, dry, old-fashioned Rioja Reserva with a vinegary edge.

Sparkling

£5–8

AUSTRALIA

Seaview Rosé Brut, £6.49   15/20

Off-dry 🍷🍷🍷 🍴

Gluggable, strawberry-scented fizz from Australia's biggest and best sparkling wine producer. Enjoyable party bubbly.

FRANCE

Clairette de Die Tradition, £6.45   15/20
Medium sweet 👜👜 ▮
Grapey, fresh, sweetish Rhône Valley fizz with a sherbety tang, made from Muscat grapes by the méthode ancestrale. France's answer to Asti Spumante.

Over £8

FRANCE

Waitrose Blanc de Blancs Champagne, F. Bonnet, £13.95   15/20
Dry 👜👜 ▮
Fruity, big-bubbled, savoury-rich Chardonnay with a chocolatey undertone.

Waitrose Brut Rosé Champagne, Union Auboise, £14.95   16/20
Dry 👜👜👜 ▮
Frothy, malty, complex pink fizz with super length and flavour, from the Union Auboise co-operative.

1989 Waitrose Champagne Brut, F. Bonnet, £15.95   16/20
Dry 👜👜👜 ▮
Yeasty, nutty, mature vintage Champagne with a creamy mousse and good length of flavour. Stylish stuff.

Fortified

£5–8

SPAIN

Pando Fino, Williams & Humbert, £5.25   16/20
Dry 👜👜👜 ▮
On current form, this is one of the best Fino sherries. Fresh, savoury, tangy and full of flavour, it's also generously full-bodied at 17 per cent alcohol.

Waitrose Solera Jerezana Dry Amontillado, £5.25   15/20
Off-dry 👜👜 🍶
A bit light for an Amontillado, but this is still attractively nutty and fresh. Good value at just over £5.

Waitrose Solera Jerezana Rich Cream, £5.25   15/20
Very sweet 👜👜 🍶
Raisiny, sweet Pedro Ximenez Sherry in a rich, Oloroso style, with a kick on the finish like Sancho Panza's mule.

Over £8

PORTUGAL

Churchill's Dry White Port, £8.99   16/20
Sweet 👜👜 🍶
The sort of wine normally drunk only in Portugal, this is an intense tawny Port-meets-Madeira-style fortified white with loads of character. Dry, however, it is not.

Churchill's Crusted Port (Bottled 1987), £11.49   17/20
Full-bodied 👜👜👜 ━
Lusciously sweet and aromatic vintage-style Port with masses of firm, concentrated fruit, peppery tannins and great balance.

SPAIN

Apostoles Oloroso Muy Viejo, Gonzalez Byass, half-bottle, £9.95
                                               18/20

Medium dry 👜👜👜 ━
A venerable Palo Cortado from one of Gonzalez Byass' oldest soleras, this is an almondy Sherry with tangy complexity and astonishing length of flavour.

The *Grapevine* Guide to Independent Wine Merchants

Introduction

For a decent evening out most of us can content ourselves with a meal at a Pizza Express or a Café Rouge. Stifle that yawn for a moment. Now that restaurant dining has become an accepted part of the 1990s' good life, expectations have grown and gastronomic horizons expanded. Responding to demand, restaurants offering fresh food and eclectic cooking with the personal stamp of the individual chef or owner have shot up like shiitake mushrooms on a Tesco shelf.

As with dining at Pizza Express and its ilk, one-stop shopping in supermarkets, topped up by occasional visits to the local off-licence, may be enough to keep us liquid and reasonably happy. Today the overall standard of wines in the high street is better, after all, than it ever was. But we were born free, so if we don't have to do all our eating and drinking in chains, why do we have to do all our wine buying in them? The answer is that we don't.

Anyone who's paid a bit more for a bottle of wine and experienced the thrill of true quality or character will have had a glimpse of a vinous Nirvana beyond the supermarket and high-street chain. This is where the independent wine merchant comes in. It gets to the parts, so to speak, that the chains can't reach, with a range of quality wines and a level of personal service and attention that even the likes of Oddbins can't hope to replicate.

Something for everyone

There may be a lurking grain of truth in the view of the independent wine merchant as an old-fashioned institution dealing in expensive wines for a well-heeled, but dying élite. Ultra-traditional wine merchants such as Berry Bros & Rudd, Justerini & Brooks and Corney & Barrow play to such a gallery when they flaunt the royal seal and the creaking stairs to the cellar. For every traditional merchant, though, there are half a dozen professional, modern companies, catering for the tastes and lifestyles of a generation for whom claret, Port and Burgundy are not the be all and end all.

Experience gleaned from combing vineyards on and off the beaten track gives the independents a level of expertise and enthusiasm that is second to none. Large or small, traditional or modern, specialist or generalist, upright or downright quirky, the sector encompasses an immense variety of type and style of operation, each stamped with the hallmark of its own personality.

If you're a customer, it doesn't matter if you live in Truro and your wine

Independent Wine Merchants

merchant is in Edinburgh. With a list as its shop window, a phone or PC through which to communicate, and transport to deliver to your door, the independent wine merchant is as accessible as, and in some instances more so than, any high-street chain. So what, more precisely, does the independent wine merchant have to offer over and above Tesco or Bottoms Up? If you are the customer of a wine merchant, you'll be familiar with the type of thing.

The advantages of specialisation

No high-street retailer can match Noel Young for his peerless Austrian line-up, Valvona & Crolla for its splendid Italian range, Moreno or Laymont and Shaw for their Spanish wines, Vin du Van or the Australian Wine Club for their extensive Aussie portfolios. By devoting themselves to specific areas, they know their onions and they're well positioned to unearth the best. Even within countries, you'll find regional specialists such as Yapp Bros or Gauntley's of Nottingham in the Rhône or Howard Ripley in Burgundy.

Specialisation doesn't have to be by country or region. There's a handful of organic specialists, for instance, such as Vintage Roots and Vinceremos. And with one or two exceptions, supermarkets are not terribly good at selling mature or expensive wines. Independent wine merchants are. Most traditional merchants carry stocks of mature vintages that simply can't be found in the high street. At the really pukka end of the market, fine and rare wines are a speciality of, among others, Farr Vintners, Peter Wylie and Reid Wines (1992) Ltd.

Thanks to regular personal contact with suppliers, independent wine merchants are often able to understand and communicate the passion of the grower. Take Burgundy and California, for instance, two regions where quality begins at price levels too risky for most supermarkets and high-street chains. Authentic grower's Burgundy is wonderful stuff, likewise Pinot Noir and Chardonnay from top Californian estates. To enjoy the stuff, however, you have to pay more. And get on the books of the likes of Haynes, Hanson and Clark, Morris & Verdin, or Raeburn Fine Wines – merchants, that is, who thrive on visiting their suppliers.

The lone ranger syndrome

As we pointed out last year, the number of urban, suburban and country-based lone rangers is increasing. Howard Ripley, Noel Young, Nick Brookes of The Vine Trail, Michael Pollard of Chippendale Fine Wines and Ian Brown of Vin du Van typify the new breed of one-man band. They are not greedy or ambitious, but they know what they like and they know their customers' tastes, too. Firms such as Chippendale Fine Wines or Vin du Van may come across as the Harry Hills of the wine trade, but all the more power to their nostrils if they can do it as professionally as Mr Hill.

Delivered to your doorstep

Mail order is an expanding area of operation for independent wine merchants. It's an art to sell a wine off a page, and the best, such as Adnams' offers, for instance, can have you drooling at the mouth-watering descriptions. Customers of the biggest of the mail-order merchants in Britain, Bordeaux Direct, receive a steady stream of informative literature along with their cases of wine. In its safer, more staid way, the Wine Society offers a similar service. Increasingly, independents are producing better, more informative literature, to entice customers into buying. Delivery, especially if you live outside a town or city, is a sine qua non of the service.

Services rendered

Like the little cheese shop or fishmonger who's survived the supermarket onslaught, there's no substitute for the personal touch, despite moves in some supermarkets to involve customers more. Personal attention, a range of services and good relationships with customers set the independents apart. In the age of the computer, the need for human interaction is all the more important. Dispensing expertise and advice in a smiling, no-nonsense manner, about what to drink with what or the optimum moment for drinking a particular wine, is part and parcel of the service. Equally, opportunities to meet producers at wine tastings or festivals or to go on wine trips and visit vineyards add immeasurably to the personal flavour.

I shall be released

Pre-release offers before bottling of the new vintage of, typically, Bordeaux, are one of the staples of the independent's business. Following the revival of interest in futures with the 1995 Bordeaux vintage, the offer of 1996 Bordeaux en primeur, and up to a point, 1995 Burgundy, was a great success in the early summer. On the back of such offers, a number of independents are now regularly offering Burgundy, Rhône and German wines on a pre-release basis. As long as this type of offer is popular with customers, it may not be long before we see the service extended to Italy and the New World.

Deliciously different

The great virtue of the independent sector is that it doesn't conform to stereotype. Often built up through the personality of an individual or family, what the successful wine merchant has to offer its customers is a point, or several points, of difference from the increasing standardisation of the supermarket and high-street chains. Basically, being an independent is about being different, playing to its strengths and personalised service. Long live independence!

Adnams

Address: The Crown, High Street, Southwold, Suffolk IP18 6DP

Telephone/fax: 01502 727220 (general enquiries); 01502 727222 (mail order); 01502 727223 (fax)

Number of branches: 3

Opening hours: Mail order: 9.00am to 5.00pm Monday to Friday, and 9.00am to 12.00am Saturday; Southwold Wine Shop, Pinkneys Lane, Southwold, IP18 6EW: 10.00am to 6.30pm Monday to Saturday; The Grapevine, 109 Unthank Road, Norwich, NR2 2PE: 9.00am to 9.00pm Monday to Saturday; The Cellar and Kitchen Store: 10.00am to 6.30pm Monday to Saturday

Credit cards accepted: Access, Connect, Switch, Visa

Discounts: 5 per cent on orders of five cases or more

Facilities and services: In-store tastings; glasses and ice; advice; cellarage; Adnams Wine Course; gift packs; wine search (for wines not on the list); corporate supply; wine list compilation; lectures and tutored tastings; bacchanalia supplement (fine oils, kitchenware, etc.)

Mail order: Free delivery on any order over £100, or for two cases or more, to any mainland UK address

Areas of specialisation: French country wines, Loire, Alsace, Bordeaux, Burgundy, Germany, Italy, Australia, California

In January of this year, one half of the *Grapevine* team shared a car touring the vineyards of southern Italy and Sicily with the ear-ringed chairman of the Adnams Board, Simon Loftus. From this unique vantage point, we were able to observe at first hand the Loftus buying technique, which combines a ready camera, pen and palate with an unnerving ability to charm and haggle. It's a technique that rubs off on the buying team of Alastair Marshall and Rob Chase, who are dispatched to every corner of the vinous globe in search of fresh vinous treasures.

The result is one of the best-produced, most entertaining lists in the country, the key to which is enthusiasm and a sense of adventure. You may not always like an Adnams' selection, but you have to admire its inclusion, because there's always passion and genuine interest behind the choice. Adnams' buying staff are not interested in me-too brands and safe choices. Nor, it seems, are its customers. Their raison d'être is in venturing to off-the-map places and returning with hand-selected, occasionally off-the-wall gems from the heroes of the wine world – the growers.

Adnams is the place for the mail-order wine lover with a taste for the idiosyncratic, the characterful and the exotic. It also deserves praise for its willingness to champion unfashionable local grapes and unusual wine styles, which don't conform to the straitjacket of Chardonnay or Cabernet Sauvignon. Like the list, Adnams' special offers, illustrated in creative prose and art-house photos, are always mouth-wateringly tempting. And if you ever did get tired of the wines, there's always a pint of bitter to refresh the palate.

White

£3–5

SPAIN

1996 Basa, Rueda Blanco, £4.45   15/20
Dry 💰💰💰 ▌
Made for Adnams by pin-up winemaker Telmo Rodriguez, this is a Verdejo-based Spanish white with small quantities of Viura and Sauvignon Blanc. A zesty, modern, pleasantly grapefruity white with good weight.

£5–8

AUSTRALIA

1997 David Wynn Unwooded Chardonnay, Eden Valley, £6.95
                                                                      16/20
Dry 💰💰 ▌
Made by Adam Wynn, one of Australia's leading Chardonnay specialists, this is a ripe, textured, tropical fruity Eden Valley Chardonnay with notes of melon and peach and plenty of impact and flavour on the palate.

FRANCE

1996 Pech-Céleyran Viognier, Vin de Pays des Côtes de Pérignan, £5.95   16/20
Dry 👜👜👜 |

Full-flavoured, southern French Viognier with more weight and depth than many examples of the Languedoc's second trendiest grape (after Chardonnay). Attractive apricot fruit and fresh acidity make this an enjoyable drink.

1996 Domaine des Forges, Coteaux du Layon, Claude Branchereau, £6.95   17/20
Sweet 👜👜👜 ➡

Rich, appley, honeyed Chenin Blanc from an excellent vintage, with enough acidity to stop the wine cloying and delightful balance and length.

1996 Beaujolais Blanc, Domaine des Terres Dorées, £7.20   16/20
Dry 👜👜 |

An unusual white Beaujolais made from the Chardonnay grape, with mealy, unoaked flavours in a mini Pouilly-Fuissé mould. Fresh and delicately honeyed with good length of flavour and acidity.

GERMANY

1996 Riesling Kabinett, Carl Aug. Immich Batterieberg, Mosel, £7.95   16/20
Medium sweet 👜👜 ➡

Very tight and youthful at the moment, but this stylish Mosel Riesling is going to be extremely impressive in a year or two. For the time being you'll have to be content with crisp Cox's apple fruit and a tangy bite of acidity.

NEW ZEALAND

1996 Forrest Estate Sauvignon Blanc, £7.95   16/20
Dry 👜👜 |

Well-made Marlborough Sauvignon with classic green-bean and elderflower flavours and decent concentration and balance. A little pricey, but then Marlborough often is.

Over £8

FRANCE

1996 Alsace Gewürztraminer, P. Blanck, £8.45   17/20
Dry 🛍🛍🛍 ▐
If anything is going to get you excited about Gewürztraminer, this is it. Rich, abundantly aromatic, lychee and rose-petal-like white with everything in balance. Weighty and super-ripe.

Red

£3–5

FRANCE

1996 Mas des Chimères, Oeillade, Vin de Pays des Coteaux du Salagou, £4.95   15/20
Full-bodied 🛍🛍 ▐
From a little-known vin de pays area, this is a soft, peppery, alcoholic, Grenache-based southern French red from Guilhem Dardé. Miles better than most basic Côtes du Rhône.

1996 Carignan, Domaine Henry, Vin de Pays de l'Hérault, £4.95
16/20
Full-bodied 🛍🛍🛍 ▬
Ultra-concentrated, old-vine Carignan with robust tannins, vibrant fruit and powerful alcohol. A classic Adnams' find, with masses of character for your francs.

ITALY

1995 Montepulciano d'Abruzzo, Roxan, Cantine Sociale di Montepulciano, £4.85   16/20
Full-bodied 🛍🛍🛍 ▐
Robustly peppery, liquoricey Abruzzo red with sweet-and-savoury characters and ripe blackberry fruit. Very well balanced with a thirst-quenching snap of acidity.

SPAIN

1996 Baso Navarra Garnacha, Vinos de la Granja, £3.99   14/20
Medium-bodied 👜👜 ▮
The companion bottle to the Basa (sic) white, this is a simple, blackberry and
liquorice-like red with a herby twist, from Telmo Rodriguez.

£5–8

FRANCE

1995 Faugères, Les Jardins, Domaine St Antonin, £5.35   17/20
Full-bodied 👜👜👜 ▬▬
Chunky, herb-infused Faugères with come-hither blackberry fruit, cigar-box
spice and meaty, sinewy tannins. Still youthful, but already a very impressive
wine.

1996 Château du Grand Moulas, Côtes du Rhône, £5.40   16/20
Full-bodied 👜👜👜 ▬▬
Made by one of our favourite southern Rhône producers, this is a seriously
chunky, Grenache-dominated red with good concentration and weight and
sweet red-fruit flavours.

ITALY

1995 Eloro Rosso, Cantina La Elorina, £5.95   16/20
Full-bodied 👜👜👜 ▬▬
From the Noto hills in Sicily, this is a youthful, deeply coloured red made from
the Nero d'Avola grape, with spicy, warm-climate fruit, weighty black cherry,
plum and raisin characters and a bitter chocolate twist.

1994 Sangiovese di Toscana, Conti Contini, £5.95   16/20
Medium-bodied 👜👜👜 ▮
Vinified at Tuscany's respected Capezzana estate, this is a soft, black cherry
fruity wine made in a very modern style with refreshing acidity and smooth,
lingering tannins. Very well priced.

UNITED STATES

1994 Madrona Zinfandel, Sonoma, £6.20   16/20
Full-bodied 🍷🍷🍷 ▬

Tobaccoey, cedary, youthful California Zinfandel matured in American oak and showing liquorice and bramble fruit and plenty of sappy personality.

Over £8

FRANCE

1995 Châteauneuf-du-Pape, Vieux Mas des Papes, H. Brunier, £10.85   18/20
Full-bodied 🍷🍷🍷 ▬

Made by the Brunier family of the celebrated Domaine du Vieux Télégraphe, this is a powerfully concentrated, chocolatey, Grenache-dominated red with delightful, savoury spice and layers of flavour and intensity. Still young.

1995 Bourgogne Côte Chalonnaise, La Digoine, A. et P. de Villaine, £10.95   16/20
Medium-bodied 🍷🍷 ▮

Ripe, cherry and raspberry fruity Côte Chalonnaise Pinot Noir made at the family domaine of the co-owner of Vosne-Romanée's ultra-prestigious Domaine de la Romanée-Conti. Finishes on the firm side.

UNITED STATES

1994 Sangiovese, Rabbit Ridge, Sonoma, £9.95   15/20
Full-bodied 🍷 ▮

Charry, substantially oaked Sonoma Sangiovese, which doesn't bear much resemblance to Chianti as we know and love it. At this price, you'd be better off buying the real thing.

1995 Garnet, Saintsbury, Carneros, £9.95   16/20
Medium-bodied 🍷🍷 ▮

From one of California's leading Pinot Noir specialists, this is a soft, ripe, almost heady Carneros Pinot Noir, with supple loganberry fruit and more than a hint of sweet oak.

Rosé

£5–8

FRANCE

1996 Château Lacroix, Merlot Rosé, Bordeaux, £5.95   15/20
Dry 🍾 ▮
Made by an English winemaker at Château Teyssier, this Merlot-based rosé is a
refreshing, summer pudding-like number with plenty of flavour. £1 cheaper at
Fuller's.

Fortified

Over £8

ITALY

1989 Primitivo, Dolce Naturale, Pervini, £8.60   17/20
Full-bodied 🍾🍾🍾 ▮
Recioto-style Puglian red with concentrated, Porty alcohol, sweet raisiny fruit
and a damsony bite. Highly idiosyncratic, but worth a punt, especially with plain
chocolate or dried figs.

The Australian Wine Club

Address: Freepost (WC5500), Slough, Berks SL3 9BH

Telephone/fax: 0800 716893 (freefone order line); 0800 856 2004; 01753 591369 (fax)

E-mail/Web: sales@austwine.demon.co.uk; www.australian-wine.co.uk

Opening hours: 9.00am to 6.00pm Monday to Friday; 9.00am to 2.00pm Saturday

Credit cards accepted: American Express, Mastercard, Visa

Discounts: Active members of the club's subscription-case schemes receive a 10 per cent discount off all purchases; bulk purchase (5 cases or more) by arrangement

Facilities and services: AWC catalogue published 10–11 times a year; export sales to the Channel Islands; annual 'Great Australian Wine Tasting' featuring an extensive selection of the AWC's wine range, together with over 100 others exhibited by the individual wineries

Mail order: Free delivery to any mainland UK address

Area of specialisation: Australia

After its departure from a dingy basement below South Australia House in the Strand to become a fully fledged mail-order operation in suburban Datchet, the AWC continues to sell what it calls 'mainstream and sought-after wines from many of Australia's top small to medium wineries, with an emphasis on the more unusual varieties'. Under the Buckleys, Laraghys, Apex and Cornerstone labels, it also sells specially commissioned wines. A verbal diarrhoea of newsletters, irreverent comment and banter (or insult, if you're a journalist) comes with the territory.

The focus is largely on South Australia and, in particular, good to excellent estates such as Tim Adams, St Hallett, Heritage, Veritas, The Willows, Primo Estate, David Traegar and Pam Dunsford's Chapel Hill. Apart from much drinking of Cooper's sparkling ale and boat trips down the Murray River, forays to Oz by Craig Smith, formerly of the Drunken Mouse, bring in occasional new crops of interesting stuff. After the latest such outing, the lads from Datchet are touting Torbreck, Koppamurra and Riley's Cottage as names to watch out for.

The Australian Wine Club

The AWC's prices aren't the cheapest, but with delivery, newsletters and a slice of attitude thrown in for good measure, the service is excellent. Although Australian prices have gone up, wines in the £6 and £12 price bracket continue to represent pretty good value and this is the AWC's strength. According to the AWC, 'Smaller wineries have a more realistic view of what can be achieved in the UK, as opposed to chasing perceived opportunities in some of the more esoteric export markets.'

If you want single bottles, try Tesco or Thresher, to whom the AWC supplies a fair bit of wine. But for Aussie 'estate wines' by the case, the AWC, with its expertise and relaxed approach, remains the best place to buy mail-order Aussie wines in Britain. Its predictions for the coming year? 'We are confident that we will get approximately one year older.' A bit rash, boys?

White

£5–8

AUSTRALIA

1997 Primo Estate Colombard, £6.99   16/20
Dry 👛👛 🍷
Tropical, guava and passion fruity Colombard from Joe Grilli's vineyards on the Adelaide Plains. Like a super-charged Gascon white.

1996 St Hallett Riesling, Eden Valley, £7.99   17/20
Dry 👛👛👛 ➡
Elegant, almost European-style Eden Valley Riesling with refreshing acidity and subtle, mineral and lime-zest characters. A very successful first release from St Hallett in a defiant Mosel flute bottle.

1996 Eldredge Riesling, Clare Valley, £7.99   17/20
Dry 👛👛👛 ➡
Rich, floral, lime-infused Clare Valley Riesling from the Watervale district, which is still tight and youthful at the moment. Has the weight and concentration to develop in bottle.

Over £8

AUSTRALIA

1996 St Hallett Semillon Select, Barossa Valley, £8.99   17/20
Dry 🍷🍷🍷 ▬
Classic Barossa Valley Semillon from Big Bob McLean, with typical flavours of lemon butter and herbal undertones, balanced by spicy oak. Should age very well into something a little more complex.

1996 Tim Adams Semillon, Clare Valley, £8.99   17/20
Dry 🍷🍷🍷 ▬
Stylish, well-made Semillon, which is beginning to mature into something smoky, complex and refreshing. Cleverly oaked and an improvement on the 1995.

1994 Galah Chardonnay, Adelaide Hills, £8.99   15/20
Dry 🍷 ▮
Mature, golden-hued, cool-climate Chardonnay from the Adelaide Hills, with hefty alcohol and oak handling and a slightly coarse finish.

1995 Penley Estate Chardonnay, Coonawarra, £9.50   16/20
Dry 🍷 ▮
Smoky oaky, richly textured Coonawarra Chardonnay from Kym Tolley, with a faintly bitter finish. Well made without being particularly enjoyable.

1996 Geoff Weaver Sauvignon Blanc, Lenswood, £9.99   17/20
Dry 🍷🍷🍷 ▮
From Geoff Weaver's Stafford Ridge Vineyard in the cool Adelaide Hills, this is an intense, grapefruity, tightly focused Sauvignon Blanc, which is among the best examples of the variety in Australia.

1994 Geoff Weaver Chardonnay, Lenswood, £9.99   18/20
Dry 🍷🍷🍷 ▮
Same producer, same vineyard, different grape variety. This delightfully complex, barrel-fermented Chardonnay with its intense melony elegance and buttery, lees-derived complexity confirms Geoff Weaver's standing as one of Australia's best winemakers.

1996 Chapel Hill Reserve Chardonnay, £10.99 17/20
Dry 👛👛 ▮
A barrel-fermented blend of Padthaway, McLaren Vale and Coonawarra fruit
made by the talented Pam Dunsford. The oak is subtly done, with the emphasis
on richness and citrus-fruit complexity.

Red

£5–8

AUSTRALIA

1996 Laraghy's Cabernet/Shiraz, £5.50 15/20
Full-bodied 👛👛 ▮
Blended specially for the Australian Wine Club, this is a juicy, berry fruit and
spicy oak glugger with lots of flavour and sweetness.

1996 Buckley's Grenache, Clare Valley, £6.99 15/20
Full-bodied 👛 ▮
Sweet and faintly soupy Clare Valley red, with pleasant, brambly fruit and a hint
of sweet oak. Falls a little short and hard on the finish.

1996 Buckley's Shiraz, Clare Valley, £7.99 16/20
Full-bodied 👛👛 ▬
Cinnamon spicy Clare Valley Shiraz with smooth, chocolatey tannins, attractive
berry fruit, well-handled oak sweetness and refreshing acidity.

1995 Primo Estate Shiraz, £7.99 17/20
Full-bodied 👛👛👛 ▬
Smooth, aromatic, sweetly oaked Aussie Shiraz, which displays the suppleness
of a Pinot Noir combined with the blackberry fruit intensity of a Shiraz.
Deliciously drinkable, voluptuous stuff from Joe Grilli, with a dry, grippy
aftertaste.

Over £8

AUSTRALIA

1994 David Traeger Shiraz, Victoria, £7.99   15/20
Medium-bodied 🍷 |
From Victoria's Goulburn Valley, this is an American oak-aged Shiraz with a malty, Ovaltine-like quality, decent blackberry fruit and an undertone of mint and tannin.

1996 RBJ Mourvèdre/Grenache, £8.50   14/20
Full-bodied |
A southern Rhône-style blend of Mourvèdre and Grenache, which trades on its would-be cult image rather than its quality. Hot and hollow.

1995 Galah Shiraz, Clare Valley, £8.99   15/20
Full-bodied 🍷 ➤
Youthful, spearminty, tightly focused Clare Valley Shiraz with lots of flavour and very firm tannins, which may soften with age.

1996 Tim Adams, 'The Fergus', Clare Valley, £8.99   18/20
Full-bodied 🍷🍷🍷 ➤
A Grenache-dominated Clare Valley stunner with homeopathic doses of Cabernet Sauvignon, Cabernet Franc, Shiraz and Malbec. Rich, minty, beautifully textured stuff, which manages to combine power with elegance and style. A lingering delight.

1996 Apex Riverside Vineyard Merlot, Barossa Valley, £9.99   15/20
Medium-bodied 🍷 |
A new discovery for the AWC, this is a small-volume find from the Barossa Valley with mint and lavender aromas, robust, faintly raisiny fruit flavours and a curious loganberry note.

1996 Cornerstone Grenache/Shiraz/Mourvèdre, £9.99   16/20
Full-bodied 🍷 ➤
Ripe, minty, damson fruity blend with vibrant, youthful sweetness, a sheen of new oak and chunky, dry tannins. We find the acidity a little clumsy here.

1994 St Hallett Blackwell Shiraz, £9.99   15/20
Full-bodied 🍷 ▯
Named after St Hallett's winemaker, Stuart Blackwell, this is a smooth, substantially oaked Aussie Shiraz with liquorice and blackberry flavours and puckering acidity.

1994 St Hallett Old Block Shiraz, £13.50   17/20
Full-bodied 🍷🍷 ▬▬
The price may have gone up in recent years, but this is one of the best Old Blocks we've had, with more backbone than previous vintages. Ripe, succulent Barossa Shiraz with exuberant blackberry fruit and stylish American oak.

1995 Primo Estate Joseph Cabernet/Merlot, 'Moda Amarone', £13.99   17/20
Full-bodied 🍷🍷 ▯
Made using the Amarone method of drying the grapes before crushing to concentrate their sugar and flavour, this is a super-rich, concentrated, sweetly oaked Bordeaux-style blend with masses of alcohol, vanilla sweetness and smooth tannins. Very powerful and idiosyncratic.

1995 Tim Adams The Aberfeldy, £14.99   18/20
Full-bodied 🍷🍷🍷 ▬▬
A big, deeply coloured Shiraz from Tim 'Bonecrusher' Adams, with attractive, minty aromas, chocolatey oak and lashings of flavour. Spicy, soft and powerful, with concentrated aromatic power. One of the best 1995 Aussie reds we've had.

Avery's

Address: Orchard House, Southfield Road, Nailsea, Bristol BS19 1JD

Telephone/fax: 01275 811100 (sales office); 01275 811100 (general enquiries); 01275 811101 (fax)

Number of branches: 2

Opening hours: Sales office 9.00am to 5.15pm Monday to Friday; Avery's Shop, 8 Park Street, Bristol (tel. 0117 921 4145): 10.00am to 6.00pm Monday to Saturday; Avery's Wine Cellar, Culver Street, Bristol (tel. 0117 921 4146): 10.00am to 7.00pm. Monday to Saturday

Credit cards accepted: MasterCard, Visa

Discounts: By negotiation on special orders

Facilities and services: Glass hire; tutored tastings; group tastings; delivery; storage of customers' reserves; sale of customers' reserves at auction; newsletters and en primeur offers; in-store tastings in Culver Street Wine Cellars, Bristol; monthly newsletters and special offers; quarterly 'Automatically from Avery's' mixed cases of wine; the Avery's Bin Club

Mail order: Free delivery to any mainland UK address for two cases or more; otherwise, £5.50 per consignment

Areas of specialisation: Burgundy, Bordeaux, Italy, the New World, Port

Avery's is one of the country's most traditional merchants, making its name from nearly two centuries of bottling claret and Burgundy in its Bristol cellars. If Ronald Avery developed his firm's reputation for the traditional staples of the wine world, such as Port, and the French classics, then his son John's pioneering interest in Australia, South Africa, California and New Zealand has added a number of New World strings to the Avery's well-endowed bow.

Today, Avery's business is three-pronged. First, as a wholesaler, it supplies hotels and restaurants. Second, it has an agency rôle, representing a variety of growers for their sales into the UK. And third, it sells to private customers from its two shops in Bristol and via its nationwide mail-order service. Hallgarten is the parent company, and Michael Druitt, which specialises in supplying hotels and restaurants, is the latest addition to the group.

The broad selection in its 1,000-strong list is something of a mixed bag. There's plenty of New World interest in Tyrrells of Australia, Nobilo of New Zealand, Norton of Argentina and Klein Constantia of South Africa, along with Swanson, Sonoma-Cutrer and Far Niente in California, Inniskillin in Canada and Echeverria in Chile. Enate in Somontano and latterly Aguirre in Chile (Undurraga has been dropped) add focus to the Spanish and Chilean ranges.

Over the past year, the main area of expansion has been Italy, with a massive raft of new producers, Carpineto, Torrevento, Badia a Coltibuono, Basilium, Pellegrino, Duca di Castelmonte, Castellani Vini and Pubrida. The Bordeaux and Burgundy sections of the list remain resolutely old-fashioned however. And we're still not convinced by Avery's cosy relationship with some of its suppliers, notably South Africa's Rustenberg and Remoissenet in Burgundy.

The programme of modernisation and expansion, of which Averys' Culver Street Wine Cellars are part, continues. Relocating the offices and warehouse to Nailsea has resulted in the more effective management of stocks and the ability to store customers' reserves in a temperature-controlled warehouse. By October, in line with John Avery's promise last year, Avery's aims to be offering next-day delivery nationwide.

White

£3–5

CHILE

1995 Aguirre Tierra Arena Sauvignon Blanc, £4.70   13/20
Dry 🜶 |
Nettley, bog-standard Chilean Sauvignon Blanc with a note of sweetness. The sort of thing that supermarkets can do for £1 cheaper.

£5–8

AUSTRALIA

1996 Taltarni Fiddleback White, £6.90   14/20
Dry 🍷 🍶
Clean, zesty, refreshing, if rather soft and neutral Aussie white from Frenchman
Dominique Portet; £2 over-priced.

CANADA

1995 Inniskillin Chardonnay, £7.05   15/20
Dry 🍷 🍶
Decent, unoaked, cool-climate Canadian Chardonnay with refreshing acidity. A
Lake Niagara take on Petit Chablis.

FRANCE

1995 Avery's Fine White Burgundy, £6.40   13/20
Dry 🍶
Very basic, faintly gluey white Burgundy with a sharp edge of acidity. Poor value,
given what you can find from Chile and even France at this price.

ISRAEL

1995 Yarden Golan Heights Chardonnay, £8.00   14/20
Dry 🍶
Hefty, clumsily oaked Israeli Chardonnay with a bitter appley edge. Like a
coarse Mâcon Villages. At least it's kosher, Moshe.

NEW ZEALAND

1996 Nobilo Fall Harvest Sauvignon Blanc, £6.65   14/20
Off-dry 🍶
Sweetish, commercial, faintly tropical New Zealand Sauvignon Blanc in a silly
bottle, with tinned pea and gooseberry notes.

1996 Nobilo Poverty Bay Chardonnay, £6.65   15/20
Dry 🍾 🥄
A wine that is justifiably popular with British Airways' passengers, this is a soft, commercial, peach and pineapple style-North Island Chardonnay with no oak.

Over £8

ITALY

1994 Sella del Boscone Chardonnya, Badia a Coltibuono, £12.70
16/20
Dry 🍾 🥄
From one of Tuscany's best red-wine estates, this is a rich, well-made, toasty, nutty Chardonnay with well-integrated new oak and elegant acidity. Ought to be under £10.

Red

£5–8

CHILE

1996 Aguirre Palo Alto Cabernet Franc, £5.30   15/20
Medium-bodied 🍾🍾 🥄
Lively, grassy, capsicum fruity Chilean Cabernet Franc with soft fruit and summery, thirst-quenching acidity. A good alternative to Loire Valley reds.

FRANCE

1995 Avery's Fine Claret, £5.55   14/20
Medium-bodied 🍾 🥄
'Fine' is a bit of an exaggeration for this firm, rustic quaffer. This really ought to be under £5.

1995 Bouchard Aîné Mâcon Rouge Supérieur, £5.95   14/20
Medium-bodied 🍷 ▮
Faintly peppery Mâcon thirst-quencher from a slightly pointless appellation.

1994 Château Gamage, Bordeaux Supérieur, £7.30   15/20
Medium-bodied 🍷 ▮
A grassy, forward, Merlot-based claret from the reasonable 1994 vintage, with smooth tannins and a hint of succulence.

1995 Jaffelin, Brouilly, £7.75   15/20
Light-bodied 🍷 ▮
Pleasant, if uninspiring, cru Beaujolais, with notes of bubblegum and strawberry and crisp acidity. Typical Gamay, really.

ITALY

1994 Ulysse Etna Rosso, Duca di Castelmonte, Pellegrino, £6.25
15/20

Medium-bodied 🍷 ▮
A Sicilian blend of 70 per cent Nerello Cappuccio with Nerello Mascalese, this is a smooth, Mediterranean red with pruney fruit, dryish tannins and a hint of sweet oak.

1994 Castel del Monte Rosso, Il Pedale, £6.65   15/20
Medium-bodied 🍷 ▮
Simple, fruity, surprisingly youthful Puglian red with pleasant raspberry and cherry fruit and no great complexity.

1991 Capitel San Rocco Rosso, Tedeschi, £7.65   16/20
Full-bodied 🍷🍷 ▬
Made by the traditional ripasso method (whereby young Valpolicella wine is re-fermented on the lees of a Recioto), this is a vibrantly fruity, concentrated Veronese red with lovely balance, acidity and freshness, especially for a six-year-old wine.

SPAIN

1995 Enate Tinto Cabernet Sauvignon/Merlot, £5.65   15/20
Medium-bodied 🍷 ▮
From the cool-climate Somontano region, this is a refreshing, oak-aged Bordeaux blend, which promises a little more than it delivers.

1993 Enate Crianza Tempranillo/Cabernet Sauvignon, £7.40   16/20
Medium-bodied 👜👜 ▮

Rioja-like Somontano red with lots of charry oak and strawberry-jam fruitiness. A well-structured tinto with some cool-climate elegance.

Over £8

FRANCE

1993 Avery's Fine Red Burgundy, £10.05   15/20
Medium-bodied 👜 ▮

Chunky, traditional Hautes Côtes red Burgundy with a dry finish and chewy tannins. We expect better from a Burgundy specialist in a vintage like 1993.

1995 Domaine du Grand Tinel, Châteauneuf-du-Pape, £10.95
17/20

Full-bodied 👜👜👜 ▬

Ripe, savoury, concentrated, Grenache-based red from one of our favourite Châteauneuf producers. Powerful, but not overwhelming stuff, with plenty of oomph and alcohol for winter meditation.

SPAIN

1991 Ondarre Rioja Reserva, £8.10   16/20
Medium-bodied 👜👜 ▬

Youthful for a 1991 Reserva, with nicely integrated oak, sweet blackcurrant fruit and a firm backbone of tannin. Should continue to age well.

UNITED STATES

1992 Clos du Val Cabernet Sauvignon, Napa Valley, £16.70   16/20
Medium-bodied 👜 ▮

Frenchman Bernard Portet, who hails from Bordeaux, is at his confident best working with Cabernet Sauvignon. This silky, structured, age-worthy Californian red has fine and attractive cedary oak characters and may benefit from another year or two in bottle but is starting to dry a little.

Sparkling

Over £8

FRANCE

Avery's Champagne, £15.10   14/20
Dry 🍾 ▮
Youthful, gassy Champagne without much in the way of bottle-aged complexity. A decent aperitif fizz.

Fortified

£5–8

UNITED STATES

1995 Quady Essensia Orange Muscat, half-bottle, £6.20   13/20
Very sweet ▮
Barley sugar and orange-blossom-scented California sticky with a hard, spirity edge. Someone must like this kind of thing, but we're not sure who.

Berry Brothers & Rudd

Address: 3 St James's Street, London SW1A 1EG

Telephone/fax: 0171 396 9600 (general enquiries); 0171 396 9669 (order number); 0171 396 9611 (fax)

Number of branches: 4

Opening hours: 3 St James's Street, London: 9.00am to 5.30 pm Monday to Friday; Berry's Wine Warehouse, Hamilton Close, Houndmills, Basingstoke, Hampshire RG21 6YB: 10.00am to 6.00pm Monday to Thursday, 10.00am to 8.00pm Friday and 10.00am to 4.00pm Saturday; Duty Free Wine Shop, Terminal 3 Departures, Heathrow Airport, Middx TW6 1JH: 6.00am to 10.00pm daily; Duty Free Wine Shop, Terminal 4 Departures, Heathrow Airport, Middx TW6 3XA: 6.00am to 10.00pm daily

Credit cards accepted: Access, American Express, Diners, JCB, Mastercard, Visa

Facilities and services: Regular and ad hoc mailings; broking; cellar advice including Tailor Made Cellar Plans; storage; tastings; glass hire; sale or return; gift vouchers; wedding lists; laying down as a present for children, etc.

Mail order: Free delivery to any mainland UK address for orders over £100; £7.50 delivery charge for orders of less than £100; express next-day delivery £12.50 for the first case and £6.00 for each additional case; overseas delivery arranged

Areas of specialisation: Bordeaux, Burgundy, Germany and Vintage Port

Number 3 St James's Street is the most famous address in the wine trade and its occupant, Berry Brothers and Rudd, the nearest thing a wine merchant gets to an institution. Founded at the same time that corkscrews were invented at the end of the seventeenth century, it still occupies the same venerable oak-panelled premises, whose 1922 frontage features on the Berry Bros label. It's impossible, in fact, to walk into Berry Bros without feeling a frisson of the ghosts of the famous people whose London-bottled claret and Burgundy originated at Berry's. Berry Bros only stopped bottling wines in 1993.

If the carefully cultivated Olde Worlde facade conveys the impression that not much has changed in the last hundred years or so, nothing could be further from the truth. First, Berry Brothers has entered the modern world via Basingstoke, which is the hub of its mail-order operation. Second, it has

470

successfully established two seven-days-a-week airport shops at Heathrow's Terminals Three and Four, where the status symbol of a Berry Bros label combined with a minimum 20 per cent tax-free saving enables it to sell massively expensive wines and other luxury products to American and Far Eastern travellers.

The Berry's list of over 1000 wines and spirits includes own-label and fine wines and is sent out to over 35,000 mail-order customers, most of them in the 40, 50 and 60-something age range. Increasingly though, through its youthful Masters of Wine, David Roberts, buying director, and Alun Griffiths, wine director, young growers and more modern styles from traditional areas of Europe are being grafted on, along with a growing New World selection. Berry Bros is not the place to go if your main objective is cheapness. The varied professional services it offers, however, along with the cachet of the Berry Bros name, make it a unique set-up in an increasingly standardised business.

White

£3–5

SOUTH AFRICA

1996 Berry's South African Chenin Blanc, Simonsig, Stellenbosch, £4.95   14/20
Dry 🍾 ▮
Basic, ripe pear-like Cape white with a hint of aniseed, some spritz and an appley bite. About £1 over-priced.

£5–8

CHILE

1996 Berry's Chilean Sauvignon Blanc, Carmen, Rapel Valley, £5.30   15/20
Dry 🍾🍾 ▮
Weighty, well-made Chilean Sauvignon Blanc from Alvaro Espinoza, with a rounded, almost buttery texture and ripe gooseberry notes. Fuller than most Chilean whites.

FRANCE

1996 Domaine de Farelles Chardonnay, Vin de Pays dOc, £5.95
14/20

Off-dry ▌
Golden-hued, almost Australian-style southern French Chardonnay from Jeanjean, with masses of oak and pineapple-chunk fruit flavours. A parody of an Australian wine.

PORTUGAL

1995 Quinta de Pedralvites, Bairrada, Sogrape, £6.45
16/20
Dry 👜👜 ▌
Made exclusively from the Maria Gomes grape in the northern Portuguese region of Bairrada, this is a creamy, full-bodied, herb and lemon-meringue-like white, which reminds us of a good Aussie Semillon.

Over £8

FRANCE

1994 Berry's Puligny-Montrachet, Gérard Chavy, £16.45
15/20
Dry 👜 ▌
Not the best example of what Puligny-Montrachet has to offer. The nose is a little coarse, although the wine is better on the palate, with butter and banana fruitiness and fresh acidity filled out by oak-fermented complexity.

1993 Chassagne-Montrachet, Chenevottes, Domaine J. Pillot, £26.50
14/20
Dry ▐
Gluey, rather disappointing, oak and rice pudding-like white Burgundy with an alcoholic finish. A very poor example of a Premier Cru wine.

GERMANY

1992 Scharzhofberger Riesling Spätlese, Von Kesselstatt, £9.75
16/20

Medium sweet 👜👜 ▬–
Mature, delicately refreshing Mosel Riesling with crisp, amazingly youthful green-apple fruitiness and a hint of petrolly maturity. Still in Lederhosen.

Red

£5–8

CHILE

1994 Berry's Chilean Cabernet Sauvignon, Central Valley, Carmen, £5.30   15/20
Medium-bodied 👜👜 🍾
Grassy, refreshing, capsicum-like Chilean Cabernet Sauvignon for easy drinking, with juicy, blackcurrant fruit and a nip of tannin.

FRANCE

1995 Château de Cazeneuve, Pic St Loup, Coteaux du Languedoc, £6.65   16/20
Full-bodied 👜👜👜 ▬
From the fashionable Pic St Loup appellation, this is a heady, highly aromatic Languedoc red from André Leenhardt, with masses of Grenache and Syrah spice backed up by powerful, blackberry fruitiness.

1993 Château Corbin, Montagne St Emilion, £6.95   15/20
Medium-bodied 👜👜 🍾
Well-priced St Emilion satellite red, with attractive Merlot-based maturity and a firm edge of tannin. Good luncheon claret, as they say in St James's.

Over £8

AUSTRALIA

1996 Simon Hackett Old Vine Grenache, £8.65   15/20
Full-bodied 👜 🍾
Minty, perfumed, old-vine McLaren Vale Grenache, with intensely peppery aromas and powerfully alcoholic raspberry and cherry fruit.

1992 Elderton Command Shiraz, Barossa Valley, £24.75   17/20
Full-bodied 👜 ▬
Thick, concentrated Barossa Shiraz with sweet, nicely handled spicy oak, lots of old-vine concentration and rich, sweet, liquorice and berry fruit. A brash, upfront red. Shame about the price tag.

FRANCE

1990 Château Plaisance, St Emilion Grand Cru, £11.10   17/20
Medium-bodied 🍷🍷🍷 ▮
Rich, spicy, blackberry fruity Merlot-based claret, whose aromas remind us of a
northern Rhône Syrah, believe it or not. Attractively mellow claret at a nice
price for a 1990.

Berry's Pomerol, £11.25   16/20
Medium-bodied 🍷🍷 ▮
Smooth, silky, elegantly mature Pomerol made by Berry's know whom, showing
supple, brown-sugar and fruitcake Merlot characters and a veneer of sweet
oak.

Berry's St Estèphe, Lafon-Rochet, £12.85   16/20
Full-bodied 🍷🍷 ▬
Youthful, chunky, deeply coloured claret with classic St Estèphe chunkiness,
from classified Château Lafon-Rochet. Needs time for the oak and fruit to
soften.

1991 Savigny-Lavières, Premier Cru, Domaine Tollot-Beaut, £16.15   15/20
Medium-bodied 🍷 ▮
Lavishly oaked Burgundian Pinot Noir in a typical Tollot-Beaut style. Starting to
dry on the palate. Catch it before it rolls downhill to meet its maker.

1993 Volnay Premier Cru, Santenots, Domaine Jacques Prieur, £23.75   16/20
Medium-bodied 🍷 ▬
From one of the biggest domaines on the Côte d'Or, this is a rich, deeply
coloured Pinot made with the American critical palate in mind. The fruit
character is smothered by oak, in our view, but it may all come together, given
another year.

ITALY

1993 Villa Cafaggio, Solatio Basilica, £15.75   16/20
Medium-bodied 🍷 ▮
From a rapidly improving Tuscan estate, this is a well-oaked, concentrated
Sangiovese with pure cherry and mulberry fruit flavours. Good, but not good
enough at the rather inflated price.

UNITED STATES

1992 Hedges Red Mountain Reserve, Columbia Valley, £20.95
17/20

Full-bodied

Hedges is one of the best wineries in Washington State, as demonstrated by this coconutty oaky, almost Rioja-like, Columbia Valley warm-climate blend. It also knows how to charge high prices.

Sparkling

Over £8

AUSTRALIA

1993 Berry's Australian Quality Sparkling Wine, Taltarni, £10.25
16/20

Bone dry

Well-made Aussie fizz, made from Pinot Noir and Chardonnay grapes by Frenchman Dominique Portet. Cool-climate Tasmanian grapes make this a refreshingly austere, elegant sparkler with good length and a tangy bite.

FRANCE

1990 Berry's United Kingdom Cuvée Champagne, Binet, £17.95
15/20

Dry

Better on the nose than it is on the palate. Still youthful, but we're not convinced there's enough fruit richness on the palate here. Finishes a tad green.

Fortified

£5–8

PORTUGAL

St James's Fine Ruby Port, Warre's, £7.90   15/20
Full-bodied 🍷🍷 ▬
Fiery, youthful, well-made Ruby with a rasp of alcohol and sweet, chunky blackberry fruit and cinnamon spice.

SPAIN

Berry's Fine Dry Oloroso Sherry, Barbadillo, £7.35   16/20
Dry 🍷🍷 ▮
Nutty, tangy, traditional Oloroso with notes of coffee and crème brûlée and a dry, chewy finish.

Over £8

PORTUGAL

**1990 Berry's Own Selection, Late Bottled Vintage, Churchill
Graham, £11.25**   16/20
Full-bodied 🍷🍷 ▮
Smooth, sweet, chocolate and raisin-like LBV Port with heady alcohol and spicy, liquoricey fruit concentration.

Bibendum

Address: 113 Regent's Park Road, London NW1 8UR

Telephone/fax: 0171 916 7706; 0171 916 7705

Number of branches: 1

Opening hours: 10.00am to 6.30pm Monday to Thursday; 10.00am to 8.00 pm Friday; 9.30am to 5.00pm Saturday

Credit cards accepted: American Express, MasterCard, Switch, Visa

Discounts: Not available

Facilities and services: Comprehensive party service; glass loan; cellar management and storage; fine-wine desk; en primeur offers; gift service; corporate service; quarterly newsletter; regular in-store tastings, both tutored and untutored; Bibendum Direct subscription wine club; Bibendum Card account and reward scheme

Mail order: Free delivery in mainland England and Wales (minimum order one case); for London addresses, delivery within 24 hours; for all other addresses within mainland England and Wales, delivery usually within three days; delivery service to other parts of the UK available on request

Areas of specialisation: A good generalist, with particular strengths in Italy, France, California, Australia, South Africa and South America; also good on fine wines

If Berry Bros epitomises the old wine trade, Bibendum presents its well-scrubbed modern face. There's an element of young fogeyishness still lurking about the Primrose Hill premises, but a restless quest for quality and interest in Europe and the New World makes it one of Britain's most dynamic forces in wine. In not much more than a decade, Bibendum – not to be confused with the Conran restaurant of the same name – has established itself as one of the liveliest, most open-minded and good-humoured wine merchants in the country.

Simon Farr is the bespectacled éminence grise who seems to spend all his time charging between the two hemispheres to taste, blend and buy the goodies for Bibendum's busy collage of a list. New agencies joining Bibendum's expanding portfolio in 1997 included, among others, Bodegas Santo from

Bibendum

Mexico, Casal Baio and Lageder from Italy, Cottin Frères from Burgundy, Domaine des Chandelles from Corbières and Calera from California. The company also sells large quantities of wine to high-street chains and supermarkets, and acts as a front-line agent for producers in Europe and the New World, steering them towards more modern, consumer-friendly styles.

The past year has seen an expansion of the Bibendum Fine Wine Desk. Fronted by Farr and the irrepressible Willie Lebus, Bibendum runs a busy events calendar, including some of the best-tutored tastings, sometimes with the grower present, in the capital. The programme in 1997 included 12 vintages of Château Latour, a super-Tuscan dinner at the ultra-trendy River Café and an evening of tasting 10 vintages of Château Le Pin, the world's most expensive wine. The annual Bordeaux and Burgundy en primeur evenings are always enjoyable scrums of fine wine and North London gossip. If you're looking for fine wine and fun combined, Bibendum wouldn't be a bad place to start.

White

£3–5

ITALY

1996 Casa Bianca, Tenuta Casal Baio, Puglia, £3.50　　　　14/20
Dry 👛👛 |
Basic Puglian blend of Bombino Bianco and Verdeca, with apple and pear fruitiness. A decent house white, as it were.

MEXICO

1996 Santo Tomás, Mision Blanco, Bodegas Santo Tomás, £4.50
　　　　14/20

Dry 👛 |
Faintly bitter, herbaceous Mexican white, which gets brownie points for rarity value rather than quality. Mission Impossible?

£5–8

AUSTRALIA

1996 Deakin Estate Alfred Chardonnay, £6.00   16/20
Dry 🍶🍶🍶 ▮
Intense, richly oaked Chardonnay made in a modern style, showing flavours of
citrus fruits and toffee popcorn and a buttery texture.

ITALY

1996 Brunori Verdicchio dei Castelli di Jesi Classico, £5.50   16/20
Bone dry 🍶🍶🍶 ▮
Nutty, characterful, lemon-zesty Italian white from the under-rated Verdicchio
grape, with a citrus-peel twist of acidity. A seafood classic.

1996 Alois Lageder Pinot Bianco, £6.95   15/20
Medium-bodied 🍶 ▮
Fresh, unoaked, middle-weight Alpine Pinot Blanc with refreshing acidity and a
mountain air purity.

Over £8

ARGENTINA

**1995 Catena Agrelo Vineyard Chardonnay, Bodegas Esmeralda,
£9.00**   17/20
Dry 🍶🍶🍶 ▬
The top Chardonnay from Argentina's leading wine group, this is a ripe, super-
concentrated white with intense melon and pineapple fruit, lovely oak and
remarkable winemaking complexity. A wine that hangs around on the palate.

FRANCE

1996 Sancerre, Le Manoir, Vieilles Vignes, André Neveu, £9.75
                                                                16/20
Bone dry 🍶🍶 ▮
Textured, slightly old-fashioned Sancerre, with minerally intensity, piercing fruit
and good length. How's your uncle?

1995 Mâcon Solutré, Clos des Bertillonnes, Domaine Robert-Denogent, £9.75   16/20
Dry 🥂🥂 ▮

Honeyed, oaky, ultra-ripe, late-picked Chardonnay from southern Burgundy, with an idiosyncratic edge. A wine lover's wine or a one-glass wonder? You tell us.

NEW ZEALAND

1996 Te Kairanga Barrel-Aged Sauvignon Blanc, Martinborough, £8.50   17/20
Dry 🥂🥂🥂 ▮

Fresh, toasty, passion fruity Marlborough white from a much-improved winery. The oak is so subtle here that it glides effortlessly past you on the palate.

UNITED STATES

1995 Edna Valley Chardonnay, Paragon, Chalone, £9.95   17/20
Dry 🥂🥂🥂 ▮

Ultra-rich, toffee-fudge-like, California southern central coast Chardonnay, with delightful elegance and nutty complexity.

Red

£3–5

AUSTRALIA

1996 Lonsdale Ridge Shiraz/Cabernet, Wingara, £4.50   14/20
Medium-bodied 🥂 ▮

Minty, faintly herbaceous Aussie blend with light spicy oak. A £3.99 wine if ever we've tasted one.

CHILE

1996 Valdivieso Merlot, £5.00   15/20
Medium-bodied 👛👛 🍾
Abundantly aromatic, lusciously fruity, green-pepper-like Chilean Merlot, with a nip of thirst-quenching acidity. A really good summer quaffer from Chile.

FRANCE

1995 Antoure Merlot, Vin de Pays d'Oc, £5.00   12/20
Full-bodied 🍾
Cooked, jammy, heftily alcoholic, southern French Merlot, which is already on the way out. We hope the wine isn't supposed to taste like this.

ITALY

1996 La Piazza Rosso, Tenuta Casal Baio, Sicily, £4.00   15/20
Medium-bodied 👛👛👛 🍾
A blend of Nero d'Avola and Sangiovese made in a modern, cherry fruity style, with restrained alcohol and soft, well-balanced tannins.

£5–8

ARGENTINA

1995 Alamos Ridge Malbec, Bodegas Esmeralda, £5.50   15/20
Medium-bodied 👛👛 🍾
Intense, savoury, lightly peppery Argentine red made from the country's most widely planted, quality red grape, with a hot, alcoholic finish.

FRANCE

1996 Domaine de Font-Sane, Côtes du Ventoux, £5.75   15/20
Full-bodied 👛👛 🍾
Lightly coloured, white-pepper-scented, southern French white with appealing juicy fruit richness and full-bodied alcohol. Lots to get your tongue round.

MEXICO

1994 Bodegas Santo Tomás Barbera, £5.95   15/20
Full-bodied 👤👤 ▮
More interesting than the same winery's white wine, this is a rich, coconutty oaky red made from Piedmont's Barbera grape, with robust tannins and a sweet core of fruit.

Over £8

CHILE

1996 Valdivieso Malbec Reserve, £9.95   17/20
Full-bodied 👤👤👤 ▬
Scented, French oak-aged Malbec from the Valdivieso winery with notes of tar and sage and delightful, refreshing acidity. Still young, but already on the way to being a stunning red wine.

ITALY

1995 Talenti Rosso di Montalcino, £8.50   17/20
Medium-bodied 👤👤👤 ▮
As you'd expect from one of the top names in Montalcino, this is a stylish, savoury Sangiovese with perfectly judged tannins, youthful acidity and voluptuous, liquid cherry fruit.

NEW ZEALAND

1996 Lawson's Dry Hills Pinot Noir, Marlborough, £10.00   14/20
Medium-bodied ▮
From a winery better known for its Sauvignon Blancs, this is an oaky, faintly beetrooty Pinot Noir with rather coarse tannins. Stick to the whites, guys.

SOUTH AFRICA

1995 De Trafford Cabernet Sauvignon, £8.75   17/20
Full-bodied 👤👤👤 ▬
Intense, minty, almost Napa Valley-like Cape Cabernet made in a commendably modern style, with chocolatey oak, vibrant blackcurrant fruit richness and structured tannins.

UNITED STATES

1994 Calera Jensen Vineyard Pinot Noir, Mount Harlan, £25.00

16/20

Medium-bodied 🍷 |

Well-made Californian Pinot Noir from Burgundy nut Josh Jensen, with mature, wild-strawberry notes and harmonious oak. Our only quarrel is with the price.

Rosé

£5–8

FRANCE

1996 Domaine de Pujol, Coteaux du Languedoc, £5.50   16/20
Dry 🍷🍷🍷 |

A serious, dry, concentrated French rosé with a herby, redcurranty feel and lively acidity. One of the best rosés we've had this year.

Sparkling

£5–8

AUSTRALIA

1996 Deakin Brut, £6.00   15/20
Dry 🍷🍷 |

Big-bubbled, tropical fruity Aussie sparkler with notes of pineapple and lime zest and a broad, sherbety mousse. Enjoyable, but not very subtle.

Bordeaux Direct

Address: New Aquitaine House, Paddock Road, Reading, Berkshire RG4 5JY
Telephone/fax: 0118 947 1144 (orders); 0118 946 1953
E-mail: orders @ bordeaux-direct.co.uk
Number of branches: 5
Opening hours: 9.00am to 7.00pm Monday to Friday; 9.00am to 5.00pm
Saturday; 10.00am to 4.00pm Sundays and public holidays (apart from
Christmas Eve afternoon, Christmas Day, Boxing Day and New Year's Day)
Credit cards accepted: American Express, Diners, MasterCard, Switch, Visa
Discounts: On all case purchases
Facilities and services: Free glass loan from retail outlets; cellaring service for
customers' wines introduced in 1997 at £4.50 per case; regular in-store
tastings throughout the year, plus bottles always open for tasting; monthly
special offers to selected customers; comprehensive tasting notes with most
mixed cases; wine tours; annual Vintage Festival in the spring
Mail order: Minimum order one bottle; 14 wine lists sent out each year;
delivery to a single address at £3.99 per order; average delivery time is 3.2
days; next-day delivery available
Areas of specialisation: Bordeaux, individual domaines, French regional wines
and malt whisky

When Bordeaux Direct started in 1969, it began, as the name suggests, as a
mail-order-cum-retail operation specialising in the wines of the Gironde. Things
have changed a bit since founder Tony Laithwaite shipped his exciting finds
home himself in the back of a van. For one thing, he has a Bordeaux château
named after him, Château La Clarière-Laithwaite, in the Côtes de Castillon. For
another, Bordeaux Direct is now the largest mail-order operation in the
country, with over 185,000 active customers, sales of over 800,000 cases and
a turnover of £40 million.

Bordeaux Direct doesn't just deal in Bordeaux. On the contrary, it has cast
its net wide, first to other parts of France and Europe and more recently to
the New World. There has been a strong emphasis on developing the range,
particularly in the areas of fine wines and pre-release offers, both from the
traditional regions of France and from new areas such as Chile and Australia.
Bordeaux Direct can take the credit for pioneering the concept of flying
winemakers, by introducing Australian oenologists and their bags of tricks to
sleepy southern French co-operatives in the mid-1980s. Today, it still uses flying
winemakers to produce bespoke blends for its customers.

The full range runs to around 600 wines, most of them exclusive, and a proportion of which is available by the bottle from Bordeaux Direct's five retail shops, as well as by the mail-order case. Prices are not always the cheapest, but they're compensated for by the level of service and the basic quality of the wines, which is consistently good. There are also ten full-time wine advisers to give advice over the telephone.

The quality of the wines is reflected in Bordeaux Direct's voluminous and well-presented, informative literature, which its customers receive each month, along with information packs and helpful tasting notes. Selling most of its wines direct means that the Reading-based company can choose wines 'which have a great story behind them', says managing director, Greg Hodder. Having outgrown its Paddock Road premises, Bordeaux Direct plans to up sticks in the spring of 1998 and expand into purpose-built premises at Theale to the west of Reading. Junction 12 may not be the most romantic of addresses, but it will provide the launchpad for the next ambitious phase of development.

White

£3–5

AUSTRALIA

1996 Pioneers Raisined Muscat, Bin 168, Miranda, £4.99   16/20
Very sweet 🛍️🛍️🛍️ |
A luscious, marmaladey Aussie sticky from Griffith in New South Wales, with unctuous, peach and orange-peel characters balanced by fresh acidity. Well balanced, but hang onto your fillings.

£5–8

AUSTRALIA

1997 Yarrunga Fields Special Reserve, Bin 303, South East Australia, £5.39   14/20
Dry 🛍️ |
Simple, slightly confected, banana and sawdust-style Aussie white. The kind of thing the supermarkets do cheaper and better.

CHILE

1997 Viña Tarapaca Chardonnay, Colchagua, £6.39   16/20
Dry 🍾🍾🍾 ▮

A mixture of oaked and unoaked Chardonnay from a much-improved Chilean estate, with elegant, melon and ginger spicy characters and barrel fermentation-derived complexity. Very drinkable.

FRANCE

1996 Domaine des Cassagnoles, Vin de Pays des Côtes de Gascogne, £5.29   15/20
Bone dry 🍾 ▮

Crisp, grapefruity Gascon white from the Baumann estate, made in a tingling, mouth-watering style, with an appealing citrus-fruit tang. A little pricey.

1996 Château Haut-Reygnac, Entre Deux Mers, Haut-Benauge, £5.39   15/20
Bone dry 🍾🍾 ▮

Modern, stylishly turned-out Bordeaux white with Semillon and Sauvignon Blanc flavours jostling on the palate. A refreshing, unoaked style.

1996 Les Grandes Pallières, Vermentino, Côtes de Provence, £5.69   15/20
Bone dry 🍾🍾 ▮

Substantial, southern French Vermentino with herby, liquoricey, Mediterranean characters and a typical punch of bracingly dry acidity.

1996 Laithwaite Sauvignon Blanc, Oak-Fermented, Bordeaux, £6.45   16/20
Dry 🍾🍾🍾 ▮

Toasty, sweetly oaked Bordeaux white with impressive Graves-like weight and concentration and crisp, nettley fruit flavours. The oak is really well done.

1996 Viognier, Vin de Pays des Coteaux de l'Ardèche, £6.79   16/20
Dry 🍾🍾🍾 ▮

Aromatic, American oak-aged Viognier with sumptuous apricot and nectarine fruit flavours and a broad texture, tapering to an appetisingly tangy finish.

1996 Bourgogne, Domaine Touzot, £6.99   16/20
Dry 🍾🍾🍾 ▮

Modern, New World-influenced white Burgundy, with fresh, lemony fruit intensity and well-handled oak. A refreshing house-white Burgundy.

Over £8

FRANCE

1996 Chablis, Vieilles Vignes, Emmanuel Dampt, £9.99   17/20
Bone dry 👛👛 ➦
Rich but youthful, lemon butter-style Chablis showing old-vine concentration and a citrusy, zippy tang. Not quite as good as the 1995, but still very enjoyable.

1995 Château de la Saule, Montagny Premier Cru, Alain Roy-Thevenin, £12.29   17/20
Dry 👛👛 ▮
Rich, buttery, golden-hued Côte Chalonnaise Chardonnay with attractive, balancing acidity and a surprising degree of complexity for a Montagny.

GERMANY

1989 Wehlener Sonnenuhr Riesling Spätlese, Mosel, Weingut Licht-Bergweiler, £8.29   16/20
Medium dry 👛👛 ▮
Light, elegant, pleasantly mature Riesling, which is on the dry side for a Spätlese. A delicate, finely judged Mosel that is starting to develop classic, kerosene-like characters.

Red

£3–5

ITALY

1996 Farnese Signifero, Montepulciano d'Abruzzo, £4.99   15/20
Medium-bodied 👛👛 ▮
Bright, juicy, lightly spicy Montepulciano from the Moro Valley, with soft, approachable tannins. Bordeaux Direct's best-selling red, which is rather ironic, given that it comes from Italy.

£5–8

AUSTRALIA

1996 Tatachilla Partners Cabernet Sauvignon/Shiraz, £6.79   16/20
Full-bodied 👜👜👜 ▬
Ripe, sweetly oaked Aussie blend with supple tannins and attractively smoky, chocolatey fruit, which is complemented by Shiraz pepper and liquorice spice.

FRANCE

1996 Domaine de Buadelle, Minervois, £5.45   15/20
Full-bodied 👜👜 ▬
From a domaine whose name looks like a typing error, this is an aromatic, thyme-infused red with good aromatic power, Mediterranean spice and robust tannins. A superior barbecue red.

1995 Côtes du Rhône, Cuvée André Roux, Les Abeilles, £6.55
16/20

Full-bodied 👜👜👜 ▬
Made at the quality-conscious Chusclan co-operative by André Roux of Château du Trignon, this is a winning combination of Grenache and Syrah grapes, with the former providing the richness and alcohol and the latter the aroma and blackberry fruit backbone.

1995 Château Mouquet, Bordeaux Supérieur, £6.79   16/20
Medium-bodied 👜👜 ▬
Youthful, modern-style claret with soft tannins, smooth oak, a hint of green pepper and thirst-quenching blackcurrant fruit. Very drinkable.

ITALY

1994 Fattoria di Basciano, Vigna Il Corto, Toscana, £7.99   17/20
Medium-bodied 👜👜👜 |
A super-Tuscan blend of 90 per cent Sangiovese with 10 per cent Cabernet Sauvignon from a Tuscan estate based in Chianti Rufina. Savoury and spicy with delightful cherry and damson-fruit definition.

SPAIN

1996 Cariñena, El Bombero, £5.15   15/20
Full-bodied 💰💰 ➡–

Rich, chocolatey, plushly alcoholic Spanish red with softer tannins than many wines from the appellation. Still, you'll want to be standing somewhere near a steak or barbecued rib when you drink this. Make sure there's someone to catch you when you keel over.

Over £8

AUSTRALIA

1996 The Farms Merlot, Barossa Valley, £16.15   17/20
Full-bodied 💰💰 ➡–

Huge, densely fruity Merlot from Jim Irvine at the Yaldara winery, with sweet, luscious oak and cassis and eucalyptus fruit characters. Full-frontal stuff.

FRANCE

1995 Château La Clarière-Laithwaite, Côtes de Castillon, £8.89
17/20

Full-bodied 💰💰💰 🍶

Vibrantly coloured, very youthful claret with masses of elemental berry fruit and dark, chewy oak tannins, which comes with the personal imprimatur of Bordeaux Direct founder, Tony Laithwaite. Tuck this away and come back in three to five years.

1995 Hermitage, Domaine Fayolle, Les Dionnières, £20.45   18/20
Full-bodied 💰💰💰 🍶

From an outstanding northern Rhône vintage, this is an intense, finely balanced Syrah with refreshing acidity, a brushstroke of sweet oak and elegant blackberry fruit. Stylish stuff, which is worth the outlay.

1995 Domaine Amiot, Aux Combottes, Gevrey-Chambertin Premier Cru, £21.45   16/20
Medium-bodied 💰💰 ➡–

From grower Denis Philibert, this is a rich, concentrated, strawberry fruity Côte de Nuits Pinot Noir, with toasty, well-handled oak and robust tannins. Needs time.

489

Eldridge Pope

Address: Weymouth Avenue, Dorchester, Dorset DT1 1QT

Telephone/fax: 01305 258347; 01305 258155

Number of branches: 7 wine shops and 4 Reynier Wine Libraries

Opening hours: Generally 9.00am to 6.00pm Monday to Saturday

Credit cards accepted: American Express, MasterCard, Switch, Visa

Discounts: Case discounts generally 5 per cent per case, but differs with the wine type

Facilities and services: In-store tastings; free local delivery; glass hire; cellarage; wine advice; en primeur and other regular special offers; bin-end sales; good beers by the bottle and the cask

Mail order: Telephone 01305 258347 at head office for details

Areas of specialisation: France, fine and rare wines and, increasingly, Australia and South Africa

If you're familiar with Eldridge Pope, it's probably thanks to beer, rather than wine. Royal Oak and Hardy Country Export are the staple fare of this famous Dorchester-based brewer and pub owner. Wine is no after-thought, however. In fact, with a flourishing mail-order business and 11 retail shops dotted about West Country market towns like Sherborne, Shaftesbury and Wincanton, as well as a presence in London, Eldridge Pope makes one-third of its turnover from wine. The shops include four wine libraries in Bristol, Exeter and London, where you can choose a bottle from the helpful Eldridge Pope list (adding £1.50 for corkage) and enjoy it with a plate of wine-bar food.

There have been lots of changes at Eldridge Pope in the last year. Wine buyer Robin Kinahan has departed, to be replaced by Matthew Cooper as manager of retail wine, and his old department split into two halves, retail and wholesale. Sue Longman is now in charge of wholesale buying. Cooper's arrival has sparked off a number of innovations. The wine shops and the mail-order side of the business have been integrated as part of the retail division, wine prices have been standardised and a first, easy-to-use retail wine list has been introduced, with the addition, also for the first time, of Eldridge Pope's beers and vintage ales.

Despite the company's traditional strengths in mature clarets and Burgundies, not to mention fine German estate wines, the company has been moving towards good-value wines from the New World, in particular Chile, South Africa, Argentina and Australia, in recent years. Eldridge Pope now lists no fewer than 50 wines from the Cape alone, and has sprinted off the mark in South America with wines from Norton, Etchart and Vistalba in Argentina, and Santa Carolina, Villard and Casa Lapostolle in Chile.

Eldridge Pope remains proudly francophile, though. 'The fact remains,' says chairman Christopher Pope, 'that when God made the world, his most loving finger paused on the soil and climate of parts of France.' (Several of these French wines come with Mr Pope's name on them. His Chairman's Selection wines are the most popular with customers, apparently.) But the French list is changing. 'We haven't removed anything,' says Cooper, 'but we've added lots of new wines.' The Alsace list, for example, used to come almost entirely from Dopff & Irion. Now it's been spiced up with Trimbach, Schlumberger and Zind-Humbrecht.

Alsace notwithstanding, most of the recent signings (50 per cent of the list, according to Cooper) have come from the New World, Spain and Italy. The pace of change is unlikely to slacken in the next 12 months, with more additions to the range and development of the company's Website. Mr Cooper has another ambition, too: 'persuading a journalist to make the trip down to Dorset'. Does he mean us?

White

£3–5

CHILE

1996 Viña Gracia Chardonnay, Cachapoal Valley, £4.99   14/20
Dry 🜹 ▮
Made in the southern part of Chile's Central Valley, this is a ripe, New World-style Chardonnay with lots of alcohol and pineapple-chunk characters.

FRANCE

1995 Domaine Loubadère, Cuvée Coup de Coeur, Gros Manseng, Vin de Pays des Côtes de Gascogne, J.C. Fontan, £4.99   15/20
Off-dry 👜👜 ▮
Peachy, quite old-fashioned Gascon white with an exotic note of melon sweetness balanced by refreshing acidity. Bizarre.

1995 Montlouis Sec, Clos de Cray, £4.99   15/20
Dry 👜👜 ▮
Rich, fruity Chenin Blanc in a ludicrous, heavy-duty designer bottle. Appley, intense and well made, with steely acidity on the finish.

ITALY

1996 Terme I Cortese, Alto Monferrato, Viticoltori dell'Acquese, £4.99   16/20
Dry 👜👜👜 ▮
Made from one of Italy's best white grapes, this is an ultra-fresh, ripely textured white with apple and pear fruitiness, a hint of aniseed and a refreshing spritz. A good alternative to more expensive Gavi.

£5–8

AUSTRALIA

1994 Hunter Valley Verdelho, Draytons, £5.99   14/20
Off-dry ▮
Strange, cheese-rindy, Hunter Valley white with pronounced sweetness and rather heavy alcohol. Not very well balanced.

FRANCE

1995 Jurançon Sec, Grain Sauvage, £5.85   14/20
Dry 👜 ▮
Made at the local Jurançon co-operative from Gros and Petit Manseng grapes, this is a waxy, honeyed Pyrenean white, which is starting to tire a little on the palate.

1995 The Chairman's Fine, Fresh, Crisp White Burgundy, A.
Rodet, £6.25   15/20
Dry 👜👜 |
Better than the 1993, which we tasted last year, this is a clean, fruity, well-made
Chardonnay with pleasantly crisp acidity.

GERMANY

1987 Hallgartener Hendelberg Riesling, Grüngold, Fürst
Löwenstein, £6.75   13/20
Medium sweet |
Bright, golden-hued Rheingau Riesling, which is mature to the point of senility.
Needs to be drunk before it falls over the top of the Zimmer frame.

Over £8

AUSTRALIA

1996 Capel Vale Unwooded Chardonnay, £8.20   16/20
Dry 👜👜 ➖
Full-flavoured, concentrated, unoaked Chardonnay with masses of buttery fruit
and power underpinned by good acidity. Western Australia's answer to Chablis.

FRANCE

1993 Domaine des Baumard, Savennières, Clos du Papillon, £8.65
                                                                    16/20
Bone dry 👜👜 ➖
From a small and often rather over-priced Loire appellation, this is a nettley,
complex, honeyed, mature Chenin Blanc, which will continue to age for some
time yet. An ideal white for fish dishes.

1993 Alsace Gewürztraminer, Clos Windsbuhl, Zind-Humbrecht,
£12.99   18/20
Dry 👜👜👜 |
Made by French Master of Wine, Olivier Humbrecht, this is a concentrated but
beautifully balanced Gewürztraminer with classic lychee and exotic spice-box
fruit. Still surprisingly zesty and fresh for a four-year-old wine. About as good as
dry Gewürz gets.

NEW ZEALAND

1994 Giesen Marlborough Riesling, £8.99   17/20
Dry 🍷🍷🍷 ❘

The Giesens are German ex-pats, so they ought to know how to make good Riesling. This is pretty good stuff, with dry, lime-like fruitiness and a ripe, honeyed texture. Well made, very much with food in mind.

SOUTH AFRICA

1996 Stellenzicht Semillon Reserve, £10.99   16/20
Dry 🍷🍷 ❘

Unusual to find a Semillon in South Africa, a country where Chenin Blanc, Sauvignon Blanc and Chardonnay hold sway. Still, this is rather good in a smoky, herby kind of way, with attractively dry, elegant fruit flavours and a charry bite.

UNITED STATES

1994 Grgich Hills Chardonnay, Napa, £20.55   16/20
Dry ❘

Made by Mike 'the beret' Grgich, this is an optimistically priced Californian Chardonnay with bright, apple and citrus-fruit flavours and an overlay of oak. Ought to be half the price.

Red

£3–5

FRANCE

1996 Laroche Pinot Noir, Vin de Pays de l'Île de Beauté, £4.99
                                                                14/20

Full-bodied 🍷 ❘

Jammy, prominently oaked Pinot Noir from Corsica, with a core of raspberry fruit and slightly cooked, robust tannins.

1996 Domaine de Montpertuis, Counoise, Vin de Pays du Gard, £4.99 15/20
Medium-bodied 👜👜 🍷
Made by Counoise specialist, Paul Jeune, this is a juicy, peppery red, which is like a cross between a Beaujolais and a Côtes du Rhône. A characterful quaffer at a good price.

PORTUGAL

Vinha Nova Tinto, Caves Aliança, £3.99 13/20
Full-bodied 👜 🍷
Old-fashioned, leathery Portuguese red with chewy tannins. You can do much better than this from the Iberian Peninsula at under £4.

SPAIN

1996 Aran Garnacha, Campo de Borja, £3.99 14/20
Medium-bodied 👜👜 🍷
Made by Rioja's Telmo Rodriguez, this is a soft, juicy, raspberry and plum fruity red conceived in a modern style, without oak or much in the way of complexity.

1994 Lar de Barros Tempranillo, £4.75 15/20
Medium-bodied 👜👜 🍷
An unoaked Tempranillo from Extremadura in western Spain, with savoury, cherry fruitiness and a faintly rustic, tobaccoey edge.

1995 Viña Bajoz, Toro, £4.99 12/20
Full-bodied 🍷
Densely coloured, Tempranillo-based red from western Spain, with cooked fruit flavours and an old-fashioned, vinegary edge.

£5–8

FRANCE

1995 Château St Martin-Baracan, Bordeaux Supérieur, £5.79 15/20
Medium-bodied 👜 🍷
Supple, chocolatey, Merlot-based claret with attractive, chocolatey richness and a faintly drying finish. Quite advanced for a two-year-old wine.

ITALY

1988 Taurino Notarpanaro, Rosso del Salento, £6.39   16/20
Full-bodied 🏺🏺 ▮
Made from Negroamaro in the hot heel of Italy, this is a rich, raisin and damson red with a pleasantly sweet, gamey edge. Good, mature quaffing.

SOUTH AFRICA

1995 Die Krans Pinotage, Klein Karoo, £5.45   13/20
Full-bodied ▮
Baked, jammy, fruitless Cape red with masses of dry tannins. A wine that chews you before you chew it.

Over £8

CHILE

1996 Vina Casablanca, Santa Isabel Estate Merlot, £8.49   16/20
Medium-bodied 🏺🏺 ▬–
Intense, vibrant Merlot from Chile's star winemaker, Ignacio Recabarren, with beautifully judged oak and sweet, blackcurrant fruit flavours. Lots of character, but not much complexity at the price.

Justerini & Brooks

Address: 61 St James's Street, London SW1A 1LZ

Telephone/fax: 0171 493 8721; 0171 499 4653

Number of branches: 2, London and Edinburgh (45 George Street, Edinburgh EH2 2HT)

Opening hours: 9.00am to 5.30pm Monday to Friday

Credit cards accepted: Access, American Express, Connect Card, Diners, Visa

Discounts: Contact head office for case-rate details

Facilities and services: Selected Cellar Plan and Personal Cellar Plan for laying down wine; broking; storage; regular en primeur offers; in-store tastings

Mail order: 8–10 mail-order offers each year posted to all customers; free delivery for two cases or more to any address in mainland UK and Northern Ireland

Areas of specialisation: Bordeaux, Burgundy, Germany, Australia

With its close links to J & B Rare whisky, its eight royal seals and its smart St James's address, Justerini & Brooks has the delivery van to make your neighbours go bottle-green with envy. Even the driver comes wearing a jacket and tie. J & B also takes care of the royal cellar, which presumably involves buying large quantities of German wine and caseloads of gin.

Justerini's patrician buyer and Master of Wine, Hew Blair, rightly prides himself on the company's 2,000-strong wine list, in which each page bangs a large bass drum for 'the fine wines of Justerini & Brooks'. As you'd expect, J & B's major strengths lie in the traditional regions of France and Germany. But wines such as California's Chalk Hill and Saintsbury, Scotchman's Hill, Neil Paulett and Cape Mentelle from Australia, Thelema and Kanonkop from South Africa and Ata Rangi, Palliser and Dry River from New Zealand show that J & B's idea of a fine wine extends far beyond Europe's borders.

J & B's smart shopfronts in London and Edinburgh are the window dressing for a largely mail-order business, selling wine to well-heeled private customers described by Hew Blair as 'combining the enjoyment of fine wine and the possession of substantial amounts of spare cash'. If many of J & B's wines are expensive, they are also surprisingly good value for money and are often wines that J & B has gone out and found itself.

The focus here is very much on the top echelon of the wine world, but the prices are fair – and sometimes better than that. (To prove that he hasn't entirely overlooked cheaper wines, Hew Blair has also developed an affordable southern French and country wine range too, with very good wines such as Château Tour des Gendres and Domaine du Vieux Chêne.)

The J & B agency list is impressive and growing. The last year has seen a number of impressive signings, including Domaine Leroy from Burgundy (for the London area) and two new Australian estates, Dalwhinnie and Clarendon Hills. There has also been a lot of activity in Piedmont, an area in which J & B was already strong, thanks to Domenico Clerico and Poderi Bertelli.

At a time when independent wine merchants are under threat, J & B continues to take the high road between Edinburgh and London. Its offers of en primeur claret and Burgundy are among the best in the country and its wine selection is generally superb. With its 250th anniversary only two years away, J & B looks set for the next millennium. We (and possibly the Windsors) will raise a glass to that.

White

£3–5

FRANCE

1996 Domaine Montrose Chardonnay, Vin de Pays de l'Hérault, £4.95   15/20
Dry 🍾🍾 |
Ripe, honeyed, fruity Mâcon-style Languedoc white with a soft texture and just enough acidity for balance.

£5–8

AUSTRALIA

1996 Paulett's Chardonnay, Clare Valley, £7.90   15/20
Dry 🍾 |
Prominently oaked, eucalyptus and ginger spicy Australian white. Very idiosyncratic.

FRANCE

1996 Côtes du Rhône Villages, Domaine du Vieux Chêne, £6.95

17/20

Dry 🍶🍶🍶 ▮

Made by Jean-Claude and Béatrice Bouche, this is a fresh, pear-like, southern Rhône white with mealy, complex fruit flavours, herby freshness and superb weight and balance.

1995 Mâcon-Uchizy, Domaine Talmard, £6.95

16/20

Dry 🍶🍶🍶 ▮

A consistently good Mâcon Chardonnay from Paul and Philibert Talmard, made in an ultra-ripe, grapefruity, unoaked style with clean, refreshing acidity.

Over £8

AUSTRALIA

1995 Scotchman's Hill Chardonnay, Victoria, £9.95

16/20

Dry 🍶🍶 ▮

Oaky, developed, densely flavoured Victorian Chardonnay with crisp acidity and toffee-fudge characters and underlying cool-climate elegance. Exciting stuff.

FRANCE

1996 Pouilly-Fumé, Serge Dagueneau et Fille, £8.50

17/20

Dry 🍶🍶🍶 ▮

Complex, nettley, low-yielding Loire Valley Sauvignon Blanc with minerally intensity and superb poise. Shows you what the ideal combination of climate, harvest and grape variety can achieve.

1995 Petit Chablis, Dauvissat-Camus, £8.90

17/20

Bone dry 🍶🍶🍶 ▬

From one of the best family domaines in the Yonne, this is an intense, unoaked Petit Chablis, which is better than most people's Chablis. Minerally, fresh and buttery with a steel girder of cool-climate acidity.

1995 Sancerre, La Grande Côte, Domaine Cotat, £16.00   16/20
Dry 🛍 ▮

A little pricey, even for Sancerre, this is an ambitious, but ultimately rather fruitless attempt at a late-picked cuvée made from super-ripe grapes.

1995 Gewürztraminer, Cuvée Théo, Clos des Capucins, Domaine Weinbach, £16.50   18/20
Off-dry 🛍🛍🛍 ▬

Powerful, ultra-ripe, pot-pourri of a wine with immense richness, and honey and rose-petal intensity. Despite the concentration, this is commendably elegant and poised. Make sure there are six of you when you open the bottle.

1992 Sauternes, Cru Barréjats £38.00   15/20
Very sweet ▮

Rather ordinary, barley-sugared sweet white from a not terribly impressive vintage. Very much aimed at the St James's customer with money to incinerate. Lacks the complexity, but not the price, of a top Sauternes.

GERMANY

1995 Riesling Kabinett, Joh Jos Prüm, £9.45   16/20
Off-dry 🛍🛍 ▬

Prüm is one of the most famous names in the Mosel Valley, and this spritzy, intense, surprisingly dry Riesling shows you why. A classic aperitif style, with crisp acidity and lingering green-apple fruitiness.

UNITED STATES

1995 Saintsbury Unfiltered Chardonnay, Carneros, £12.00   16/20
Dry 🛍🛍 ▮

Dick Ward and David Graves have established an enviable reputation for Pinot Noir, but their Chardonnays can be just as good. This is a ripe, toffee-fudge and buttered popcorn-like white, with well-handled oak and nutty richness.

Red

£5–8

FRANCE

1996 Beaujolais Villages, Les Larmoises, Vincent Lacondemine, £7.95　　　　　　　　　　　　　　　　　　　　　17/20
Light-bodied 🛍🛍🛍 |
Juicy, concentrated Beaujolais Villages, which is as good as most cru Beaujolais. An exuberant, cherry and strawberry fruity red, with a refreshing lift of acidity and no hard edges.

Over £8

AUSTRALIA

1994 Charles Cimicky Signature Shiraz, Barossa Valley, £9.50
15/20
Full-bodied |
Porty, alcoholic, massively oaked, faintly vinegary Aussie Shiraz, which takes no prisoners. Something has gone awry between the vineyard and the bottle here.

1995 Leconfield Cabernet Sauvignon, Coonawarra, £9.95　　17/20
Medium-bodied 🛍🛍🛍 ▬
Intense green-pepper and berry-like Bordeaux blend from one of Australia's best red-wine regions. Classically elegant Coonawarra red with pure blackcurrant fruit flavours and exciting intensity. A bit of a find.

FRANCE

1992 Château Tour de Marchesseau, Lalande de Pomerol, £8.95
16/20
Medium-bodied 🛍🛍 |
From a light vintage in Bordeaux, this is a decent, Merlot-based claret with well-judged oak, dry tannins and a core of cassis and vanilla oak sweetness. Pretty good, given the year.

1993 Crozes-Hermitage, Château Curson, £9.50   15/20
Medium-bodied 🍷 ▮

For a 1993 (a wet year in which some producers declassified their red wines) this is reasonably impressive, with some juicy, spicy, blackberry fruit. Only the dry finish is a give-away.

1993 Nuits St Georges, Robert Chevillon, £16.50   17/20
Medium-bodied 🍷🍷🍷 ▬▬

Showing the structure of the 1993 vintage, this is a perfumed, wild-strawberry fruity Pinot Noir with a savoury, chocolatey undertone and chunky, youthful tannins.

1992 Château de Monthelie, Monthelie Sur La Velle, Eric Suremain, £18.50   17/20
Medium-bodied 🍷🍷🍷 ▬▬

Sweetly oaked, savoury spicy Pinot Noir from low-yielding vines, which outperforms its comparatively humble appellation. Perfectly pitched.

1994 Côte Rôtie, Clusel-Roch, £19.00   16/20
Medium-bodied 🍷 ▬▬

Youthful, prominently oaked Syrah from a modern-style domaine. Our feeling is that the oak spice rather smothers the quality of the fruit.

1994 Gevrey-Chambertin, Les Cazetiers, Bruno Clair, £28.00
18/20

Full-bodied 🍷🍷🍷 ▬▬

Made by one of the best young growers on the Côte d'Or, this is a powerfully structured, liquid cherry and raspberry-like Pinot Noir, with lots of sweet vanilla oak intensity and tannin.

NEW ZEALAND

1995 Dry River Pinot Noir, Martinborough, £17.95   17/20
Medium-bodied 🍷🍷 ▬▬

Made by the eccentric, Pinot Noir-obsessed Neil McCallum, this is up there with Ata Rangi and Martinborough in the pantheon of New Zealand's leading Pinot Noirs. An intense, vanilla oaky red, with flavours of cherry and wild strawberry and beautifully handled tannins, especially for the vintage.

1995 Ata Rangi Pinot Noir, Martinborough, £18.00   16/20
Medium-bodied 🛍 ⏐

Consistently one of New Zealand's best Pinot Noirs (although it can't yet
compete with top red Burgundy), this is a sweetly oaked, lightly structured red
from a tricky vintage. You'd be better off waiting for the 1996 vintage, or buying
village Burgundy, in our view.

UNITED STATES

1993 Chalk Hill Cabernet Sauvignon, Sonoma, £12.95   17/20
Full-bodied 🛍🛍 ➡

A supple, attractively textured Cabernet Sauvignon with small proportions of
Merlot and Cabernet Franc, showing mature, almost gamey fruit complexity
and smoky vanilla oak, underpinned by good structure.

Lay & Wheeler

Address: Gosbecks Road, Gosbecks Park, Colchester, Essex CO1 9JT

Telephone/fax: 01206 764446; 01206 560002

E Mail/Web: laywheeler@ndirect.co.uk; http://www.layandwheeler.co.uk

Number of branches: 1, The Wine Centre, Colchester

Opening hours: 9.00am to 7.00pm Monday to Saturday; 10.00am to 4.00pm Sunday

Credit cards accepted: American Express, MasterCard, Visa

Discounts: Wholesale terms for 5-case (may be mixed) orders; collection discount of £3 per case

Facilities and services: Wine workshops; en primeur offers; Saturday wine course; bin-end sales; bi-monthly customer newsletter; wine racks; sale or return; free glass loan; ice; additional party equipment (ice buckets, punchbowls, etc.); waiter service and food for cocktail parties; gift vouchers; in-store tastings; cellarage; twice annual wine list

Mail order: Nationwide, call Lay & Wheeler for terms and details; free delivery to any mainland UK address for consignments of £150 and more; other areas on application

Areas of specialisation: Good everywhere, but with strengths in Bordeaux, Burgundy, Rhône, Alsace, Loire, Germany, California and Australia

At first glance the predominantly male, suit-wearing dramatis personae smiling out from the front pages of Lay & Wheeler's sumptuously colourful wine list could be taken for the management of a small, provincial building society. The faces are kind faces. If Lay & Wheeler were to enter a competition to find Britain's friendliest and most dependable company, it would almost certainly win the award. The personnel, from paterfamilias and chairman Richard Wheeler down, are a big part of Lay & Wheeler's enduring success.

Just as important is the mouth-wateringly extensive wine list. Enquire within, and behind the holiday-snap photos of anonymous vineyards and growers cut off at the knees, you'll find one of the best-endowed wine lists, perhaps the best-endowed list in fact, in the country. Every wine gets a tasting note, every wine region a first-hand introduction. And the selection is extremely good in almost every corner of the viticultural globe.

Lay & Wheeler may be a fairly traditional merchant, with its feet planted in the classic regions of Bordeaux, Burgundy, Piedmont, Port and Champagne, but the company has not been slow to discover value for money in the south of France and to explore the brave New World of Australia, California, South Africa, Chile and New Zealand. The list of New World producers includes the likes of Henschke and Kym Tolley in Australia, Te Mata and Fromm in New Zealand, Duckhorn and Frog's Leap in California and Buitenverwachting and Hamilton Russell in South Africa.

Lay & Wheeler is also keen to educate its customers. As we've mentioned before, its wine workshops are among the most informative in the country, often tutored by high-profile visiting winemakers, who are now accommodated in Lay & Wheeler's 100-seat tasting theatre in Colchester. The Saturday wine course is highly recommended, too.

Those producer tastings are a major focus at Lay & Wheeler. Bruno Prats of second-growth Château Cos d'Estournel in Bordeaux and Stephen Henschke are already scheduled to appear in the coming months. Tastings are not restricted to Colchester, either. London and Edinburgh are regular venues, with the likes of Angelo Gaja of Piedmont and Anne-Claude Leflaive of Burgundy already in the guest book. The company has also recently opened a tasting area beneath one of its City wine bars on Ludgate Hill for City-based customers (by appointment).

Sales in 1997 have been dominated by 1996 en primeur claret, according to Master of Wine Hugo Rose, which 'went mad'. This underlines Lay & Wheeler's reputation as a good and very reliable source of classic wines (something to bear in mind, along with solvency, when choosing an en primeur merchant). But the company is also looking to the future. The Lay & Wheeler Internet site, called The Intelligent Wine List, allows you to choose the wines that reflect your preferences and look up background information on individual growers and producers. You can also leave e-mail messages for members of Lay & Wheeler's staff. Knowing them, they'll almost certainly get back to you.

White

£3–5

FRANCE

1996 Lay & Wheeler Blanc de Blancs, Cuvée Prestige, Côtes de St Mont, Plaimont, £4.65 15/20
Dry 👜👜 ▮
Fresh, bracing, unoaked Gascon white showing the richness of a good vintage and a ripe, buttery texture.

£5–8

AUSTRALIA

1994 Terra White, Hollick, Coonawarra, £6.99 16/20
Dry 👜👜👜 ▮
An unusual blend of 85 per cent Riesling with Sauvignon Blanc, with zesty lemon and lime-peel flavours and a refreshing tang of acidity. Could this be the start of a trend?

AUSTRIA

1996 Heinrich Chardonnay, Burgenland, £7.24 17/20
Dry 👜👜👜 ▮
Bright, complex, partially barrel-fermented white from Austria's Burgenland region, made by red-wine specialists, Heinrich, showing citrus-fruit intensity and a hint of butterscotch with an elegant finish.

FRANCE

1995 Alsace Pinot/Auxerrois Vieilles Vignes, Albert Mann, £7.45
16/20

Dry 👜👜 ▮
Spicy, old-vine Alsace white, which smells like a Pinot Gris, with peachy, almost tropical fruit flavours and a hint of angelica spice. Very moreish.

SOUTH AFRICA

1996 Brampton Chardonnay, Stellenbosch, £6.99   16/20
Dry 🍾🍾🍾 ╎
The first vintage from Rod Easthope's new winery, this is a well-priced, well-made Cape Chardonnay with delicate oak handling and a lemon butter undertone. Crisp and clean.

Over £8

FRANCE

1995 Mâcon Villages, Tête de Cuvée, Verget, £8.95   17/20
Dry 🍾🍾🍾 ╎
Toasty, youthful, structured, barrel-fermented Chardonnay made by the négociant side of Jean-Marie Guffens' excellent, if eccentric, domaine. Belies its humble appellation.

**1995 Tokay Pinot Gris, Hinterburg de Katzenthal, Meyer-Fonné,
50 cl., £10.95**   19/20
Sweet 🍾🍾🍾 ▬
A dense, botrytis-intense Alsace Pinot Gris with plenty of colour and weight, good acidity and layered flavours of peach and mango. Fabulous balance and freshness, despite the richness.

**1995 Savigny-lès-Beaune, Les Montchenovoy, Javillier-Guyot,
£15.95**   18/20
Dry 🍾🍾🍾 ▬
Golden-hued, traditional Côte de Beaune white with notes of honey and beeswax and superb old-vine concentration. A good wine in spite of itself.

NEW ZEALAND

1996 Le Greys Chardonnay, Marlborough, £8.95   17/20
Dry 🍾🍾🍾 ╎
From John and Jennifer Joslin, this is a ripe, sweetish, peach and melon-like Marlborough Chardonnay with subtle oak influence. Stylish and concentrated, with remarkable purity of fruit and a clean, elegant finish.

Red

£3–5

ITALY

1995 Montepulciano d'Abruzzo, Roxan, £4.99 16/20
Full-bodied 👜👜👜 ❘
Robustly peppery, liquoricey Abruzzo red with sweet-and-savoury characters and ripe blackberry fruit. Very well balanced with a thirst-quenching snap of acidity.

£5–8

ITALY

1995 Eloro Rosso, Villa Dorato, £6.54 16/20
Full-bodied 👜👜👜 ➖
From the Noto hills in Sicily, this is a youthful, deeply coloured red made from the Nero d'Avola grape, with spicy, warm-climate fruit, weighty black cherry, plum and raisin characters and a bitter chocolate twist.

Over £8

AUSTRALIA

1994 Hollick Wilgha Shiraz/Malbec/Cabernet, Coonawarra, £8.20
15/20

Medium-bodied 👜 ❘
Faintly herbaceous, green-pepper-like red with hints of fennel and liquorice and an overlay of smoky, dry oak. A little bit overworked.

1995 Veritas Shiraz, Heysen Vineyard, £9.50 16/20
Full-bodied 👜👜 ➖
Dense, almost opaque Barossa Valley red with masses of sweet, smoky oak, rich plum and blackberry fruit and extracted, chewy tannins. Good in a head-banging, full-frontal kind of way.

1994 Henschke Keyneton Estate Shiraz/Cabernet, Eden Valley, £13.95   19/20
Full-bodied 👝👝👝 ▬

A stunning Shiraz-dominated red from the Eden and Barossa Valleys, made by one of Australia's outstanding red-wine producers, combining intense aromas and flavours in a mulberry and blackberry fruity package. Rich but elegant, with beautifully handled tannins and definition. Wow!

FRANCE

1994 Château Charmail, Cru Bourgeois, Haut-Médoc, £8.45 17/20
Medium-bodied 👝👝👝 ▬

Modern, muscular claret at a terrific price, with well-handled oak and a core of dense cassis fruit. Needs another five years to reach its peak, but already very drinkable.

1995 Domaine de Bourgueneuf, Pomerol, £11.20   17/20
Medium-bodied 👝👝👝 ▬

Not to be confused with Château Bourgneuf, this is a new Lay & Wheeler discovery, showing classic Merlot succulence and well-handled oak. Very drinkable, even for a two-year-old Right Bank wine, but will improve for at least another five years.

1994 Santenay Premier Cru, Clos Tavannes, Domaine de la Pousse d'Or, £14.75   17/20
Medium-bodied 👝👝👝 ❘

From the under-rated village of Santenay in the Côte d'Or, this is a stylish, comparatively forward Pinot Noir with sweet oak, succulent tannins and mulberry fruit flavours from a brilliant Volnay-based domaine.

ITALY

1993 Gaja Sito Moresco, Vino da Tavola delle Langhe, £15.94
                                                                        17/20

Full-bodied 👝👝 ▬

From Angelo Gaja, one of the stars of Italy's Piedmont region, this is a comparatively cheap offering (believe it or not), with stylish, vanilla oak, elegant plum and cherry fruit and the classic tannic backbone we associate with Barolo's Nebbiolo grape.

NEW ZEALAND

1996 Fromm Pinot Noir, La Strada, £11.95   16/20
Medium-bodied 🍷🍷 |

From an exciting Swiss-owned winery in Marlborough, this is really concentrated by the high standards of New Zealand Pinot Noir (just wait for the 1996 Reserve), with tightly bound, youthful tannins and notes of black cherry and sweet oak.

UNITED STATES

1994 Pedroncelli Zinfandel, Pedroni-Bushnell, £9.95   16/20
Full-bodied 🍷🍷 ➖

From the warm Dry Creek Valley in Sonoma, this is a throaty, full-on Zin, with masses of fruit concentration, brambly fruit, sweet oak and chunky, tobaccoey tannins.

Lea & Sandeman

Address: 301 Fulham Road, London SW10 9QH

Telephone/fax: 0171 376 4767; 0171 351 0275

Number of branches: 3; also at 211 Kensington Church Street, London W8 7LX (tel. 0171 221 1982) and 51 High Street, Barnes, London SW13 9LN (tel. 0181 878 8643)

Opening hours: 9.00am to 8.30pm Monday to Friday; 10.00am to 8.30pm Saturday

Credit cards accepted: Access, American Express, MasterCard, Switch, Visa

Discounts: On cases, including mixed cases

Facilities and services: Glass loan; cellarage through Elephant Storage; party service; en primeur offers; wine advice; regular mailings

Mail order: Free delivery in central London (or close to the shop in Barnes) for a case or more, and on any order over £200 elsewhere in mainland UK south of Perth; elsewhere, or in smaller quantities, by arrangement (delivery to the Isles of Scilly is usually free)

Areas of specialisation: France, Italy, en primeur offers

It's been nearly a decade since Charles Lea and Patrick Sandeman boldly opened their first Fulham Road store in November 1988, at a time when independent wine merchants, especially ones specialising in fine French and Italian wines, were said to be in decline. But, somewhat against the prevailing trends towards New World wines and supermarkets, the venture has been an evident success. With the acquisition of the Barnes Wine Shop two years ago, the well-spoken duo extended their London wine empire to three roomy, well laid-out shops.

The shops are in pretty ritzy bits of London and tend to be frequented by the sort of people who don't worry about the pounds, never mind the pennies. There is much talk of 'shooting claret', which sounds like a scene from the film Trainspotting, but is only a harmless country pursuit. Only one-third of Lea & Sandeman's business is retail, however. The bulk is mail order, serviced by regular, well-written bi-monthly offers and a slim, blue, inside pocket-sized list.

This is not the place to come for a two-litre bottle of vin de table, in other words. Lea & Sandeman specialises in carefully selected, largely exclusive, top-quality growers' wines from the classic regions of France and Italy, the palate-blowing Sherries of Miguel Valdespino (Sandeman's uncle), and regular en primeur offers of claret and Burgundy. There are also a few cheaper wines from the south of France.

Both business partners are self-confessed traditionalists, and although Charles Lea has admitted he's not desperately keen on the stuff from Down Under, more than a token presence of Australian, Kiwi, Californian, South African and Argentine wines has crept into the posh premises of Fulham Road, Kensington Church Street and Barnes. There is even an Aussie wine or two from Pike's in the Clare Valley, these days.

Lea & Sandeman prides itself on buying parcels of wine that are too small to sell in high-street off-licence chains. 'Most of the people we deal with are small enough to satisfy our needs,' says Sandeman, 'and don't really want to deal with the larger chains.' Even though the Fulham Road shop has to compete with a boisterous Oddbins over the road, customers clearly enjoy the personal touch and the boyish enthusiasm of the Lea & Sandeman staff.

In a high street that is increasingly standardised, it's encouraging to find a range which, although not inconsiderably priced, as former prime minister John Major might have put it, is never short on personality. Lea & Sandeman deserves praise for pursuing quality and individuality. We could do with a few more independents like it.

White

£3–5

FRANCE

1996 Chardonnay, Domaine de Valensac, Vin de Pays d'Oc, £4.85
14/20
Dry ☻ ▐
Fruity, easy drinking, unoaked southern French Chardonnay with crisp, lemon butter fruitiness and pleasantly refreshing acidity.

£5–8

FRANCE

1996 Château Tour des Gendres, Cuvée des Conti, Bergerac Sec, £5.95
16/20

Dry 👝👝👝 ▮

Well-made, nettley, dry Bergerac with good weight and a hint of oak, made in a mini-Graves style and showing the concentration you'd expect from a high proportion of Semillon.

1996 Viognier, Domaine La Condamine l'Evêque, Vin de Pays des Côtes de Thongue, £6.95
17/20

Dry 👝👝👝 ▮

Made by wine consultant-cum-academic Guy Bascou on the shores of the Bassin de Thau, this is a fragrant, apricot and rose-petal-like Viognier with unoaked fruit concentration balanced by pithy acidity. Sumptuous stuff.

ITALY

1996 Montescudaio Bianco, Tenuta del Terriccio, £5.95
14/20

Dry 👝 ▮

Off-the-wall, ginger and angelica spice-like Italian white with a bitter, faintly herbaceous twist.

1996 Pinot Grigio, Vigneti di Castagnari, Cantina Sociale della Valdadige Veronese, Alta Riva, £6.95
15/20

Dry 👝👝 ▮

Appealing, unoaked Italian white with notes of crisp apple and fresh pear and a herby twist. Well made, if a little lacking in complexity. A decent, food-friendly white.

1996 Bolgheri Bianco Vermentino, Vigneto Le Contessine, Le Macchiole, £7.95
17/20

Bone dry 👝👝👝 ▮

Rich, spicy, herby, bracingly dry Mediterranean white made from the characterful Vermentino grape. When Vermentino is good, benefiting from low yields and careful winemaking, it's very good.

Over £8

FRANCE

1996 St Véran, Tête de Cuvée, Verget, £9.95   16/20
Dry 🌑🌑 ▮
Modern, richly textured Mâconnais Chardonnay from an excellent producer, with honeyed spice balanced by subtle oak and lively acidity. A welcome preview of the delights of the 1996 vintage in Burgundy.

1994 Château Tirecul La Gravière, Monbazillac, 50 cl., £11.95
16/20

Very sweet 🌑🌑 ▬
From Claudie and Bruno Bilancini, this is a toasty, barrel-fermented white, which oozes mango, barley sugar and honeyed richness. About as good as Monbazillac gets.

1995 Auxey-Duresses Blanc, Domaine Comte Armand, £12.95
17/20
Dry 🌑🌑🌑 ▬
Made at a domaine that is better known for its stunning Pommard reds, this is a toasty, substantially oaked white Burgundy with good complexity and youthful, citrus-fruit flavours and excellent intensity.

1995 Coteaux du Layon Rochefort, Les Rayelles, Château Pierre Bise, 50 cl., £12.95   18/20
Very sweet 🌑🌑🌑 ▬
Unctuous, botrytis-thick Loire sticky, which is so dense and honeyed that it's difficult to stop swallowing. Marmalade and crystallised pears are the dominant flavours on this stunning, super-concentrated white.

ITALY

1996 Con Vento, Tenuta del Terriccio, £8.95   17/20
Dry 🌑🌑🌑 ▮
There may only be a touch of spicy Gewürztraminer in this stylish Sauvignon Blanc-dominated blend, but the aromatic quality of the Alsace grape is very much in evidence on the nose and palate. A smart Livornian coast table wine, with well-defined acidity and delightful flavours of greengage and gooseberry. One of the best Sauvignon Blancs in Italy.

1996 Le Terrazze della Fattoria di Manzano, Vino da Tavola Toscano, £9.95   17/20

Bone dry 🍷🍷🍷 ▮

Modern, smartly oaked blend of Sauvignon Blanc, Chardonnay, Viognier and Grechetto, which combines the four grapes to good effect in a nutty Graves-like white with a zesty, refreshing tang of acidity. An outstanding Italian white, which combines local and international flavours in a stylish package.

Red

£3–5

FRANCE

1996 Saumur Rouge, Réserve des Vignerons de Saumur, £4.95
                                    15/20

Light-bodied 🍷🍷 ▮

Classic green-pepper and lead-pencil-like Loire Cabernet Franc with the soft tannins you'd expect from the 1996 vintage and juicy, quaffable fruit. Perfect for Indian-summer picnics.

£5–8

FRANCE

1995 Château de Lascaux, Coteaux du Languedoc, £6.75   17/20
Full-bodied 🍷🍷🍷 ▬

Elegant, blackberry fruity, predominantly Syrah-based red with vivid flavours and supple, spicy tannins. If you want to know what all the fuss is about in the south of France, get hold of a bottle of this.

1995 Château des Tours, Côtes du Rhône, £7.95   16/20
Full-bodied 🍷🍷 ▬

Made by the nephew of the late Jacques Reynaud of Châteauneuf-du-Pape's Château Rayas, this is a spicy, powerfully aromatic, essence of Grenache-style red, which Reynaud himself would have admired. A connoisseur's Côtes du Rhône.

1995 Bourgogne Rouge, Domaine Roger et Joël Remy, £7.95 16/20
Medium-bodied 🛍🛍 ⬤–

Peppery, fragrant, faintly chewy red Burgundy with a core of strawberryish Pinot Noir fruit. Pretty good at the price and should age for a year or two yet.

ITALY

1995 Chianti Classico, Querciabella, half-bottle, £5.75   16/20
Full-bodied 🛍🛍 ⬤–

From an ultra-modern winery in the town of Greve, this is a consistently impressive Chianti, with tight, youthful, faintly unyielding plum and black cherry fruit and dense, inky tannins. Needs time.

Over £8

AUSTRALIA

1995 Pike's Clare Valley Cabernet Sauvignon, £9.95   16/20
Medium-bodied 🛍🛍 ⬤–

Australian wines are scarce at Lea & Sandeman, so it's good to see this Clare Valley red establishing itself on the list. A smooth, cassis and mint-like Cabernet Sauvignon, blended with Cabernet Franc and Merlot and aged in French oak for good measure, which is a very successful Australian attempt at a European-style Bordeaux blend.

FRANCE

1995 Château Petit Bocq, St Estèphe, £12.95   15/20
Full-bodied 🛍 ⬤–

Not a typing error: Bocq is indeed the name of the wine. Massively oaked, chocolate and coffee-bean oaky Médoc red with rather extracted tannins. May soften in time, but we're not convinced.

1994 Chassagne-Montrachet, Domaine Henri Germain, £14.50
                                                           16/20

Medium-bodied 🛍 ⬤–

Powerfully oaked, densely structured red Burgundy from a Meursault-based grower best known for his white Burgundies. Finishes rather chewy and astringent.

ITALY

1994 Vino Nobile di Montepulciano, Dei, £9.95   17/20
Full-bodied 👜👜👜 ●—

Dense, concentrated Sangiovese with a delightfully supple core of sweet cherry, plum and blackberry fruit and quite firm tannins. Almost cheap for Vino Nobile.

1996 Podere Il Vescovo, Gamay di Toscana, Fattoria di Manzano, £9.95   17/20
Medium-bodied 👜👜👜 ●—

An Italian Gamay that is more expensive than almost anything you'd find in Beaujolais. Taste the wine and you can see why: a dark, brooding, super-concentrated red with liquid cherry fruit and a firm structure of tannin.

1995 Tassinaia, Tenuta del Terriccio, £16.95   16/20
Medium-bodied 👜 ●—

Oaky, Cabernet Sauvignon-based super-Tuscan red with assertive aromas of mint, vanilla spice and liquorice and stylish, herby concentrated fruit flavours. Over-priced, but that's Italy for you.

Tanners

Address: 26 Wyle Cop, Shrewsbury, Shropshire SY1 1XD

Telephone/fax: 01743 232007; 01743 344401

Number of branches: 4

Opening hours: 9.00am to 6.00pm Monday to Saturday; 10.00am to 4.00pm Sundays (in December)

Credit cards accepted: All major credit cards accepted, but Access, Switch and Visa preferred

Discounts: 5 per cent off collected wines of a case or more, 7.5 per cent off ten cases or more; for delivered orders, 2.5 per cent off three cases, 5 per cent off five cases, 7.5 per cent off ten cases

Facilities and services: Goods on sale or return; free glass loan; waiter service; valuation and purchase of rare and interesting wines; gift packs; gift vouchers; monthly payment cellar scheme; regular newsletters and offers

Mail order: Free delivery within local area for orders of 12 or more bottles and nationwide for orders over £75

Areas of specialisation: France (particularly the classic areas and the Languedoc-Roussillon), Germany and the New World

Family-owned and still proudly independent, Tanners is a Shropshire institution. Take a stroll along Wyle Cop, situated on one of the bends in the River Severn, and its antiquated shop front stands before you. Behind the façade lies an equally Dickensian warren of offices and cellars, which have remained virtually unchanged for the last 155 years. The pictures of prize-winning Shropshire sheep on the office walls further underline the Tanners lineage – gentleman farmers and wine merchants to Middle England since 1842.

A former winner of *Grapevine's* independent wine merchant award and a very strong contender again this year, Tanners continues to run one of the best wine businesses in the country, offering everything from Ata Rangi Pinot Noir to Swiss Chasselas, Austrian Sämling to Montilla. It is difficult to find a bad wine on the list. Some producers have been with Tanners for generations, others have joined the extended family this year. But the quality is invariably first-rate.

Although conservative by nature, Richard and son James Tanner are never afraid to embrace change. (Anyone who has seen James skiing will know that here is a man who relishes speed, excitement and the challenge of a black run.) Their line-up of New World wines, for example, contains a number of top-notch wineries, such as Stoneyridge in New Zealand, Bannockburn in Australia and Au Bon Climat in California. All the same, France remains the focus of the business, where domaine- and château-bottle wines are sourced with care.

The new, full-colour Tanners' list is evidence of James's growing impact on the business. He has introduced photographs to the list (half of them taken by himself), as well as adding information and a clearer layout, without sacrificing the clear, tightly written prose we've praised in previous editions. The same clear-eyed focus is apparent in Talking Tanners, the company's regular newsletter, and in its unhurried approach to the business of selling wine in general. Prices are extremely competitive across the board, service is polite and efficient and (most important of all) the wines are some of the best in the country. A model independent wine merchant.

White

£3–5

FRANCE

1996 Château de Tiregand, Bergerac, £4.95   16/20
Dry 🍷🍷🍷 ▮
Owned by the Comtesse de St-Exupéry, a cousin of the late author of *Le Petit Prince*, this is a rich, weighty, full-bodied Semillon-based white with impressive balance and poise. The former aviator would be proud of this one.

£5–8

FRANCE

1996 Muscat à Petits Grains, Domaine de l'Arjolle, Vin de Pays des Côtes de Thongue, £6.30   15/20
Dry 🍷 ▮
From a region better known for its fortified Muscats, this is a full, dry, expressive white with floral fragrance and nice balancing acidity. A little pricey.
1995 Vouvray, Château Gaudrelle, £7.40   17/20

Off-dry 👜👜👜 ➡–

From a very good year for white wines in the Loire, this is a concentrated, aniseed-scented Chenin Blanc with honey and apple-like intensity, fermented in old casks for added complexity.

1996 St Véran, Christian Collovary et Jean-Luc Terrier, £7.60

16/20

Dry 👜👜👜 ➡–

Clean, buttery, unoaked and slightly nutty Chardonnay from the Mâconnais made by two dynamic brothers-in-law. The perfect house-white Burgundy, which shows that France can deliver value for money when it tries.

SOUTH AFRICA

1996 Vriesenhof Chardonnay, Stellenbosch, £6.50   16/20
Dry 👜👜👜 |

From former hard-tackling Springbok flanker, Jan Coetzee, this is a well-made, smoky oaky Cape Chardonnay, which is a lot subtler than it appears at first – a bit like the man who made it – with a lemony bite.

Over £8

FRANCE

1995 Coudoulet de Beaucastel, Côtes du Rhône, £10.60   17/20
Dry 👜👜👜 |

A blend of Viognier, Marsanne, Clairette and Bourboulenc, made by the Perrin brothers of Châteauneuf's Château de Beaucastel, which proves that the south of France can make really good white wines. Honeysuckle and apricot are the dominant flavours in this stylish, weighty, complex white.

1992 Château Doisy-Daëne, Bordeaux, £10.60   17/20
Dry 👜👜👜 |

Mature, Graves-style blend of mainly Sauvignon Blanc, with Semillon, Muscadelle and (unusually) Riesling and Chardonnay. Ripe, concentrated, toasty and extremely complex. A bargain.

1995 Coteaux du Layon, Chaumes, Domaine des Forges, Les

Onnis, £13.20 18/20
Very sweet 👛👛👛 ▬
Super-rich, but stylish Loire sticky from Claude Branchereau, with luscious, honeyed, botrytis fruit flavours balanced by fresh acidity. Pooh Bear heaven.

1992 Chablis Premier Cru, Les Lys, Daniel Defaix, £15.80 18/20
Dry 👛👛👛 ▬
Traditional, unoaked Chablis with a rich, lees-derived texture and honeyed complexity underpinned by firm acidity. Daniel Defaix's wines seem to go on for ever. We're very glad they do.

GERMANY

1995 Wehlener Sonnenuhr Riesling Auslese, Kerpen, £13.20 18/20
Sweet 👛👛👛 ▬
Minerally, racy, peachy, intensely concentrated Mosel Riesling from one of Germany's best vineyard sites, which is just beginning to develop a kerosene-like character – as long as its 6'7" owner's king-sized bed.

Red

£5–8

ARGENTINA

1992 Weinert Carrascal, Mendoza, £7.30 16/20
Full-bodied 👛👛 ▮
A blend of Malbec, Cabernet Sauvignon and Merlot from one of Argentina's most traditional wineries. Sagey, tarry and concentrated with sweet, leathery maturity.

FRANCE

1995 Faugères, Gilbert Alquier et Fils, £7.10   17/20
Full-bodied 🍷🍷🍷 ▬
A blend of Syrah, Grenache, Carignan and Mourvèdre from one of the Languedoc's leading red-wine appellations, showing chunky, old-vine concentration and spicy, brown-sugar fruitiness.

1994 Crozes-Hermitage, Domaine des Entrefaux, £7.10   17/20
Medium-bodied 🍷🍷🍷 |
Supple, essence of Syrah-like Crozes-Hermitage from Tardy et Ange, with heady, aromatic complexity, silky blackberry fruit and good length. A wine for hedonists.

Over £8

AUSTRALIA

1995 Vasse Felix Cabernet/Merlot, Margaret River, £9.00   18/20
Medium-bodied 🍷🍷🍷 ▬
Made at one of Margaret River's pioneering estates, now owned by the Holmes à Court family, this is an intense, beautifully made Bordeaux-style blend with masses of fruit, beautiful concentration and clarity and delightful elegance. Stunning value.

1995 Coriole Shiraz, McLaren Vale, £9.20   17/20
Full-bodied 🍷🍷🍷 ▬
From the warm-climate McLaren Vale region south of Adelaide, this is a rich, but beautifully defined Shiraz with extremely fine tannins, supple blackcurrant fruit, sweet vanilla oak and a warming finish.

FRANCE

1995 Santenay, Clos de la Confrérie, Vincent Girardin, £12.80
                                                                     16/20
Medium-bodied 🍷🍷 ▬
Modern, youthful red Burgundy with charming red-fruit characters and lots of spicy tannins and new oak, from one of the best producers in this Côte d'Or commune.

1993 Auxey-Duresses, Premier Cru, Michel Prunier, £13.00   17/20
Medium-bodied 🍷🍷🍷 ▬

From a superb red Burgundy vintage, this is a dense, concentrated red with the tannic structure and backbone of the year, but with a lovely underlying core of sweet fruit.

1993 Réserve de la Comtesse, Pauillac, £14.50   17/20
Medium-bodied 💰💰 ➖

A very respectable second wine from top Bordeaux château, Pichon-Lalande, with elegant, vanilla oak and green-pepper intensity. A wine to drink in its voluptuous youth.

1994 Côte Rôtie, Cuvée du Plessy, Gilles Barge, £17.30   19/20
Medium-bodied 💰💰💰 ➖

Gilles Barge is one of the best producers in Côte Rôtie, even though he's less well known than the likes of Guigal and Jasmin. This superb, herb-infused Syrah comes predominantly from the Côte Blonde, and shows silky tannins, refreshing acidity, mulberry and blackberry fruit and a twist of spice. Stunning wine.

SPAIN

1992 Marqués de Vargas Reserva Rioja, £9.95   16/20
Medium-bodied 💰💰 ▮

Herby, Tempranillo-based Rioja made by Pomerol's Michel Rolland, with supple tannins, intense blackberry fruit and spicy, well-integrated American oak.

UNITED STATES

1988 Niebaum Coppola Rubicon, Napa Valley, £17.00   18/20
Full-bodied 💰💰💰 ➖

From film director Francis Ford Coppola's home vineyard in the Napa Valley, this is a blend of Cabernet Sauvignon, Cabernet Franc and Merlot, which has barely moved in the last nine years. Brooding like Marlon Brando, with thick, inky tannins and masses of cedary concentration. Come back in another decade.

Sparkling

£5–8

FRANCE

Saumur Brut, Domaine de la Paleine, £8.00   16/20
Dry 🍾🍾🍾 ▮
Mature, attractively honeyed Chenin Blanc-based Loire fizz with good weight, from an estate owned by Joël Levi, a Parisian publisher-turned-winemaker. Serious for Saumur.

Fortified

£3–5

SPAIN

Jerez-Cortado, Vinicola Hidalgo, half-bottle, £4.65   17/20
Bone dry 🍾🍾🍾 ▮
Nutty, tangy, traditional, burnt-toffee-like Palo Cortado, midway between an Amontillado and an Oloroso in style. This comes from a Solera that dates back to the eighteenth century. Complex stuff.

Over £8

PORTUGAL

Douro Bake, Churchill, half-bottle, £11.60   17/20
Full-bodied 🍾🍾 ▬▬
Traditional Douro Valley-aged Tawny Port bottled specially for Tanners, with plenty of colour and fire and rich, sweet, peppery date and raisin-like fruit.

The Wine Society

Address: Gunnels Wood Road, Stevenage, Herts SG1 2BG

Telephone/fax: 01438 741177, 01438 740222 (order office); 01438 761167 (fax)

Opening hours: 8.30am to 9.00pm Monday to Friday; 9.00am to 2.00pm Saturday; out of hours there is an answering machine on which members can leave orders that will be dealt with the next working day

Credit cards accepted: MasterCard, Visa; accounts are debited only when the order is dispatched

Discounts: £1.20 per case of unmixed dozens; £3 per case from The Society's Showroom in Stevenage; bulk delivery discounts also available

Facilities and services: The 'Cellar' Showroom in Stevenage holds small stocks of older vintage wines and bin-ends, as well as a range of accessories and food items; glass loan (if collected and returned to Stevenage); sale or return on large orders; gifts; three main lists per year and regular mailings and newsletters; Wine Without Fuss scheme; regular tastings in Britain, Ireland and France; open days in Stevenage once a month; en primeur offers; temperature-controlled cellars

Mail order: Free delivery to any UK address, usually within a week of receipt of order, on orders of 12 bottles or more

Areas of specialisation: A good generalist

It's been well over a century since a 'committee of gentlemen' met in the Albert Hall (of all places) to discuss setting up a 'co-operative company' to source and buy wine in 'unadulterated condition'. But the aims and ideals of The Wine Society's founders are alive and well in Stevenage. It is still run along co-operative lines for its 80,000 active members, with any profit reinvested in the business for their benefit.

'It's a virtuous circle,' according to wine buyer and Master of Wine, Sebastian Payne. 'The more people buy, the more we can bring the prices down.' Buying is exactly what The Society's members have been doing over the last 12 months, to the tune of £35m. 'We've done a hell of a lot of business,' says Payne. 'We're going to look cheap by the autumn.' Exchange rates have helped.

Nearly 60 per cent of The Society's wines come from France, with another sizeable chunk from Italy and Spain, so the strength of the pound has been a boon for members.

The Society doesn't advertise: any new members learn about it through friends, family or colleagues. They clearly find the co-operative set-up to their liking. More than 9,000 people have joined in 1997, the highest total in The Society's distinguished history. What attracts them? The service, the service, the service, as Peter Mandelson might put it. The Society offers free delivery, lots of events, tastings and offers, excellent cellarage, a shop in Hesdin, near Boulogne, and increasingly competitive prices.

Most of The Society's members are fairly traditional in outlook, with the professional classes heavily represented. They like buying Bordeaux en primeur (20,000 cases were sold of the 1996 vintage), but they're also big fans of the Rhône (10,000 cases of 1995 Rhônes were sold en primeur in 1997, which is a huge quantity of fine wine), Spain, Italy and the New World.

The Society's selection is generally reliable at the bottom end and much more than that at the top, with particular strengths in France, Germany, Sherry, Port, Champagne, New Zealand, California and Australia. The list looks fairly conservative, but there's plenty of exciting stuff within its pages. It's also a good source of glasses, olive oils, wine racks and hand-made chocolates.

So onwards and upwards. The Society is busy investing in its computer systems and generally making it easier for members to buy wine. That's what it's there for, after all. The next milestone for The Society is 1999, when it will celebrate its 125th anniversary in conjunction with the millennium. It's going to be quite a party in Stevenage. Perhaps they should hire the Albert Hall as well.

White

£3–5

ARGENTINA

1995 Alamos Ridge Chardonnay, Mendoza, £4.95   16/20
Dry 🍾🍾🍾 ❘
Ultra-commercial (in the best sense) Argentine Chardonnay from the Catena group, with ripe melon-fruit flavours and a hint of subtle oak. One of the best Chardonnays on the market at this price.

FRANCE

1996 Domaine du Bosc, Muscat Sec Perlé, Vin de Pays d'Oc, £4.25
15/20

Dry 👜👜 ▯

Spritzy, ultra-refreshing southern French Muscat with crunchy, grapey fruit and good balancing acidity.

1995 The Society's Vin d'Alsace, Hugel, £4.95   15/20
Dry 👜👜 ▯

Floral, weighty, well-made Alsace blend, which is justifiably popular with Wine Society members. Good value at under £5.

£5–8

FRANCE

1996 Menetou-Salon Morogues, Henry Pellé, £6.65   16/20
Dry 👜👜👜 ▯

Crisp, assertive, well-priced Loire Sauvignon Blanc with grapefruit and passion-fruit intensity. A good-value alternative to Pouilly-Fumé.

1995 Mâcon Viré, André Bonhomme, £7.50   17/20
Dry 👜👜👜 ▯

From one of the Mâconnais' most celebrated producers, this is a ripe, exuberantly buttery Chardonnay with creamy, vanilla oak and honeyed richness. Much more flavour than you're entitled to from a Mâcon.

GERMANY

1995 Graacher Himmelreich Riesling Spätlese, Moselland, £5.25
13/20

Medium sweet ▯

Flat and rather boring Riesling, which ought to be a lot more interesting at this price. You can buy good German estate wines for less than this.

NEW ZEALAND

1996 Villa Maria Chardonnay, Gisborne, £6.25 15/20
Dry 🌢🌢 ▮
Ripe, peachy, tropical fruity Chardonnay, which stops short of over-indulgence.
A typically well-crafted Villa Maria white.

Over £8

AUSTRALIA

1996 Madfish Bay, Western Australia, £8.50 17/20
Dry 🌢🌢🌢 ▮
Made by John Wade, one of Western Australia's veteran winemakers, this is a
fresh, attractively balanced Chardonnay with a brilliant label, crisp, citrus-fruit
concentration and attractive vanilla oak.

FRANCE

1995 Domaine Cauhapé, Jurançon Sec, £8.75 13/20
Dry ▮
Flat, ageing, oxidised white Jurançon. This is usually a good wine from an
excellent domaine, so we can only assume this was a bad bottle.

1994 Meursault-Genevrières, Premier Cru, Remoissenet, £22.50
17/20
Dry 🌢 ▮
Nutty, concentrated, traditional white Burgundy from a top Côte de Beaune
village. Well made, but rather pricey at over £20.

Red

£3–5

CHILE

1995 Carmen Cabernet Sauvignon, Central Valley, £4.75   14/20
Medium-bodied 🍾🍾 ▮
Straightforward, blackcurrant pastille-style Chilean red with green pepper and blackcurrant fruit and four-square tannins. Not the best wine we've had from Carmen this year.

FRANCE

The Society's French Full Red, Vin de Table, £3.50   13/20
Full-bodied 🍾 ▮
Robust, fruity, well-made southern French glugger made in a modern style. A good, cheap party red with muscular tannins.

SOUTH AFRICA

1995 Stormy Cape Dry Red, £4.50   14/20
Full-bodied 🍾 ▮
Baked, sage and mint-scented Cape red with savoury tannins and a chewy finish.

SPAIN

1996 Negre Scala Dei, Priorat, £4.95   15/20
Full-bodied 🍾🍾 ▬
From one of Spain's most fashionable regions, this is a chunky, sturdy, Garnacha-based red with the emphasis on fruit, alcohol and tannin, rather than on oak or complexity.

£5–8

FRANCE

1995 Z de Zedé, Bordeaux, £5.95   15/20
Medium-bodied 👛👛 ▬
The second wine of Château Labégorce-Zédé, made in an elegant, modern style for early drinking. Grassy and well made, with refreshing blackcurrant fruit and a slightly stalky finish.

1995 Domaine Cros de la Mûre, Côtes du Rhône, Michel et Fils, £5.95   15/20
Full-bodied 👛👛 ▬
Rich, youthful, chocolatey red with smooth tannins and pure blackberry and violet characters. Finishes with a robust bite.

1995 Juliénas, Les Foillouses, Domaine Pelletier, £6.95   16/20
Medium-bodied 👛👛👛 ▮
Classic cru Beaujolais from one of the best producers in the appellation, with sweet, concentrated cherry fruit and crunchy, refreshing acidity.

ITALY

1995 Chianti Classico, Montecchio, £6.25   17/20
Medium-bodied 👛👛👛 ▬
From the heart of the Chianti Classico zone, this is a silky, luscious, pure Sangiovese red with well-integrated oak and supple, liquid cherry fruit. Attractively moreish.

PORTUGAL

1994 Duas Quintas, Douro, Ramos-Pinto, £5.25   15/20
Full-bodied 👛👛 ▬
A Douro blend of Tinta Roriz and Touriga Nacional made in a chunky, but surprisingly modern style, with good concentration and a core of black-fruit flavours. A wine that grabs you by the tongue and doesn't let go.

Over £8

AUSTRALIA

1993 Balgownie Estate Cabernet Sauvignon, Bendigo, £8.95   15/20
Full-bodied 🥃 🍾

Sweet, chewy, densely coloured Aussie Cabernet Sauvignon with lashings of chocolate and vanilla oak. Rather old-fashioned in an unsubtle and distinctly alcoholic way.

FRANCE

1990 Leroy Bourgogne, £9.95   12/20
Medium-bodied 🍾

Vinegary, old-fashioned, shagged-out Bourgogne rouge from a trendy négociant. A Pinot Noir that is some way past its sell-by date.

1990 Château Lestage Simon, Cru Bourgeois, Haut-Médoc, £9.95
                                                             17/20
Medium-bodied 🥃🥃🥃 ▬—

From the best Bordeaux vintage of the last ten years, this is a perfumed, concentrated red with beautifully integrated oak, showing the richness and cassis fruit flavours of the year. Stylishly balanced.

Sparkling

Over £8

FRANCE

The Wine Society's Private Cuvée Champagne, Alfred Gratien, £15.95   16/20
Dry 🥃🥃 🍾

Elegantly traditional, bottle-aged Champagne from Wine Society stalwart, Alfred Gratien, with a mouth-filling mousse and a nutty, dry tang.

SPAIN

Agusti Torelló Mata Cava, £8.75   15/20
Dry 🜂 |

Mature, well-made Cava with good bottle-developed characters and a nice creamy texture. Our only quibble is with the optimistic price.

Grapevine's Best of the Rest

John Armit Wines

Address: 5 Royalty Studios, 105 Lancaster Road, London W11 1QF

Telephone/fax: 0171 727 6846; 0171 727 7133

Number of branches: 1

Opening hours: 9.00am to 6.00pm Monday to Friday

Credit cards accepted: Access, American Express, Switch, Visa

Discounts: None

Facilities and services: Cellar planning; cellarage; wine broker; en *primeur* offers; wine investment advice; major annual tasting in October; regular tutored tastings; private customer tastings on request

Mail order: Free delivery for orders of three cases and over

Areas of specialisation: Bordeaux, Burgundy

Fashionable, West London wine merchant catering for the capital's rock stars, film producers and assorted glitterati. Particularly good for growers' Burgundies, clarets from the Left Bank négociant house of Jean-Pierre Moueix, boutique California wineries and, appropriately enough, the never knowingly undercharged Angelo Gaja from Piedmont. Seresin Estate from New Zealand, owned, appropriately enough, by a cinematographer, is a good new find this year. Armit hosts an annual lunch or dinner with American wine guru Robert Parker and seems to spend as much time at the Groucho Club as in Notting Hill Gate.

Butlers Wine Cellar

Address: 247 Queens Park Road, Brighton, East Sussex BN2 2XJ

Telephone/fax: 01273 698724; 01273 622761

Number of branches: 1

Opening hours: 10.00am to 6.00pm Tuesday to Wednesday; 10.00am to 7.00pm Thursday to Saturday

Credit cards accepted: American Express, JCB, MasterCard, Switch, Visa

Discounts: Apply to monthly special offers

Facilities and services: Monthly special offers; regular tastings; free glass loan; newsletter

Mail order: National and international delivery (ask for details of carriage charges); free local delivery on orders of 1 case and over

Areas of specialisation: Bordeaux, Burgundy, Italy

The Butlers, father Geoffrey and son Henry, are English eccentrics. From their small Brighton shop, they've established an excellent reputation along the south coast and further inland. The list is large and intriguing, with specialisms in venerable bottles from Bordeaux, Burgundy and Germany at good prices, and other curiosities. The Butler's Journal, distributed to BWC Club members, is an amusing source of spleen and strongly held opinions.

D. Byrne & Co.

Address: Victoria Buildings, 12 King Street, Clitheroe, Lancashire BB7 2EP

Telephone: 01200 423152

Number of branches: 1

Opening hours: 8.30am to 6.00pm Monday to Wednesday; 8.30am to 8.00pm Thursday and Friday; 8.00am to 6.00pm Saturday

Credit cards accepted: None

Discounts: £2 per mixed and unmixed case

Facilities and services: Sale or return; free glass loan; party planning; cellar planning; storage; free delivery within 50 miles; regular free tastings and free annual tasting each autumn

Mail order: By arrangement only

Area of specialisation: Bordeaux

A local, family-owned institution run by brothers Andrew and Philip Byrne from a nineteenth-century shop in the heart of Clitheroe. The line-up of wines here is amazing, as are the malt whiskies. The Byrnes produce a huge, if rambling, telephone directory of a list, with nothing in the way of tasting notes or information to guide the punter. Perhaps these aren't necessary, as the Byrnes are usually on hand to provide advice and (most Saturdays) to conduct tastings in their cellars. The sort of merchant that every English town would be more than happy to have.

Chippendale Fine Wines

Address: 15 Manor Square, Otley LS21 3AP

Telephone/fax: 0943 850633; 0943 850633

Number of branches: 1

Opening hours: 10.00am to 5.45pm Monday, Tuesday, Thursday and Friday; 9.30am to 5.00pm Saturday

Credit cards accepted: Access, Switch, Visa

Discounts: 5 per cent case discount (mixed and unmixed) on orders of one to five cases, 7 per cent case discount on orders of six cases and over; 'Discount Club' members receive a basic discount of 3 per cent, even on single-bottle purchases, with discounts of 4–7 per cent on monthly newsletter 'specials', and case discount increases to 6 per cent on orders of one to five cases and 8 per cent for six cases and over

Facilities and services: Sale or return; free local delivery on orders of 6 bottles or more; free glass loan; party planning; weekly in-store tastings; tutored tastings on request; free 'Discount Club'

Mail order: Nationwide delivery (ask for details of carriage charges)

Areas of specialisation: Australia, southern France

The author of one of the most amusing wine lists in the country, supplemented by regular, soapbox-style outpourings in monthly newsletters, Michael Pollard is an *écrivain manqué*, who appears to have one eye on Robin Yapp's title as the Marcel Proust of the British wine trade and the other on a book of Ogden Nash poems. We particularly enjoyed the introduction to the latest Chippendale tome, with typical tasting notes ('only good for shifting mildew from bathroom grouting' and 'like drinking lemon and sugar pancake with a dash of pencil shavings') and well-aimed tirades against cheap Bordeaux and anything else that gets his Yorkshire goat. His Otley-based operation is a one-man Punch and Judy show with particular strengths in Australia, the south of France and, latterly, Argentina. An idiosyncratic delight run by an appealing nutter.

Connolly's Wine Merchants

Address: Arch 13, 220 Livery Street, Birmingham B3 1EU

Telephone/fax: 0121 236 9269; 0121 233 2339

E-mail: connowine@ao1.com

Number of branches: 1

Opening hours: 9.00am to 5.30pm Monday to Friday; 10.00am to 2.00pm Saturday

Credit cards accepted: American Express, MasterCard, Switch, Visa

Discounts: On unmixed and mixed cases of wine when orders are paid by cheque, cash or debit card

Facilities and services: Free local delivery for one case or more; free glass loan; sale or return; gift packaging; regular tutored tastings, often featuring winemakers

Mail order: Orders accepted both by telephone and fax for single-bottle and case sales (ask for details of carriage charges)

Areas of specialisation: Burgundy, Italy, California

A dynamic Midlands wine merchant run by enthusiast and William McGonagall wanna-be, Chris Connolly ('Said Mr Clever, "Don't despair, I'll get us out of trouble. Give those Connolly's chaps a ring, they'll be here at the double."') Connolly's holds lots of tastings and wine-and-food evenings, with the emphasis on the New World. But the main treat is the chatty, well-chosen list, called The Book of Bacchus, which covers the world's wine regions in just the right depth and throws in a good range of malt whiskies and Riedel glasses for good measure. Connolly's personal favourites are Italian wines ('as elegant, graceful and classy as Ravanelli at a fraction of the price') and some excellent Burgundies from the likes of Pousse d'Or, Lafarge and Comte Armand. The Midlands is well served by Mr C.

Corney & Barrow

Address: 12 Helmet Row, London EC1V 3QJ

Telephone/fax: 0171 251 4051; 0171 608 1373

Opening hours: 9.00am to 6.00pm Monday to Friday

Number of branches: 4

Also at: 194 Kensington Park Road, London W11 2ES. Telephone/fax: 0171 221 5122; 0171 221 9371. Opening hours: 10.30am to 8.00pm Monday to Saturday

And: Belvoir House, High Street, Newmarket, Suffolk CB8 8OH. Telephone/fax: 01638 662068; 01638 560255. Opening hours: 9.00am to 6.00pm Monday to Saturday

And: Corney & Barrow with Whighams of Ayr, 8 Academy Street, Ayr KT7 1HT, Scotland. Telephone/fax: 01292 267000; 01292 265903. Opening hours: 9.00am to 5.30pm Monday to Saturday

And: Corney & Barrow with Whighams of Ayr, 26 Rutland Square, Edinburgh EH1 2BW. Telephone/fax: 0131 228 2233; 0131 228 2243. Opening hours: 9.00am to 6.00pm Monday to Friday

Credit cards accepted: Access, American Express, Visa

Discounts: By negotiation

Facilities and services: Cellarage; corporate services; gift packaging; wine broker; regular in-store tastings; cellar planning; sale or return; advice for weddings; contactable on e-mail; *en primeur*, broking lists and newsletters

Mail order: Delivery throughout mainland UK (ask for details of carriage charges)

Areas of specialisation: Bordeaux, Burgundy

The kind of place where it helps to have a double-barrelled surname to get onto the mailing list, never mind onto the staff, Corney & Barrow is the City wine merchant *par excellence*. Its close links with the ultra-expensive Domaine de la Romanée-Conti, Christian Moueix and his Château Pétrus and other Pomerols are a good indication of the style of operation, but there are less expensive wines on the list, too. Those from Domaine Dujac and négociant Olivier Leflaive are especially noteworthy.

Direct Wine Shipments

Address: 5–7 Corporation Square, Belfast, BT1 3AJ

Telephone/fax: 01232 238700 and 01232 243906/01232 240202

E-mail: dws@dial.pipex.com

Number of branches: 1

Opening hours: 9.30am to 6.30pm Monday to Wednesday and Friday; 9.30am to 8.00pm Thursday; 9.30am to 5.00pm Saturday

Credit cards accepted: Access, Delta, MasterCard, Switch, Visa

Discounts: Up to 10 per cent case discount on mixed and unmixed cases; quantity discount by negotiation

Facilities and services: Free glass loan; *en primeur* and ex-cellar offers; tutored tastings with slide presentations by request; regular customer tastings featuring winemakers and Masters of Wine; 6-week wine appreciation courses available

Mail order: Through the wine club 'Home Direct' (ask for further details)

Areas of specialisation: Australia, Bordeaux, Burgundy, California, Italy, Spain

Alongside James Nicholson, Direct Wine Shipments is the place that wine drinkers head for in Northern Ireland. The emphasis, as with Nicholson, is on winemaker tastings (Dr Tony Jordan of Green Point, Michel Laroche of Domaine Laroche and Piero Antinori are all recent speakers) and good selection. DWS is particularly strong in the New World, but its Old World wines are interesting, too. The pocket-sized list includes interesting essays on subjects as diverse as phylloxera and the historical development of wine production, written by owner Peter McAlindon.

Farr Vintners

Address: 19 Sussex Street, London SW1V 4RR

Telephone/fax: 0171 821 2000; 0171 821 2020

Number of branches: 1

Opening hours: 9.00am to 6.00pm Monday to Friday

Credit cards accepted: All major credit cards

Discounts: On orders over £2,000 ex. VAT

Facilities and services: Cellarage; advice; valuation

Mail order: Minimum order £500 ex. VAT (ask for details of carriage charges)

Areas of specialisation: Fine and rare wines

Short of a bottle of 1961 Château Latour? Run out of 1990 Château d'Yquem or 1983 Grange? Then call Farr Vintners, Britain's leading fine- and rare-wine brokers, whose thriving business has been rewarded with a Queen's Award for Export Achievement. (This gives you an indication of the international spread of Farr's customers.) At times, the owners are a little too dependent on scores given by American wine writer Robert Parker and *The Wine Spectator* when it comes to choosing wines, but there's no denying the depth of knowledge and expertise here. They also make a lot of money for themselves as well as some of their clients, as the high-profile Andrew Lloyd Webber sale at Sotheby's this year confirmed. A minimum order of £500 keeps the hoi polloi – but not necessarily the Japanese, Americans and Swiss – away.

Gauntley's of Nottingham

Address: 4 High Street, Exchange Arcade, Nottingham NG1 2ET

Telephone/fax: 0115 911 0555; 0115 911 0556

Number of branches: 1

Opening hours: 9.00am to 5.30pm Monday to Saturday; (11.00am to 4.30pm Sunday during the Christmas period only)

Credit cards accepted: Access, Switch, Visa

Discounts: 5 per cent case discount

Facilities and services: Sale or return; free glass loan; free local delivery; gift boxes; in-bond transfers and storage; tutored tastings; bi-monthly newsletter and special offers

Mail order: Worldwide for single bottles and cases (ask for details of carriage charges)

Areas of specialisation: Alsace, Loire, Languedoc-Roussillon, Rhône

The still amazingly youthful John Gauntley is often to be found truffling through the vineyards of France in search of new wines from his beloved Rhône, Loire and Languedoc-Roussillon. We can't fault the man's choice of specialist regions, or his choice of growers within them. He's also branched out into top estates in Australia, California, New Zealand and South Africa. Not a place for claret lovers, but a very good place to come if you're a Rhône Ranger. If you're based in Nottingham, make sure you go along to one of Gauntley's regular tastings in the shop or the University's Derby Hall.

Gelston Castle Fine Wines

Address: Gelston Castle, Castle Douglas, Scotland DG7 1QE

Telephone/fax: 01556 503012; 01556 504183

Opening hours: 9.00am to 6.00pm Monday to Friday; 24-hour answerphone service

Number of branches: 2

Also at: 45 Warwick Square, London SW1V 2AJ. Telephone/fax: 0171 821 6841; 0171 821 6350. Opening hours: 9.00am to 6.00pm Monday to Friday; 24-hour answerphone service

Credit cards accepted: MasterCard, Visa

Discounts: 5 per cent case discount on Champagne; £2 case discount on wine orders of 5 cases and over; 5 per cent case discount on wine orders of 10 cases and over

Facilities and services: Gift packing and delivery; cellarage; menu planning; in-store and private tutored tasting; fine-wine dinners and wine weekends; cellar planning and evaluation; fine-wine broking and auction sale/purchase

Mail order: Orders may be placed by telephone, fax and post; free delivery in mainland UK for orders over £200, otherwise a fixed charge per drop

Areas of specialisation: Burgundy, Germany, Loire, the Midi, Rhône

In with a shout for the title of Scotland's best independent wine merchant, Alexander Scott's turreted operation produces a stylish, well-written and hugely informative wine list and sends out regular offers of off-beat wines from regions such as Jurançon, Lombardy and Tokay. Scott is strong in Burgundy and the Midi and is also one of the few merchants who takes a sensible approach to the annual *en primeur* circus.

Peter Green

Address: 37a/b Warrender Park Road, Edinburgh EH9 1HJ

Telephone/fax: 0131 229 5925; 0131 229 5925

Number of branches: 1

Opening hours: 9.30am to 6.30pm Monday to Thursday; 9.30am to 7.30pm Friday; 9.30am to 7.00pm Saturday

Credit cards accepted: Access, Switch, Visa

Discounts: 5 per cent unmixed case discount

Facilities and services: Free glass loan; free local delivery; gift packaging service; cellarage; regular in-store tastings; tutored tastings nine times a year; frequent organised group tastings; *en primeur* offers; bin-end sales

Mail order: Delivery throughout the UK (ask for details of carriage charges)

Areas of specialisation: Australia, New Zealand, South Africa, Chile, Argentina, and so on around the world in 80 days

Scotland's very own A–Z of wine is housed in Michael Romer's Warrender Park Road shop, which combines the feel of a traditional wine merchant with the stack-it-high, browser-friendly ambience of a wine warehouse. The range is so big that it's bound to be stronger (especially in the New World) in some areas than others, but if you're looking for a bottle from Oregon, Argentina or Zimbabwe, the chances are that Peter Green will be able to help. There are even 15 Romanian wines and eight vintages of the Lebanese Château Musar.

Richard Harvey Wines

Address: Bucknowle House, Bucknowle, Wareham, Dorset BH20 5PQ

Telephone/fax: 01929 480352; 01929 481275

Number of branches: 1

Opening hours: 9.00am to 6.00pm Monday to Friday; 9.00am to 1.00pm Saturday

Credit cards accepted: None

Discounts: 5 per cent case discount on orders of six unmixed cases and over

Facilities and services: Free local delivery for three cases and over; free national delivery for 7 cases and over; free glass loan with order; cellarage; tutored tastings

Mail order: Mail order only

Areas of specialisation: France (*domaine*-bottled wines)

With the closure of his shop in Cherbourg earlier this year, Master of Wine Richard Harvey is once more a West Country-only wine merchant. The restricted, but well-chosen selection that made the French shop one of the best in the Channel ports is now available solely by mail order from Bucknowle House in Dorset. The emphasis is on French *domaines* and estates, many of which seem to be owned by British ex-pats, with a cursory nod in the direction of the New World.

Haynes, Hanson & Clark

Address: 25 Eccleston Street, London SWIW 9NP

Telephone/fax: 0171 259 0102; 0171 259 0103

Opening hours: 9.00am to 7.00pm Monday to Friday; 10.00am to 6.00pm Saturday

Number of branches: 2

Also at: Sheep Street, Stow-on-the-Wold, Gloucestershire GL54 IAA. *Telephone/fax*: 01451 870 808; 01451 870 508. Opening hours: 9.00am to 6.00pm Monday to Friday; 9.30am to 6.00pm Saturday

Credit cards accepted: Access, MasterCard, Switch, Visa

Discounts: 10 per cent case discount on mixed and unmixed cases

Facilities and services: Free local delivery; free glass loan; ice; gift packaging service; wine bins made to order; cellar planning; regular tastings

Mail order: Free delivery throughout the UK on orders of 5 cases or more, or over £450

Area of specialisation: Burgundy

Haynes, Hanson & Clark draws on the knowledge of Master of Wine and Burgundophile-in-chief, Anthony Hanson, whose book, *Burgundy*, is by far the best tome on the subject. Hanson is not averse to rattling a few cages outside, as well as inside, Burgundy. His 1996 *en primeur* offer was one of the most critical of the absurd prices being asked for ultra-fashionable châteaux. Still, Burgundy is the focus here. Haynes, Hanson & Clark is one of a small handful of places that sells really fine, limited-production wines from the Yonne and the Côte d'Or. If you enjoy Chablis from Raveneau, Volnay from De Montille, Chambolle-Musigny from Roumier or Meursault from François Jobard, this is the place to open your cheque book and close your eyes. H, H & C also does a good job in the Loire, Bordeaux, Beaujolais and California.

J.E. Hogg

Address: 61 Cumberland Street, Edinburgh EH3 6RA

Telephone/fax: 0131 556 4025; 0131 556 4025

Number of branches: 1

Opening hours: 9.00am to 1.00pm Monday to Saturday; 2.30pm to 6.00pm Monday, Tuesday, Thursday and Friday

Credit cards accepted: Switch

Discounts: Only with special offers

Facilities and services: Sale or return; free glass loan; delivery in Edinburgh

Mail order: Ask for details

Areas of specialisation: A generalist

A popular address with canny, wine-drinking Scots, Jim Hogg's cramped, old-fashioned shop is home to diverse malt whiskies, spirits and fresh coffee, as well as a huge range of very competitively priced wines. After years of writing everything out by hand himself, whether it be invoices or the annual list, Hogg has finally entered the computer age, we are sorry to say. A good place to buy most things, especially cheaper clarets and Australian wines, which Hogg did so much to pioneer in Scotland.

Laymont & Shaw Ltd

Address: The Old Chapel, Millpool, Truro, Cornwall TR1 3PF

Telephone/fax: 01872 270545/01872 223005

Number of branches: 1

Opening hours: 8.30am to 5.00pm Monday to Friday

Credit cards accepted: None

Discounts: £2.50 discount per case on all wines collected from the premises at Truro; other quantity discounts available

Facilities and services: Free glass loan with local orders

Mail order: Minimum order one case; free delivery to the UK mainland

Area of specialisation: Spain

The original Iberian independent, run by Spanish enthusiast, John Hawes. If you're a fan of Cava, Rioja, Sherry or the less well-known delights of Rias Baixas, Bierzo and Priorato, it's worth taking a holiday in Cornwall just to visit L & S. Mail-order customers are kept informed on matters Iberian with a quarterly newsletter. As Spain reasserts itself as a wine-making nation, thanks to a new generation of wineries, or *bodegas*, it's good to have access to such passion and expertise.

Laytons Wine Merchants

Address: 20 Midland Road, London NW1 2AD

Telephone/fax: 0171 388 4567; 0171 383 7419

Opening hours: 9.30 to 6.30pm Monday to Saturday

Number of branches: 5

Also at: 50–2 Elizabeth Street, Belgravia, London SW1W 9PB. Telephone/fax: 0171 730 8108; 0171 730 9284. Opening hours: 9.30am to 7.00pm Monday to Saturday

And: 21 Motcomb Street, Knightsbridge, London SW1X 8LB. Telephone/fax: 0171 235 3723; 0171 235 2062. Opening hours: 9.30am to 6.30pm Monday to Friday; 10.00am to 1.00pm Saturday

And: 23 Elystan Street, Chelsea Green SW3 3NT. Telephone/fax: 0171 581 2660; 0171 581 1203. Opening hours: 9.30 to 6.30pm Monday to Saturday

And: 77–8 Chancery Lane, London WC2A 1AB. Telephone/fax: 0171 405 0552; 0171 405 0553. Opening hours: 9.30am to 6.30pm Monday to Friday

Credit cards accepted: Access, American Express, Diners, Switch, Visa

Discounts: 'Rare', apparently

Facilities and services: Free delivery on orders over £150; wedding list service; gift delivery service; regular customer tastings in London, Oxford, Cambridge, Manchester, York and Leeds/Bradford

Mail order: National and international deliveries available (ask for details of carriage charges)

Areas of specialisation: France (particularly Burgundy), Italy

So farewell then, Graham Chidgey, the only wine merchant we know of to have scored a first-class century. Chidgey had had a good innings but decided to sell the business and retire to France earlier this year. The company he took over in 1965 is in good hands after a mangement buy-out. It remains a traditional, pinstripes and braces operation, which concentrates on Bordeaux and Burgundy, specialising in *en primeur* offers and fine-wine bin-ends, sold through mail order and its four André Simon shops. The Layton's house Champagne is well worth a detour.

Moreno Wines

Address: 23–5 Praed Street, Paddington, London W2

Telephone/fax: 0171 723 6897; 0171 724 3813

Opening hours: 9.00am to 5.30pm Monday to Friday; 10.00am to 8.00pm Saturday

Number of branches: 2

Also at: 11 Marylands Road, London W9 2DU. Telephone/fax: 0171 706 3055. Opening hours: 2.00pm to 10.30pm Monday to Wednesday; 12.00pm to 10.30pm Thursday and Friday; 10.00am to 10.30pm Saturday; 12.00pm to 8.00pm Sunday

Credit cards accepted: MasterCard, Switch, Visa

Discounts: 5 per cent discount on one to three cases; 10 per cent discount on over three cases

Facilities and services: Free local delivery; corporate account facilities; in-store and tutored tastings; Spanish wine club

Mail order: £7 per case within the UK

Areas of specialisation: Spain, Oregon, United States, New Zealand, South America

Hispanophiles who find *tapas*-bar fare as dull as the Gypsy Kings tend to gravitate towards academic-turned-wine-merchant Manuel Moreno's quirky West London shops. Hand-selected bottles from estates such as Guelbenzu, Marqués de Alella and Valdespino, as well as a broad selection of older vintages from the likes of Vega Sicilia and La Rioja Alta, make this one of the two best Spanish specialists in the country (Laymont & Shaw being the other). Chilean wines from Viña Casablanca and Viña Porta and the Argentinian Vistalba are worth a punt, too, as are Giesen from New Zealand and Rex Hill from Oregon, both new agencies this year. Moreno sells quite a few wines to supermarkets and high-street chains, so you may come across them there.

Morris & Verdin

Address: 10 The Leathermarket, Weston Street, London SE1 3ER

Telephone/fax: 0171 357 8866; 0171 357 8877

Number of branches: 1

Opening hours: 8.00am to 6.00pm Monday to Friday

Credit cards accepted: None

Discounts: 10 per cent on unmixed cases

Facilities and services: Glass loan; tutored tastings; free delivery within inner London

Mail order: Orders taken both by telephone and letter

Areas of specialisation: Burgundy, California

When the new Burgundy vintage is released onto the *en primeur* market in the spring each year, Morris & Verdin's Leathermarket base is the first place the *Grapevine* team tends to head for. Master of Wine Jasper Morris's mouth-watering selection of growers' wines, from good-value house red and white Bourgogne to Premier and Grand Cru stunners from the likes of Bonneau du Martray, Dominique Lafon, Daniel Rion and Pousse d'Or, is a delight for Burgundophiles. He also buys well in Bordeaux and acts as an agent for some increasingly good wines from Californian producers such as Au Bon Climat, Ridge (in London only), Qupé and Bonny Doon. They've also taken on the agency for Vega Sicilia, Spain's most famous red wine, and the Portuguese Quinta de la Rosa in the last year or so.

James Nicholson

Address: 27a Killyleagh Street, Crossgar, County Down, Northern Ireland BT30 9DG

Telephone/fax: 01396 830091; 01396 830028

Number of branches: 1

Opening hours: 10.00am to 7.00pm Monday to Saturday

Credit cards accepted: Access, Switch, Visa

Discounts: Case discount between 7 and 10 per cent on mixed or unmixed cases of wine

Facilities and services: Sale or return; free glass loan; regular free in-store tastings and occasional themed or winemaker tastings and dinners; gift packs; bi-monthly special offers; cellarage and free delivery of one case or more within Northern Ireland

Mail order: 48-hour delivery service available throughout the UK

Areas of specialisation: Bordeaux, Burgundy, Germany, California

The best wine merchant in Northern Ireland, and one of the finest in the UK to boot, James Nicholson's Crossgar operation is the model of an independent specialist. Nicholson is proud of having earned thousands of Air Miles in his search for new wines and his first-rate judgement is apparent on every page of his stylishly designed, ring-bound list, coloured in New Labour red for 1997. This year's haul includes new wines from the Loire, Burgundy, New Zealand and Australia. Nicholson's standing with winemakers ensures that many of the world's biggest names can be found tutoring tastings for the citizens of Crossgar and Kildare. If you're in the vicinity, Randall Grahm of Bonny Doon, Paul Draper of Ridge and Olivier Humbrecht of the Domaine Zind-Humbrecht in Alsace are all coming your way.

Christopher Piper Wines

Address: 1 Silver Street, Ottery-St-Mary, Devon EX11 1DB

Telephone/fax: 01404 814139; 01404 812100

Number of branches: 1

Opening hours: 9.00am to 1.00pm and 2.00pm to 5.30pm Monday to Friday; 9.00am to 1.00pm and 2.30pm to 4.30pm Saturday

Credit cards accepted: MasterCard, Visa, Visa Delta

Discounts: 5 per cent case discount on mixed and unmixed cases; 10 per cent discount on orders of three cases and over

Facilities and services: Free glass loan; sale or return; in-store tastings; account facilities; cellarage; bi-monthly newsletter; *en primeur* offers

Mail order: Free local delivery on orders of four cases or more; free delivery throughout the UK on orders of six cases or more

Areas of specialisation: Beaujolais, French country wines, Burgundy

One of the few British wine merchants with a degree in oenology (and the experience of making Beaujolais at Château des Tours in Brouilly every year), Chris Piper is an opinionated and dynamic Devon wine merchant, whose Noble Rot newsletter is always crisply argued and thought-provoking. His literate, well-upholstered list is strong on Burgundy and Beaujolais, as you'd expect, as well as the New World. And regular offers of traditional, *en primeur* wines ensure a strong West Country following. Locals and visitors alike can take advantage of the annual tasting in Ottery St Mary and of regular wine weekends.

Terry Platt

Address: Ferndale Road, Llandudno Junction, Gwynedd LL31 9NT

Telephone/fax: 01492 592971; 01492 592196

Opening hours: 8.30am to 5.30pm Monday to Friday

Number of branches: 2

Also at: World of Wine, 29 Mostyn Avenue, Craig-y-Don, Llandudno LL30 1YS. Telephone: 01492 872997. Opening hours: 10.00am to 8.00pm Monday to Saturday; 12.00am to 5.00pm Sunday

Credit cards accepted: MasterCard, Switch, Visa

Discounts: By negotiation

Facilities and services: Sale or return; glass hire; corporate gifts; valuations; wine list preparation; in-store tastings every Friday and Saturday; free local delivery; tutored tastings; newsletter; themed dinners, often with the winemakers; party planning

Mail order: 48-hour delivery throughout the UK mainland (ask for details of carriage charges)

Areas of specialisation: Burgundy, Spain, Italy, Australia, South Africa, New Zealand, California

The leading wine merchant in Wales and a regular award-winner, Jeremy (son of Terry) Platt offers a broad, well-chosen range with highlights in Burgundy, Beaujolais and Bordeaux and an increasing presence in Australia, California, New Zealand and South Africa. The weirdest wines on the list are Wales' very own Monnow Valley Vineyards (full marks for patriotism, boyo), but non-Gaelic-speaking customers would be better served drinking Martinez Bujanda from Rioja, Quinta do Carmo from Portugal or Vavasour from New Zealand. The list gets bigger and better each year, with 33 wines from California, 70 from Burgundy, 70 from Australia, 38 from Spain, 35 from Italy, 51 from South Africa and 25 from New Zealand to choose from.

Raeburn Fine Wines

Address: 21/23 Comely Bank Road, Edinburgh EH4 1DS

Telephone/fax: 0131 343 1159; 0131 332 5166

Number of branches: 1

Opening hours: 9.00am to 6.00pm Monday to Saturday; 12.30pm to 5.00pm Sunday

Credit cards accepted: Access, American Express, Delta, JCB, MasterCard, Switch, Visa

Discounts: 2.5 per cent discount on mixed cases; 5 per cent discount on unmixed cases

Facilities and services: Tutored tastings; corporate tastings; free glass loan; *en primeur* offers

Mail order: Available throughout the UK (ask for details of carriage charges)

Areas of specialisation: Burgundy, Bordeaux, New World

Five minutes from the Firth of Forth, Raeburn is the only wine merchant in Britain that also sells lilies, carnations and roses. This florist-cum-off-licence is run by wine nut, Zubair Mohamed, who confesses that he's not a 'great guy for lists'. (His last publication was in January 1995.) The 500-strong range is consistently of high quality, whatever the price, with one of the best growers' Burgundy lists in Scotland and an eye for idiosyncratic estates in the New World, such as Joseph Swann, Dry River, Warwick Estate and Moss Wood. Mohamed also has a well-chosen, eclectic selection from Italy, Spain and Germany and hosts regular dinners and tutored tastings. More fun than selling chrysanthemums, we reckon.

Reid Wines (1992) Ltd

Address: The Mill, Marsh Lane, Hallatrow, Bristol BS18 5EB

Telephone/fax: 01761 452645; 01761 453642

Number of branches: 1

Opening hours: 10.30am to 5.30pm Monday to Friday; weekends by arrangement

Credit cards accepted: MasterCard, Visa, with a 3 per cent surcharge on the total cost of each order

Discounts: None

Facilities and services: Occasional in-store tastings; free local delivery; glass hire

Mail order: Ask for details of carriage charges

Areas of specialisation: A generalist, with an emphasis on fine and rare wines

Peppered with wine quotes and Bill Baker's humorous asides, Reid Wines' laconic but authoritative list is a good place to find rare and mature bottles snapped up at the auction houses and described with self-deprecating honesty. (Our favourite is 'should never have been put into bottle: your risk' about a 1963 Château Latour.) So good are some of the fine wines that Reid suffered a break-in this year, losing 50 cases through a window in the men's lavatory. The 'fine and rare' tag shouldn't be overstated, however, as Reid Wines lists plenty of things from more recent vintages, too, including traditional Burgundy, Bordeaux and Rhône, as well as Calera, Clos du Val and Niebaum Coppola from California, Taltarni from Australia and Wairau River from New Zealand. You may see some of these on the lists of Conran restaurants, such as Quaglino's and Bluebird Café, following Baker's appointment as a part-time wine consultant.

Howard Ripley

Address: 35 Eversley Crescent, London N21 1EL

Telephone/fax: 0181 360 8904; 0181 351 6564

Number of branches: 1

Opening hours: 9.00am to 10.00pm Monday to Friday; 9.00am to 12.00am Saturday; 9.00am to 12.00am Sunday

Credit cards accepted: None

Discounts: None

Facilities and services: Free glass loan; free local delivery; private tastings on request

Mail order: International and national delivery (ask for details of carriage charges); minimum order one case

Area of specialisation: Burgundy

One man, one region. Dentist and wine merchant Howard Ripley's single-minded focus on top-quality, *domaine* Burgundy shows considerable commercial derring-do. But if you're interested in the finest names of Chablis and the Côte d'Or, such as Ramonet, Leroy, Leflaive, Lafarge, Raveneau and Rousseau, and money isn't too tight to mention, this is a warren of the world's best Pinot Noirs and Chardonnays. We're not sure how Ripley funds his fact-and wine-finding visits to the cellars of Vosne, Pommard and Chassagne-Montrachet, but gold fillings could have something to do with it.

Roberson Wine Merchant

Address: 348 Kensington High Street, London W14 8NS

Telephone/fax: 0171 371 2121; 0171 371 4010

E-mail: wines@roberson.co.uk

Number of branches: 1

Opening hours: 10.00am to 8.00pm Monday to Saturday

Credit cards accepted: American Express, Delta, Diners, MasterCard, Switch, Visa

Discounts: 5 per cent on mixed cases; 10 per cent on umixed cases

Facilities and services: Free local delivery; cellarage; free glass loan; in-store tastings; regular tutored tastings; *en primeur* offers

Mail order: Ask for details of carriage charges

Areas of specialisation: Pretty good in most places, but best for fine wines

The smartest, most outlandishly designed wine shop in the capital (and a useful watering hole during the annual London Wine Trade Fair), Cliff Roberson's Gaudi-esque emporium is stocked with one of the most eclectic ranges in the country. The place to go if you're looking for a single bottle of something truly special, Roberson's carries good stocks of mature and unusual wines, such as Jura whites, and expensive Burgundies and clarets. It also does regular *en primeur* offers and has a fine-wine mailing list. Expect to pay Kensington rather than Kennington prices, however.

House of Townend

Address: Red Duster House, 101 York Street, Kingston upon Hull, East Yorkshire HU2 0QX

Telephone/fax: 01482 326891 and 01482 586582 (order office); 01482 218796

Number of branches: 12 in East Yorkshire

Opening hours: Order office: 9.00am to 5.30pm Monday to Friday and 24-hour answerphone; shops: 10.00am to 10.00pm Monday to Saturday, 5.00pm to 10.00pm Sunday

Credit cards accepted: Delta, MasterCard, Switch, Visa

Discounts: 5 per cent on mixed and unmixed cases; quantity discounts by negotiation

Facilities and services: Sale or return; free glass loan; free local delivery; tutored tastings; regular in-store tastings; cellarage; gift packaging service

Mail order: To UK mainland and and Northern Ireland (ask for details of carriage charges)

Areas of specialisation: A generalist

Owned by prominent Eurosceptic John Townend (who is obviously happier buying wines from foreigners than sharing a currency with them), the House of Townend is one of Yorkshire's best traditional wine merchants. As you'd expect, the list is on the conservative side. It manages to cover all of the world's major vineyard areas, but seems most comfortable in France and Germany. Perhaps there's hope for EMU after all.

Ubiquitous Chip

Address: 12 Ashton Lane, Hillhead, Glasgow G12 8SJ

Telephone/fax: 0141 334 5007; 0141 337 1302

Number of branches: 1

Opening hours: 12.00am to 10.00pm Monday to Friday; 11.00am to 10.00pm Saturday

Credit cards: Access, American Express, Diners, MasterCard, Switch, Visa

Discounts: 5 per cent case discount

Facilities and services: Free glass loan; ice; free local delivery; tutored tastings; gift vouchers

Mail order: Ask for details of carriage charges

Areas of specialisation: Good general specialist, with an interesting list of fine and rare wines, malt whiskies and interesting and unusual spirits and liqueurs

The title of Arnold Wesker's play, *Chips with Everything*, lives on in the name of this popular Glasgow media haunt, which serves good-value food as well as having the best wine list in the city. Presented in a no-frills, printer-paper format, the wines are a palate-watering selection from traditional and out-of-the-way regions of France, as well as Italy, Spain and the New World. The Australian, Californian and South African selections are particularly good.

Valvona & Crolla Ltd

Address: 19 Elm Row, Edinburgh EH7 4AA

Telephone/fax: 0131 556 6066; 0131 556 1668

Number of branches: 1

Opening hours: 8.00am to 6.00pm Monday to Wednesday and Saturday; 8.00am to 7.30pm Thursday and Friday

Credit cards accepted: Access, American Express, Switch, Visa

Discounts: 10 per cent on unmixed cases; 5 per cent on mixed cases

Facilities and services: Daily in-store tastings; regular informal tastings; regular tutored tastings; regular wine and food events; free delivery in Edinburgh for orders over £30; free glass loan; sale or return

Mail order: Ask for details of carriage charges

Area of specialisation: Italy

If you like Italian food and wine, it's hard to walk through Valvona & Crolla's Elm Row deli without salivating. The Contini family's famous shop is a showcase for the best of Italy – north, south and central – stocking wines, olive oils, hams, salamis and fresh pasta. This is a meeting place for Edinburgh's Italian community and assorted Italophiles, who come here for gossip, tutored tastings, dinners, cookery demonstrations and an annual fungi foray. It's also a great place to choose from 600 different Italian wines, with good stocks of older vintages and the best of modern Brunello, Chianti, Amarone and Barolo, as well as a growing range from Puglia and Sicily. And just to make the place even more enticing, Philip Contini has opened an on-site Caffè Bar. We bet he gives good espresso.

La Vigneronne

Address: 105 Old Brompton Road, London SW7 3LE

Telephone/fax: 0171 589 6113; 0171 581 2983

Number of branches: 1

Opening hours: 10.00am to 8.00pm Monday to Friday; 10.00am to 6.00pm Saturday

Credit cards accepted: Access, American Express, Delta, Diners, Switch, Visa

Discounts: 5 per cent case discount

Facilities and services: Gift packaging service; regular tutored tastings; newsletter; *en primeur* offers; free delivery within the UK for orders of £250 inc. VAT and over

Mail order: Ask for details of carriage charges

Areas of specialisation: Regional France, especially Rhône, Alsace, Bandol, Madiran, Languedoc-Roussillon, and old and rare wines

Master of Wine Liz Berry and husband, Mike, may have decamped to Provence on a semi-permanent basis (and who can blame them), but their retail shop and tasting programme are still thriving, helped by the Berrys' endless flow of new finds from France's less traditional regions. If you're more interested in Bandol and Buzet than Bordeaux and Burgundy, this Old Brompton Road institution is a must. There are on average two customer tastings a week, regular newsletters and a well-written list full of rare wines and older bottles that are hard to find elsewhere. One of our favourite independents.

Vinceremos

Address: 261 Upper Town Street, Bramley, Leeds LS13 3JT

Telephone/fax: 0113 257 7545; 0113 257 6906

E-mail: vinceremos@aol.com

Number of branches: 1

Opening hours: 8.45am to 5.45pm Monday to Friday

Credit cards accepted: American Express, Delta, MasterCard, Switch, Visa

Discounts: 5 per cent on orders of 5 cases or more; 10 per cent on orders of 10 cases or more; trade discounts available

Facilities and services: Free local glass loan; cellarage; tutored tastings; wine clubs

Mail order: Nationwide delivery free on orders of 5 cases or more and to Leeds LS postcodes

Areas of specialisation: Organic, vegetarian and vegan wines, Hungary, Morocco, Russia

Taking its name from a revolutionary song, Jerry Lockspeiser's politically correct shop has outgrown its original focus on organic and vegetarian wines to list bottles from such diverse sources as Morocco, Hungary and the Ukraine. A large part of the business goes through Bottle Green, which sells mainly Hungarian, southern French and Moroccan wine to British supermarkets and off-licence chains, many of which have been blended or made by in-house Australian, Nick Butler. But Vinceremos was where it all started, and it still has one of the best vegetarian ranges in the country. Look out, in particular, for James Millton's bio-dynamic Kiwi wines and Guy Bossard's Muscadets.

The Vine Trail

Address: 266 Hotwell Road, Hotwells, Bristol BS8 4NG

Telephone/fax: 0117 921 1770; 0117 921 1772

Number of branches: 1

Opening hours: 9.00am to 7.00pm Monday to Saturday; 24-hour answerphone

Credit cards accepted: None

Discounts: 2 per cent case discount on orders of five cases or more; 3 per cent on 10 cases or more; 5 per cent on 25 cases or more; trade discounts negotiable

Facilities and services: Cellarage; sale or return; free glass loan; free local delivery; ice; gift packaging service; regular tastings; tutored private tastings; special food and wine events; fine-wine broking, newsletter

Mail order: Delivery throughout the UK (ask for details of carriage charges)

Areas of specialisation: Small *domaine* wines, especially from the Rhône, Beaujolais, south-west France and Languedoc

Bristol-based accountant-turned-wine-merchant Nick Brookes is a one-man promotional board for La France Profonde, specialising in small *domaine* wines from off the beaten (vine) trail. His list is restricted to only 80-odd wines, but you get the impression that Brookes knows them all personally and would be happy to have them round for dinner. Each wine comes with a tempting explanatory tasting note. The quality is high here, with wines from *domaines* such as André Perret in Condrieu, Château Thivin in Côte de Brouilly, Sylvain Bailly in Sancerre, Clos Thou in Jurançon, Pierre Gonon in St Joseph, Larmandier-Bernier in Champagne and Daniel Brusset in Cairanne. Highly recommended.

Vintage Roots

Address: Sheeplands Farm, Wargrave, Berkshire RG10 8DT

Telephone/fax: 0118 9401222; 0118 9404814

E-mail: roots@ptop.demon.co.uk

Number of branches: 1

Opening hours: 8.30am to 6.00pm Monday to Friday; answerphone service out of office hours

Credit cards accepted: Access, Visa

Discounts: 5 per cent on all orders of five cases or more

Facilities and services: Occasional in-store tastings

Mail order: Telephone for details

Areas of specialisation: Organic and biodynamic wines

Based at the appropriately bucolic Sheeplands Farm, Lance Pigott and Neil Palmer's organic wine business is now well into its second, muck-spreading decade. We can see why it's done so well – most of the world's best organic and bio-dynamic wines are stocked here, from Huet and Domaine de Marcoux to Millton in New Zealand and Fetzer in California. The list is extensive (running to ten different countries) and well illustrated. It also shows a genuine commitment to the organic cause, with useful information on each wine. Britain's best organic specialist.

Vin du Van

Address: Colthups, The Street, Appledore, Kent TN26 2BX

Telephone/fax: 01233 758727; 01233 758389

Number of branches: 1

Opening hours: 9.00am to 5.00pm Monday to Friday; 24-hour answerphone

Credit cards accepted: Access, MasterCard, Visa

Discounts: None

Facilities and services: Free glass loan; free local delivery; sale or return for functions; tutored tastings

Mail order: Orders taken by telephone only; delivery within 48 hours in the UK, except for the Highlands and Islands (ask for carriage charges)

Areas of specialisation: Australia, New Zealand

Ian Brown's background in advertising is gloriously apparent in his surreal, pun-infested list. What is the man on? Vying with Chippendale Fine Wines for the title of Britain's most eccentric wine merchant, Brown and his collection of cats focus almost exclusively on Australia and New Zealand. Prices are keen and the selection impressive, mixing the familiar (Penfolds, Wynns, Seppelts, Hardy's and Orlando) with the esoteric (Rockford, Mount Mary, Coriole, Bass Phillip and Trentham Estate). One of the two best Australian lists in the country.

Yapp Brothers

Address: The Old Brewery, Mere, Wiltshire BA12 6DY

Telephone/fax: 01747 860423; 01747 860929

Number of branches: 1

Opening hours: 9.00am to 5.00pm Monday to Friday; 9.00am to 1.00pm Saturday

Credit cards accepted: Access, Switch, Visa

Discounts: Various case discounts (ask for full details)

Facilities and services: Daily in-store tastings; tutored tastings for groups, either at The Old Brewery or private venues; wine lunches at restaurants throughout Great Britain; free glass loan

Mail order: £5 surcharge on single case or less; next morning delivery for orders received before noon (except Scottish Highlands)

Areas of specialisation: Rhône, Loire, Provence, the Midi

The original one-man wine merchant, launched in 1969 by dentist and purple-hued travel writer, Robin Yapp. Being first in the queue enabled Yapp to sign up most of the best growers in his specialist areas, such as Chave in Hermitage, Alain Graillot in Crozes-Hermitage, Druet in Bourgueil, Vatan in Sancerre, Filliatreau in Saumur-Champigny, Clape in Cornas and Domaine de Trévallon in Les Baux de Provence. The business has expanded over the years, but retains the quirky, cartoon-strewn list and characterful touches that made Yapp such an important pioneer. Robin's son, Jason, is now taking an increasingly important role in the business.

Noel Young Wines

Address: 56 High Street, Trumpington, Cambridge CB2 2LS

Telephone/fax: 01223 844744; 01223 844736

Number of branches: 1

Opening hours: 10.00am to 9.00pm Monday to Saturday; 12.00am to 2.00pm Sunday

Credit cards accepted: Delta, MasterCard, Switch, Visa

Discounts: 10 per cent on mixed and unmixed cases; 7 per cent case discount when paying by credit card

Facilities and services: Sale or return; glass hire; free delivery within 25 miles; free tastings every Friday evening and all day Saturday; regular winemaker evenings and tutored tastings as advertised in the newsletter

Mail order: National and international delivery (ask for details of carriage charges)

Areas of specialisation: Fine and rare wines, Austria, New World (especially Australia, California and New Zealand), Italy, quality French

Frequented by thirsty dons and well-to-do students, Noel Young's Cambridgeshire shop has established its alarmingly youthful, goatee-bearded owner as one of the most interesting wine merchants in the east of England, since it opened four years ago. The information-packed list runs to nearly 1,000 wines, with strengths in regional France, Austria (the best selection in Britain by far), Italy and the New World. An impressive, go-getting wine merchant who really seems to understand quality and individuality.

The *Grapevine* Guide to Cross-Channel Shopping

Cash-and-carry city

'Dave, there's a bloke here who wants to know if you'll give him a discount if he spends over £1,000.'

'Tell him,' came the considered reply, 'that I wouldn't give him the droppings off the end of my nose.' Dave West, the lovable, stubble-chinned proprietor of EastEnders, and his barking Alsatian were enjoying the Sunday afternoon throng at West's new 5,000-square-foot cash-and-carry in Calais' Zone Industrielle.

Down on the warehouse floor, the queue snaked past the tasting table ('Anyone who opens a bottle without purchase will be charged and then shot'), past the huge stacks of Conquistador White and Liebfraumilch, and into the fine-wine selection at the back of the warehouse, where West has accumulated an outrageous job-lot of top German wines. The customers we saw on our annual foray across the Channel were more interested in buying sugary Hock at £1 a bottle than fine Rieslings – but that's Calais for you.

West reckons this has been his best-ever year, thanks to the exchange rate, 'Kill the Competition Prices' and his growing celebrity. The new premises are a magnet for thirsty Brits, with large 'Prime Wine' and 'Biggest British in Europe' signs visible from the motorway. By all accounts, wine, beer, tobacco and successive UK chancellors have made him a millionaire. One of these days he might invest in a few razor-blades and a new pair of carpet slippers.

EastEnders is not the only successful business in Calais. The Zone Industrielle has another four or five outlets, catering to holidaymakers, day trippers and the odd illegal beer runner. ('Beer running is in decline,' West says with a hint of nostalgia. 'People have moved into tobacco, which is more profitable.') Add Sainsbury's, Tesco, Franglais, Beer Lovers, Le Chais, Victoria Wine and the various French-owned supermarkets and you have what is almost certainly the biggest concentration of cheap booze in the world.

Onwards and upwards?

Calais has become the focus of the cross-Channel booze boom. One survey estimates that we'll be buying 20 per cent of our drink in continental outlets by the end of the century, pointing out that the flow of beer and wine (most of it from Calais) has more than trebled in the last four years. With the opening of the Channel Tunnel and increasingly competitive deals from the ferry companies, more people than ever are buying their booze in France.

The *Grapevine* Guide to Cross-Channel Shopping

Things may not be quite as manic as they were on that foam-splashed day in January 1993, when a million corks popped to the sound of 'Auld Lang Syne'. But cross-Channel shopping has become a way of life in Britain, and is likely to remain so, unless there's a significant reduction in UK duty rates or the French Treasury does the unthinkable and increases French alcohol duty. Imagine the demonstrations and street protests if that happens.

Thanks to the continuing difference between UK and French duty rates, our love affair with cross-Channel shopping shows no sign of abating. And the exchange rate has encouraged even more Brits to buy on the other side of the Channel. Over the past year, the pound has picked up against the franc, breaking through the FF10 barrier for the first time in ages. Two years ago it stood at FF7.40. No wonder those electronic tills are buzzing.

Farewell to The Grape Shop

Everyone, it seems, is coining it in France at the moment. Well, almost everyone. On a more pessimistic note, the last year has seen the closure of two of the best independent cross-Channel operations: The Grape Shop in Boulogne and Calais and La Maison du Vin in Cherbourg. It's not easy for the smaller operators to compete with the big boys, especially if their shops are located away from the Calais throng. 'The whole thing is more Calais-focused than ever,' says Katrina Thom, formerly of The Grape Shop and now at EastEnders. 'There's so much more traffic coming through here.'

Things are not quite as bad as they appear, however. As we went to press there was a strong possibility that The Grape Shop's outlet in Boulogne's Gare Maritime was about to reopen. New owners Hoverspeed will run the store, but Martin Brown, The Grape Shop's previous owner and one of the best palates in the business, will buy the wines. Let's hope so. For La Maison du Vin there will be no such reprieve.

The duty game

Duty on alcohol increased in Gordon Brown's June 1997 budget, but the changes will not come into effect until 1 January 1998. For the time being, the differences between UK and French duty rates remain the same. UK duty stands at £12.64 a case, excluding VAT, on table wines (compared to FF2.04 in France) and £18.06 a case on Champagne, sparkling wines (FF4.92 in France) and fortified wines of between 15 and 22 per cent alcohol. That's a saving (on duty alone) of just over £1 a bottle on table wine and £1.50 on fizz, Port, Sherry, Madeira and fortified Muscats.

In 1998 UK table-wine duty will go up by four pence a bottle to £1.09 (£13.12 per case), but sparkling and fortified-wine duties will be unchanged. One thing to bear in mind is that French VAT, at 20.6 per cent, is higher than ours, so the more you spend per bottle, the more French VAT you pay. This means that the biggest savings tend to be at the cheaper end of the spectrum.

The prediction that Britain will one day follow the likes of Denmark, Canada and Ireland by cutting duty rates to stem cross-border sales looks less likely than ever. The Treasury is still not convinced that lower duty rates would produce a corresponding increase in drink sales and, with it, revenue, despite the fact that the duty increases in previous budgets have resulted in falling UK sales of whisky and beer.

Bootleggers and booze bandits

Customs and Excise are increasingly active when it comes to discouraging bootleggers, stopping 5,000 smugglers in the last year. Illegal imports (of beer and rolling tobacco, rather than wine) remain a substantial problem, but the occasional seven-year jail sentence for big-time smugglers clearly acts as a deterrent. The French authorities have also started to clamp down on the spivvier end of the business, particularly in Calais.

Life is getting harder for the bootlegger. The incidence of so-called booze bandits stealing illegally imported alcohol on the south coast of England, before it has reached its final destination, is on the increase, too. Several gangs have lost their hauls to local criminals while sleeping in nearby bed-and-breakfast accommodation. Others have had their transit vans hijacked. Autoglass in Dover is a busy place these days.

What's your limit?

The rules governing cross-Channel buying have not changed since last year. The first and most important thing to remember is that as long as you are buying wine for your own use (and that includes parties, weddings and other celebrations), you can bring as much booze into the country as the axle on your vehicle will bear.

If the alcohol is not for your consumption, or that of your family, you are breaking the law by carrying smuggled goods. Bootlegged booze (the first smugglers used to hide drink inside their boots, apparently) is anything you plan to sell to someone else without paying duty. In 1995, the owners of Death Cigarettes lost a test case designed to show they could run a business bringing tobacco across the Channel without having to pay duty. The courts nipped that idea in the bud, along with any plans that more enterprising members of the booze trade may have had to try the same thing with wine.

Customs can stop you while you're travelling and ask whether the wine or beer you're carrying is really for your own consumption. If you don't want them turning up at the wedding like the proverbial bad one-pence piece, carry some evidence of any impending celebration with you (a packet of streamers and a party hat is unlikely to satisfy Her Majesty's Customs officers).

The limits – or, to use the jargon, Minimum Indicative Levels – are the point at which Customs start to ask if the goods cross the dividing line between personal and commercial use. The current limits are 90 litres of table wine (of which not more than 60 may be sparkling), 20 litres of fortified wine, 110 litres of beer and 10 litres of spirits. If you want to bring back more, the burden of proof is on you.

What and where to buy

There's no dearth of outlets in France, but they vary enormously in terms of service, range and wine quality. The best places put on tastings, offer advice and stock wines that you won't find back home. The worst are dives, or just cynical operations designed to fleece know-nothing tourists. In a two-day visit to Calais this year, we tasted some truly appalling wines, as well as some undoubted bargains.

Our advice is to stick to the outlets we've selected below. If convenience is your main concern, you're probably best-off at Tesco or Sainsbury's. But don't overlook the smaller outlets, such as Le Chais, Nicolas, Perardel, Milles Vignes, The Wine Society and Bar à Vins, where you can take your pick of estate wines and growers' Champagnes.

Without wishing to be too chauvinistic, we still think it pays to buy from British-owned supermarkets, although French outlets such as Leclerc and Auchan have some attractive deals on Grande Marque Champagnes and classed-growth claret. In general, however, the French hypermarkets are struggling to keep up.

The problem is that most of them seem to regard quality as a secondary issue. The day may come when the French hypermarkets prove a match for the likes of Sainsbury's or Tesco, but so far it's the British who have taken the cross-Channel initiative. Which is why this year, with the exception of Franglais, Perardel and Bar à Vins, we have again concentrated on British-owned retailers.

Santé!

So, all in all, this is a very good time to buy wine in France. Significant savings can still be made, especially on cheaper wines, where the difference in duty represents a larger percentage of the price, and on Champagne. And there are some good deals to be had on more expensive French wines at places like Perardel. Time to book a berth on a ferry or Le Shuttle? We reckon so.

Grapevine's Top Ten Cross-Channel Outlets

If calling from the UK, prefix the following nine-digit telephone numbers with 00 33; if calling from France, prefix them with 0.

Bar à Vins ☆☆☆☆
52 Place d'Armes, Calais
Tel: 321 96 96 31
Opening hours: 9.00am to 7.00pm; closed Wednesday
Small, quirky, French-owned wine shop with an interesting collection of vinous artefacts. Doubles as a bar for locals. A super range of domaine-bottled French wines and a good place to practise your Franglais.
Best buys: White Burgundies and southern Rhône reds

EastEnders ☆☆(☆)
Zone Industrielle Marcel Doret, 62100 Calais
Tel: 321 34 53 33
Opening hours: 24 hours a day, seven days a week
The biggest cash-and-carry in Calais with lots of bargains, some of them extremely drinkable. A gigantic booze emporium, which is worth visiting just to meet Dave West.
Best buys: Cheap and cheerful German wines and 'millennium' Champagne

Franglais ☆☆
62185 Fréthun
Tel: 321 85 29 39
Opening hours: 9.00am to 7.00pm Monday to Friday; 9.00am to 6.30pm Saturday; 9.30am to 6.00pm Sunday
A large, French-owned outlet that has recently changed hands. The biggest range of wines for tasting. Quality variable, so stick to Bordeaux, Beaujolais, Fitou and fizz.
Best buys: Sparkling wines

Mille Vignes ☆☆☆(☆)

90–4 Rue Carnot, Wimereux

Tel: 321 32 60 13

Opening hours: 10.00am to 7.00pm Tuesday to Saturday; 10.00am to 1.00pm Sunday; closed Monday

Closer to Boulogne than Calais (no bad thing), this is a small, English-run operation specialising in middle to top-of-the-range French wines. Flanked by a couple of good restaurants.

Best buys: Champagne and domaine-bottle French reds and whites

Perardel ☆☆☆☆(☆)

Zone Industrielle Marcel Doret, 62100 Calais

Tel: 321 97 21 22

Opening hours: 8.00am to 8.00pm Monday to Saturday; 9.00am to 8.00pm Sunday

The best range of wines in Calais now that The Grape Shop's premises have closed. Well-selected bottles at every price level, ranging from basic vins de pays to top Burgundies and clarets. Very good for Champagne. Limited New World range.

Best buys: Champagne, Burgundies and regional French wines

Sainsbury's ☆☆☆

Auchan Centre, Route de Boulogne, 62100 Calais

Tel: 321 82 38 48

Opening hours: 8.30am to 9.00pm Monday to Saturday; closed Sunday

French off-shoot of JS, stocking around half the full range. Auchan (formerly Mammouth) is next door if you want to load the car with cheese and charcuterie. Cheerful staff.

Best buys: New World wines and French generics, such as claret, Beaujolais and Champagne; see the main Sainsbury's entry on page 272

Tesco Vin Plus ☆☆☆☆

Unit 122, Cité de l'Europe, 62231 Coquelles

Tel: 321 46 02 70

Opening hours: 9.00am to 10.00pm Monday to Saturday; closed Sunday

Enormous booze-dedicated supermarket with nearly 1,000 wines. Lists Tesco's UK range as well as a few extra (French) goodies.

Best buys: Champagne and New World wines; see the main Tesco entry on page 327

The *Grapevine* Guide to Cross-Channel Shopping

Victoria Wine ☆☆☆☆
Unit 179, Cité de l'Europe, 62231 Coquelles
Tel: 321 82 07 32
Opening hours: 10.00am to 8.00pm Tuesday to Sunday; closed Monday.
Smaller than Tesco round the corner, but a bit more personal. Takes the entire range from Cellars, Victoria Wine's upmarket UK chain. Good bilingual staff with a sense of humour.
Best buys: Champagne, sparkling and mid-priced wines from the New and Old Worlds; see the main Victoria Wine entry on page 402

The Wine and Beer Company ☆☆(☆)
Zone Industrielle Marcel Doret, 62100 Calais
Tel: 321 97 63 00
Opening hours: 7.00am to 10.00pm, seven days a week
Majestic-style wine warehouse with three branches in and around Calais. Loud music, enthusiastic staff and wines stacked to the ceiling. Better in the New World than the Old.
Best buys: Chile and Australia

The Wine Society ☆☆☆(☆)
Rue Fressin, 62140 Hesdin
Tel: 321 86 52 07
Opening hours: 8.00am to 6.00pm Monday to Saturday; closed for lunch 12.30–1.45pm, Sundays and French public holidays
A pick-up point for members of the Stevenage-based Society, just off the main square of Hesdin, a pretty town inland from Boulogne. Stocks a limited range of wines, but also holds excellent tastings and dinners.
Best buys: Champagne, claret and the New World; see the main Wine Society entry on page 525

Other Supermarket and Wine-Shop Addresses

Amiens

Nicolas, 1 Rue de Beauvais, 80000 Amiens (322 91 83 15)

Boulogne

Auchan, Route Nationale 42, 62200 Saint Martin Les Boulogne (321 10 11 12)

Le Chais, Rue des Deux Ponts, 62200 Boulogne (321 31 65 42)

Intermarché, 62360 Pont de Briques (321 83 28 28)

Prix Gros, Centre Commercial de la Liane, 62200 Boulogne-sur-Mer (321 30 43 67)

Les Vins de France, 11 Rue Nationale, 62200 Boulogne (321 30 51 00)

Caen

Nicolas, 10 Rue Bellivet, 14000 Caen (231 85 24 19)

Calais

Auchan, Route de Boulogne , 62100 Calais (321 34 04 44)

Beer Lovers, Rue de Verdun, 62100 Calais (321 97 72 00)

Le Chais, 40 Rue de Phalsbourg, 62100 Calais (321 97 88 56)

Intermarché, 42–6 Avenue Antoine de St-Exupéry, 62100 Calais (321 34 42 44)

Pidou, Zone Industrielle Marcel Doret, 62100 Calais (321 96 78 10) and Quai de la Loire, 62100 Calais (321 46 07 67)

Prix Gros, Route St-Omer, 62100 Calais (321 34 65 98)

Le Terroir, 29 Rue des Fontinettes, 62100 Calais (321 36 34 66)

Cherbourg

Auchan, Centre Commercial Cotentin, 50470 La Glacerie (233 88 13 13)

Continent, Quai de l'Entrepôt, 50104 Cherbourg (233 43 14 11)

Leclerc, 5 Rue des Claires, 50460 Querqueville (233 03 55 43)

The Wine & Beer Company, Centre Commercial Continent, Quai de l'Entrepôt, 50100 Cherbourg (233 22 23 22)

The *Grapevine* Guide to Cross-Channel Shopping

Deauville
Nicolas, 31 Rue de Breney, 14800 Deauville (280 49 94 04)

Dieppe
Auchan (including Sainsbury's), Centre Commercial Belvédère, 76371 Dieppe (232 90 52 00)

Intermarché, 76370 Rouxmesnil Bouteilles (235 82 57 75)

Leclerc, 76370 Etran-Martin Eglise (235 82 56 95)

LC Vins, 1 Grande Rue, 76200 Dieppe (235 84 32 41)

Le Havre
Nicolas, Les Halles Centrales, Rue Bernardin St Pierre, 76600 Le Havre (235 42 24 63)

The Wine & Beer Company, 16 Quai Frissard, 76600 Le Havre (235 26 38 10)

Roscoff
Les Caves de Roscoff, Zone de Bloscon, Ateliers 7–9, 29680 Roscoff (298 61 24 10 and 0171 376 4639 in UK)

Rouen
Nicolas, 18b Place du Vieux Marché, 76000 Rouen (235 71 56 10)

Useful Telephone Numbers
Brittany Ferries: 299 82 80 80 (France); 0990 360360 (UK)

Customs & Excise Single Market Unit: 0171 620 1313 (UK)

Hoverspeed: 321 46 14 14 (France); Freephone number: 0590 1777; 0304 240101 (UK)

P&O Ferries: 321 46 10 10 (France); 0181 575 8555 (UK)

Sally Line Ferries: 328 26 70 70 (France); 0800 636465 (UK)

Le Shuttle: 321 00 61 00 (France); 0990 353535 (UK)

Stena Sealink: 321 46 80 00 (France); 01233 647047 (UK and European head office)

SILVER WINGS, SANTIAGO BLUE

The jocular voices and the back-slapping camaraderie going on didn't include her, as pilots milled about the ready room, playing cards or chatting idly, puffing on endless cigarettes. She wanted to be part of the living world, not an onlooker.

Mary Lynn couldn't put a name to the force that made her turn around so that she saw Walker when he came in. His officer's cap was raked to the back of his head, showing the heavy brown hair that grew with such unruly thickness. His leather battle jacket hung open and the tails of the white scarf draped around his neck were dangling loose.

Walker paused to draw a match across the abrasive strip of its match cover and cup the flame to his cigarette. Over the fire, he caught sight of the small, silent woman watching him from a corner of the room. Her dark eyes were on him, rousing him fully.

For an instant, she became the only living thing in the room for him. Slowly, he lifted his head, staring at her as he shook out the match. Steadily, she returned his gaze, not looking away or showing reluctance.

There was a message in that – one he wanted to explore . . . to be sure of its meaning.

About the Author

Janet Dailey, a former farm girl from Iowa, USA, is one of the world's bestselling romantic novelists, best known for her magnificent CALDER saga. In SILVER WINGS, SANTIAGO BLUE she tells her most ambitious tale yet: the story of the first WASPs, the Women Airforce Service Pilots who risked their lives, and the censure of their peers, to help the war effort during World War II.

It is a memorable celebration of the courage of women at war and of the unparalleled glory of women in flight.

Janet Dailey lives with her husband Bill in Missouri, USA, and they travel extensively.

SILVER WINGS, SANTIAGO BLUE

Janet Dailey

CORONET BOOKS
Hodder and Stoughton

Copyright © 1984 by Janet Dailey.
First published in Great Britain by
Hodder & Stoughton Ltd in 1985.

Coronet edition 1985.

British Library C.I.P.

Dailey, Janet
   Silver wings, santiago blue.
   I. Title
   813'.54[F]   PS3554.A29

ISBN 0-340-37770-4

Printed and bound in Great Britain for
Hodder and Stoughton Paperbacks, a
division of Hodder and Stoughton Ltd.,
Mill Road, Dunton Green, Sevenoaks,
Kent (Editorial Office: 47 Bedford
Square, London, WC1 3DP) by
Cox and Wyman Ltd., Reading, Berks.
Photoset by Rowland Phototypesetting Ltd.,
Bury St Edmunds, Suffolk.

To Jerry, my flight instructor back in 1968 when I earned my private pilot's license,

and to Frank, the F.A.A. pilot who gave me my "up check,"

and to Bill, my husband, manager, friend, and lover, but more important in this case, the man who showed me the skies and encouraged me to fly in them myself. Now I know what it's like to be high above the earth, rocking a plane and singing at the top of your lungs from the sheer joy of solo flight.

With special thanks to former WASP Harriett "Tuffy" Kenyon Call, for her memories and mementos of those years.

Author's Note

The parodies of song lyrics appearing on the pages delineating the Parts of this book are the actual songs the Women Airforce Service Pilots (WASPs) sang while they marched to and from the flight line, their classes, and their barracks. In their own way, the songs tell much of the girls' story.

HIGH FLIGHT

Oh! I have slipped the surly bonds of earth,
    and danced the skies on laughter-silvered wings;
Sunward I've climbed and joined the tumbling mirth
    of sunsplit clouds – and done a hundred things
You have not dreamed of – wheeled and soared and
    swung – high in the sunlit silence.
Hov'ring there, I've chased the shouting winds
    along,
    and flung my eager craft through footless halls of
    air.
Up, up the long, delirious, burning blue, I've topped
    the windswept heights with easy grace,
Where never lark or even eagle flew.

And, while with silent, lifting mind I've trod the high
    untrespassed sanctity of space,
Put out my hand, and touched the face of God.

John Gillespie Magee, Jr.

In December 1941, Pilot Officer Magee, a nineteen-year-old American serving with the Royal Canadian Air Force in England, was killed when his Spitfire collided with another airplane inside a cloud. Discovered among his personal effects was this sonnet, written on the back of a letter at the time he was in flying school at Farnborough, England.

PROLOGUE

She sat amidst a framework of canvas and piano wire, her long skirts tied around her knees and her legs extended full length in front of her. No doubt her thudding heart competed with the reverberations of the 30-horsepower motor spinning the two propellers. When the wire anchoring the Wright Brothers flying machine to a rock was unfastened, the *Flyer* was launched five stories into the air, and in that wildly exhilarating moment Edith Berg nearly forgot to hold on to her seat.

Beside her Wilbur Wright was at the controls, dressed in his customary high starched collar, gray suit and an automobile touring cap. The flight over the Hunaudières race track in Le Mans, France, lasted two minutes, three seconds, and Edith Berg entered the pages of aviation history as the first woman to ride in a flying machine. It was all a publicity stunt to promote the reliability of the new Wright flyer, an idea concocted by her husband, Hart O. Berg, a sales representative for the Wright Brothers.

The year was 1908 and Edith Berg was an instant sensation, her courage and daring applauded. The press loved the stunt. The French shook their heads and whispered among themselves, 'That crazy American woman! And imagine her husband's letting her do it!'

She wore a stunning flying suit of plum-colored satin, from the hood covering her raven hair to her knickers and the cloth leggings, called puttees, which wrapped her legs from knee to ankle. It was understandable that the all-male members at the Aero Club of America's headquarters on

11

Long Island would look at twenty-seven-year-old Harriet Quimby with open mouths, especially when she asked to be licensed as an aeronaut – a woman! (The government had not gotten around to accepting responsibility for licensing pilots and wouldn't until 1925.)

The green-eyed writer for *Leslie's Magazine* suggested the members let her demonstrate her flying skills. With considerable skepticism they watched Harriet Quimby climb into her gossamer biplane and take off. She flew over a nearby potato field, then banked the plane back to the field and set her aircraft down within eight feet of her takeoff point – setting a new record for the club in landing accuracy.

The date was August 1, 1911, and Harriet Quimby became the first woman to be licensed as an aeronaut. In a wry comment to reporters she said, 'Flying seems easier than voting.' Not until 1920 would the Nineteenth Amendment be ratified, giving women the right to vote.

She sat cross-legged in the doorway of the fuselage while the flame-red, tri-motored Fokker airplane with gold wings, the *Friendship*, floated on its pontoons in the harbor off Burry port, Wales. Her short-cropped hair was the color of the dune grass on Kill Devil Hill, site of the Wright Brothers' first powered flight.

Captain Hilton Railey rowed alongside the *Friendship* and shouted to her, 'How does it feel to be the first woman to fly the Atlantic? Aren't you excited?'

'It was a grand experience,' Amelia Earhart replied, but she knew she hadn't flown the Atlantic. Bill Stultz had been the pilot and navigator on the flight. 'I was just baggage. Someday I'll try it alone.'

That was June 18, 1928.

Four years later, on May 21, 1932, Amelia Earhart landed her red 500-horsepower Lockheed Vega in a farm meadow outside of Londonderry, Ireland. Exhausted, she crawled out of the cockpit and said to the staring farmhand,

'I've come from America.' It was five years after Lindberg had made his Atlantic crossing.

On January 12, 1935, Amelia Earhart accomplished another first in aviation history by becoming the first pilot, male or female, to successfully fly from Hawaii to the continental United States, landing her Vega at Oakland Airport in California. That feat was immediately followed by the first non-stop flight to Mexico City, then from Mexico City to New York.

As a women's career counselor at Purdue University in Indiana, Amelia Earhart advised a group of female students, 'A girl must nowadays believe completely in herself as an individual. She must realize at the outset that a woman must do the same job better than a man to get as much credit for it. She must be aware of the various discriminations, both legal and traditional, against women in the business world.'

Amelia had already encountered them in 1929 when Transcontinental Air Transport, later to become Trans World Airlines, asked her to become a consultant for them along with Lindbergh. While he flew around the country checking out new air routes, she traveled as a passenger, talking with women and lecturing various women's clubs on the safety and enjoyment of flying.

At the Bendix Transcontinental Air Race in May of 1935, Amelia Earhart had the chance to meet newcomer Jacqueline Cochran, whose story would rival any tale by Dickens. As an orphan, her birth date and parents unknown, she was raised by foster parents in the lumber towns of northern Florida. It was a hardscrabble existence, and little Jacqueline often went shoeless. When she was eight years old, her foster family moved to Columbus, Georgia, to work in the local cotton mills, and Jackie worked, too, on the twelve-hour night shift. A year later, she had charge of fifteen children in the fabric inspection room.

She left the cotton mill to go to work for the owner of a beauty shop, doing odd jobs. A beauty operator at the age of thirteen, Jackie was one of the first to learn the technique of giving a permanent wave. She began traveling to demonstrate the technique in salons through Alabama and Florida, until a customer persuaded her to go to a nursing school even though she only had two years of formal education.

As a nurse, she worked for a country doctor in Bonifay, Florida, a lumber town, so much like the places where she'd been raised. A short time later, after delivering a baby under wretched conditions, she abandoned her nursing career and went back to the beauty business. She became a stylist for Antoine's at Saks Fifth Avenue, both in his New York and Miami salons. In 1932, at a Miami club, Jacqueline Cochran met Floyd Bostwick Odlum, a millionaire and a Wall Street financier. She told him of her dream to start her own cosmetics company. Odlum advised her that to get ahead of her competition and to cover the kind of necessary territory she would need wings. Jackie used her vacation that year to obtain a pilot's license, and subsequently the equivalent of a US. Navy flight training course.

At the same time that Jacqueline Cochran Cosmetics, Incorporated, was born with Odlum's help, Jacqueline Cochran aviatrix came into existence. In 1934, this striking brown-eyed blonde made her debut in air-racing circles with the England-Australia competition. Engine troubles forced her to land in Bucharest, Rumania.

In the Bendix Transcontinental Air Race of 1935 which saw both Earhart and Cochran competing, Earhart took off in the middle of the night with the rest of the starters. Cochran's Northrop Gamma was next on the ramp for takeoff, when a heavy fog rolled over the Los Angeles airport. The plane ahead of her roared down the runway and disappeared into the thick mist. The sound of a distant explosion was immediately followed by an eerie light that backlit the fog. Her reaction was instinctive, her nurse's training taking over. Jackie jumped in her car and followed the fire truck down the runway. Both arrived too late to do the pilot any good. By the time the fire was put out, the pilot was dead.

Jackie stood beside her aircraft while the tow truck dragged the burned and twisted wreckage off the runway. The fatal crash left everyone a little stunned, including her. A government aviation official was standing not far away from her and she heard him say he thought it was suicide to take off in that fog. The realization that she was next in line sent her running behind the hangar so no one would see her when she vomited.

When her legs quit shaking, she placed a long-distance call to New York and talked to her ardent backer and now her fiancé as well, Floyd Odlum. 'What should I do?'

But Odlum couldn't tell her, ultimately advising her that it came down to 'a philosophy of life.' At three o'clock that morning, Jacqueline Cochran made a blind takeoff, her fuel-heavy aircraft barely clearing the outer fence which ripped off the radio antenna hanging below the plane's belly. She spiraled up through the fog, flying by compass only, to gain altitude to clear the seven-thousand-foot mountains inland from the coast.

Amelia Earhart came in fifth in the race, but an over-heated engine and dangerous vibrations in the tail of the Northrop Gamma forced Jackie back to the starting line at Los Angeles.

May 10, 1936, was the wedding day for the slim-built, sandy-haired Floyd Odlum and the glamorous and gutsy blonde Jacqueline Cochran. The homes she'd never had as a child became a reality as they purchased an estate in Connecticut, a ranch near Palm Springs, and an apartment in Manhattan overlooking the East River. Aviation had long been a love of Odlum's, so his interest went beyond being merely a supporter of his wife's career. Among his many holdings were the Curtiss-Wright Corporation and the Convair Aircraft Company. So it wasn't surprising that the Odlums helped finance Amelia Earhart's around-the-world flight.

On June 1, 1937, they were in Miami to see her off

on that last, fateful trip. Before she left, Amelia gave Jacqueline a small American flag made of silk – which became a symbolic 'transfer of the flag,' in military jargon, when Amelia Earhart vanished without a trace. Speaking at a tribute to the famous woman aviator, Jacqueline said, 'If her last flight was into eternity, one can mourn her loss but not regret her effort. Amelia did not lose, for her last flight was endless. In a relay race of progress, she had merely placed the torch in the hands of others to carry on to the next goal and from there on and on forever.'

That year, Jacqueline Cochran won the women's purse in the Bendix Air Race and finished third overall. On December 4, 1937, she set a national speed record, traveling from New York to Miami in four hours and twelve minutes, bettering the previous time set by the millionaire race pilot Howard Hughes. The following year, Jacqueline Cochran won the Bendix Race, covering the distance of 2,042 miles in eight hours, ten minutes and thirty-one seconds – nonstop! Her plane was the P-35, a sleek, low-winged military pursuit-type aircraft. She set a new cross-country record for women, and in 1939 broke the women's altitude record. She received her second Harmon Trophy, the highest award given to any aviator in America, presented to her in June by the First Lady, Eleanor Roosevelt. She kept flying, setting records, and testing new designs and new equipment.

But events in Europe were dominating the world scene. The Axis held control over Czechoslovakia, Albania, and Spain. In September, Hitler sent his German Panzers into Poland. On the 28th of September, the day after Warsaw fell, Jacqueline Cochran sent a letter to Eleanor Roosevelt, expressing her view that it was time to consider the idea of women pilots in non-combat roles and implying a willingness to do the advance planning for such an organization. Beyond expressing gratitude for the suggestion and stating her belief that women could make many contributions to the war effort should they be called upon to do so, there was little Eleanor Roosevelt could do.

16

Throughout 1940 and the first half of 1941, Jacqueline Cochran continued to expound on the idea of establishing a women's air corps to free male pilots for war duty. After she had lunch with General H. H 'Hap' Arnold, Chief of the US. Army Air Corps, and Clayton Knight, who directed the recruiting of pilots in America for the British Air Transport Auxiliary, General Arnold suggested she should ferry bombers for the British and publicize their need for pilots. Knight thought it was a splendid idea.

But the Air Transport Auxiliary headquarters in Montreal wasn't as enthusiastic. Their response was, 'We'll call you,' and they didn't. Undeterred, she got in touch with one of her British friends, Lord Beaverbrook, who just happened to have recently been appointed minister of procurement, formerly called aircraft production. During the second week of June, Montreal did indeed call and ask her to take a flight test – Jacqueline Cochran, the holder of seventeen aviation records, twice recipient of the Harmon trophy, and the winner of the 1938 Bendix Race.

After three days of grueling tests that seemed more intent on determining her endurance than her flying skill, Jackie made the mistake of joking that her arm was sore from using the handbrake when she was accustomed to toe brakes. The chief pilot stated in his report that while she was qualified to fly the Hudson bomber, he could not recommend her since he felt she might have a physical incapacity to operate the brakes in an emergency situation.

His objections were deemed petty and overruled by ATA headquarters, and Jacqueline Cochran received orders to ferry a Lockheed Hudson bomber from Montreal to Prestwick, Scotland, with a copilot/navigator and radio operator as her crew. But her troubles weren't over. Vigorous protests were made by the ATA male pilots, who threatened to strike. Their objections ranged from concern that ATA would be blamed if the Germans shot down America's most famous woman pilot to complaint that an unpaid volunteer – and female to boot – flying a bomber across the Atlantic belittled their own jobs. A compromise was ultimately reached whereby Jacqueline Cochran would be pilot-in-command for the Atlantic crossing, but her copilot would make all the takeoffs and landings. On June 18, 1941, Jacqueline Cochran became the first woman to fly a bomber across the Atlantic Ocean.

On July first, she returned from England. In her Manhattan apartment, with its foyer murals showing man's early attempt at flight and a small chandelier designed to resemble an observation balloon hanging from the ceiling, she held a news conference and talked about her trip to Britain. After the reporters had gone, Jackie received a phone call inviting her to lunch with President and Mrs Roosevelt.

The next day, a police escort drove her to the estate at Crum Elbow, the famous Hyde park mansion with its majestic columned entrances. She spent two hours with the President. The meeting resulted in a note of introduction to Robert Lovett, Assistant Secretary of War for Air, in which the President stated his desire that Jacqueline Cochran research a plan creating an organization of women pilots for the Army Air Corps.

Her subsequent interview with the Assistant Secretary early in July resulted in Jackie's becoming an unpaid 'tactical consultant,' with office space for herself and her staff in the ferry Command section. Using the Civil Aeronautics Administration's files, she and her researchers found the records of over 2,700 licensed women pilots, 150 of them possessing more than 200 hours of flying experience. When contacted, nearly all were enthusiastic about the possibility of flying for the Army.

Jacqueline Cochran put forward a proposal to her former luncheon partner, Army Air Corps General 'Hap' Arnold, to utilize not just the 150 highly qualified women pilots but to give advance training to the more than two thousand others. Hers was not the only proposal regarding women pilots the Army received. Nancy Harkness Love, a Vassar graduate and commercial pilot for the aviation company she and her husband owned in Boston called Inter-city

Airlines, had also contacted the Ferry Command of the Army Air Corps with a plan to use women pilots to ferry aircraft from the manufacturers to their debarkation points.

But in July 1941 such drastic measures seemed premature to General Arnold. The United States was not at war, and there was an abundance of male pilots. He wasn't sure that it ever would be so dire that they would need women.

Then Pearl Harbor happened. By the spring of 1942, the Army was 'combing the woods for pilots,' and the plans of the two women were resurrected. Jacqueline Cochran was in England recruiting women to fly for the British ATA when she learned that Nancy Love was putting together an elite corps of professional women pilots, ranging from barnstormers to flight instructors for the Ferry Command. Jacqueline Cochran raced home to argue with the Army Air Corps commander, General H. H. Arnold, for her training program, offering him more than a few pilots – promising him thousands, and assuring him she'd prove they were every bit as good if not better than men.

The situation *was* dire. The Allies were losing the war on all fronts in September 1942. General Arnold agreed to Jacqueline Cochran's proposal. The following month, she was busy locating a base where she could train her 'girls.' Facilities were finally provided for the first two classes of trainees at Howard Hughes Field in Houston, Texas, but it soon became apparent that the Houston base wasn't big enough to hold her plans.

Her girls were learning to fly, and they were doing it 'the Army way.'

Part One

We are Yankee Doodle pilots
Yankee Doodle do or die.
Real live nieces of our Uncle Sam
Born with a yearning to fly.
Keep in step to all our classes
March to flight line with our pals
Yankee Doodle came to Texas
Just to fly the PTs.
We are those Yankee Doodle gals.

CHAPTER ONE

Late January, 1943

In her parents' Georgetown home, Cappy Hayward sat on the sofa cushion, her shoulders squared, her hands folded properly on her lap, and her long legs discreetly crossed at the ankles. On an end table sat a framed photograph of her father wearing his jodhpurs and polo helmet and standing beside his favorite polo horse. The picture of the proud, handsome man smiling for the camera bore little resemblance to the career military man confronting her now. Her face was without expression, emotions controlled the way Army life had taught her, while she watched her father's composure disintegrating in direct proportion to his rising anger.

Dropped ice cubes clattered in the glass on the bar cabinet. The golden leaves on the shoulders of Major Hayward's brown Army jacket shimmered in the January sunlight spilling through the window. Major Hayward was not accustomed to having his authority questioned, and certainly not by a member of his family.

'I thought we had discussed all this and it was agreed you were not going to pursue this highly experimental program. It is a damned stupid idea to train women pilots for the Army.' He pulled the stopper out of the whiskey decanter and splashed a liberal shot of liquor into the glass with the ice cubes.

'You "discussed" it and reached that conclusion,' she corrected him smoothly. Her shoulder-length hair was dark, nearly black, a contrast to the startling blue of her eyes. Her poise was unshakable, giving a presence and authority and an added sense of maturity to this tall, long-legged brunette.

'Now, don't go getting smart with me, Cappy.' A warning finger jabbed the air in her direction.

As a small child, she'd always begged to wear her father's hat. He'd been a captain then. Subsequently, she had been dubbed his 'little captain,' which had become shortened to Cap, and eventually expanded to the nickname Cappy.

'I'm not,' she said evenly. 'I am merely informing you that I have been accepted for this pilot training program and I'm going.'

'Just like that, I suppose.' Displeasure made his voice harsh. Its lash could be much more painful than any whipping with a belt. 'What about your job?'

Wartime Washington, DC, paid high wages for moderately skilled typists, but Cappy didn't consider the work to be much of a job. It demanded nothing from her, and provided no challenge at all. There was a war on and she wanted to make some meaningful contribution, no matter how trite it sounded. She wasn't doing that, typing interoffice memos nobody read, in some dreary 'tempo' – one of more than two dozen prefabricated office buildings the government had erected for temporary quarters. After sweltering all summer inside the gray asbestos walls, Cappy couldn't face an entire winter shivering in them.

'I've already given them my resignation.' She glanced down at her hands, then quickly lifted her chin so her father wouldn't get the impression she was bowing under the dictatorial force of his arguments. 'I'm not going to change my mind, sir.' She slipped into the childhood habit of calling him 'sir,' a throwback to the days when a gangly, white-pinafored, pink-ribboned little girl had trailed after her tall, handsome 'daddy' and been sternly ordered to call him 'sir.'

With a sharp pivot, he swung away from Cappy to face the meekly silent woman anxiously observing the exchange

24

from the cushion of a wing chair. He lifted the glass and poured half the contents down his throat.

'This is all your fault, Sue,' he muttered at his wife. 'I never should have allowed you to persuade me to let Cappy move into an apartment of her own.'

'Don't blame this on Mother,' Cappy flared. 'She had nothing to do with it.'

Not once during her entire life could Cappy recall her mother taking a view opposing her husband. She was always the dutiful Army wife, ready to pack at a moment's notice and leave behind her friends with never a complaint. With each move to a new post, her mother painted, papered, and fixed up their housing into beautiful quarters, only to leave them for someone else to enjoy when they moved again. She observed all the Army's protocol, treating the colonel's and the general's wives with the utmost kindness and respect, and taking their snubs without a cross word. Her mother was either a saint or a fool, Cappy couldn't decide which.

'Women in the cockpits of our military aircraft is positively an absurd idea,' her father ranted. 'It will never work. Women are not physically capable of handling them.'

'That's what they said about welding and a half dozen other occupations supposedly only men could do. Rosie the Riveter has certainly proved that isn't so,' Cappy reminded him. 'You should be glad about that. If it weren't for women like Rosie, you wouldn't have all your war machinery coming off the assembly lines now.'

Rosie the Riveter's occupation was the antithesis of what her father saw as suitable for a female. If they had to work, women could be teachers, nurses, secretaries, and typists. In truth, her father wanted her to get married and give him a grandson to make up for the son he'd never had, Cappy being their only child. Dissatisfied with her choices, he'd even picked out a future husband for her – Major Mitch Ryan.

Cappy hated the Army – the way it submerged personalities in its khaki sea and imposed discipline on almost every facet of her life. As far as her father was concerned, the Army was always right. The Army was right to move them every four years, never allowing attachments to people or places to form, and it was right to discourage socializing between officers' families and those of enlisted personnel. When she was nine years old, her father had caught her skipping rope with a sergeant's daughter. Cappy still remembered how much fun Linda was and all the variations she knew. But the Army caste system had been violated, and Cappy had been forbidden to see her little friend again, and had her skip-rope taken away. And her mother had not said a word in her behalf – accepting, always accepting.

Cappy had been too well trained by Army life to ever openly rebel. But the minute she reached her majority and legally could live apart from her parents, she had moved out. It was a case of serving out her hitch. From now on, she made her own decisions and her own friends. And if they happened to be someone like Rosie the Riveter, she didn't care even if her father did.

'Don't cloud the issue,' he answered contentiously. 'Learning manual skills does not mean a woman is capable of the mental and physical coordination required to fly long distances. Why on earth would you even entertain the idea?'

'Maybe you shouldn't have taught me how to fly,' Cappy murmured with a small trace of mockery.

It was the one time she'd felt close to her father, that summer of her seventeenth year when she'd been going through that awkward, coltish, long-legged period. She and her mother had been watching from the ground while he performed beautiful and exciting aerobatics in the sky. After flying he had always seemed relaxed, more approachable, and less the stern disciplinarian. A few questions from her had led to a ride in the plane.

Suddenly her childhood god began to look upon her with favor; her father taught her to fly. For a while they'd

26

had something in common, experiences to share and things to talk about – until the novelty had worn off for him. It had been cute to teach his daughter to fly, like teaching a dog a new trick. Later, he hadn't understood why she wanted to continue such an unfeminine pursuit. Always she'd been a disappointment to him, too tall and striking to ever be the petite, pink-and-white little girl he envisioned for his daughter, and not the son she knew he wanted.

Typically, he ignored her reminder of his role in her flying as his jaw hardened, his blue eyes turning steel-hard, so similar in color and quality to hers. 'Young women on military bases are going to be ogled by every noncom around. How can a daughter of mine subject herself to that kind of leering humiliation?'

'I was raised on military bases,' she reminded him. 'I can't see that there's any difference.'

'There damn well is a difference!' His neck reddened with the explosion of his temper. 'You are my daughter. If any man so much as looked at you wrong, they answered to *me*! A single woman on base is just asking to be rushed by every man jack there.'

'It doesn't say very much for the men, does it?' Cappy challenged.

'Dammit, I want you to be practical,' he argued. 'If you're determined to make some use of your pilot's license, join the Civil Air Patrol instead of traipsing halfway across the country to attend some fool training in a godforsaken Texas town.'

'That's a joke and you know it,' she retorted angrily. 'You've told me yourself that it's ridiculous to even suppose there will be an invasion of the East Coast. And the chance of any long-range bomber strike is equally remote.'

'No daughter of mine is going to take part in any pilot training program for women! I won't have you getting involved with any quasi-military organization that is going to send unescorted females to male airfields around the country. Why, you'd be regarded as no better than tramps.'

27

Outwardly, she showed a steely calm, all those years of disciplining her emotions coming into play and keeping her from giving sway to her anger. 'You no longer have any authority over me. You may still have Mother under your thumb, but I'm not there any more. I came to inform you of my plans. Now that I have' – Cappy picked up her coat and scarf from the chair back – 'I see no reason to stay any longer.'

'Cappy.' Sue Hayward sprang to her feet, dismayed by this open break between father and daughter.

'Let her go, Sue,' Robert Hayward ordered coldly. 'If she has so little respect for her parents that she would deliberately go against our wishes, then I don't care to see her again.'

Briefly, Cappy glared at her father for demanding his wife's undivided loyalty, then she started for the door, knowing well whose side her mother would choose. She caught the silent appeal in the look her mother gave her unrelenting husband before she turned to Cappy. 'I'll walk you to the door.'

Waiting until they were out of earshot, Cappy said, 'I'm not going to apologize, Mother. I'm not sorry for anything I said.'

'He meant it, you know that.' She kept her voice low as they paused by the front door. 'Don't go into this program just to spite him, Cappy.'

'It's what I want to do,' she insisted. 'I don't think you ever understood that. I don't deliberately do things to upset him. There are things I want to do because they give me pleasure. Haven't you ever done anything that you wanted to do? Has it always been what he wanted, Momma?'

'I love him. I want him to be happy.' Every discussion on the subject brought a look of vague confusion to her mother's face.

'Haven't you ever wanted to be happy?' But Cappy didn't wait for an answer. Her mother was too much a reflection of her husband, even to the extent of reflecting

28

his happiness. 'What do you have, Momma? You have no home, no friends – you haven't seen your family in years.'

'It hasn't been possible. The Army –'

'Yes, the Army.' Cappy struggled with the toe-tapping anger she contained. 'It's no good, Mother. I won't change. I won't be like you.' She sensed the faint recoil and realized how her thoughtless remark had hurt. 'I'm sorry.'

'This is what you want?' her mother asked quietly. 'To fly?'

'Yes.'

There was a moment's hesitation while her mother searched Cappy's face. 'Then go do it,' she said.

The encouragement, however reluctantly given, was totally unexpected. Misty-eyed, Cappy gave her a brief hug. 'Thank you,' she said softly, then became knowingly wary. 'But I promise you, I'm not going to set foot in this house again until *he* invites me.'

From the living room came the harsh, commanding voice, calling, 'Sue? Susan!'

'I'm coming, Robert,' she promised over her shoulder, then exchanged a hug with Cappy.

Cappy tucked the ends of her loosely knotted long wool scarf inside her coat and reached for the doorknob. 'Goodbye, Mother,' she said.

Outside, Cappy paused a moment on the stoop, then walked carefully down the snow-shoveled steps to the sidewalk. The visit had turned out almost the way she had expected it would. She had anticipated her father's anger, his lack of understanding. She breathed in the cold, sharp air and started off.

With head down, she turned at the juncture of the main sidewalk and walked in the direction of the bus stop. At the crunch of approaching footsteps in the snow, she lifted her glance and tensed at the sight of the Army officer in a long winter coat – Major Mitchell Ryan.

'Hello.' His breath billowed in a gray, vaporous cloud as he smiled at her in puzzlement. 'Am I too late? I thought the Major told me dinner would be at six this evening.' It

29

was typical of her father to invite the bachelor major to dinner without mentioning it to her. She had been foolish enough to go out on a few dates with him after her father had introduced them. Now both of them seemed to believe Mitch Ryan had some sort of proprietary rights over her.

Cappy reluctantly stopped to speak to him. Dusk was gathering, sending lavender shadows across the white townscape. She looked out across the snow-covered lawns and bushes rather than meet the narrowed probe of his dark eyes. 'I wouldn't know. I'm not staying for dinner. Father and I had a falling-out over my decision to join the training program for women pilots.'

'General Arnold's new little project. Yes, I remember you mentioned it to me.' His head was inclined in a downward angle while he studied her closed expression. 'There is some skepticism toward it.'

'I've been accepted.' She tilted her head to squarely meet his gaze, since he was a head taller than her five-foot-seven-inch height. The rich brown shade of his eyes had a velvet quality, and there always seemed to be something vaguely caressing about the way he looked at her, a definitely disconcerting trait – all the more reason to stay clear of him now that these last few months had shown her she could like him. Major Mitchell Ryan was career Army.

'Are you going?' His eyes narrowed faintly.

'I report to Avenger Field in Sweetwater, Texas, next week.' She started walking and Mitch Ryan swung around to fall in step with her, the wool Army coat flopping heavily against his long legs. Like Cappy, he looked straight ahead.

'For how long?'

'Twenty-six weeks, if I make it the full distance.'

'What then?'

'Then I'll be assigned to the Air Transport Command, I expect, ferrying planes around the country,' she said.

'And where, exactly, does that leave us, Cap?' His head turned in her direction, the bill of his officer's hat pointing down.

'I wasn't aware there was any "us."' Her mouth was

becoming stiff with the cold, but it seemed to match her mood.

His leather-gloved hand caught her arm, stopping Cappy and turning her to face him. 'Don't go.' He held her gaze, their frosty breaths mingling.

'Why?'

The line of his mouth became grimly straight. He was struggling to conceal the frustration and annoyance he was feeling. 'Surely the Major advised you of the negative image associated with women and the military.'

'Yes, I heard the whole lecture, but this happens to be a civilian group.' She stayed rigid in the grip of his hands.

'I suppose I can't change your mind about going.' The muscles along his jaw stood out in hard ridges.

'No,' Cappy replied evenly, without rancor. How many times had she seen Mitch since her father had introduced them three months ago? A half-dozen times maybe, but no more. Yet she must have turned down thrice that many invitations from him. Her rejection only seemed to add to his determination. It was just as well she was leaving before his persistence wore her down and she became involved with him despite her better judgment.

Through the thickness of her winter coat, she could feel his fingers digging into her arms. 'There's a war on, Cappy.'

'Washington is loaded with man-starved girls. You aren't going to miss me for long, Mitch. Not in this town.' The approaching rumble of a bus was a welcome intrusion on a scene that was becoming very uncomfortable to Cappy. 'Here comes my bus, Major. I won't have a chance to see you again, so we might as well say goodbye to each other now. It's been fun.'

He flicked an impatient glance toward the oncoming bus, then brought his attention back to her face. 'Fun. Is that all it's been to you?'

'Yes.'

For an instant longer, his dark gaze bored into her while his mouth tightened. With a roughness he'd never shown her before, Mitch dragged her closer and bent her head

31

backwards with the force of his kiss. It was hard and short, briefly choking off her breath. When he abruptly released her, Cappy gave him a stunned look.

'Go,' Mitch ordered roughly with a jerk of his head toward the braking bus.

'That achieved nothing, Mitch.' The tactic was so typically military – to overpower and control. Cappy wanted him to know it had failed. He might be like her father, but she was not like her mother.

'Then there's nothing to keep you here, is there?' The hard gleam in his eye challenged her.

Behind her, the bus crunched to a full stop next to the snow-mounded curb. Cappy hesitated only a split second. Long ago she had resolved not to let herself be open to hurt. It was better to know what she wanted. In the long run, it would spare her a lot of pain and heartache. She waved for the bus to wait for her and left him standing in the snow.

The clickety-clack of the iron wheels clattered in the background as Cappy gazed at the Texas buttes to the south. They were the only landmarks in an otherwise monotonous landscape of mesquite and dull red earth beneath a gray sky. Yet she observed it all with a controlled eagerness.

There was a movement in her side vision, followed by an outburst of raucous laughter. Cappy let her attention stray from the dust-coated train window to the group of servicemen at the front of the car. It was a motley assortment of passengers on board, weighted heavily on the side of soldiers either heading home on leave or reporting for duty.

Everybody was going somewhere. It had been that way for over a year – ever since Pearl Harbor. Cappy glanced at the family from the Arkansas hills, seated across the aisle from her. The woman and her three children were on their way to California. She had confided to Cappy earlier in the journey that her husband had 'gotten hisself a right fine job at one of those aeroplane plants.' Cappy had surmised from the woman's wide-eyed look of wonder that he was making more money than his family had seen at one time before.

'Momma, I'm hongry.' The oldest child made the hushed comment which carried to Cappy's hearing. The girl looked to be about seven although the mother didn't appear to be much older than Cappy's twenty-two years.

Cappy's head bobbed slightly with the rocking sway of the train while she observed the family with idle curiosity. For all the woman's apparent inexperience of the world, the blue eyes above those hollow, boned cheeks possessed a knowledge of life's more basic realities.

The woman removed a wax-paper-wrapped sandwich from the satchel at her feet without disturbing the toddler sleeping on her lap. The middle child, a five-year-old boy, stared at the sandwich with big eyes, but didn't say a word. When the woman pulled the sandwich into two more-or-less equal halves, the older child made a faint sound of protest.

'Now, Addie, you share this with your little brother,' the woman admonished with a warning look that silenced the girl, but Cappy noticed the resentful glance she gave the boy.

The sandwich didn't appear worthy of a fight. The thick slices of bread almost hid the thin slice of cheese trapped between them, yet the children ate it slowly, savoring every mouthful, and carefully picking up any crumb that fell. The woman bent across the sleeping child again to rummage through the satchel, and this time came up with a small, slightly withered-looking apple. As she straightened, she noticed Cappy watching her. She darted a quick, self-conscious glance at the apple in her hand.

'Would ya care fer an apple?' the woman offered hesitantly. 'They're right sweet ones growed from our own tree in the back yard. They kept real fine in the cave this winter.'

'Thank you, no.' Cappy noticed the faint show of relief

33

in the woman's expression. 'I'm getting off at the next stop.'

Cheese sandwiches that were more bread than cheese, old and wrinkled apples – Cappy mentally shook her head in a kind of wry pity. She couldn't recall ever eating plain bread and cheese in her life. Army life had insulated her from much of the Great Depression. Food had always been plentiful in her family, purchased at PX prices. They had never lacked for anything.

A man in a Marine uniform approached, deliberately catching her eye. He paused by the aisle chair next to the window seat she occupied and braced his feet against the rock of the train.

'Anyone sitting here?' He indicated the vacant aisle seat.

Cappy gave a negative shake of her head. 'Help yourself.' Such advances had occurred so many times during her long train ride, they had acquired a certain monotony. As the young marine dropped into the seat, she asked, 'Are you heading home on leave or on your way back?'

'Reporting for duty in California,' he said. 'Rumor has it we'll be shipping out in a few weeks. Destination – some "nowhere" in the pacific.' His mouth twisted in a rueful grimace, intended to elicit sympathy.

'Somebody has to go, I guess.' Her sidelong glance mocked his pity-me look.

He laughed shortly, unsure whether she was joking or making fun of him. He eyed her, faintly puzzled by the aloof poise she maintained, so at odds with the vibrant image of her long dark hair, curled at the ends, and her vivid blue eyes.

'My name's Andrews, Benjamin T. Ben to my friends.' He tried to smile. Usually the uniform did the trick for him with girls but he could tell she wasn't at all impressed by it.

'Hayward, Cappy.' She mimicked his military phrasing.

'Cappy, eh.' He seemed to search for a topic that would give him control of the conversation. 'Well, where are you bound . . . Cappy?'

34

The clackety-clack of the train became louder as the connecting door between the passenger cars was opened. The conductor entered and started down the aisle. 'Swee-eetwater! Next stop, Swee-eetwater!' He made the rhyth-mic announcement as he walked through the car.

'This is where I leave you – Avenger Field, Sweetwater,' Cappy said to the Marine and glanced briefly out the window. The flat-topped mesas to the south that had dominated the landscape since Abilene were gone. All she could see now was flatly undulating country beneath a gray and bleak sky.

The train began to slow as it reached the outskirts of the Texas town. Another young woman in the front of the passenger coach stood when Cappy did and took her suitcase from the overhead rack. Their glances met across the heads of the other passengers, and recognition flashed between them – recognition of the shared purpose for which they'd traveled to this west Texas town.

'I'll get that for you.' The Marine reached for the blue suitcase bearing Cappy's initials and lowered it down.

'Thanks, I can manage.' She started to take it from him, but he eluded the attempt.

'No doubt you can,' he agreed with a rare show of humor that put them on equal footing. 'But my mom taught me to carry heavy things for a lady.'

Unexpectedly liking him, Cappy shrugged and laughed. 'Suit yourself.' They made their way to the end of the coach with Cappy gripping each passing seat-back to retain her balance against the slowing lurch of the train. The grinding screech of the brakes put an end to any further conversation as the train rumbled to a stop. 'Good luck to you, Ben.' She stuck out a friendly hand to say goodbye to him.

'Yeah.' He looked at her hand for a second, then at her face, and leaned forward to plant a kiss on her surprised lips. Grinning, he handed her the suitcase. 'A fella never knows if he'll get another chance to kiss a pretty girl.'

Cappy smiled widely. 'Liar,' she mocked the trite sentiment, as a barrage of wolf whistles rose from the other servicemen in the car.

Wartime had a crazy effect on people, a fact she had noticed before. It became an excuse for them to throw aside convention and do what they pleased – and they usually did.

The door opened and Cappy turned to leave. Her glance locked with the other girl also waiting to disembark. There was a bold and reckless quality about her – an earthy zest. Cappy had a distinct feeling this girl would do anything on a dare. About the same height as Cappy, maybe an inch shorter, she had sand-colored hair, bobbed short into a mass of loose curls that needed little attention, and her eyes were an unusual gray-green, very frank in their gaze.

The conductor took their luggage and carried it down the steps. He left it sitting on the platform of the Texas and Pacific train depot and came back to give them a hand down. A raw wind lashed at their cheeks as Cappy followed the other girl. She looked down the track, but no one else had gotten off the train. All the townspeople seemed to have been chased inside by the blustery wind of this gray, February day. Their glances met again as they reclaimed their respective suitcases.

'I heard you tell that private you were bound for Avenger Field.' The girl's voice had a pleasant rasp to it, husky and warm, yet as bold as she was. 'Since we're both going to the same place, we might as well share that lone taxi.' She nodded in the direction of a navy-blue sedan that had just driven up to the train station.

'Why not?' Cappy couldn't argue with the practical suggestion.

The numbing wind chased away idle chit-chat and hurried them both to the waiting taxi. The driver stepped out, his collar turned up, a cowboy hat pulled low over his forehead. He angled his body into the wind while he took their suitcases.

'Reckon you two are wantin' to go to Avenger Field with the rest of those females,' he surmised, sizing them up with an all-seeing glance while he juggled their luggage and opened the trunk.

'That's right,' came the whiskey-rough reply as the girl didn't wait around for the car door to be opened for her, but bolted into the rear seat. Cappy followed and shut the door. Finally sheltered from the bitter wind, the long and lanky girl suppressed a shudder. 'It's cold out there. I always thought Texas was warm,' she grumbled.

'Texas is infamous for its "blue northers."' Cappy opened her purse and removed a cigarette from a pack. 'Want one?'

'No thanks.' Gray-green eyes were on her as the match was struck and the flame held to the tip of the cigarette. 'Are you from Texas?'

'No, but I've lived here.' Exhaling a cloud of smoke, Cappy settled into her corner of the back seat. 'My name's Cappy Hayward, by the way.'

'Marty Rogers, from Detroit, Michigan.'

'My last address was Washington, DC.' She flipped open the car's ashtray, glancing at the driver when he slid behind the wheel. 'I'm an Army brat, so – you name it, I've lived there.'

When the taxi pulled away from the depot, the Rogers girl leaned forward to ask the driver, 'How far is it to the field?'

'Not far.' He shrugged as if to indicate the distance was of little import and not worth his time figuring.

'A couple of miles.' Cappy supplied the information she had gleaned from inquiries within the Army system.

'How do you know? Have you been to this air base before?'

'Actually it isn't a military air base. It's a municipal field converted to military use to train pilots.' She took a drag on her cigarette and exhaled the smoke while she added, 'The town named it Avenger Field last year – to train pilots to "avenge" the attack on Pearl Harbor.'

'You're a veritable fountain of information. I thought I'd done well merely locating Sweetwater on a Texas map.'

The husky gravel of her voice had a taunting pitch of self-mockery, a wry humor always lurking somewhere to poke fun at something.

'We had some British flyboys out there. Last of 'em left last summer.' The driver volunteered the information, tossing it over his shoulder to his passengers in the back seat. 'Got some American boys out there now,' he told them in a voice that was thick with the local twang.

'They only have a few more weeks before they finish their training. Then, rumor has it, Avenger Field will be strictly female.' Cappy sensed the questioning look and acknowledged it. 'I did some checking after I received my telegram from Jacqueline Cochran ordering me to report here. Only half of our class will be training at Avenger Field. The other half is reporting to Howard Hughes Field in Houston.'

The taxi had already passed the last buildings on the edge of town. From the little she'd seen of Sweetwater, it hadn't struck Marty Rogers as being a place filled with action, whereas Houston at least conjured up images of a big town. Oh, well, she decided with a mental shrug, she had come here to fly, not to party. A good thing, too, because about all she saw out the window was a heavy gray sky and a lot of desolate country.

'I don't care. I just want to fly,' Marty asserted a little more strongly than was necessary.

'Don't we all,' Cappy murmured and stabbed out the fire in her cigarette.

'I suppose your father's a pilot in the Air Corps.'

'He has a desk job in Washington. He's been posted to the Pentagon – the new building in Washington they built to house the military command. He flies, but strictly for his own pleasure.'

'Is that how you learned?'

'Yes.' Cappy didn't elaborate on her answer to the first truly personal question put forth. She could have told this Rogers woman that her father now rued the day he'd ever taught her to fly. Sharing information was one thing, but giving confidences to strangers – 'telling all' in the space of five minutes – was another.

Over the years, she had lost count of the number of new homes she'd lived in, new towns, new friends – the pathetic eagerness to be liked. She had made the mistake of confiding things about herself to those she thought were new-found friends only to have them blab it all over school. She'd learned the hard way to keep things to herself – problems, fears, and desires. It was better to be self-sufficient; then people couldn't hurt you.

'How did you learn to fly?' Cappy switched the focus to Marty Rogers.

'When my older brother, David, took up flying, I had to give it a whirl. One time up and I was hooked.' Her wide mouth quirked in wry remembrance. 'My folks bought David a plane, a little Piper Cub. I mean he's the number one son so he gets everything, right? I turned out to be an afterthought in more than one way.'

David had always had center stage from the time she could remember. She had grown up in her older brother's shadow, worshiping him sometimes and violently resenting him other times. The competition between them was strong – as strong as the sibling love that bound them.

'Anyway –' Marty took a deep breath and plunged on. 'David let me use his plane as long as I paid for the fuel. It was a helluva good deal for me.' She swore naturally and casually, managing to make it inoffensive. 'You should have heard him when he found out I'd qualified for this flight training program the Army's giving us. He was so damned green with envy.'

'Why is that?' Cappy knew she was expected to ask.

'With that plane of his, he thought he was going to have a leg up on everybody when he joined the Army. He figured with all his hours and experience he'd be a shoo-in for pilot training, but he couldn't pass the physical.'

'I think we all sweated that.'

'Yeah, well, David's on his way to Fort Bragg in North Carolina for paratroop training. He decided if he couldn't fly planes for the Army, jumping out of them was the next best thing. Hell, I'm twice the pilot he ever thought of being and I know it.' Marty bragged without apology. 'Not that my parents are ever likely to notice anything I do.' She paused a second, an indignant anger surfacing. 'You know, David left a couple of weeks ago for camp, and for his last night home my mother used all of her meat-ration coupons on a steak for him! You know what I had my last night? Macaroni. It isn't fair.'

'I know what you mean,' Cappy said with empathy.

'Do you have any brothers?'

'No, I'm an only child.'

'Lucky you. Your parents probably think anything you do is wonderful. Do you know how my father reacted when I told him I was going to take this training? I got this whole lecture that proper young women should be content to stay on the ground. He just couldn't get it through his head that I'm twenty-four years old. I don't need his permission.'

'I was forbidden to come,' Cappy replied.

'You're kidding! I figured an Army father would be all in favor of it. Isn't that something?' She sat back in her seat. 'You ought to hear my folks carry on about the way I smoke and drink and date guys. Their precious son certainly is no saint. Where do they think I learned everything? Hell, I'm probably not an ideal daughter.' She hit a flat note. 'But I can't be what I'm not. Besides, there's a war on.' Marty came back to her old form, husky and uncaring. 'It isn't fair that David gets to go and have all the excitement while I'm supposed to sit around and twiddle my thumbs.'

The driver slowed the taxi and Cappy glanced out the window at the guardhouse marking the entrance to the field. 'Looks like we're here.'

The taxi stopped in front of a long, slant-roofed building, squatting low to the ground and painted gray as if to match the clouds overhead. Military paint came in only three colors: battleship gray, olive drab, and khaki brown. Beyond were the barracks buildings, six of them marching by twos facing each other lengthwise in a north-south line. The hump-backed roofs of two hangars were visible. Atop one there was a tower of sorts that reminded Cappy of a widow's walk, a flight of steps leading to it from the outside.

In addition, the recreation/dining room and ground school classroom buildings made the third side to the triangular layout of the field buildings with the hangars for a base line. A long stretched-out building ran parallel to one of the two intersecting runways. Windows lined the front of one end where the pilot's 'ready room' was located, the place where the trainees would await their turn to fly. The other end was divided into classrooms for their ground school courses. All the wooden, gray buildings were huddled by the runways, intertwined by taxi strips linking the ends of the runways with the flight line and hangars as well as with each other. From the air, Avenger Field resembled a crudely drawn map of Texas.

The driver set their suitcases on the hard-packed ground spotted with a few tufts of tenacious buffalo grass. Splitting the fare, Cappy and Marty each paid their share. He pocketed the money and gave them a wondering look. 'It beats me why you gals would think you could take up this flying business. It ain't natural, ya know.'

'I guess we're all just a little crazy,' Marty informed him with mock seriousness at his male prejudice against females and flying.

It sailed right by him as he turned away, shaking his head. When Marty glanced at Cappy, she was wearing the same slightly exasperated expression. The common bond brought a smile to each of them. A feeling of adventure and excitement ran high in Marty's veins. As the taxi rumbled away, it suddenly ceased to matter how cold and forlorn the day was. This was the chance of a lifetime and there wasn't a damned thing that was going to stand in her way. She could tell Cappy Hayward felt the same way.

41

'This is it.' Marty looked at the administration building before them.

'Let's go in.' Cappy hoisted her heavy bag and started for the door, her deeply blue eyes agleam.

Accustomed to being the one in the lead, Marty faltered a second before she followed the calmly assertive brunette. As Cappy opened the door, the cold wind rushed inside to announce their arrival to the large group of women already gathered in the big room. The sudden draft swirled through the blue-gray smoke hanging in layers close to the ceiling. Heads turned toward the door to protest the gust of cold air, then remained in the same position to eye the newcomers. But the lull in the conversation didn't last long as Cappy and Marty were quickly absorbed and the buzz of female chatter reached its former level.

It seemed natural that since they had arrived together, they would stay together. They worked their way through the massed clusters of women until they found a patch of unoccupied floor and set their suitcases on it.

Throughout the room, luggage was put to a variety of uses – racks for coats to be draped on, backrests for those seated on the floor, and narrow seats for others to sit on. Marty shed her heavy winter coat and laid it across the top of her suitcase while she glanced at a trio of women only a couple of feet away.

'Hi.' She wasted no time getting acquainted, untroubled that Cappy Hayward exhibited no such eagerness. 'Marty Rogers from Michigan.'

'Hey, I'm from Chicago,' piped up a girl with dark hair. 'Whereabouts did you fly?'

'Out of Detroit mostly.'

'Where are you from?' The question was directed at Cappy, acknowledging her presence on the periphery of the group.

'Cappy Hayward, Washington, DC.' She identified herself with the close-mouthed crispness Marty had already begun to expect from her.

'Is that where you did your flying?'

'No. I logged most of my hours out of Macon, Georgia,' she replied.

'Oh?' The dark-haired woman nearest to Marty had been an interested listener, half sitting and half leaning on her suitcase. Marty blocked her view of Cappy, so she straightened to look around her. 'Are you from there originally?' The girl's soft, drawling voice revealed her southern upbringing, silky and sweetly refined. But it was her size that startled Marty – she was so much shorter than the rest of them.

'I'll be damned,' Marty exclaimed under her breath. 'You must have just made it above the minimums.'

'I squeaked through by an eighth of an inch.' She laughed. 'Five foot two and five-eighths. It was a good thing they measured me in the morning or I wouldn't have made it.'

'How do you see over the control panel? Hell, for that matter, how do those short legs of yours reach the rudder pedals?' Marty poked fun at her in a jesting manner. 'You must sit on a stack of pillows.'

'Only two.' She pointed to a pair of cushions, secured with a strap to her suitcase handle.

Noticing the initials *MLP* on the suitcase, Marty couldn't resist asking, 'What does MLP stand for – Mighty Little Pilot?'

'Mary Lynn Palmer,' she corrected, offering an apple-cheeked smile at Marty's razzing yet managing to convey a ladylike air.

'Hello, Mary Lynn.' With her handshake, Cappy managed to inject a modicum of manners. 'My father was stationed in Macon five years ago. He's career military, a major in the Army Air Corps.'

'In that case' – Chicago spoke up – 'let me officially welcome you to the Three hundred nineteenth Women's Army Air Forces Flying Training Detachment – more familiarly known as the Three hundred nineteenth WAAFFTD.' They were designated as Class 43-W-3, meaning they would be the third class of women to graduate during the year 1943.

'God, what a mouthful,' Marty commented, then informed the others,' If you want the lowdown on anything, just ask Cappy here. She knows just about everything.'

'How soon do you think they'll make us a branch of the military? They're talking of bringing the WAACs in – and the Navy women, too.' The girl from Chicago took Marty at her word.

It was on the tip of Cappy's tongue to say, 'When hell freezes over if my father is to be believed,' but she suppressed that urge and responded with military tact. 'So far, we're only an experiment. The two classes that started ahead of us three months ago in Houston haven't graduated yet. On paper, it looks good to train women pilots to ferry aircraft so men can be released for combat duty. Until we prove we are capable of doing that, the jury is out.'

'It gripes me the way men think we can't fly as well as they can, given the same training,' Chicago complained, but there was a hint of reservation in her voice, as if she might have some misgivings of her own.

'Don't you know it's because all females are scatter-brained, too flighty to fly?' Marty retorted.

'Well, I'm just glad an airplane doesn't know whether it's being flown by a man or a woman,' the third member of the trio said, a comely blonde who slouched in an attempt to diminish her nearly six-foot stature.

Just then, Marty's eye was caught by the sight of a tall, very fashionably dressed woman threading her way through the lounging clusters of females. Marty had always believed that she carried her height well, but this auburn-haired woman moved with an almost regal grace.

'Who is she?' Marty discreetly gestured toward the stately redhead with a small nod of her head.

'She's really something, isn't she?' the shy blonde replied with a trace of envy in her voice.

'She looks like she stepped out of the pages of a Paris fashion magazine,' Marty murmured.

A second later, the woman stopped beside two huge steamer trunks set next to the wall. A full-length leopard-skin coat was draped negligently across one of them. The woman used it as a cushion to sit on and crossed her long, silk-clad legs.

'Good God,' was Marty's stunned, blasphemous comment. When the woman slipped a cigarette into the end of a long silver holder, it was too much for Marty. 'I've got to meet her. She can't be for real.' She looked expectantly at the others. 'Are you coming with me?' she challenged them, but didn't wait for a reply.

Curiosity prompted all of them to trail after her, assuming a guise of nonchalance. A wide bracelet glittered with jeweled brilliance around the woman's wrist, and the blonde whispered to Chicago, 'Do you suppose those are real diamonds?'

No one, not even for a minute, believed anything about her was phony. When she noticed them strolling so casually her way, her glance slid away as if to snub them. Then she turned back, her chin lifting a fraction of an inch while a cool smile edged her red, red lips.

'Hello.' A very cultured and smooth voice greeted them.

'Hi, I'm Marty Rogers. We couldn't help noticing you sitting over here by yourself.' Her glance went to the big trunks in obvious question.

'I'm Eden van Valkenburg from New York.' She extended a slim, manicured hand in greeting. Her long nails were painted the same bright red shade as her lipstick.

For a second, Marty wondered if she was supposed to curtsy over the proffered hand. But when she shook it, the returning pressure was firm and definite. It gave Marty a second's pause.

'Let me introduce you around. This is Cappy Hayward. We arrived on the same train,' Marty explained. 'Her father's an Army man so if you have any questions, just ask her.' There were no more handshakes, just exchanges of polite and curious smiles. 'Mary Lynn Palmer is from

Mobile, Alabama. And – Chicago, I don't know your name.'

'Gertrude Baxter, but everybody calls me Trudy.' She ran a hand over her limp hair, a self-conscious gesture in reaction to the stylish and obviously very sophisticated woman before her.

'I'm Agnes Richardson – Aggie.' The awkwardly tall blonde bobbed her head in quick introduction, then couldn't keep from gushing, 'I just love your outfit.' She gazed enviously at the powder-blue wool dress with its padded shoulders and full, draping skirt.

'Thank you. Actually, I feel slightly overdressed.' The frank admission caught them all by surprise.

None of them thought she would say what they were all thinking, but the proud gleam in Eden's brown eyes should have warned them. She knew it was better to verbalize their thoughts for them than to let them talk behind her back.

'Do you?' Marty replied, always quick with a whiskey-voiced retort. 'It's the cigarette holder. It's a bit too much, don't you think?' It was a gibe meant to sting. Marty had never cared for people who thought they were somehow better than everyone else. The air crackled briefly with a sparking antagonism.

'Are both these trunks yours, Miss van Valkenburg?' Cappy quietly inserted the question between them.

She was slow to turn her attention away from Marty. 'Yes, they are.' She met the pleasantly interested look and found nothing threatening in the inquiry. 'I felt I should bring only what I absolutely needed.'

For a stunned second, no one could say anything. Even Marty waited for the redhead to smile at the little joke she had made, then realized the woman was dead serious. The discovery seemed to hit them all at the same time. Beside her, Chicago choked on a gasp of laughter that brought on a coughing spasm.

'You did bring an evening gown, didn't you?' Marty asked with a straight face.

'No.' Eden van Valkenburg appeared taken aback by the question as she warily searched the faces of the other women. 'Will I need one?'

'Oh, God,' Marty muttered, and she swung away, missing the flare of anger in the redhead's expression.

A hush was spreading across the long rec hall. When it reached their small group, they all turned to find the cause of it. An officer in an Army uniform had entered the building. Once he had the attention of the entire room, he introduced himself as the base commander, and told them what to expect over the next twenty-six weeks while they learned to fly 'the Army way.' It wasn't a heartening speech as he ominously warned that two out of three would 'wash out' – fail to graduate. It became very clear they were going to be subjected to military rules and disciplines, with demerits issued for any infringements.

As he briefly listed some, he came to '. . . profanity will not be tolerated . . .'

'Oh, damn,' Marty murmured under her breath, and the blond-haired Aggie Richardson tittered with laughter.

CHAPTER TWO

By the time the five girls retrieved their luggage and joined the queue at the linens window, they were near the end of the line. In a definite break with what Cappy Hayward regarded as Army tradition, the women were being allowed to choose their roommates – or baymates, since the barracks were divided into bays, each with six bunks. The five of them – Cappy, Marty Rogers, Mary Lynn Palmer, Trudy 'Chicago' Baxter, and Aggie Richardson – had decided to share a bay and take potluck on who would make up the sixth.

'I guess we have to get used to shuffling in these damned lines,' Marty muttered.

47

'That's the Army way,' Cappy replied.

Aggie inched closer. 'I wonder where that rich van Valkenburg girl is?' She looked down the line of females to see if she could find her.

'She's probably trying to find a bellboy to take her trunks,' Marty joked, then shook her head. 'Can you believe her? If it wasn't so damned funny it'd be pathetic.'

'You didn't give her much of a chance.' The accusation was made in the softly drawling Alabama accent of Mary Lynn Palmer.

From anyone else, Marty might have bridled at the reprimand, but from this dark-haired, dark-eyed woman, she didn't take offense. Despite their brief acquaintance, Marty was ready to swear there wasn't a mean or spiteful bone in Mary Lynn's body.

After thinking it over, she conceded, 'Maybe I was quick to judge her. But I wasn't really trying to make fun of her.'

'Oh, weren't you?' Chicago chided.

'Maybe I was, but the situation was so damned comical.' Marty defended her behavior while hinting that she sometimes went for the joke without considering the feelings of the person who was the butt of it.

'Maybe she plans to write a book on what to wear when you go to war,' Chicago suggested with a quick laugh.

As the line moved along, they each had their turn at the linens window and received their sheets, pillowcases, and blankets. Loaded down, they headed for the row of barracks.

'All the bays are alike,' Cappy Hayward informed them. 'Anybody have any preference for location?'

'It doesn't make any difference to me,' Marty said and the others nodded their agreement. 'Lead on, Cappy,' she declared, then shivered. 'And get us out of this damned wind.'

'You're going to have to start watching your language,' Cappy advised her. 'They start issuing demerits tomorrow.'

The barracks were new, hastily constructed frame buildings, covered with cheap clapboard siding, and roofed with

48

asphalt shingles, painted a dingy Army gray. Red dust clung to every groove, evidence of the pervasiveness of the dry Texas soil. A narrow, roofed walkway fronted the long buildings, pairs of double-hung windows alternating with bay doors.

As they neared the end of a long walkway, Cappy opened the door to an empty bay and the others trooped in behind her. They stopped inside and stared at the austere quarters. The plasterboard walls had received a coat of white paint, but gouges, scuff marks, and telltale yellow water stains warning of a leaky roof took away any sense of newness, although every building on the field, except for one hangar, had been constructed within the last year.

Six narrow Army cots roughly three feet apart stood one end against the wall in a long line. A thin mattress covered with blue-and-white-striped ticking lay atop each metal-framed bed together with a lumpy-looking pillow in the same material. At the foot of each was a large-sized foot-locker, taking up more room on the bare wood floor. A wall switch by the door turned on the overhead light, housed in a dark green metal shade. The windows also sported green window shades, but no curtains.

'Be it ever so humble' – Marty walked to the cot nearest the end wall to dump her linen on it and set her suitcase on the floor – 'there's no place like home sweet home.'

Cappy made no response as she chose a cot of her own, taking the next-to-last on the other end. She laid her things on it in advance of settling in. The other three followed suit more slowly.

'These cots aren't even as wide as the studio couch in my apartment back home,' Chicago offered in a distant voice.

'You hadn't better roll over in your sleep at night or you'll wind up on the floor,' Aggie predicted. All of them could feel the grittiness of the floor beneath their shoes, that fine dust pulverized into the boards.

'Mighty little Mary Lynn is the lucky one,' Marty surmised. 'These cots are just her size.'

'I'm not that small,' she protested, claiming the second cot, next to Marty's.

But Marty was already investigating the footlocker that would serve as closet and bureau, and paid no attention to the reply. A raspy laugh came from her throat, a brief burst of humor. 'Can you imagine that van Valkenburg dame trying to fit her two trunks of clothes into this?'

Her question was met with faint smiles as each tried to adjust to her spartan environment. All five of them came from different parts of the country, different backgrounds. Yet, the fact that they were at Avenger Field meant it was likely they had all enjoyed a measure of affluence in their lives or they never would have been able to attain a pilot's license nor accumulate the number of hours necessary to meet the requirements. Flying was an expensive hobby. Few women had the desire to fly and even fewer had the opportunity.

Choosing to explore her new surroundings rather than unpack, Marty closed her locker and straightened to look around the room. A door was at the other end.

'Where does that lead?' she asked, already heading down the length of the room to find out.

'It's probably the bathroom,' Cappy guessed and followed to see if she was right.

Marty entered and came to an abrupt stop, startled by the sight of a strange female washing her hands at one of the two white porcelain sinks protruding from the wall, their pipes exposed below. 'Sorry, I –' she started to apologize.

'No problem. I'm finished.' The girl shook the excess water from her hands and reached for a towel to dry them.

Besides the two sinks, the small, communal lavatory contained two showers and two stalls, lighted again by a ceiling fixture with a green-painted metal disc. Marty noticed the second door and frowned. 'I thought this was our bathroom.'

'It looks as if we have to share it with the girls in the next bay,' Cappy said.

'That's what we were told.' The gangly brunette finished drying her hands and cast a wry glance at the limited facilities.

'You're kidding!' Marty protested. 'Twelve girls sharing *one* bathroom – and *one* mirror?'

'It's absurd, isn't it?' the other girl said in a commiserating tone as she walked through the door to the adjoining bay.

'Absurd isn't going to be the word for it when tomorrow morning comes and we're all trying to get in here at the same time.' Marty foresaw the room would become a battleground with each girl fighting for her turn. Cappy didn't disagree as they re-entered their bay. 'Better set your clocks early if you want a crack at the bathroom before the stampede starts in the morning,' she warned the others.

They were all busy unpacking or getting their beds made, but Marty didn't feel like tackling hers yet. She sat on her cot and spread her fingers across the blue-striped mattress to test its softness. Mary Lynn Palmer had taken the cot next to hers. Her suitcase lay open atop it while Mary Lynn transferred her clothes to the footlocker. Marty spied the framed photograph lying among some lingerie.

'Who's the picture of – your fella?' she asked.

'You could say that.' Mary Lynn lifted it out to show Marty the photograph. 'It's my husband.'

Belatedly, Marty noticed the gold wedding band on Mary Lynn's left hand. The gold-edged frame held a photo of an Army pilot, an officer's cap sitting jauntily on his head, thick dark hair waving close to his ears. He had on a fleece-lined leather flying jacket, unzipped at the throat, and dark, smiling eyes stared at Marty from a lean, handsome face.

'Is he ever damned good-looking.' Marty read the inscription scrawled across the bottom of the picture: 'To my darling wife, Mary Lynn, All my love always, Your adoring husband, Beau,' then passed the picture back to Mary Lynn. 'He flies, too,' she observed.

'Beau is a B-17 pilot – stationed in England.' She spoke in a very low and soft voice that managed to convey the strength of a deep emotion. 'He flies the big four-engine bombers they call the Big Friend.'

'Lucky guy. I'd love to crawl into the cockpit of one of those someday.' Marty rested her hands on the edge of the cot and casually leaned forward, noticing the caressing way Mary Lynn touched the photograph.

'Flying is how I met him.' She laughed softly and corrected herself. 'Well, that isn't exactly *how* I met him. A big air show was held at a field outside of Mobile and my daddy took me to see it. That's where I saw Beau for the first time and found out he was a flying instructor. I persuaded my daddy to let me take lessons so I could meet him. You have no idea how hard it was to fly an airplane when he was talking in my ear.' Her laughter invited Marty to join in. 'After we were married, Beau used to tease me that it was the flying bug that bit me – not cupid's arrows.'

'How long have you two been married?' Marty guessed they had to be newlyweds since Mary Lynn hadn't lost that dreamy-eyed look. Sooner or later she'd wake up, Marty knew. With the war on, it was likely to be later, though.

'Ten years.'

'Ten . . . Wait a minute. How old are you?' Stunned, Marty frowned in disbelief. 'Were you a child bride or something?'

'No. I was seventeen when Beau and I were married.' Mary Lynn smiled at Marty's reaction and set the free-standing frame upright on the footlocker. 'But I knew from the start he was the only man for me.'

'It must be nice to know you belong like that to somebody.' Long ago Marty had become resigned to her single state. She'd been born without the nesting instinct, lacking homemaking skills and the yen for a settled existence. She craved action and excitement too much. Once, during her early college years, she'd let a man try to tame her wild streak and show her a sample of domestic bliss. The only part that hadn't bored her was the bedroom. Within a week they were at each other's throats, he insisting that she settle down and stop carousing and Marty refusing to change her nature. After they split up, she had joked to her friends that she should have known it would never work. Even as a child, she had enjoyed playing doctor, but hated playing house.

So Marty had fun. Looking at Mary Lynn, Marty knew she could never be like her. Petite, dark-haired and softly feminine, she was the type men wanted, not Marty.

'I miss him.' Mary Lynn traced a finger across his picture. 'When Beau was sent overseas I couldn't stand being in the house without him, and I moved back home with my parents. That was a mistake, I'm afraid.'

'You don't get along with your parents either?'

'It isn't that exactly. I mean, my daddy is a sweetheart. He insisted on driving me to the train station in his car when I could have taken the bus and saved him precious gallons of gasoline. And he knew I had to pay my own fare here to Sweetwater, so he slipped me five dollars to be sure I had spending money on the train. He spoils me.'

'Must be nice.'

'It is.' Her dark, lively eyes sparkled with the admission, a smile highlighting her cherub-round cheeks.

'Then what was your problem living at home?' Marty asked curiously.

'My mother and I had trouble getting along. I guess I'd lived away for too long. I didn't always do things the way she wanted them done.' Her shoulders lifted in a vague shrug. 'And I was restless. I wanted to do something – to contribute in some small way to the war effort – to do my part. Outside of being a wife, the only skill I had was flying. I knew how badly they needed pilots . . . so I decided that if they'd take me, I'd go. Mother thinks I'm foolish.'

'Why?' Marty demanded.

'She felt I could contribute a lot more by going to work at one of the defense plants and get paid better for it too.' Sometimes Mary Lynn felt her mother hadn't wanted her to leave because she didn't want to lose the money Mary Lynn paid for her share of the household expenses. She knew what a struggle financially it was for her parents and she felt bad for having such mean thoughts about her mother. 'She couldn't understand that flying makes me feel close to Beau. When I'm up in a plane, I feel that I'm near him.'

'What does Beau think of all this?' Marty wanted to know.

'He's in favor of it,' Mary Lynn assured her. 'He knows how much the Army needs good pilots, and naturally he knows I am one since he taught me. He feels as I do –' Her drawling voice took on an earnest tone, catching Chicago's attention in the next cot. 'We all must do what we can to shorten the war and bring our men home sooner.'

'That's true,' Chicago inserted while Aggie, in the adjacent cot, listened in. 'The more women we can put in the air, the more men can be sent overseas and the more planes can be sent over Germany. What we're doing here is vital.'

'I know all this is important to the war effort.' Tall, gangly Aggie glanced at her fellow baymates somewhat hesitantly, unsure of her welcome in the conversation. 'But for me, it's the flying – the chance to do something I really love. Up there, with the sky and the clouds – the exhilaration – the sense of power – it's like nothing else.' She became caught up in the struggle to express her feelings. 'There's nothing to hold you back. You're free, totally free. It's a kind of delirious joy and awe all mixed up together. Flying is a physical, emotional, and spiritual experience.' When she paused, she noticed the silence and the way everyone was staring at her. Her chin dropped quickly in a self-conscious gesture. 'I guess I sound crazy.'

It was a moment before anyone spoke. 'No, you don't,' Mary Lynn said quietly. 'I think we all share those feelings you just described. But some of us have never heard another woman say them.'

'Oh, I don't know. I think Aggie did get a little carried

54

away,' Marty suggested wryly. 'She's made flying sound better than kissing.'

The atmosphere immediately lightened as smiles spread across their faces. 'You're right, Marty,' Chicago agreed. 'It's the next best thing, maybe, but not better.'

They laughed dutifully at Chicago's small joke, but underneath her soft laugh, Mary Lynn felt a twinge of guilt. No matter how much she justified her decision to enlist in the training program the underlying reason was the same as Aggie's – she loved to fly. How a blue sky beckoned to her, tugged at her soul and urged her to come away and experience the ecstasy of its heights. She knew the power of its call, that wild sense of freedom that was so exhilarating, and the feeling that Beau was with her – right beside her, flying through the same clouds. When she was up in that sky, nothing else existed – not the war, not her fears for Beau, her parents' problems – nothing. She could leave them behind when she flew, but they were always waiting for her when she came back down on the ground.

Next to the end of the row of bunks, Cappy Hayward stood up. 'Let's get unpacked and the beds made,' she said, prompting the others to return to their tasks, then she went back to the opened suitcase lying on her cot. The precisely folded clothes were arranged in an orderly fashion. She'd had ample experience at packing in her lifetime.

Cap. There was such irony in the nickname she'd been given. But, of course, the others didn't know of her abhorrence for the military, its cold impersonality and demand for unquestioning obedience. Never would she live the life her mother had. She had hated it, never having any sense of roots, any friends, or any control over her existence. Perhaps the latter was what had addicted her to flying. In an airplane, she possessed that control. And Aggie was right – there was no sensation like it.

The hard rap of a hand rattled the bay door in its frame. Aggie made a start toward it, then glanced at Cappy.

'There are some guys in uniform out there. I noticed them a minute ago through the window. Do you want to get the door, Cap?'

Cappy's hesitation lasted only a split second as the knock sounded again. 'Sure.' She replaced the folded blouse on the pile of clothes still in the suitcase and crossed the room to the door. She scanned the khaki uniform of the man standing outside, noting the chevrons on his sleeves. 'Yes, Sergeant?' Standing to one side of the door, out of sight of the others, was the tall redhead in the leopard coat. One steamer trunk was sitting on the walkway while a second soldier waited by it, his breath clouding in steamy vapors.

'Is there room in this bay for another occupant?' The sergeant's broad, flat features wore a thin-lipped expression that suggested his patience had been tested. The redhead didn't appear to be in a much better mood.

'We have an empty cot.' It was the last one in line, next to hers and closest to the bathroom, a dubious advantage since it was like sleeping next to an elevator. The barracks' thin partitions did little to mask the sound of clanging water pipes, flushing toilets, or chattering occupants. Just as Cappy started to move out of the doorway so they could enter, Marty Rogers shouldered her way in.

'What does he want, Cap?' A second after she asked the question, Marty noticed the auburn-haired female huddled deep in the warm fur of her coat.

'If you'll hold the door open, we'll carry this trunk inside.' The sergeant ignored her question as he signaled the waiting soldier to pick up his end of the trunk.

Eden van Valkenburg's hands, gloved in expensive black leather, bunched the collar of the leopard-skin coat tightly around her neck as she took one look at Marty Rogers and turned to the sergeant. 'I want to check another . . . bay.' It took her a second to recall the proper terminology.

'The accommodations are the same in every one, miss.' Exasperation threaded the sergeant's voice as he picked up an end of the trunk.

'I think it's the company, not the accommodations, that she wants to change,' Marty suggested wryly.

The sergeant wasn't interested in their clash of personalities. 'Please move out of the way, ladies.' There was a strained politeness in the order as he backed toward the doorway lugging his end of the trunk. Marty had no choice but to move out of his way or be bowled over.

With a grudging acceptance of her fate, Eden followed the trunk-toting men into the barracks. Her dark challenging gaze made a sweep of the other faces in the room, making it clear that she liked the idea of sharing the quarters with them no more than they did. Cappy could empathize with that feeling of alienation, of being an outsider, unwanted and unwelcomed. How many new school classrooms had she entered, looking at cold-faced strangers who stared back? Too many.

The two men deposited the large trunk on the floor next to the empty cot. As they turned to leave, Cappy noticed the van Valkenburg woman open her purse and riffle through the contents. When the sergeant walked past her, she stopped him and pressed something into his hand. 'Thank you,' she said, snapping her purse shut, missing the man's initial start of surprise at the folded bill he held.

'Keep your money, miss.' He pushed it back into her hand with a look of vague disgust. 'This isn't a suite at the Waldorf.'

He was shaking his head as he walked out the door. A flush darkened her cheeks with hot embarrassment. Cappy could well imagine that the wealthy socialite was so accustomed to tipping bell-boys and porters for carrying her luggage that she had passed the money to the sergeant out of habit. While the enlisted man might have accepted it, the sergeant appeared to have had a bellyful of high-toned females.

When the door shut behind the sergeant, a heavy silence overtook the room. The staccato click of Eden's heels seemed to punctuate it as she walked briskly to the trunk, peeling off her leather gloves, finger by finger.

'What happened to your other trunk?' Marty made a sauntering foray over to the vicinity of her Army cot.

'I made arrangements to have it shipped home.' She swept the hat off her titian hair and lifted the ends with a push of her fingers, not bothering to look at Marty. 'It seems there were a great many items that I regarded as necessities which weren't required here.'

'That must have been tough to do,' Marty suggested in a faint taunt.

Anger was seething just below that cool surface. That vague self-mockery was all a pose to conceal how painfully foolish she had been made to feel. Granted, she had made a rather large mistake but she had no intention of letting this tawny-haired, raspy-voiced female rub her nose in it.

'Actually, it wasn't difficult at all,' she retorted, smiling sweetly. 'One of the staff helped me go through my trunks and weed out the nonessentials.' The leopard-skin coat joined the hat, purse, and gloves already adorning the bare mattress.

'Some weeds,' Aggie murmured, staring at the coat that was again serving as a cushion for its owner as Eden sat down on the narrow Army bed. Cappy moved past Marty and returned to her cot, situated between Aggie's and Eden's.

'All this reminds me of a fairy tale,' Marty declared with a sweep of her hand in Eden van Valkenburg's direction. 'I have a feeling the princess is going to wake up in the morning and complain to us about sleeping on a pea.'

Eden opened the black leather purse and removed a gold cigarette case. Determinedly ignoring Marty, she took out a cigarette and tapped it on the metal to more firmly pack the tobacco. 'Does anybody have a light?' she inquired. Cappy tossed her a book of matches. Eden took one and raked its sulfur head across the sandpaper-rough strip. She carried the naked cigarette to her mouth while she held the match flame to it, the fancy holder abandoned. Making a face, Eden picked the loose bits of tobacco from her red lips.

Because of her gross misunderstanding of both the training situation and the type of accommodations available, Eden knew she was off to a bad start, both with the flying staff and her fellow trainees. But it only made her all the more determined to stick it out. Besides, roughing it for a while would be a lark. It wasn't as if she had to live under these spartan conditions forever. She took another puff of her cigarette, then crushed it out while she tried to pick the shreds of tobacco off the tip of her tongue.

As the flurry of interest her arrival had created faded, the others went back to their work. At the next cot, Cappy was drawing her sheets tightly across the mattress. Eden watched her a few minutes, then smiled to herself. She had never made a bed in her life . . . nor unpacked a trunk and put away her own clothes, for that matter.

'Hey, Cap.' Chicago frowned as she watched the brunette tightly tucking the ends in. 'Did your father teach you to make a bed like that? I bet you really could bounce a coin on it.'

'You can, I promise.'

'Would you show me how to do mine?' she asked.

Eden watched while Cappy instructed the others in the art of making beds the 'Army way,' then made an attempt at doing her own. The results were less than encouraging.

'Want some help?' Cappy asked, offering but not forcing her assistance on the redhead.

Eden straightened, faintly surprised by the friendly yet reserved gesture. 'Yes. Thank you, Miss Hayward.'

A wry smile quirked Cappy's mouth. 'Better make that Cappy, or plain Hayward. In the Army, manners and formality go by the wayside about as fast as privacy, so you'd better not wait for someone to pull out your chair or hold the door for you,' she advised as she showed Eden how to pull the bedsheets and blanket taut.

'I'll remember that,' Eden replied with a determined nod and worked to make the precise fold in the corner ends.

After some initial mistakes and ineptitude, Eden stepped back from the cot in satisfaction, the dark wool Army blanket stretched tightly, the covers turned precisely back, and the pillow situated squarely in the middle. She reached for her purse, now sitting atop the trunk with her fur coat and hat.

'Let's see if a coin will bounce on it.' She took out a dime and dropped it onto the cot. It hit the blanket and bounced into the air, then landed again with a small hop. The sense of triumph was followed by the sobering thought, 'I suppose we'll be expected to make the beds every day.'

'Every morning and checked before every inspection. The Army loves inspections,' Cappy warned dryly. 'Their motto is "A place for everything and everything in its place." And the Army doesn't have any place for personal mementos – photos, little keepsakes, or the like. They'll expect this bay to be spotless, and they'll inspect with white gloves to find out if it is.'

'I don't suppose they have –' Eden paused in mid-sentence as she looked around the narrow confines of the long bay, then responded to her own unasked question. 'No, I guess the Army wouldn't have cleaning ladies that come in and tidy up. We are they, I suppose.' She smiled in irony and joked, 'And Mother complains about the shortage of servants since the war started. They keep quitting to go to work in the factories.'

Cappy's mouth curved in a warm line, liking that self-mocking humor and what it told her about the redhead's character despite her privileged and affluent life style. 'Everyone wants to do their bit for the war.'

'God, don't I know it. Mother was always volunteering me for some new war project of hers,' she declared. 'Whether it was rolling bandages for the Red Cross, collecting "bundles for Britain" or . . . once, I even helped her haul wheelbarrows of dirt up to our penthouse apartment so she could have a victory garden on the balcony.'

'No blood donations?' Cappy grinned.

'Oh yes. Me, and every one of my friends as well as a few distant acquaintances,' Eden assured her. 'Dear Ham insisted he was becoming anemic from giving so much blood.'

'Ham?'

'Hamilton Steele.' Eden had an instant image of the unprepossessing man nearly twice her age with dark, thinning hair and gold wire glasses. The scion of an old established New York banking family, he had much to recommend him, no matter how staid and conservative he was. 'He's a dear man and a good friend. I probably would have married him if I hadn't met Jacqueline Cochran at the Christmas party my parents gave. At twenty-five, what else is left? I've done practically everything. Made my society debut, attended Vassar, and toured Europe. The only occupations someone of my social status is supposed to seek are marriage and motherhood – in that order. I was nearly bored and desperate enough to take the plunge.'

It was an empty life Eden described. Cappy could well understand her dissatisfaction with it. 'Is that how you found out about this flight training program for women – from Jacqueline Cochran?'

'Yes. As a matter of fact, her exploits are what prompted me to get my pilot's license. Flying is about the only thing that makes me feel alive.'

'I think all of us feel that way.'

For Eden, it was a feeling to which she clung. Her life had become much too riddled with cynicism, living as she did in a moneyed world. Everything, it seemed, had a purpose other than the one purported – even where the war was concerned. Like the 'Buy Bonds' drive, which was not really an attempt to fund the war. The intent of the Series E bonds, as her father was wont to assert, was to absorb the 'little man's dollars' and curb inflation. She saw the way the big businesses profited from defense contracts because they had the factories, the assembly plants, and the workers already in place to grind out the war machinery. The government had to make pragmatic decisions, and Eden could see that the rich got richer and the poor did a little better than before.

'Jacqueline Cochran painted an exciting picture of her program at the party,' Eden recalled while casting a disparaging glance at her stark quarters. 'But she did mislead me. She indicated I would be taking my training in Houston instead of some cowtown in the middle of nowhere. Our chauffeur is arriving with my car next week. Where will I go in it?'

'I don't know. But you can always look at it another way. Without the car, you'd be stuck here,' Cappy suggested, a small smile edging the corners of her mouth.

'You're absolutely right,' Eden agreed, laughing and liking the woman she'd be sleeping beside for the duration.

By late evening, nearly all talking had died. It was a travel-weary group that lounged on their cots. From the shower, Eden entered the bay wearing a rose satin robe with matching mules.

Cappy was the only one in the group not busily scribbling a letter. 'Not writing home?' Eden sank onto her cot and picked up a nail buff to shine her long, professionally manicured fingernails.

'No one to write to.' Cappy shrugged with apparent indifference. She had dropped her mother a short note, informing her that she had arrived safely, but she had no longtime friends.

'No one?' Eden frowned, vaguely curious. 'I thought you had a father in the Army.'

'I have a father but he doesn't have a daughter,' she replied, then paused to meet Eden's confused glance. 'He disowned me.'

'Good lord, why?'

'Because I came here.' Cappy hesitated, then with false indifference, continued. 'No daughter of his was going to fly for any quasi-military corps. Never mind that he taught me how to fly himself.'

'He'll get over it. Parents always do.'

'You don't know my father,' Cappy dryly countered. 'He couldn't have been more horrified if I had told him I was joining a traveling bordello.'

A smile briefly twisted Eden's mouth. 'That attitude isn't confined to your father. I've often heard mine say that intelligence is wasted on women. I suppose it harks back to that old belief that we can't be taken seriously – as pilots or anything else. Men might teach us how to fly as a cute novelty – rather like training a dog to sit up and beg – but they only want the trick performed when they say.'

'How true,' Cappy murmured with a very clear mental image of her father.

'And as for the military,' Eden continued, 'it's obviously a corrupting influence, because from what I hear in New York, a woman in uniform is somehow immoral.' Her dark eyes were agleam with mocking laughter. 'You put those two things together and this *is* about the equivalent of a traveling bordello in a lot of people's minds.'

Cappy laughed in her throat, losing some of her bitterness over the situation with her father. Still, the clash of personalities had been inevitable. Both of them were too strong-willed, and her father was too accustomed to imposing his authority. It was a long time since she had been the blindly obedient daughter, never questioning his orders.

From her cot, Marty paused in her letter-writing to watch the friendly interplay between Cappy and Eden down the row. They were talking in low tones so she hadn't heard what they were saying. What a group, Marty thought. Three cots down, Aggie was tying her hair in rag curlers, using a mirror propped on her cross-legged lap. This side of her, Chicago was lying on her back atop her cot, a knee bent and one leg bobbing in the air, matching the rhythm of her popping gum while she added pages to the voluminous letter she was writing home.

Eden van Valkenburg, Marty noticed, had slipped out of her satin robe and tossed it carelessly on top of the footlocker. As she turned back the covers on her cot, she kicked off her feathered mules. The matching rose satin nightgown could easily have passed for a low-cut evening gown. When Marty saw her slip on a ruffled sleeping mask in the same rose satin material, she couldn't help but shake her head.

'What a well-dressed trainee wears to bed,' she murmured under her breath, untroubled by her own plain blue pajamas.

In the next cot, Mary Lynn Palmer, petite and feminine in her baby-doll pajamas, looked up from the writing pad balanced on her knee. 'Did you say something, Marty?' She frowned.

'No.' The strong north wind sifted through the cracks around the windows and door, creating sudden drafts of cold air. 'God, this place is drafty,' Marty complained, suppressing a shiver.

'When summer comes, we'll probably be glad of that,' Mary Lynn predicted.

'Listen.' Marty cocked her head as the wind carried the sound of deep, singing voices. 'Do you hear that?'

'Yes.' Mary Lynn listened a minute. 'It must be those cadets in the next barracks.'

'I guess,' Marty agreed.

For long seconds, they listened to the indistinguishable melody until it trailed away on the wind. 'So far away from home,' Mary Lynn murmured in a subdued tone. Marty wasn't sure if she was referring to her husband overseas in England, the trainees next door, or themselves, but it didn't seem important.

'Yes,' she said simply and turned her attention back to the half-finished letter to her brother.

CHAPTER THREE

The sudden shrill blast of noise woke Eden from a deep sleep.

She sat bolt upright in bed and ripped off the satin

sleeping mask that covered her eyes. For an instant, the completely alien surroundings threw her; she didn't know where she was. Someone hit the light switch, and a pillow went sailing across the room at the culprit as Eden shielded her eyes against the sudden glare.

In the next cot, Cappy Hayward threw back the covers and swung her feet to the floor. 'Come on, you guys. Reveille. Rise and shine.'

When Eden tried to move, muscles stiffened by sleeping on the wretchedly uncomfortable cot ached in protest. Blinking at the still bright light, she forced her body to turn so she could sit on the side of the cot. Behind the green shades, the window panes were black.

'It's still dark outside.' The sleeping mask dangled from her hand. 'What time is it?' She flexed her shoulders and neck, arching them to ease the stiffness.

'Six fifteen,' someone answered, but Eden's mind wasn't functioning well enough to identify the voice.

Her groan was involuntary. Under her breath, she muttered, 'This is uncivilized.' Either no one heard her comment or else they all agreed with it.

'The bathroom!' It was Chicago who issued the panicked reminder of the facilities they shared with six other women. As she and the tall blonde charged the bathroom in their pajamas, Eden couldn't help thinking that the pieces of cloth tied in Aggie's hair resembled little white propellers all over her head.

'Better start getting dressed,' Cappy advised her, when Eden continued to sit on the edge of her cot, waiting for the grogginess to leave. 'We have to get the beds made and the bay cleaned up for inspection.'

'What time is that?' With a weary effort, Eden tilted her head back to blearily gaze at the brunette who seemed so knowledgeable about the routine.

'Breakfast formation is at six forty-five.'

She was slow to calculate the time. 'A half hour?!' Her eyes opened wide. 'But it takes me an hour just to put on makeup and do my hair!'

'It can't anymore,' Cappy replied with a look of sympathy.

With an effort, Eden stifled the impulse to declare it was barbaric to expect anyone to function at this hour of the morning, and pushed herself off the cot. No one else was complaining, so it seemed wisest to keep her own mouth shut.

In the mess hall proper, the women trainees filed by the steaming service troughs for their cafeteria-style breakfast, and proffered trays, sectioned by indentations to separate the food, to the kitchen help. As Aggie Richardson carried her trayful of food to one of the long tables, she paused to let the shorter Mary Lynn Palmer catch up with her. 'Real butter,' she marveled to her baymate. 'There's no rationing in the Army.'

'I know. I think I've forgotten what it tastes like.' Mary Lynn set her tray on the table and stepped over the bench to sit down.

The others in their group were only a few steps behind them. There was a lot of scraping and table-bumping before all of them were seated. Chicago looked around at the corps of female trainees occupying the mess hall.

'I thought we might see some of those cadets at breakfast this morning.' Disappointment edged the curiosity in her remark.

'Yeah. Where do you suppose they are?' Marty swept the mess hall with a frowning glance.

'You have about as much chance of seeing them as you do of catching a snipe,' Cap declared with indulgent mockery for their wishful thinking.

'Why?' Aggie wanted to know.

'Because the staff is going to arrange the schedules to keep us separated. You can bet if we're at one end of the field, they'll be at the other,' Cap predicted with a knowing light in her keen, blue eyes.

'I've never heard of anything so damned ridiculous.' The gravelly protest had escaped Marty's lips before she realized what she'd said. She cast a quick, guilty look around to see if she'd been caught swearing, but there was no one in authority within hearing. Marty continued with her thought. 'It doesn't make sense to make such an effort to keep us apart. Good heavens, their barracks are right across from ours.'

'But it's a no-man's-land in between,' Cap cautioned.

'Or maybe you should say "no woman's,"' Chicago suggested with a short laugh.

'Ha. Ha.' Marty forked a mouthful of scrambled eggs from her tray. Eden van Valkenburg was sitting across the table from her, nursing a cup of coffee and ignoring the lone piece of toast on her tray. 'Is that all you're eating?'

'I'm not hungry in the mornings.' She shrugged indifferently and fingered the unappetizing slice of toasted bread.

The tall, big-boned Aggie Richardson gazed at the sleekly fashionable redhead with undisguised envy. 'Gosh, you look fabulous this morning.'

Eden smiled in pleased surprise at the compliment. 'Thank you.'

'It's no wonder,' Marty inserted. 'You should have seen the mess she left in the sink when it finally was my turn to use it.'

'Sorry.' Her apology was slightly abrupt. Cleaning dirty sinks had always been the maid's job. She was expected to do more than make her own bed, she realized, and sobered at the thought of how much adjusting she had to do.

No dawdling over breakfast was allowed as the day began in earnest. At breakfast formation, the seventy-five women trainees were split into two groups, called flights. From their ranks, a flight lieutenant and section marchers were elected for each group. It was a flight lieutenant's duty to call her flight to breakfast formation in the mornings and command the section marchers who drilled them in columns, marching every place they went on the field.

Individuality was further smothered by the issuance of regulation flight gear. In addition to the leather battle jackets, the parachutes, flight caps, and goggles, they received standard Army knaki flight coveralls.

When they returned to the barracks later that day, Eden shook out the jumpsuit given to her and looked at the inside tag. 'These are men's coveralls,' she protested to the rest of her group.

Aggie had already unzipped the front of hers to try it on. As she stepped into it and pulled it up so she could put her arms through the sleeves, the others stared at the way it fit her six-foot frame. The shoulder seams extended two inches past the width of her shoulders and the material sagged around her legs and hips like a deflated balloon.

'It's too big,' Aggie said in surprise, while everyone else hastily tried on their own.

'Good grief, they look like those outlandish "zoot suits" the Mexicans are wearing in California,' Marty complained as she watched Eden struggle to tighten the belt on her flight suit so it would at least look as if she had a waist.

'Do you suppose they'll shrink?' Mary Lynn suggested hopefully.

'Maybe they will –' As Marty caught sight of the petite brunette, laughter exploded from her. The sleeves were so long they hid her hands, and the crotch hung down around her knees. Mary Lynn tried to take a step and tripped on the bottoms of the pants.

'They don't really expect us to wear these, do they?' Eden wondered for all of them.

Only Mary Lynn's appeal for a smaller suit was granted. The rest had to make do with what they were issued. The smaller-sized coveralls didn't improve the baggy fit of the style when Mary Lynn tried them on.

'Just call us the glamour girls,' Eden joked feebly while she fastened the straps of her parachute, which ran uncomfortably between her legs.

For the time being all they could do was grumble about the fit of the jumpsuits as they were again called to fall into formation. In ragged columns, they marched toward the flight line, slowly making the transition into a military unit.

A large, circular pool was located in the middle of the base. Its low sides were constructed of stone with a cement cap around the lip. In the center of the reflecting pool of water, a fountain rose out of a stone base. Word spread through the ranks identifying the pool as the Wishing Well. A scattering of coins shimmered in the bottom where the sunlight caught them. The male trainees here before them had tossed the coins for luck to ensure a satisfactory check ride.

But it was the planes parked along the flight line that generated the most excitement. The ready room, where they gathered to wait for the instructors to call them individually, had windows all along the front, facing the parked planes. A motley assortment of tables and chairs was scattered about the room for the use of the thirty-plus women trainees in the flight group, and a Coke machine stood in the corner to ease their dry-mouthed excitement. Marty's heart thumped against her ribs, betraying her eagerness. She'd never flown anything more powerful than her brother David's Piper Cub.

'Martha Jane Rogers!' A deep, male voice boomed her name, and she came to her feet, flinching at the dreaded use of her given name.

'Martha Jane?' Chicago laughed and slapped at Marty's leg when she passed by.

But it seemed unimportant as her legs stretched into long, eager strides to carry her across the ready room to the huskily stout man who had called her name. He was standing by the door with a clipboard in his hand, chewing on an unlit cigar. The earflaps on his cap were turned up, the straps dangling to create a comical sight, but the tough and unrelenting expression on his round, bulldog features didn't invite a smile.

'You Rogers?' He swept her with cold eyes.

'Yes, sir.' Marty pushed her chin out, refusing to be intimidated by his gruffness. 'Everyone calls me Marty.'

'I'm not everyone, Rogers,' he said flatly.

'No, sir.' She lowered her chin a fraction while her jaw

tightened and she struggled to contain the quick retort she wanted to make.

His attention appeared to shift to the clipboard. 'How come you sound so hoarse? Have you got a cold or something?'

'No, sir. I always sound like this,' Marty informed him.

He gave her a hard, short glance, then looked back at his clipboard. 'My name's Turner Sloane, and I'm going to be your instructor for this primary phase of your flight training. Any objections?'

'No, sir.' But she pulled in a deep breath to hold on to her patience and forced a pleasant smile on her mouth when he looked up.

'It wouldn't do you any good if you did.' He tucked the clipboard under his arm, then pushed his hands into his pockets.

'That's what I thought.' Marty's smile grew wider and lost its pleasantness as in silent disgust she watched him manipulating the fat cigar to the other side of his mouth. All the instructors were civilians, mostly pilots who were too old to qualify – like Turner Sloane – or who couldn't pass the stiff Army physical.

'That smart mouth is going to get you in trouble, Rogers.' He tilted his head back, his gaze narrowing, and Marty realized she was a good inch taller than he was.

'Yes, sir.' It was very difficult to keep her mouth shut. Even that response had a hint of sarcasm. Marty had a strong suspicion that he was deliberately needling her.

'Are you ready?' That cigar held between his teeth made every sentence come out in a kind of sneer.

'Yes, sir.' Her own militarily correct responses were beginning to grate on her nerves. But she wanted to fly, whether this man wanted to teach her or not.

He took the cigar out of his mouth to bark gruffly, 'Then get going.' As if this whole conversation had been her idea.

Swallowing the hot rush of temper, Marty used that fire of energy to push herself out the door ahead of him and into the coolness of a west Texas winter day. Outside, she pulled up to wait for him, her gaze running impatiently to the rows of nose-high aircraft parked on the hangar's apron, nearly thirty that Marty could see. The area was astir with activity, planes taxiing while instructors and trainees made their walk-around, or ground inspection to visually check the plane's airworthiness.

With a wave of his hand, Turner Sloane singled out the trainer they'd be flying. Marty suppressed the urge to run ahead and shortened her stride to keep pace with her slow-walking instructor, but her gaze devoured the plane.

That spurt of antagonism she'd felt toward her argumentative instructor was forgotten as she listened intently while he described the features of the Fairchild PT-19, its takeoff and landing speeds, its stalling characteristics, its cruising speed, fuel consumption and range. Marty stared at the low-winged plane with its open cockpits, the forward one for the pilot and the rear cockpit for the passenger, or in this case the instructor. A high charge of nervous excitement had her stomach churning and her hands itching for the feel of the stick. She trailed a hand along the edge of a wing. The metal almost seemed alive.

'Are you going to stand here gawking at the plane all day or what?' Sloane challenged her belligerently.

Stung by his mockery of her awe for the plane, Marty made a sharp denial. 'No.'

'Well, what are you waiting for? Climb up there in the front seat.' He jerked a hand toward the open cockpit.

Closing her mouth, Marty climbed onto the low wing and walked forward to the front seat. Awkwardly, she maneuvered herself into it, hampered by the bulky flight suit and the parachute straps between her legs. By the time she had buckled herself in, Sloane was standing on the wing. After he had shown her the location of the instruments and gone over the operations with her, he made sure she had on a helmet and earphones so she could hear his instructions from the rear seat above the engine noise.

'But what if I want to talk to you?' There was no microphone for her use.

'I am the teacher and you are the student. I do the talking and you do the listening,' he stated and didn't crack a smile. Marty held her tongue and stared at the instrument panel. It was becoming clear that this was not going to be fun. But if Turner Sloane thought that was going to dampen her enthusiasm for flying, he was greatly mistaken.

Within seconds after Turner Sloane climbed into the back seat of the open cockpit, he was barking in her ear. When the 175-horsepower engine roared to life, so much more airplane than she'd ever flown before, the vibrations added to the excited trembling of her own nerves. All her senses were alive, her perceptions heightened.

As they taxied away from the apron under Sloane's pilotage, Marty felt the movement of the jointly controlled rudder pedals under her feet. The tail-wheel aircraft had a typically nose-high attitude which made it next to impossible to see anything in front. He S'ed the plane down the taxi strip, curving left and right in order to have a view of what was ahead of them.

The hammering voice in her ear constantly reminded Marty that she wasn't along for the ride. But she was all concentration as he aimed the plane down the center of the runway. The roll was begun, the engine thundering with full throttle and the wheels bouncing roughly over the ground as the plane gathered speed. Her throat tightened as she kept watching the airspeed indicator.

Then came that moment when the vibrations stopped and as the plane lifted off the ground the engine roared smoothly. All the anxieties and tensions seemed to fall away from her. Marty smiled with the utter calm and confidence that filled her.

The sensation of speed abated as the plane climbed effortlessly into the high, gray sky, staying well below the cloud ceiling. The altimeter needle rotated, marking off the altitude they gained in hundreds of feet. The small, dusty town of Sweetwater lay to the east. Marty spied the gypsum plant and a small refinery, highly visible landmarks in this west Texas terrain of mesquite and greasewood.

The stick pressed against her knee as the plane banked to the north. Below her, all the roads seemed to have been laid by a compass, running either north-south or east-west. It was a country meant for flying, with a lot of open sky.

After the plane had attained the desired altitude, Turner Sloane leveled it out. They had reached one of the practice areas. Two other PT-19s were already in the vicinity, doing maneuvers.

'All right, Rogers, you take the stick,' ordered the rough voice in her earphones. 'I want you to make a simple, slow turn to the right.'

There was a surge of adrenaline through her system as her hand gripped the stick between her legs. That exhilarating sense of power was nearly all-consuming when Marty gently banked the plane to the right and felt its instant response. When the turn was complete, she smoothly brought the wings back level with the horizon.

'What's the matter, Rogers?' came the caustic voice. 'Was that too hard for you? You lost thirty feet in altitude, and the ball never saw the center of the turn-and-bank indicator. Try it again, and this time use some rudder.'

So it went, with Turner Sloane finding fault with everything she did. Marty felt as green as a raw beginner. It was one of the most frustrating experiences in her life.

Less than an hour later she heard, 'That's enough for today, Rogers,' ordered in a voice that sounded riddled with exhausted patience. 'Take a heading back to the field.' For a split second, Marty froze. Her head swiveled in panic while she tried to get her bearings. 'What's the matter, Rogers? Are you lost?'

'When he said that to me' – Marty's hands were doubled into fists as she recounted the story to her baymates – 'I wanted to take those earphones and jam them right up his –'

'Careful, Marty,' Mary Lynn cautioned her.

'– butt,' she offered as a concession.

'Did you know where you were?' Aggie questioned.

'I knew the field was somewhere to the south, so I just turned the plane in that direction and crossed my fingers. Luckily, I saw the smoke from the refinery and managed to zero in on the field after that,' Marty explained with a rueful expression for the whole misadventure. 'I think I would have flown in any direction before admitting to Sloane that I wasn't sure where the field was. I don't know why I ended up with such a hard ass for an instructor.'

'My instructor made it quite clear that I shouldn't expect any special treatment just because I'm a woman.' Cap tapped the ash off her cigarette. 'They're probably going to go to the opposite extreme to make sure they aren't accused of it.'

'Do you think that's it?' Eden curled a leg beneath her as she sank onto her cot. 'I wondered if the problem was the fact that we aren't paying for our own training. If we were customers hiring them to train us, we'd be treated with more respect.'

'But it wouldn't make them like us any better,' Marty pointed out.

'I don't know.' Chicago frowned and shifted uncomfortably, appearing slightly self-conscious. 'I didn't have any trouble with Mr Lentz. He was real nice to me.'

'Yeah, I saw you two when you taxied back to the hangar.' Aggie poked the short-haired brunette in the ribs. 'He helped her down off the wing and everything,' she told the rest of the girls with a big wink.

'Look! Chicago is blushing.' Marty drew everyone's attention to the dots of color in her cheeks.

'Come on,' Chicago protested. 'He was just being polite.'

'You seemed to have an awful lot to talk about,' Aggie teased. 'You stood out there in the cold a good ten minutes.'

'He used to live in Chicago when he was a little boy – in the same suburb where I live. He was just asking me about some of the old places he remembered.'

'Is he married?' Marty asked.

'No –' Chicago stopped abruptly when she saw the glints of laughter in their expressions. She reddened even more. 'He just happened to mention it,' she insisted.

'Just happened to mention it,' Marty repeated with teasing mockery. 'What does this paragon of gentlemanly virtue look like? Tall, dark, and handsome, I'll bet.' When Chicago showed signs of reluctance, Marty urged, 'You tell us, Aggie.'

'Well, he's about five foot eight or nine. He's got a good build, not too skinny and not too stout,' Aggie began. 'With that cap on it was hard to tell, but I think his hair was brown. His eyes were brown, too . . . or were they blue? I can't remember. Which were they, Chicago?'

It was an obvious trap. Chicago glanced around the room, then a faint smile touched her lip corners. 'Blue,' she said and they all laughed. 'But for all the good it does, they might as well be purple. They made it pretty plain to us today that we aren't allowed to socialize with our instructors.'

'Rules are made to be broken, honey,' Eden inserted in a silken voice. 'The trick is, don't get caught.'

'Is that the voice of experience talking?' Marty challenged.

'Of course.' Eden tipped her head back, exposing the creamy arc of her throat, and blew a stream of cigarette smoke upwards.

'Getting into trouble is a lot easier than getting out of it . . . I suppose, unless you can buy your way out of it,' Marty retorted with acid sweetness.

'Don't be so testy, Marty,' Cap inserted grimly.

'How come you're always sticking up for her?' Marty demanded.

'I'm not,' she retorted impatiently, then noticed Mary Lynn pulling on her flight suit. She took advantage of the chance to change the subject. 'What are you doing?'

'I'm going to find out whether this thing will shrink.' She zipped the oversized garment all the way up to her chin, and looked at the others. 'Anyone for the showers?'

'Hey! That's a great idea!' Chicago seized on the suggestion and hauled out her own flight suit to put it on.

Before it was over, six pairs of coveralls were hanging on the clothesline in back of the barracks. Judging by the number of dripping wet khaki coveralls already hanging on other lines, the idea wasn't a unique one.

CHAPTER FOUR

Four days later bay doors were standing open, crowded with female trainees. More women were hanging out the double-hung windows, bottom sashes fully raised. Their low, laughing voices had a conspiratorial sound as they made jocund comments, looking across the Texas-red ground, sparsely covered with scrub grass between the long gray barracks.

A deeper rumble of voices came from the direction of the opposite barracks. The roofs were extended into wide overhangs that shielded the concrete walkways abutting the buildings to create a military version of galleried walks. A straggly male group of enlisted trainees shuffled toward their assigned bays, dressed in their flight suits with parachute packs slung over their shoulders. There was a dragging tiredness about them that didn't stop them from smiling and flirting across the distance with the bevy of women who were making their own assessment of the men.

'Say, girls!' A tall, lanky airman with a thatch of light brown hair all askew from his helmet and goggles called to them. The long white scarf tied around his neck gave him a somewhat dashing air. 'Why don't you come over?' The invitation was seconded by a chorus of his buddies.

'Yeah, birds of a feather should flock together,' another shouted.

Another one added his voice. 'Wanta flock?'

'Can't.' Marty's distinctive voice lifted in answer. 'We aren't allowed to socialize.'

'That's a rotten shame,' the first retorted.

'it sure as hell is,' she agreed. Beside her, Cap groaned under her breath.

Then, suddenly, a stern voice was saying, 'You just earned your first demerits, Rogers.' A quick pivot and Marty found herself confronted with a staff officer. With a stern clap of the hands, all the trainees were called to order. 'Okay, girls, fall in. Volleyball time.'

As they trudged into marching columns, stifling groans, Marty glanced across the way at the tall cadet who lingered in his bay doorway to watch. Her shoulders lifted in a barely perceptible shrug of resignation. His mouth curved upwards at the corners.

By the conclusion of the first full week, a grueling pattern had begun to take shape. The new trainees attended five hours of ground school daily, the primary phase consisting of courses in mathematics, physics, aerodynamics, engine operations, and navigation. They also spent four hours daily on the flight line. And their spare time was taken up with a regimen of calisthenics, volleyball, or baseball.

Exhaustion was dulling some of the shiny newness of the adventure, but their enthusiasm for flying was undampened. It was a quiet group that lounged about the bay preparing for an early night, their hangar-flying talk finished. The initial discomfort about undressing in front of each other was a thing of the past; Chicago pattered around the bay in her underclothes and bare feet, carrying the robe she had intended to put on and forgot. Mary Lynn was curled up on her cot, busy writing her nightly letter to her husband.

Sitting cross-legged on her cot, Cappy was sectioning off strands of her silky brown hair and wrapping them around her finger into tight curls, then securing them to her head with one of the war-precious bobby pins she held clamped between her lips. Eden gathered up her towels and cosmetics case with its jars of creams and lotions, and headed for the bathroom for her nightly beauty routine.

Marty observed her departure. 'She's so soft and squeaky clean, I don't know how she stands the rest of us.' Her arm was hooked around her upraised knee, pulling it to her chest while she puffed on a cigarette. Then her thoughts drifted to another pet peeve. 'I thought this was supposed to be a civilian organization, so what's all this Army discipline about?' she grumbled, indirectly grousing about what was rapidly becoming known as Marty's 'damned demerits.' 'We march here and we march there; it's regulation this and regulation that. Orders, all the time.'

'How else are they going to keep control without a punishment system?' Cap reasoned, removing the bobby pins from her mouth long enough to talk. 'We've got them outnumbered. They need something to hold over our heads to keep us in line.'

'I hate logic.' Marty, already in her pajamas, flopped backwards onto her pillow and blew smoke at the ceiling.

There was a rustling of sound outside the window, soft scurrying and whispering. Marty sat up on her elbows to stare at the door, her head cocked at a listening angle. The others, too, had heard it and strained to identify it. There was a very faint, light tap on their door, a single knuckle knocking. Marty was on her feet in an instant, pulling on her robe as she strode to the door, the half-smoked cigarette dangling from one side of her mouth. With her hand on the knob, she leaned close to the door jamb.

'Who is it?' she demanded in a low murmur.

'Turn out the light and let us in,' came the roughly whispered response.

'Lights out, everybody,' Marty warned before she plunged the bay into darkness. Aggie squealed in protest. 'Shh,' she hissed, then carefully opened the door a crack. Three figures sprang out of the darkness and slipped in quick succession through the narrow opening.

'Who is it? Who's there?' Chicago demanded and pulled

out her flashlight to shine it on the trio who had dropped down to hug the wall just inside the door.

The beam illuminated the dirt-darkened faces of three grinning cadets, centering on the lean-faced ringleader with his shock of sun-bleached brown hair. 'Don't get scared, girls. We thought with all this training we ought to practice a little nighttime reconnoitering in case we find ourselves bailing out over enemy territory.'

'Good thinking.' Amusement riddled Marty's voice.

'It's lucky that we found friendlies straight off, wasn't it?' His audacious smile broadened, creating parenthetical grooves in his lean cheeks. 'I'm Colin Fletcher. The guy on the right is Art Grimsby, and the other one's Morley Tyndall.'

Their initial surprise over, the girls crowded around the door next to which the men squatted. There was a confusion of hand-shaking as they introduced themselves, talking over each other in a jumble of voices.

'We raided the kitchen before coming here,' Colin said, and he produced a cloth-covered basket. 'Since you couldn't come over for drinks with us the other day, we thought we'd share this little snack with you.'

The cloth was turned back and a warm smell drifted upwards. Chicago breathed it in. 'Hamburgers,' she declared in a mock swoon.

The basket was ceremoniously passed around for each to help herself. 'Where did you get them?' Marty asked, taking the first bite.

'Mom fixed them for us,' the dark-haired, pale-skinned Art Grimsby replied. 'She's a sweet old lady. Calls us her "boys."'

'A regular dear heart,' Morley agreed. 'Even gave us some Cokes. I'm afraid we'll have to drink it out of the bottles, though. She wouldn't spring for any glasses.'

'Here you go.' Colin opened one of them and handed it to Marty. His hazel eyes seemed to single her out from the others. It piqued her interest as she made a closer study of his face in the dim pool of light cast by the flashlight. A

79

shock of wheat-brown hair fell across his high forehead, nearly hiding it. The straight bridge of his nose was long and narrow, matching the high ridges of his cheekbones. But she was more attracted by the devilish glint in his eyes than by his aristocratic features.

'Do you do this sort of thing often?' Marty wondered if other bays had entertained these cadets.

'We had no reason until you girls moved onto base,' he acknowledged. 'We couldn't believe our luck. How many cadets get to share an airfield's facilities with female trainees?'

'Right. We celebrated when we heard you were coming,' Art Grimsby asserted.

They lapsed into a discussion of planes, flying techniques, instructors, and ground school courses, with the cadets warning the girls of the difficulties in the advanced stages of training. When their eagerness to share knowledge and show experience had passed, the conversation took a personal turn, delving into lives and backgrounds.

'I'm from Pensacola,' Colin said in response to a question. 'My parents still live there . . . in a big old house on the Gull. That's where I learned to fly. But you know the Army. They sent me over to England, had me on a ground crew, then decided maybe they could use my flying talents and sent me back here for training.'

Mary Lynn spoke from the shadowed edge of the light pool. She leaned into view, her features subdued. 'My husband is assigned to a squadron stationed at an airfield somewhere in England. He's a bomber pilot. B-17s.'

'What's his name?' His thoughtful look narrowed on the petite southern woman, a hint of compassion showing in its depths. 'Maybe I know him.'

'Beau. Beau Palmer.' In a breathless rush, she gave him the squadron group.

He let it run through his mind, then slowly shook his head. 'Sorry. I don't think I met him.'

All week Mary Lynn had seemed subdued, spending most of her time gazing at the photo of Beau. Of the whole lot, Mary Lynn was unquestionably the most lonely. But, then, she was the only one who had a husband far away. No one else in the group had a steady boy friend, except Eden, if Hamilton Steele could be called that.

The connecting door to the bath opened, spilling light into the bay. The tall, shapely form of Eden van Valkenburg stood silhouetted in the opening, motionless at the blinding darkness of the room.

'What is this? Who turned out the lights?' she demanded.

'For godsake, keep your voice down.' Marty rasped the warning. 'Hurry up and shut the door.'

As soon as Eden shut out the light from the bathroom, Chicago directed the flashlight beam at her so she could see to cross the room and join the group. Her face was bare of any makeup and a turban was wrapped around her head, hiding her russet-red hair. Marty groused to herself over the way Eden could look so wretchedly perfect, so nakedly beautiful in her shimmering satin robe.

'Well, well. Why didn't someone tell me we had visitors?' Eden remarked, smiling vaguely as she sank gracefully onto the floor beside an Army cot, using it as a back rest. Introductions were made, then apologies rendered since all the hamburgers and Coca-Colas had been consumed. Stories were reiterated, including Colin's. 'You were in England?' Eden remarked.

Colin nodded. 'Yes.'

'I adore London.' When she took a pack of cigarettes from her cosmetic case, the three Army cadets scurried through their pockets in search of a match.

'Have you been there?' Art Grimsby scored the victory, struck the match and suddenly illuminated the semidarkness.

Eden bent her head to the flame, then straightened to blow aside the inhaled smoke. 'Dozens of times. Not recently, of course. I think the last time' – she paused to recall – 'was shortly after I almost eloped with Nicky, our chauffeur. I used to go to a great nightspot – some crazy pub on the waterfront along the Thames. It was called the Boar and Hound, or some such thing. Do you know it?' she asked Colin, a nostalgic gleam in her eye.

'The one with the stuffed boar's head behind the bar, a huge tusker?' At Eden's affirmative nod, he said, 'I believe it was called simply the Boar's Head.'

'What an incredible coincidence! You've actually been there, too!' she said with amazement. 'I used to close that place nightly –'

'*Was* called the Boar's Head?' Marty picked up on Colin's past tense usage and the solemnness of his expression. Eden paused to stare at him as the significance of Marty's comment penetrated.

'That whole section of the waterfront was bombed out by the Jerries,' he stated.

The bay fell into silence. Eden suppressed a shiver at the icy cold finger that ran down her spine. The war suddenly had a reality beyond the headlines and the newsreel footage, or even her mother's many war-related social activities. So many ecstatic memories had been wrapped up in that English pub. To learn it no longer existed, the entire block destroyed, never again to be visited, leaving only mental images which would eventually fade from the mind, was sobering. War killed – people, places, feelings.

Colin looked at his watch. 'It's getting late.' He glanced at his buddies. 'It's time we were getting back.'

'Yes, before they do a bed check and discover we're missing.' Morley tried to inject some levity into an atmosphere that had grown heavy.

Marty untangled her long legs and pushed to her feet. 'Let me check and make sure it's all clear.'

They doused the flashlight as Marty opened the door and stuck her head outside. The sky was ashine with stars, thousands glittering on a velvet blue backdrop. The night's silence had settled on the column of barracks. She looked up and down the long row of buildings that faced each other. The only visible signs of life were the yellow patches of light gleaming from the windows, isolated spots of brightness in the dark shadows of the covered walkways. Nothing stirred.

Marty motioned for their forbidden male guests to join her at the door. With silent stealth, they came to her side and took their own cautious look out the door. One by one they squeezed through the narrow opening and immediately ducked down to hug the shadows. Colin was the last to leave. His narrow features were a blur in the darkness, but Marty sensed he was looking at her when he paused half in and half out of the doorway.

'Be careful,' she urged in a hoarse whisper.

'We'll do that,' he murmured. 'With your permission, we'll pop over again some time.'

His buddies were hissing at him to hurry. 'Sure.' Marty gave him a little push out the door, then rejoined her quiet baymates still huddled on the floor. She eyed Eden curiously. 'Were you serious about eloping with your chauffeur?'

'Unfortunately, yes.' Her mouth curved with a faint smile. 'I was going through what my father called my "plebeian" phase.' Her self-mockery was so evident, it encouraged the others to smile along with her. 'Luckily I realized that I was only marrying him to make an anti-money statement. But the more I thought about it, the more unwilling I became to give up my charge account at Saks . . . so I changed my mind about running away with him.'

'What happened?' Aggie was all agog over this peek into Eden's past.

'Daddy found out and fired him.'

'How insensitive can you get?' Marty demanded in mild outrage. 'A man loses his bride and his job all in one blow.'

'Anyway' – Eden liked a shoulder in a dismissing shrug – 'after that sobering experience, Daddy sent me off to Europe.'

'Alone?' Chicago asked.

'Yes.'

'I'm surprised he trusted you,' Marty murmured dryly.

'We flew to London first –' Eden began.

'Wait a minute,' Marty halted her. 'You just said you went alone. Who is "we"?'

'My maid and my secretary, of course,' she replied very matter-of-factly, as if it should have been obvious. A second later, Eden realized how very snobbish that sounded. 'I always traveled with a small retinue . . . until I came here. I haven't been very successful at getting you girls to wait on me.' She laughed at her own joke.

'It isn't all that funny,' Marty asserted when the others laughed with her. 'Thanks to her, our bay hasn't passed inspection yet, or have you forgotten? She's always leaving things lying around somewhere, expecting one of us to pick up after her.'

'Old habits die hard.' Her light response made a joke out of Marty's criticism. 'As I was saying, we flew to London, where I met Rinaldo, my expatriated Italian count. Three days later he proposed. It was another abortive engagement, however, but great fun while it lasted.'

'You were engaged to a real count?' Again it was Aggie who asked, expressing a typically American awe at a title.

'Yes. In this case, the tables were turned though. You see, Rinaldo's properties and bank accounts had been confiscated by the Italian Fascist Government for some trumped-up reason. And he wanted to marry me so he could live in the style to which *he* had become accustomed.' Eden dropped the burning butt of her cigarette into a Coke bottle, hearing it sizzle when it encountered the scant liquid in the bottom.

'That was a bit cheeky of him, wasn't it?' Cappy suggested dryly.

'The last I heard he was consort to one of Britain's titled ladies, who shall remain nameless,' Eden jested.

During the next week, Eden's chauffeur arrived with her car, a canary-yellow roadster with a convertible top and white leather interior. Unfortunately they weren't permitted off the field yet, so they couldn't take it out for a ride. And the cadets made two more late-night visits to the bay, staying later each time. After the last, Mary Lynn stumbled to her cot, weak with fatigue.

'The next time, tell your midnight Lotharios to come earlier,' she complained to Marty. 'Some of us would like to get some sleep.'

When reveille sounded the next morning, Mary Lynn pulled a pillow over her ears. It seemed as though only a few minutes had gone by before Cap cracked one eye open to look at the clock. She yelped the alarm as she sprang out of bed. But it was too late. All of them were late for formation.

As far as Cappy was concerned, the day went downhill after that. She wasn't prepared for the physics exam, which she was certain she failed. And there were no letters for her at mail call. Her mother had written once but that was all. It was a lonely feeling not to be remembered while others were exclaiming over their letters from home. But she didn't let it show, and if anyone guessed, it was Eden. The two of them stood off to one side and smoked, listening while others read aloud snatches from their letters.

Things seemed just as bleak when she took to the air. She was either using too much rudder in her chandelle maneuvers or not enough. She was not quick enough applying throttle in her stall recoveries. All she heard from Rex Sievers, her instructor, was criticism; never once did he raise his voice to her, but his grim tone of disapproval couldn't have been more crushing. When he cut the session short and ordered her to make a full stop landing, Cappy knew her incompetence had finally exasperated him. Utterly dejected, she taxied to the hangar area.

With the switch off, the spinning propeller blade slowed its revolutions to a stop. Cappy made slow work of going over the checklist to shut down the plane, dreading the moment when she had to literally face her instructor.

When he walked up the wing to the forward cockpit she occupied, Cappy didn't give him a chance to tell her what an abominable job she'd done. 'I don't know what's the matter with me,' she said in self-disgust. 'I can fly better than that.'

'I know you can, Hayward,' he agreed. 'And you're going to have to do it, starting now.'

'I know,' she murmured, her head still hanging low.

'From this moment, Hayward,' he re-emphasized his last phrase.

She lifted her head to stare at him, hardly daring to believe the implication. 'Solo?' The smiling glitter in his eyes confirmed her guess. All the poise that usually protected her disintegrated to expose her insecurities.

'You can do it, Hayward.' He winked and slapped the edge of the cockpit. 'She's all yours.'

A wide smile broke across her face as she unconsciously snapped him a salute. 'Yes, sir!'

Minutes later, she was skimming through the skies in the sleek, low-wing trainer. The blood in her veins pounded with the roar of the engine as the singing wind rushed by the open cockpit. All alone with the clouds, Cappy was filled to bursting.

It was like a dream. Right rudder down, stick back and eased to the right, the PT-19 soared into a steep climbing turn. At the top of it, when the wings grew heavy with a near-stall, Cappy gently straightened out of the turn and let the nose come down, and again, she and the plane were sliding effortlessly through the air. Chandelles. Lazy eights. Soaring and swooping in graceful turns like a leaf curling in the wind. Up here in the open-cockpit trainer, she was alone, completely alone with the wind and the sun on her face while she touched the sky. The solitude felt good and full, not lonely. An intimacy existed between her and the plane, the sleek trainer responding to her slightest touch. There was an ecstasy in it that could not be explained, only experienced.

When the runways of Avenger Field came in sight, Cappy contained a sigh and entered the traffic pattern. Her hands grew sweaty on the stick, and she wiped first one, then the other, on the baggy pants of her zoot suit. As she turned on her base leg, perpendicular to the runway, a family of tumbleweeds rolled onto the strip. She extended her turn onto final rather than risk fouling her landing gear or prop with the errant tumbleweeds.

The windsock sat at an angle to the runway, indicating a crosswind. The runways at Avenger Field did not seem to be laid out with the prevailing winds in mind. Takeoffs and landings were rarely made squarely into the wind. It seemed to always come at an angle, as now. On her final approach, Cappy crabbed the plane into the wind to hold a straight line to the runway. She kept her eyes alert for the appearance of a dust devil, those tiny cyclones capable of tipping a wing. The wheels of her landing gear touched down and rolled smoothly onto the ground while her tail slowly settled until its wheel met the ground in a textbook-perfect landing.

Back at the hangar area, Rex was waiting for her. His freckled face was split with a smile that went ear to ear. Hardly able to contain her own excitement, Cappy scrambled out of the plane and hopped off the wing, taking off goggles and helmet to shake her dark hair out to the wind. With swift, running strides, she hurried to her instructor, beaming with that inner thrill of accomplishment.

'I did it.' She stopped in front of him, her body straining with the urge for physical contact.

'You sure did. Congratulations, Hayward.' He took her hand and squeezed it between both of his, then held on to it. 'You are one of the best damned natural pilots I've ever seen. You try too hard once in a while, but you're going to be one of the best.'

Tears stung her eyes. For a minute, she couldn't see. She turned her head aside, lowering it while she blinked to clear away the blur.

It hurt that she had no one with whom she could share that compliment or the elated pride she felt. It would mean nothing to her mother, and her father wouldn't care. Yet, if she'd been a boy, right now he would have been bursting with pride. It wasn't fair.

'Thank you.' But her voice rang hollow. With her head

lifted once again, Cappy pushed her chin out and managed a distant smile. Puzzlement flickered across Rex's expression. But doors always closed when anyone saw too much or came too close to Cappy.

Mary Lynn soloed that same afternoon. When the rest of the trainees learned of their milestone, the two girls were dragged from their bay and hauled to the Wishing Well for a baptismal dunking.

Cappy was the first to be thrown into the three-foot-deep water, dumped head first, zoot suit and all. 'Grab some money!' one of the girls shouted as Cappy was going under. According to custom, the coins thrown into the pool for luck could be retrieved by those who had earned the privilege of being dunked. She surfaced, gasping with the shock of the cold water. When she opened her hand, a copper penny lay in her wet palm. Shivering, she scrambled out, aided by Eden's helping hand, which had also pushed her in. Then it was Mary Lynn's turn. In her letter to Beau that night, she wrote:

. . . They wanted to throw my two pillows in the pool with me, but Marty rescued them before they got wet. I managed to scoop up a dime and a British pee or pence, I guess they call it. One of the cadets from the UK must have thrown it into the well before a check ride. It immediately made me feel I was sharing the moment with you, darling. I'm going to keep the coin for luck – luck for me and for you.

Tomorrow we're finally going to be allowed to go into town. They've had us confined to the Field. I have some shopping I want to do, and I hope I can find some little souvenirs of Texas that I can send home.

I miss you, Beau.

All my love,
Mary Lynn

CHAPTER FIVE

Downtown Sweetwater, Texas, was only a few streets wide. The women trainees from Avenger Field flooded the business district of the small cattle community, splintering into groups composed of baymates.

'Lord God above, please let there be a hairdresser in this town,' Eden murmured as the six of them piled out of her bright yellow car and headed down the street.

'To hell with a hairdresser,' Marty retorted. 'If you're going to ask for something, make it worthwhile.'

'Like what? A drink?' Chicago suggested with a laugh.

'This may be a dry county, but you can bet there's some bootleg to be had if you know who to ask,' Marty declared. 'Colin's hinted as much to me.'

'I want to go in here.' Mary Lynn headed for the entrance to a small shop, and the others trooped along with her. 'You don't have to come with me, if you don't want to.'

'Maybe the clerk will be able to tell me where I can find someone to fix my hair,' Eden said.

All six of them invaded the shop, splitting to go down the aisles and investigate the merchandise. On the street outside, a big truck lumbered to a stop at the corner, pulling close to the curb. The trailer of the semi was fitted with long board seats to haul its human cargo and its slatted sides for ventilation earned it the nickname 'cattle truck.' As it disgorged its occupants, Marty recognized the tall sandy-haired cadet.

'Colin's in town.' She nodded to direct Cappy's attention to the handful of cadets coming their way.

Colin was in the middle of the boisterous, laughing group as it drew level with the gift shop. His hands were hitched in the side pockets of his trousers. Marty rapped on the glass window that separated them, attracting his attention, and waved. Given to impulsive behavior, she never thought twice about the possibility that a friendly gesture might be considered too forward. This nonsense about waiting for the man to make the first move had never made sense to her.

When Colin saw her, a crooked smile immediately broke across his features. He came up short, back-pedaling a step or two while the group flowed around him. Voices were raised in razzing comments that Marty couldn't quite hear when Colin separated from the group and approached the shop entrance.

The bell above the shop door tinkled when he entered. Marty turned expectantly to meet him, but before he could take a step in her direction, he was intercepted by the brown-haired salesgirl.

'Colin Fletcher, I was hopin' you'd stop in.' Her voice fairly gushed with delight, its nasal twang thickening with the dripping sweetness.

Quickly recovering from his initial start of blankness, Colin flashed her one of his winning smiles. 'Hello, Sally,' he said warmly, but his glance flitted by her to Marty, his eyes betraying a dry patience at the interruption. Marty's eyebrows arched in amusement over his situation.

'Momma would like you to come over tonight for supper.' All that eagerness in the invitation was positively cloying, as far as Marty was concerned. It was all she could do to conceal her reaction, steadfastly looking away so she wouldn't break into chortling laughter. 'We're havin' some friends over for homemade ice cream. I . . . Momma . . . knows how much you like it so she said for me to be sure and ask you over if I saw you today.'

'That's most thoughtful of your mother,' Colin acknowledged, and Marty glanced sideways so she could see how he was going to handle it. That dry, dashing charm was in evidence as he smiled at the girl. 'Unfortunately, some of us have already made other plans for the evening.'

'Oh.' Disappointment seemed to sag through her. 'You

will come to Sunday dinner tomorrow after church, as usual, won't you?'

'Naturally, I will.' He inclined his head in an affirmative nod, warmly polite but sufficiently aloof to discourage too much familiarity. 'I couldn't let a weekend pass without enjoying your mother's cooking, now could I?'

'No.' But it was plain, his explanation was not the one she wanted to hear. After a short hesitation, she added, 'If you change your mind about tonight, you're welcome to come anyway.'

'Thank you.'

There was an awkward moment while the sales clerk waited for Colin to say something more to continue the conversation, but he remained silent, regarding her with obvious forbearance. Mary Lynn stepped over to the cash register, giving the girl an excuse to move away. Colin looked after her for a moment with an expression of amused indulgence before he leisurely strolled over to Marty.

At the counter Mary Lynn was asking, 'Do you have a box or something I can pack these in for mailing?'

There was an attractive glitter in his hazel eyes when Colin stopped in front of Marty. 'We finally meet in broad daylight,' he remarked softly. 'With no dark corners the flashlight can't reach.'

'No slinking through the shadows.' Marty went along with his thought, but she was conscious of the hotly jealous look she was receiving from the sales clerk. Obviously Sally regarded Colin as her property, and Marty was poaching.

'The sunlight becomes you.' His mouth slanted with a crooked smile.

'Enough flattery, Colin, or I'll start to believe you.'

'Since this is your first trip to town . . . ladies' – he expanded his comment to include her other baymates within earshot – 'you should have an escort to show you the sights.'

'Sorry.' Eden was the first to turn down his invitation. 'I have the name of a woman who fixes hair. If I'm lucky, she'll

91

be able to do something with these nails of mine, too.'

Mary Lynn begged off with the excuse she had more shopping to do. Aggie and Chicago had some errands to finish, which left only Marty and Cappy to accept the invitation. Eden submitted to arm-twisting and promised to catch up with them later at the Bluebonnet Hotel.

'Where is it?' she asked.

'You can't miss it,' Colin replied. 'It's the only hotel in town.'

With Cappy on one arm and Marty on the other, Colin went swinging out of the shop as the little doorbell tinkled merrily. Their tour of the town, what there was of it, was periodically delayed by groups of cadets or other female trainees they met along the way. The size of their party fluctuated as others joined them for a block or two, then parted for some other destination.

The downtown businesses were grouped around the courthouse square – Sweetwater was the seat of Nolan County. Once they had strolled the square's perimeters and wandered its peripheral feeder streets, they stopped at the USO Club, but Marty and Cappy were refused entrance. All three of them left and ventured into more residential areas. After Colin had pointed out six of Sweetwater's ten churches, Marty suggested they save the remaining four for another time. He took them to the city park located at the north edge of town on Lake Sweetwater. He assured them they would hallucinate about this man-made body of water when the mercury soared to one hundred degrees in April and stayed there until September. Where the scrub growth encroached on the park, he regaled them with tales of dark-of-night assignations with the local bootlegger, a seedy old granny, as his story went.

The sun was resting on the lip of the horizon, igniting the sky with its copper-pink glow, when they arrived at the Bluebonnet Hotel. One of the cadets had rented a suite at the Bluebonnet where they could all congregate. The suite, as it turned out, consisted of two adjoining rooms with a connecting door.

92

Word spread of a party in progress. Soon there was a constant flux of trainees and cadets flowing in and out of the rooms and spilling into the outer hall. Cigarette smoke thickened the air while Coca-Cola bottles clanked. A cadet from Colin's barracks arrived with a bottle of clear liquid tucked inside his jacket. He produced it with a little flourish amidst the cheers of those who recognized the illicit liquor for what it was. While the bottle made a cola-spiking circle of the room, the cadet told them the spooky story of his eerie meeting in the mesquite brush with the lady bootlegger.

As many as eight or nine crowded onto the hotel beds at one time, virtually the only sitting area in the rooms. More camped on the floor, sitting cross-legged or with knees pulled up to their chests, while others leaned against walls. There was no clear pathway, so any movement meant stepping over bodies. Competition for the softer seats on the bed was keen. To leave the bed was to lose your place and free-for-alls erupted intermittently as others vied to claim space.

The roisterous clamor of loud, laughing voices filled the smoke-heavy hotel rooms. Marty was one of the lucky ones to have a seat on the bed, curled at the top with the headboard at her back. The pillow was long gone, in use somewhere as a cushion against the hard floor. Colin had a narrow edge of the bed near her, his long legs drawn up under him.

Marty poked a finger into her cigarette pack but it was empty. 'Damn.' She crumpled the pack with a mixture of irritation and disgust. 'I never smoked so much until I came here,' she said to Colin. 'My mother would have a hissy-fit if she saw the way I puff on them. She's very midwestern. According to her, nice girls don't smoke. 'Course, according to her, nice girls don't do a lot of things.'

'Parents are like that. They'd like us to believe they never did anything improper.' He dug into his breast pocket and took out a stubby, thin, hand-rolled cigarette, the paper ends twisted. 'Want to share one of these?'

'Sure.' Marty watched him place the crude cigarette between his lips, her glance lingering on his strong mouth. They were close, their bodies brushing, his back and shoulder pressing against her thigh as her arm hooked her legs and pulled her knees up under her chin. Neither attempted to carve out more space on the bed, preferring the physical contact.

With typical self-honesty, Marty recognized the wayward direction her thoughts were taking, which had nothing to do with the potent spirits that laced her Coca-Cola. Passion was a natural stirring of her body in response to the closeness of an attractive male. Her physician father had been frank in his early talks with her about sexuality so she had always regarded her own urges as normal. If she liked and respected a guy, she did not believe in holding back. As long as a consenting couple took the necessary precautions to prevent pregnancy, she saw no reason why they shouldn't make love and satisfy those natural urges. So after enjoying Colin's company for the better part of the day, it seemed logical for her to wonder whether she'd enjoy the embrace of his arms.

After the match flame had ignited the paper-wrapped tobacco, Colin pulled the smoke deep into his lungs and held it while he passed the cigarette to Marty. A smile twitched her mouth as she inhaled it. She was reminded of an old Bette Davis movie she'd seen once. This seemed a variation on the corny romanticism of that scene.

As the smoke's cloyingly sweet smell infiltrated her nostrils, Marty drew her head back to frown skeptically at the homemade cigarette. 'What is this?'

'Hemp weed.' His hazel eyes studied her with a certain bemusement. 'One of the cowboys from a ranch outside of town put me on to it. It makes you feel all loose and relaxed. It's a great tension-easer on those nights before a check ride.'

'Really?' Beyond the acridly sweet taste, Marty felt no soothing effect.

'The trick is to hold it in your lungs and slowly exhale it.' Colin took the cigarette from her fingers and demonstrated the procedure.

Marty tried it again, wrinkling her nose at the taste. She made the mistake of trying to swallow the smoke, and a spasm of racking coughs convulsed her as she waved a hand in front of her face to clear the smoke from the air she breathed. Laughing at her attempts, Colin persisted. Finally, squeezing the last drag out of the cigarette Marty managed it and nearly burned her fingers in the process as the fire neared the end of the butt.

With an air of expectancy, Marty sat quietly and mentally checked out her system. Beyond a deliciously liquid sensation, she didn't feel a thing.

'What did you say that was made from? Hemp weed?' she questioned Colin.

'Yes. It's a plant that grows wild around here.' He gazed steadily into her unusual gray-green eyes.

Soon the party began breaking up. They left in groups of threes and fours, segregated by sexes, some assisting their slightly inebriated friends. Cappy paused beside the bed where Marty and Colin were sharing another hand-rolled cigarette.

'We're leaving now, Marty. Are you coming with us?' She attempted to prod her baymate into action.

'I'll be along.' Marty impatiently waved her away.

Cappy turned to the others and shrugged. Together, Cappy, Eden, and Mary Lynn made their way to the hall door. The crowd in the connecting rooms had thinned to only a handful of people. Colin swung around to sit next to Marty, using the headboard for a backrest. He passed her the cigarette and she took a long drag, not paying any attention to her departing friends.

'This isn't very sanitary.' She gave him the cigarette that had just been between her lips and watched Colin carry it to his mouth.

'Neither is kissing,' he pointed out.

She chuckled. 'Now I know what this has all been about. You're trying to fuddle my thinking so you can take advantage of me.'

'You've found me out.' He acknowledged his guilt with a properly remorseful expression, but a wicked twinkle gleamed in his eyes. 'What a damned shame – and just when things were looking so good, too.'

Marty turned her head to study him. 'Did you really believe you'd have to resort to such tactics with me, Colin?'

'You're so damned forthright, I don't know for sure how to handle you,' Colin remarked with a rueful smile.

'I'm no simpering Sally, that's for sure.' After the oblique reference to the girl in the gift shop, Marty dropped the smoldering butt into her spiked drink.

'I guess that's it.' He tilted his head back and stared absently at the ceiling. 'I'm not interested in becoming some woman's husband, which is what the Sallys of this town are seeking. A few of the guys in my class want wives they can impregnate to ensure their immortality before they go off into enemy skies.'

'But you don't want marriage and all the things that go with it.' Marty studied his profile in a sideways glance, her head, like his, resting against the headboard. A long, patrician nose and slightly receding chin were his prominent features beneath that thatch of sand-brown hair.

'With you, Marty, I don't feel I have to pretend that I do,' he said, turning his head slightly to bring her into his vision.

'When I was in college, the girls who *did it* always seemed to convince themselves they were wildly in love with the guy. It was as if they needed the justification to avoid any feelings of guilt or immorality.' She sighed as her fingers made a slow trail up and down the slick sides of the squat pop bottle. 'As far as I was concerned, it was enough if I liked the guy and we respected each other.'

Marty had never bewailed her lost virginity, nor wept over the man who had taken it. To her, it seemed neither

96

wrong nor unusual. After all, her brother certainly didn't practice celibacy. Whenever David could make it with a girl, he did. Her sexual urges weren't that much different than his, and if he could do it, so could she, albeit more selectively. She felt sorry for David with his indiscriminate ways, having discovered for herself how much more pleasurable it was to make love to a person than a body.

With a turn of her head, she looked into his eyes. 'I respect the hell out of you, Colin.'

Uncertainty kept him motionless while he tried to decide whether her choice of words had been deliberate. She took pity on his wary confusion and, with a laugh, she leaned over to kiss him. His fingers glided into her hair to cup her head and keep the pressure of her lips on his mouth.

'It's almost curfew,' he told her in a half-muttered complaint. 'We don't have much time to get back to the field.'

'Mmmm.' It was a conceding sound, made while she nuzzled his smoothly shaven cheek. 'It would be awful if we were late.'

Colin knew he was being mocked. When she slipped off the bed, he stayed, uncertain what her next move would be. Everyone had cleared out of the hotel suite with the exception of two cadets who were arguing vociferously the merits of the Spitfire over the Thunderbolt in a sky duel with a Focke-Wulf or Messerschmitt. With the long-legged stride of an athlete, Marty crossed to the connecting door and closed it. She also shut and locked the hallway door before she turned to face him, the suggestion of a lazy smile barely touching the corners of her mouth. Colin had the impression of a stalking lioness, all sleek and purring with power.

'On the other hand, it would be a shame to let this bed go to waste,' she suggested huskily.

His mouth quirked. 'A damned shame.'

When she came to him in the darkness seconds later, her nude, long-limbed form gliding against him, Colin recognized she was a rare woman. Bold and assertive, Marty was sure of what she wanted. While their bodies strained together in passion, it escaped Colin that it required a rare man not to be intimidated by her aggressive instincts.

In the bay, Mary Lynn sat on her cot, a pillow propped behind her and a writing pad angled on her legs. She had written no more than two sentences in her nightly letter to Beau. The words simply wouldn't come. She read his last letter over again, hearing the intonation of his voice, that familiar speech pattern coming through the written words. The lonely ache inside her grew stronger.

Tonight had been the first social evening she'd spent in the company of other men since Beau had left. She had laughed and talked and been flattered by their attentiveness, always feeling safe with the gold wedding band around her finger.

When she tried to tell Beau about it in the letter, her pen hovered over the paper, making no marks. It had all been so innocent yet there was a sense that she had betrayed him by having a good time with other men. She had enjoyed herself, but now that the night was ending, she felt emptier and more alone.

She heard a scuffle outside the bay door. It opened quickly as Marty darted inside, laughing and breathless from running. The lively glitter in her silver-green eyes seemed to match the vibrancy she exuded.

'You lucky devil.' Cappy shook her head in mild disbelief. 'You just made it by the skin of your teeth.'

'I know.' Marty crossed the room and flopped onto her cot, winded yet subtly exuberant. 'Some tobacco-chewing cowboy gave us a ride in the back of his pickup. We had to keep ducking every time he spit out the window. It was the wildest ride I've ever had.'

No one asked who her companion was, all silently guessing it was Colin. As Mary Lynn studied the silkily contented look on Marty's face, loneliness and frustration welled in her chest. She knew that look, recognizing it from the times she'd seen her own reflection in the mirror after Beau had made love to her. Desire was a feeling she had suppressed, successfully, until this moment. She ached for Beau's touch, for the play of his hands on her body and the warmth of his mouth on her skin.

She flipped the tablet closed and attempted to push aside the urges clamoring within. With unreasoning logic, she blamed them on the evening she'd spent surrounded by other men, as if such needs had not been simmering below the surface for some time. Beau was her first and only lover.

'Hey, how come you aren't finishing your letter to Beau tonight?' Marty noticed the break in Mary Lynn's nightly ritual.

A dark flush stained Mary Lynn's cheeks while a tautness claimed her expression. 'I'm tired,' she asserted stiffly, and put away the tablet in preparation for bed.

Marty reclined on her cot, stretching languidly, like a satisfied cat. 'So am I'

Mary Lynn made no response as she slid under her bed covers away from Marty and rolled onto her side.

The next morning, many a cadet and trainee sat in church pews around the town and winced at the heavy-handed playing of an organ or piano, their heads splitting from too much celebration the night before. Most of the cadets were invited to the homes of local residents for Sunday dinner, but few of the women trainees had such invitations. Most regrouped after attending church.

Word of the party did not elude the field staff. The trainees were sternly lectured about their conduct and reminded that they were, at all times, representatives of the flight training program for women. How they comported themselves would affect the entire program's reputation.

Again, there was an attempt to strongly discourage any socializing with the cadets. Their classes and activities at Avenger Field were so well segregated they rarely saw each other. They didn't even have the chance to mingle on the flight line since the men did all their flying out of an auxiliary field in Roscoe, a small town not far away. This stepped-up attention to the problem severely curtailed Colin's visits to the bay. Others didn't understand and Marty didn't try to explain her lackadaisical attitude about seeing him less often. She and Colin were good friends who had become lovers; romance had very little to do with their relationship, so she wasn't thrown into a mope when she didn't see him.

After the weekend's respite, it was back to training full tilt. Ground school had their heads awhirl with carburetors and manifolds, learning, memorizing and transcribing the International Code, which was changed monthly, discussions and tests, as well as map and chart work. Then it was out to the flight line for dual instruction, two and three of the open-cockpit PT-19s taking off at a time, piggyback, and solo flying, the best-loved time of all in the air. Sandwiching the training were physical games and body-conditioning calisthenics, and evenings in the rec hall were filled with hangar talk.

After the evening meal one night, they dragged their bone-weary bodies back to the bay. Inside they sprawled on their cots and made a stab at conversation.

'Did you think the stew tasted funny tonight?' Chicago put the question to the group. Her hands were clasped behind her head, ruffling the ends of her short, brown hair.

'Not that I noticed,' Eden replied, reclining full length on her cot with a hand draped over her eyes to shield out the light. Her nails were short and unpolished and her red hair was hidden under a bandanna turban – the stylish socialite of three weeks ago had been absorbed into the group. 'But I don't think it was intended to tickle the palate. Ragout, it is not.'

'What's the matter? Isn't stew good enough for you?' Marty, tired and irritable, was quick to issue the taunting inquiry.

'A change would be nice.' Unmoving from her languid pose, Eden failed to rise to the bait, as usual.

'I heard' – Chicago paused to garner their attention, and sat up on one elbow – 'that they put saltpeter in it.'

There was an instant of silence while everyone digested the outlandish rumor, not fully disbelieving it. Eden removed her hand from across her eyes and lifted her head to stare at Chicago. 'Are you serious?' she said.

'Forget it.' Humor was laced in Cappy's mildly derisive tone. 'They don't have to do that. Just look at us. We're all too tired to even contemplate anything remotely strenuous. If a man held me in his arms, I don't know about the rest of you, but I'd probably fall asleep.'

Agreeing sounds of laughter came from the row of cots, not too loud and not too forceful. Smiles required less energy.

CHAPTER SIX

Flying was the all-consuming focus for the girls; anything else became relegated to the background as of minor importance. Their world was the sky above Avenger Field. When they weren't flying in it, they were looking into it, taking automatic note of wind directions and ceiling heights, or watching fellow trainees in the traffic pattern making touch-and-go landings while they waited for their turn in the air.

After almost a month, they had become familiar with the routine occurrences around the field. When a jeep from the motor pool went dashing off to the old hangar, everyone knew the line dispatcher was making a check of the anemometer to find out the wind velocity. The actual control tower was still under construction, and the temporary one, located atop the hangar next to the office building, housed little equipment in its second-story cubicle.

The grumblings of the maintenance mechanics enroute

to right an airplane that had ground-looped on landing were largely ignored. Little attention was paid, as well, to the firing of the biscuit gun. Construction always seemed to be in progress somewhere, rendering runways and taxi strips inactive. Sometimes the construction made landings dicey, but usually it was merely the frustration of blowing red dust that choked the lungs and coated the skin and powdered everything in sight.

There were rare interludes in the middle of the hectic pace when all seemed perfect. The sky would be that incredible blue, stretching to forever. A beatific stillness would claim the land, hushing everything except the bursting song of the meadowlark.

In the sky, aircraft performed lazy and graceful aerobatics, climbing high into the blue and spiraling down out of a full stall, then sliding into level flight. Pilots picked out the navigationally straight roads to practice their 'S' curves against, snaking along a line and changing their angle of bank in a turn to compensate for the changing push of the wind. Many a rancher's windmill was selected as an imaginary axis for seven-twenties, also called turns-around-a-point, consisting of two complete three-hundred-sixty-degree revolutions. The aerial patterns always appeared to be effortlessly executed, a series of slow, lazy curves, circles, and spirals, flowing languidly one to the other. Yet all of them were potentially lifesaving maneuvers.

All this practicing and honing of skills these past nearly six weeks was in preparation for that 'check ride' day. They were at the end of the primary phase of training. Their individual instructors had flight-tested them, but to advance to the next phase of basic training and fly the more powerful BT-13, they had to go up with Army pilots who would 'check' their skills. If they failed that test, they were through. There was no second chance – no next phase of training. They were dropped from the program.

As the time neared when they were either ready or they'd never be, the tension became palpable along the flight line, charging tempers and numbing senses. When the Army check-pilots arrived, anxiety levels reached their peak.

In the ready room, cigarettes were virtually chain-smoked. It was a subdued group of trainees who massed inside, conversing either in mumbles or in voices grown shrill with nerves. Their glances kept straying out the windowed front of the building to watch the takeoffs and landings of the planes piloted by their fellow trainees. Soon they would be up there, but the agony was in not knowing when your name would be called.

As Eden tore the paper off her pack of Lucky Strike Greens, her fingers trembled. She lit the cigarette with an unnatural clumsiness. She exhaled the smoke in an impatient rush while her thumbnail resumed its nervous flicking of her fingernail, making little clicking sounds.

'For crissake, will you stop that?' Marty Rogers snapped. 'It's getting on my nerves.'

'Sorry.' She stilled her thumb, but the ticking went on inside her. Her auburn hair was caught in a confining snood at the back of her neck, its richly deep red lustre toned down. The flight suit bagged all over her slim figure, creating a shapeless silhouette. Never had anything fit her so atrociously, yet she had become so accustomed to wearing it every day that she never gave it a thought.

On occasion, Eden was conscious that her standards were changing; she was judging people less from their outer appearance and more for their inner qualities. All her life, things had been hers for the asking; wealth and privilege gained her access to the most prestigious schools; name and position granted her entry into elite circles; money and power allowed her to indulge in nearly any whim. This was the first time she'd ever had to work for something – the first time she'd ever been treated the same as those around her – and she liked it.

The marching, the drills, the military inspections were a bore. It still didn't make sense to her why demerits were given because there was litter in the wastebasket; where else was she supposed to have put it? Yet the camaraderie, the closeness, the sharing of desires with her baymates, more than made up for the sacrifice of creature comforts and the hardships she'd endured.

She had worked hard to reach this point, so she appreciated the struggle some of the other trainees were going through. Eden knew she was a damned good pilot. Yet, while she had confidence in her ability, she wanted to pass this check ride so badly, she was a bundle of nerves. It was the first time in her life anything had meant so much to her.

Only minutes ago, she had watched the pale-faced and drawn Mary Lynn walk out of the ready room behind an Army officer. The petite woman had lost the natural color that usually highlighted her round cheekbones. Her dark eyes had become haunted with apprehension. But Eden looked with envy at the two pillows Mary Lynn had clutched to her breast like a shield.

'There goes Number Thirty-seven lifting off,' Chicago observed in a low, taut voice, referring to the aircraft number of the low-winged PT-19. 'Isn't that the plane Mary Lynn's flying?'

'I think so.' Cappy was the only one of the group who didn't appear to be a victim of the intense pressure weighing on them all. Looking calm and unflappable, she puffed on a cigarette. Eden grinned to herself when she noticed there was already a cigarette burning in the ashtray. Cappy wasn't as poised as she looked.

Earlier in the day, they'd all paid their ritual visit to the Wishing Well and thrown their coins into the pool, making a wish for an 'up-check.' Some even added a prayer to Fifinella, the Disney-designed, female gremlin who was the mascot for the women pilot trainees.

At the time, Eden had joked about the half dollar she had tossed into the pool, laughing at her own extravagant gesture and declaring that she was buying the fulfillment of her wish.

'Van Valkenburg.' A flat, deep-toned voice called her name.

Her head jerked around, and her heart plummeted

to her toes, turning her legs into rubber. Somehow she managed to crush out her cigarette despite the shaking of her hand, and scrambled to her feet, the parachute pack banging against her legs.

The military officer at the door was searching the room for a response to the name he'd called. When Eden stood up, his gaze stopped on her. With a cold, cocky arrogance, he looked her over. How much would it take to bribe him? Money, power, prestige, all the commodities that had cushioned Eden all her life had no value in this situation. It was a chastening thought to one accustomed to acquiring what she wanted through one means or another.

With her head held unnaturally high, she unknowingly made a comical sight as she crossed the room. All the grace inherent in her regal carriage looked gauche and ridiculous in the flappy, out-sized flight suit. Her long, leggy strides were reminiscent of a galloping giraffe. The amused smirk on the officer's face was understandable when she stopped before him.

'I'm Eden van Valkenburg,' she said.

When she followed him onto the flight line, she was a quivering gel of nerves. As she made her walk-around ground check of the assigned aircraft, Eden knew she was going to make some stupid mistake. All his questions seemed snide and tricky while all her answers sounded uncertain, even when she was positive of them. Was he trying to trip her up, or was it merely her imagination?

In the forward cockpit of the trainer, Eden wiped repeatedly at her sweaty palms before she pulled on her gloves. She was so scared, she was close to tears. As she went through the preflight checklist, anger started to build in her. Who did this man think he was, intimidating her in this manner? She had studied and trained long hours for this moment. She'd gone through too much and worked too hard to blow it now. Dammit, she was a fine pilot!

Later, when she crawled out of the cockpit and hopped off the wing of the primary trainer, she confronted the close-faced military inspector. She took off helmet and goggles along with the hairnet. She shook her head with a exhilarating sense of freedom and brought her hands to rest on her flight-suit-padded hips in an unconsciously challenging stance.

'Well?' Eden prodded him for a reaction. Despite all her confidence in her ability, she needed to hear the confirmation from an unbiased – or better yet, negatively biased – source. 'How did I do?'

'I'm giving you a satisfactory mark.' Although he made it sound as if he were doing her a favor, rather than giving her a mark she had earned, he couldn't diminish the importance of it.

With an unrestrained squeal of joy, Eden left him standing on the flight line and sprinted for the big fire bell that hung outside the administration building. She yanked on the rope, ringing out her triumph in the tradition of the successful trainee, laughing and crying in elation.

Not long afterwards, Eden learned that Mary Lynn had rung the bell before her. One by one, over the next two days, her baymates went up for their check rides. On the second afternoon, Marty charged into the bay like a crazy woman and did a mock war dance in the center of the room, whooping and carrying on.

'I flew that little baby the best that I knew how. Not even the big, bad Army can stop me now!' She sang while she danced around an imaginary point on the floor, then stopped, out of breath and elated, to share her victorious moment with them. 'I made it!! It's the old lucky thirteen for me.' She had advanced from the Fairchild PT-19 to the more powerful BT-13 aircraft.

But when she finally looked around the room, she noticed that none of her baymates' faces mirrored her jubilation. Instead, they looked uncomfortable and their glances skittered away in a grim and almost embarrassed fashion. Marty briefly had the feeling Eden would have enjoyed throttling her but her look didn't last long either before it was directed to the side and downward.

Bewildered by their reaction, Marty felt the silence

106

weighing on the room. Chicago shifted her position, enabling Marty to see behind her. Aggie was sitting on her cot, dressed in a skirt and blouse. Her curly blonde head was bent over the handkerchief she was twisting in her lap. Marty opened her mouth to tease Aggie about wearing civilian clothes. Then the significance hit her and her shocked gaze flashed to Mary Lynn. A small nod confirmed that Aggie had failed her check ride.

'Aggie –' Overwhelmed with guilt, Marty struggled to find the words that would make up for the salt she'd unknowingly rubbed on Aggie's wound. '– I'm sorry.' It sounded so inadequate. 'I didn't know,' she finished lamely.

'How does your foot taste, Rogers?' Eden asked angrily.

Marty turned on her, lashing out in anger. 'How the hell was I supposed to know she washed out?'

'God, I don't believe it.' Eden sent a heavenward glance at the ceiling.

'Somebody could have warned me when I came in,' Marty protested, still guilt-faced while she searched for a way out of the awkward situation.

'Why don't you just shut your mouth?' Chicago suggested.

It seemed the best advice. Marty's lips came together in a straight line. Sniffling loudly through her nose, Aggie stood up slowly, her six-foot frame all hunch-shouldered.

'It's all right. Marty didn't mean anything by it.' Her eyes were red-rimmed and swollen from crying. 'She has a right to be glad she made it. You all have. But . . .' Aggie blew her nose, and the sobs began to sound in her throat when she finally finished the sentence. '. . . I can't help feeling sorry for myself. I wanted so much to –'

The rest was choked off as Aggie abruptly turned away from them. For a minute, none of them moved, trapped by an awkward embarrassment. Finally, Mary Lynn went over to console her.

Marty sank onto her cot, thinking how odd it was that Mary Lynn had gone to Aggie's side rather than Chicago, who had been Aggie's best friend. An unnatural silence hung over the room while Aggie removed her belongings from the footlocker and packed them in her suitcase. Like all of them, Agnes Richardson had paid her own fare to Sweetwater and she'd pay her own way back home.

When the moment of leave-taking came, they all felt an odd reluctance to get too close to her, as if they were afraid her bad luck would rub off on them. They had trouble looking her squarely in the eye. Aggie understood and didn't linger. She didn't belong there any more.

The empty cot in the bay haunted them for days after Aggie had left. There were empty cots in other bays, too. Roughly twenty percent of their class had washed out in the first cut, beginning the weeding process. At the end of the week, Eden switched cots, occupying Aggie's former bed and vacating the noisy location next to the shared lavatory. It helped.

Only one letter came for Mary Lynn. Mail from England was spotty at best. Sometimes two weeks would go by without her getting a single letter from Beau, then a half dozen would come in one day with pieces snipped out of them. For a long time it had bothered her that their mail was being read and censored. But there was a war on, even if it did seem far, far away from Sweetwater, Texas.

She read her letter for the third time while she sat at a table in the recreation hall. The trainees often gathered there in the evenings to study, write letters, hangar-fly, socialize, and escape the small, stark bays, so militarily uniform and devoid of personality. It was strictly informal, chairs pulled around in casually formed clusters, girls wandering around with their hair wrapped in curlers, dog-eared magazines scattered around. The March issue of the *Sweetwater Reporter* was opened to the latest list of sinkings of Allied ships in the Battle for the Atlantic. The much-frequented Coca-Cola machine stood in the corner, wooden cases for the empty bottles stacked beside it. On the wall, a bulletin board posted announcements of church events and other activities, pertinent newspaper cartoons, and pinned messages.

A hot Ping-Pong match was in progress at one end of the rec room, Marty and Chicago against a pair of trainees from another bay. The slap-pop of the paddles and ball punctuated the chatter in the room as the game grew intense in a battle for match point. Marty's low-driven slam-shot won it.

Flushed and exhilarated, the pair of them returned to the table where Mary Lynn sat with Cappy and Eden. The five of them were rarely apart. Since Aggie's departure, they had taken to calling themselves 'The Inseparables,' hoping in some superstitious way it would mean they'd stay together through the completion of their training. Aggie's failure had sobered all of them. Their training was taken more seriously than before and their resolve to succeed deepened.

Marty pulled out a chair and plopped onto it, kicking back to rock the chair on its rear legs. 'Hey, kid, what are you reading?' she said to Mary Lynn.

Although Mary Lynn was the oldest, she was treated as the baby of the group, partly because of her size and cherub-cheeked face, but mostly because of her inexperience. She had married so young she'd never been on her own before.

'A letter from Beau.'

'I should have guessed,' Marty declared.

Cappy looked up from her meteorology textbook and glanced at the tablet in front of Mary Lynn. All this time she'd been hearing Mary Lynn's pen scratching across the paper, she thought Mary Lynn was taking notes from her own book, but she could see it was a letter. 'Hey, you're supposed to be studying,' Cappy reminded her. She was the unappointed captain of the bunch, naturally taking charge and handling everything from making sure their bay was ready for inspection to getting all of them up and ready for class on time.

'I will – as soon as I finish this letter to Beau. I'm telling

109

him about the new planes we're flying now.' She needed to tell him all the small details of her life, to share with him the things that were happening to her so she could feel their lives were still linked no matter how many miles separated them.

So she told him all about the basic training aircraft, the BT-13. Like the PT-19 they'd been flying, it was a low-winged, tail-wheeled airplane. But at that point the similarities ended. Called the 'Valiant' by its manufacturer, the Vultee Company, the BT appeared enormous with its powerful 450-horse engine. It had a front and rear seat, but unlike the open-cockpitted Fairchild, it had an enclosed canopy top. Another major difference, Mary Lynn wrote, was that the BT-13 had a radio. For the first time, the trainees were in communication with the control tower.

The operators in the tower gave the pilots their taxiing instructions and takeoff and landing positions. Mary Lynn told Beau that although some of the trainees had to learn a new language in communication, none of them minded being told what to do and when. They finally had a microphone attached to their headsets, and they could talk back.

'Leave her alone, Cap.' Marty could be counted on to defend Mary Lynn, invariably sticking up for the loyal, trusting girl she idealized. She seriously doubted that there was a mean, unkind bone in Mary Lynn's small body. No one dared say a thing against her in Marty's presence. 'A wife is supposed to write her husband every day when they're apart.'

'I'm not stopping her.' Cappy shrugged, but it made her think about how the Army separated couples, and not just during a war. When she married, her husband was going to come home to her every night. Under no circumstances were they ever going to live apart.

'Are you going to see Colin this weekend, Marty?' Chicago wondered.

'Sure.' She took it for granted. On weekends there was a casual mixing of the enlisted cadets and the women trainees in town, but mainly it was a friendly group thing.

110

Few routinely paired off the way Marty and Colin did. A wicked light danced in her silver-green eyes as Marty looked sideways at Chicago. 'Are you going to see Mr Lentz this weekend?' Always the agitator, she couldn't resist stirring up a little trouble by mentioning Chicago's former instructor in primary training. She knew her baymate had a crush on the man.

'No.' Chicago turned red.

Restless with this inactivity, Marty set her chair down hard on all four legs. 'Let's do something besides study,' she urged.

'You're right. This place needs some livening up.' Eden unexpectedly agreed with her.

'Her hignness has spoken,' Marty said mockingly. 'Someone fetch the court jester.' She gibed at Eden, her favorite target when she wanted to pick a fight, because Eden was the only one who fought back.

'You do such a good job of it, Marty, we don't need another one,' she retorted coolly and closed up her study papers. Standing, Eden paused to motion them to follow her. 'Come on.'

After a second's hesitation, Cappy shrugged and put away her papers, too. The rest followed suit and trailed after Eden as she crossed the room to the upright piano. Used to commanding attention and occupying center stage, Eden sat down at the keys and began rumbling out a boogie-woogie beat that gathered a crowd.

By the time the weekend rolled around, the girls had discovered the basic training phase had a few twists besides new ground school courses, more powerful aircraft, and radios. But the most grueling and mentally strenuous was the concentration required to fly the plane by instruments alone. A black curtain enclosed their cockpit, shutting out any visual reference point. It was brutal on the nerves and on the senses.

'I could have sworn I was in the steepest right turn you've ever seen.' Marty was slumped in the chair, fatigue etched in her features. Colin listened sympathetically, his chair across from hers at the table in the hotel's restaurant, where they usually met on weekends. 'Those damned instruments showed straight-and-level flight, but it felt so real that I was sure they were wrong. Then that flaming Frye started yelling in my ears.' A tired sigh broke from her, heavy with self-disgust.

'Vertigo is something you just have to learn to ignore. You'll overcome it,' Colin insisted calmly.

'Yeah.'

'I agree.' Cappy was at the big table, too, along with Mary Lynn, Eden, and Chicago. 'Flying blind is no picnic. After two hours of it, my eyes feel like they're connected to my head with little springs, and they're going to pop out.'

'You girls better get used to it,' Colin advised. 'One of our guys got a look at your curriculum. You're going to be flying more instrument time than the cadet training calls for.'

'That isn't fair,' Marty protested.

'As ferry pilots, you'll potentially be flying in worse weather conditions than we will as combat pilots,' he reasoned. 'We have more emphasis on aerial acrobatics. It's natural.'

There were skeptical murmurings around the table. Instrument flying was definitely not a favorite among them, the five who had once believed anything connected with flying was a joy. Over the course of the last months, they had changed, too, but the determination remained, growing stronger as flying got tougher.

Seeing their expressions, Colin added, 'Wait until you do some night flying. Then you'll really find out what disorientation is like.'

'We start this coming week,' Cappy said.

'I haven't figured out when we're supposed to sleep yet,' Eden complained.

'And without her beauty sleep, Eden reverts to a witch,' Marty taunted, never able to resist a gibe at her rich baymate.

'Have any of you had your trainer into a spin yet?'

112

Chicago asked, uninterested in the ongoing but minor feud.

'It scared the hell out of me.' Marty confirmed her experience with it, while the others nodded a mutual agreement. 'I thought the plane was going to shake apart. I mean, it shuddered so violently I thought this was *it*.'

'I used up more than two thousand feet of altitude before I could level her out,' Cappy admitted.

'Instead of the Valiant, they ought to call her the Vultee Vibrator,' Eden suggested dryly, tapping her cigarette on the ashtray in the middle of the table. A black-haired woman in a tight-fitting dress walked by their table. The exaggerated sway of her hips caught Eden's eye. An eyebrow arched in dry, cynical humor. 'Speaking of vibrators,' she murmured.

Marty turned in her chair and looked over her shoulder. 'She really thinks she's a hot number, doesn't she?' It wasn't the first time she had noticed a member of that woman's profession in the vicinity, especially at the Bluebonnet Hotel.

'It's a pretty dress,' Mary Lynn said admiringly. 'It's a pity it's so tight.'

There was a slight break as everyone looked at Mary Lynn to see if that softly drawled remark was meant seriously. Her dark eyes blinked innocently back at them.

A staccato laugh came from Marty. 'For a married lady, Mary Lynn, you have certainly led a sheltered life. Can we blame it on your magnolia-white upbringing.'

Mary Lynn looked around the table, feeling ignorant but unsure why. 'What did I say wrong?'

In exaggerated mimicry, Marty copied her southern accent. 'Honey, I believe you would refer to that woman as a "lady of the evening," or perhaps a "soiled dove."'

Mary Lynn's dark eyes rounded as she craned her head to stare after the woman, then she paused to look at the group long enough to ask, 'Is that what they look like?'

Amid the laughter that followed, Marty declared, 'We'll corrupt you yet.'

113

Avenger Field wasn't equipped with runway lights. As the long shadows of twilight stretched over the field, it became customary to see the truck loaded with flare pots drive down the runway, depositing the burning oil pots at regular intervals.

What with 'flying blind' beneath a black curtain, hours spent on the ground boxed in the Link trainer to simulate instrument flight, and night flying, the girls were convinced the basic training courses were designed to test their sanity and their endurance. Cold showers and pots of Mom's black coffee kept them going – the showers taken before reporting for night flights and the coffee consumed in the ready room while they waited for their turn to fly – usually until two in the morning.

On takeoffs, Mary Lynn had still not gotten used to the sensation of charging down the midnight-dark runway, the yellow flames from the burning pots flashing in her side vision while she watched her airspeed indicator to know when to pull back on the stick. After liftoff, all was instantly swallowed into the blackness. It unnerved her every time.

Landing was equally tricky, the darkness lousing up her depth perception. She had to depend on her altimeter, virtually to the point of touchdown, and watch her airspeed to keep the plane above stalling speed. She couldn't remember making a smooth landing. Invariably, she hit with a thud and a bounce before skittering onto the runway like a wounded duck.

Endless time was spent in the traffic pattern around Avenger Field, making touch-and-gos – landing, applying full power, and taking off again. Other planes were mere pinpoints of light – the red and green navigational lights on their wings and the white beams of their headlights shining like sightless eyes on final approach to landing.

Once they left the traffic pattern to practice navigation by radio beam, Mary Lynn's infatuation with night flying surfaced. There was a magical quality in the utter blackness of a Texas sky sparkling with stars. Beneath the moonlight the airplane's wings appeared dusted with silver. The glass canopy over her cockpit sometimes seemed to reflect the moonbeams, bathing her in the silvery glow.

The odd ranch light shining in the bottomless black below her plane became an eye-catching sight. Mary Lynn filed away its location, so she could find the friendly source in the daylight. Passenger trains, with their many windows of lights crawling through the dark void, reminded Mary Lynn of caterpillars. In her ear the steady hum of the signal, beamed from the navigational radio beacon, confirmed that she was on course. If she strayed off the transmission quadrant, the sound changed to Morse Code beeps. *Da-dit*, which was the letter *A*, was repeated if she was to the left of her course; and *dit-da*, which was *N*, if she strayed to the right.

Each radio beacon had its own assigned frequency on which it transmitted. Its location was marked on maps so a pilot could fly from one beacon to another, changing from one frequency to the next. When a pilot flew directly over the transmitter, there was a cone of silence, allowing her to pinpoint her exact location on the map. The cessation of sound lasted for only a short interlude. An ear always had to be attuned to it or it would be missed.

The droning stopped for those ticks of seconds. Mary Lynn changed the frequency and made the turn toward the second beacon, following orders previously given by her instructor. Above the *da-dit, da-dit* that was beeping in her ears the instructor barked, 'What do you think you're doing, Palmer? I told you not to fly to the second beacon until you'd flown over the first. Haven't you got ears?'

The sarcasm made her bristle on her cushion of pillows. 'Yes, sir, and I heard the cone of silence.' Very sweetly, 'Didn't you?'

His failure to respond immediately was immensely satisfying. Marty had told her some of the instructors had only a few more hours in the BT-13s than they themselves had. 'The blind leading the blind,' she had joked. Mary Lynn had suspected Marty of exaggerating but it was beginning to ring true. On two other flights, she'd followed his directions and they'd wound up lost.

Finally, her instructor came back to claim defensively, 'I was just testing you.'

With a warm feeling of satisfaction, Mary Lynn headed the BT into the star-studded blackness. Minutes later, a sense of unease stole over her. The engine wasn't running right; it was a feeling rather than an actual change in its rhythm. She began checking the gauges.

The roughness began as a vibration. Her instructor started yelling at her. Then a tongue of flame leaped out from the whirling propeller, dancing, darting, and disappearing. Then it came again. Fire. The engine was on fire! The instructor screamed obscenities and yanked the controls from Mary Lynn; the stick banged against her knee. Mary Lynn was fighting her own waves of panic at the sight of that deadly yellow fire spilling backwards from the nose of the plane toward the front cockpit where she sat.

It was after 2 a.m. when Marty and Chicago staggered into their bay, physically exhausted, their heads whirling, still seeing the streamers of light from the flare pots in their side vision. Cappy was just climbing into bed, and Eden was already stretched out on her cot, the satin sleep mask over her eyes.

'I could sleep for a week,' Marty complained. She flopped onto her cot, letting her tired head sink into her hands.

'Couldn't we all.' Cappy pulled the covers up around her shoulders and turned onto her side, snuggling into the pillow.

With an effort, Marty raised her head. The cot next to hers was empty, the blanket stretched tautly across it. 'Where's Mary Lynn?' She frowned.

'I guess she isn't back yet,' Cappy said without bothering to open her eyes.

Chicago had wasted no time shedding her flight suit and

climbing into her pajamas. Late-night conversation was the last thing she was interested in.

'Good night.' She hauled her tired body onto the cot and slipped under the covers.

Marty was now the only one still up. She eyed the empty cot for another several seconds, nagged by Mary Lynn's absence. Then she shrugged her shoulders and announced to no one in particular, 'That stupid instructor probably got her lost again.' She reached for the zipper of her flight suit. 'You know, I don't know why we should bother to undress. We'll be getting up again in four hours.'

Eden, who had given every semblance of being sound asleep, finally said, 'Shut up, Rogers.'

The next morning the cot was still empty. Mary Lynn's absence could no longer be shrugged aside. Worry was a knife in each one of them.

'What do you suppose happened?' Marty probed each of their faces with her hard glance, afraid but unwilling to show it.

'I don't know.' Cappy shared the anxiety written in the expressions of her baymates, although it glimmered only in the blue confusion of her eyes. 'Like you said last night, Marty, they might have gotten lost. They probably landed at another field and decided to wait until daylight to fly back,' she reasoned. Until they were told differently, she felt it was wisest to maintain a positive outlook. She smiled to encourage optimism. 'We're all probably worrying for nothing.'

'Yeah.' But Marty wasn't convinced.

After reporting for morning formation, they skipped breakfast and went directly to operations. Marty shouldered her way to the front of the quartet and demanded to know what had happened to Mary Lynn Palmer.

'Please. We're her baymates,' Cappy said, attempting to temper Marty's belligerence.

There was a telling hesitation on the part of the establishment officer. 'I'm sorry, but the wreckage of her BT-13

117

was found this morning on a ranch north of here. The plane appears to have exploded on impact. A search is under way for the bodies now.'

'No.' The small negative came from Marty, who went numb with shock. It wasn't possible. They had made some mistake, her mind kept insisting. Mary Lynn couldn't be dead. Not her. Marty met the news with a raw and wild disbelief.

While the others reeled from the news, Cappy retained her presence of mind. 'Thank you,' she murmured to the solemn-faced woman. They walked out in a close bunch, shoulders rubbing, arms supporting waists, all of them needing the physical contact with one another. Chicago was the only one crying, sobbing softly while tears slid down her cheeks.

Outside, the sun shone down out of an incomparable Texas sky. Spring was bursting around them, birds trilling. It was a perfect day for flying, a gentle wind blowing, but the four were too stunned by the news to notice.

'I don't believe it,' Marty repeated.

Her expression was stark with the shock of it, her face drained and pale. Marty was taking it the hardest of all of them; she had been the closest to Mary Lynn.

They stood huddled together, grieving in silence. Beyond the loss of a baymate, there was the shock of coming face to face with their own mortality. Regardless of the cause – instrument malfunction, engine failure, pilot error, it could have happened to any of them. Chicago started crying again, smothering the sobs with a hand clamped over her mouth.

If they stood around much longer, Cappy feared they'd become paralyzed. 'Come on,' she urged quietly. 'We have to report to the flight line.' Her reminder seemed to fall on deaf ears, so she added, 'Have you forgotten? There's a war on.'

The stony look left Marty's eyes as she glared at Cappy. 'Hayward, you make me sick! You can take your stiff upper lip and shove it!' She stalked away, rigid and hurting, unable to find a release for the pain that clutched her throat.

Later, Marty cut off her instructor Bud Hanson's expression of sympathy as she walked with him to the airplane parked on the ramp. She didn't want to hear the words, more confirmation of Mary Lynn's death.

'I don't want to talk about it, Bud,' she informed him in a hard, cold voice.

His glance skidded over her. 'Sure.'

Climbing into the cockpit of the trainer and buckling in was a strange sensation. She caught herself wondering what Mary Lynn had felt when the plane was going down. Had there been time for fear . . . or pain?

'FF eighty-one.' She depressed the microphone button to call the tower. 'This is sixty-two on the ramp requesting taxi instructions. Over.'

A tear slid down her cheek, followed by a second, and a third. Marty heard the reply, but she just couldn't seem to act. The tears turned into a steady stream, washing down her face and into the corners of her mouth.

'Marty?' Bud Hanson's voice came over the earphones. 'The tower gave you clearance to runway seventeen. Didn't you hear it?'

'Yes.' She sniffed loudly. 'I'm going.' With a check on either side for other aircraft, Marty pushed the throttle forward and stepped her foot down on the right rudder.

It was the poorest job of flying she'd ever done. She almost resented the patience Bud exhibited with mistakes usually made by beginners. Inside, Marty felt sick and dulled. On the ground, she paused to look at the chubby-cheeked man without quite meeting his eyes.

'I'm sorry, Bud,' she said.

'We're all entitled to our bad days.'

Her legs seemed to be made of lead as she headed across the concrete apron to the hangar. She spotted Chicago standing by a jeep parked near the hangar and immediately bent her head, not wanting to give any sign that she had noticed her baymate. The pain and grief were too fresh and too new. She didn't want to face any of them and listen to them talk about Mary Lynn. It hurt too much.

'Hey! Marty!'

It was too late. Chicago had seen her. Marty considered ignoring the shouted call, then grudgingly turned her gaze toward the girl and altered her direction when Chicago waved her over to the jeep. The knot in her throat got thicker as Marty guessed Chicago probably wanted to tell her the bodies had been recovered. Doll-sized Mary Lynn, all broken up and battered.

'Marty!' A familiar voice called her name.

All at the same time, Marty observed the short, baggy-suited girl waving at her, the crumpled parachute in the back of the jeep and the wide smile on Chicago's face.

It was Mary Lynn – very much alive despite the scratches from being dragged by the parachute when she had landed. Laughing and crying, Marty broke into a run. When the hugs and the laughter subsided, Mary Lynn explained how she and her instructor had both bailed out of the burning plane before it crashed. The wind had carried her slight weight farther, separating her from the instructor, who had broken his leg in the fall. After shivering through the night's cold, Mary Lynn had set out walking at dawn and met up with a cowboy.

'When he hauled me onto the back of that horse and it started bucking, I thought I was really doomed.' Mary Lynn laughed in retrospect. But the laugh faded as she glanced at the handle to the parachute ripcord, a souvenir she still gripped in her hand. 'I guess this makes me an official member of the Caterpillar Club, doesn't it?' This was an exclusive club whose membership was limited to pilots who had bailed out of an airplane and had the parachute handle as proof.

'It makes you the luckiest devil on earth,' Marty retorted.

'I know.' It would be a long time before she'd forget the sensation of that night – cracking the canopy and shoving it back, the rushing push of the wind and fiery heat from the flames blowing on her, hurtling into that black void and feeling that abject terror, pulling on the ripcord and waiting those agonizing seconds for the chute to open, the crack of the billowing silk and the sight of the burning plane spinning in its death throes. A long time.

'Hot damn! This calls for a party!' Marty declared, unable to blink back the tears in her eyes. 'Let's round up Cappy and Eden and go to the canteen. The Cokes are on me!'

'Yeah, we need to celebrate,' Chicago agreed. 'The Inseparables are all together again!'

CHAPTER SEVEN

Her neck and shoulder muscles ached with tension, but Cappy couldn't spare the few seconds it would take to relax them and ease some of the painful stiffness. All her concentration was focused on the instrument panel in front of her. Her hands gripped the stick between her legs and her feet operated the rudder pedals as she performed the maneuvers instructed by the voice on the headphones. The air inside the closed cockpit was becoming suffocatingly close. It seemed to add to the dull throb in her head.

'Okay, that's enough for today,' the voice said, then added, as an afterthought, 'Good job.'

All the instruments went dead, but Cappy was slow to loosen her grip on the stick. It seemed a permanent part of her. Sighing, she arched her shoulders and back, turning her neck into them in a flexing maneuver, then reached up to unfasten the hatch.

Whenever she first stuck her head out of the cockpit she always experienced that disoriented pause. She felt she'd been flying a plane this last hour, but she was climbing out into a classroom. Cappy swung over the side of the Link trainer and stepped down to the floor. The 'voice' was sitting at a table. He could communicate by phone with the 'pilot' and observe the pilot's performance as it was recorded by the automatic stylus.

With her feet on the floor, Cappy looked at the flight simulator that had tricked her once again into believing it was real.

The Link trainer was such an absurd sight – a boxlike structure with stubby mock wings and a ridiculous tail. It always reminded Cappy of a cartoon caricature of an airplane, something that belonged in a carnival. All it lacked was a fake propeller. But she supposed for all its comical appearance it accomplished its purpose, which was to give the trainees plenty of practice in instrument flying.

At the end of a Link class, Cappy always felt frazzled and worn out, as if her brains had been fried and scrambled. This time wasn't any different. It had been raining steadily since morning, so there would be no flying. With the day's classes over, the trainees were at loose ends.

Like herd animals, the five from Cappy's bay naturally coalesced into a group as they headed for the door. They all wore that same sense-dulled expression and that blank look in their eyes.

'Hell has to be a Link trainer,' Marty declared. 'It got so stuffy in there today I thought I was going to suffocate. Can you imagine what it's going to be like in the summer when the temperature hits a hundred in the shade . . . and us trapped in that sweatbox for hours on end? There isn't a muscle in my body that doesn't ache. And my head – the damned thing is pounding so, I'd just as soon cut it off.'

'Please do.' Eden's smlle was thin with sarcasm. 'Then the rest of us wouldn't have to listen to you bitch all the time.'

Marty curled a lip at her but didn't respond as they filed through the door. The rain was coming straight down in obscuring sheets. They huddled under the overhang of the building with the steady drum of the falling rain above them and the runoff from the roof creating a water screen in front of them. An incongruous evergreen, short and squat, stood beside the post, one of a scattered row that dotted the front of the classroom building. Evergreens seemed out of place in this red Texas landscape.

'Hell, I need a cigarette. Let's go over to the canteen for Cokes and smokes,' Marty suggested and looked to Cappy for agreement.

'Okay, but somebody has to go back to the bay and empty the pans.' Their barracks was not only notoriously drafty, but the roof also leaked. They had scrounged up a half-dozen containers and strategically positioned them to catch all the drips. Cappy had organized a system where they each set their alarm clocks for a different hour of the night so the pans would be emptied at regular intervals.

'I did it last,' Marty asserted. 'It's Chicago's turn.'

With a grimace, Chicago accepted her fate. 'I'll see you all later.'

'Aren't you going to join us at the canteen?' Cappy asked.

'Nawh. I got some washing I need to do.' There was a troubled and sad look in Chicago's eyes before she turned away and raised the collar of her battle jacket up around her head. 'See you later.' With her head down, she dashed into the rain. Cappy felt a twinge of pity for the girl as she watched her leave.

'What's the matter with her?' Marty frowned.

'I think this instrument flying is giving her problems.' Cappy shrugged to indicate it wasn't really any of their business.

'Some days it gets to all of us.' Mary Lynn hunched her shoulders and looked out into the downpour. Water was already pooling on the ground, the pelting drops splattering when they hit. 'A gloomy day like this naturally makes you moody.'

'It's definitely ruining my hair.' Eden hooked her finger

around a limp strand and let it fall. 'Look at the way it's drooping. Do you know what I keep fantasizing about? Getting a hot oil treatment for my hair, and a facial, then stretching out on a massage table and sipping twelve-year-old Scotch while trained hands rub away all the muscle aches and tension.'

'It sounds wonderful,' Cappy murmured.

'Especially the Scotch,' Marty agreed in her raspy, amused voice.

'This rain isn't letting up a bit. Why are we standing here?' Mary Lynn wanted to know.

'She's right. Come on.' Marty loosened her jacket and pulled it up over her head.

In follow-the-leader style, they all ducked their heads under their raised jackets and splashed across the compound toward the canteen. The rain drenched them.

'Hey, look!' Marty pointed to the administration building while water dribbled down her face. The local taxi was parked in front while its well-dressed, umbrellaed passengers waited to claim their luggage from the trunk, their heads turning in every direction as they gawked at everything they saw. The women looked bewildered, decidedly out of place, but eager to belong. 'It's the new class of trainees. Do you suppose we looked that green?'

'Probably,' Cappy replied, smiling faintly. That gray day almost a month and a half ago when they arrived at Avenger Field seemed years away.

'I think we need to show them the ropes.' There was a devilish glint in Marty's eyes.

'What does she mean?' Mary Lynn turned her head to look up to the taller Cappy, and got a faceful of rain in the process. Cappy tried to hide her smile at Mary Lynn's inexperience.

Come sundown, the clouds rolled away and a rainbow came out to compete with the fresh-washed brilliance of a scarlet sunset. The containers were emptied for the last time and stored away for a future rainy day. Then the Inseparables waited until Marty decreed the time was ripe.

Outside they joined other trainees of the first Sweetwater class and sloshed through the red mud to the barracks of the new recruits. Mary Lynn was swept along with the pack as they burst into the first bay. Marty was at the front of the assault, barking out orders and acting tough.

'Attention!' she shouted to the startled trainees, who were lounging on their new beds, writing their first letters home. After they scrambled off their cots, the giggling started as they realized they were being hazed by their 'upper classmen.' 'What's so funny?' Marty demanded without cracking a smile, but her light-colored eyes were gleaming with wicked humor. 'Stand up straight. Shoulders back, chest out, stomach in!'

The raucous spirit of the initiation went against everything Mary Lynn had been taught about kindness and courtesy, all the mannerly things that should be done to make a new person feel welcome. But the new trainees seemed to take the harassing and the sometimes cruel ridicule all in good fun. Obediently they marched to the confusing set of orders and attempted to sit in chairs they knew would be pulled away at the last second. When a few of them were selected to be thrown in the showers, they squealed with a kind of laughter.

At first, Mary Lynn wasn't certain she liked this brand of fun; it seemed a little too much. But gradually, as the hazing flowed from one bay of trainees to the next, she got the hang of the new game and joined in the mischief. In the last bay, she succumbed to an impish urge and turned off the cold water tap to the shower spray. Someone shouted the warning, and the fully clothed and saturated trainees managed to elude the scalding hot water that came from the shower head.

When it was over, they tramped back to their bay, laughing gleefully. Mary Lynn sprawled on her cot, mindless of the mud splattered on her slacks and caked on her shoes. She felt gloriously relaxed, all the pent-up frustrations and tensions gone.

'Did you see the way they jumped when I reached for

that cold water faucet?' She laughed in remembrance and looked at Marty, one of the instigators of the night's outing.

'It was the damndest sight I ever saw.' Marty snorted with laughter.

But it wasn't so funny the next morning when their entire class was sternly reprimanded for their sophomoric antics. The base commanding officer announced that any future hazing of new trainees was expressly forbidden. A girl from one of the other barracks had suffered a fractured tailbone after falling on the floor when a chair had been pulled out from under her. It was too soon to know if the injury would wash her out of the program.

'My momma always told me no good ever comes out of taking pleasure from making someone else miserable,' Mary Lynn remembered, too late.

'No one was supposed to get hurt,' Marty insisted in a subdued defense of their action.

'Zero thirteen, you are cleared to land.'

Eden compressed the mike button. 'Roger, FF eight one. Zero thirteen is cleared to land.'

Below the low-winged trainer, mesquite and scrub cedar dotted the ground. Eden lined up her BT-13 with the runway and adjusted her rate of descent. The ground seemed to rush up at her, blurring as she flew lower. Her wheels greased the runway, and the tingle of satisfaction she felt at the textbook-smooth landing was something that couldn't be bought.

As she braked to make the turn onto the taxiway, a voice came over the radio. 'This is Jacqueline Cochran.' Eden was instantly alert. 'I'm coming in for a landing. Clear the area,' the woman's voice ordered.

Eden taxied to the hangar, watching the sky. Planes swung out of the flight path of the stagger-winged Beechcraft approaching the field, climbing to circle at a respectful distance while the director of their women's pilot training program made a straight-in approach.

When the plane touched down, Eden had climbed out of the cockpit and jumped to the ground. After two hours of solo work, her time in the air was finished for the day. Eden made no move to walk to the hangar, waiting instead to greet her famous commanding officer and wondering whether Jacqueline Cochran would remember their meeting at that party the previous December.

With the airfield and the skies above it virtually empty of traffic, Eden couldn't help being amused. Long ago, she had been taught the value of making an entrance. There was no doubt that the director of the Women's Flying Training Detachment had accomplished it in style.

The big plane taxied by her, its propeller nearly touching the concrete. After braking to a stop, the engine was cut. Eden approached the Beechcraft, unconscious of the grime on her face and the ratty pigtails of auburn hair, as the familiar blond aviatrix emerged from the cockpit.

'Hello, Miss Cochran.'

Her greeting barely rated a glance as the director headed toward the hangar. 'Carry this for me.' She tossed a full-length mink coat to Eden.

Eden came to an indignant stop, stunned at being treated as some sort of servant. Outrage bubbled as she looked down at the mink coat in her arms. But she also saw the wrinkled clothes and dusty grime that covered her. She touched a hand to her absurd pigtails and broke into a laugh.

At the sound, Jacqueline Cochran slowed her steps and swung around to regard Eden with a commanding hauteur. 'Do you find something amusing?'

'I just realized my own mother probably wouldn't recognize me,' Eden replied, unabashed.

A finely drawn brow arched in question, creating a furrow in the smooth forehead. 'Have we met?' she asked, then immediately broached an explanation that was polite and aloof, fitting her rank as commander. 'I have interviewed many girls. I can't be expected to remember all their faces. I'm sure you understand that.'

'Of course, Miss Cochran.' Their meeting had been memorable to Eden, but it had been merely one of a multitude for the blond aviatrix. 'I'm Eden van Valkenburg. We met last December in New York at a party my parents were giving.'

'Yes, of course.' The significance of the name registered although Eden seriously doubted that Jacqueline Cochran actually remembered her.

And Eden's social equality with her commander had little effect but to temper her supercilious attitude into something a shade more condescending. She turned and headed again toward the hangar, expecting Eden to follow, her strides long and smooth, almost leisurely compared to her previous sweeping rush.

'Tell me, Miss van Valkenburg, how are you getting along?' she asked. 'Any problems or complaints?'

'No.' There was a whole list, from a leaky barracks roof to harassment by a rare few of the instructors, but Eden guessed she didn't really want to hear about it. Still relegated to carrying the mink, she absently burrowed her fingers into the dark fur, stroking its sleek softness and savoring the almost forgotten sensation. 'Besides, Miss Cochran, I've already learned the Army response to complaints is a very simple "That's tough."'

A low, melodic laugh came from Cochran's throat. 'How very true,' she agreed, and paused to face Eden when they reached the hangar. The smile softened her features and harked back to her southern upbringing. The look in her eyes when she studied Eden was both serious and sincere. 'If you ever do have a serious problem, I want you to come directly to me. You, or any of the other girls.'

'Yes, ma'am.' But it made Eden curious about the purpose behind this visit, although she was well aware their director regularly called on the base to check on the operations. 'What brings you here this time, Miss Cochran? Is it just a routine stop?'

'Not quite.' A self-satisfied gleam came into her eyes. 'You girls are going to have more company. We'll be

128

shutting down the Houston operation and moving the entire training program here to Avenger Field. The demand for qualified pilots is outstripping the supply, and more men need to be released for combat duty, which means more women in the air. Houston doesn't have the facilities to allow an expansion, so we're taking over here.'

'The whole field?' Eden stared. The war. She'd almost forgotten about it. Flying, flying, all the time it was flying. The war, it was some remote thing that didn't really mean much to her. Newspapers – who had time to read them? Oh, sure, she knew Marty got letters from her brother, a paratrooper in the 101st Airborne Division stationed in North Carolina, and Mary Lynn heard regularly from her bomber pilot husband in England. She knew it, yet it didn't really touch her.

'The last class of Army cadets will be leaving next week, and we'll move in – lock, stock, and airplanes.' She smiled with a hint of pride. 'I can't stress enough the important contribution you girls will be making, stepping in for the men so they can go off and fight.'

'Yes.'

'I'll take my coat.' The prodding statement snapped Eden out of her reverie.

'Of course.' Unwittingly, she had been clutching the mink so tightly in her arms that the fur was being crushed. She attempted to smooth it with a caressing stroke of her hand while she reluctantly returned it to its owner. 'It's funny. At home I have a mink stole, a mink bolero jacket, and a coat like this, but I'd almost forgotten how soft they feel.'

Jacqueline Cochran took the coat and merely smiled at the comment. 'Good flying,' she said and walked away.

The light from a full moon spilled through the window of the darkened hotel room and cast a diffused glow over the interior. Colin lay in bed on his side, one arm crooked under his head on the pillow while the other rested along his length. The bedsheet covered his hips and left his chest bare, the muscled flesh gleaming pale in the moonlight.

Lying next to him, Marty broke into a mocking song, 'The stahs at night . . . are big and bright . . .' She clapped her hands. '. . . deep in the haht of Texahs!' She had deepened her voice to mimic his earlier singing.

'Enough.' Colin clamped a hand over her mouth to smother any future mangling of the song.

Her shoulders shook with the laughter he smothered. The husky chuckles continued in her throat when she finally pulled his hand down. The sheet slipped, exposing her breasts, but Marty felt no need for false modesty with Colin. His hands and lips had fondled them often. She brought his hand down to the valley shaped by the rise of her breasts, not to be provocative, but simply because it was the natural place to let it rest.

'I can't believe you actually sang that song to the towns-people. It took a helluva lot of nerve.' Her voice continued to croak with humor. 'It's practically been adopted as the national anthem of Texas.'

' 'I think they were rather pleased by our gesture,' he informed her, the corners of his mouth pulled in, suggesting a smile was lurking somewhere in warning of retribution to come.

'Oh, were they?' Marty mocked him again.

'Yes.' A warm, admiring glint appeared almost reluctantly in his eyes. 'They recognized we were expressing our appreciation for the way they've taken us into their homes –'

'And into their beds,' Marty interrupted.

'Ah, but gentlemen don't speak of such things.'

'How interesting.' Marty turned her head to get a better look at him. 'What do gentlemen speak about?'

'Other things,' he said. He withdrew his hand from beneath the slightly pinning weight of her hands and reached up to smooth the toasted gold strands of her hair against the white pillowcase. He curled the end of a lock around his finger, testing its silkiness. 'Your eyes remind me of the color of the water in the English Channel.' A

130

certain drollness touched his mouth. 'I expect I'll be taking a dunking in it sooner or later. I'll write and let you know if it's the same shade up close.'

'I wish I could go in your place.' More than once when she was out flying alone, Marty had wondered what it would be like to be locked in the throes of an aerial dogfight.

But it was an experience she was denied, because she had the misfortune to be born female. She was allowed to make brief forays into the male world, but only with its permission. It had always rankled her to see how much more her brother, David, could experience and do than she could. It wasn't fair. Right now he was in training at Fort Bragg, jumping out of airplanes as one of the 'Screaming Eagles' – the 101st Airborne Division.

'I'll bet you do.' Colin chuckled and rolled onto his back, smiling at the shadow patterns on the ceiling.

With a turning lift of her body, Marty propped herself up on one elbow, facing him. The sheet slid down to her waist. 'I suppose you think I couldn't do it.'

'You? You could probably be the Joan of Arc of the skies, the warrior maiden with wings,' Colin retorted smoothly and caught her hand, carrying it to his mouth to kiss the center of her palm. His look became slightly serious as he gazed at her. 'I'm going to miss you, Marty. I didn't expect to say that, but it's true.'

'Please, let's don't get all sloppy and sentimental and spoil everything,' she urged.

'I'm not. I promise you.' He turned his lazy, smiling glance on her. 'No emotional entanglements for either of us – just good friendship. But I will miss you all the same.'

She leaned down to kiss his mouth. 'I'm going to miss you, too. These last weeks have been fun.'

The hanging fullness of her breasts invited the caress of his hands. Colin cupped the weight of one in his hand and rubbed his thumb back and forth across the hardening nipple.

'You're a rare one, Marty,' he declared. 'I doubt I shall

ever have the good fortune to meet a woman like you again.'

'We've been damned good together, haven't we?' She stroked the ridge of his shoulder with her fingers. 'I'm glad we've had this last time together for – what shall I call it? – our farewell fuck?'

Laughter rumbled from deep within as Colin caught her by the waist and twisted her back onto the mattress while he hovered above her. A wide, laughing grin split his face.

'Has anybody ever told you that you have a definite way with words?' he chuckled. 'You cut right through all the drivel and get straight to the heart of it.'

Her hands slid down his torso and under the sheets, gliding over his pelvic bones and continuing downward into the springy nest of hairs. 'In that case . . .' Marty peered at him through her lashes with deliberate provocation while her fingers deftly encouraged his hardening with caressing strokes. '. . . why has there been so much conversation tonight, and so little action?'

'Is that right?' Colin asked with a deepening smile. His hand pushed at the bend of her knee to open her legs, then he filled the opening with his body and lowered himself onto her. 'Well, if it's fucking you want, babe, it's fucking you shall get,' he promised in a voice husky with affection and desire.

Her hand cupped the back of his head to drag his mouth down onto hers. Marty kissed him, secure in the mutual respect and admiration they shared. Theirs was a caring relationship in which neither would be hurt. Marty sought nothing deeper than that, and, for once, she had found a man who wanted the same. Yes, she would miss him.

Later, the big April moon rode high in the sky, silvering the landscape and silhouetting the two, who faced each other outside the gates to Avenger Field. Marty gazed thoughtfully into the eyes of the lanky airman.

'I probably won't have a chance to see you again before we leave,' he said.

'I know.' There were no tears, just a twinge of regret at

the necessity of parting. As there was no need for tears, there was also no need for clinging embraces or a flood of words. Yet some final gesture, some appropriate remark, some hint of contact seemed to be required. After a long minute's pause, Marty offered him her hand. 'Good flying, Colin.'

He took it, gripped it warmly, and smiled. 'Same to you, Marty.'

CHAPTER EIGHT

In straight lines, the column of baggy-suited trainees marched toward the flight line. Out of step, Chicago skipped to get back into stride with the others while the section marcher called out the cadence.

'Hup, two, hree, hor. Hup. Hup.'

Someone started the singing, picking out the tune to 'Bell-Bottom Trousers.' It had become routine to sing while they marched. And they had a whole medley of songs to which they'd made up their own lyrics.

> *Zoot suits and parachutes*
> *And wings of silver, too.*
> *He'll ferry planes like*
> *His mamma used to do!*

While they were singing the fourth and last verse to the song, Marty noticed the formation of Army BT-13 aircraft approaching the field from the south. She missed the line about never trusting 'a pilot an inch above your knee' as she watched the basic trainers peel out of formation to enter the traffic pattern.

By the time they reached the flight line, everyone in the column had noticed the outsider planes preparing to land at their field. The column broke up and waited in front of the ready room for the arriving planes.

'It must be the Houston trainees,' Cappy said, the five of them grouped together again. 'I heard they were getting to fly their BTs here so they could have a taste of cross-country flying.'

'What an experience that must have been,' Marty grumbled with envy.

One by one, the planes roared in, the pilots showing off with their wheel-greasing touchdowns. 'I'll bet they think they're something.' No one disputed Marty's disparaging comment as the planes taxied up to the flight line and the women trainees tumbled out. They all unconsciously disassociated themselves from the arriving trainees, even though they were members of the same class, trained at different fields.

The invasion of strange faces wasn't at all like the arrival of the new trainees a couple weeks ago. Those had been novices, under-classmen so to speak, but these women were their equals, the other half of 43-W-3. While Houston had been the site where the women's flight training program had begun, with the very first two classes remaining there to complete their training, the Sweetwater half of the third class had been the first occupants of Avenger Field. They had a proprietary feeling toward it. Now they were expected to share it with strangers – outsiders. A sense of rivalry was inevitable.

Jimmy Ray Price, Cappy's instructor in the basic training phase, paused alongside their group, giving them a glowering, long-jawed look. 'Ya better quit gawkin' and get yourselves into the ready room. You're here to fly. Remember?'

Dragging their attention away from the tired but ecstatic Houston trainees greeting each other on the ground after their long flight, Cappy, Eden, Mary Lynn and Chicago filed into the ready room with the rest of their flight group. The flying side of them wanted to know what it had been like to make that cross-country trip from Houston to

Sweetwater, yet there was also a matter of pride which made it difficult to admit the Houston trainees had done something they hadn't. Besides, all the cliques were already formed, so that didn't leave much room for outsiders.

While the Houston group went through the orientation process at Avenger Field, the Inseparables flew with their instructors, getting in more instrument practice. The new arrivals were nowhere around when they landed, but their BT-13s were parked by the hangar, evidence of their presence on the base.

They were called into formation and marched to their barracks, then dismissed. They fell out of formation in a chatter of voices, disassembling and assembling into bay groups.

'It was really a sight to see – those two formations of planes barreling through the sky,' Chicago declared to the others.

The door to the bay was pulled open and they began filing through. Mary Lynn didn't notice the pile-up ahead of her and ran right into Cappy's back. Behind her the door swung shut, hitting her in the rump.

'Hey, what's going on?' she protested.

There at the back of the group with all their bodies blocking her view, Mary Lynn couldn't see what was causing all this consternation. Finally, Marty, who had been the dam-block, moved, and Mary Lynn saw a tall, slim woman sleeping on the far cot that Eden had once occupied. Her shoulder-length hair was a pale shade of biond, all touseled and mussed.

'What the hell is she doing here?' Marty wondered in a stunned outrage.

Her gruffness caused Mary Lynn to snicker behind her smothering hand. At the accusing look she received from Marty, she explained, 'This sounds like Goldilocks and Who's been sleeping in my bed.'

No one else seemed amused by her analogy. Mary Lynn decided they hadn't read that particular bedtime story as many times as she had, or they would have seen the humor

135

in it. For the moment, however, they were intent on the stranger in their midst.

'She's probably one of the trainees from Houston,' Cappy guessed as they drifted toward the cot.

'Well, that doesn't explain what the hell she's doing here.' Marty purposefully stalked to the cot and roughly shook the woman's shoulder. 'Wake up, Goldilocks.'

A violent toss of the arm threw off Marty's grip and a female voice snarled, 'Leave me alone.'

'Just what the hell do you think you're doing here?' Marty appeared incensed at the opposition she was getting as she hovered beside the cot.

This time the blond head moved a fraction. 'Sleeping. What the hell does it look like?'

'All right, *who* are you?' Marty challenged with hot sarcasm.

'One damned tired Woofted.' The woman made an attempt to burrow deeper into the cot and huddle into a smaller ball.

'A Woofted,' Marty repeated, then looked blankly at the others, still sarcastic. 'She's a Woofted, whatever the hell that is.'

The woman on the cot appeared to give up. In long, fluid moves she sat up on the edge of the narrow Amy bed, her shoulders bowing in tired lines and her head drooping with weariness. But there was plenty of fight in her voice, and her eyes were so violet as to appear almost purple-black.

'Women's Flying Training Detachment, stupid,' she said to Marty. 'Woofteds. W-F-T-D, Woofteds, that's what we call ourselves.'

'Woofteds, I should have guessed,' Marty said mockingly. 'We go by a much simpler term – trainees.'

The blonde raked Marty with a scathing glance. 'It figures.'

Marty was ready to claw those unusually dark eyes out of her head, but Cappy stepped in. 'Would you mind telling us what you're doing here?' Her tone had an authoritative ring, which didn't appear to sit any better with their Houston counterpart.

'I was assigned to this bay and this cot. Believe me, I don't like it any better than you do,' she stated flatly.

'I suppose the place isn't good enough for you,' Marty retorted.

'As a matter of fact, this place is the Taj Mahal compared to some of the living quarters we had in Houston. We lived in moldy, bug-infested tourist courts before they finally got barracks built for us. The food they served us was fit only for the garbage can. They finally installed a rest room. Before that, the nearest one was half a mile away. We wore the same clothes from dawn to dusk, because there was no place to change, so we walked around all day, dusty, dirty, and stinking with our own sweat.' Her sweeping glance encompassed all of them. 'You don't know how good this place is.'

'Isn't it wonderful, girls?' Marty piped sarcastically. 'Now we have our own resident expert. Instead of our parents telling us how rough *they* had it, we have a Woofted.'

'You don't like me and I don't like you,' the woman informed Marty. 'Let's leave it at that. Now I happen to have flown practically across the whole state of Texas, so if you don't mind, I'd like to get some rest.'

Marty backed away from the cot in mock deference. 'Forgive us for disturbing you. Just because this happens to be our bay it's really of little consequence. Why should we care who's sleeping in it?'

'Rachel Goldman from New York. Do you feel better?' she said sarcastically.

'New York,' Chicago repeated and nodded toward Eden. 'Eden's from New York, too.'

'Yeah?' She eyed the redhead, sizing her up with a wary, yet interested look.

'We live on Fifth Avenue just across from the park at Seventy-fifth,' Eden volunteered.

'Well, I'm from the Lower East Side,' she said and began

shifting in preparation to lie down again. She had slapped away the friendly hand that had belatedly been extended to her. Again, she stretched her long, feline body on the cot, and turned her back to them. In her stockinged feet, she missed being six feet tall by a fraction of an inch, so there wasn't much room left at either end of the cot.

Slowly they all moved toward their own Army cots, unsettled by this sudden intrusion of a stranger among them. The five of them had been a complete unit; they hadn't needed or wanted another.

'Someone probably had the bright idea of integrating the two classes,' Cappy suggested in an undertone.

'Well, it stinks!' Marty declared.

Mary Lynn winced at the loudness of her friend's remark. 'Marty, keep it down,' she advised quietly. 'She's trying to sleep.'

'So? I'm not going to tiptoe around here because of her!' Marty belligerently made no attempt to lower her voice, but the figure on the cot didn't appear to care.

It wasn't that Rachel Goldman was not used to defending herself. She had the sharp claws required to do it. They had been honed over the years of being picked on. As a Jew, she had often been made to feel unwanted, the victim of subtle persecutions and sometimes not so subtle ones.

There were only two things that had ever enabled her to escape, even briefly, from that. Dancing and flying. Despite her natural talent and years of training, there simply weren't many male dancers capable of lifting a six-foot ballerina, and her height made it equally difficult to get a job on a Broadway chorus line. So, mostly she had worked in nightclubs as a showgirl.

The first time Rachel had ever been in an airplane, it had been a transatlantic flight to Austria to visit her grandmother in Vienna. Of course, that was years ago, before Austria was occupied, when Hitler was merely a pompous-sounding fanatic, spouting his theories about the master race.

She'd spent a glorious month with her grandmother.

138

After corresponding for so many years, first at her parents' insistence, then because her grandmother seemed to really understand her love for the classic theater. Her grandmother had been wardrobe mistress at the Vienna opera house. At first, communicating was difficult; her grandmother's English was not good. Rachel's Yiddish was equally faulty, and her German nonexistent.

She had been fresh from flight when they met, enthralled with the sensation of it. She had talked about the experience for days on end until her grandmother had finally proclaimed, 'If you love flying so much, learn to do it yourself.' That, unfortunately, required lessons, which required money, and Rachel already had a big investment in dance.

Her parents had never been enthusiastic about her theatrical career, but her grandmother's support had always swayed the balance. When it came to flying, they had been even less thrilled to let their daughter try it. 'Marry, settle down, raise children. Forget all this nonsense,' her mother had urged. But Rachel had preferred her grandmother's advice. Ultimately, her parents had thrown up their hands, and Rachel had earned her own money for the flying lessons.

Along the way, she had learned some things, some bitter truths. If you want to be accepted outside your own community, don't be Jewish; if you want to get a job in a nightclub, don't look Jewish; if you want friends and lovers outside your faith, don't act Jewish. In some circles, it was even claimed the Jews were responsible for starting the war so they could profit from it. Some of the things 'Lucky Lindy,' Charles Lindbergh, had said still made Rachel cringe when she thought about them.

Since that awful day in 1938 when Austria was virtually handed over to Hitler on a platter, communication with her grandmother had become sporadic. A letter smuggled out of Europe by a fleeing family shortly after Warsaw fell was the last her family had had. Later came the vague stories of persecution, properties confiscated, arrests, roundups, then the work camps – some said death camps.

Way back in the beginning her father's group had lobbied Congress and the State Department in Washington to allow more Jewish refugees into the country. Hitler had offered to send the Jews to whatever country would take them, but almost no one had accepted – not even the United States.

Bitter – yes, she was bitter. And she hated, too, with a passion that would have made the Zealots proud of her. So when she had slapped away the one friendly overture made by Eden, it had been with the wariness of a cat many times burned, who now circled the beckoning flames but stayed well away from the warmth. Rachel's features had a hardened look to them that suggested all of her twenty-six years hadn't been easy ones. But Rachel was wiry and tough – a survivor. And right now, she needed a cat's short sleep.

The following day the last class of Army cadets left Avenger Field, Colin Fletcher among them. Just as their daily schedules had been regimented to keep the cadets separated from the trainees, so it was with their departure. The girls had no opportunity to wish them 'good luck and good flying.' They never actually saw the cadets leave. They were simply gone.

After an afternoon on the flight line, they returned to the bay to shower and change before evening mess. The vacant barracks across from theirs seemed faceless and forlorn. There had always been that underlying excitement of knowing men slept just across the way. Now that presence was gone, and with it, the little forbidden thrills it had conjured. The bays wouldn't be occupied until the next class of female trainees arrived in a couple of weeks.

'I'm going to miss those guys.' Chicago sent a glance in the direction of the opposite barracks as she opened the door to their bay.

'Yeah,' Eden agreed. 'No more late night visits from Colin and his cohorts. No more conversation by flashlight.'

Halfway through the doorway, Cappy stopped and bent to pick up a note lying on the floor.

'What is it?' Marty crowded ahead of Mary Lynn and Chicago.

'It's a note.' Cappy's curiosity was aroused as she moved into the long room and studied the small envelope in her hand. 'Addressed to all of us,' she added with a sweeping look.

'I'll bet it's from Colin. Hurry up and read it, Cap,' Marty urged impatiently, unzipping her flight suit the rest of the way down.

The connecting door to the bath facilities opened and the new baymate, Rachel Goldman, came in. Fresh from the shower, she was wrapped in a long blue chenille robe. Her wet hair had a silvery look to it as she rubbed the dripping ends with a towel. There was a slight break in her motion when she saw the five of them, then she continued toweling her hair dry as she walked to her cot.

Cappy removed the feather-thin note paper from the envelope, effectively directing the group's attention to it. 'It's from Colin, Grimsby, and the rest,' she said after a quick glance at the signatures at the bottom of the short message. 'We wanted to thank you' – she read – 'for all the nights you made less lonely for us, and for the warm memories we will be taking with us. Mary Lynn, we promise we'll keep an eye out for your Beau if we get to merry old England. We'll hope he understands when we give him your love.'

'Those rats,' Marty interposed with a chuckling laugh.

'They wouldn't?' Mary Lynn wasn't sure whether to laugh or not. No one answered her.

'To prove we aren't four-flushers, not by half, we have left one last treat for you to enjoy, a last cup of kindness.' A frown creased Cappy's forehead as she and the others tried puzzling out the meaning. 'Since we couldn't say goodbye to you, we won't say it now. Just "Good flying." . . . Signed, Colin, Arthur, Morley, and Henry.'

'What last treat?' Chicago asked, as they all looked

around the bay to see if something had been left – a package or a box. There was nothing in sight.

'Hey, Goldman?' Marty called, somewhat combatively. 'When you came in, was there anything sitting out here?'

'It'd still be there if it was,' she retorted.

'I'll bet they've hidden it somewhere,' Eden surmised. She gazed about the room for a logical hiding place.

'"A cup of kindness" . . . you drink it for Auld Lang Syne.' Distracted by Eden's musings, Marty started putting pieces together. 'You don't suppose?' she began, then a gleam of an idea spread the beginnings of a grin across her mouth. 'Half of a four-flusher – I think I know where they put it. Come on.'

'Where they put what?' A bewildered Mary Lynn followed the group, led by Marty, as they charged into the bathroom.

Marty went straight for the two stalls, unoccupied at the moment. She lifted the tank lid of the first commode, but it was the second one which contained the bottle of bonded whiskey. She held up the wet bottle in triumph while the others gathered around her.

'I can't believe it.' Eden almost fondled the bottle of aged liquor. 'Who did they bribe to get this?'

'How did they smuggle it in here – that's what I'd like to know,' Cappy murmured.

'Who cares?' Marty replied.

'But if we get caught with it on base, we're automatically thrown out of the program.' Mary Lynn saw nothing to rejoice about in that.

'That's true,' Marty agreed, but there was a wild sparkle in her olive-gray eyes. 'We don't have a whole lot of choice, girls,' she said. 'We'll just have to drink the evidence.'

Mary Lynn was the only one skeptical of the solution; the rest heartily endorsed the plan. Chicago was dispatched for a round of Cokes. Half of each bottle was poured down the sink to make room for the whiskey. In a conspiratorial huddle, they re-entered the bay carrying their spiked

Cokes. The capped whiskey bottle was tucked inside Marty's flight suit.

As they passed Rachel's cot, Marty nudged Chicago and stopped. In their absence, Rachel had dressed in slacks and a blouse. The thick mass of her blond hair was nearly dry.

'Thirsty, Goldman?' With a wide-eyed look of absolute innocence, Marty extended the extra Coke bottle to her, seemingly in a peace offering. 'You're welcome to drink this. Mary Lynn didn't want it.'

On the verge of refusing, Rachel appeared to reconsider and wavered for a skeptical minute before wanly accepting the bottle. 'Thanks.'

'Cheers.' Marty lifted her own bottle in a mock toast and watched with barely disguised glee as Rachel tilted the bottle to her mouth to take a swig of the Coke.

A second later, Rachel was choking on burning whiskey, coughing and spitting up the liquid her convulsing throat muscles refused to swallow. Despite her cupping hand, some of the liquid dribbled onto the clean blouse she'd just put on.

They all tittered with laughter, even Mary Lynn. Rachel Goldman was the only one who didn't see the humor in the prank. Anger glittered in her indigo-violet eyes as she shoved the bottle back into Marty's hand.

'Very funny.' Her voice still rasped on the edge of a coughing spasm.

'We thought so.' Marty's voice naturally matched the sound. 'The drink's yours, if you want it.' She offered her the Coke again. 'Mary Lynn doesn't drink anything but mint juleps.'

'Keep it.' Her look swept them all with contempt. 'You might have come here to party, but I'm here to fly.'

As Rachel stalked from the bay, Marty quirked an eyebrow, unperturbed by the denunciation. 'Little Mary Lynn isn't the only tee-totaler in our midst.'

Chicago looked apprehensively after their departing baymate. 'What if she reports us?'

'She won't,' Eden replied coolly. 'She wouldn't dare.' The implied threat in her remark was unmistakable.

'Here's to our guys.' Marty lifted her glass. 'May they never drink the water in the Channel.'

By the time lights out came, the 'evidence' had been consumed and the bottle was broken into non-incriminating pieces. All that remained of the label was a charred, curled mass of ashes. None of them had gotten drunk; they had more sense than that. But they slept deeply and soundly that night.

Too soundly. They missed reveille. And if Rachel Goldman hadn't yelled at them as she was heading out the door, they would have missed breakfast formation. Heavy-eyed, they staggered into line and tried to shake off the drugged sensation of sleep. They looked at Rachel, so alert and impassive, with a mixture of gratitude and resentment.

Outside morning mess, they dawdled to grumble before joining the cafeteria line. But the aroma of freshly made doughnuts invigorated their senses.

'I'd kill for them,' Marty declared as she piled four of them onto her tray.

As they reached the end of the line, Chicago stopped. 'Look. They've taken our table.'

Stunned by the announcement, they stared at the far end of the long table they had occupied since their very first meal at the base.

Part of the Houston class, including Rachel, was now seated in the space they considered reserved for them. Others in their class had always respected their right to it.

'I'll handle this,' Eden asserted and strode to the front, leading them across the room to the table. Their arrival barely rated a glance. 'Excuse me. This is our section.' Her cool hauteur implied all would be forgiven if they would vacate immediately – a tone guaranteed to make a *maître d'* bow, very low.

'What's your name?' Helen Shaw, a doe-eyed woman with a set of dimples carved in her cheeks, asked the question.

'Van Valkenburg. Eden van Valkenburg.' The self-importance was evident.

'Funny.' The woman looked around the table. 'I don't see your name anywhere.' The others in her group laughed to themselves.

A tremor of anger stiffened Eden. 'Very funny indeed,' she retorted. 'This happens to be our table. We have always sat here in this corner.'

'I guess you'll have to find another place this morning,' Rachel stated. 'Because this one is already occupied.'

Marty pushed her way to the forefront. 'You wanna bet, cookie?' she threatened.

'Forget it.' Cappy laid a restraining hand on Marty's arm.

'Why should we forget it?' Marty shook it off. 'We were here first. They're the ones who don't belong.'

'I think you have that turned around,' Rachel coldly corrected her. 'Maybe you came to Sweetwater before we did, but the Houston classes before you pioneered this whole program. We Woofteds were the guinea pigs.'

'That makes you something special, I suppose,' Marty answered mockingly.

Their dispute was attracting the attention of the other trainees in the room. Cappy could tell the Houston group would vacate the table only through force. There was no diplomatic solution to the situation.

'Come on, Marty,' she urged quietly. 'You can't afford any more demerits.' For the time being, they had to retreat.

But the battle lines were drawn. Possession of the table became the symbolic center of their dispute. Eden, Marty, Cappy, and the others regarded the Houston class as interlopers on the base, while their Houston counterparts saw themselves as heir apparents of the very first classes in the pilot training program for women.

What had begun as a personality conflict in the bay between Rachel and Marty became part of a larger rivalry. The Sweetwater half of the class assumed a proprietary attitude toward everything on the base, and the Houston half contested it.

145

Having Rachel in their bay made the situation more awkward. An armed truce existed; her presence was tentatively accepted. But for Marty it was a case of accepting under strong protest.

CHAPTER NINE

The day was glorious; sun-drenched skies stretched lazily to the flat horizons. On the ground the air was hot and dry, but at four thousand feet it was pleasantly warm. Bored with her solo practice of the requisite maneuvers, Eden decided to play a little aerial hooky and enjoy some of this afternoon sunshine.

She pushed open the canopy of her BT-13 to let in the day. In preparation, Eden trimmed the aircraft until it was practically flying itself. The skies around her were empty and blue when she unbuttoned her blouse and shrugged out of it, taking care not to bump the stick held between her knees.

The lacy brassiere supporting her breasts was one of those 'nothing' creations that barely covered her rose-brown nipples. It was designed to be worn under garments with plunging necklines, but Eden had found the flimsy and scanty bra ideal since its softness never chafed and its brevity allowed more freedom of movement. It was also perfect for sun-bathing.

With her blouse neatly folded and tucked behind her, Eden leaned back and closed her eyes against the sun shining on her face. The enveloping warmth was blissfully relaxing. The pleasant heat seemed to caress her bare skin; it was so soothing and sensuous. She basked in the cockpit, unconcerned, listening to the reassuring level pitch of the engine and the steady rush of air spilling over her aircraft.

Suddenly, a roaring noise intruded. Eden opened her eyes to scan her instruments, but her side vision caught the reflection of sunlight on metal off her left wing. Another trainer was flying beside her, piloted by a grinning cadet. With a sudden shock, Eden realized he had a clear view inside the cockpit of her trainer and the lace brassiere revealed much more than it concealed.

She ducked lower, trying to make herself small, and banked the plane away from him. She had expected his pursuit, but she hadn't counted on the additional support he picked up. Within minutes, it seemed, she was surrounded by a swarm of buzzing aircraft, all vying for a glimpse inside her cockpit.

Her usually unshakable poise was fast forsaking her. Desperate, Eden tried to hold the plane steady with her knees while she struggled with her blouse. The whipping wind kept tugging at it and defying her efforts to find the opening of the sleeves. She had to keep grabbing the stick to straighten the erratic weaving of the airplane. Suddenly, the wind tore the blouse from her hands. She tried to grab it before it went sailing over the top of the canopy but failed. She swore she could hear the surrounding pilots cheer at the sight.

Hot with embarrassment, Eden crouched low in the cockpit and swung her plane into a steep turn, making a mad dash for the 'off-limits' safety of Avenger Field. As she neared her destination, one by one the pursuing aircraft peeled away.

Touchdown signaled the end of that ordeal and the start of another. With all the mechanics and instructors on the flight line, how on earth was she going to make a dignified exit from the plane when she was half naked?

Sneaking looks, Eden taxied to the hangar area and shut the plane down. When she peered cautiously out the side, she noticed a group of trainees in front of the ready room. Swallowing a big chunk of pride, she called to them. 'Hey! Will one of you bring me a jacket or something?' She risked one more look to see if they had heard her, then ducked back down.

In short order, someone was climbing the wing of her

trainer. As a shadow fell across her cockpit, Eden looked up with relief. Her expression froze into a kind of stiffness when she found herself looking into the almond-shaped eyes of Rachel Goldman. Any hope she'd had that this humiliating incident could be kept quiet died.

Later, in the bay after evening mess, Eden fumed at the unfairness of it. 'It was bad enough that it had to be one of those damned "Woofteds," but Rachel?!' she ranted to the barely disguised but sympathetic amusement of her four baymates. 'You should have seen the way she gloated when she handed me that blanket.'

'At least she gave you the blanket,' Mary Lynn pointed out. 'Come on, Eden, you have to admit there's some humor in it.' Marty had seen the regal redhead when she crossed the flight line, swathed in the blanket as if it was some royal robe, her head held unnaturally high and her cheeks flaming. If Eden hadn't already been the butt of all the Woofteds' comments, Marty would have poked some fun at Eden herself.

'Oh, it's very funny,' she returned sarcastically. 'On top of everything, that blouse happened to be one of my favorites. It cost the earth, too! Now some mesquite brush is probably wearing it.'

As Rachel entered the bay, there was an instant silence. The tall, supple blonde moved into the room, a catlike gleam in her dark amethyst eyes as they swept over Eden.

'How's the sunburn?' she queried maliciously.

'I don't have one.' Eden pushed the sweetly voiced comment through her clenched teeth.

'Really? Your face seemed very pink at mess tonight,' Rachel replied with feline slyness. 'I thought for sure it was because you had too much sun today.'

Eden found herself caught in one of those irritating moments when she wanted to make some really scathing response, but her mind deserted her. She simply couldn't think of anything. It would come in the middle of the night, when it was too late.

A new facet was added to the instrument-flying phase of their basic training when the trainees were informed they would be flying with a 'buddy' of their choice. The pairing was almost a natural selection. Mary Lynn and Marty elected to fly together while Cappy and Eden teamed up to make a unit, and Chicago paired up with Jo Ann North, a fellow trainee from the adjoining bay.

As they walked to their BT-13, Cappy thought nothing about the arrangement until she was strapped into the rear cockpit seat. Then the jitters shook her. All her instrument time under the black hood had been under the supervision of her instructor. Now she would have to trust Eden to correct any mistake she might make and to keep watch for any aircraft in their immediate vicinity to avoid a midair collision. She was literally trusting Eden with her life.

After taking off, Eden flew the plane to the designated practice area. Cappy fought the flutterings of unease in her stomach when Eden volunteered to go first. While the black curtain was being pulled in place, Cappy took the controls. As soon as Eden was ready, she surrendered them to her again.

Nervously, Cappy scanned the instruments and the skies around their plane, and kept an eye on the attitude of the aircraft's nose to the horizon while Eden practiced turns, descents, and climbs. She felt a strange urge to override the controls before Eden could unwittingly put the plane in a dangerous attitude where it might stall and spin out, but gradually, Cappy came to recognize her buddy's competence. Instrument flying was a precise skill, requiring the utmost in concentration. A calm began to settle her raw nerves as Cappy saw that Eden could fly as well as she could.

When it came time to switch, Cappy pulled the hood over herself without any reservation. She was confident of Eden's ability in an emergency. It was a rare experience to place her life in someone else's hands – to rely on another to keep her safe – yet that's exactly what she was doing. What's more, it filled her with an elated kind of relief.

149

After that first flight when they tumbled out of the aircraft, they looked at each other with new eyes. 'Has anybody ever told you you can fly, Hayward?' Eden remarked with a hint of amazement.

'So can you,' she replied.

A second later, they were laughing and companionably hooking an arm across each other's shoulder as they headed back to the ready room. Cappy felt near to tears. These last weeks they had eaten together, studied together, griped together, and shared the same sleeping quarters, but nothing had forged the closeness she now felt. It was respect and admiration, coupled with a hard-won trust.

Spring storms raised havoc with the flying schedules. The trainees were forced to fly when the weather permitted in order to get their required time in the air, which meant they gave up most of their April Sundays.

In May, the base command was thrown into a turmoil by the news that General George C. Marshall, Chief of Staff of the United States Army, as well as General Henry 'Hap' Arnold, Commanding General of the United States Army Air Forces, would be visiting Avenger Field on an inspection tour. The rumor of their impending arrival swept the barracks like a fire storm.

'I don't understand what all the fuss is about,' Eden shrugged, unimpressed by their titles.

'The Commanding General of the Air Forces and the Chief of Staff, no less. How blasé can you get?' Marty threw her arms in the air in a show of exasperation.

'You have to talk to Eden in terms that she understands,' Cappy said, good-naturedly ribbing her friend. 'You see, it's like this, Eden. Generals expect to review the troops – and we don't have a thing to wear.'

'What do you mean?' Eden asked cautiously.

'While the government was issuing us our battle jackets and zoot suits, they failed to include a Class A – in civilian terms, a dress uniform,' Cappy explained.

'Can you see us parading past the reviewing stand in our fatigues?' Mary Lynn laughed.

For the rest of the week, rumors abounded that frantic phone calls were being made to obtain a standard outfit for all the trainees. A short three days before the generals were to appear, the outfits, consisting of tan slacks, short-sleeved white blouses, and boat-shaped flight caps, arrived. Alterations had to be made in order to ensure proper length and fit, and with so little time left, the girls had to do it themselves. They were all in a mad rush to get it done.

Perched on her cot, Eden struggled with a needle and thread, trying to hem the legs of her tan slacks. The tip of her tongue was poked out the corner of her mouth, a study of concentration, as if facial contortions could assist the wayward needle.

'Ouch!' She jabbed herself in the thumb and quickly raised the injured finger to her mouth to suck on it.

Exasperation was showing in her expression as she studied the wound for any red dots of blood. Her bay-mates, all busy with their own alterations, barely gave her more than an amused grunt.

'My thumb has more holes in it than a pincushion,' Eden announced bitterly, then looked at the slacks on her lap. No more than a half-dozen stitches had been sewn. Yet, for all her painstaking care, they were irregular and uneven. In disgust, she tossed the pants aside and swung off the cot. 'This is ridiculous. I have no business taking a needle and thread in my hands. I've never done any sewing in my life and I'm not about to start now.'

'There aren't any maids here,' Marty reminded her dryly, struggling with her own ineptitude at anything more than the cursory sewing of a button on a blouse.

'Somebody has got to help me,' Eden insisted and looked around the room for a candidate, but all heads were bowed over their own tasks. She zeroed in on Mary Lynn, the only one of their group who had any skill with a needle. 'Mary Lynn?'

'I'd do it for you but I have to finish my own.' Mary Lynn's work entailed a major alteration of the waistline, length, and hips in order for the slacks to properly fit her petite frame.

At the hint of possibly forthcoming assistance, Eden crossed to Mary Lynn's cot to press her appeal. 'Please,' she urged. 'I'll pay you five dollars. Ten.'

'Don't say anything, Mary Lynn,' Marty advised. 'Maybe she'll make it fifteen.'

'Fifteen, twenty – I don't care,' Eden declared impatiently. 'These pants legs practically drag the ground. I'll stick out like a sore thumb.' The remark reminded Eden of her many-times poked thumb and she made another biting suck on it.

They all looked sympathetic to her problem and slightly amused by it, too. Then, from the last cot, an unexpected offer was made. 'If you want, I'll hem them for you.'

They had been for so long in the habit of ignoring the sixth member of their bay that when Rachel Goldman reluctantly offered to help, initially they could only stare at her. The ongoing feud between the two factions prompted Eden to question the offer before she jumped at it.

'Can you sew?' She retrieved her pants from the cot and warily approached Rachel, who was putting the finishing touches on her own slacks.

'My grandmother taught me.' With a series of dexterous flicks of the wrist, the needle flashed through the cloth. Rachel tied the thread in a knot, and bit the thread in two with her teeth. Eden was impressed with the entire process.

But her skepticism returned when Rachel, having neatly folded her slacks by the creases and laid them aside, reached for Eden's. She held on to them. 'Why are you doing this for me?' She had absolutely no reason to trust Rachel.

'For *you*?' The pronoun was stressed with contempt. 'I personally don't care how you look, but we march in the same squad, and I'm not going to have you drag all of us down because you look like a sad sack of shit.'

The response made perfect sense, but Eden's mouth thinned just the same as she handed over her slacks. 'They're already marked for the proper length.'

After surrendering the pants, Eden stayed by the cot to watch, playing it safe. With her shoulders pressed against the wall and one leg bent while the other braced her, Eden folded her arms in front of her. She kept an eye on the darting needle as it stitched the thread with precision. Her own proven ineptitude gave her a greater appreciation of the skill.

'Is your grandmother a seamstress in New York?' She considered passing the information to her mother. It could be worth knowing, especially now that no more designs were coming out of occupied Paris.

'No.' The sylphlike blonde didn't let her attention stray from her work.

'Where does she work?' Eden stubbornly persisted in the quest for information, mostly to irritate the uncommunicative Rachel.

'Vienna.'

The answer sounded so preposterous, Eden laughed. 'You're kidding?'

The blond head lifted, and those intensely violet eyes, like pansies with black centers, focused on Eden with cold challenge. 'She was the wardrobe lady for the opera company there.' She returned to her sewing.

Sobering, Eden realized that Rachel was serious. 'Was?' she said with a slight frown.

'My grandmother is in one of the Nazi work camps in Poland.' Rachel didn't look up.

The others had been listening in on the conversation. Rachel's last remark roused Mary Lynn's curiosity. 'What's this about work camps? I don't remember hearing anything about them before.'

'From what I've read, they're Hitler's version of our detention camps for Japanese,' Eden replied, then belatedly turned to Rachel. 'Isn't that right?'

'Maybe they look alike,' Rachel conceded derisively.

'Both have high barbed-wire fences and guards with dogs and machine guns. But the Jews who have escaped have told us they go there to die. The ones that don't starve to death, the Nazis slaughter.'

'That's absurd,' Marty scoffed from the other end of the room.

'Why?' Rachel was quick to challenge. 'In the last two thousand years, many countries have made some kind of attempt to do away with the Jews. Why should it come as any surprise that Hitler intends to try?'

'I think you're taking an extreme view,' Eden suggested.

'I am?' Her needle seemed to fly more swiftly in and out of the material, stabbing and surging. 'What do you call the White Shirts, the Lindberghs, the Henry Fords? What about Father Coughlin and his Christian Front? Or didn't you hear about the attacks on Jewish school children after the Irish Evacuation Day exercises in Boston just two months ago in March? Don't you think their anti-Semitic views are extreme?'

Her impassioned words prompted Cappy to inject some calm and reason in the heated air. 'Eden never meant to offend you.'

'No one ever does.' Her voice was quieter, flatter. 'Jews just make a good scapegoat. You can take all your fears and frustration out on us; blame the Jews for the Depression, the war – everything.'

At the end of her bitter words, there was an awkward silence. Her head remained bent to her task. Uncomfortable, Eden watched Rachel's hands and avoided the blonde's face.

'I'm sorry,' Eden voiced the feeling in the room, the phrase seeming inadequate.

'Being sorry is worthless.' A knot was tied and the thread was broken with a small snap. Then Rachel lifted her glance to Eden. 'When I was a little girl, I remember listening to my father during his morning prayers. One of the Old Testament verses he sometimes recited said, "Blessed art Thou, O Lord our God, King of the universe, who hast not made me a woman." I used to be sorry I was a girl because there were so many things I couldn't do. Being sorry doesn't change anything. If I can't be a soldier and fight the Germans, then I'll fly planes so a man can go. In my own way, I'll fight.'

'We all will,' Mary Lynn agreed in a low, tight voice.

Rachel handed Eden the finished pants. 'Thanks,' Eden said as she took them from her. Rachel's hand remained outstretched.

'Ten dollars is what you said you would pay,' Rachel reminded her coolly.

For a shocked instant, Eden was stunned that her offer had been taken seriously. Her reaction became tempered with cynicism. 'So much for *esprit de corps*,' she murmured and went back to her cot to fetch the money from her purse.

With the impending visit of the big brass, they managed to fit into their free time between ground school and flying not only the uniform alterations but also hours of drilling. Marching to and from the flight line, or mess, or the barracks took on a new significance. They practiced until their columns were as knife-straight as the creases in their new tan slacks. Then the word came.

'They aren't coming?' Mary Lynn wailed. 'After all I went through to get these damn pants to fit me!'

'Tsk, tsk, such language,' Marty said mockingly.

'There was a change of plans at the last minute,' Cappy informed them. 'That happens often in the Army.' Cappy knew this well, but she'd been all caught up in the excited furor, too.

'Is that it?' Eden demanded. 'I mean, they simply aren't coming – no apologies, no explanation, nothing?'

'That's it,' Cappy replied, then shrugged. 'Oh, there was talk of some low-level officer being sent around in the next few days to look around.'

Eden pulled off the turban that had enwrapped her red hair and slammed it on her cot, then flounced down beside it, simmering. 'I feel as if I've just been stood up by my date. No one has ever dared to do this to me before.'

They all shared the feeling, and none of them liked it any better than Eden did.

The hush of the classroom was broken by the scratch of lead pencils on the test sheets, the rub of erasers to strike a reconsidered answer and the soft shuffle of papers. Cappy was bent over the essay-type meteorology quiz, the tension throbbing in her temples.

Define the difference between cirrostratus, cirrocumulus, and stratocumulus and the type of weather or associated fronts related to each. Cappy read the question and wanted to groan aloud.

As the lead pencil-point touched the paper, the door to the classroom clicked resoundingly into the near silence. Briefly, the class was distracted by the opening of the door.

It lasted long enough for most of them to surmise that the rather good-looking officer, escorted by one of the training staff, was the Army major sent on the unofficial inspection tour. Rumor had reported his arrival at Avenger Field earlier in the morning, so his appearance wasn't totally unexpected.

Except by Cappy. She stared at him, indifferent to the meteorology instructor, who joined him by the door to converse in whispers. That angled profile and strong jaw-line, that proud way of carrying himself, she'd know them anywhere. Cappy didn't need to see the confirmation of the name tag, on his breast pocket. It was Major Mitch Ryan.

Her throat felt tight and strangled by an emotion she was reluctant to name. Until she saw Mitch standing there, in the same room with her, she hadn't realized how home-sick and lonely she'd been. Cappy felt the excited rush of her pulse, the joy that soared inside her. Mitch was a slice of home. The remembered warmth in his dark eyes and the hard feel of his arms came rushing back.

Her fingers released their grip on the pencil and it

clattered onto the tabletop. Impulse nearly pushed Cappy out of her seat to cross the room to Mitch, but it died the instant he turned his gaze in her direction and she saw the hard, impersonal look in his expression. She realized how wide her smile had been and felt the sting of a rebuke for allowing her emotions to be seen in public. He was here in an official capacity, she reminded herself, and quickly lowered her gaze.

Her intense dislike for the requisite military discipline resurfaced as Cappy picked up her pencil and attempted to concentrate on the meteorology test, but she was conscious of all that went on at the classroom doorway. She recognized the familiar tread of his footsteps as he wandered into the room and strolled behind the test-taking trainees.

When Mitch paused by her chair, all her nerves went tense. Her pencil remained poised above the paper the whole time he was there.

Her mind refused to function or come up with a single, intelligent answer to any of the easy questions. In the edges of her vision, she could see the sharp creases of his trousers and the polished brown of his shoes. He stood next to her for so long that Cappy wondered if he expected her to acknowledge his presence. She started to look up, but he resumed his leisurely pace, moving by her.

A few more hushed words were exchanged with the instructor, then Mitch left the classroom. Cappy stared at the door for a long time, feeling hurt without being sure why.

Later, on the floor of the ready room, Cappy sat hunched over her bent knees, subdued and silent in the afternoon bustle of the flight-line area. She listened to her more talkative baymates with only half an ear.

'I don't know why we couldn't have multiple choice,' Marty complained. Then brightening, 'Now, if I'd been given my choice, I would have picked that rugged-looking major. I wouldn't have objected if he wanted to make a closer inspection of the troops.'

'Marty, you're incorrigible,' Mary Lynn protested with a laugh.

'Attention!' A voice barked the command that sent all the trainees scrambling to their feet.

As Mitch Ryan walked into the ready room with his entourage of base personnel, Cappy kept her gaze to the front, resisting the urge to look at him. 'As you were.' His richly timbred voice released them to return to their former casual informality.

Despite the order, Cappy couldn't fully relax. Her glance kept darting to locate him as he wandered through the room, smiling aloofly at the eager and admiring looks that greeted him and steadily coming closer to the side of the room where she stood. Then he was towering beside them, his few extra inches adding to the commanding aura.

'Cigarette?' He shook some partway out of the pack and offered one first to Marty.

'Thanks.' She took one while Mary Lynn refused.

The pack was offered to Cappy and she withdrew a cigarette. 'Have you been up flying today?' Mitch addressed the question generally as he took a pack of matches from his inside pocket.

'Not yet,' Marty answered while he lit her cigarette. 'It should be a good day for it, though.'

His hand cupped the match flame to Cappy's cigarette. She bent her head to it, her gaze straying over his long fingers, conscious of the strength in them. When Cappy straightened to blow the smoke to the side, her response was automatic. 'Thanks, Mitch.'

Silence seemed to thunder about her for a lightning-struck second while Marty and Mary Lynn stared at her. But Cappy had already felt the hard, accusing thrust of his look. She met it without outwardly flinching.

'It is Major Ryan to you, trainee.' The rough reprimand discouraged any further familiarity.

'My mistake, sir,' Cappy shot back at him, cold and angry. 'I thought I knew you.'

She dropped the cigarette and ground it into the floor

with her heel before she stalked onto the flight line, her visage frozen into an emotionless expression. She faced into the wind, letting the hot May air blow over her.

CHAPTER TEN

Minutes after Cappy had walked onto the flight line, Mitch came running out of the building accompanied by one of her classmates. As they crossed the apron to a waiting aircraft, it was clear Mitch intended to fly with the trainee to see for himself the type of training the women pilots were getting. He didn't so much as look Cappy's way.

She wished fervidly that he was flying with her instead. What a pleasure it would be to pop the stick and snap his Army neck. The propeller churned the air, blowing up the ever-present red dust. As the plane made its turn to taxi to the runway, the stinging dust cloud was kicked back at Cappy. She narrowed her eyes, blinking them to get rid of the smarting dust while she watched the plane leave the hangar area.

The lyrics to one of their marching songs, the one patterned after the Georgia Tech tune, kept flitting through her mind. It seemed to match this bitter and confused resentment she was feeling.

If I had a civilian check, I know just what I'd do;
I'd pop the stick and crack his neck, and probably get
  a U.
But if I had an Army check, I'd taxi across the grass.
I'd flip the ship upon its nose, and throw him on his
  . . . Ooooo
Oh, I'm a flying wreck, a-risking my neck and a
  helluva pilot too —

The noise from the roaring engine of the BT-13 receded as it taxied away from the flight line. Marty and Mary Lynn emerged from the ready room and joined Cappy in the hangar's shade. Avid curiosity lurked behind Marty's close study of her baymate.

'It's obvious you know him, Cap. Aren't you going to tell us?' Marty prodded.

'I *knew* him.' All her attention seemed to be on the aircraft taxiing toward them. 'That's my plane coming in. See you later.' With a little skip, she broke into a slow jog to meet the basic trainer.

'Did you see that look in her eye when we first came out?' Marty said to Mary Lynn while she watched their departing baymate.

'What do you mean?'

'She was dirty-fighting mad.' Marty was willing to bet on it. 'It's kind of hard to believe, isn't it? Calm, competent Cappy was riled, but good.'

Mary Lynn didn't comment. The relationship between a man and a woman was a private thing, not to be aired in public. She respected Cappy's desire for silence on the matter. If she didn't want to talk about the major, then they had no right to ask.

After three hours of dual instruction, part of it hood time, Cappy landed the BT-13 and taxied to the hangar, where the rest of the planes sat scorching in the rays of the late afternoon sun. Fatigue from the strain of endless concentration left her feeling dull as she climbed out of the cockpit onto the wing-walk.

'Your mind wasn't on flying today.' The hard criticism came from her instructor, Jimmy Ray Price. He knew full well she could have done much better.

'I know.' Hot and tired, she pulled off the snood and ran ruffling fingers through her nut-brown hair.

'It's a cardinal rule for pilots – don't take your problems up in the air with you. Leave them on the ground. Up there, you need all your concentration on flying.' As always

160

he was harsh with her, always demanding the best from the best.

Tears of exhaustion and self-pity threatened to spill over but she kept them at bay. Why was it the men she knew all seemed to be callous and demanding – her father, her instructors, everyone? She might try to deny it, but – damn, she did want their approval. Always she was expected to excel and even when she did, she received only faint praise for it.

Tired and miserable, Cappy walked toward the ready room with her head down. Her instructor kept pace with her, his silence merely weighting his previous tongue-lashing. Just let the day be over, she kept thinking. Before they reached the building, the base commander, his aide, and Mitch Ryan walked out the door and paused directly in their path. Cappy attempted to avoid Mitch's watching eyes as her glance skimmed the dark brown of his uniform jacket and, on its shoulders, the gold leaves signifying his rank. The hard bill of his officer's cap obscured his look, but the set of his mouth and jaw hadn't softened at all.

'Good flying today, Price?' The base commander directed his question at her instructor, his tone hearty. Then he turned to offer an aside to Mitch. 'This young woman is one of our best pilots.'

Obliged to stop, Cappy paused beside her instructor, stiffly tense. She forced a certain pleasantness into her expression for the benefit of the Army Commander of Avenger Field and kept her attention focused on him rather than Mitch.

'Very good, as usual,' Jimmy Ray Price lied. Cappy was convinced it was the kindest gesture he'd ever made, even if it hadn't been to spare her.

'I'm glad to hear it,' Mitch replied, and Cappy was equally certain that was a lie. So far, no one had addressed a comment directly to her. The omission wasn't corrected as Mitch turned to the commander. 'This trainee happens to be the daughter of a friend of mine.'

Surprised that he should choose this moment to acknowledge her, Cappy stared at him. He looked back, aloof and vaguely challenging. 'With your permission, Major,' Mitch continued, going through the motions of observing proper channels, 'I would like to take Miss Hayward to dinner tonight, off the post. I know the Lieutenant Colonel and his wife are anxious to learn how she's getting along.'

Lieutenant Colonel. The news of her father's promotion barely registered. Uppermost in her feelings was a raw resentment at his presumption that she would want to spend an evening with him. Cappy's response was tempered by the presence of the base commander.

'You'll have to excuse me this trip, Major Ryan. It has been a very long and exhausting day –'

His low voice cut across her polite refusal. 'I don't recall asking whether you wanted to come, Miss Hayward.'

She wanted to rail at him, to scream and stomp her feet in an uncontrolled protest, but it all lodged in her throat. She had been too well schooled against such outbursts. After a few seconds of hesitant uncertainty, the commander interpreted her ensuing silence to mean an acceptance of the invitation.

'If Miss Hayward is agreeable, naturally you have my permission,' he qualified his answer, giving Cappy an opportunity to protest. She didn't. Whatever their differences, she wasn't going to make them a public issue – and Mitch had known that.

'Good.' Satisfaction settled smoothly onto his features. 'I'll need the use of a vehicle from your motor pool.'

'Of course.'

'Can you be ready by eighteen hundred hours, Miss Hayward?' He leveled another glance at her, then swept her with it to indicate a change of attire was required.

'Yes, sir.' She had to agree, but her blue eyes glared at him.

Promptly at six o'clock, Mitch knocked on the bay door. Eden went to answer it while Cappy fastened the clasp on

162

the scrimshaw necklace her father had brought her from Alaska. His presence in the room seemed to alter the atmosphere, sending an undercurrent of tension through it. Cappy listened to the brisk pitch of his voice as Eden made the introductions, but she didn't look around as she gathered up her purse.

When she finally turned, Mitch was standing just inside the door, his hat tucked under his arm. Without a cap, he looked more mature and masculine, less like a recruiting poster of a roguishly handsome officer.

'Ready?' The one word managed to convey the impression of a challenge.

Cappy simply nodded, and lowered her lashes to conceal the flaring surge of pride that wanted to defy him. Avoiding the glances of her baymates, she crossed to the door and brushed past him as he opened it for her. She caught the tangy scent of some aftershave lotion drifting from his smoothly shaven face before the hot, dusty air chased it away.

The impersonal pressure of his hand at her elbow guided her to the olive-drab jeep parked in front of the barracks and helped her into the seat. Mitch walked around the rear of the vehicle to the driver's side and hopped behind the wheel.

His hand paused on the ignition key while he sent her a sideways look. 'I've been told the Bluebonnet Hotel is the place to go in Sweetwater.'

'The dining facilities are probably the best in town,' she agreed stiffly.

'Then you have no objections if we go there?'

'None.' Cappy tied a scarf of sapphire blue silk around her head so her dark hair wouldn't be blown into total disarray in the open vehicle.

The jeep was not known for its smooth ride. Cappy gripped the side when they turned onto the main road and picked up speed. The roar of the engine made it impractical to talk and the rush of air would have swept the words away if they had tried. In silence, with their eyes to the front, they sped down the highway, traversing the short distance to Sweetwater, bouncing roughly over the bumps and ruts.

Within the town limits, they slowed and Cappy directed him to Sweetwater's lone hotel. The stiffness and awkwardness between them persisted as they parked in front of the six-story tan brick building. Mitch escorted her into the hotel lobby with its pink walls and art deco light fixtures. In addition to a small sitting area and writing desks in the lobby level, a set of three steps led to a separate sitting area for hotel guests.

'The dining room is this way.' Cappy indicated the direction and Mitch guided her to it.

The hotel dining room repeated the art deco theme and color scheme they'd seen in the lobby. The cloth-covered tables all were set with silverware and glasses, but few diners were seen.

'Not very busy,' Mitch remarked.

'It's relatively quiet during the week. You have to wait until the weekend for things to liven up.' Cappy was conscious of his body leaning over her as he pushed her chair up to the table.

'Do you come here often?' He placed his hat on the seat of a side chair and sat down opposite her, combing fingers through his hair to rumple its flatness.

'Yes, sometimes.' She opened the menu and pretended to study its familiar fare.

'What will you have?' After she told him, Mitch gave their order to the waitress. 'Do you have a good burgundy?'

The waitress gave him a blank look, and Cappy stepped in to inform him dryly, 'You aren't in Washington, Mitch. This is a dry county – no wine, no beer, nothing . . . except for some potent moonshine if you know the right people to ask.'

A curt nod of dismissal sent the waitress away from their table. Cappy felt the hard probe of his gaze. 'And do you?' he asked tersely.

'Let's say a friend of a friend does,' she countered, and

opened her purse to take out a cigarette. Ignoring his offer of a light, Cappy struck her own match, and dragged the smoke deeply into her lungs before exhaling it.

Finally, Mitch lit his own cigarette. For long minutes there was only silence at the table, broken intermittently by the tap of a cigarette on the shared ashtray.

'Aren't you going to ask me about your father's promotion?' Mitch inquired with a grim-lipped look. 'It only came through last week.'

'Did he ask you to mention it to me?' Cappy studied the lipstick – stained tip of her cigarette.

'No.'

'Then I don't have to bother to offer him any congratulations, do I?' she retorted, the hope dying that he might have sent her the message as a conciliatory gesture. 'How's Mother?'

'I think she's finding it awkward being caught in the middle between you and Colonel Hayward.'

'She isn't in the middle. She's on his side.' She shied away from further discussion on the subject of her father and their feud. 'Let's talk about something else.' Conversation, however stilted, was preferable to the strain of a continued silence.

But talking, instead of easing the tension, merely increased it. As the meal progressed, their exchanges became more staccatolike, as if each was trying to outdo the other's clipped sentences. When Mitch picked up the bill for their meal, Cappy nearly bolted for the door in her eagerness to have this wretched evening end.

Outside the sun had gone down, taking with it some of the searing heat. A handful of evening stars glittered in the purpling blue sky while a waning moon turned a sleepy eye on the occupants of the jeep speeding back to the airfield.

A guard at the entrance waved them through the gate. But Mitch didn't stop at the barracks. Instead he continued on to the criss-crossing air strips and followed an access road to the end of one of them. Flarepots had been set out on the adjacent active runway for that evening's group of night flyers.

The jeep bounced to a stop and Mitch switched the motor off. Frowning, Cappy turned to look at him. Both his hands grasped the wheel as he gazed out the front windscreen. In the deepening shadows of night, the muscles along his jaw stood out, catching the faint sheen from the moon and intensifying the grim and angry set of his features.

'Why did you bring me here?' Cappy demanded impatiently.

The blunt question seemed to prod him into action. A hard glance was thrown her way, as if he suddenly remembered she was there, then Mitch was swinging out of the jeep.

'Let's walk.'

Obedience to a command was almost a conditioned reflex. Cappy was out of the jeep and taking a step to follow the tall, uniformed figure whose hands were thrust into the side pockets of his creased trousers, before she realized what she was doing.

'No.' She came to a stop. 'I don't have to take orders from you.' Mitch halted and half turned to look at her, his face shadowed by the brim of his cap. 'You can go for a walk if you want, but I'm going back to the barracks.'

With her rebellion announced, Cappy swung away and aimed for the distant set of low buildings beyond the curved humps of the hangar roofs. As she started for the barracks, she heard the trotting thud of his footsteps break into a quick pursuit. When his hand caught the crook of her arm she tried to shrug it off, but his fingers tightened their grip and she was pulled around, held by her upper arms.

'You're not going anywhere, Cap, until I find out what's happening here. You've changed and I don't like it.' Mitch bit out the words, his teeth flashing whitely in the shadowed planes of his face.

'*I've* changed?' she repeated in stunned anger.

'You openly admitted tonight that you frequent the Bluebonnet Hotel. Do you think I don't know what's going on there? Do you think the talk hasn't gotten around?'

At first she frowned at him in puzzlement, then impatience swept it aside. 'You aren't making any sense.' Cap flattened her hands against his beribboned breast pockets to push him away.

His hands tightened their grip, giving her a hard shake. 'The word has spread to every air base in the area. At each stop before coming here, I was told by everyone from mechanic to lieutenant – if I wanted a good time, go to the Bluebonnet Hotel in Sweetwater where one of those "pretty little women trainees" would take care of me.'

'That's a lie,' Cap answered emphatically.

'From one source, maybe two, I would have questioned it.' His voice was tight and low. 'But it was all up and down the line, and several could personally vouch for the truth in it.'

'I don't believe it.' Her lips came firmly together in solid resistance to what she was hearing.

'Come on, Cap. Are you trying to tell me you don't know what's going on?' he taunted.

She pulled back to stare at him. 'What are you thinking, Mitch? That I'm one of these trainees supposedly bestowing her favors on any soldier that comes by?'

'I must have amused the hell out of you.' He ground out the words, his jaw tightly clenched. 'Always so damned proper and respectful – holding your hand and kissing you at the door when I really wanted . . .' Mitch hesitated a split second. '. . . to take you to my bed and make love to you till morning. Why aren't you laughing, Cap? It's very funny.'

'What's funny is how happy I was to see you when you walked into that classroom today –' Bitterness thickened her voice. '– and now, how I can hardly wait for you to leave.'

'Dammit, Cappy, tell me it isn't true.' He shook her

shoulders, whipping her head back, exposing the creamy arc of her throat.

'No.' Tears stung her eyes at his perfidy. 'You come here with a host of accusations and insinuations. It's up to you to prove them, not me.'

Cap felt the loosening of his hands, the withdrawing from her, and wrenched her shoulders slightly to twist out of his hold. She walked away, and this time no footsteps came after her. Anger and pain were all wrapped up in one another. The barracks looked so far away, long rectangular shapes a shade blacker than their dark backdrop. She wanted to break into a run, but pride and the impracticality of trying to run in high-heeled shoes kept her at a fast walk, her shoulders squared and her head high.

After she'd gone about a hundred yards, Cappy heard the motor of the jeep start up. Soon its headlight beams were sweeping the rough track in front of her and she moved to the side at its approach. When it pulled up alongside her and slowed to a crawl, she refused to look around.

'Get in the jeep, Cappy,' Mitch ordered, somewhat tiredly.

'I'll walk, thank you,' she retorted without slackening her pace or turning her head.

With a rough shifting of gears and a tromping on the foot-feed, the jeep lurched ahead of her and screeched to a stop. Mitch pushed out of his seat and vaulted over the low door to stand directly in her path.

'You're going to ride in the jeep, Cappy,' he said flatly.

'What's the matter, Mitch? Are you afraid someone might see me walking back to the barracks by myself?' she taunted. 'They just might figure that you got fresh with me – and what would they think of the major then? After all, he couldn't even make time with a so-called whore.'

'Shut up, Cap,' Mitch ordered through his teeth.

'I hope you don't expect me to believe for one minute that it's my reputation you're worried about.' She doubled

168

her hands into rigid fists at her side. The jeep's engine idled in a steady growl while the headlamps cast twin trails of light piercing through the darkness beyond them.

'If you don't get in the jeep, Cappy, I'll pick you up and put you there. You'll fight me, but I'll win. Let's spare each other all that physical wrestling.' Again, he sounded tired.

His reasoning was inarguable. With a small dip of her head, Cappy conceded and walked to the passenger side, climbing in unaided. Behind the wheel again, Mitch shifted gears and the jeep lunged forward. They had nothing to say to each other, not then and not later when he dropped her off at the barracks.

In the bay, Cappy managed to elude most of the questions with a plea of fatigue. After morning reveille, too many other things crowded in to distract her baymates' attention from her outing the previous evening.

At noon mess, Marty was late in arriving so they saved her a place in line. When she joined them, Marty's gray-green eyes were bright with speculation.

'I just heard your major is going to be staying here a few days, Cap.'

'He isn't my major,' she said in an expressionless voice. 'He's a friend of my father's, not mine.'

Eyebrows were raised in skepticism, but no one pursued the topic. It was her coldness and closed-in look that told them the major was a touchy issue, so they didn't probe.

The following day, rumor raced through the base. Chicago carried it to her compatriots: 'I heard they're going to make the Bluebonnet off-limits.'

'What? Why?' Marty protested.

'There's been some complaints of some sort.' Chicago indicated her lack of more specific knowledge with a shrug of her shoulders. 'I think Cap's major has something to do with it.'

Marty turned, cocking her head to the side, wheat-colored strands of hair escaping from under the bandanna. 'Do you know anything about this, Cap?' She narrowly eyed the brunette who had been so uncommunicative about the visiting officer.

'No.' Though it was a flat denial, Marty had difficulty believing it.

When Cappy arrived at the flight line on the third day of Mitch's extended tour, she saw the sleek, twin-engined AT-7 being given a preflight ground check – Mitch's plane. Good riddance, she thought, but with regret for the lost illusion of the warm, strong man she had believed him to be.

'Hayward.' Her instructor, Jimmy Ray Price, peremptorily summoned her with a wave of his hand.

'He sounds like his usual friendly self, doesn't he?' Eden murmured in dry mockery.

Her mouth briefly quirked in a smile of agreement before Cap split away from the group to jog over to her waiting instructor. She was ready to do some flying, hoping it would shake off some of this flatness she was feeling.

'You wanted me, Mr Price?' She crisply reported to him.

'Nope. But the major wants to see you before he leaves.' He jerked his head in the direction of the twin-engine.

Her glance skipped past the short bulldog of a man to the parked aircraft. Cappy wanted to refuse outright, but every instinct warned against it. Her credo of survival was not to let the other person know you'd been hurt.

It was a full minute before Cappy noticed the odd way the instructor was staring at her and realized how long she had been standing there. Self-consciously she let her glance fall away from his stare.

'Thanks,' she mumbled and headed across the hangar apron to the twin-engined transport.

As she walked in front of the airplane's nose, she spied Mitch in conversation with his pilot. She ducked under the wing tip, conscious of the little drum of her pulse. At almost the same instant, Mitch observed her approach and said something to the pilot, dismissing him. He came forward a few steps to meet her while the pilot climbed into the plane.

'I understand you wanted to see me, sir.' She kept her gaze level and her expression bland, but her teeth were gritted.

His gaze was narrowed and thoughtful while the corners of his mouth deepened in a line of regret. 'I was wrong, Cappy. I owe you an apology,' he said. 'I had the right place – the Bluebonnet – but I was mistaken about the women involved. It seems some . . . camp followers, shall we call them . . . set up business in the hotel. They have been telling the soldiers they're part of the contingent of female pilots training here at Avenger. I jumped to conclusions, Cappy, and I'm sorry.'

'Apology accepted. And it's Miss Hayward to you,' she countered with icy calm.

His look became impatient. 'I admit I made a mistake, and I'm sorry. Dammit, what more do you want?' Mitch demanded roughly.

'I could forgive a simple mistake, and even overlook the fact you were willing to take the word of other men. But I can't forgive that you wanted to believe it was true about me.' She observed the faint recoil, proving she'd hit the target dead-center.

With a smart pivot, Cappy turned to walk away. The air shimmered with heat, making the distant concrete look wet. That's the way her eyes felt, so hot and bright, yet they were painfully dry. She hadn't gone five steps when Mitch caught up with her, and swung her back around to face him. His expression was hard with anger.

'You're damned right I wanted to believe it,' he admitted. 'Ever since I've known you, you've never let me get close to you. I wanted to believe that behind your coolness there was some kind of passion. And I was jealous as hell that someone had tapped it before I could. Maybe that makes me a rotten bastard, but I don't care.'

Cappy was thrown by his totally unexpected admission. She stared at him in confusion as a propeller chopped the

air, caught, and revved into full power. They were blasted
by the prop-wash, dust swirling around them in eye-
stinging clouds. Mitch pulled his cap down tighter on his
head and hooked an arm around Cappy to draw her out
of the driven wind to the end of the wing.

'Nothing's changed, Cappy,' Mitch practically shouted
to make himself heard above the engine noise. 'You're
going to see me again.'

While she was scraping her wind-blown hair away from
her mouth to deny it, Mitch took advantage of her momentary distraction and covered her lips with his own in a
long, hard kiss. She tasted his hunger and frustration, the
wanting to stay and having to go. Just for a minute, she
leaned into him. The desire was strong to reach out to
him, but she wouldn't give in to it, torn by the feelings he
aroused and the bitter truths she knew. The Army was a
rival that would always win. In the end, she pulled away
from him, fighting the ache inside. His eyes were like dark
velvet when he looked at her.

Above the roar of the engines, a cheering sound could
be faintly heard. Both of them became aware of their
audience of trainees, vocally offering their approval of the
romantic scene they had just witnessed. Mitch smiled and
winked at her, amused by it, but Cappy backed away from
him, averting her gaze and striking out for an empty
hangar.

From the coolness of its shade, Cappy watched the
powerful twin-engined transport lift off the runway, its
wheels retract into its belly, and its flap-setting change.
She tensed at the sound of footsteps approaching her from
behind. With a backward glance, she recognized the deep
red-brown color of that pigtailed hair. Eden was the only
one who sported that particular shade.

'Missing him already?' Those dark eyes were a little too
keen in their inspection.

'Not hardly,' Cappy answered with a short laugh.
'No one in their right mind falls in love with an Army
man.'

'But you fall in love with your heart – not your head,' Eden reminded her.

'Not if you're smart, you don't.' Cappy pushed herself away from the post she'd been leaning against. 'It's time to do some flying, isn't it?'

CHAPTER ELEVEN

Word came down from the control tower to the waiting press corps that the powerful AT-6s and the twin-engine AT-17s were entering the traffic pattern and would be landing shortly. Off to the side, dusty zoot-suited figures watched the scurry of activity. Unlike the reporters and photographers, they were interested in the planes themselves rather than the pilots.

'It won't be long before we'll be flying them.' Eden observed a sleek, single-engined advanced trainer zoom onto the runway. Beneath the certainty in her tone, there was also an eagerness.

Graduation ceremonies were scheduled on the following day for the 43-W-2 class of women pilots who had completed their training in Houston, staying behind when Rachel's group had transferred to Sweetwater. The long cross-country flight was the last one they'd be making as trainees. Tomorrow they would be full-fledged ferry pilots.

'Not all of us,' Chicago corrected her with a certain dullness. All of them went through the motions of denying her claim, but from one source or another, they'd all heard about her lack of proficiency in instrument flying. 'We all know it's true. I'll never pass my check ride.'

'You can't be sure of that,' Marty insisted, but she also had a hunch it would take a miracle.

The big planes came wheeling up to the hangars, the roaring engines churning clouds of dust. While newsreel cameras cranked the footage and photographers aimed their lenses at them, the pilots, one by one, bounded out of their planes and pulled off their nets to let the wind blow their hair. These female pilots were pictures of beauty and confidence with their bright eyes and shining faces.

'I wish that was us.' Marty expressed the envy all of them were feeling. Not because of the attention they were receiving, but for successfully completing the rigorous and demanding training program. 'I want it so bad I can taste it.' Her husky voice vibrated with the near ferocity of her desire.

No one replied or commented. It was a feeling that went too deep to articulate. Flying was an all-consuming passion for them. They wanted it so fiercely that, even in the beginning, they had gone against convention, defied the disapproval of parents or left behind families, and ignored the raised eyebrows of friends to have what they wanted. It was a bit like being horse-crazy. High flight had an addictive power and excitement to it that nothing else could match. They'd willingly go through the hotbox hell of the Link trainer and the brain-scrambling confusion of instrument flying for those moments of supreme exhilaration in the lofty solitudes of the sky.

Shortly after the last graduate landed, a stagger-winged Beechcraft came shooting down the runway. Eden recognized it and nudged the others. 'That's Jacqueline Cochran.'

After the women's director of flying climbed out of her aircraft, she headed toward the operations building. This time she was accompanied by another woman, her French-speaking maid, as the group later learned. Almost instantly she was engulfed in the wave of Houston graduates who gathered around her to pay homage. Eden shook her head in mild amusement at another spectacular entrance.

The 'cattle trucks' arrived to transport the Houston group into Sweetwater for a night's stay at the Bluebonnet Hotel. And the flurry of excitement passed.

The graduation ceremonies for the Houston class gave

174

all the Avenger trainees a chance to wear their new regulation dress uniforms and to show off the marching skills
they had practiced for the generals who had never come.
A flag-carrier and two flight lieutenants led the long,
straight columns past the reviewing stand. Behind them,
the Big Spring Bombardier School Band played with
drum-pounding exuberance.

Since the graduates weren't officially Army, regulation
wings couldn't be presented to them. A pilot without wings
was unthinkable, so bombardier's 'sweetheart' wings were
redesigned. A shield and ribbon, engraved with the squadron and class designation 43-W-2, were soldered to the
middle of the 'sweetheart' wings.

Elated and high-spirited, the Inseparables swept into
their bay, all of them talking at once, filling the room
with their impressions of the ceremony. The graduation
exercises had reaffirmed the sense of importance of their
flight training, ennobling it with duty and honor and pride.
Men were needed on the war fronts and they would be
performing a vital service by relieving them of the home
duties so they could go fight.

With continuing chatter back and forth, they began
changing out of their uniforms of tan slacks and short-
sleeved white shirts. Dawdling in various stages of undress,
some in bra and slacks and some bottomless in shirts, they
roamed the bay.

'You can bet there'll be an article in the *Sweetwater
Reporter* tomorrow.'

'Do you suppose they'll have pictures, too? I know I
was in one of them. The photographer was right there in
front of me when he snapped it.'

'It depends on the background. They can't publish a
photograph if there are more than two planes in the picture. The censors won't allow it. No mention can be made
of the base, where it's located, or how many trainees are
here.'

'I'm sure the enemy is anxious to learn all about us
female flyers. We're such a threat.'

Laughing along with the others at the thought, Mary Lynn bent a bare knee to the floor in front of her footlocker and opened it to take out a change of clothes. Lying on top, Beau's smiling face looked back at her from the gilt-framed photograph. It jolted her. The smile, the laughter, died. Mary Lynn slowly reached to pick up the photo, then carried it to her cot, where she sat silently staring at it, indifferent to the continuing barrage of voices behind her.

'Has anybody looked inside Eden's locker?' Marty stopped beside the opened footlocker, and saw the rumpled clothes and underwear tumbling over the sides. 'It's worse than Fibber McGee's closet. Don't you ever fold your clothes before you toss them in there?'

'Butt out, Rogers.' Eden shouldered her out of the way and bent to dig through the mess for a change of clothes, further disheveling the contents.

'What's the matter, Miss van Valkenburg?' Marty razzed. 'Are you jealous 'cause Cochran gets to bring her maid along and you don't?' Laughing, she ambled back to her cot. 'God, Mary Lynn, you should take a look at her footlocker.' The lack of response, the absence of any sign her comment had been heard, drew Marty's full attention. She tipped her head to the side, trying to get a glimpse of the brunette's downcast face. 'Hey, Mary Lynn, is something wrong?' The more direct question seemed to pierce through Mary Lynn's absorption with the photograph of her husband.

Her expression was troubled and her eyes were dark with near panic. 'All this talk about Army censors and the enemy – we joke about it and none of it is funny. There's a war on. Men are fighting and dying.'

'Nobody meant anything by it,' Marty hastened to assure her, at a loss for the right words to comfort and reassure her friend. She sat beside her on the cot, awkwardly touching Mary Lynn's small-boned shoulder.

The others, including the tall, sleek Rachel Goldman, noticed the changed tenor of the conversation and glanced

176

curiously at the huddled pair, discreetly listening in.

'Beau is over there.' Mary Lynn stared at the photograph. 'What if something happens to him? What if he's hurt or killed? What would I do without him? He's got to come back to me, Marty. I'll die without him.' She was scared for him and frightened by the thought of a future without him. The loneliness was awful now, but at least she could look forward to his letters and the distant tomorrow when he'd come home. 'I should be with him. I don't belong here.'

'That isn't true,' Rachel inserted. Usually there was minor resistance to any inclusion of her in their conversations. Marty stiffened at her unexpected participation, wary of Rachel yet willing to let her speak as long as she said the right things. 'We are at war, and your husband is over there fighting to protect all the things we believe in. At a time like this, we all have to make sacrifices – put aside our personal wants and do what is right.'

Mary Lynn raised her head, drawn by the forceful argument being put forth. The militance in Rachel's expression convinced her of the blonde's sincerity.

'Hitler and his Fascist armies have to be destroyed. We all have to fight in the ways that we can to protect our homes and the ones we love,' Rachel declared. 'You can do it by flying, by freeing a male pilot for combat and maybe to fly fighter escort for your husband's bomber. We are at war and this is where you belong – for his sake and everyone else's.'

For long seconds her words lingered, ringing in their minds. The rationalization, the justification was the assurance Mary Lynn needed.

'Thanks,' she murmured to Rachel, who was already self-conscious about her impassioned outburst.

Later, with the half-light of night coming through the barracks' windows, Mary Lynn lay on her cot, listening to the even breathing of her sleeping baymates. An awful, aching loneliness knifed through her as she strained to recall those nights of marital closeness with Beau.

Her lips could almost feel the pressure of his kiss. She closed her eyes, trying to make the ghostlike sensation more real. Months had passed since he had held her. She rubbed her arms, seeking to remember the feel of his muscles, flexed and hard. It had been so long. She caught her lower lip between her teeth, biting down on it while she tried to keep the wanting at bay.

She trembled with longing. Beau. She mouthed his name as her hand slid to the underside of her breast, feeling its rounded firmness. The sensation stimulated a driving ache. She turned her face into the pillow to smother any sound she might inadvertently make. Doubled into a fist, her hand pushed its way between her legs where her thighs clamped themselves on her wrist to hold it there.

Long-ago childhood memories came rushing back. She could hear her mother's voice again, so strident and condemning. 'Mary Lynn, what are you doing? You get your hand out of your panties this instant!' The censure and the stinging slaps for a wrong she didn't understand. 'Nice little girls don't do such things. Don't ever let me catch you doing that again.' Words that drove her to secrecy – in the darkness of night and the hiding cover of blankets – and the ultimate easing of that terrible tension.

'Beau,' she whispered in near apology as her body sagged in relief against the thin mattressed cot.

Check-ride time came around for the basic training stage of their flying program. Those who passed civilian rides with their instructors went for their Army check rides. When it was over, the ranks of the trainee class were thinned considerably. Chicago was among the group who washed out.

The mattress of her empty cot was rolled up, and all her personal belongings had been removed from the premises.

'Do you suppose she's gone already?' Mary Lynn wondered.

'Yes,' Cappy replied.

'I bet she was out of here within a couple of hours. They

don't let them hang around long once they're out of the program.' By the ubiquitous *they*, Marty meant the command staff at Avenger.

'I suppose she failed the instrument flying.' Eden sank onto her cot and drew a knee up to her chest.

'I suppose.' Cappy shrugged an agreement, aware they would never know for sure.

Some of the military inspectors had been known to wash out a student for no more cause than the check pilot's decision that the trainee wasn't strong enough to handle a plane in difficulty. Even being female was reason enough for some.

'Remember when they caught those two girls in bed together?' Marty recalled. 'They were packed up and off the base within an hour.'

There was a nod from Eden, but no one said anything. The Inseparables were no more. The empty cot was a mute testimony of that.

The hot Texas summer found the combined Houston and Sweetwater class of 43-W-3 just entering the advanced phase of training, cut almost in half. This was the final stage.

No more BT-13s; instead they were flying the AT-6, known as the 'Texan,' built by North American Aviation. The advanced trainer had 150 more horses in its engine than the 450-horsepower BT-13. For the first time, the girls had to deal with retractable landing gear, which not only gave the single-engined plane, with its pushed-in nose, a very sleek look on takeoffs but also gave the aircraft a cruising speed of 145 miles an hour.

The training concentrated on long-distance navigation, cross-country trips that would be invaluable experience for future ferry pilots. Many lessons were learned the hard way, as attested by red-faced pilots who knocked at the doors of ranch houses after running out of gas and making forced landings in someone's pasture or cotton field.

A triangle that went from Sweetwater to Odessa to Big Spring and back to Sweetwater was flown countless times by the trainees, both solo and with their instructors. After a while, most of them swore they could fly it blindfolded.

With the summer sun sending temperatures soaring into the hundreds regularly, any chance to crawl into a Texan AT-6 and climb into the sky was welcomed. For every thousand feet of altitude, the temperature dropped three and a half degrees. The air blowing through the plane's ventilators was about as refreshing as a fan blowing across a block of ice.

Rachel leveled her advanced trainer off at eight thousand feet and adjusted the trim tab for straight and level flight. The rush of cool air was directed squarely at her, ruffling the map she tried to study. In a break from the usual routine, she had elected to fly a different cross-country route, going to San Angelo, then to Abilene and back to Sweetwater.

The flight leg from Sweetwater to San Angelo had been fairly routine. After Rachel had turned north to Abilene, she'd had trouble locating her first few checkpoints. Taking out her little round-wheeled flight calculator, she refigured her airspeed and flying time to approximate the distance, then plotted it on the map. The wind velocity would affect her groundspeed, but, even allowing for that variance, Abilene should have been in sight.

Craning her neck, Rachel strained to see out the front of the mullioned canopy. There was no sign of a town on the hazy horizon. She tipped the plane on its wing to look below and behind, in case she'd overflown it. Nothing.

Without a radio frequency to turn to, she couldn't cross-check her position. Her uneasiness grew as she considered the possibility she was off course. It was too soon to panic. The winds aloft might be stronger than she'd been told. It would be silly to turn back, especially if her destination was just ahead. Rachel decided to fly her heading a while longer.

Another twenty minutes in the air and she knew something had gone wrong. Somehow she had missed Abilene and she was lost. Below her, there was nothing but mesquite brush covering the dark red earth. Then she spied the iron tracks of a railroad leading into a small town. Immediately, Rachel angled the AT-6 into a steep descent and buzzed the train depot. FREDERICK, the sign on it read.

Not knowing the frequency, she was unable to call the control tower as she entered the traffic pattern on the downwind leg. A combination of nervousness over her situation and limited experience with this faster and more powerful ship caused her to land the AT-6 about twenty miles an hour faster than the recommended speed. It was a 'hot' landing, the kind usually made by highly experienced fighter pilots.

Her confidence was being chipped away – first, because she strayed off course, second because this airfield wasn't shown on her maps, and third because the power-on landing made her question her mechanical flying skills. Men in uniforms were hurrying out of the operations building to meet her as Rachel taxied her plane to the flight line.

The searing heat of the afternoon hit her as she crawled out of the cockpit and stepped onto the wing. The looks on the faces of waiting soldiers weren't too friendly. Rachel took a deep, silent breath and walked down the edge of the wing, shaking her long pale blond hair loose.

Their expressions took on a stunned look when she hopped onto the ground in front of them. The officer, a captain, stepped forward to eye her with wary and angry suspicion. 'Just who the hell are you? And what are you doing with that plane?'

Rachel retaliated in self-protection. 'Since I'm the pilot, I guess I'm flying it.'

Just about then, a jeepload of MPs came charging onto the scene. It suddenly hit her that they really had no idea who she was. They were probably ready to believe she was some kind of saboteur, a possibility that was reinforced when the MPs crowded around her and the plane with their rifles at the ready.

'That's an Army plane you've got,' the captain pointed out.

There she was, standing beside the AT-6, her six feet making her the tallest one present, a striking blonde with sloe eyes, and surrounded by armed men. This was no time to react in kind.

'Yes, sir.' Rachel schooled her voice to answer with terse calm. 'I'm Rachel Goldman, a trainee with the 319th Army Air Force Flight Training Detachment at Avenger Field in Sweetwater.'

'You surely don't expect me to believe that?' He challenged her harshly. 'The Army doesn't have any women flying planes.'

'Excuse me, but you are wrong, sir. As a matter of fact, there are a couple hundred of us at Avenger Field – and we all fly Army planes.

'If you would just tell me where I am . . .' Rachel struggled to hold her temper. 'I'm a little confused because my map doesn't show an air base outside of Frederick, Texas –'

'That's because you're in Frederick, Oklahoma.'

It was all she could do to keep her mouth from falling open. More than off course, she had been lost. She didn't even have maps that went this far.

'Now you know why the Army doesn't have any women flying its planes,' the captain jeered. 'A woman has no business behind the wheel of a car, let alone at the controls of a plane.' He waved a hand at the milltary police. 'Check out the plane.' Then he turned to the young officer next to him. 'Get a hold of the CO, Crawford, and let him know about this. And you' – he faced Rachel and reached for her arm – 'are coming with me.'

She yanked her arm out of his hold. 'Listen, Captain.' She managed to put a wealth of sarcasm in the reference to his rank and resisted the urge to call him a sawed-off little punk. 'All you have to do is call Avenger Field in Sweetwater and they can verify who I am.

'I'll call them,' he promised her, certain he was calling her bluff as well.

'Don't you think we ought to see if she's armed?' one

182

of the MPs suggested. 'There's no telling what she might be concealing in the baggy suit she's wearing.'

'You're right.' The captain nodded.

Protest screamed through her nerves, but Rachel gritted her teeth and said nothing. Unmoving as a statue, she stood there submitting herself to the indignity of a physical search. All the while the hands were unzipping her flight suit, sliding under her arms, down her waist and hips, and brushing her tautly held breasts, she glared at the captain.

'Nothing, sir,' the MP concluded.

'This will be reported, Captain,' Rachel assured him with icy stiffness. Yet she knew that in the face of his belief that she was some kind of enemy agent, he was probably following the proper military procedure.

She was escorted to his office in the operations building, where she was again questioned and her story challenged. Her repeated efforts to have him call Avenger were brushed aside. Everything was being checked, he told her.

Half an hour had passed since she'd taxied her plane up to the building. Rachel was beginning to think they'd lock her in the guardhouse next when the phone on the captain's desk rang. Evidently, the call was from his commanding officer, judging by his almost subservient manner. Rachel caught a glimmer of displeasure in his expression when the conversation ended.

'It seems there *is* some sort of training program for female pilots at Avenger Field,' he acknowledged reluctantly as he pushed himself out of his chair. 'You are free to go, trainee Goldman. May I suggest the next time you keep your mind on flying instead of daydreaming and you'll be less likely to get lost.'

There were no apologies, and no attempt to hide his contempt for her sex in the cockpit of a plane. It required all her self-control not to tell the captain precisely what her opinion of him was.

'Yes, sir.'

With considerable satisfaction, Rachel straightened up to tower over the shorter man, then walked out of his office, aware that he was following. An MP was standing guard by her AT-6 when she emerged from the operations building. He started to block her access to the plane, until he caught the signal from the captain to let her pass.

Rachel was in the cockpit with her belt fastened before she realized she had been given neither a map nor a heading back to Sweetwater. She was determined she'd fly the plane into the ground before she'd ask that captain for anything.

'Clear!' she shouted out the side of the opened canopy, then turned the switch that brought the propeller blades churning to life.

After taking off from the Oklahoma airfield, Rachel picked up the railroad tracks that had guided her to this strip and followed the reliable iron beams south. The encroaching darkness of night was about to obscure the landmarks on the edge of Sweetwater. Seconds later, she spied the runway at Avenger Field, outlined with flare pots.

Her instructor, Joe Gibbs, was waiting for her on the flight line when she landed. He chewed her out, but not too roughly, sensing that she'd suffered enough for her mistake. Rachel didn't tell him all that had happened. It was enough that she'd gotten herself lost.

After he'd left her, Rachel's friend Helen Shaw came out of the ready room to meet her. The ex-Hollywood actress eyed her curiously. 'What happened?'

Before she was through, Rachel ended up telling her fellow Woofted about the entire incident, her treatment in the hands of the insolent captain, and the blind-luck flight back to Sweetwater.

'Men,' Helen said, commiserating with Rachel's sentiments.

'To paraphrase an old quotation – "Men are bastards ever,"' she replied, and meant it.

At the barracks, Rachel and Helen parted company to go to their separate bays. There was the usual confusion, everyone trying to shower and change before evening mess, when Rachel entered. Her late arrival didn't escape Cappy's notice.

'Where've you been, Goldman?' she inquired with idle curiosity. 'Did you have plane trouble or something?'

After a second's hesitation, Rachel told them the whole story, chastened by the experience but still seething over the way she'd been treated.

Marty's initial reaction had been to scoff, 'Oklahoma?! How could you have made a mistake like that?' By the time Rachel had finished, she was saying, 'Officer or not, I think I'd have punched him in the nose.'

CHAPTER TWELVE

There was no relief from the hundred-degree July heat. The rows of barracks were lined up in a north/south direction, the same as the prevailing summer wind, allowing for no cross-ventilation in the bays.

In the suffocating stillness of the night, Marty lay on her cot, hot and sweating. Her legs were spread apart to keep her thighs from sticking together with the prickly dampness of perspiration, and her arms were flung over her head to avoid touching her sides. Nothing seemed to offer any relief from the miserable, oppressive heat, not even the wet towel she had draped over herself.

From outside the barracks came the tantalizing whisper of a breeze. It danced by the opened windows and the screened door. Not once did it come inside. Marty listened to it, feeling so sweaty and irritable.

'Oh, hell.' She sat up. 'How can anybody sleep in this hot hole?'

'Shut up, Rogers.' Eden's voice was half muffled by the mattress on which she was lying face down, motionless with her arms away from her body as Marty's had been.

'You can stay here if you want, but I'm moving.' Marty piled out of her bed and grabbed the end of her cot. The legs made an awful scraping sound as she started dragging it across the floor. 'Somebody want to give me a hand with the door?'

'What the Sam Hill are you doing?' Cappy rose on an elbow to glare at her.

'I'm going to sleep outside where at least there's a breeze,' she declared.

Within minutes, they were all dragging their cots outdoors and setting them up between the barracks. As other bays heard the commotion, they joined them until cots were strung out the full length of the buildings. It wasn't much of a breeze, but it moved the air and revived them.

'Would you look at all those stars?' Marty lay on her back and gazed at the millions of rhinestone lights in the black velvet sky, each one so individually brilliant. She glanced at Mary Lynn with a wry look. 'Now where's that cowboy who wanted to show me the Big Dipper?' She chuckled in her throat at the memory of the amorous cowhand she'd met at the rodeo-barbecue given the girls by a local rancher on the Fourth of July.

'It is a beautiful night,' Mary Lynn sighed and pillowed her head in her hands.

On the other side of them Cappy mused, 'It won't be long until they start checking us out in the AT-17s.' Flying the twin-engined aircraft would be the last stage of their advanced training, giving them a multiengine rating before graduation the first week of August.

'The good ole "Bamboo Bomber,"' Eden joked dryly, referring to the plywood construction of the airplane, dubbed the 'Bobcat' by its Cessna manufacturer.

Marty overheard their talk. 'You mean the "Bunson Burner"?' she mocked. 'The damned thing looks as if it would go up like a matchstick.'

Lying silently on her cot, Rachel listened to the low discussion about the twin-engined plane. She remembered hearing Woofteds in classes ahead of hers talking about the AT-17. The plane had a seat behind the pilot and copilot that was low and seemed to be sunken in a well. Even those who weren't prone to airsickness had grabbed for paper bags when they'd sat in that seat.

Somewhere down the line of cots came a shriek. 'A snake! A rattlesnake!' The cry went up. 'Somebody kill it!!'

In a wild scramble of bodies, some girls sought the safety of the barracks while others perched atop their cots to peer over the edges, and more searched for a weapon. The rattler, which had so foolishly crawled onto the walkway, was subsequently clubbed to death.

'Poor snake,' Marty said in absent pity.

'It was a rattlesnake,' Eden protested.

'I've heard they always travel in pairs,' a trainee down the way offered.

A moment of silence followed. Then a clamor began anew as a search was started for the mate of the dead snake. Some of the trainees gave up and hauled their cots back into the bays, but Marty yawned and stretched out more fully on her cot. A second snake was never found, but most of the trainees spent a restless night, listening for the slightest rustle of grass that might betray the presence of a snake beneath their cots.

Before graduation, each trainee was required to make a long, solo cross-country flight to a destination prescribed by her instructor. It was sheer chance that Mary Lynn was assigned to fly to her own home town of Mobile on Alabama's Gulf Coast. Midway, she stopped to refuel her AT-6 and wire her estimated time of arrival so she could squeeze an hour or longer visit with her family.

On the last leg, favoring winds added another hour to her allotted ground time in Mobile. Upon landing, she called to say she was on her way and disregarded her mother's veiled complaints over having her sleep interrupted. Working the graveyard shift meant that her mother slept during the day while her father had the coveted day shift at the shipyards. Unfortunately, she wouldn't get to see him on this trip.

Outside the air base, she caught a bus into town. The giant cranes of the shipyards ranged across the skyline, by their presence transforming the sleepy Gulf seaport of Mobile, Alabama, into a boom town. Coal smoke drifted in layers, held aloft by the sea winds, its smell tainting the salty air. The city sidewalks were crowded to overflowing.

Mary Lynn got off the bus to connect with the line that went to her neighborhood and waited impatiently at its stop. At first, she didn't notice the trio of young girls dawdling outside the corner drug store. Dressed somewhat alike in blouses and skirts, bobby socks and saddle shoes, they wore heavy makeup, garish paint on young faces, slashing lips an unkind scarlet red. They eyed Mary Lynn, in her tan gabardines, white short-sleeved shirt, and perky general's cap on her midnight-dark hair, with the mistrust of the young toward the older, and of the female toward another of her own gender. Mary Lynn seriously doubted if any of the three had celebrated her sixteenth birthday.

Looking away, she glanced down the street to see if the bus was coming and debated whether it would be faster to find a cab. After nearly six months in Texas, she was unused to the hot, humid climate of the Deep South – a sticky heat that not even the breeze coming off the Mexican Gulf could alleviate. She felt its oppressive weight as she looked down the busy thoroughfare. No bus was in sight. Mary Lynn turned back to the trio of bobby-soxers.

'When's the next bus due?'

Her inquiry was met with shrugs and one politely drawled, 'I don't know, ma'am. Soon, I expect.'

Mary Lynn smiled briefly in response and suppressed a deep sigh, resigned to waiting for the bus to make its appearance. A sailor came strolling up the street, setting the young girls to tittering and giggling behind their hands while they eyed him with flirtatious interest. Mary Lynn was absently amused by their adolescent silliness over a young serviceman, until she saw the brazen way they approached him.

'Where are you from, sailor?'

'Gee, you're cute. I'd be proud to keep you company if you're lonely.'

'Wanta buy me a soda?'

The three girls practically threw themselves at the sailor, pressing close with the straining urgency of their young bodies. Such behavior from seemingly well-brought-up young ladies was scandalous to Mary Lynn. The sailor was being virtually offered his pick of them. Each seemed to melt when he looked her over to make his choice.

'What's your name, honey?' He familiarly slid a hand around the waist of the chosen one and let it ride down low, resting suggestively near the curve of her bottom.

'Donna May.' Adoration dominated her expression, not even a hint of objection showing at the near-intimate contact.

The sailor bent down and whispered something in Donna May's ear, then straightened to say, 'I'll take you to a movie. How's that?'

'I'd love it just fine.' She was atremble with some kind of wild excitement, triumphant while the other two girls started to drift away, disappointed yet already looking down the street in anticipation of another chance.

When the young girl started to move off in the company of the sailor, it was more than Mary Lynn could tolerate. 'Does your mother know you're doing this?' she demanded. 'How old are you?'

The girl turned, angry and defensive, clutching the sailor's arm as if she was afraid she might lose him. 'It's none of your business, lady.'

Mary Lynn glared at the sailor, finding him equally to blame. 'She's hardly more than a child.' The sailor was unmoved by her protest.

'I'm old enough,' the girl, Donna May, insisted, and jerked her head in the direction of the oncoming bus. 'Why don't you get on your bus and leave us alone. No one asked you to butt in.'

Brake shoes screeched against the drums as the bus rattled to a halt at the curb stop. Mary Lynn hesitated a second longer, staring at the sailor and the child-woman, then swung aboard. The crowded bus reeked of sweaty, unwashed bodies and stale tobacco smoke, odors made all the more objectionable by the hot and humid July air. A small space was available on a front seat and Mary Lynn wedged her hips into the narrow section between two seated passengers as the bus lurched forward.

Through a dust-filmed window, Mary Lynn watched the sailor and the girl stroll along the sidewalk, acting more like lovers than the strangers they were. Mary Lynn's apple-cheeked features wore an unusual expression of stern disapproval. The woman passenger on her right, dressed in the garb of a factory worker, noticed it and the object of its censure.

'Disgusting, isn't it?' she agreed.

'She's too young to know what she's doing.' It was a frustrated protest.

'Khaki-wacky, they call it,' came the dryly cynical response. 'Some of these young kids go crazy over anyone in uniform. I've seen them in drug stores trying to buy . . . you know . . . protection. This war, it's doing things to all of us.' She lit a cigarette, something manly about the way she exhaled the smoke and pinched out the match. 'I don't know. Maybe they're right and we should grab everything we can today.'

Mary Lynn fell silent rather than continue the depressing conversation. As long as the bus moved, a wind swept through the opened windows and offered the passengers some relief. But it was short-lived, dying down at every block corner while the bus let passengers out and took more in, letting the stifling close air fill the interior. Old, mansard-roofed homes with vine-choked iron grillwork and tall colonnades lent a shabby elegance to the city gone wild with the war boom, which crowded its streets with

190

people and littered its gutters with fly-attracting trash.

Outside a movie house, jammed around the ticket booth, were children of all ages, from a sleeping toddler held in the aching arms of a seven-year-old to a cigarette-smoking nine-year-old dictator keeping his brood of siblings close by. Few adults were in sight.

'Lock-outs, most of them,' the woman said.

'What?'

'They're locked out of their houses. Their mothers are working somewhere and don't want their kids alone in the house so they lock them out and send them to the movies – a cheap babysitter,' the woman announced. 'Doorkey children are the other kind. They wear the key to the front door around their necks so they don't lose it. It's sad. It's really sad.'

They moved past the theater and the wind was once again blowing through the windows. The bus turned onto a tree-shaded street and Mary Lynn strained to see the white frame house with its long front porch.

Her mother's welcome was less than warm when Mary Lynn reached the house. A more pinched and worn-out look marked her mother's features, but her eyes remained dark, burning coals of light – angry and hungry for something, Mary Lynn knew not what. She was taking in boarders now, renting out the spare rooms.

'You're working too hard, Mama.' Pity rose at the driven weariness she sensed in her mother. There were four boarders, she'd learned, occupying the spare beds in shifts. 'Holding down a night job plus keeping up this house and renting out rooms . . .'

'Sleeping space is at a premium in this town,' her mother declared. 'If this war will just last a few more years, your papa and I will be able to pay off the mortgage on this house and have some money set aside for our old age as well.'

The greed she heard in her mother's voice twisted her insides. To wish for the war to continue because of the money that could be made from it struck Mary Lynn as selfish and callous. Beau was fighting in this war. If it was prolonged, his exposure to danger would be that much longer.

But while she bitterly resented her mother's greed, Mary Lynn could understand it. Her parents had lost a lot during the Depression, barely managing to keep the family home. Her mother had hated being poor and doing without. It had soured her and made money an obsession.

Without thinking, Mary Lynn took a cigarette from the pack in her small purse. She tapped it on the table to pack the loose tobacco. With a jaundiced eye, her mother observed the action.

'What other dreadful habits have you picked up in Texas besides smoking and wearing men's pants?' she asked reproachfully.

'Mama, it's difficult to climb in and out of planes in a skirt.' Mary Lynn defended the practicality of her attire, but made no attempt to justify the cigarette in her hand.

'It's certainly not ladylike.'

She lit the cigarette and took a drag from it. Trails of smoke were released as she responded to the remark. 'Maybe it's time you looked at yourself in the mirror, Mama.'

The visit with her mother wasn't a pleasant one. It was almost a relief when it was time to return to the airfield and make the long flight back to Sweetwater. The next time she came home, her stay would be longer and a pair of silver wings would be pinned to her uniform.

The incessant hot wind flung dust at Rachel's face, making her eyes smart with the fine particles, but it provided some relief from the blistering temperatures on that early afternoon in late July. She stood outside the ready room with Helen Shaw and two other Woofteds, waiting for their instructors to arrive. The twin-engined Cessna Bob-cats were parked on the flight line, all serviced for an afternoon of radio navigation practice. Graduation was so close all of them could taste it.

'My parents are catching the train from Oklahoma to be here when I get those silver wings pinned on me,' Helen said, adding wryly, 'presuming, of course, that I pass the check rides.'

'You will,' Rachel replied confidently.

A shirt-sleeved instructor stepped out of the building behind them. 'All right, let's cut the gabbing and get the plane checked out.' The order was directed at Helen and her flightmate that day, Carla Ellers.

'It looks like we'll be the first off the ground. You can follow us in your Bunson Burner. That way you won't get lost on your way to Big Spring,' Helen gibed at Rachel, and winked as she headed for the planes with the boxy fuselage, constructed of plywood.

Despite the five-minute head start Helen had, Rachel had her AT-17 in sight shortly after taking off from Avenger Field. Both had successfully bracketed the radio beam to Big Spring and had the unbroken hum of its signal droning in their ears. Helen's twin-engined aircraft kept the lead. It was always within Rachel's range of vision as she flew the beam with her instructor in the copilot's seat and Barbara Frye, a fellow trainee, sitting in the unenviable position of the rear seat.

That low, irregularly shaped hill, the landmark she always associated with Big Spring, jutted onto the horizon. Their destination was just ahead. Rachel reached to turn down the volume of the radio signal so her hearing would be attuned for that brief cone of silence when they passed over the beacon.

Out of the corner of her eye, she caught the flash of something in the sky just ahead of her. Rachel looked up as the AT-17, the notorious 'Bunson Burner' flying the lead, exploded into a yellow ball of flowering flame that turned quickly into smoke and fiery chunks of debris.

'My God.' The whispered words came from Joe Gibbs, her instructor.

Rachel's throat was paralyzed; nothing could come out. In silent horror, she watched bits and pieces of burning, smoking debris scatter through the sky while the main core spiraled to the ground – a slow, tortuous death spiral. There was no need to look for parachutes; there hadn't been time for anyone to bail out.

Mesmerized by the nightmarish sight of the burning wreckage falling to earth, Rachel stared at it, turning to watch as they flew over it. It had been consumed by flames within seconds. Death had come swiftly to the occupants, maybe right after they heard the explosion or saw the first flames. One charged second of fear, surrounded by fire, and it had been over.

Sweat ran from her pores, drenching her skin. She was afraid to close her eyes; already she could see engulfing flames leap around her in yellow glee. Rachel started shaking with fear as the first sob rose in her throat.

'All right, snap out of it, Goldman,' Joe Gibbs ordered harshly. 'Pay attention to what you're doing. You're way off the beam. What kind of a pilot are you? No wonder you're always getting lost.'

His harsh criticisms forced her attention away from the smoke trailing from the crash site. The *da-dit, da-dit* in her earphones confirmed she had strayed to the left of the beam, but she couldn't have cared less. She turned an embittered look on her instructor, tears blurring her eyes.

'That was my friend in that plane.' Her teeth were clenched together in a combination of intense pain and anger.

'Are you piloting this plane or not?' he challenged coldly.

'Yes!' Rachel flashed, and grimly turned the plane back on course, locating the beam, while he radioed a report of the accident to the base at Big Spring.

It wasn't until later that evening that Rachel remembered Helen's instructor, Frank Lawson, had been a close friend of Gibbs's. Likely as not, he'd been yelling at himself as much as at her, but she couldn't forgive his callousness at that moment, any more than she could forget the fire in the sky.

Avenger Field was stunned and shaken by the deaths of the two trainees and their instructor. The tragedy transcended the petty feud between the Houston half of the class and the Avenger pioneers. Flying had always been an exciting challenge to them, something of a thrill. On this eve of graduation, they were forced to face the reality that it was also dangerous. Flying might seem a glamorous duty to be performed for the war effort, but they were also risking their lives in doing it.

That night in the bay, Cappy urged Rachel to tell them what had happened. Rumor had already circulated the base that she had been a witness to the midair explosion.

When she had finished, Rachel lowered her head and bitterly recalled, 'On the flight line, Helen jokingly referred to it as the "Bunson Burner." We all called it that, I guess.' The cockiness had been knocked out of them.

On graduation day, the class of 43-W-3 marched by the single-engined Texan toward the reviewing stand where Jacqueline Cochran waited to pin on their wings, while four more classes undergoing staggered training looked on. All women pilots, those in the Army Air Force, in training, or in the ferry division of the Air Transport Command, were now under the sole jurisdiction of the Director of Women Pilots, Jacqueline Cochran, whose offices were located in the newly built Pentagon. Nancy Harkness Love would continue as the Director of the WAFs in the Air Transport Command.

On August 5, 1943, the women pilots and trainees were finally given an official designation: the Women Airforce Service Pilots. From that day forward, they would be known by their acronym, the WASPs.

CHAPTER THIRTEEN

Proudly sporting her hard-earned silver wings on the collar of her white shirt, Marty hefted her suitcase and walked away from the taxicab backing out of her parents' driveway. Detroit had changed. The numerous war plants had attracted thousands of workers to the city, a large number of them 'po' whites' from the South. On the drive from the train station, Marty had noticed the increased number of tents and tarpaper shacks, and the dank basements of houses that would never be built, called 'foxhole homes.'

She climbed the porch steps of the rambling two-story house, conscious of the sweltering August heat. A service flag hung in the window, white with a red border and one blue star which signified the occupant had one child in the service. The front screen door opened under the turn of her hand and Marty walked in, the heavy suitcase banging against her leg.

'Hello! Anybody home?'

'Who is it?' a woman's voice answered in imperious demand.

'Surprise! It's me. I'm home,' she called in a rasping and happy voice.

'You aren't supposed to be here until tonight.' Her mother appeared in the molded archway to the entry hall.

'I caught an earlier train. Remember that rich girl I told you lived in my bay? Her family chauffeur was driving her car back to New York and I hitched a ride with him as far as Dallas and managed to catch a different train.' She set her suitcase down by the newel post of the staircase and stood proudly at attention, her chest out and the boat-shaped general's cap perched atop her short, sand-colored curls. 'Well, what do you think of them?'

Althea Rogers checked the embrace she had been about to give her daughter and frowned. 'What?'

'My wings!' Marty said in exasperation and grasped the collar of her shirt to show them to her mother. 'See.'

'They are very nice,' the small and slender woman said with some enthusiasm, but Marty detected the perfunctory note in it. Age had lightened her mother's dark hair to an iron shade of gray and she wore it in a matronly bun, long sweeping waves softly framing her face before being drawn back to the nape of her neck. Dark eyes critically surveyed Marty's attire. 'Martha Jane, you didn't travel in that outfit, did you? Slacks in public?'

'You know how I hate that name. I wish you wouldn't call me that,' Marty protested, her elated spirits flattening. 'And, yes, I wore this on the train. It's our uniform, until we get an official one.'

'Is that right?' Her physician father came into the foyer, tall and ramrod straight, a stern-faced man accustomed to withholding his emotions and not allowing himself to become too personally involved with others.

'Dad.' Marty hugged him and received a kiss on the forehead. 'We've been officially named the WASPs by the government,' she went on to explain, '– which is short for Women Airforce Service Pilots. So now you have two children in the service and you can put another star on that flag in the window.'

'I'm afraid we can't do that,' he replied with a distantly kind look. 'Those stars are supposed to represent those in service in one of the armed services. You're in a civilian organization attached to the Army but not a part of it.'

'We will be,' Marty insisted. 'Right now we have officer status and all the privileges of rank. If David was home, he'd have to salute me because he's just an enlisted man.'

'I wish you could have been here when he was home on leave the last of June. He looked so handsome in his uniform,' her mother declared and took her arm. 'Come. I want to show you the pictures we took while he was here. He had so many ribbons and little badges he wore on his

197

uniform – sharpshooting medals and things.' She led Marty into the living room. 'The heat was terrible while David was here. Here he was, home on leave, and wanting to go out and have a good time, and Detroit was under martial law with curfews and federal troops patrolling the streets. It ruined his furlough.'

'I heard about it.' Resentment swelled in her; the conversation was already centering on David and she'd barely been home five minutes.

'Did your mother write that David shipped out?' Her father lowered his long, lanky frame into an armchair while her mother sat down on the matching sofa and opened a leather-bound photo album. 'The entire Hundred-and-first Airborne Division has been sent to a staging area in England.'

'I'm supposed to report to Jacqueline Cochran in the Pentagon. A bunch of us got the same orders, so we don't know what we'll be doing. It's kind of mysterious.'

'I expect David will be going into action soon,' her father said.

'Look at this photo of David. It was taken the very day he came home.' Her mother lifted the photo album onto Marty's lap and pointed out the picture. 'You can't see it very well, but we had a big Welcome Home sign strung across the front porch.'

The pages of the photo album were filled with pictures and her brother David was in the center of every one of them. Bitterly deflated, Marty realized that while Detroit might have changed, nothing was any different at home.

Surrounded by thick, white carpeting, the black marble tub sat in the middle of the room, filled with hot, scented water and mounded with bubbles. Reclining along the full length of it, Eden let her body go limp. Her hair was piled on top of her head in a mass of sorrel curls, its length sleeked away from her neck to avoid the dampness of the perfumed bubbles.

Through slitted eyes, she saw the maid enter, an older

woman with muddy gray hair who didn't appear entirely comfortable in the starched, black uniform. She approached the marble bath, raised by two steps onto a platform.

'Your drink, miss.'

With a motion marked by languor, Eden removed the glass of iced Scotch from the proffered tray. 'Thank you.' She couldn't recall the maid's name. In her absence there had been almost a complete turnover of servants in her parents' Manhattan apartment. She took a sip of the aged liquor and felt the velvet fire burn her throat.

'Miss?' The maid continued to hover by the tub, and Eden unwillingly opened an eye to acknowledge her. 'There's a gentleman to see you. What should I tell him?'

'Tell him I'm indisposed and to call later. No, wait!' Eden lifted the glass of Scotch in a detaining gesture. 'Who is it?'

'A Mr Steele, miss.'

'Ham?! Show him in,' she insisted, instantly delighted at the thought of seeing her faithful suitor again.

There wasn't much about Hamilton Steele to make her heart beat faster, but he was a dear friend. She ignored the maid's stiffnecked disapproval as the woman withdrew from the spacious bath. Eden took another drink of Scotch and savored its smoothness going down.

Scant minutes had passed before the maid returned with the scion of a New York banking family in tow. Conservative to the core, Hamilton Steele was dressed in the requisite dark pin-striped suit and silk tie. Wire-rimmed glasses snugly hugged his head, their thick lenses magnifying his shrewd but kindly eyes. Short of stature, he was trimly built despite his staid life style and forty-plus years, revealed by his fast-thinning hairline. Eden laughed at his briefly disconcerted expression when he saw her lounging in the tub full of bubbles.

'Ham, darling, come in.' The hand holding her drink gestured toward the dainty brass chair in the corner of the bathroom, its cushioned seat covered in white velvet. His hesitation was momentary before he turned to give his hat to the maid. 'When the masseuse comes, have her wait,' Eden informed the maid, then cast an amused glance at Hamilton. 'Would you like something to drink, Ham?'

'No. I think not.' He watched the servant leave the bathroom, then with a hitch of his trousers he sat on the delicate chair to face the marble bath. Recovering his aplomb, he managed a touch of wry humor. 'My grasp of history may be faulty, but I don't believe ladies have entertained gentlemen callers in their boudoirs – let alone their baths – since before the Victorian era.'

Eden laughed in her throat and sank a little deeper into the tub, luxuriating in the sensation of bathing in scented bubbles and nearly two feet of hot water. 'If you only knew how I have fantasized about this moment after six months of lukewarm showers,' she murmured. Then, in the middle of a sip, 'I nearly forgot to thank you for the flowers. They were waiting for me when I arrived yesterday. It was especially nice since neither Mother nor Father was on hand to welcome me home.'

'I'm sorry. If I had known, I would have picked you up at the station.'

She gazed at him across the frothy clouds of bubbles, aware he meant it. It was funny how time had a way of altering the memory of a person. His dark hair was thinner than she remembered, although it was artfully combed to conceal the encroaching baldness. At the same time, she'd thought of him as being shorter, when he was actually the same height that she was. The gold-wire glasses gave him a very studious look, but she had forgotten the way his eyes could sometimes twinkle. For all his staid character, he was a good man. She could certainly do worse than marrying him. Eden almost laughed out loud when she realized what she was thinking.

'If you had really wanted to be thoughtful, Ham, you would have had a case of the best Scotch in New York waiting for me,' she declared. 'You can't know how I've missed all this. I've already warned Father that I intend to make the most of my leave. I've earned myself some time on the town and I'm going to have it. The theater, the best restaurants, the fanciest clothes – and dancing until dawn.' On the last, she lifted her glass in a salute to her plans. 'No more jukebox music, Texas bootleg, or stew!'

Her avowal eased the concerns that had been bothering him while she'd been away. The glamor and excitement associated with flying had not supplanted her love of life's creature comforts. What he lacked in virility and charm, he made up for in patience. He had weathered her affair with the chauffeur and that dalliance with the impoverished Italian count, and other would-be lovers who didn't have his staying power. Always, she'd come back to him. Hamilton Steele was confident that she would ultimately marry him.

If basically she was selfish and spoiled, she was also a caring woman. Hamilton understood that, just as he understood that her dream of a *grande passion* still lingered, whether she acknowledged it or not. He could have told her that was all so much romantic nonsense. He was older, by some eighteen years, and wiser, so he knew.

A sound, lasting marriage was founded by two people of similar backgrounds and tastes, such as they shared, with differing personalities to spice their joint existence. Her outgoing, uninhibited nature kept him from becoming too dull and unadventurous, while his stability prompted her to be more circumspect about her behavior. They were a good match – his maturity and experience, and her vitality and youth.

'I am so glad to hear you say that, my dear Eden.' Hamilton reached inside the jacket of his suit to remove the small envelope from the inner breast pocket. 'Because I happen to have two tickets for this evening's performance of *Oklahoma*! The critics have been giving it rave notices, and I was hoping to persuade you to accompany me tonight.'

'Ham, you darling! Of course I will. And afterwards we can have dinner at Twenty-One or maybe the Stork Club, then to the Copacabana, the Latin Quarter . . . Who's at the Wedgwood Room? We could go there. I want to visit them all!' Eden finished with a rush of enthusiasm.

His gaze slipped from her face, distracted by the tantalizing glimpses of her milk-white body. A patient man he might be, but a saint he wasn't. It was impossible to sit calmly and view her growing nakedness without being stirred by it, nor could he affect nonchalance.

'I hate to inform you on this point, Eden, but your . . . cover of bubbles is dissolving,' he murmured discreetly.

'Poor Ham.' She laughed at his demand for modesty, but acquiesced to it. 'Fetch me another drink while I climb out of the tub.'

Nearly every night of her leave, Hamilton Steele escorted Eden somewhere – to the blacked-out district of Broadway or the garishly plush nightclubs with their elaborate floor shows. He ignored the crowds of shirt-sleeved war workers, flush with their big paychecks, sitting in front-row seats, and the multitude of servicemen crowding the dance floors at the clubs, fully aware they cut a more dashing figure than he did.

As long as he was willing to pay scalpers' prices, he could obtain tickets to any show in town, and a hundred-dollar bill would get him the best table at any nightspot. They were sitting at one such table, surrounded by two-inch-thick pile carpeting, velvet-covered walls – the ones not studded with mirrors – and satin drapes, all the extravagance and waste an escape-hungry public could want.

'It stank.' Eden sipped at her twelve-year-old Scotch while she offered her opinion of Moss Hart's *Winged Victory*. 'God help us if our combat pilots are as brainless as the ones in that play.'

'I could sympathize with the wives,' Hamilton ventured. 'Especially when one of them complained that all her husband talked about was flying.'

'Are you implying that I do that?' she asked innocently.

'My dear, you have talked of little else. I probably know as much about the idiosyncrasies of an AT-6 as you do,' he replied dryly. 'For someone who has complained as vociferously as you have about the hardships you endured, you show a remarkable affection for it. If you hated it as much as you pretend, you would have quit.'

'I loved it,' Eden admitted. 'Sand, sun, and all.' With a rare bit of honesty she added, 'Of course, I knew it was only temporary, too, which added to the feeling of adventure.'

'That's true.' Hamilton relaxed.

'You don't like to fly, do you?' She studied him with a sideways glance.

'If man were meant to fly . . .' He didn't bother to finish the obvious thought. 'Let's find another subject to discuss tonight.'

'Such as?' Nothing interested her as much, so she looked away, seeking a diversion. Her eye was caught by a tall, willowy blonde just emerging from the backstage area by a side curtain. Without the familiar flight togs, it was a full minute before Eden recognized the glamorous woman. 'Rachel!' She blurted out the name, their sometimes less-than-cordial relationship momentarily forgotten in the surprise of seeing a fellow flyer.

Hearing her name called, Rachel turned to glance around the luxurious club. When she spied Eden, she appeared to hesitate before she finally approached their table. Hamilton politely stood up, self-conscious as Rachel towered over him with her six-foot height.

Eden glossed over the introductions, then cloaked her curiosity with an idle remark. 'I never expected to run into you. I guess it proves New York is just a small town after all.'

'I was visiting some friends backstage.' Rachel was aloof and defensive under Eden's prying look. 'I used to dance in the floor show here.'

'Would you care to join us for a drink?' Hamilton gestured toward the empty chair.

'I'm with someone.' As if on cue, a man wound his way through the crowd of tables to Rachel's side. He had jet-black hair and piercing blue eyes; though he was shorter than Rachel by two inches, his stature was oddly not diminished by her.

'More friends of yours?' he said, prompting Rachel to introduce them.

She did so with reluctance. 'Eden, Zach Jordan, a friend of mine.' She seemed none too certain of that.

'Eden van Valkenburg. Rachel and I flew together at Sweetwater,' Eden informed him while she appreciatively eyed the darkly handsome man in the Army uniform, a little surprised by his enlisted status since theoretically WASPs weren't supposed to fraternize with enlisted men. 'This is Hamilton Steele.'

'A pleasure.' With a certain arrogance in his style, Zach Jordan shook hands with Hamilton, bowing slightly.

Hamilton began to repeat his earlier invitation. 'I was just suggesting we all have drinks –'

'I explained we were leaving,' Rachel pointedly interrupted him, while Zach Jordan appeared amused by the assertion.

'Another time, perhaps,' he suggested to temper the curtness of Rachel's refusal.

Thoughtfully, Eden watched them work their way through the packed house to the club's exit. When they disappeared from her sight, she took an absent sip of her drink and noticed the way Hamilton was eyeing her.

'Is something wrong?' she wondered.

He lifted a shoulder in a dismissive shrug, then commented, 'He is a handsome soldier.'

A smile spread slowly across her scarlet lips. 'Ham, I do believe you're jealous.'

'Jealous.' He seemed to consider the possibility. 'Perhaps. But I know the day will come when you'll discover you can love me.'

For a long minute, she simply looked at him, at a loss for a reply that wouldn't hurt his feelings. She was fond of him, but it was the kind of attachment one had for a pet. The kind thing would have been to end their relationship years ago, but she selfishly wanted his friendship.

Behind a diaphanous curtain a big band struck the opening note of a song, signaling the start of the flashy costumed floor show, and the need for a response was eliminated.

Outside, it was a warm, summer's night in Manhattan. An occasional breeze found its way amid the canyons of tall concrete structures. With the lithe stride of a dancer, Rachel walked along the sidewalk, ignoring the soldier who effortlessly kept pace with her. People were sitting on building stoops, young and old alike, enjoying the night air.

With a turn of his head, Zach Jordan inspected the rare beauty of her profile. 'Why are you ignoring me?'

Rachel stopped and swung around to challenge him. 'Look, I didn't ask you to come along with me tonight. You invited yourself. All you do is talk about Palestine. And all my father does is pray.'

She had an immediate image of her father with his black-and white prayer shawl about his shoulders while he rocked and talked with his God. As more stories about Hitler's persecution of fellow Jews filtered through to the United States, her father seemed to become that much more religious. For Rachel, the little knot of fear in her heart for her grandmother's safety grew tighter.

'No lectures.' A smile etched itself into the corners of his mouth, deepening them. 'You and I are alike, Rachel. The things that drive your father to prayer fill us with the need to fight.'

The man bothered her, irritating her with his arrogance, that glitter in his eyes stirring up a restlessness which contradicted all her dislike. She'd met Zach Jordan two days after she'd returned. Homeless, he was spending his leave with a Jewish family whose son was a friend of his in the Army.

They lived in the same neighborhood as Rachel's parents. In that first accidental meeting, their chemistries had mixed with instant results.

'I don't fight. I fly planes.' She seized on the small detail to deny any common calling. 'The Army doesn't believe a woman can fight.'

'They have never heard of Deborah,' he replied smoothly.

'What does it matter?' Impatiently, she would have turned away and resumed walking, but his hands caught her shoulders. His touch was warm against her skin, firm without being hard. That crazy ambivalence kept her motionless, struggling between two conflicting emotional responses.

'It matters,' Zach said. 'After the war is over, you and I are going to marry.'

'No!' The shocked denial rushed from her at the preposterous suggestion she would marry a virtual stranger.

But he continued as if she had said nothing. 'We will go to Palestine. No more will we be wandering Jews without a homeland.' His hand cupped the side of her face, his thumb stroking the point of her chin in an idle caress while his gaze roamed her features and came to a stop on her lips. 'Our children will be born there, true sabras.'

With fingertip pressure, he urged her to him. Before their lips met, Rachel caught the warmth of his breath and the male scent that drifted from his lean cheeks. Then her senses were engrossed in the persuasion of his mouth as it moved against her. She liked the taste and feel of the kiss, the confident ardor that solicited her response.

When he drew away, his gaze ran over her face to gauge her reaction. A small smile of satisfaction appeared on his mouth, that intense light in his blue eyes darkening a little. Zach Jordan was so damned sure of himself Rachel wished she hadn't found so much pleasure in his kiss.

The hard shell snapped back in place to cover up her vulnerability as she turned away and began walking down the street again, looking straight ahead. 'You presume an awful lot, Zach Jordan,' she said mockingly. 'What makes you think I care about any of those things?'

He matched pace with her, eyes to the front as well, with that smile still etched in the corners of his mouth.

'Because we are alike, you and I. We want the same things – including the freedom to be a Jew, and we are willing to fight for it.'

'Such idealism.' But her tone of voice scorned him. 'Am I supposed to believe all this nonsense?'

'I mean every word of it,' he insisted smoothly.

'In other words' – Rachel threw him a sidelong glance – 'you are asking me to marry you?'

Blandly he met her skeptical gaze, taking note of its challenge, and answered simply, 'Yes.'

Startled by his easy reply when she had expected to catch him out, Rachel stared wildly straight ahead once again. 'Do you feel safe in saying that because you know I'll refuse?' Her voice accused him.

'Partly. But believe this, we will marry and you will have my sons,' Zach said with calm assurance.

Rachel was shaken by how much she wanted to believe him. A door opened as they passed, momentarily throwing light onto the sidewalk. Her side vision caught the tan color of his Army uniform.

'You're a soldier going off to war,' she tersely reminded him.

He caught her hand as his smile deepened. 'I promise you I'm not going to die.'

It irritated her that he should treat the possibility with amusement. 'You joke,' Rachel accused.

'You care,' Zach replied, that arrogantly pleased look spreading across his darkly good-looking features. His claim was suddenly impossible to deny. 'Rachel, Rachel.' He murmured her name with such longing and tested patience. 'My leave will be up soon, and I'll have to be reporting back to my company. Let's spend what time I have left together.'

The windows of the darkened hotel room stood open, letting in any vagrant breeze that happened by. Bedsheets rustled as their bodies moved, their heads turning on pillows to gaze at one another through the dimness of night. The sounds of the city street below – the blare of a horn or the shout of a reveler – intruded not at all.

Studying his face, its thick black brows and unbelievably blue eyes, Rachel felt all warm and loose, blissfully spent. The moment had an intimacy to it that exceeded the sexual closeness they had enjoyed only moments ago.

'Didn't I tell you it would be good?' Zach boasted. He leaned over to kiss the rounded point of her shoulder, then stayed close, his hand sliding around to rub the smooth ridges of her lower spine.

'Do you know I don't remember agreeing to any of this?' she countered, the bemused smile of satisfaction never once leaving her mouth.

'That's because I didn't ask.'

In this present whipped-cream mood, it was impossible for Rachel to take offense at that very male remark. Especially when Zach followed it with a nibble of her sensitive shoulder ridge, a sensual foray that eventually lowered to nuzzle a small breast. Her fingers curled through his black hair and dug into his scalp as she arched her body forward. That darting tongue encircling her erect nipple was arousing her again.

The weight of his hard, muscled body pressed her backwards while his hair-roughened legs entwined with her long limbs. Talk was unnecessary, but they murmured to each other, meaningless love words, as hands roamed and caressed all the intimate places. Soon the spiral of desire had them straining for an even tighter embrace, bodies moist, tongues tangling and mating.

The looming shadows of the war lent an urgency to everything. Each moment of happiness had to be snatched and savored. If she was letting herself in for a big hurt, Rachel didn't care. For all his promises, Zach couldn't guarantee he would survive the war. It was only a matter of days before he would be leaving – possibly never to return. This time together had no right or wrong to it. Its very impermanence made it all the more cherished.

As dawn's first light was tinting a gray sky, Zach walked

Rachel to the front steps of her parents' home. 'I'll speak to your father about us.'

'No.' Rachel wasn't going to pretend there was a future for them. 'Do you think the Army will send you to the Pacific?'

'The Seventh is fighting in Sicily,' he replied after a small pause, then went on. 'The beachheads of the Pacific belong to the Navy and the Marines. Artillery fighting is a war of nerves. The big stuff will be sent to Europe.' He angled his body closer to her, his hand gliding down her arm in an absent caress that seemed to say he couldn't get enough of her. 'We only have two days left.'

So little time, Rachel wanted to cry, but there was a war on. In her heart of hearts, she wished only that she could go with Zach and fight at his side. She looked at the door of her parents' house, then suggested, 'Let's go eat somewhere.'

Everything was crowded in Washington, DC. The plush Mayflower Hotel on Connecticut Avenue was no different. The patrons in the dining room were elbow to elbow; tables and chairs were jammed to fill every available inch of space, leaving little room for walking. Military uniforms of every style and branch colored a room otherwise populated with dark-suited men, an assorted collection of government officials, 'dollar-a-year' men, and 'five percenters.' The latter were so called because that was their cut of the government contracts they negotiated for a business. The dollar-a-year men received that amount as their government salary, supplemented by their own companies while they held down government jobs and used their influence on behalf of their company whenever they could. Spicing the dining-room atmosphere were the foreign accents of visiting dignitaries and their resident diplomatic corps.

Exhaling the last drag of smoke, Cappy crushed the cigarette in the ashtray and glanced across the table at her mother. 'I can be as stubborn as he is,' she said, regretting that her mother was caught in this tug of war between her father and herself. 'I'm not coming home until he invites me.'

'He's a proud man.' She pleaded with Cappy to be reasonable. 'He doesn't own a monopoly on pride,' she countered stiffly. Then she signed the check, charging it to her room. With the restaurant check and her purse in hand, Cappy pushed away from the table. 'Shall we leave?'

Without waiting for her mother's nod of agreement, she rose to wend her way through the labyrinth of tables and chairs to the cashier. After she'd shown her room key to the cashier and left the check, Cappy continued into the richly appointed hotel lobby, typically packed with people. Once there, she paused to let her mother join her.

'I don't see how you can afford to stay here.' Sue Hayward looked about her surroundings with a dubious expression.

Actually she couldn't, but Cappy didn't admit that to her mother. She had been lucky the first two weeks of her leave, staying at the apartment of a friend who was between roommates. But no one in Washington could afford the rent being charged. Cappy had contributed her share during her stay at Annie's, but when her friend had a chance for a permanent roommate, she had to take it. And Cappy had checked into the Mayflower.

'It's only temporary,' she reminded her mother. 'I have to report to my new assignment in two days.'

Her stay at the hotel was more temporary than her mother knew, since hotel policy limited an individual's stay to three days. Cappy had just used the last night. If she couldn't persuade the management to bend the rules a little, she'd have to find a room at another hotel.

'I'm so glad you're going to be stationed close by,' her mother said. 'I was afraid they'd send you to California or some other place far away.'

'I know.' Despite an earlier denial by her mother, Cappy suspected that her father had pulled some strings to arrange this assignment for her, stationed at an air base just outside of Washington. It sounded like something he'd do to keep an eye on her.

A minor stir was created in the lobby as a tall, gorgeous redhead swept into the hotel, followed by a small entourage consisting of a well-dressed but self-effacing man, a maid carrying hatboxes, and three porters with an equal number of trunks. A smile of recognition flashed into Cappy's expression.

'Eden!' She hailed her friend and dragged her mother across the lobby to meet the woman chicly suited in blue linen. 'Talk about making an entrance,' Cappy chided after they had clasped arms in a laughing embrace of surprise. She glanced at the steamer trunks. 'You didn't learn a thing at Sweetwater, did you?'

'Oh, no, I'm not about to make that mistake again,' Eden assured her. 'Two of these trunks will be shipped right back to New York *before* I report. Ham and I decided to come down a couple of days early, and I wanted to be sure I had plenty of clothes to wear,' she explained with a sly smile at her extravagance. 'Who knows when I'll get another chance to wear all of them again.'

A moment was taken for introductions. After Cappy presented her mother, she was introduced to the older man accompanying Eden. She recognized Hamilton Steele's name and curiously eyed the man who, Eden had said, wanted to marry her. Cappy wondered if there was any significance to their traveling together – if perhaps absence had made the heart beat faster. But Eden seemed to treat her companion very casually.

'Excuse me while I make certain our reservations are in order.' Hamilton Steele smiled politely to Cappy and her mother, then withdrew.

'He seems nice.' But Cappy's glance at Eden was quietly speculating.

One shoulder lifted in an elegant shrug. 'They're either too young or too old,' she said wryly. 'I decided old was better.'

'That's not very kind.' She was surprised by Eden's apparently callous attitude.

'No,' she agreed. 'But then I'm not very kind to Ham.'

The significance of these remarks seemed to escape Mrs Hayward, whose interest was focused on her daughter. 'Are you going to be assigned to the same base with Cappy, Miss van Valkenburg? After flying together at Sweetwater, it would be wonderful if you could continue together.'

'I don't know anything about my assignment,' Eden replied. 'It's all very secret and mysterious. My orders simply said to report to Jacqueline Cochran, room 4D957, the Pentagon. As a matter of fact, everyone in our bay – except Cappy – received the same instructions.'

'How strange,' Mrs Hayward murmured.

'Yes. Have you had lunch?' Eden inquired, changing the subject.

'Yes, we have,' Cappy replied as her mother glanced at her watch.

'It's time I was catching the bus home if I want to avoid being caught in the late afternoon crush. It was a pleasure meeting you, Miss van Valkenburg. Cappy.' She kissed her daughter's cheek.

As she left them, Eden surmised, 'You still haven't patched things up with your father?'

'No,' Cappy admitted without remorse.

'Where are you staying?'

'I had a room here.' Cappy explained her predicament, the hotel's policy, and the uncertainty about where tonight's lodging might be.

Despite considerable persuasion on Eden's part, and that of her friend Hamilton Steele, the management wouldn't budge, insisting they didn't dare make exceptions. In the end, Cappy packed her suitcases and had the bellboy carry them down to the lobby for her.

'I know some of the staff at the Carleton,' Hamilton Steele volunteered when Cappy rejoined them. 'If you would like, I –'

'Cappy!' The anger and exasperation in the male voice

calling her name was evident in its explosive quality. Cappy turned to see Mitch Ryan in his major's uniform pushing through the lobby crowd to get to her. Along the way he was forced to pause now and then to perfunctorily salute a superior officer. The irritated snap stayed in his voice when he reached her. 'I've been trying to get hold of you for the last three days. What are you doing here? You were supposed to be staying at Annie Kramer's apartment. I finally went over to where she works and she tells me you're staying here.'

Cappy briefly explained her situation, then belatedly introduced Eden and Hamilton. Mitch acknowledged them and attempted to stifle some of his impatience.

'I've been on an inspection tour these last two weeks,' he began. His glance strayed beyond Cappy as he paused, coming to military attention, and threw a salute at a set of general's stars on an Army brown uniform. Then he relaxed. 'I've been trying to reach you ever since I got back.'

'I didn't know,' she said a shade defensively.

'Is this your luggage?' He indicated the set stacked next to Eden, and began grabbing it up when Cappy nodded in the affirmative. 'I've got a jeep out front,' Mitch said, tucking a hand under her arm and excusing them from Eden and Hamilton's company. As he guided her toward the door, another officer, this time a colonel, passed him, requiring another salute from Mitch. 'Let's get out of here,' he muttered near her ear. 'I've never seen so many caps with scrambled eggs on them in one place before.'

Outside, Mitch helped her into the open jeep and stowed her luggage in the rear. 'I haven't had time to make a reservation at another hotel,' Cappy warned him.

'Never mind. I know where you can stay.' He vaulted into the jeep and slipped behind the wheel, his hat pulled low on his forehead.

The heavy traffic on the capital's streets demanded Mitch's undivided attention. Cappy didn't distract him with questions about their destination as he drove through the snarled jams of cars and assorted motor vehicles. With

213

the Lincoln and Washington Memorials behind them, they crossed the Potomac and approached the National Cemetery at Arlington.

Nodding his head, Mitch directed her attention to it. Burial services were being held on a hill slope, a dark rectangle of exposed earth cut into the summer-yellow grass.

'There will be more of those before it's over,' he said flatly. Cappy knew it was true, but the remark didn't warrant a comment. Shortly, they passed the huge Pentagon building, and Mitch turned the jeep off the main road onto a residential side street. When he stopped they were parked in front of an apartment building.

'Who lives here?' Cappy asked, studying the well-built complex as she climbed out the jeep.

'I do.' Hefting her luggage under his arm, Mitch started for the entrance.

'I'm not staying here.' She followed him to the apartment door, stunned and not altogether sure of his intentions.

'It beats a high-priced hotel room,' he said and unlocked the door, knocking it open with her suitcase.

'Where are you staying?' Cappy demanded as she entered the compact two-room apartment. It was hot and stuffy from being shut up all day, but the accommodations did appear to be very comfortable, especially the big sofa with its thick seat cushions.

Having deposited her luggage on the floor, Mitch began unbuttoning the dark brown military jacket and shrugging out of it. 'Why don't you open those windows so we can get some circulation going through here?' He was already heading for another set, stretching his neck to unfasten the shirt button at the throat and strip off his tie.

Within minutes, a fan was blowing, Cappy had a cold beer in her hand and Mitch was lighting her cigarette. As she breathed out the smoke, he settled back against the sofa cushions and propped his feet onto the long, low table in front of it. In all the times she'd seen him, he'd never been out of uniform. Her glance strayed to the tanned

214

hollow at the base of his throat, and those springy chest hairs poking out from the edges of his white undershirt. She found such details vaguely unsettling.

'Are you still angry with me over that mixup in Sweet-water?' Mitch wanted to know, quiet and intense in the way he studied her.

'No.' She stared into the amber liquid in her perspiring glass.

'Have I gone about this all wrong, Cap?' Mitch mused, continuing to regard her from his lounging position. 'Have I courted you when I should have been making passes?'

His questions were too close to her own thinking. She straightened from the couch and wandered over to a screened window. 'What's this transport assignment I've been given going to entail, do you know?'

Behind her, Cappy could hear him set his feet on the floor, then he was rising and walking over to where she was standing. Her fingers tightened their grip on the slippery sides of the beer glass.

'You'll be flying generals, colonels . . . and some majors . . .' His hands settled onto her shoulders and absently rubbed them. '. . . to various bases in the area. It'll be real rough duty – staying in the best hotels, eating at the Officers' Club.'

'Was my father responsible for getting me this assignment?'

'What makes you think that?' Mitch bent his head and began nuzzling at the lobe of her ear.

Her breath seemed to get caught in her throat, and Cappy jerked away from the stimulating nibble of his teeth to face him. 'Did he?' She kept to the subject, trying to ignore the suddenly erratic beat of her pulse. All his attention seemed to focus on her lips. She quickly lowered her chin and turned back to the window to take a puff on her cigarette.

'I think I would have heard if he had,' Mitch said. 'Only the best pilots draw this kind of duty, Cap, and you rated the highest among all the graduates at Avenger Field.'

'How do you know that?' She was conscious of his breath stirring the ends of her hair.

'I made it my business to know.' A long sigh came from him. 'Cappy, what's it going to take for you to look at me? I was ready to tear this town upside down to find you. I ended up dragging Annie out of a meeting and I had to throw some Army-weight around to do that.'

Upset, Cappy swung around to face him. 'Mitch, stop it.'

'No.' He wouldn't hear any more of her denials. He covered her lips with his mouth, rocking over them with hungry force.

He took the cigarette and beer glass from her hands and shoved them somewhere so he could gather her into his arms. Cappy didn't attempt to deny the pleasure she found in his driving kiss, but she didn't want him taking control of her emotions. When he untangled his lips from hers and drew a mere inch away, she felt the hot, sweet rush of his breath on her face.

'Cappy, I want you.' His voice was husky and rough with need.

Wrapped in the hard, lean force of his body, she understood that and the hands that moved restlessly over her waist and hips, pressing and urging their message on her. She pulled away from him.

'I just remembered –' Cappy had her back to him, her head angled partly in his direction. An awareness licked through her nerves, creating a thready tension. '– you never did answer my question when I asked where you were staying.'

Mitch studied the tenseness, the wall of reserve she erected against the world. Behind it, she was fire and striking passion. He struggled with his heavy urges, bringing them into check.

'I'll find a bed somewhere.'

'There's no need. I can get a hotel room –' she began.

'No.' Mitch swung her around, but he was careful to keep the circle loose. The smile that pulled in the corners of his mouth had a trace of tautness about it, an ease that was forced. 'Stay here. I want to know where you are.'

'All right.' She seemed to relent, but cautiously.

'Since your father's booted you out of the nest, the least I can do is take you under my wing these last two days before you have to report for duty.' There was something jesting in his comment, an attempt to make light of the arrangement, and disguise the personal, selfish motives behind it.

The deep blueness of a glacier colored her look. 'In case you haven't noticed, I have my own set of wings.'

Again, there was that assertion of independence, that hinted denial of any need for another person.

'You're doing it again.' He closely studied her expression. 'You're always flying away before I get too close. Why, Cap?'

'There's no great mystery to it.' She attacked his question head-on. 'I'm not interested in becoming romantically involved with you. There's a war on, and we each have a job to do.' Her tone was very matter-of-fact.

'We also have off-duty hours,' Mitch reminded her. 'What's the harm in spending them together?'

'None, I suppose – as long as you realize I'm not one of those Washington typists caught up in the glamor of the uniform and the glory of the war, living for today and leaving the regrets for tomorrow.' She seemed all cold and angry with him.

'All of us are sorry about something in our lives. The saddest is not living it.' Mitch struck closer to the target than he knew. He moved away from her to light a cigarette and missed the flicker of longing that briefly broke through her closed expression.

'How about dinner? Where would you like to go?'

They dined at a quiet, out-of-the-way Italian restaurant, one of the few uncrowded places in the capital. Afterward, they strolled under the cherry trees and sat on the steps of the Lincoln Memorial, talking and sharing a rare moment of peace. It was a companionable evening, without contact.

Mitch doubted that he could maintain this platonic posture for long. And while Cappy enjoyed his undemanding company, she wondered how long she'd be content with it before she wanted more.

Part Two

Oh, I'm a flying wreck, a-risking my neck,
*   and a helluva pilot too –*
A helluva, helluva, helluva, helluva,
*   helluva pilot too.*
Like all the jolly good pilots, the
*   gremlins treat me mean;*
I'm a flying wreck, a-risking my neck,
*   for the good ole three-eighteen.*

CHAPTER FOURTEEN

When they entered the new Pentagon, billed as the world's largest office building, the two dozen graduates from Avenger Field still had no idea of the future roles they were to play for the war effort. The last two days had been spent sightseeing around Washington, except for the bus trip to Bolling Field in Virginia, where they were tested in a high-altitude chamber and certified to fly up to 38,000 feet.

Upon entering, they were given clearance badges to pin to their shirts, after which a guide led them into the corridor maze. The Pentagon was deserving of its reputation, since it held the population of a small city within its walls, thirty-five thousand workers. Carved into niches the length of the hallways were offices, creating a multitude of doors and openings.

'It's worse than a rabbit warren,' Marty said in a husky undertone. She peered at a painting of a general who was completely unknown to her and mildly shook her head. Mary Lynn's absent glance was the only response to her remark.

Their curiosity had escalated to almost uncontrollable excitement, and brought with it the certainty that all this was leading up to something important. Over the last two days, they had considered and discarded so many possibilities that no assignment seemed too far-fetched now.

There was a slowing toward the front, which indicated that either their guide was lost or they were nearing their destination, Eden decided wryly. A door opened just ahead of their group and an officer appeared. He waited, with a hint of impatience, for the young women to pass.

After coming this far through the military complex, Eden was just about convinced that all men in uniform looked alike. But there was something familiar about this tall, hatless Army officer with his dark, gleaming hair.

'Major Ryan. I didn't expect to see you.' Eden paused to speak to him, her dark eyes alight with interest as she looked at him, all the while making sure the group didn't get too far ahead of her.

The shutters were closed on his expression, his lean, square-jawed face revealing none of his feelings. 'Miss van Valkenburg.' He inclined his head in greeting, polite but aloof.

'I never heard from Cappy. I was hoping she'd call so we could all get together for dinner. Did she find a room at another hotel?'

'She found suitable accommodations.' One side of his mouth twitched in a bland facsimile of a smile. 'I believe your group is going into the conference room. Perhaps you should join them.'

'Thanks.' She started to take a step to rejoin them, then paused. 'Do you know what all this is about, Major?'

Behind those smooth looks and the cool Army discipline, she sensed a keen intelligence – and a power that operates behind the scenes. She had been around her father too much not to recognize that. Perhaps he worked at a war desk, but he did more than push papers. She was almost sorry he belonged to Cappy, but then the strictures of an Army life weren't really for her anyway.

To her question, he merely replied, 'You'll be briefed.'

A typically military response. Hurrying, Eden caught up with the last of the group. They were ushered into a conference room, dominated by a large, long table around which they were seated by their director, Jacqueline Cochran. The padding of wine-red leather seemed a definite break with the usual Army drab of olives, khakis and browns.

The slightly awed silence was broken when the general arrived and chairs were pushed quickly back from the table while they automatically stood to attention. Tall with a rocklike solidness, General 'Hap' Arnold had an infectious smile that seemed to reach out from his strong face to all of them. His eyes had a glint to them, close to both humor and battle fire, and his hair was a distinguished white.

After greeting them, the general congratulated them. Only the top pilots in their graduating class had been selected to participate in this program, he informed them, without actually telling them what this special program was. Eden couldn't help wondering why Cappy had been excluded from their number, but there wasn't time to dwell on it as General Arnold introduced Jacqueline Cochran, who now held the title of Director of Women pilots.

When she stood, she leaned her hands on the table as if to impress each and every one of them with the importance of this moment. Then she began talking, stressing first that this was a top-secret mission which would entail flying planes bigger and faster than women had ever piloted.

They would not be ferrying airplanes, which they had trained for the last six months to do. Their new duty was one of the most crucial assignments of home-based pilots in the Army Air Force. How well they performed would determine whether female pilots would be able to venture into other flying fields and free up more men for combat roles.

Mitch was in the outer chamber with a sheaf of new directives in his hand when the general returned to his office at the conclusion of the meeting. As he stopped at the desk to look them over, Mitch's glance strayed to the open door and the young, attractive women filing past outside. General Arnold followed the direction of his look.

'You did tell me they could fly, Major,' the general remarked in a mocking vein, as if belatedly seeking confirmation of that fact.

'Yes, sir.' A faint smile edged his mouth, but Mitch

223

remained vaguely distracted, his thoughts not fully focused on the moment.

'This isn't going to be the most popular decision I've ever made,' the general sighed grimly. 'Towing targets for green air gunners and ground artillery to practice on is not the safest flying job around, but it's one of the most war-essential domestic duties we've got.' He released a short, harsh laugh. 'These combat-hungry male pilots with their dreams of achieving ace status will resent the hell out of me even more when they learn I've demeaned their job by assigning women pilots to do it.'

'Yes, sir. It's rough either way, sir,' Mitch agreed blandly.

'I need those pilots for combat missions. If this experiment works, I'll have more men to fill the ranks.' He paused to eye his young staff officer. 'You don't have much faith in the program, do you, Major?'

'I think it's a fine program, sir,' Mitch assured him after the smallest start of surprise.

'I noticed you pulled that Hayward woman from the group and had her orders changed. She was one of the top-rated pilots in that class. It's obvious you didn't want her up there while a bunch of raw recruits shot up the sky trying to hit the muslin target she would be towing.'

'Transport needed a well-qualified pilot. As you said, sir, WASP Hayward is one of the best in her class,' Mitch responded and steadily met his general's probing glance.

'Of course,' the general remarked finally, a knowing light in his eyes as he gave the directive back to Mitch and turned his attention to more pressing matters.

The view of the sunset from the windows of the DC-3, the passenger version of the Army's C-47 cargo transport, was spectacular, the green, rolling grasslands of Virginia's Piedmont Range awash with the reds and golds of a dying sun. Rachel wondered about their destination as the plane flew south with its two dozen WASPs aboard, heading

224

toward their new assignment as pilots of tow-target planes. All their faces showed the same hopeful enthusiasm for the challenge and adventure this new duty might afford.

Always the loner, Rachel sat aloof from the others, not drawn in by their speculating conversations. Out of the twenty-five WASPs who had been picked for this assignment, three were her former baymates – Marty Rogers, Eden van Valkenburg, and Mary Lynn Palmer. But they had never really become close friends, and Rachel was just as glad Eden hadn't tried to follow up that chance encounter in New York.

During the long flight Rachel absently listened to the excited chatter around her and gazed out the window. As dusk spread, darkening the skies, she noticed the glistening waters of the Atlantic. Below were the barrier islands of North Carolina's Outer Banks, treacherous shoals that had claimed hundreds of ships and lives over the centuries. The long stretch of beach along the coast was a pale finger against the gleaming black ocean. The watery graveyard of ships had taken more vessels to its bosom in recent months, as cargo ships were torpedoed by German U-boats and sunk within sight of the American coast. Rachel searched for the silhouette of a darkened ship following the route that hugged the eastern seaboard, but saw none.

Somewhere down there was Kitty Hawk, the site of man's first powered flight. Rachel looked, wondering which island hill had been the takeoff point for the Wright brothers' flying machine.

The plane veered inland, flying over blacked-out settlements, and began a descent. 'Camp Davis, just ahead,' one of the pilots in the cockpit shouted back to his passengers.

No runway lights were allowed on this coastal base, located near Cape Fear. Rachel could barely make out the airstrip. The big twin-engine flew in low, skimming over the cypress thickets of a swamp before dipping onto the runway.

'I guess this is it,' someone said.

* * *

Camp Davis was one of the oldest and largest training bases for antiaircraft artillery. Inland from Wrightsville Beach to the north of Cape Fear, it was almost surrounded by swamps; Holly Shelter and Angola Swamp to the north and east, Green Swamp to the west and southwest. Farther up the coast was Wolf Swamp.

Quartered in the nurses' barracks, Marty awakened the next morning and sat on the edge of her cot, flying to shake the grogginess out of her head. Outside, the vibrating roar of an airplane engine came closer and closer until it was rattling the windows of the barracks. Marty charged out of the small private cubicle, certain the plane was going to crash into the building. It roared over the roof. A nurse looked at her wide-eyed expression and smiled in sympathetic understanding.

'You'll get used to it,' she assured Marty.

'It sounded like it was taking off right over the barracks.'

'It was.' The nurse confirmed her suspicion. 'We sit at the end of a runway.'

With their new quasi-officer status, the WASPs breakfasted in the officers' mess, then reported to the flight line for duty. The male pilots in the ready room greeted them with looks of scorn and skepticism. Marty bristled at the barely veiled contempt they were shown.

The commander of the tow-target squadron to which they were assigned was a short, balding man with a thickset body. Major Stevenson spoke with a heavy southern accent and his attitude revealed much of the southern view of women and their traditional roles. Mary Lynn doubted that his opinion of them as pilots was any better than what their male counterparts had shown them.

As they followed the commander down the flight line in the sunshine of a bright Carolina morning, he walked them past dive bombers, twin-engined bombers, and transports. When he reached the row of small piper Cubs, he stopped and informed them that, after they had checked out in the L-4s and 5s, he might let them fly some administrative missions.

'He's kidding,' Marty said in disbelief.

'I don't think so,' Mary Lynn murmured.

'My God, doesn't he know we've been flying AT-6s and twin-engined 17s?' Eden protested. 'These are kiddie planes.'

'I think someone forgot to tell him the program,' Marty declared grimly and headed for the nearest Cub. Griping wouldn't accomplish anything. It appeared they would have to prove all over again to another set of Army personnel that they could fly virtually anything with wings.

She felt a tug of nostalgia as she climbed into the cockpit of the piper Cub. She hadn't flown one since she'd gotten her license in the L-4 her brother David had owned. Aware that other WASPs were following suit, Marty taxied to the active runway and took off. After the fast, sleek Army trainers, the little plane seemed like a putt-putt. She stayed in the traffic pattern to circle the field and practice touch-and-gos.

When she came in for her first landing, Marty set her feet on the rudder pedals. A little warning bell rang in her mind, but the reason for it was vague. The instant the wheels touched the runway and Marty attempted to steer the plane with the rudder pedals, she remembered the unusual characteristics of this plane. The brakes, instead of being at the tops of the pedal shoes, as had been the case in all the Army trainers she'd flown for the last two hundred hours, were located at the base of them.

With the first screech, she corrected the mistake, steering with her toes and avoiding the heel brakes. Applying power, Marty liked the plane off the runway again and went around. From the air, she watched her friends land their Cubs, unaware of this major difference. The planes jerked, bounced, and came close several times to nosing over. They unquestionably looked like the worst bunch of pilots ever given wings. Marty watched them and groaned, wishing she had remembered about the brakes in time to warn the others.

It was a subdued and chagrined collection of women

227

who regrouped at the flight line. The male pilots were standing around, openly laughing at them. Most of the other WASPs were merely exasperated at their inability to show themselves well, but Marty was bitter, feeling they'd been tricked. Her teeth were clenched together and her fists were jammed into the pockets of her flight suit. The look in her gray-green eyes was as turbulent as the stormy Atlantic Ocean they resembled as she strode into the ready room with Mary Lynn and Eden.

'It looks like those Cubs turned out to be more than you girls could handle,' a freckle-faced pilot spoke up, a mere boy by Marty's standards.

She stopped and leaned toward him, topping him by a good inch, to belligerently challenge him. 'I can take any plane out there on that flight line and fly circles around you any day of the week.'

But he simply drew back in mock respect and laughed with his buddies. 'We've got ourselves a hot pilot here.'

Struggling with that awful feeling of impotence, Marty turned away and muttered bitterly to Mary Lynn, 'I wish I could haul off and hit him.'

Outside on the flight line, they saw more of their number buck-jumping the Piper Cubs on landing and struggling with the ignominy of not being able to master the little airplane. They had been expected to fail as pilots, and they had, but they were determined to conquer the plane and show the male pilots they were every bit as qualified. In the meantime, they had a peculiar gauntlet to run, a combination of wolf whistles and male jeers.

By the third day, Eden was just about ready to throw in the towel. This was not the reason she'd joined the WASPs, and she didn't like being the object of ridicule. Another L-5 was taxiing toward the flight line, so Eden waited on the hot and muggy flight line, rather than enter the ready room alone and endure patronizing remarks from her male counterparts.

After the Cub had stopped neatly in line with the others, she watched the long-legged blonde emerging from the cockpit. 'Nice job,' she complimented Rachel Goldman on her handling of the heel-braking airplane.

Rachel gave her a brief look of surprise before she lowered her head to shake a hand through her long hair, freed of its bandanna turban, and continued walking in the direction of the ready room, showing indifference when Eden fell in step with her.

'You should have seen me,' Eden said with a short exasperated sigh. 'I did just fine, perfect in fact, right up to taxiing to the flight line until I had to stop the Cub. And I tried to brake with my damned toes. I had to circle the plane around and bring it back into line with the others.'

'That's tough,' Rachel offered in vague sympathy.

Far off in the distance, they could hear the low rumble of artillery fire shooting at the muslin-sleeved targets towed by planes. It was a bitter reminder of the job they'd come to Camp Davis to do, before they had been relegated to flying Piper Cubs, just about the lowest rung on the ladder.

The roar of a powerful engine attracted their attention to the Beechcraft taxiing to the flight line. Eden thought she recognized the stagger-winged aircraft with its huge, churning propeller nearly grazing the ground, and paused. Catching her lower lip between her teeth, she chewed thoughtfully on it, and watched for the pilot to climb out of the cockpit.

'If that's who I think it is,' she murmured to Rachel, whose curiosity was more idle, 'maybe they'll make some changes around here.'

Sure enough, Jacqueline Cochran stepped from the plane. When she saw the two waiting female pilots, she walked over to greet them, her large brown eyes studying them with interest. Her expression was aloof, but pleasant, warming slightly as she recognized Eden.

'Hello. How are you getting along down here?' She plainly wasn't prepared for Eden's frank answer.

'We're not.' The hardships of their previous training, the spartan living conditions of the Sweetwater barracks, and the lack of creature comforts there still had held a degree of glamour and adventure. But this situation had none. Eden found it humiliating and degrading, and she refused to be stripped of her pride.

'What do you mean?' the Director of Women Pilots demanded.

'Major Stevenson has us checking out in Piper Cubs.' At that moment an L-5 landed with a screech of grabbing brakes and jerked down the runway. 'Here comes one of our group now,' Eden said dryly and observed the sharply interrogatory look from her superior. 'None of the Army trainers have heel brakes.'

Their director's lips came together in a grim line. 'I'll speak to him,' was all Jacqueline Cochran said before she turned away from them to stride toward the operations building.

'I think we'll see some changes,' Eden mused.

A military transport truck came roaring and rattling by them. Its back end was loaded with GIs in uniform and full gear. When it skidded to a stop in front of the ready room, an officer hopped out of the cab and went inside. As Eden and Rachel approached, the whistling GIs hung out the open sides of the truck to ogle them with good-natured, if lascivious, interest.

None of the girls had quite gotten used to receiving so much attention from the tens of thousands of men on the base. The best course was to ignore it. Eden would have done the same this time, except one of the soldiers sparked a glimmer of recognition. She stared for a full second, then turned an amazed glance on Rachel.

'That guy in the truck looks just like the Army private you were with that night at the club. I'd almost swear it's him,' she declared. 'His name was Zach . . . something or other.'

'Zach Jordan. It can't be him, because he was shipping out ov –' Rachel broke off her denial in midword. Zach was in the back of the truck.

Through the hiya-honeys and what-are-ya-doin'-

tonight-babes, his voice pierced the jumble of remarks and whistles. 'Rachel, what are you doing here?'

She wouldn't – she couldn't – answer him. At first, she simply felt betrayed. Then she realized she'd fallen for the oldest line in the Army. He had let her think he was going overseas, that she might never see him again. How could she have been so gullible?

As they passed the rear of the transport truck, Zach called to her again. 'Hey, Rachel. Wait up.'

Rachel ignored him as best she could, conscious of the speculating look she was receiving from Eden. Inwardly, she kept berating herself for being so stupid. As they headed for the door to the ready room, there was a clatter of boots scrambling out of the truck and a thud as they landed on concrete.

'Rachel, I can explain.' Zach came running after her, catching her by the arm and making her stop to face him.

'Let go of my arm, soldier,' Rachel warned.

'Jordan!' An officer stepped out of the ready room, barking Zach's name in sharp reprimand. 'Get back in that truck.'

'In a minute, sir.' His dark gaze continued to probe Rachel's face.

'Now, soldier.'

'Look, Lieutenant. She's a friend from back home. Just give me a few minutes to explain something to her.'

'Not on the Army's time, Private. Back on the truck before I put you on report.'

Rachel said nothing as Zach reluctantly backed away and moved toward the truck. Bitterly, she called herself a fool again. It was a hot August day, sticky and miserable. The burning humiliation and hurt only made the rest seem worse.

CHAPTER FIFTEEN

Cochran's visit to Camp Davis achieved its objective. No more Piper Cubs. The WASPs were checked out in the Douglas Dauntless dive-bomber, the A-24. Eden's ride had been less than instructive. The rear cockpit, which was actually the gunner's seat, had no working instruments, so she could only guess at what the pilot was doing and when.

Her head was still sore where she'd hit it on the gunsight when the plane had been pulled up so abruptly an instant before landing. It throbbed as she sat in the cockpit, familiarizing herself with the position of the gauges and going over the operations manual for the Dauntless. The instructor had walked off and left her, without bothering to see if she had any questions.

Irritated, Eden looked around, but the only person passing by her aircraft was an Army mechanic in a pair of greasy fatigues. 'Hey!' She whistled shrilly. 'Come here a minute!'

He stopped, and looked uncertainly in her direction. 'You talkin' to me?' His voice was thick with a Texas twang, as he pointed to himself with a slightly skeptical expression.

'Yes, you,' Eden confirmed, her patience thinning. But it was difficult to be irritated with the tall, lanky Army sergeant who hopped onto the wing of her plane and walked up to the cockpit. Everything about him was wide – as wide as Texas – his jaw, his mouth, and his smile. Smile lines ran up his face to his eyes, like spreading ripples in a pond. And when he smiled, he put his whole heart into it. The result was decidedly likable.

'What can I do for ya, ma'am?' That warm politeness and respect was ingrained by his western upbringing. It

232

had nothing to do with Army training.

'Can you tell me something about this plane?' She looked again at the panel of instruments, the corners of her mouth deepening in a kind of grim exasperation.

The lanky mechanic tried not to show his surprise that the question would be asked of him, but his nut-brown eyes looked at her askance while he explained. 'The dive flaps act as a kind of brake. Ya see, the Dauntless was designed mainly for Navy use – to land quick and short on the flattops. When you're comin' in, ya aim that nose right at the runway, then pull up jest before the wheels touch.'

He showed her how the hydraulic flaps operated, extending from the trailing edge of the wings, and informed her about takeoff, landing and stalling airspeeds, and other pertinent information. His cooperative attitude prompted Eden to ask more questions about the idiosyncrasies of the Douglas Dauntless.

'Have you checked Form One on this plane?' the mechanic asked after Eden ran out questions.

'Form One?' At Avenger Field, the instructors had taught them to always check the form in the cockpit to verify the plane's airworthiness and note any repairs recommended by the previous pilot and the subsequent work done. It was such a perfunctory thing Eden hadn't given it a thought. It was hardly more than routine procedure, but for the mechanic's benefit, she got it out.

'You're in luck,' he drawled in mild amazement.

'Why?' Eden sensed something was wrong.

'This plane's in pretty good condition. A lot of them here are red-lined.' When a plane was determined to be unfit to fly, a red X was marked on the airworthy form. But half an X, or diagonal red line, indicated the plane could have something wrong with it yet could still be flown. 'Sometimes if the wings and tail are attached and the engine runs, that's all it takes.' The mechanic grinned with his ear-to-ear smile.

'That's just great.' Eden wasn't sure whether she should believe him or not. It could be just an attempt to scare her a little. The men around here didn't seem to be very receptive to the idea of women in cockpits.

'Is that it, ma'am?' He straightened, wiping his big hands on a greasy rag that had been sticking out of the pocket of his fatigues.

'Yes, I think so.' Then she remembered one other thing, and removed a plastic packet she'd found stowed in a side flap in the cockpit. 'What is this for?'

'You don't need that, ma'am.' He took it from her and stuffed it back in the pocket, so flustered he was actually blushing underneath his tan.

'But what is it?' Eden persisted.

'It's a . . . it's a pressure release valve,' the mechanic mumbled, scowling and uncomfortable, and hopped off the wing before she could come up with any more questions. As he backed away from her plane, he called to her. 'Land as easy as you can, ma'am. Those tires are gettin' kinda worn.'

'Can't you put on new ones?'

'Ma'am, there's a war on,' he reminded her patiently. 'Practically every rubber tire is bein' shipped overseas to combat zones. We jest don't have a surplus of them sittin' around. It's best ya be cautious with the tires on these planes.'

That night in the barracks, they sat around the common room and exchanged experiences, some of them harrowing. Eden had been lucky. Except for a rough-running engine, her flying had been without incident. Others had not been so lucky.

'My engine failed. It just coughed and quit. I barely had enough altitude to glide back to the runway and land.'

'I had just landed. There I was whipping down the runway when all of a sudden, it was as if somebody yanked the plane to the right. I braced myself away from the panel and jammed on the rudder pedal, but it just wouldn't answer. There I went, tearing off the runway into the grass. I thought, This is it, I've had it now. But the plane finally stopped. When I crawled out, I saw I'd blown a tire. You wanta talk about somebody being scared shitless, that was me.'

'These planes aren't safe,' Marty protested, sitting astraddle a chair facing the back. 'I'm beginning to understand what the CO meant when he said the planes were dispensable – and so are we. Hell, he didn't want us here to begin with – and now he's found a way to get rid of us.'

'The men have to fly these planes, too.' That was small consolation.

'There's a shortage of spare parts and tires. The combat planes have the top priority on all that.' No one was impressed with that justification either.

'Speaking of parts,' Eden inserted, 'did any of you figure out how that pressure release valve works?' None of them knew what she was talking about so Eden described the plastic packet.

Marty let out a hoot of laughter. 'Don't you know what that is? It's a pressure release valve all right. It's a urinal tube for men.'

'No wonder that poor mechanic was so embarrassed when I asked him about it.' Eden remembered his expression and broke into laughter.

An Army nurse stuck her head into the room. 'Hey, is there a pilot here named Rachel Goldman?'

From her listening post on the edge of the jagged circle, Rachel lifted a hand. 'What is it?' She sat on the floor, her long legs folded in a half-lotus position.

'A soldier waylaid me outside and asked me to give you a message,' the nurse said, and Rachel came to her feet in a gracefully fluid motion, ignoring the interested looks the announcement attracted.

The soldier had to be Zach. She had been half hoping he'd attempt to contact her. She thought it would prove he had some feelings for her and it hadn't all been a ruse to get her in bed. At the same time, she was still hurt and angry, unwilling to forgive him for his trickery. The last thing she wanted was to have any of her peers learn the way she'd been taken in by this Jewish Romeo, especially her former baymates at Sweetwater. So she had no intention of allowing Zach's message to be relayed in their presence.

In the relative privacy of the outer hall, Rachel confronted the young nurse. 'What did he want?'

'He's waiting outside to talk to you.' The nurse eyed her with a mildly disapproving look. 'Both of you could get into a lot of trouble if an officer catches you together. You're not supposed to fraternize with enlisted personnel.'

'I'm still a civilian,' Rachel asserted, although she knew it was a moot point.

The nurse shrugged, 'It's nothing to me if you want to meet this guy, but there's others who won't see it that way. I'm just giving you a friendly bit of advice – don't get caught.' With the officers' privileges the WASPs had acquired, there also came restrictions.

'Thanks.'

Blackout curtains darkened the barracks windows. Nowhere on the coastal base were lights allowed to be seen. Rachel stepped out into the August night, its warm humidity tempered by a sea breeze. She scanned the black shadows beyond the walkway. The swamps, the tall sea pines and moss-draped cypress, came right up to the edge of the field, filling the air with the songs of their night creatures. A dark shape loomed in front of her, and Rachel was barely able to conceal her start of surprise.

'Rachel.' His voice reached out to her in pleasure, and she had to remember to harden herself against him. 'I wasn't sure whether you'd come.'

'Weren't you?' she countered; she'd caught the satisfaction and confidence that had entered his tone.

'I decided there were three possibilities – you wouldn't come, you'd have me arrested for making improper advances to an officer, or . . . you'd meet me.' Zach moved to take her into his arms, but Rachel turned out of them, his arrogance riling her.

'You didn't know where they'd be sending your outfit,'

she mocked him bitterly. 'But you were almost sure it would be Sicily. It's funny, but this doesn't look like Sicily.'

'I never said I was going overseas right away,' Zach reminded her with unabashed ease.

'Not in so many words, maybe,' Rachel conceded angrily. 'But you implied it. You were going off to war, and we might never see each other again.'

'I promised you I'd survive,' he reminded in an almost teasing fashion, amused instead of chastened by her icy temper.

'But you knew that's the way I would think,' she accused.

'I hoped you would,' Zach admitted. 'I wanted you, Rachel. I still do.'

'I'm sure you'd like to pick up where we left off.' She wouldn't look at him, too aware of how persuasive his charm could be. 'What kind of fool do you think I am?'

'I stretched the truth a little bit, but as soon as we finish our gunnery training here, we will be shipping out.'

'Zach, I'm not going to fall for that line a second time,' Rachel warned him.

'I was going to write and tell you I'd been sent here for more training,' he insisted.

'I'll just bet you were.' Her doubt was impregnable.

'How can I convince you it's true?' A beguiling smile played with the corners of his mouth as Zach urged her to believe him. The night's shadows brought out the strong planes of his handsome features.

From her left came the low murmur of voices, men's voices, and the sound of footsteps. When Rachel turned, she could barely make out the dark shapes of two figures. As they came closer, the silhouette of their caps warned they were officers.

'Someone's coming,' she whispered and pushed Zach toward the deep shadows off the walkway, following on his heels.

The large trunk of a tree offered them some concealment, but its narrowness forced them closer together, shoulder against shoulder. As she strained to catch the sound of the officers passing, all her senses were heightened. She was conscious of the muscled feel of his body and the spicy scent of some shaving cream lingering on his skin. His handsome face, his dark brows and jet black hair, were very near. What was more, Zach was leaning into her, pressing the advantage of this forced closeness.

'You aren't as mad at me as you pretend,' he murmured into her ear.

'Shh, they'll hear you,' Rachel whispered.

His arms circled her body while Rachel tried to stand rigid within them, but Zach wasn't deterred. His hand wandered over her arm and shoulder, traveling up to her neck and tracing the line of her throat. She had no doubt that he was enjoying the situation.

The minute the officers were out of hearing, Rachel demanded, 'Will you let me go?' She refused to struggle with Zach and give him an excuse to be more aggressive.

'You really do care about me, don't you?' he said.

'I'm sure you're conceited enough to believe that,' Rachel retorted.

'It's true. If you really wanted to get rid of me, you'd have let those officers find us together. And maybe,' he challenged her lazily, 'you'd like to explain why you hid with me?'

'I'm not going to let you use me again.' It was the only defense she had against him, but it was a weak one.

'You silly fool, Rachel.' Zach laughed softly at her and moved in closer until his dark features filled her vision. 'Don't you know I love you? My daughter of Deborah.'

His mouth sought the outline of her lips. The deep, thoroughly satisfying kiss assuaged her hurt pride. She felt all atingle inside, warm and glowing with life. There was no trickery involved in the love she felt for him. It was genuine and fierce.

Ensconced in the cockpit of the Dauntless, Eden made a last survey of the panel, conscious of a little flutter of nerves. She switched the radio to the intercom position and pressed her fingers to the throat mike.

'Are you strapped in back there? What's your name? Frank?' Eden frowned with the effort to recall the name of the extremely apprehensive enlisted man who was acting as her tow-target operator.

'Yes, sir – ma'am.' He stammered out the correction.

Eden supposed the affirmative reply was to both her questions but she didn't bother to obtain a clarification. The private was in the rear cockpit under obvious duress. She'd heard all about the mass demand for transfers by the cable operators the minute they learned they would be flying in planes piloted by females.

'We'll be rolling in a minute, Frank,' she said and took her hand away from her throat.

After an all-clear check, Eden started the powerful Curtiss-Wright engine. A ground crewman removed the wheel chocks and scampered away from the plane. Eden applied the throttle to initiate the roll. The engine rumbled with deafening noise and vibrated roughly until the whole plane seemed to be shaking. Eden didn't like the sound of it.

With the radio switch on intercom, she depressed her throat mike again. 'Something's wrong with this plane. I'm taking it back to the hangar, Frank.'

'Yes, ma'am!' The voice coming through her earphones was unmistakably relieved by the decision which seemed tantamount to granting him a stay of execution.

She taxied back to the flight line and ordered her tow-target operator to fetch a mechanic. She kept the engine running to see if it wouldn't smooth out, but it continued its ominous rumble. Frank came back with a young gum-chewing mechanic, barely in his twenties.

'What's the problem?' He sauntered up to the plane, and walked the wing to the front cockpit. Eden slid the canopy open and he leaned on the edge, giving her the eye.

'Listen to that engine.' It was vibrating the stationary plane so noticeably that she didn't see how the mechanic could ask such a stupid question.

'It's running a little rough,' he acknowledged with gum-cracking indifference. 'They all do.'

As he turned away, Eden couldn't believe he would summarily dismiss her complaint. 'Aren't you going to check it out?' she protested.

'Look, lady, I got better things to do with my time. If you're too scared to fly it like that, mark the problem on the form and find yourself another plane.' He hopped to the ground.

Furious at his attitude and his insubordination, Eden shut the plane down with lightning precision and piled out of the cockpit before the propeller blade stopped turning. The mechanic had stopped to make some comment to her cable operator. When he saw Eden charging toward him, he looked more amused by her anger than anything else.

'Okay, lady –' he began.

'That is not the way you address an officer.' And she was entitled to that status of respect.

'Yes, sir . . . ma'am,' he snidely corrected himself.

'I want that engine checked, and I want it checked now.' She jabbed a stiff finger at the parked Dauntless, her feet planted apart in a challenging stance and her arms akimbo.

'And I told you there was nothing to worry about. The engine's just running a little rough, that's all. I know my job.'

'A little rough, huh? Would you stake your life on it? Why don't you climb into that plane and fly with me a couple times around the field?' Eden challenged.

The invitation was plainly not to his liking, as he took a step backward, eyeing this red-haired female who was easily his height if not taller. 'I can't do that, ma'am,' he protested vigorously.

Their raised voices had attracted the attention of other members of the ground crew. Some ignored them after first locating the source, but most watched with ill-disguised amusement. One mechanic left a plane undergoing repairs in the hangar and came out to investigate the cause of the disagreement.

'What seems to be the trouble, ma'am?' That drawllng, respectful voice had a familiar ring.

As Eden swung around, she recognized the strong, wide face, sobered now with a frown, but capable of a Texas-size smile. He was grease-smudged from his overalls to his face, even to the billed cap on his head, but he was unmistakably the mechanic who had helped her become familiar with the Dauntless dive-bomber.

'I want the engine of this plane checked. And this so-called mechanic won't look at it. He claims there's nothing wrong with it.'

'It's just running rough –' the accused mechanic attempted to defend his position.

'Why don't you finish puttin' that plane back together in the hangar, Simpson, while I check out this lady's engine?' It was less a suggestion than an order.

'Yes, sir.' Disgruntled by the outcome, the mechanic moved off in the direction of the hangar.

This time the Texas mechanic was smiling when Eden glanced at him. 'I jest can't get it through that boy's head that the customer is always right.' The conciliatory remark brought a grudging smile to Eden's mouth. 'I'll look at your plane.'

'Thanks.' Eden intended to be there when he did. It wasn't that she didn't trust him; she simply didn't want someone going through the motions with the idea of pacifying her fears. Before she followed him to the plane, she instructed her cable man, 'You might as well wait in the ready room and have some coffee. Let them know we have a mechanical delay.'

He showed his disappointment at the word 'delay,' implying that he would have preferred an aborted mission. 'Yes, ma'am.'

The experienced sergeant quickly located the problem, and drained more than a cup of water from the carburetor. 'I figured that was the trouble,' he said. 'Somebody on the ground crew might have forgotten to top the fuel tanks last night and the water vapor condensed. Or they might

241

have filled it from an almost empty fuel drum that could have had some condensed water in it,' he suggested.

'That sounds awfully careless to me.' But she'd seen more than one example of that kind of indifference from the overworked ground crew. 'None of these planes are safe to fly.' It was an angry protest at the appalling conditions of the aircraft they were expected to fly. 'The instruments don't work half the time, so you don't dare rely on them. The seats are broken. The radios are usually so full of static you can't hear most of the time.' The list was endless.

'I can't argue with anything you say, ma'am,' the mechanic admitted. 'Even if we could get all the spare parts we need, we don't have the manpower to keep the planes in top shape. All we can do is keep the engines running so these tow-target missions can be flown. The base doesn't even get enough fuel. Sometimes we have to put in a lower octane than the manufacturer requires for proper engine maintenance.'

Eden realized just how dangerous this assignment was. No wonder the men pilots balked at taking this kind of non-combat risk – towing targets for artillery practice in marginally safe airplanes.

'What's your name?' she demanded suddenly.

He gave her a briefly startled glance. 'Sergeant William Jackson, but my friends call me Bubba.' His eyes narrowed. 'Why?'

'Bubba, I'm Eden van Valkenburg.' She shook hands with him, then scrubbed at the grease that came off on them, using an embroidered handkerchief from her pocket. 'Before I climb into the cockpit of one of these planes, I want you to check it out, so at least I can know the kind of trouble to expect and make a judgment on whether I want to fly that particular plane or not.' When he showed signs of hesitating, Eden hastened to add, 'I'll make it worth your while, Bubba.'

'I'll be happy to look 'em over for you, ma'am. And you don't have to give me any money for doin' it either. I don't reckon your pay is much better than mine.'

'Believe me, I can afford it, Bubba.' She laughed at the suggestion that she had to watch her pennies. She had never worried about the price of anything in her life.

Her reply seemed to trouble him. 'I don't know as I'd feel right takin' money from you, ma'am.'

'We'll worry about that another time,' she said. 'And the name is Eden.'

'Yes, ma'am,' he drawled in his ever-respectful way.

It was an idyllic August morning with the sun glistening diamond-bright off the waters of the Atlantic and the surf rolling onto the beaches of the outer bank of islands on the Carolina coast. But the scene was marred by the presence of the antiaircraft batteries that occupied more than a mile-long stretch of sandy beach.

Still some distance from the artillery range, Rachel activated the throat mike with her fingers. 'It's just ahead of us,' she told her cable operator. 'I'm going to see if they're ready for us.'

'Okay,' came the nervous response.

With a grim smile, Rachel recalled the way the private had gawked at her six-foot-tall frame. No doubt he believed he had been assigned to fly with some Amazon. He had acted afraid of her, the plane, and probably his own shadow.

She turned the radio key and contacted the gunnery officer, reporting her position and eight-hundred-foot altitude. As they approached the artillery range, she could begin to see little clusters of men moving about the big guns. She wondered if Zach was down there. The officer responded to her call with an order to reel out the target and bring it on.

'Roger,' she replied and flipped the switch to intercom. 'Did you monitor that?'

'Target going out,' her operator confirmed.

The target was a long muslin sleeve attached to a cable which the operator cranked out by means of a winch. As

243

he let the target out, the A-24 began to slow. Rachel advanced the throttle to maintain her airspeed, conscious of the little frissons of tension she was feeling on her first mission.

Luckily, today the wind conditions were ideal. She would have to make few corrections for crosswind drift. She tried to shut out her thoughts and concentrate on the long line of anti-aircraft guns on the beach. The big three-inch guns were first in line, followed by the .40- and .35-millimeter artillery, and lastly the small-arms range, which would require her to fly at a lower altitude for the rifle fire to hit her target.

The huge barrels of the heavy guns lacked maneuverability. The gunners were unable to track their target while the barrels swiveled clumsily in their casings, their snouts fifteen to twenty feet in the air. They were being taught how to lead their target and shoot at a spot ahead of it.

With the white target trailing behind her Dauntless, Rachel made her run down the beach. She watched the burps of white smoke from the guns and heard the thudding explosions. Her glance darted to the altimeter to make certain she was holding her pattern altitude. The prop of her plane sliced the air with a roar, and its powerful vibrations seemed to travel up the stick through her hand and into her body.

The plane began bumping through some turbulence. It seemed the noise of the guns was getting louder. Then Rachel noticed the black puffs of smoke punctuating the air in advance of her plane. That was flak! The realization hit her with sobering force. She felt that first shiver of alarm as she discovered what it was like to fly in combat. Along with the taste of fear came the rush of adrenaline and that crazy sense of excitement.

With fingers to her throat mike, she called the ground command. 'That flak is bouncing us around the sky,' she warned.

A few seconds later, the air around her plane cleared of the telltale black puffs and the explanation came back,

'Sorry. Some of the gunners thought they were supposed to take a lead on the plane instead of the target. We've got them straightened out.'

'Roger.'

The small-arms range was coming up and Rachel swooped the plane to a lower altitude for their rifle fire, leaving the explosions of the big guns behind her. The soldiers were lined up like little stick-men on the sand, the supervising officers stationed to the rear of their positions, some of them pacing. Beyond were the dunes, hairy with waving stalks of sea oats, and below, the ocean colors ranged from the aqua blue of the shallows to the turquoise green of the deep. To Rachel, the wild beauty of the coastline seemed an incongruous setting for artillery practice.

At the end of the gunnery range, she executed a slow, banking turn and made another pass. Upon completion of the pass, ground command ordered her to drop the target in the designated zone. Her tow-target mission was over.

Flying low over the drop area, she told her quiet operator to release the target. The cone-shaped sleeve was unfastened by a lever near the gunner's seat, which the tow-target operator occupied. There was a sudden lurch of the plane as it was released from the drag of the target.

As she banked the plane into a climbing turn, Rachel saw a jeep speeding across the beach to the drop zone to recover the target and check the accuracy of the gunners. In the briefing, she had learned that each gun was loaded with bullets marked with a different dye, so the color as well as the number of hits would be checked by the officers.

'What's your name again?' the artillery officer radioed.

'Goldman, WASP Goldman.' She experienced a moment of apprehension that somehow she had fouled up her first mission.

'Well . . . good job, Goldman.' The praise was grudgingly given, tainted with a bit of surprise.

'Thank you, sir.'

CHAPTER SIXTEEN

In that first week, it only took a few missions for the
WASPs to realize what they had let themselves in for.
These missions at Camp Davis bore little resemblance to
the idealized image they'd had of their roles in this war
upon graduation at Sweetwater. They weren't ferrying
spanking new planes cross-country for the Army. They
were flying the dregs of the Army Air Force, and in
exercises that practically put their life on the line every
time they went up.

After morning flight, a handful of subdued women pilots
clustered on the flight line, lingering in the shade of a
hangar building on the summer-hot August day. The low
morale was evident in lowered chins and drooping heads.

'You should see my plane.' One of the WASPs, a former
Olympic diver from California named Betty Cole, dragged
nervously on her cigarette, trying to hide the tremor in her
hands. 'There's a half-dozen holes in the fuselage, less
than a foot from the fuel tanks. Do you realize how close
I came to going up in flames?'

'I think I've got it all figured out,' Marty declared, the
only one among them not unnerved by the situation. 'This
is a trapshoot and we're the clay pigeons.'

'Brother, is that ever the truth!' another agreed.

'Half of those fools on the beach don't know how to aim
the guns and the other half don't know where.'

As Marty crushed a cigarette beneath the heel of her
shoe, she glanced sideways at Eden, crouched beside her,
her weight balanced on the balls of her feet. 'Your Jacqueline told us this assignment was an experiment.'

'And we're regular guinea pigs,' Betty Cole complained
grimly.

'It's funny.' Mary Lynn studied the sky overhead, watching the planes in the pattern. 'I always wondered what it was like . . . for Beau to fly through flak. Now I know.'

The noise, the violent shudders and hard rocking of the plane, the smell of brimstone, all were fresh impressions on her senses. She chain-smoked, nervously puffing on a cigarette and twisting it in her fingers. The experience had left her badly shaken. It was small consolation that she wasn't alone.

'I don't know about the rest of you' – another of their number spoke up – 'but the thought of going up again in another red-lined plane so a bunch of green soldiers can use me for target practice – I get all sick inside just thinking about it.' Her declaration was followed by a forced laugh, a brittle attempt to make light of her feelings. 'Maybe I'm losing my nerve,' she joked very weakly.

Others faked smiles to go along with her pretense of humor. The area was aptly named Cape Fear. The smell of it was in the air, enveloping them in a chilly dread that made their skin clammy and set their blood to pounding.

'Let's get a Coke,' someone suggested.

There were a lot of dry mouths, but the sweltering afternoon heat was not to blame. No one was comfortable with the subject of conversation. In a loose group, they drifted toward the ready room.

A poker game was – perpetually it seemed – in progress in a shadowed corner of the room. The whirring blades of a rotating fanhead moved the hot, smoke-stale air to offer some relief. The players at the table, all young male pilots, looked up when the sober bunch of flight-clad women wandered in. Their collective unease was almost tangible. The freckle-faced pilot spied Marty in their midst and rocked his chair onto its back legs.

'Look who made it back, fellas – it's our hot pilot,' he taunted.

Marty didn't miss a beat. 'I haven't seen you on the flight line lately, Freckles. Don't tell me a big, brave boy

247

like you has been ducking his missions and letting a female take them?'

'I had a mechanical problem,' he retorted stiffly.

'Called what? No guts?' she derided.

Mary Lynn pressed a squatty Coke bottle into Marty's hand, protesting in an undertone, 'That isn't fair.'

'You notice he isn't denying it,' Marty declared with cutting scorn.

'If you're stupid enough to crawl in the cockpit of one of those planes and be a sitting duck for a bunch of artillery gunners, I'm not going to stop you,' Freckles said. 'You survive in this man's Army by letting the other guy – or gal – get his head blown off. You wanted a man's job. Now you've got it, so what's your complaint?'

'You're brave as hell, aren't you?' she sneered.

'I'm alive.'

'That's really something to brag about, isn't it?'

A pilot burst into the ready room. 'Dusty went down! We're all ordered up in the air!'

Cards were discarded and chair legs scraped the floor in an instant reaction to the summons. Pilots, male and female alike, ran out of the ready room onto the flight line, fanning out to seek out their aircraft.

An air search for a downed pilot was fairly routine for the men in the squadron, but it was still new to the WASPs. Each pilot was assigned a certain quadrant to fly, criss-crossing a given area and watching for the glitter of metal wreckage in the tangle of cypress and swamp grass that surrounded the camp. The proper procedure in the event of a forced landing was to pancake the plane in the swamp so it would leave a wide path that could be spotted from the air. If possible, a parachute was to be spread on the ground to aid in the spotting. Above all, a pilot was to stay at the crash site.

After better than an hour's search, Mary Lynn felt the eyestrain and the tension that ridged her neck muscles. She hadn't seen anything but the white dots of herons in her section of swamp. Subconsciously, she was always listening to the sound of her plane's engine in case it started giving her trouble.

Finally, the downed plane was located in another quadrant. The message was radioed to the search planes that the pilot and his cableman had been found and all aircraft were ordered back to the field. Mary Lynn turned her plane onto a heading for the strip, relieved yet conscious of the jangled tearing on her nerves.

That evening, all of them were slightly strung out. At mess, lack of appetite was blamed on the heat. The August weather was held responsible for a lot of the frayed tempers and irritable moods. Marty was the only one who seemed to have some immunity to the common condition. It didn't take much urging on her part to persuade Eden and Mary Lynn to have a drink at the Officers' Club and unwind a bit.

Male officers at Camp Davis outnumbered the women a hundred to one. The three of them walked in. The base band was playing a Glen Miller tune while another major pushed his chair into the circle that surrounded their table.

After an hour of being plied with drinks and urged onto the dance floor at every song, they escaped to the powder room for a breather. Eden sat at the mirrored vanity to freshen her lipstick. 'Two weeks ago, I was complaining at the lack of eligible men. Out there, a girl can have her pick.'

'Ah, but why settle for one when you can have a whole squadron,' Marty countered as she fluffed the short curls of her honey-light hair.

'They all seem so lonely.' Mary Lynn supposed Beau felt the same. 'You get the feeling they're happy just to have a woman to talk to.'

'It's more than talk they want.' Marty shook her head at Mary Lynn's innocent interpretation of a man's needs. 'Ready to go back among the wolves?'

'Yes.' Eden stood up, joining them as they moved toward the door. 'They drink a lot, have you noticed?' Her observation drew little comment beyond affirmative nods.

Later, Eden discreetly covered her mouth to hide the yawn she couldn't suppress. She tried to appear interested in the ramblings of the officer with the silver oak leaves on his uniform, so confident of his ability to impress her that he couldn't see her boredom.

Her glance strayed to the dance floor where Marty was tightly entwined in the arms of her partner, a devastating lieutenant with sun-gold hair. For a fleeting instant, she wished for Marty's sense of freedom with men, then changed her mind. Its very impermanence lacked style. She turned back to her lieutenant-colonel and faked an attentive smile.

In an Army camp capable of housing ten thousand soldiers, innumerable hiding places existed for those who had reason to need them. It was in such a forgotten corner of the base that Rachel and Zach lay on a scratchy Army blanket, mostly clothed even though few of the buttons were fastened.

Rachel rested her head on the pillow of Zach's muscled shoulder while he stroked the silken strands of her hair. She was turned toward him, her hand lying on his chest where it could feel the heady thud of his heart. There was a languor about the warm night air that soothed and put distance between Rachel and the half-known fears of her assignment.

'You and your artlllery buddies almost got me today,' she informed Zach from the secure comfort of his embrace. 'You shot the cable in two just three feet from the tail of my plane.'

'We're a trigger-happy bunch.' A smile was in his voice.

'This is ridiculous, you know that,' Rachel murmured, casting an eye at their surroundings. 'We'll probably be carried off by the mosquitoes.'

'The facilities are on the primitive side,' he conceded, his voice rumbling deep in his chest and vibrating against her ear. 'But it's the best I can offer right now. Marry me, Rachel.'

For a little second, she let the fanciful words turn around her before she faced the reality. 'You can't marry without the Army's permission. They'd never give their consent to a marriage between an officer and an enlisted man. Even though we aren't officially a branch of the Army, we do have officer status.'

'Who said anything about asking? We don't need them,' he countered evenly. 'We'll marry the ancient way. Find two witnesses and vow before them, "Behold, thou art consecrated unto me according to the law of Israel."'

'Zach, you talk such nonsense.' But for all her denial, it filled her with a warm glow to hear him speak like that, simplifying everything.

His fingers fitted themselves to the point of her chin and lifted it so he could see her face, glowing in the pale light. 'Why is it nonsense to love you, Rachel?' His handsome looks were so dark and devastating they took her breath away, that ebony-black hair, those azure-blue eyes, and those nobly chiseled features.

'Maybe because there's so much uncertainty around.' She curved her fingers along the back of his neck. 'I love you, Zach. Sometimes . . . I just don't know what I'd do if anything happened to you.' There was an underlying fierceness in her low voice.

A frown flickered across his expression. 'I keep telling you,' he insisted, 'nothing is going to happen to me.' He rocked a hard kiss across her mouth in a sealing promise, then rolled her out of his arms and sat her up so he could light a cigarette. 'Want one?' He offered her a Camel from the squashed pack in his breast pocket.

'Thanks.'

When the match flared suddenly in front of her, the brilliant yellow flame coming toward her, Rachel recoiled in a terror that seemed instinctive. It shook her, and she turned from it.

'What's wrong?' Zach looked at her, puzzled by her reaction. 'It was too bright. It hurt my eyes.' She came up with this plausible explanation and pushed the unlit cigarette at him. 'Light it for me, will you?'

The match went out and he had to strike another. Zach saw her turn her head rather than look at the fire. It puzzled him as he passed her the burning cigarette and bent his head to light his own. She circled her knees with her arms and drew them up to her chest, hunching over them in a tight ball.

'What is it, Rachel?' he asked gently, sensing the fear in her that she didn't want him to see. 'You seemed afraid of the match flame.'

'I wasn't.' She sounded impatient with him. 'It hurt my eyes. I told you that.'

For a long minute, Zach stayed silent and studied the white spiral of smoke rising from his cigarette. 'In the barracks, some of the guys talk a lot about what it's like in the fighting . . . some of the things they've heard . . . what happens to guys on the front. It's as if they have to talk their fears out – in case they're the one who gets hit by an artillery shell and blown into so many bits they can't even find his dogtags.' His glance flickered to her, measuring and keen. 'I've heard pilots are afraid of fire.'

A tension seemed to electrify her. For an instant, Zach expected to hear an explosive denial. Then a sudden sigh loosened her, although a twisting agitation remained.

'It doesn't have anything to do with flying, not really.' Her mouth was grim-lipped and tight, a frustration seething somewhere inside. 'A girlfriend of mine – she was an actress in Hollywood for a while – just before graduation, she was flying an AT-17 to Big Spring. I was following her in another plane. All of a sudden, there was a big, blinding ball of flame where her plane should have been.'

'Rachel –'

'But I had this . . . aversion before that.' Impatiently, she broke in to reject any possible sympathy. 'When Helen was killed, I thought it was a premonition of her death, but it hasn't gone away.' Finally, she looked at him in the darkness, her face all white and rigid with tension. 'I'm

afraid to look into the flame – afraid I might see you . . .
or maybe my grandmother.'

The haunted depth of her strangely violet eyes was more
than Zach could stand. He looked away. Words seemed
inadequate comfort. The burning tip of his cigarette
glowed in the dark, the red heart growing hotter and
pulsating with an eerie life. He ground it into the dirt, then
reached for the tight ball Rachel had made of herself and
gathered her into his arms.

'What are you doing?' Rachel protested when he took
the freshly lit cigarette from her fingers and threw it into
the night.

'No cigarette. No fire. No flames to see faces in.
For now, there is only love.' A smile was on his mouth
as he lowered it onto her lips. His body followed it
down, its weight gently driving her backwards onto the
blanket.

The hot, drugging kiss lasted long seconds before Zach
lifted his head to study her face and see if he'd driven the
fear aside. The heady sweetness of her was on his tongue,
adding to the high run of pleasure he felt.

Rachel fingered the black silk of his hair, absently combing through its sleek thickness. 'You are crazy.' Her lips
lay softly together, all the previous tension eased.

'I must be to love you,' he agreed smoothly. Their
embrace had pushed her blouse apart where the lower
buttons were unfastened, exposing the pale flesh of her
stomach. Zach bent to kiss it, feeling her skin quiver under
the caress of his mouth. 'I'm waiting for the day our baby
will grow inside you.' When he lifted his head to look at
her, his hand lovingly rubbed her flat stomach. 'Why don't
we start making one now?'

'Zach, no. What am I supposed to do with a baby while
you go off to fight?' Her words resisted his suggestion, but
her face appeared warm.

'What's the matter? Can't you fly a plane with a baby
on your hip?' he mocked and began nibbling on the sensitive cord along her neck.

'Zach.' Her hands tightened around him to press him closer. 'Love me.'

CHAPTER SEVENTEEN

OUTSIDE THE pilots' ready room, all was black. After sundown, no lights were permitted; the field was under blackout orders and even the runways were darkened.

Yet in the battle zones the war was fought by night as well as by day. Radar trackers and searchlight operators had to be trained in the skills they would need in their combat roles, skills which required night practice . . . and pilots were needed to fly the planes for them to track on their screens or with their lights.

'Cigarette?' Eden shook a Lucky Strike from the green pack and offered it to Rachel.

The tall blonde refused with a shake of her head and turned away as Eden snapped a flame from her lighter and held it to the end of her cigarette. She pulled the smoke deeply within her lungs, then exhaled in a nervous rush. The hastily crushed butt of her previous cigarette still smoldered in the ashtray.

There was little Eden could do to rid herself of the tension that honed all her senses to a razor-fine edge of animal keenness. Danger lurked out there – stalking around the darkened field.

There was no mission to fly. Tonight was merely a check ride to test their night-flying proficiencies. In a way, it was a compliment to the female pilots that they'd done so well on the tow-target missions they were now being considered for other assignments, but Eden was too conscious of the added risks to feel flattered by the commanding officer's show of faith.

'I'd feel better if we were going up in multiengine planes.

At least if an engine failed, we'd have a back-up.' It was the closest Eden could come to admitting the trepidation she felt. Accustomed all her life to the best, she still had trouble accepting the junky craft she flew.

At night, the land was shrouded in darkness, making it difficult – if not impossible – for a pilot to determine wind direction and select a safe landing site in an emergency. The airfield was surrounded by swamp, and the thought of going down in its snake-infested marsh was even more harrowing.

Rachel was never very communicative. If she shared any of Eden's apprehensions, she kept them to herself. Taking a drag of smoke deep into her lungs, Eden guessed at a great many of Rachel's secrets. She'd already figured out that Rachel slipped away in the evening to meet her handsome, enlisted lover. With a twinge of envy, she'd identified the look of love she had sometimes glimpsed in Rachel's expression. Naturally, she didn't let on that she knew about the trysts, and Rachel was hardly likely to confide in her about them.

The instructors arrived to give check rides to the group of WASPs ordered to report to the flight line. The inaction and the inability to talk about the misgivings they all shared were finally put behind them as they went about the business of checking out the individual aircraft they'd be flying. But they kept reminding themselves that male pilots had been flying these night missions all along, and they were here to replace them.

In the warm, languid air of late summer, Eden read the Form One sheet of her aircraft's log. The only defect listed on the form was a broken seat, a very minor item in Eden's opinion. Other than that, her plane was in good flying condition. Still, when she saw Bubba Jackson going over her A-24, it gave her added reassurance.

The lanky mechanic waited by the wing to give her a hand up while her instructor spent a last few minutes conferring with one of his colleagues. 'You're working awfully late, aren't you?' Eden observed, smiling and aware of the strength in the hand that assisted her onto the wing. Usually, only the ground crew was around the flight line for the night missions, the mechanics long gone.

'Had to check the planes out for you ladies; make sure they were safe for you,' Bubba replied with a warm, wide smile. There was about him a generous, loving nature, sparked with an easy humor, steadied by a solid will, and tempered by an iron strength.

'No major problems?' Eden climbed into the front cockpit. Bubba followed her onto the wing and helped her get settled in the seat.

'None, not in any of them,' Bubba stated, then qualified his words. 'It's all fairly minor – broken seats like yours, static problems with radios, a sticky canopy latch, but no trouble with the engines on any of the planes.'

'Thanks,' she said and meant it. Just knowing that Bubba had checked out her plane eased her fears. She tried to tell herself that tonight would be no different from the many times they'd practiced night-flying in Sweetwater.

With a wink, Bubba slapped the metal skin of the plane in a kind of farewell pat and hopped off the wing. Her instructor took his place in the gunner's seat. Down the shadowed row of aircraft, Eden saw the shimmer of something white, then the small silhouette of Mary Lynn crawling into the cockpit of an A-24 with the pillows which enabled her to reach the foot controls.

Engines sputtered and coughed, then revved into a steady roar. When they taxied away from the ramp, Eden followed the plane Rachel was piloting down the darkened taxi strips to the unlighted runway. She closed her canopy and made her run-ups while she awaited her turn. As soon as Rachel's Dauntless cleared the runway, Eden started her roll, hurtling her plane down the blacked-out airstrip. It was like flying blind, relying solely on her instruments to direct her liftoff.

Airborne, they were to stay in the pattern and practice takeoffs and landings from the darkened field. In order to see the dimensions of the strip, they were forced to fly low, always keeping in mind the swamp pines that loomed so close to the foot of the runway.

On her first circuit, Rachel wasted a lot of runway before setting her plane down by coming in too high, an error her instructor pointed out as she went around to try again. It was difficult to distinguish the long, black shapes of the camp buildings below, but one of them was the barracks that housed Zach. The thought of him stabbed into her concentration, bringing a momentary break in focus – and a smile to her lips.

'Bring it in low this time, Goldman,' her instructor advised from the rear gunner's seat. 'You can't see where the runway starts if you come in like a cautious old woman.'

'Yes, sir.' She bridled at the slur of female timidity and aggressively attacked the pattern, swooping down to make her approach.

In the changing colors of darkness, the runway lay before her, a wide swath of gray-black. With all her concentration focused on setting up the A-24 for a turn down the center of the strip, Rachel failed to see the trees rushing up to meet her. Suddenly the plane was jolted, the wheels snagged by the treetops.

Rachel heard a cry, but didn't recognize it as her own. There was barely time to brace herself as the Dauntless tumbled forward, nosing for the ground. On impact, there was a wrenching tear of metal, a violent jarring that bounced her from side to side. When the crashing, crunching noise stopped, it was a dazed instant before Rachel realized she was still alive.

Then she saw it – the leap of yellow flame from the engine, a searching serpent's tongue, flicking and darting and disappearing, only to show itself again. Terror sucked at her throat. Her fingers tugged frantically at the buckle to free herself from the seat, then turned their efforts on the canopy.

GET OUT!

She jerked at it, but the latch was stuck. Panic flashed through her mind as she remembered the Form One sheet had warned the canopy could only be opened from the outside. The fire blossomed into a roar, sweeping back from the engine while Rachel screamed and beat on the mullioned canopy.

GET OUT!!

She clawed at the latch in a frenzied attempt to escape as the yellow flames swirled through the cockpit. The fire trapped her inside its searing net, and rolled her up inside its life-snatching heat.

On her downwind leg, Eden saw Rachel's plane shudder to a stop in midair, hang there for interminable seconds, then topple into the swamp at the edge of the field. The impact snapped it in two, separating the front cockpit from the gunner's seat. She saw the yellow tongues of flame lick over the engine as it caught fire.

The landing pattern took her directly over the burning wreckage. In horror, she looked at the scene below her. Time and space seemed to stand still, hovering, while she heard Rachel's screams and watched the figure in the blazing cockpit make a last desperate attempt to push open the canopy before the fire consumed her.

Then she'd flown past, the screams ringing in her ears and the sight of a fiery figure, arms, legs, and body all aflame, emblazoned in her mind. Afterwards, Eden didn't remember landing the plane or taxiing it to the flight line.

One of the first things she did upon landing was to open the canopy of her A-24 and drink in great globs of air. Distantly she heard the wail of sirens as rescue trucks and fire engines raced to the crash site. She was sweating, but she felt cold and shivery.

Vaguely she became aware that someone was calling her name. Still encapsulated in a kind of dazed shock, she became aware of someone standing on the wing outside her cockpit. He reached in to switch off the engine and shut down the systems.

'Eden.' Bubba's strong, wide face was close to hers, examining it in the night's darkness. 'Are you all right?'

258

In the strain of the moment, Bubba had dropped the formality of 'ma'am.'

The deep caring and concern she saw in his anxious expression broke the paralysis of shock. 'I saw it, Bubba. I saw it all.' Her gaze clung to his big-jawed face. 'She hit the trees.'

'I know.' He was very matter-of-fact as he urged her out of the cockpit. 'Come on.'

Mechanically, she climbed from the plane. Her instructor was on the ground, but she paid little mind to him. It was Bubba she turned to as she tried to shake off the dazed terror that gripped her. The instructor hovered uncertainly until Bubba indicated he should leave.

'I'll look after her. They'll probably want you in operations,' he said quietly and kept a hand on Eden. In an absent gesture, she took off her scarf and let her shiny auburn hair tumble free, as if releasing it would rid her of the dreadful images.

'I could hear her screaming,' she told Bubba in a flat voice as the instructor moved away. 'The engine caught fire. She couldn't get the canopy open and –' She couldn't get the rest of it out, the horror of it too much for speech.

'My God,' Bubba said, softly at first, then in a clearer, flatter voice. 'My God.' He remembered the canopy with the faulty latch that could only be opened from the outside.

'Bubba, it was awful,' she said with a sob.

When his arm circled her shoulders, she gratefully turned into his body and buried her face in the hollow of his shoulder. He held her tightly against his lanky frame, absorbing the violent shudders that racked her body. His low, softly drawled voice murmured near her ear, dulling the memory of those terrifying shrieks while he suffered pangs of remorse and guilt. 'If only I had . . .' but he hadn't.

The night was a din of noise – the strident wail of an ambulance, the shrill sirens of fire trucks, and the roaring engines of other planes landing and taxiing back to the flight line. The check rides had come to an abrupt end; the planes landed on the air strip one after another. Eden stayed hidden in the shadows of her plane and isolated in the island of Bubba's arms.

'I didn't even like her,' she said in an odd mixture of guilt and regret.

'Shh.' He cupped his hand to the back of her head and pressed it more tightly to his shoulder while he gently rocked her.

By the time the fire trucks could put out the fire, Rachel's body was charred beyond recognition. In fate's strange way of working, her instructor had been thrown clear of the fire-engulfed front section. The ambulance whisked him away.

Within minutes of the crash and the first shriek of sirens, word of the accident swept through the Army barracks. Zach joined the cluster of soldiers outside his bay and stared at the odd light reflected in the sky.

Nearly all party invitations in Washington, DC, included instructions on which bus to take. Mitch Ryan, however, had a military vehicle at his disposal, a mark of his status regardless of his rank.

When they reached the exclusive Washington suburb of Chevy Chase, Mitch had no difficulty locating the manor-sized home. Lights blazed from virtually every window of the two-and-a-half-story structure, throwing long, rec-tangular streamers into the night, sometimes spotlighting glimpses of the partying crowd beyond the sheer drapes. Cappy couldn't help regarding it as an extravagant display.

'Will they let me in like this?' she asked when he left the vehicle parked in the drive. Mitch ran a quick glance over her uniform of tan slacks and white shirt, a tan boat-shaped cap sitting atop her midnight-dark hair. Women in slacks were still frowned on in a great many circles.

'We're at war. It would be unpatriotic to turn away an officer in uniform,' he returned glibly. Then he assured her, 'We won't be staying long – whatever time it takes to make my presence known – then we'll go off by ourselves.'

'Okay.' Even though she was stationed close by, flying out of a base on the outskirts of Washington, she'd only been out with Mitch on two occasions since starting her new assignment almost two weeks before. Each time she found herself looking forward to seeing him more and more.

The hectic pace of wartime Washington made it socially acceptable for guests to arrive in street clothes or office garb. But Cappy's uniform slacks did succeed in raising a few blasé eyebrows. However, the plethora of military uniforms, especially field grades, took much of the strangeness out of her appearance.

Caterers circled the rooms with trays of drinks balanced on their hands. Cappy was holding a glass within minutes of entering the house. Either there weren't any shortages in Chevy Chase or the black market was the popular shopping place, she decided, upon seeing the silver platters of canapés and hors d'oeuvres, which were not only plentiful but also stuffed with an array of meats rarely obtainable.

While Mitch squired her through the noisy, laughing clusters of guests, Cappy quietly observed the avidly gossiping crowd, spreading the latest rumors. This scene was all too familiar to Cappy, the currying of favor and the back-stabbing She'd seen all these games played; she'd seen the advancements and promotions that had nothing to do with merit.

She had become so inured to the sight of Army uniforms that she almost didn't notice the gold stars adorning the shoulders of the officer now receiving Mitch's respectful attention. Then she heard Mitch introduce her and the broadly smiling general turned an interested glance on her.

'WASP Hayward, at last I have the pleasure of meeting you.' He warmly clasped her hand, the gleam in his eye hinting at the many things he'd heard about her. The glance he sent Mitch revealed the source.

'You're very kind, General Arnold.' She inclined her

head to him, respectful of his rank but unawed by it. Protocol and pettiness too often walked hand in hand. She was well schooled in the ways of paying lip service to rank. 'Please forgive my less-than-feminine appearance,' she said, drawing attention to the gabardine pants tailored to her slim hips and long legs. 'But I'm afraid I came straight from the flight line.'

'I wouldn't worry about it,' he replied easily. 'I'd wager half the women at this party wished they looked as attractive as you do in slacks.'

'Now you are being gallant, General,' Cappy demurred with practiced ease.

His chuckle held approval as he glanced at Mitch. 'No wonder you're so taken with this young lady. She'd be an asset to any man.'

'That's always supposing I would want to be,' she murmured. Pride straightened her shoulders and lifted her head as she gave him the full strike of her gaze. She refused to exist in a man's shadow the way her mother did.

On an amused intake of breath, the general glanced again at Mitch. 'The trouble with letting women wear pants is getting them to take them off.' His attention returned to Cappy. 'You're Lieutenant Colonel Hayward's daughter, aren't you? He's a crack polo player, I've heard.'

'Yes, sir.'

'He must be very proud of you,' General 'Hap' Arnold remarked.

'I wouldn't know, sir.' Her smile was reserved as she turned military on him, clipped and opinionless.

An aide approached and discreetly called the commanding general of the Army Air Forces aside. The content of the whispered message caused a frown to furrow the general's wide forehead. He looked soberly from Cappy to Mitch, lingering on the latter as if he had half a mind to call him away, too.

'Excuse me, I . . . have a phone call. You'll be around for a while yet, won't you, Major?' The polite inquiry was an indirect order to remain.

'Yes, sir.' Mitch confirmed with a small nod of his head. 'We'll be here.'

'Good.'

After the general had gone off to some private room to take the phone call, Cappy sipped at her drink and surveyed the gaggle of guests over the rim of her glass. 'I thought you said we wouldn't be staying long,' she mockingly reminded Mitch.

'I'd like to think you're complaining because you want to be alone with me.'

'Maybe I do.' When she turned to look at him fully, her eyes were big and blue, demanding in their keen brilliance.

'What do you want from me, Cappy?' There were many meanings to his question, but Mitch knew she'd pick the one that suited her, as usual.

This time she surprised him. 'I don't know. I've been asking myself that lately, too.'

It was a subject he would have preferred to pursue, but the party made it impossible. Someone came up to speak to him and the conversation was sidetracked. They became caught up in the social chatter of the war, the endless talk and speculation and the hinted-at secrets.

Twenty minutes later, Cappy observed the general's return. He was an imposing figure, solidly packed and vigorous as he moved through the room, always in their direction. The congenial smile that came so readily to his lips seemed distant and preoccupied, an automatic response while more serious matters dominated his mind. He stopped when he reached them and looked at Mitch, a serious light in his hazel-colored eyes.

'Would you excuse us for a moment?' The perfunctory request was addressed to Cappy as General Arnold drew Mitch aside.

No response was expected from her beyond an agreeing nod while she pretended to focus her attention elsewhere and not listen to the words spoken in undertones. But when Cappy heard 'WASP' and 'crash' mentioned, followed by the location, 'Camp Davis,' she did the unforgivable – she intruded.

'Whose plane crashed?' she demanded and watched the general's thin lips come together to hold back the information. Impatience and agitation swept across her features, writing an unbearable tension and strain all over her expression. 'I heard you say a WASP crashed at Camp Davis in North Carolina. please, I have friends there.'

'Sorry, sir,' Mitch muttered and tried to silence Cappy with a look as he reached for her arm to lead her away.

'No.' She refused to be removed, aware that her actions were attracting the unwanted attention of those around them. A false calm steadied her. 'General, you did say a WASP crashed. Who? Was she . . . hurt?'

For a long span of seconds, he merely looked at her, then a gently sad quality suffused his hard visage. 'Positive identification has not been made. There was a fire,' he explained, and had to say no more. Cappy's jaw was tightly clenched as a kind of paralysis gripped her throat. 'At this time, it's believed the victim was a young woman named Goldman – Rachel Goldman.'

The shock of recognition broke the superficial barrier of calm. Tears sprang into her eyes and Cappy quickly lowered her head to hide them.

'Did you know her?' the general probed.

'We were baymates at Sweetwater.' She lifted her head, stunned and shaken. 'I never thought it might be her.' Her fears had been for Eden, Mary Lynn or Marty.

'Come with me.'

This time Cappy didn't protest against being led away, letting the hand at her elbow guide her across the room. A set of pocket doors was slid open and closed after they walked through. The chattering noise of the party didn't intrude inside the paneled den. General Arnold motioned his aide toward a liquor cabinet while he paused to inspect the titles of the books lining the wall shelves.

'I love books,' he remarked in a deliberate change of subject. He looked around to be sure he had an audience.

'Have you seen those new, small-sized books with paper covers? A publishing company named Pocket Books is putting them out. Handy for the soldier to carry with him. But when it comes to reading, I like the solidness of a hard-bound book.'

A wave of vertigo made Cappy sway and she felt Mitch's hands steady her. She leaned into the support he offered, finding a warmth and a strength that she needed. The general's aide brought her a snifter of brandy, but she didn't really want it.

'Drink up,' General Arnold urged.

'Yes, sir.' Perforce, she was obliged to take a sip.

'It was an unfortunate loss,' he said, referring to the crash. He didn't inquire as to the closeness of her relationship with Rachel, nor did he invite her to confide.

'Yes, sir.'

To Mitch he said, 'There'll be a board of inquiry looking into the crash. I'd like you to be there . . . in an unofficial capacity.' In other words, as his eyes and ears, with the findings to be reported directly back to him. 'Perhaps' – he seemed to consider the suggestion he was about to make, before actually saying it – 'Miss Hayward could fly to Camp Davis with you . . . as your pilot.'

'Thank you, sir.' Cappy was grateful for the favor granted, a cynical part of her aware that it was given out of an Army loyalty to one of their own, daughter of a respected Army officer and girlfriend to one of the general's prized staff members.

'I must be getting back to the party,' the general said, taking his leave of them.

Alone in the den, Mitch asked, 'Were you close to this Rachel Goldman?'

'No,' Cappy admitted. 'Is it all right if we leave the party now?'

'Of course.' An instant later, a guiding hand rested on her waist to direct her through the maze of people and rooms.

The night air was summer-warm and still. Cappy rode

in the passenger seat without talking. Her fears about the fate of her friends had been eased, but there lingered an unsettling feeling that gnawed at her. She turned her gaze from the traffic on the capital's streets and the lighted windows of its houses and buildings to look at Mitch. The present route would take them to Bolling Field, where she was stationed.

'Please, I'd rather not go back to the barracks right away.' Cappy felt him looking at her, wary and curious while he searched her expression. 'Could we go to your place for a drink?'

'If that's what you want,' Mitch consented.

An odd silence lay between them for the rest of the ride as Mitch changed directions, crossing the Potomac to the Virginia side, where his apartment was located. Once they had entered the apartment, the long silence was interrupted by short questions and one-word responses, all very correct and polite, as Mitch fixed them each a drink.

A restlessness moved Cappy about the room, finally drawing her to a window where she looked out into the starry night, but she could see little beyond her own reflection in the windowpane. When she turned back to the room, Mitch was standing the width of it away from her, watching her.

'Why are you standing clear over there?' Cappy tried to make light of her question, needing to alleviate the heavy mood.

'If I come any closer, you might bite,' Mitch replied with a vague shrug of his shoulders.

'That's ridiculous.' She was suddenly impatient with his answer.

'It's the truth,' he insisted, with no glint in his eye. 'Whenever anybody gets too close to you, you start snapping until you drive them away.'

'Is that what you think?' A small, hurt frown entered her expression.

'It's what I know. Do you want to see my scars?' Behind

266

his half-smile was a hard deep hurt. 'You remember the old saying, Once bitten, twice shy? I'd hate to count the number of times I've reached out to you and received the cutting edge of your tongue instead.'

She shook her head, trying to dismiss a subject she was reluctant to discuss. Tears were stinging the back of her eyes, and she opened them wide to try to dry them out. He spoke too quietly, his jest was too piercing.

'How could you room with someone for nearly six months without being close to her?' Mitch wondered at the way she could hold people away from her. 'Why are you afraid to let anyone get near you, Cap?'

'None of us got along with Rachel. I don't know why.' She looked at her drink, not really seeing it. 'The Army takes. Haven't you noticed that, Mitch? The Army is always taking things. I'm tired of it. I want it to be my turn.'

Cappy was aware of the selfishness in her needs. But the crash that had taken Rachel's life had brought her face to face with her own mortality, and she wanted to grab at the things she wanted and hold them for as long as she could.

Mitch stood, silent and unmoving. It was difficult for her to cross the room – she, who had always contained her feelings and kept them bottled inside where no one could see or know how vulnerable she was. But the fear that maybe there wouldn't be a tomorrow pushed her. She'd been alone and lonely for so long. This time she was going to do the taking.

Halfway across the room, she deposited her drink on top of a table so her hands would be free when she reached Mitch. His stance was unchanged, a stone-statue stillness about him, his lidded gaze veillng his thoughts. With a downcast head, Cappy took the drink from his unresisting fingers and set it aside. A rigid pulse hammered along her throat.

His expression remained unchanged, silence his only response while she lifted her hands and curved them to

267

the rigid muscles standing out tensely along the back of his neck. Slowly his muscles gave in to the pressure she exerted to bring his head down the few inches so her lips could reach his mouth. Her contact with the unyielding line of his lips was tentative, warming gradually from the heady taste of him and the stimulating male scent that clung to his skin.

For long seconds, he was immobile and it was Cappy doing the kissing. When the lines of restraint broke, it was a violent break. His arms pressed her closer to him while his mouth ground down upon her lips with punishing ardor. Cappy didn't complain.

When he pulled back from the kiss, her hands tightened around his neck. 'Hold me, Mitch,' she urged in that tight voice, afraid to let go of her emotions. 'I don't want to be alone tonight.'

The inviting push of her hips, the hot urgings of her lips, and the stirring roundness of her breasts all made their impressions on him, but it was the pooling blue of her eyes that pulled him down.

'Where you're concerned, I swear I'll always be the fool,' he muttered thickly. With a scoop of his arms, he picked her up and carried her into the bedroom. 'I won't let you go tonight.'

In the faint light that spilled into the room from the hallway, they watched each other undress. Their uniforms were cast aside, until they were stripped bare of clothes, facing each other as only man and woman.

On the bed, the closeness was savored. The hungry deepening of kisses and stroking of bodies was slow but eager as their needs pushed them, and they tried not to rush the wonder of it. Their play – the erotic sucking of nipples and fondling of bodies – was drawn out as long as possible.

When the moment could no longer be prolonged, he mounted her and penetrated the last barrier. Still, Mitch murmured to her, 'Let me in.'

Later in the night, while Cappy slept curled up like a

kitten in his arms, Mitch reflected on the shared ecstasy. A keen disappointment knotted the pit of his stomach. She had given him her body and her willingness, but she had kept her feelings apart and not allowed him to get too deeply under the surface of them. Yet they were there; he could sense their wanting.

She confused him – her silence, her fear, her lack of trust.

His hands knew her body, roaming over every crest and crevice of it; his lips knew the taste and texture of her flesh; and his body had rocked with the rhythm of hers, matching and mating. He had gotten into her, and known her physically. But she had not allowed words, had silenced anything he tried to say. She had wanted him and he had satisfied her. But he wanted more than that.

CHAPTER EIGHTEEN

Eden prowled the room like a cage-crazy tigress. A tense, restless energy permeated the air, the strain and tension showing on both Mary Lynn's and Marty's faces. None of them looked as though she had slept a wink since last night's crash. Cappy had difficulty assimilating the changes that had been wrought in her friends within such a short space of time. She had expected shock and a certain amount of grief over Rachel's death, but not this bitter anger. Her glance strayed to Mitch as she wished she hadn't asked him to stay. She doubted that Eden understood the gravity of the charges of dereliction she was throwing about.

'Eden's upset,' she said to him, calmly coming to the defense of her friend.

'You're damned right I am,' she snapped.

'Maybe I should leave,' Mitch suggested, aware that his uniform was a less-than-welcome presence in the room.

Tempers had been whipped raw, resentment ran high.

'No. Stay,' Marty insisted with belligerence. 'Somebody from the top brass oughta hear what we think. No one else is interested enough to listen, so why not you, Major Ryan.'

'Mitch isn't here in an official capacity.' Cappy held back the knowledge that he was at Camp Davis to observe and report his findings to General Arnold. But she didn't want him carrying tales back about her friends either.

'Official or not, he's Army, and somebody in command needs to know the kind of rotten business that's going on down here.' Eden joined with Marty to insist that Mitch stay. The flash of her dark eyes was hard and her lips were thinly compressed. 'You don't see our leader anywhere around, do you? The great Jacqueline Cochran is conferring with that red-necked commanding officer – as if he's going to tell her what's been going on around here.' Her sarcasm and bitterness was thick. 'Of course, she has agreed to speak to us – tonight at seven. I beg your pardon – at nineteen hundred hours,' she corrected in mock deference to Mitch.

To hear Eden make such snide comments about their director when she'd always expressed such an admiration for Jacqueline Cochran added to Cappy's surprise. Beside her, Mitch seemed to settle back, those dark eyes and that quick mind not missing anything.

Cappy thought Eden would have learned from the Sweetwater experience that the Army's attitude toward complaints was 'Tough.' Whatever their gripes about conditions here, it would do them no good to tell Mitch. It would merely put them in a bad light.

'Rachel's death was a tragic accident.' Cappy had seen the preliminary report, identifying the faulty canopy latch as a contributing factor to her death, although pilot error had been the obvious cause of the crash.

'The tragedy is it could have happened to any of us.' Eden paused, plainly agitated. 'You don't know the deplorable conditions of the planes we're expected to fly.'

'Eden –' Cappy began, but never got any further.

'She's right.' Marty sided with the New Yorker, one of the rare times in Cappy's memory. 'Yesterday, two engines failed and the pilots had to make a forced landing. Since we've been here, we've flown air search for eleven planes that went down in the swamps. And the tires on these planes are so worn, there were five blowouts in one day. Those are just the major things; this has nothing to do with the radios that don't work, the flap levers that won't stay locked in position – or canopies that won't open from the inside.' Stormy-eyed, she ran a hand through her touseled, light brown curls. 'Some experiment, huh?'

'Are you serious?' Cappy was appalled by the charges.

'It isn't just the planes.' Mary Lynn appeared more subdued, less inclined to critical outbursts, but the strain was evident in her pale cheeks and worn expression. Her eyes were very dark, without their usual inner light. 'Most of the instructors here know less about the planes than we do, yet they're giving us check rides.'

'They're rejects – all of them.' Marty was more sweeping in her condemnation. 'You can almost bet that they were assigned to this tow-target squadron because they washed out of some other program. If they were such hot pilots, they'd be flying missions overseas in the combat zones.'

'Do you realize the seriousness of the charges you are making?' Cappy believed them, yet she was stunned by what they were telling her too.

'Don't take our word for it.' Eden stopped her pacing to challenge both Cappy and Mitch Ryan. 'Just ask any of the mechanics.'

'Yeah,' Marty agreed. 'They've told us more than once that all they try to do is keep the engines running. It's a waste of time to write anything on the Form One sheets. They don't make the repairs.'

'They can't get the parts,' Eden inserted. 'That flight line out there is filled with junk aircraft and we're expected to fly them.'

'Or kill ourselves trying, the way Rachel did,' Mary Lynn offered quietly.

271

A long silence followed, which no one tried to fill. Eden took another cigarette from her pack and tamped the tobacco in it, hitting it on the side of the pack with short, incisive taps that bespoke her impatience. She carried it to her lips, letting it dangle there while she struck a match to light it.

Her glance sliced to Mitch. 'What's your recommendation, Major?'

'Go through channels,' he replied easily, not rising to her challenging tone. 'Tell your story to Cochran when you meet with her at nineteen hundred hours tonight.'

'Will you be there, Major?' Mary Lynn asked, accustomed to her southern world where men played the dominant roles.

'No.' The answer was simple and direct, emphasizing his detached observer status.

When the conversation became a rehash of complaints already covered, Mitch excused himself. Cappy hesitated before she accompanied him to the door, wanting a private word with him. Outside the building, an August sun broiled the Army grounds. The air was still and heavy; disciplined columns of men marched through it with sweaty backs and perspiring lips, constantly drilling until they could act without thinking. In the Army, a soldier didn't think – he obeyed. Someone else did his thinking for him.

Cappy knew this, yet she turned to Mitch, troubled by all she'd heard. 'What do you think, Mitch?'

His handsome face, chiseled in such strong, clean lines, was devoid of expression. 'I think there's a war on and there isn't always time to do things the right way.'

'I don't want an Army answer!' she flared.

'Maybe not,' Mitch conceded with a smooth, dismissing shrug. 'But it's likely that's all you'll get.'

She knew better than to argue the point, and asked instead, 'Where are you going?'

'Between you and me?' An eyebrow lifted to extract her promise of silence, and received her affirmative nod. 'To ask a few questions on my own. Then, I'd better sit in on the inquiry.'

At precisely nineteen hundred hours, the women pilots met with their director in the operations building. It had been nearly twenty-four hours since Rachel's plane crashed near the end of the runway; time for the seething anger to come to a rolling boil. Every incident was recapped, every rumor retold, and every fact related. Agreement was unanimous among them.

After the meeting, when the trio of Mary Lynn, Eden, and Marty arrived at the Officers' Club, Cappy was relieved to see they had calmed down considerably. But the tension hung about them, the waiting air of expectancy.

'What did she say when you told her?' Cappy asked after drinks were ordered round.

'She promised she'd check out the planes herself.' Mary Lynn answered the question about Jacqueline Cochran.

In the early cool of the following morning, a short memorial service was held for Rachel Goldman. Mitch escorted Cappy to the small chapel on the base. Mary Lynn had saved a space for them on the wooden pew where she sat with Marty and Eden.

They felt a closeness to her in death that they'd never known in life. Rachel, tall and feline-sleek with a cat's grace, passionately giving back whatever she got – friendship or hostility. Rachel, the proud and the wary. Rachel, the stranger.

For Mary Lynn, there was regret that she hadn't been kinder. Eden couldn't shake the horrifying image of yellow flames swirling around Rachel while she flew by overhead. A sense of obligation and duty brought Cappy to the chapel, and Marty was there to pay her respects to a fellow flier, a lover of the sky.

As they were filing quietly out of the chapel at the conclusion of the service, Eden noticed the man sitting in the back row, wearing an enlisted man's uniform. His head was bowed, a crown of thick, black hair absorbing the shine of the sunlight streaming through a stained glass window. His hands were folded in his lap, tightly clutching his soldier's cap. Although she couldn't see his face, Eden was sure she knew him.

'Excuse me.' She sent the others out of the chapel while she stayed behind to move quietly into the pew. After a second's hesitation, she sat on the smooth-worn seat, angling her body toward him.

'You're Zach Jordan, aren't you?' she guessed in a low voice, and watched him stiffen. 'Rachel introduced us in New York. I'm Eden van Valkenburg.'

With a small turn of his head, he cast an identifying glance in her direction. 'I remember.' The deep, haunting blue of his eyes glistened with a contained wetness while his patrician, proud features had the pinched-in look of grief to them, feelings sucked in tight.

'I can't tell you how sorry I am . . . about Rachel.' Some of Eden's bitterness came through – the resentment at the jeopardy all their lives were in because of slipshod maintenance and a poorly equipped staff of mechanics.

'I stood outside my barracks last night and watched the light the fire made in the sky.' His tightly clenched hands could not disguise the tremors that vibrated through him, but his expression remained stony. 'A plane had crashed and burned, they told me. And I hoped Rachel hadn't seen it. She was afraid of fire – afraid of seeing faces in the flames.'

His words made the image she carried in her mind even more horrifying. 'She shouldn't have died,' Eden insisted in a trembling, emotion-riddled voice, her anger resurfacing.

'After the war, we were going to have children . . . lots of children. We were going to go to Palestine – to Jerusalem. After the war.' His voice faded into the blankness the future held out for him.

His throat worked convulsively, then Zach turned from her and stood. He walked out of the chapel, still clutching the folded length of his cap.

The morning inspection of the aircraft was conducted by Jacqueline Cochran, her executive assistant, the squadron commander, Major Stevenson, a representative from the Air Safety Board, and the chief maintenance officer. From the sidelines, Mitch watched the group going over the engine logs for all of the A-24s.

Pragmatically, Mitch decided on another course to obtain the information and wandered into a hangar. A soldier slogging through the mud had a better knowledge of road conditions than a general flying over it at a thousand feet. A tall, rangy mechanic was bellied over the engine of an A-24. Perspiration made a wet stain on his greasy fatigues, ringing his underarms and making a dark patch between his shoulder blades. It took Mitch a minute to discern the chevrons amidst all the dirt and grime.

'Hello, Sergeant.'

The mechanic glanced backward in his direction. 'Sorry, sir,' the mechanic drawled. 'It's kinda hard to salute when you got a wrench in your hands and a bolt half loosened. Be through here in a minute.'

'No hurry.' Mitch waited, observing the man's clean, decisive actions.

'I suppose you'll be wantin' your plane rolled out.' The sergeant talked as he worked, occasionally punctuating his words with grunts of energy exerted.

Judging by the man's apparent competence and rank, Mitch wasn't surprised that the sergeant knew generally who he was. 'No. Just some information.' Something clicked in his memory. 'By any chance you wouldn't be Sergeant Jackson?'

'Yes, sir.' He looked again at Mitch, silently questioning how he had known.

'Eden mentioned you.'

'Miss van Valkenburg? Yes, I know her, sir.' There was a small pause, almost deliberate as if considering the next words. 'How is she? She was tore up the other night . . . saw the crash and . . . everything.'

'Fine.' Mitch couldn't really comment on Eden's emotional state, so he glossed over his answer. 'The investigation going on now – what do you think they're going to find?' The sergeant stopped to wipe his hands, his wide, strong-boned face serious with concern. 'It's likely that they'll find most of the planes are overdue for an engine overhaul – according to combat standards.'

'What do you know about the plane that went down?'

'It had five hundred hours on the engine – maybe two hundred tow-target missions flown,' he admitted.

'And?' Mitch prompted.

Bubba gave a telling shrug, and avoided stating an opinion. 'Our orders are to keep 'em flying. Most of the time we accomplish that, even when we don't have the spare parts, or the gas allotment gets shorted.' His head dipped for an instant, his glance darting away. 'That canopy latch, it was such a small thing. Hell.'

'Right.' Mitch agreed with the mechanic's assessment.

That afternoon, another meeting was convened by Jacqueline Cochran to relay the findings to her pilots. But it wasn't to be the informal gathering of the previous night. She was accompanied by some of the top brass from the base. Eden had the feeling their director had chosen sides, and it wasn't theirs she was on.

Brisk and businesslike, the dark-eyed, blond director of the women's flying program read the engine time logged on the A-24s her girls were flying. The implication was clear that the aircraft were not as poorly maintained as they had believed. While it was true many of them were past due for overhauls, that criterion was mainly applied to combat planes. It wasn't practical to expect that degree of maintenance on the planes flown at home.

As Eden realized they were being given the official explanation, she looked down the row of seated women pilots. Few liked what they were hearing but they seemed perforce to accept it. The Army officers were very plainly supporting their director, so there was no place to appeal the decision.

But Eden was in no mood to be bought off by a

bunch of officers, no matter how much brass they carried. 'That's a whitewash, and you know it,' she called out, in open criticism of the aviatrix she had once admired.

Marty was quick to take up the cry. 'The mechanics don't pay attention to those engine logs. I doubt if they're even up to date.'

But their protests were ignored. No one acted as if they'd even heard them as the commander of the base got up to speak, expressing his delight at having the women at his camp. After he had given his little spiel, it was the chief surgeon's turn, then the public relations officers', who promised them publicity.

When they filed outside after it was over, Cappy was waiting to hear the results. Their sullen faces told her almost as much as their words as they recounted what Eden regarded as a betrayal by their leader.

'The chief surgeon gets up there and says we have his permission to use the nurses' quarters. It's obvious the old fart doesn't know that we're already living there,' Marty muttered in her whiskey-rough voice.

'It was another one of the Army's famous snafus,' Mary Lynn concluded, less bitter than the others.

'Do you know what snafu stands for?' Marty asked her in wry mockery. 'Situation Normal – All Fucked Up.'

No one spoke of resigning as a protest to the Army's response. They had been warned the assignment would be tough and dangerous, and long ago had learned they had to be better than the average male pilot. They couldn't quit; it was a matter of pride.

Late that day, the UC-78 Cappy was piloting lifted off the ground, following in the wake of the AT-17 flown by Jacqueline Cochran. Mitch occupied the right seat, letting her silence run its course. They had barely exchanged five words beyond the requisite communication prior to takeoff.

His sideways glance studied the mutinous set of her jaw and the hard sparkle in her blue eyes. Her ire was aroused, and Mitch was fascinated by the animation it gave her face. She so rarely allowed her feelings to show.

'Why, Mitch? Why?' Cappy demanded once the aircraft was trimmed to its angle of climb. Flying over Cape Fear, they banked to the north. Far out to sea, ships steamed in a convoy, hugging the coastline. 'Eden wasn't lying about the shoddy condition of those planes.'

'No, I don't think she was lying,' he agreed.

'Then surely something can be done.' It was a protest, and an expression of frustration. 'You've been here. You've seen what's going on. Surely you –'

'Why?' Mitch interrupted, reacting to the disparaging emphasis she placed on him, as if he was some tin god she despised. 'Because I have the general's ear? What would you have me suggest? That he detour a shipment of spare parts and reassign mechanics from the battlefront? Maybe I could just have him call off the war while I'm at it.'

For an instant she didn't respond. 'Are you saying it can't be helped?' There was a steely quiet to her voice.

'Yes, that's what I'm saying.' He sighed heavily. 'I'm not telling any tales out of school when I admit our planes are getting shot out of the sky faster than we can replace them. Maybe we have managed to drive Rommel out of Africa, but we're still fighting a defensive war in the Pacific.'

'Why didn't Cochran say that?' Cappy answered, subdued but still angry. 'Why did she try to whitewash the whole situation?'

'It's simple, really,' Mitch said, his gaze automatically searching the sky for air traffic. 'She wants "her girls" to obtain a lot of flying assignments besides ferrying aircraft around the country. You have no idea what she went through to persuade command to let those girls into the tow-target flying. Now she can't admit it might be too dangerous, any more than she can admit that "her girls" might not have the guts to take such risks. If this experiment fails – for whatever reason – her whole plan to broaden the women's flying program will be set way back.'

'I see,' Cappy murmured, understanding yet not liking the situation any better.

'Satisfied?' A dark brow was quirked in her direction.

'Yes.'

'Well, I'm not.' He reached across the space between their seats and turned her head toward him. He saw the protest beginning to form as he leaned across to kiss her. His vision narrowed, like a camera lens closing in its focus on one object, until all he could see clearly was the unbroken line of her lips. His mouth moved onto them, meeting initial stiffness that soon gave, and the warm pressure was returned. Mitch suspected it was not so much a giving in to his wants as it was a giving in to her own.

When he pulled away, he saw her lashes lower to conceal the look in her eyes. But he welcomed such a concealment from Cappy, since it meant he had aroused some feeling she didn't want him to see.

'I was beginning to wonder if you weren't tired of me already,' Mitch said complacently. 'I wondered whether you were regretting the other night.'

'I never do anything I'll regret later,' Cappy stated emphatically.

His narrowed glance skimmed her, but he kept his response light. 'Then you're obviously a better man than I am.'

'Obviously,' she agreed and leveled the wings of the twin-engined craft as they attained the desired altitude.

CHAPTER NINETEEN

Leaving her car parked on the firm shoulder of the beach road, Eden wandered across the dunes to the outer shore-line. The chauffeur had arrived with her car about two weeks before, two days after Rachel died in the crash.

Overhead, the morning sky was a sharp blue. Not even the brightly burning sun could warm the cool air that blew in from the sea. Her high-necked sweater of biscuit-colored wool held in her body warmth. The loose sand sifted over the tops of her shoes and collected inside them. On the hard-packed beach, Eden stopped and emptied them, standing cranelike, first on one foot, then on the other.

The tide had left windrows of seaweed, driftwood, and broken shells tangled together. Interspersed in the wrack were fragile treasures: the jewel-colored wing of a butterfly, a chip of emerald-green glass, and the pure white of a gull's feather. The wet sand of the beach was crossstitched with the prints of birds' feet, the patterns running every which way on the spume-speckled shore. The restless ocean matched her mood and she turned her face to the salty breeze, letting it muss her red hair. Swooping, soaring gulls seemed to be everywhere, their strange cries punctuating the rhythmic rush of the waves onto the beach.

Two weeks had passed since the fatal crash. For the first part of the time, the women pilots had been grounded. Then it was back in the air for all of them, the same as before, checking out in the little L-4 and L-5 Cubs and graduating to the A-24s and tow-target missions. A new group of WASPs from the class behind them had arrived fresh from Sweetwater, ignorantly eager. Nothing had changed. They were flying under the same perilous conditions. Rachel's death had served no purpose.

The solitude of the beach reached to her as she walked along the waterline, pensive and silent. The churning sea threw its waves at the shore, pounding the sand into hardness, then retreating to gather strength and come again. As the waters ran away, leaving their spume behind to melt into the sand, a few of the plovers, sanderlings and funny boat-tailed grackles gave chase.

Lifting her head, Eden looked far out to sea where a smoky haze obscured the horizon. Fear gripped her, made her ache and put a haunted look in her deeply brown eyes. Never in her life had she been confronted by this kind of mortal fear. So she walked, waiting for the quietude and the wild beauty of the coast to ease the rawness of her nerves.

Birds flew up, startled into the air by her leisurely approach. She watched them wheel and turn and land farther down the beach, lowering their landing-gear legs and back-flapping their wings. She dragged the windblown strands of hair from her face and continued plodding up the beach, mindless of the sea spray that dampened the legs of her fine wool slacks.

Twenty yards ahead of her a surf fisherman was casting his line into the foamy waves. Eden hesitated, nearly changing course to avoid contact with another human, but she continued on. Almost idly she observed his actions, the narrowing distance still giving her enough room to watch without appearing rude. With the line out, the rod was set butt-end on the sand and propped at an angle by a forked branch, relieving the fisherman of the burden of holding it.

He was wearing a pair of tough denim Levi's, boots, and a water-resistant jacket, half unzipped. Nothing covered his head, and the wind was making free with a shaggy crop of dark hair. As the tall, lanky man lowered himself onto the sand behind his pole, something seemed familiar about him. The rumble of the surf onto the shore and the screech of the herring gulls overhead masked the sound of her approach. Eden was still trying to decide whether she knew him when he saw her and promptly came to his feet.

'Hello, ma'am.' He drawled the greeting, a keenness in his look.

'Hello, Bubba.' She smiled. 'I almost didn't recognize you without those greasy coveralls.'

'I know what you mean, ma'am.'

Eden avoided his gaze and looked out to the building waves, scraping the wind-twisted strands of hair from her cheek. 'How come you aren't in town with the rest of your buddies? I thought all you soldiers made a beeline there the minute you were given a pass.'

'After spendin' nearly every wakin' hour breathin' in exhaust fumes and smellin' oil, I get to needin' some fresh air. And when you live on top of one another like you do in a barracks, there isn't much allowance made for privacy. So it's kinda nice just to come out here and be alone with your thoughts for a while.'

'I know what you mean,' she agreed with a wry, fleeting smile. Her hands were shoved into the side pockets of her jacket while she idly watched the tremor at the tip of his fishing rod. 'Are you catching anything?'

'Naw, but I'm not really tryin' yet. I only want to catch what I can eat, and if I do that too soon, I won't have any more reason to stay here,' Bubba replied, a smile twinkling his eyes at such logic.

'That sounds reasonable to me.' Humor laced her answer, the shared kind that was so enjoyable. 'What about you, Bubba? Where's your home in Texas?'

For a moment, he appeared surprised by her show of personal interest. But his skepticism disappeared as he searched her friendly, open face.

'I come from a little town along the Gulf. It's not likely you ever heard of it – a place called Refugio.' At his questioning look, Eden shook her head, admitting her ignorance of his home town. 'There's more cows than people there. But I was always fascinated by motors. I grew up tinkerin' with cars – anybody's. My momma swore I was born with grease under my fingernails. I been diggin' it out ever since.'

She laughed, but her eyes were noticing how different he looked from his usual workaday appearance. Without its usual grime, his sun-leathered face had a healthy vigor. And his thick, rumpled hair had a sheen to it now, instead of looking dull and flattened by his cap. Without the bulk of his fatigues to conceal it, his long body was flatly muscled, all sinew, tough and hard. There was an earthy aura to him that seemed to do away with all pretense and hone things down to the basics. He was so straightforward – and intelligent. Eden eyed him with close curiosity.

'Where did you get a name like Bubba?' she wondered, because it seemed to fit some hulking, dumb brute – not this man.

'Now, I tell you. I picked it myself,' he admitted with his head tipped back and one leg bent, putting all his weight on one foot.

'Why?' Eden laughed her surprise.

'Well, where I come from, a fella just never gets called by his right name. I was christened William Robert Jackson. Now, when I was growin' up, I figured I had a choice of bein' called either Billy Bob or after the General Jackson. I didn't much like either one, but my daddy had a friend named Bubba who always used to let me mess around with his car. I liked him, so I took his name.'

'Is that true?' She eyed him skeptically.

He drew back in pretended dismay. 'Would I pull your leg, ma'am?'

She studied him with wondering interest. 'I don't know.'

His expression became serious; a second later his glance was falling away from her. 'Hell, ma'am, you know you can always trust me,' he insisted. But he seemed uncomfortable with her, nearly angry, and tried to conceal it by reaching inside his jacket for a cigarette. Bubba hesitated, then offered the pack to her. 'Want one, ma'am?'

'Thanks.' She carried it to her mouth and waited for a light. 'And, Bubba, please stop calling me ma'am all the time.'

'It's a habit. I've ma'amed and sirred everybody all my life.' He cupped his hands around the match flame to protect it from the blowing wind and offered the welled light to Eden.

As she bent her head, she noticed the scoured cleanness of his callused hands, the undersides of his blunted nails completely free of grime. Lifting her head, she expelled the smoke she'd dragged into her lungs and the wind whipped it away.

'Sometimes, Bubba' – she watched him light his cigarette – 'I think you put on an act with me. All that talk about dirt under your nails and just look at your hands.'

'It's no act, ma'am. I'm just a poor ole Texas boy,' he insisted with a faint grin.

'See what I mean,' Eden accused.

His hand was curled around the cigarette as he took a drag from it and idly shrugged. 'It could be, ma'am, that I'm just a sergeant, and a poor one from the country at that, whereas you're an officer and a rich city lady.' Behind his smiling study of her, there was a sober light in his eye. 'It would be foolish for a man in my position to get ideas. It could spoil a good friendship.'

Eden stared at him for a long second, realizing just how much she trusted this strong, rangy man on whose judgment she relied. The sudden nodding of the fishing pole caught her eye at the same moment that Bubba noticed it.

'Looks like I've hooked one.' He grabbed up the rod to begin playing the fish.

It was impossible to remain detached while Bubba struggled to land his catch. She found herself searching the waves, trying to get the first glimpse of the hooked fish. But neither saw what was on the line until he had reeled it in. Eden started laughing when she saw the small-sized fish that had put up such a large-sized fight.

'I'd like to see how you'll make a meal of that,' she teased.

'Watch,' Bubba replied, and gently removed the hook from the fish's mouth, then gave the small fry a toss beyond the oncoming wave. 'Swim out and tell your big brother how I saved you,' Bubba called to the fish. 'Then send him back to bite on my hook.'

'You should have kept it.' Eden chuckled to herself. 'It's liable to be all you'll catch.'

'Not a chance. That fish is going to send his big brother back. Wait and see,' Bubba assured her with a deadpan expression.

'I think I will,' she declared. She crossed her feet to sink down onto the sand.

'Hey, you can't sit down there.' He caught her by an elbow and pulled her upright before she could sit. 'You'll ruin those good slacks you're wearing.' He unzipped his jacket to shrug out of it. 'Just a minute. You can sit on this.'

The sincere and chivalrous gesture was so typical of him. 'I'm certainly not going to ruin your jacket to save my slacks,' Eden retorted, and she sat firmly down on the sand before he could stop her. 'Besides, I have a whole closet full of slacks at home even if I do ruin these.'

'Yes, ma'am.' Subdued by her remark, Bubba sank down onto the beach beside her and made a show out of checking his fishing rod to be sure it was securely positioned. She wondered why it bothered him that she was so careless about her clothes.

Twenty minutes later, there was another strike on his line. This time, when he reeled the sea bass in, it was a big one. 'See? What did I tell you? It's the big brother.' He ran a stringer through its gills.

'Why don't you throw it back and tell him to send a whale?' Eden suggested.

''Cause I figure that little fish has a bunch of big brothers and they're all gonna show up here sooner or later. So settle back and relax.' He winked broadly. 'We're gonna have us a fish fry tonight. Better start gatherin' up some driftwood for a fire.'

The sea wind scuttled the smoke from the low-burning fire. The unburned portion of a stick fell onto the hot coals when its support crumbled and the flames briefly leaped anew. The broken trunk of a huge tree cast ashore by the ocean during a fall-cleaning purge acted as a partial windbreak, both for the fire and for the couple leaning against it.

'This sea air sure does give you an appetite, doesn't it?' Bubba declared on a full sigh as he set the lid of the cooking pot, his improvised plate, onto the sand. Only fish bones were left on it. Then he noticed the way Eden was picking at the succulent flesh of the baked fish. 'Is something wrong with my cookin'? I know it's not like those fancy restaurants where they poach 'em in wine.'

'It's very good,' she assured him, then she shrugged. 'I'm just not very hungry.' Eden set her plate on the sand and rubbed her hands against each other. 'Sorry, I just can't eat any more.'

'You peck at your food like a bird. No wonder you're so thin for as tall as you are.' When he saw the troubled moodiness settle over her again, his eyes narrowed to study her thoughtfully. Several times she'd gone silent on him and brooded. 'Still thinking about the crash, ma'am?'

'No.' The denial was too quick, like the forced smile that flashed across her expression. 'I was just thinking – Water, water everywhere, and not a drop to drink,' she quoted, looking at the rush of waves onto the beach, the tide thrusting them higher and higher as the afternoon sun lowered the angle of its light.

Bubba wasn't fooled. Daydreaming she might have been, but not about anything pleasant. But since she didn't choose to confide in him, it wasn't his place to press the issue. Hell, he was just a mechanic with sergeant's stripes and she was a refined lady with the prettiest copper-red hair he'd ever seen. Why, she had more class in one little finger than he had in his whole body.

'That's not quite true, ma'am,' Bubba corrected her. 'I did bring along a drop to drink. I've just been waitin' for it to get good and cold.'

Her curiosity was aroused, deliberately, Eden suspected. Despite her initial intentions, she had never resumed her walk along the beach. She had spent practically the whole day in Bubba's company while he had entertained her with stories about his childhood and pulled her leg with a few Texas tall tales.

His skill in aircraft maintenance she'd always known, and the friendliness of his broad smile. His leadership capabilities had been indicated by the stripes on his uniform. This afternoon, he'd even let it slip that his CO had recommended him for Officer Candidate School. Naturally, he'd refused; at least, it had been natural in Bubba's way of thinking, because he enjoyed working with engines and people, and didn't see the need to give either one of them up to be some clean-nailed lieutenant. His command of logic and common sense amazed her, delivered as it was in drawled phrases. There was no doubt in her mind that Bubba was a rough diamond – completely unpolished but a genuine gem just the same.

In sand made wet by the incoming surf, Bubba pulled an anchor pin, buried deep with only its curved ring showing above the surface. Eden watched as he began coiling in the attached rope cord that was strung into the ocean. At the end of it was a fisherman's net, holding a half-dozen loose bottles. He brought his dripping catch back to the fire and knelt on the sand near the drift log.

Eden eyed the long-necked containers of brown glass. 'What is it? Beer?'

'I'll bet you haven't drunk too much of it,' Bubba surmised as he removed two bottles from the mesh trap and produced a metal opener from his pocket.

'Scotch is usually my choice,' she admitted.

'Well, let me initiate you into the fine art of beer drinking,' he said, and he settled himself back against the dead trunk so they sat side by side. 'You gotta know how to appreciate the good stuff.' He pried the top off one of the bottles. 'Now you see this cork inside the cap –' Bubba held it out for her inspection while he explained in mock-serious tones, 'Ya gotta check to see that it's in good shape and the edges haven't started to rot, 'cause that'll mean you'll have little bits of cork in your beer and you'll have to strain it through your teeth when you drink. Then you sniff the cork, too.' He lifted it to her nose so Eden could smell it while she tried to hold back the laughter bubbling inside. 'Smell good?'

'Wonderful,' she assured him, amused by the entire farce.

'Next comes the bottle.' The wet sides of the glass

container were still slippery, and Bubba waited until she had a secure hold of it before he let go. 'Carefully run your fingers around the lip to make sure it hasn't chipped. It ain't healthy to drink beer with glass chips in it.'

'No, I wouldn't think so either,' Eden agreed, her mouth twitching with the effort to hold it in a straight line.

'Now the last thing is to run the bottle past your nose so you get a little whiff of the beer,' Bubba instructed. 'What you're lookin' for is that good, malty smell you get when the grains are fermented just right.'

'How do you tell if it's aged properly?' she asked, joining in with his joke.

'When it comes out of the brewery, it's old enough to drink,' he said. 'Now give the bottle a little shake, sorta swirl it around and see if it makes a good head.' As she followed his instructions, a white foam began building inside the brown glass. 'Now, *that's* a good beer,' he promised her. 'And you got that straight from a real beer connasewer.' He clinked his bottle against hers. 'Drink up. It's only good when it's at just the right temperature.'

She took a swig of the beer and gurgled with laughter. It was such a funny parody of the wine snobbery displayed by some of her New York friends. She drank his beer, not finding it as tasty as her Scotch, but it had its place.

They talked and laughed, with Bubba doing most of the talking and Eden doing most of the laughing, until the sun lingered above the sand dunes. Its golden, glowing fire spread out to encompass sand and sea in its burnished light.

Her hand held the last bottle of beer by its brown neck while she gazed at the golden-hued waters. The fear that she had successfully blocked from her mind for a while came back, and Eden restlessly pushed herself to her feet and walked a few steps away from the fire toward the tumbling waves, all but forgetting Bubba until he appeared beside her, taller by a couple inches, his dark eyes discreetly questioning.

'You know something funny?' she began, again turning

seaward. 'The Civil Air patrol won't let women fly coastal patrols because it's too dangerous, but when we're out on a tow-target mission, sometimes we're fifty miles out over the Atlantic. And we're getting shot at, too, by our own Army. It doesn't make sense, does it?'

'The Army doesn't have to make sense. It just has to win the war,' Bubba reasoned, sensing the comment was close to the cause of her restless moods.

She fell silent once again. Bubba noticed the way her fingers flexed and tightened their grip on the bottle neck, nervously worrying it. Her glance sliced sideways to his face, apprehension widening her dark eyes.

'I think I'm losing my nerve, Bubba. Every time that plane lifts off the ground, I wonder if I'll make it back.' Although she tried to keep it steady, there was a vibration in her low voice. 'I know you check the planes over thoroughly, but . . . how many accidents do we have here a day? How many tires are blown? How many engines quit? How many planes wind up taking hits in the fuselage? I just have the feeling my number's going to come up. One of these times it's going to be me. I'm scared, Bubba.'

She tried to laugh, but the sound became choked by a sob. Looking away, she widened her eyes and blinked furiously to keep back the tears. She felt the comforting touch of Bubba's hand on her shoulder. Blindly, Eden turned into it while his arms went around her to gather her in, as he had done the night of Rachel's crash.

'Nothing's going to happen to you. I won't let it.' His rough hands made an attempt to smooth her tangled, rusty hair while the warm feel of her body filled his senses.

The instinct to live is a primitive one, potent and compelling. The physical contact made Eden subtly aware of the hard, male vigor in Bubba's lean muscled frame. It was the combination of vitality and comfort that first attracted Eden, then compelled her to seek the sustaining pressure of his mouth. As her lips grazed his cheek, she was met with an instant of stillness and hesitation. Then Bubba was turning to hasten the contact.

There was so much rawness inside her, so much built-up pressure, that it all seemed to explode as Eden strained against him, kissing him with a kind of fierce, yet desperate anger. She didn't let him be gentle, but he consumed all the force she threw at him and gave her back ease.

Once the high tension had burned itself out, she could enjoy the slow moving pressure of his mouth across her lips. It touched some needy core of her, so simple and basic in its expression of clean desire.

Bubba slowly pulled away from her lips and studied their swollen softness with heavy-lidded eyes. Eden gazed at his strong, broad features with an odd wondering. He was without guile or pretension. She was drawn by this honest, direct man with his natural intelligence and warm, wonderful sense of humor.

When she felt the pressure of his hands on her, Eden expected to be pulled back into his kiss. It was a surprise when Bubba gently set her away from him instead.

'We'd best get the fire out before the sun goes down and the beach patrol comes along to warn us about it.' After he'd made his explanation, Eden had a moment to wonder which fire he was talking about while Bubba walked to the smoldering campfire in the sand.

Mounding sand on the coals with a shoveling action of his foot, he buried the fire and Eden came over to watch him. The rumble of a motor grew into a roar as a jeep came rolling over the wave-pounded firmness of the sand, making one of its regular patrols of the beach. The sun was sinking behind a sand dune when they stopped, the motor idling, to remind the pair that no one was allowed on the beach after dark.

After the noise of the jeep's engine had faded, Bubba looked across the short expanse of sand to the hump showing where the fire had been, and held Eden's glance. 'Maybe it was a good thing they came along when they did,' he suggested.

'Maybe it was,' she conceded.

'Guess we'd better get movin'.' He seemed to push

himself into action against a feeling of reluctance, as he gathered up his tackle box and the case with his fishing rod, and hooked his arm through a strap of his knapsack.

'Do you need a ride? My car's parked down the road a ways,' Eden said, indicating its general direction with a wave of her hand.

'Thanks, but I left my bicycle just over the dunes.'

'I've got a convertible. You can throw it in the back end,' Eden persisted.

After a long minute of consideration, Bubba nodded an acceptance of her invitation, but there was a reluctance here, too, that indicated it went against his better judgment.

They reached his bicycle before they reached her car, and Bubba pushed it through the heavy sand to the road's shoulder. He took one look at the canary-yellow roadster and its white leather interior, then issued a low whistle of appreciation. He walked around it, exclaiming over every feature and asking endless questions about the engine's performance.

'I don't believe it,' Eden declared on a faintly disgusted note.

'Don't believe what?' Bubba looked up, a frown creasing his forehead.

'How many times does a girl offer you a lift and you fall in love with her car?' she challenged.

A rueful grin split his face as he scratched the back of his neck. 'Reckon I did get a bit carried away,' he agreed. 'But it is a beauty.'

'Want to drive?' Eden tossed him the keys.

'Sure.' He clambered behind the wheel with a beguiling boyish enthusiasm.

The wind tunneled through her red hair, roping it into tangled curls as Bubba put the car through its paces on the lonely beach road. The light faded and the blue shadows deepened with the coming of nightfall. The car's headlamps were hooded to keep its beams cast downward in this blackout area along the coastline.

A mile from the entrance to the Army camp, Bubba turned into a small lay-by and switched off the engine. After the roaring engine and rushing wind, the silence was vibrant.

Bubba ran his hand carelessly over the arc of the steering wheel, rubbing it with unconscious ardor. 'This car is really something.'

Amused and vaguely disgruntled, Eden sat sideways in the white leather seat and rested her back against the door. 'What about its owner?'

Bubba looked sideways at her and smiled, a deep line breaking from the corner of each eye. 'She's really somethin', too.' He paused, his look turning serious and compelling as his dark eyes took her apart. The scrutiny made Eden self-conscious about her appearance after the sun and the wind had stung color into her pale skin and the salt spray had dried it. Her clothes were gritty with sand.

'The owner's a classy number, too,' Bubba said quietly. 'Highly sensitive and temperamental, like a finely tuned racing engine. Not something you can manhandle. She needs . . . an easy touch to get the best out of her.'

'Is that right?' Eden murmured and began moving toward him, his words striking a chord deep within and drawing her to him.

'Yes –'

She pressed the ends of her fingers against his mouth. 'So help me, Bubba, if you call me ma'am I'll –' But she didn't have to finish her threat. He gathered her into his arms and murmured her name many times over.

CHAPTER TWENTY

In full uniform, Major Mitch Ryan stood at his desk in the small Pentagon office and flipped through file folders, selecting certain ones to go in his case. Behind him the door opened, and Mitch glanced idly over his shoulder, then stiffened to come to attention.

'At ease.' General Arnold waved off any salute as he briskly swept into the small room. He eyed the coffee thermos sitting atop a file cabinet. 'Is that the strongest you've got?'

'No, sir.' With the smallest of smiles, Mitch went behind his desk and opened the bottom drawer. He reached to the back and brought out a fifth of whiskey, the seal broken and a third of the contents gone. After he'd poured a shot into a coffee cup, the only available drinking vessel in his office, he handed it to the general. 'How was the fashion show?'

'You wouldn't believe it, Ryan.' There was a definite gleam in his eye as he lifted the cup to his mouth and took a quick swallow. 'It was supposed to be either the uniform the nurses rejected or else a new design out of that surplus Army green material we had left over from the WAAC uniforms.'

'That's not the way it was?' Mitch asked the question being fed to him.

'Here are these two nondescript typists from the pool wearing the uniform choices – and in walks a professional model in a blue jacket and skirt. I took one look at Cochran and knew damned well whose idea it was and which one I was supposed to choose.' He chuckled and took another sip of the whiskey. 'Those WASPs of hers are finally going to have their own uniforms – blue, like the sky they fly in. It was a pretty color.' His forehead creased with a thoughtful frown. 'Santiago blue, or something like that. After all, when you're a woman you just can't call it blue,' he joked.

'No, sir. I guess not.'

'Well, anyway, you can tell your Hayward girl that Neiman-Marcus will be sending a tailor around to get her measurements.' His look became almost fatherly as he studied Mitch's closed expression. 'Have you had a chance to see her lately?'

'As a matter of fact –' Mitch removed the bottom folder from the stack he'd been going through and inserted it in his attaché case. It snapped shut with a resounding click. '– I have.'

'She has accumulated a considerable amount of multiengine time.' The general showed an inordinate amount of interest in the liquor covering the bottom of his cup. 'I half expected her name to be on the list of candidates for this B-17 training. Wouldn't you say she's qualified?'

'Yes, sir.' Mitch set his case on the floor and picked up the remaining folders to return them to the metal cabinet.

'It isn't too late to add her name to the list,' the general remarked as Mitch opened a drawer and began stuffing the folders one at a time into it. 'Do you want me to do it?'

'*No* –' The file drawer was slammed shut, emphasizing the force of his denial as Mitch swung around to face his commanding officer. Belatedly, and in considerably modified tone, he added, 'sir.'

'Cochran is convinced her girls can handle any plane, even a Flying Fortress. Hell, I know Cochran and Love can fly anything with wings. 'Course, you know what's coming next if we get a bunch of WASPs with B-17 experience,' he said with a laughing snort. 'She's going to start agitating to let her girls fly them across the Atlantic to England. Love damned near did. I still don't know what was going through Tunner's mind when he authorized that flight.'

The general had been in England conferring with the Allied forces when he had learned of the proposed flight. Immediate orders were issued to ground the plane with its two women pilots, stopping it in Goose Bay, Labrador, before it made its oceanic hop.

'It would have been a hell of a precedent to set without any forethought as to the potential consequences. Can you imagine the uproar in Congress if the damned Jerries shot down a B-17 being ferried to England by a female crew? Talk about political hot water – they would have had my head.' He stopped, and a long, weary sigh came from him. 'They're pounding the hell out of us, Ryan.' Standing, he pushed the coffee cup onto the desk top with a prowling kind of agitation. 'I just got the losses on that last raid over Germany.'

'Not good, sir?' Mitch finally understood the purpose of the general's visit.

'We lost thirty percent; another hundred planes are grounded for repairs.' The familiar smile was nowhere in sight as 'Hap' Arnold stopped in front of his young major. 'They're sitting ducks up there. We've got to give them some damned protection . . . extend the range of our fighters.'

'Yes, sir.'

Statistics. The war was fought with numbers – casualty lists versus the percentages of expected losses. The many times Mitch had seen the war rooms in England, where uniformed British women moved markers across a map with sticks to show the progress of a raid and indicate enemy movements to counterattack, reminded him of a chess game. And the bombers, with their ten-men crews, were the pawns. In the pentagon, the war was logistics and strategy. In Europe and the Pacific, it was fighting – and killing or dying.

New orders came through, informing Martha Jane Rogers to report to Lockbourne Army Air Base, Columbus, Ohio. They weren't accompanied by an explanation of the transfer nor a description of her new duty. No leave time was given; she was to report immediately. That was the Army way.

The unknown had always sparked Marty's interest, although this time, the glitter of excitement that lighted her olive-gray eyes was tinged with regret when she looked at Mary Lynn. Marty was all packed, ready to leave. The time had come to say goodbye.

'I wish you were coming, too.' Marty hugged Mary Lynn and stepped back. The parting was awkward for her.

Almost from the time they'd met, Marty had felt like a big sister to Mary Lynn, always looking out both for and after her, cheering her up when she was down, and offering a shoulder when she needed to cry at the loneliness of being separated from her husband. Marty hated leaving her alone. She worried that Mary Lynn wouldn't be all right on her own.

'I'll be fine,' Mary Lynn assured her, but she had tears in her eyes.

'Look out for her,' Marty said to Eden, who was hovering in the background.

'Sure.'

It wasn't an idle request. Another one of their number had been killed when her plane crashed under questionable circumstances. The verdict had come back, laying the blame on a sticky throttle.

Unable to deal with the poignant feelings that tugged at her, Marty didn't prolong her goodbyes. Her wide mouth quirked with a near smile as she picked up her bags and headed out the door. Together Mary Lynn and Eden watched her go.

'She's lucky to be leaving here,' Eden remarked in a flatly serious tone while tears ran down Mary Lynn's cheeks. 'If we were smart, we'd request a transfer.'

Upon arrival at the Lockbourne Army Air Base outside Columbus, Ohio, Marty met up with five other WASPs, newly graduated from Sweetwater and members of the 43-W-6 class, whose orders read the same as hers – to report immediately to the flight operations building. The spectacle awaiting them at the flight line was awesome – a seemingly endless row of the huge B-17 four-engine bombers. Their three-bladed propellers were almost twelve feet across, in proportion with the hundred-foot wingspan. Marty longed for the chance to sit in the cockpit of one of those Flying Fortresses.

Inside the operations office, a young flight lieutenant greeted them. 'I'm your instructor, Lieutenant Winthrop.'

He was a tall, strapping man in his middle twenties, red lights burnishing the brown hair under his cap. 'I'm going to teach you ladies how to fly those Big Friends out there.'

In all, seventeen WASPs had been chosen for training in the B-17s. Looking around, Marty decided it was easy to see the reason they'd been picked. All of them were tall, an inch or two under six feet, with a couple reaching that mark.

When it was her turn to sit in the pilot's seat of the mammoth bomber, excitement thudded through her veins. The rubber earphones curved over her head like earmuffs while she went through the checklist, finally coming to that moment of power when her fingers rested on the button to start the number-one engine. She pressed it and watched the first shudder of the big prop. Four massive 1,325-horsepower engines powered the bomber. Soon, the roar of all four was vibrating the plane.

From the right seat, her instructor taxied the B-17 to the end of the runway, maneuvering the big plane with the outer engines, while Marty felt through his movements of the controls. The plane lumbered like a huge elephant and it seemed to stand about as much chance of getting off the ground.

With the instructor's voice guiding her through each procedure, Marty pushed the four throttles slowly forward and the Flying Fortress began its takeoff roll down the runway. When the airspeed indicator showed 110 miles an hour, Marty pulled back on the wheel. Smooth as silk, the giant flying machine lifted off the ground. The gear came up with a hum and folded into the plane's belly, and the airspeed increased by twenty-five miles an hour.

The sensation of raw power couldn't be matched, the engines thundering with their deafening throb until they became part of her own heartbeat. Marty became drunk with the feeling. It filled her up until she wanted to shout with the excitement of it. Wait until her brother, David, heard about this. He was still sitting out the war somewhere near Wiltshire, England, with the rest of his division.

When she wrote to Mary Lynn, which was regularly and often, she raved about the Flying Fortress, undaunted by its upwards of fifteen tons and the prospect of maneuvering a plane of that bulk and power. The required three months of intensive schooling in the operations of the complex bomber, including 130 hours of air time learning to fly it proficiently, didn't bother her either. As she told Mary Lynn, it wasn't any more grueling than it had been at Sweetwater.

Formation flying had that combination of danger and excitement that was exhilarating. Midair collisions always seemed seconds away as she learned to edge her wing tip closer and closer to another bomber, riding out the bumpy air of its prop-wash until she finally reached the smooth currents where the wings broke the air together.

Marty loved every minute she spent in the cockpit of the B-17, with its myriad gauges and dials, learning to stall and spin the monstrous plane. She was learning to fly one of the biggest and most famous bombers in the war. The thrill of it was something she knew Mary Lynn would understand. She missed having her there, missed the long talks, and missed hearing the odd fragments of the war in Beau's letters to Mary Lynn. Marty wasn't the kind to admit to being lonely – not when there were plenty of male pilots in the same B-17 training class who were more than willing to show her a good time. But none of that could make up for the closeness she'd had with Mary Lynn. So the letters came and went.

At Camp Davis, the merits of the tow-target squadron's female members – beyond the admitted decoration of pretty faces on the flight line – were finally being recognized. Artillery officers on the beachhead were asking for the women pilots to fly the tedious patterns on the gunnery range. Too many of the male pilots became bored with the constant figure-eight precision work, and either took off to practice aerobatics or else pleaded excuses not to fly the missions at all, aware some eager females would volunteer to take their places.

Sometimes, to fill the hours, Mary Lynn flew on afternoon as well as morning missions. There were only so many letters she could write to Beau or her parents – and now Marty too. Flying gave Mary Lynn many things she needed. Riding out the flak from misguided artillery fire, for those moments, made the war seem very real to her – made her feel part of it, seeing, hearing, and feeling some of what Beau went through. Temporarily she was elated by the sense of it. Flying provided an escape from the pressures of loneliness and the slow trickling time. The strain and tension of hours in the air made for an exhaustion that allowed her to fall asleep, too tired to think about the achings inside.

With a Coke and a cigarette in her hand, Mary Lynn sat on a chair in the ready room, still dressed in her droopy flying togs and bent over her legs, her forearms resting on her thighs. She noticed the operations officer glance at his watch for the third or fourth time, an irritation starting to seep into his expression.

'Something wrong?' she asked.

'Carlson was supposed to be here ten minutes ago to fly a diving mission. All the gunners are in position on the beach, just waiting for him. If I have to cancel, I'll really catch it.' The disgust in his voice was edged out by the exasperation of being caught in the middle, between the officers who had to fill their quota of gunners and the pilots who loathed missions in the 'coffin,' as they called the A-25 Curtiss Helldiver.

Two weeks ago, Mary Lynn knew who would have leaped up to volunteer – Marty – who was always ready to dare something new. It suddenly hit her that she was out from under everyone's wing – her parents, Beau, and Marty. She was truly on her own, free to do what she pleased.

'I'll take the mission.' She stood up, all five foot two and five-eighths inches of her.

Skeptically, he looked at this pipsqueak of a woman with the dark, lively eyes and rounded cheeks, a dark-haired, cherub angel. 'Have you ever flown a diving mission before?'

'No,' Mary Lynn admitted. 'But you need a pilot and here I am.'

The operations officer appeared to remember the gunners in place on the beach, and perhaps the wrath he'd incur if he failed to send a plane out to them. 'Go ahead,' he said with a gesture that seemed to say the outcome was out of his hands.

The A-25 Curtiss Helldiver was a more powerful Navy dive-bomber than the A-24 Dauntless Mary Lynn flew on tow-target missions. She managed to find a Helldiver on the flight line that wasn't red-lined, which, in itself, was unusual. Although she'd never actually flown a diving mission, she'd seen A-25s dive at the gun emplacements along the beach. Cameras were located in the gun barrels, and recorded how well the gunner followed the diving plane.

After takeoff, Mary Lynn set a course for the artillery range. As she approached the beach, she adjusted the collar with her throat microphone and contacted the gunnery officer. He instructed her to climb to 8,000 feet, then dive at the artillery positions and level off at 200 feet to simulate a strafing run.

When she had achieved altitude, she nosed the A-25 at the beach. The roaring whine of the engine seemed to be building to a crescendo. Seven tons of airplane were screaming toward the ground, and Mary Lynn had a strange, disembodied sensation of watching it all.

Out of the corner of her eye, she caught sight of the altimeter needle spinning away the feet. She pulled back on the stick to level out of the dive, and felt the resistance. Bracing herself, she pulled with all her might. The plane, bent on its headlong course, was slow to respond. The force of gravity pressed its weight on her, flattening her and blackening the edges of her consciousness. Then the plane was swooping out of the dive, so close to the breakers that she could see the frothy spume.

'That was great! Sensational!' The artillery officer's excited voice chattered in her earphones. 'Do it again!!'

'Yes, sir!' Exhilarated by the diving run, she went back up to altitude and attacked the beachhead again.

When Mary Lynn returned to base, she learned Jacqueline Cochran's experiment was soon to be put on parade. Generals from the Pentagon as well as the First and Third Air Force Headquarters, accompanied by the national press, were flying in to review the female tow-target squadron. The public relations officer's promise to generate publicity for them was about to come true.

The day before the generals' expected arrival, Mary Lynn completed an afternoon mission and landed at the field. Leaving her plane on the flight line to be serviced by the ground crew, she headed for the ready room, flight strain tearing her muscles.

'Mary Lynn, come here!' Eden called to her from the door and waved her to hurry. 'You've got to see this.'

She picked up her pace and jogged the last few yards to the building, her interest only mildly aroused. 'What is it?'

'Come on.' Eden led her up the stairs to the door of a storeroom located above the pilots' ready room.

The door stood open, and the room had been cleaned out. In place of the crates and boxes were card tables and chairs. The storeroom had become a small, private lounge. Eden pointed to the sign on the door. It used the acronym for the Women Airforce Service pilots, and made its own cute play of it to read: 'WASP Nest – Drones Keep Out or Suffer the Wrath of the Queen.'

'You're kidding,' Mary Lynn declared upon seeing it. 'Whose idea was this?'

'I have the feeling the PR officer put the idea in Major Stevenson's ear – a real catchy publicity stunt for the newspaper photographers tomorrow. It's bound to make an impression on them.' A certain grimness was in the curve of Eden's lips.

'What difference does it make?' Mary Lynn reasoned with a trace of irony. 'Let's enjoy it.'

With an agreeing shrug, Eden followed her into the new lounge where they sat at a table and smoked the cigarettes that had become almost a constant preoccupation with them. As the 'Nest' was discovered more joined them, and the talk turned to the cause of all this – the impending visit of the generals.

'I wish we had our new uniforms,' one of them griped.

'Have you been measured for yours?'

'What did you think of that tailor from Neiman-Marcus? He rattled on so . . . trying to describe what color Santiago blue is, that it took him forever to get my measurements,' a buxom pilot complained.

'I'll just bet that's what took him so long,' another said with a laugh.

'That man loves his work,' a brunette declared.

Until the new uniforms were issued, they were forced to wear their old improvised uniforms – tan gabardine slacks, white shirts, and battle jackets. The next day, they paraded past the beribboned generals and their director, Jacqueline Cochran, then came to a halt and stood at attention in their spit-shined military shoes, their columns lining up in front of two huge bombers.

The generals and their entourage approached to review the squad of women. Eden scanned the ranks of gold braid, wondering if Cappy's major was among them, but he wasn't in evidence. After the generals and Jacqueline Cochran came Major Stevenson, the commander of the tow-target squadron, and his staff.

The front row were nodded to and smiled upon by the starred Army officers while they murmured questions to the women's director of flying with her honey-gold hair and soft, southern voice. As they walked between the rows of women, the generals dawdled. Eden had the distinct impression they would have liked to get their chest decorations caught on a busty battle jacket or two.

With the review of the WASPs completed, the short,

squatty Major Stevenson slapped the last girl in line on her bottom and whispered, in good male fun, 'Get!' And they were dismissed.

As they broke ranks to be descended on by the reporters and photographers in attendance, Eden muttered to Mary Lynn, 'If he'd done that to me, I'd have punched him in the face.'

Articles about these 'brave' women pilots ran in newspapers across the country for weeks afterward. But the next morning when Mary Lynn and Eden reported to the flight line for their first mission, the WASP Nest no longer existed. The sign had been removed, as well as the tables and chairs.

Feeling used and bitter, Eden walked to her plane and with a barely controlled fury made her groundcheck of the craft. The parachute pack, strapped to her back, and her coveralls made a shapeless figure of her tall body.

The pudgy enlisted man who acted as her tow-target operator hadn't arrived to take his position in the gunner's seat. Eden wished she had a cigarette, but smoking was forbidden on the flight line, with all the high-octane gasoline around. She felt brittle and angry. Not even the sight of Bubba's long, familiar shape approaching made her feel better.

'Good morning. You look to be in fine fettle this morning.' He grinned at the snap of temper in her dark eyes.

But Eden wouldn't be cajoled out of her mood. 'What did you find when you checked out this plane?'

'The usual,' Bubba answered, watching her closely. 'The radio keeps breaking up and the engine's using oil so you might want to keep an eye on the pressure gauge. The flap handle's broken, but it's operational.'

'Wonderful,' she offered caustically.

'You're as cranky as a cow with a twisted tail,' he observed, unamused. 'What is it?'

Her hesitation didn't last long, as her complaint exploded. 'It's Stevenson and his cheap publicity stunt. I'm sick of being treated like this. I'm sick of flying worn-out planes.' Unconsciously she dug her fingers into the flesh of her arms, trembling with the force of her anger. 'I don't have to take this kind of abuse and I'm not! I'm putting in for a transfer.'

His broad features took on a closed-in look, all emotion pulled deep inside. 'If that's the way you feel, I reckon it's what you ought to do.'

She was struck by the realization that a transfer would take her away from Bubba. It drained the anger from her. After that day on the beach, they no longer met accidentally, although his noncommissioned status forced them to be circumspect in their choice of meeting places. While Eden might concede that the touch of the forbidden added some spice to their affair, it was nothing at all like the silly fling she'd had with her chauffeur. Her desire to be with Bubba wasn't based on any rebellion against money or class. And while the passion might match what she'd experienced with that impoverished count, Bubba was not shallow and selfish. He was strong and wonderful; more than that, he loved her – the person that she was – and her money and social position meant nothing to him.

'It won't change anything.' She was stiff in her attempt to convince him of that. She didn't want to lose him, not when they'd just found each other.

'If you say so, ma'am.'

'Stop it, Bubba.' Eden was irritated with his formality when they'd gone so far beyond it.

His hazel eyes bored into her, letting some raw, exposed feeling be seen in his expression. 'I don't think you know what you mean to me.' There was a wealth of emotion in the simple words. His feelings couldn't have been expressed more clearly.

'Half of all the couples in this country have been separated by the war. Why should you and I be any different?' The flight line was much too public a place for their feelings to be declared, with ground crew all around, engines revving, and pilots in their cockpits, yet their eyes locked. Their bodies strained toward one another as their emotions found a third level of communication. 'You make me feel alive, Bubba.' Stripped of all its flowery description, what she felt for him was love, passion-deep and basic.

A sexually charged tension electrified the air as Eden gazed at him, standing so close to her. She wanted to touch him, to be inside the circle of his arms, to taste the earthy flavor of his kiss.

'I wish we were somewhere else.' All his attention was on her lips.

'Can't you get a weekend pass?' Eden urged. 'We'll go somewhere – far from the Army's frowning eyes. A friend of mine has a mountain cabin. I know he'll let us use it.'

He hesitated. 'I don't know.'

'We can meet in town and take my car.' She was already making plans.

'In town.' He drew back, caution flaring in his eyes. 'There'd be hell to pay if we were seen together.'

'To hell with the Army and what they think,' Eden retorted impatiently.

'That's easy for you to say. You aren't the one who'd be facing a possible court-martial.'

Eden doubted if he'd receive any more than a stern reprimand if they should be seen, which wasn't likely. 'It's a chance to spend an entire weekend together. Don't you want that?'

'You know I do.' A muscle jumped along his wide jaw.

'Should I arrange to use the cabin?' she challenged, hurt that he hadn't jumped at the opportunity. 'Or are you going to let the Army tell you whom you are permitted to see and what you can do?'

'I'll get the pass and you get the cabin,' Bubba agreed.

Her pudgy tow-target operator came trotting up to the plane, ready for the morning's mission. His curiosity was aroused by the silence that suddenly fell between the sergeant and the red-haired pilot. He was used to hearing a free-flowing banter, a warmth and friendliness that knew no rank. But he didn't ask any questions, and simply climbed into the rear cockpit.

The sergeant helped the pilot get snugged into the front cockpit, then waited on the ground while the engine warmed. He was still standing there, watching them as the A-24 taxied to the runway.

CHAPTER TWENTY-ONE

Hamilton Steele leaned closer to the telephone, unable to subdue his pleasure at the sound of the voice coming through the receiver. 'I'm delighted to hear from you. How are you?'

'Fine.' The long-distance connection crackled into Eden's voice. 'Ham, darling. I have a favor to ask you.'

'I didn't think you called just because you missed me,' he said with a dry smile, some of the eager light fading from his eyes as his well-schooled patience came into play again. 'You have only to ask, Eden. You know that.'

'It's your mountain hideaway. You said I could use it any time I wanted. How about next weekend?' The ring of her voice brought her image vividly to his mind. Eden was a woman of passions and spirit. Her temperament, well reined through practice, was always present, its aliveness radiating from her being. 'We thought we'd slip away from the war for a couple days.'

'I'll wire the groundskeeper in the morning so he can have it stocked and ready for you,' he assured her, and settled back in his chair. 'As a matter of fact, I just may join you.'

There was a small silence on the other end of the line, followed by a throaty laugh. 'Please don't, Ham. It might prove awkward.'

Beneath that playful mockery, Hamilton recognized a trace of protectiveness. 'Ah.' He concealed a heavy sigh, having been through all this before. 'I thought perhaps

306

you and a few of your female flying friends were planning this getaway. Obviously, your companion is a male. May I inquire as to your friend? Is he a pilot too?'

'Bubba is an aircraft mechanic.'

'Bubba,' he repeated with mild disbelief.

'Ham, darling, you are sounding like a snob,' she chided. She didn't want to hear him make fun of her lover.

But Hamilton had heard more than she realized. Her voice had contained a small, possessive inflection when she said Bubba's name. It was all too familiar to him, and he breathed out a weary sound that resembled a laugh.

'What is it?' she demanded.

'I'm half tempted to gamble away all my money on the stock market and buy myself a little farm in Pennsylvania with the few pennies I'd keep back,' he declared.

'You? A farmer?' Eden laughed at the ludicrous picture of her conservative dark-suit-and-vested Hamilton Steele in a pair of bibbed overalls. 'Why on earth would you ever wish such a thing?'

'It seems . . . that you invariably fall for the impoverished or the plebeian.' His mildly mocking voice was gentle, but a sadness – which she wasn't able to see – was in his eyes.

'It's a fatal flaw in my character, I'm afraid,' she admitted and juggled the phone while she shook a cigarette from her pack of Lucky Strike Greens. 'And stop making it sound as if I always pick losers. Bubba is different.' But it seemed kinder not to discuss it with him. 'How's New York?'

'It's turning colder.'

'I had a letter from Cappy. She flew some colonel to New England last week. She said the autumn colors were spectacular this year.'

'Indeed.'

The conversation sparkled for another minute in that same false vein. Finally, Eden reaffirmed that she would use his mountain lodge the following weekend and Hamilton gave her instructions on where to obtain the key.

307

A November chill frosted the early morning air with its cool breath. Dressed in what had become regulation clothes for Cappy, the improvised uniform of khaki gabardine slacks, white shirt, and a flight jacket, she inched the zipper closure up a little higher and stepped out of the operations building at Bolling Field to proceed to the DC-3 parked on the ramp, the passenger version of the Army cargo C-47.

'How many passengers will we have this morning?' she asked her copilot, a brash man in his early twenties who couldn't quite conceal his resentment at flying second seat to a female.

'Ten.' He looked at the flight sheet. 'A light colonel's heading the group. His name's Hayward, the same as yours.' A wondering inflection entered his voice as he gave her a speculative look.

'Really.' She was struggling to conceal her dismay while wishing she'd looked at the flight orders first. It simply hadn't occurred to her that her father would be among the passengers on this flight to Republic Aviation's modification plant in Evansville, Indiana.

'I'll make the ground check,' her copilot, Lieutenant Franklin, volunteered.

The insistence that she would handle her own preflight of the aircraft died on her lips. She could hear the little triphammer beat of her pulse thudding in her ear as she watched Lieutenant Colonel Robert Hayward climb out of the Army vehicle stopped on the flight line. She hadn't seen him since that wintry day ten months earlier when she'd walked out of his Georgetown house.

'Go ahead.' She nodded permission to the copilot to make the ground preflight check.

One thing she had learned since being assigned here and repeatedly given check rides in multiengine planes was that any slacking of duty was duly noted, regardless of the reason. Every time she went up, it seemed she had to prove herself all over again to some new officer who didn't think a female was capable of piloting him anywhere.

Cappy doubted that she'd have a stiffer test than the one she'd get today from her father. She watched him approach in his Army brown jacket and tan pants, the officer's cap sitting squarely on his head, militarily precise. As he came closer, that familiar rigid-backed bearing, that face she'd known all her life, prompted a smile to start across her lips. But Cappy noticed too his coldly aloof demeanor, and her smile never got past its first beginnings.

'I've learned you are to be our pilot.' No greeting, no personal recognition.

'Yes, sir.' Cappy followed his lead, swinging around to escort him and his group to the transport. 'Lieutenant Franklin is finishing the ground check now. If you have any baggage you want stowed, the lieutenant will see to it.' She became all business, slipping into the role with ease, yet conscious of his still physically trim figure marching beside her. 'The latest forecasts indicate we should have good weather all the way.'

'Good.'

The ground time was eaten up with the usual delays involved in getting everything and everyone on board. Cappy was strapped into the pilot's seat and ready to begin the checklist when her father entered the cockpit.

'Sir?' She waited for him to explain his presence, a faint glitter of irritation showing in her china-blue eyes.

He tapped her copilot on the shoulder and motioned for him to move. 'I'll fly the right seat. You can ride in back and have yourself a nap.'

No lieutenant in his right mind argued with a lieutenant colonel. Franklin was disgruntled by the loss of logging flight time, but he complied. On the way out, he gave Cappy a look which seemed to blame her for the change.

No doubt she was the cause of it. She wished her father was joining her in the cockpit for the sake of old times and all the hours they'd flown together in the past, but she suspected it was a lack of faith in her ability to handle the big twin-engined plane.

After Lieutenant Colonel Hayward was all buckled into the right seat, Cappy made sure she had her maps and charts in order, then gave him the checklist to read off. The steady sound of his voice and the teamwork involved in the plane's start-up gave Cappy a renewed sense of nostalgia.

Unconsciously she asked, 'Ready, Dad?' before advancing the throttle to initiate a taxi roll.

'Let's keep it formal, WASP Hayward,' he replied curtly.

'Very well, sir.' Rebuffed, she silently vowed not to let her tongue slip again.

After takeoff, Cappy executed a climbing turn to put the plane on course to Wright Field in Dayton, where they'd refuel. When they had achieved the desired altitude, she trimmed the DC-3 for straight and level flight. The clouds were few and widely scattered. Below, the thinning fall colors painted the spiny ridges and slopes of the Appalachian Mountains with rusty shades of gold and orange.

Gazing out her window, she admired the burnished hills and the irregular patchwork of farm fields cut out of their elongated valleys, interspersed with small coal towns and the black taluses of mines. She didn't venture a comment on the beauty below them. With any passenger other than her father, Cappy would have drawn attention to it, but his grim-lipped silence didn't invite idle pleasantries. She had the feeling this was going to turn into a long flight.

'Aren't you going to ask how your mother is?' he inquired challengingly.

'How is she?' Cappy obliged. 'I imagine she's quite active in the Gray Ladies now.'

'Maybe if you'd call once in a while, you'd know for yourself.'

'I do call,' she retorted with a touch of anger. 'She probably just doesn't tell you.'

'I've heard you've attended some parties on the Hill with Mitch Ryan. Is it serious between you?'

'No.'

Conversation disintegrated totally after that brief combative attempt. The next hours were taken up solely with the business of flying.

In preparation for entering the traffic pattern at Wright Field, Cappy called the tower operator for landing instructions. When she received no response, she tried again – with the same results. After verifying the frequency and fiddling with the radio, she called again. In the back of her mind, she was becoming concerned that her radio was malfunctioning.

On her fourth try, a disgruntled tower operator came back, 'Will you please stay off the air, lady? This base is restricted to military personnel, and we've got some brass due to arrive any time.'

'This is a military flight, Wright tower,' she replied. 'Lieutenant Colonel Hayward and his staff are passengers. I would like landing instructions, please.' Her clipped voice demanded a response. She knew all about throwing military weight around.

'Sure, and I've got Ike's staff up here in the tower with me,' came the scoffing reply. 'Listen, missy –'

Her father broke into the talk. 'Wright tower, this is Lieutenant Colonel Hayward. I suggest you comply with my pilot's request.'

'Yes, sir!' The surprise in the man's voice was evident.

After he had related the pertinent data to Cappy – the wind's direction and velocity, the active runway number, the barometer setting, and her landing sequence – she acknowledged the information. All her attention was devoted to locating her traffic and setting up for a landing. Once on the ground, she taxied to the flight line. Her father's stern directive kept running through her mind, the words 'my pilot' echoing with an increasingly proud sound. It softened her.

'Thanks,' she said to him.

'For what?' He started reading through the shut-down list.

As he called them off to her, Cappy switched off systems

311

and double-checked others. In between, she managed to say, 'For straightening out the tower.'

'What do you expect? Women don't belong in military planes.' It was a flat statement of opinion, one that hadn't changed in nearly a year.

Cappy clamped her teeth shut and said no more, biting down hard on the waves of disappointment. Her father was Army-mule stubborn. It had been foolish to think his opinion might have changed, that a little gray might have entered the blackness of his opinion.

As soon as the aircraft was fueled, they took off again. This time Lieutenant Franklin occupied the copilot's seat and her father re joined his group in the rear passenger seats, evidently assured of her competence at the controls. Franklin kept up a steady run of patter. Oddly, Cappy found herself wishing for her father's silence.

Upon arrival at the aircraft plant at Evansville, Cappy and her copilot were taken to the cafeteria for lunch by one of the plant managers. Her father and his group of staff officers went off with one of the company heads.

That afternoon, they were given a tour of the facilities. A large percentage of the workers, Cappy noticed, were women. They were doing everything from welding to assembling parts. Cappy watched them with a sense of affinity. They all were performing jobs that had been previously regarded as a strictly male domain – and doing them well. The war was lowering many barriers that had always been raised against them. When the afternoon break signal sounded, a young woman about Cappy's age finished her weld before she turned off her torch and removed the protective goggles she wore. Cappy said something to her about the job she was doing. The woman looked at her and shrugged.

'I need the money. I can't live on the allocation I get from Ernie. He's just a private in the Army,' she explained, then sighed tiredly. 'I'll be glad when he comes home and I won't have to work anymore.'

'Yes.' Maybe if she wasn't doing something she loved

so much, she'd feel that way too, Cappy decided.

The subject didn't interest her copilot in the least, as he looked around with obvious boredom. Suddenly, he lighted up. 'Hey! Look!' His burst of excitement caught her attention.

A big, ugly plane with a large, four-bladed propeller attached to a blunt engine cowling was being rolled inside a hangar. It was the powerful P-47 Thunderbolt, a fighter plane that was earning the name 'Little Friend' to the Flying Fortresses.

'What I wouldn't give to be crawling into the cockpit of that,' Lieutenant Franklin declared.

'Me, too,' she agreed.

His look was scoffing. 'That plane's a powerhouse. They'll never let a woman at the controls of it.'

Cappy didn't argue the point, but she wondered what the young lieutenant would say if he knew the Army was teaching women to fly the B-17 bomber. It was certainly more airplane than the P-47 pursuit.

Late in the day, they were taken to the hotel where they'd be spending the night. In the short time she'd been on the job, Cappy had learned that piloting Army officers around the country also meant staying in the best accommodations available and dining at the best restaurants. The trip to Evansville was no exception. But dinner that evening proved to be an uncomfortable affair with her father glaring at her from another table the minute any male even walked close to her chair.

'Afterwards I wished I had eaten in my room,' she complained to Mitch, recounting the experience two days later. 'I know he expected me to be accosted at any minute – a woman alone in a public place. Obviously I was supposed to be fast.'

'It's a common misconception.'

A piano player was providing soft background music to the ever-louder talk in the bar. The pianist was no better than average, but with her platinum hair and a well-endowed figure, more than mediocre talent wasn't necessary. Cappy brought her attention back to the table and tapped out a cigarette from the half-empty pack. Mitch immediately offered her a light and she bent toward the match flame.

'I thought –' She stopped to exhale the smoke, then shook her head. 'Never mind.'

'You thought what?' The warm and steady regard of his dark eyes was interested and admiring. Cappy experienced that rush of pleasure his handsomely rugged looks so often evoked in her, and looked away before it became too strong.

'I thought that once my father saw what a competent pilot I was, he'd give up his stupid prejudices about a woman's place. When he got on that radio to the tower, he wasn't demanding respect for me or the job I was doing; he wanted it for his daughter. That flight proved nothing to him. If he had his way, I'd be out of the skies tomorrow.' She was impatient and resentful as bitter thoughts tangled darkly behind the blue surfaces of her eyes. 'He's impossible.'

'He loves you,' Mitch stated.

'Well, he has a fine way of showing it.' To her, love was not something that possessed and confined. It was supposed to be an acceptance and appreciation of a person's individuality, not an attempt to stifle it.

'Just the same, he does,' Mitch repeated with calm insistence. 'Whenever I see him, he always asks about you.'

It moved her, but Cappy answered, 'He still doesn't approve of what I'm doing, so don't try to convince me otherwise.'

'I won't. But you still love him.'

'He's my father.' This was an explanation rather than an answer.

'Let's dance.' Mitch slid his hand underneath her fingers and rubbed the top of them with his thumb.

Dancing was better than talking. She stubbed out her

cigarette before standing to be guided onto the crowded floor. The piano player began singing a throaty accompaniment and Cappy recognized the Frank Sinatra hit of a couple years before, 'I'll Never Smile Again.'

Other couples were making slow circles of the area as she turned in his embrace. With one arm curved around her back and lower rib cage, he held her loosely against him. Her eyes were level with his mouth, and she caught the heady scent of bay rum lotion clinging to his shaved jaw. She felt the pressure of his thighs against hers as they moved in shuffling rhythm to the slow ballad.

'Your father is a proud man, Cappy.' Mitch picked up the conversation where they'd left it at the table. 'All he has is the Army and his family –'

'In that order,' she interrupted.

A small smile touched his mouth, but he went on as if she hadn't spoken. 'I think it's normal for every man to want a son, someone to carry on the family name and tradition. I have the feeling your father regrets not having a son, although it's not something he'll admit, because he doesn't want to hurt your mother. But because he does regret it so much, it's probably the reason he doesn't want you doing the things he would have wanted his son to do. Consciously or unconsciously, he doesn't want to expect things from you that he would have expected from a son. His standards for you are very rigid because a man wants his daughter to be a certain kind of woman.'

His logic was sound, but she had her father's stubbornness. 'He wants the same blind obedience from his family that he gives to the Amy,' Cappy replied dryly. 'He isn't the least bit interested in what I want.'

'What do you want, Cap?' His head was inclined toward her, interest deepening in his expression as he tried to fathom her desires.

'I want a home of my own – and friends that I choose. I want to fly.' She heard the building pitch of her voice and stopped before the desperate longing broke through.

'Those are relatively simple things to obtain.' Mitch

drew back to study her, not quite sure what he had thought she would say, but not expecting such a basic reply.

'Are they?' she countered, a trace of mocking irony in her glance. 'Look around you and what do you see? Soldiers, traveling businessmen, secretaries from the Midwest. Impermanence. Nothing is sure. Nothing is certain.'

For a moment, he didn't say anything as he gathered her more closely to him, until his cheek was resting against her silken-dark hair, and he was breathing in its sweet smell. At last he was beginning to understand some of what kept her from caring for anyone or anything too deeply.

'It's the war,' he murmured.

And Cappy didn't contradict him.

The yellow convertible curved up the mountain heavily timbered with pine and leaf-bare hardwood. Drifts of leaves filled the ditches and carpeted the forest floor, making hiding places where the squirrels could store their winter caches. As the car breezed by, its wind whisked up the dried leaves, spinning them in a devil's whirl and leaving them to spiral slowly back to earth – in a scurry and a rush, and finally a whisper.

A blue jay took a shortcut through the trees to wait for the flashy car at the tall log chalet, nestled amongst the trees. Stained a dark brown color, the huge logs lay two-and-a-half stories tall, ringed by a galleried porch with a view of the Carolina mountains, smoky in the November afternoon.

The road came to a dead end at the lodge. Bubba slowed the car to a stop in front of it, and stared at the massive structure with a frown. Eden was busy gathering up her purse and loosening the silk scarf that had protected her hair from the tearing wind.

'I thought you said we were staying in a cabin,' Bubba stated, retreating into a thick drawl. 'Now I've never seen a cabin this size – not even in Texas, where everything's big.'

316

Eden just laughed at him and climbed out of the car. 'Come on.'

'You're really serious? This is it?' Bubba followed her skeptically, pausing by the trunk to unload the luggage.

'Leave that. Haines will bring it in.' She tucked a hand through the crook of his arm and walked him to split-log steps.

'Haines? Is that your friend?' Bubba looked down at her.

'He's the groundskeeper.' The door opened before they reached it and they were welcomed inside by a plump, matronly woman with gray hair drawn back in a bun and a chubby-cheeked smile. 'Hello, Ida Mae,' Eden greeted the woman familiarly, then breezed on by her, not bothering to introduce Bubba.

The interior walls were exposed logs, the same dark brown color as outside, but the spaciousness of the living room – with its massive stone chimney and hardwood floors spattered with bright area rugs and animal skins – eliminated any sense of darkness. The high ceilings were ribbed with wooden beams, rustic chandeliers of hurricane-style lamps suspended to light the areas below.

The kindly-faced woman had prepared the liquor trolley for Eden and discreetly withdrawn. Bubba wandered over to stand next to Eden while she fixed them each a drink.

'Who was she?' Bubba asked in an undertone.

'Ida Mae? She's the cook.' Eden handed him a drink, then touched her glass to his in an unspoken toast, the delicate ring of fine crystal making a bell-like sound.

He glanced at her face, that gleaming devil-light lurking beneath the surfaces of his hazel eyes, exciting her. Maintaining the eye contact, Eden sipped the iced Scotch in her glass, then raised herself on tiptoes to nuzzle his lips and taste the whiskey on them.

With fingers linked, she drew him with her to the Chesterfield, positioned in front of the mammoth stone fireplace. She pulled him onto the smooth cushions and sat with her legs curled beneath her. Like an orange-haired tabby cat she arched against his side. The hem of her skirt had inched up to show her silk-stockinged knees.

'Something tells me' – Bubba looked at her askance and hooked an arm around her shoulders to bring her comfortably closer – 'this weekend isn't going to be quite what I thought.'

Her smile teased him. 'I hope you weren't expecting me to do the cooking.'

'I didn't think too much about food,' he admitted.

'Oh?' She playfully walked her fingers over the ribbed white wool sweater covering his chest, up to the jutting angle of his wide jaw. 'What did you think about?'

'You and me walking through the woods, or sitting in front of a cozy fire,' Bubba replied with a kind of shrug.

'The woods are just outside and the logs in the fireplace are simply waiting for a match.' She was more interested in his mouth and the delights it could hold.

The door opened and a spare-built man entered, toting their suitcases. Not a single glance was sent in their direction as he walked through to the rustic log-railed stairs, as if he were unaware of the couple sitting so closely on the davenport.

'It's not exactly you and me.' The groundskeeper illustrated the difference between Bubba's imagined weekend and the reality. 'And this isn't exactly a little ole cabin in the woods.'

'But we're together . . . with all the comforts of home,' Eden reminded him.

'Maybe your home . . . but not mine,' he corrected her drolly. 'I'm used to doin' for myself.'

'And just what is it that you "do" so well?' she asked with her face uplifted in provocative invitation.

A half-muffled groan came from his throat as he roughly gathered her in and reached around to rid himself of the impediment of the whiskey glass, shoving it onto an end table. His mouth rolled onto her lips, heavy with the weight of his needs. She threaded her fingers into the shaggy thickness of his hair, nails digging in like a purring cat

318

flexing its claws. The driving pressure of his kiss was too demanding, yet he couldn't check it, and she seemed to revel in it. A fine sweat broke across his upper lip with the rising heat that flared between them.

'You are Eden to me.' He held himself a breath away from her softly swollen lips, a fevered huskiness in his low, trembling voice. 'All the things of paradise on earth. You are my sun, heating me with your fire – and the blackness of night, taking me into your endless reaches. God, how I love you.' His lips settled onto hers again.

A tap of footsteps on the hardwood floor brought Bubba's head up sharply. The carpet runner on the stairs had muffled the sounds of the groundskeeper's descent until he crossed the open foyer to the door. Bubba flushed darkly under his tan and pulled away from her to run a self-conscious hand through his hair. Eden couldn't completely conceal her amusement over his embarrassment.

'You'll get used to them. Eventually you won't even know they're in the room.'

But Bubba never did get accustomed to their silent comings and goings in the lodge. When Ida Mae brought them breakfast trays the next morning, she didn't bat an eye at the sight of him in the bed, stark naked under the satin sheets. Eden teased him about it until he found a mutually satisfactory way to silence her.

Against his better judgment, he let her drive him all the way back to the base, dropping him off inside the gates instead of leaving him in town to catch a ride on an Army transport. But Eden was completely unconcerned about any problems that might arise from being seen with a noncom, confident she could handle it. She had her chance when she was ordered to report to Major Stevenson.

'It's come to my attention that you were seen with an enlisted man,' the squadron commander announced accusingly, keeping the width of his desk between them so it wouldn't be so obvious that she was taller than he was. 'I want the name of this sergeant who was with you.'

'Sir, in a manner of speaking, I wasn't "with" anyone.'

In this situation, Eden was very sure of herself, drawing on the cool hauteur that could stop any man, coldly daring him to deny her word. 'I was driving back to base and saw Sergeant Jackson waiting for a ride, so I gave him a lift back to camp.'

'Sergeant Jackson?' His arched eyebrow prompted a fuller description of the man.

'He's the mechanic who's worked on some of the planes I've flown.'

'Then you admit you were with him?'

'I was *with* him,' she agreed in an implied denial. 'Sometimes I ride in the front seat with our family chauffeur. I've never regarded that as being *with* him, but I suppose you could say that.'

'I see,' he murmured.

Afterwards, Eden laughed about it to Mary Lynn. 'When I reminded him that I was a pilot and Sergeant Jackson was merely a mechanic, he was so incensed I thought he was going to burst a blood vessel. You could tell how disappointed he was that our meeting had been so innocent.' But Mary Lynn didn't laugh, causing Eden to add, 'I thought it was amusing. The major is such a pompous snob himself.'

'Yes.' Mary Lynn's attempted smile fell short of its mark. 'I was just remembering Rachel. Everybody knew she was sneaking out to meet that private.' She reached inside her jacket and took out an envelope, overseas V-mail. 'This came for you. It's from Rachel's private.'

After a small hesitation, Eden tore it open and read through the short missive from Zach Jordan. It was a reaching out, expressing his gratefulness for the words of sympathy she had tried to offer him after the chapel service for Rachel.

'He's in Italy,' she said.

Part Three

I just called up to tell you that
*   I'm rugged but right!*
A rambling woman, a gambling woman,
*   drunk every night.*
A porterhouse steak three times
*   a day for my board,*
That's more than any decent gal
*   can afford!*
I've got a big electric fan to
*   keep me cool while I eat,*
A tall, handsome man to keep me
*   warm while I sleep.*
I'm a rambling woman, a gambling woman,
*   and BOY am I tight!*
I just called up to tell you that
I'm rugged but right!
HO-HO-HO – rugged but right!

CHAPTER TWENTY-TWO

'I have denied your request for transfer.' The papers were pushed across the desk to the two women seated in front of it.

'We'll resubmit them,' Eden stated, not backing down an inch. 'It won't do you any good.' Jacqueline Cochran rose from her chair and came around to the front of the desk in the borrowed office, facing her two rebellious pilots. She did not tolerate opposition well. 'I'll simply turn them down again.'

'Then you'll have my resignation,' Eden countered.

'I won't accept it.' The director's dark eyes hardened. 'Don't you realize that your actions could jeopardize future programs for women pilots?' she argued firmly. 'Any failure to endure by any woman will be a detriment to all of us. I cannot allow the two of you to knock down what the rest of us have achieved. Conditions are perhaps not the best, but we are at war. The pilots here are performing a vital function –'

'I'm not interested in a lecture,' Eden cut in, not giving Mary Lynn a chance to talk. 'And conditions here have not improved that much. We are still flying red-lined aircraft daily. There haven't been any more fatalities because we finally got smart and started looking out for ourselves instead of depending on those in command.'

At the interruption, Jacqueline Cochran turned coldly angry. 'As your superior –'

'You are in charge, Miss Cochran, but you are not my superior,' Eden corrected her.

Mary Lynn was a silent participant in the exchange,

watching the clash of two strong wills. Her nature was quieter, but no less resilient.

Wisely, Jacqueline Cochran did not pursue her earlier remark. 'My position is unchanged; your requests for transfers are denied. If, in a month, you still feel strongly about this, we will discuss it at that time.'

'No, Miss Cochran.' Eden wasn't impressed by that ambiguous offer. 'We won't discuss it. I either have my transfer or I resign. It doesn't matter whether you accept it or not. If I walk off this base, what will you do? Have me arrested? That might make for some unpleasant publicity – and believe me, I'll make a scene.'

'That sounds distinctly like a threat.'

Mary Lynn spoke up, 'Our leaving is not going to affect the experiment here. We have proven we can fly tow-target missions. Our record is excellent. No army expects a soldier to remain on the front line for the entire war, Miss Cochran. Our request for a transfer is not unreasonable under the circumstances.'

'That is a valid argument,' the Director of Women pilots conceded.

'Does that mean you'll grant our requests for transfer?' Eden wanted a more definite response.

'I'll take them under advisement and see what can be arranged. You'll hear from me.' She retreated behind the desk, in effect dismissing them.

Eden stood, but didn't leave the office. 'When?'

With a trace of impatience and grudging admiration, Jacqueline Cochran replied, 'Within the week.'

They filed out of the office, not pausing until they were outside the operations building. The Carolina air on that December day was cold and damp, the sky overhead gray and leaden. They halted to zip their jackets against the seeping chill.

'What do you think?' Mary Lynn asked.

'She doesn't have a choice,' Eden replied complacently. 'We'll get our transfers to the ferrying division.'

A dismal, drenching downpour saturated the Carolina ground. Eden picked her way across the winter grass, taking a shortcut to the barracks, her boots squishing through the mud. She darted inside, dripping water in a trail that followed her down the narrow corridor to Mary Lynn's private cubicle.

'Mail call!' Out of breath and barely able to contain her excitement, she whipped several envelopes from beneath her rain slicker and shoved them at Mary Lynn, who was curled on her cot in the midst of her Christmas writing. 'Open this one first.' Eden indicated an official-looking envelope and watched with bright, shining eyes as Mary Lynn tore at the flap with her finger. 'New orders, right?' she guessed.

At first glance, Mary Lynn nodded affirmatively while she read a little farther. 'Yes.'

'Mine came, too.' Solid triumph put a steady gleam into her dark brown eyes. 'Can you think of a better Christmas present than getting transferred out of this place?' She didn't wait for an answer. 'Where are they sending you?'

'To the Sixth Ferrying Group in Long Beach, California.'

'Same here,' Eden said with some surprise, and sank onto the cot in front of Mary Lynn. Satisfaction radiated across her features. 'I can hardly wait to enjoy some of that California sunshine. This constant gray gloom is depressing.'

Mary Lynn's glance fell on another envelope and recognized Beau's familiar scrawl. 'It's from Beau,' she said, offering an unnecessary explanation as she eagerly ripped it open and skimmed the first few paragraphs. His letters were always read many times. 'Listen to this.' In a quick recap of the letter's opening paragraphs she explained, 'Beau was on a raid and lost two engines. He was forced to land at an RAF base. But listen to this part. "They told me luck had run out for the old girl and she was destined to be scrapped for spare B-17 parts,"' she read. '"I went to have a last look at her. Some fighter pilots were standing around. One came over and started talking to me. It turns out that he knows you.''' Mary Lynn stopped reading to tell Eden the astounding news. 'It was Colin Fletcher! Can you imagine? He and Beau are having dinner over the Christmas holidays, he said. At least he won't be alone at Christmas.' She released an excited sigh. 'Won't Marty be surprised when I write and tell her about Colin!'

An agreeing sound came from Eden, but she looked absent and preoccupied. The wet hood of her rain slicker had fallen to the back of her head. Wispy tendrils of damp, dark copper hair curled along her temples. Her dark eyes were troubled.

'Is something wrong, Eden?' Mary Lynn inquired even though the redhead hadn't shown an inclination to confide in her in the past.

A heavy sigh broke from her lips. 'Finally we have transfers that will take us out of these awful planes and away from this miserable weather – something I've wanted for months – and now I don't want to go.' Eden pushed herself to her feet on that impatient declaration, half angry. 'I don't want to leave Bubba.' She hung her head for a dejected instant, then darted a proudly assertive look at Mary Lynn. 'I'm crazy about that man.'

Hooded and coated once again to keep out the cold, dripping the rain that misted the field from low-hanging clouds, Eden splashed through the puddled water collecting on the concrete apron around the hangars. She ran with her head down and her shoulders hunched against the bone-damp chill. The massive hangar doors were shut against the inclement weather and Eden ran to a small side door, quickly rushing in out of the drizzling rain.

Pausing inside, she pushed the slicker hood to the back of her head and scanned the cavernous interior. The light patter of rain drummed a thousand finger-tappings on the corrugated metal of the hangar's roof. All sound echoed in the empty hollow of the building – the clank of metal tools, the idle call of male voices, and the thud of walking feet on the concrete floor. The humid, heavy air smelled strongly of gasoline fumes, motor oils, and grease from the disemboweled planes parked inside.

In her second sweep of the hangar, Eden spied Bubba's long, lanky figure in loose-fitting overalls, standing by a workbench along the near wall. She walked immediately toward him, her step quickening. The soft-wrapped package stowed under her raincoat for protection from the elements made a rustling sound as she moved, but it was mostly drowned by the wet swish of her slicker.

With his concentration centered on the valve lifter in his hand, Bubba failed to hear her approach. At the last minute, the sound of her footsteps reached him and his keen hazel eyes looked her way. His wide, intelligent features immediately glowed with pleasure.

'Hello.' The drawled greeting managed to convey a host of caresses. They had learned to do this – to touch and feel each other with words and looks, to mentally make love while abstaining from contact.

There was an excited quiver in the pit of her stomach. 'Hello.' Her dark gaze searched his face for an anxious second. 'My transfer came through.'

The soft expression on his face suddenly hardened. His oil-grimed fingers fiddled with the lifter. 'Are you going?' His tone was an attempt to sound offhand, yet under it was deep, painful alarm.

'It's what I've wanted,' Eden reminded him and watched him for some sign that he would insist that she stay.

'Yep,' Bubba agreed to that.

'They're sending me to Long Beach . . . in California.' Another mechanic paused at the workbench to pick up a tool, and Eden waited until he was out of earshot before continuing. 'There isn't any reason why you can't ask for a transfer.'

Bubba breathed out a sound that dismissed the thought. 'My CO has made it real plain that he isn't going to approve any such thing. I'm needed here.' His pause was short. 'Besides, I've been told if I leave this camp, it's likely to be for the Pacific. That's where they're usin' so many of these dive-bombers.'

'Not the Pacific.' That suggestion brought a cold chill down her spine. 'The Japanese scare me.' In a diversionary gesture, she brought forth the package that had been protectively hidden inside her coat, and offered it to Bubba. She wanted to remind him of the continuing patterns of life that war couldn't change. 'It's your Christmas present. I didn't know when I might have another chance to give it to you before I left.'

Self-consciously, Bubba wiped at the grime on his hands before he took the tissue-wrapped package from her, glancing around to see who might be watching.

'What is it?' he asked with a vague, boyish smile lifting his lip corners. He was trying to respond to Eden's gift-giving spirit, but not too successfully.

'Silk pajamas . . . from Saks.' She'd guessed at the size, then had Ham pick them out for her in New York and send them to her. It had all required considerable time, effort, and expense. Her dark eyes glowed with anticipation, awaiting his look of surprise and pleasure.

His brows arched high, taken aback. As always when he was in an awkward situation, Bubba retreated into a thick drawl and a country-boy pose. 'I haven't worn pajamas since I was a pup,' he joked. 'What do you aim for me to do with these?'

'You were so embarrassed about having nothing on when Ida Mae brought the breakfast tray in, I thought you should have something to wear the next time a maid brought you breakfast in bed,' Eden replied easily, warmed by the memory of that weekend.

His wide, raw-boned features grew grimly smooth and serious. 'But there aren't any maids in my house, Eden,' he pointed out with quiet pride.

Laughing, she didn't hear that underlying note. 'But there are in mine.'

*　　*　　*

On the day they left Camp Davis, Eden wangled a driver and jeep from the motor pool to take her and Mary Lynn to the train station. When the Army private picked them up at the nurses' barracks, she ordered him to stop at the flight line. No explanation was offered to the driver and Mary Lynn needed none. She sympathized with Eden's desire to see Bubba one last time.

As the jeep rolled up to the hangar area, Bubba spotted them and came trotting over to meet them. His work cap was reversed, the bill pointing down the back of his head, and he wore a wide smile at the sight of Eden. In between wipes of his greasy hands on a rag, he gave the two of them a careless salute.

'What can I do for you?' he asked, conscious of the eavesdropping private behind the wheel.

'We just came by for one last look before we left,' Eden replied, smiling too.

'The boys on the ground are gonna miss you. The place won't be the same with you gone,' Bubba said.

'We'll miss you.'

The weight of parting lay heavily between them as their smiles faded. They looked at each other with undisguised longing, memorizing details for the lonely times ahead. Mary Lynn ached for them, understanding the conflict between the love and the sense of duty they each felt.

Bubba finally broke the contact, lowering his chin and turning his head aside, and resumed the wiping of his hands. 'I guess you'd better be on your way before you miss that train.' He stepped away from the side of the jeep and stood well clear of its path. 'Good flying.'

'Take care of yourself, Sergeant,' Mary Lynn offered, aware that Eden was too choked up to say anything.

Her attempt at a salute became a tearful wave, but only Mary Lynn noticed. Except for the wetness in her eyes, Eden's poise was otherwise intact. As she ordered the private to drive on, someone in the hangar yelled for Bubba. Her last glimpse of him came as he walked away in that long, rolling gait. They'd be together again, Eden never doubted that, but she still regretted the separation.

Because of the Christmas holidays, the trains were more crowded than usual. There was always a crush of service-men and passengers in the dining and club cars. It didn't matter how discouraging the war news was in Italy and the Pacific, a holiday spirit prevailed on the train. Like Mary Lynn, Eden joined in with the caroling in the club car, each of them drawn a little bit closer to the other because of the men they missed.

As the train slowed its clacking wheels to pass through a small town, Eden absently glanced out the club-car window. A yellow convertible was stopped at a highway crossing, a street lamp shining down on it. She poked at Mary Lynn.

'Do you think that's my car?' They were past it before Eden could tell for sure. 'It looked like it, didn't it? The chauffeur is somewhere en route to California with it.'

'Wouldn't it be something if we just passed it on the way?' Mary Lynn declared.

'Many more of these cross-country jaunts and I'm going to need a new car before this war is over,' Eden joked, then she turned faintly serious.

'When we start ferrying planes, we're going to cover a lot more country than your car has.' Mary Lynn sipped at her soda-pop rickey, an innocent concoction of soda, lime juice and sugar.

'That's true,' Eden agreed.

When they arrived in California, they reported to Air Transport Command's Sixth Ferrying Group in Long Beach. New orders awaited their arrival, sending them to Palm Springs to attend the ATC pursuit school, where they would learn to fly the Army's fighters, the hottest ships around.

The first three weeks of training were spent in the rear cockpit of the AT-6 Texan, the plane they'd flown so often during their advanced flying phase in Sweetwater. The Texan's rear cockpit allowed them to simulate conditions in the nose-high 'Jug,' the pilots' nickname for the P-47 Thunderbolt because of its thick, blunt-nosed cowling. The training was intensive but it had to be. There wasn't any room in the Thunderbolt for a second pilot, so the first time up in the fighter plane had to be a solo ride.

The cockpit of the P-47 was just Mary Lynn's size, measuring roughly three feet by three feet. In that small space a mass of levers, gauges, and navigational and communication equipment was crammed, not leaving much room for the pilot. But Mary Lynn didn't take up much room.

She ran through the cockpit check, seat belt and shoulder straps fastened tight – and her heart somewhere in her throat. Thirteen separate buttons and switches had to be in position for flight preparation and Mary Lynn mentally counted them off. With the stick back and the brakes locked and the primer feeding juice to the engine, she pushed the starter switch.

A rumbling groan came from deep inside the plane, and the four – bladed propeller cranked, slowly rotating and picking up speed. So did her pulse. The rumble grew louder as the Pratt and Whitney engine took power and vibrated the aircraft with its bass-deep roar.

On the ground, her instructor gave her a thumbs-up sign, wishing Mary Lynn good luck on her first ride in the powerful plane. She scanned the dials once more – temperature and pressure gauges all reading right – and eased the throttle forward to start her taxi roll, a scared feeling in the pit of her stomach.

At the end of the runway, Mary Lynn reached up and grasped the canopy bar, located just behind her shoulder. With a squeeze of the lever, she pushed the canopy forward to close the cockpit, then locked it.

'Okay, Army Three forty-seven,' the tower operator's voice sounded in the ear sets. 'Clear for takeoff when ready.'

'Roger.' Mary Lynn depressed the button on the stick to activate her throat mike and acknowledge the clearance. She was in position, but the Thunderbolt's high nose kept her from seeing down the length of the runway.

For all her apprehensions, she was mentally committed to a take-off. Her hand slowly pushed the black throttle knob forward while the powerful engine changed from a rumbling pitch to a deepening thunder. She took her feet off the brake pedals and kept pushing the throttle forward. The Thunderbolt seemed to catapult itself down the runway, its high acceleration pressing Mary Lynn against the seat and the tremendous roar of the engine filling the cockpit. She let the stick come forward, lowering the nose and lifting the tail wheel. Applying more and more right rudder to compensate for the powerful engine torque, she kept the fighter plane pointed down the center of the runway.

She was unconsciously holding her breath as she glanced at the airspeed indicator. The needle swung past 85, then past 90, still moving. The plane wasn't fighting the controls so much now. Another glance at the airspeed and Mary Lynn gently pulled back on the stick at 110 miles an hour. The ground fell away as the pursuit surged into the air, not using even half of the runway, and the sensation turned her nervous qualms into soaring excitement.

With the gear folding away inside the fighter's belly, she trimmed the craft for a climb and the Thunderbolt streaked for the clouds like a homesick angel. Palm Springs was behind her and the blue of the Salton Sea reflected the desert sky. She put the plane through its paces, exulting in its power and high maneuverability. She was sorry when she had to return to the base.

That night her letters to Beau and Marty were filled with the thrilling experience of that first solo flight. It seemed fitting somehow that, while two of the most important people in her life were flying B-17 bombers, nicknamed the 'Big Friend,' she was now flying P-47 Thunderbolt pursuit aircraft, called by some the 'Little Friend.'

When their month of training was finished, Eden and Mary Lynn joined the Sixth Ferrying Group in Long Beach and began delivering the fast pursuits all over the country.

CHAPTER TWENTY-THREE

Jeweled turquoise waters surround the chain of islands that trail off the southern tip of Florida like stepping stones into the Gulf of Mexico. The clear barrier of the B-17's plexiglas nose was all that separated Marty Rogers from the white-capped blue waters and the sun-drenched Keys below. The February skies were clear and limitless, stretching to the end of the sea and beyond. Through them, the Army-drab B-17, painted olive green, headed to its home field at Buckingham Army Air Base outside of Fort Myers, its training mission for turret gunnery operators complete for this trip.

Belly down in the glass nose of the Flying Fortress, Marty let the panoramic view ease the tension from the previous concentrated patterns she'd flown. Her copilot took the controls for the homebound flight while she enjoyed a break. From here to the airfield, it was all fairly routine.

'It's hard to believe that a month ago I was zipped to the throat in a fleece-lined flight suit, with long underwear, a leather jacket, and wool-lined boots, trying to keep warm twenty-four thousand feet above frigid Ohio.' Her chin rested on the cup of her hand and her voice rumbled deep from her chest as she flashed a wry glance at the uniformed officer sharing the close quarters of the B-17 nose with her.

Graduation from the four-engine school at Lockbourne Amy Air Base had also signaled the end of the grueling, strength-building exercises. Marty had gladly abandoned the Bernarr Macfadden wrist developers and now picked up a newspaper only to read it, not to crumple it into a ball in her fist.

'I know what you mean,' the chestnut-haired lieutenant agreed. He was one of the many transient pilots temporarily stationed at Buckingham awaiting overseas assignments or more training in heavier bombers. Scott Daniels was a bomber pilot, but on today's flight he'd come along to observe the patterns and procedures.

The constant coming and going of pilots suited Marty. She wasn't interested in establishing any permanent relationships. Besides, it wasn't wise with so many of the pilots bound for combat overseas. Airmen had a notoriously higher mortality rate than the regular soldier. She'd had fun with all the flyboys but she'd restricted intimacies to a very few.

From the corner of her eye, she studied Lieutenant Scott Daniels, strongly attracted to his fair skin and burnished brown hair. More than once he'd looked at her with a flirting, questing gaze, making his interest in her obvious. Marty wasn't particularly bothered by the gold wedding band on his ring finger as long as he wasn't. He turned, caught her eyeing him, and smiled with a slow, knowing warmth. A second later, his glance shifted past her, locking onto something in the blue sea below them.

'Look.' He leaned closer and pointed out a small white dot in the aquamarine waters. 'Isn't that a boat? What do you suppose it is? A fishing trawler, maybe?'

'Probably.' Marty watched the bobbing speck, so small from the bomber's great height.

But her senses were picking up other messages – the slight pressure of his body making contact against her length, the warmth of his breath stirring the touseled, tawny curls of her short hair, and the spicy scent drifting from his smoothly shaven cheeks. He was very close. She turned her head slightly, feeling the little run of her pulse as her gaze darted to the full line of his mouth so near to hers.

'I wangled myself a weekend pass,' he murmured. 'A buddy of mine is lending me his car. I thought I'd drive over to Miami. Would you like to ride along?'

'Sure,' Marty agreed in her whiskey-thick voice. 'Why not?'

'Why not,' the lieutenant repeated, then he closed the space that separated their lips.

The kiss was both seeking and satisfying, a controlled exploration that invited and promised something more. Marty responded to the simple demand that didn't press. Intense passion usually required some kind of commitment. She usually backed off from that, preferring something freer, less confining.

Slowly they drew apart. Her breathing was faintly uneven, warmly aroused. Marty held his gaze while she turned onto her side and shifted so she was slightly under him.

'Tell me, Lieutenant,' she murmured, gravelly mischief lacing her voice, 'have you ever made love in an airplane before?'

A dark gleam entered his brown eyes. 'Are you a member of that famed Mile-High Club I've heard about?' he taunted, referring to the supposedly select group of female fliers who had made love at an altitude over 5,000 feet.

'Not yet,' Marty replied, then chuckled in her throat as her hand curved itself to the back of his neck and urged him down.

Miami Beach with its palm trees and endless stretches of sand was a hive of tourists, workers whose pockets were stuffed with dollars from high-paying war jobs, uniformed servicemen, and wives, stubborn in their insistence to be close to their soldier husbands for as long as they could. The beaches were a strange blend of cadets drilling in columns, sun-worshipping factory employees wading in the surf in the civilian version of a furlough, and Coast Guardsmen patrolling the shores on horseback.

Nearly all the hotels were taken over by the Army as rest and recuperation centers for the war's victims, prominent among them the Air Force pilots returning from

335

overseas with their bodies intact and their nerves shattered. Vestiges of the war were everywhere, creeping into the idyllic world of sand, surf, and sun, like a widening shadow in paradise. The shadow lurked in the corners of people's lives; their backs might be turned to it, but they were unable to banish it completely.

A bright sickle moon silvered the beach Marty strolled with Lieutenant Scott Daniels, the loose sand weighting her steps, making them slow and meandering. The salty breeze had a tangy taste, invigorating and clean. The small breakers rolled in slowly.

'I've heard ships have been torpedoed just a few miles off shore,' she remarked.

Her boat-shaped cap sat jauntily atop her short, honey-dark hair. In the moonlight, her silver wings gleamed on her semi-regulation shirt. She wore her uniform-tan pants and unbecoming but serviceable shoes. The night was warm, making a jacket unnecessary.

'Yeah, that's what I've heard, too,' Scott agreed and tipped the beer bottle to his mouth. No more than a swallow was left, and he frowned at the bottle. Hotels loomed in tall, irregular boxes close to the sand, darkened into black silhouettes. 'Want another beer?' he asked. 'There's bound to be a bar in one of these places.'

Marty shrugged, not really caring. 'Sure.' Altering their direction, they headed for the nearest blacked-out building. Where the hotel's sundeck jutted into the beach sand, Marty checked her pace. 'I'll wait for you out here.' For once, she wasn't in the mood for the noisy, smoky scene of a bar.

The pilot didn't protest. 'I'll be right out.'

While he disappeared toward the hotel's beach entrance, Marty wandered over to claim one of the lounge chairs, angular shapes in the shadows cast by the palm fronds. She stumbled over a pair of feet thrust into the walkway and nearly fell into a chair before she recovered her balance.

'Sorry,' she said to the unknown person, his outline

barely discernible in the deep shadows. 'I didn't see you sitting there in the dark.'

'The hotels are under blackout orders again.' The figure shifted, catching some of the moonlight. An officer's cap sat sideways on his head, the bill dipping over one eye and shadowing most of his features except for the smile that seemed to lurk permanently around his mouth, infected with a hard, cruel bitterness.

'I noticed the cars had the top half of their headlamps hooded' – Marty strained to see more of this stranger, wary and conscious of the hair rising on the back of her neck – 'and the blackout curtains at the windows.'

'Only on the ocean side, though,' he pointed out with dry cynicism, in case she hadn't noted how limited the precaution was.

There was something about this man Marty instinctively disliked. She couldn't name it, but she felt on edge, ready to snap. Even though she couldn't see him clearly, she could feel the slow rake of his eyes. She wished she hadn't sat down next to him, but she wasn't about to get up and leave now.

'What are those wings you're wearing?' He lifted his hand to gesture in the direction of the specially designed wings on her shirt collar, ice cubes clinking against the glass he held. The potent smell of rum came to her. 'Did your flyboy lover give them to you?'

'No. I earned them,' Marty stated in a flat, decisive voice.

He seemed to straighten with interest, and she caught the reflection of moonlight off the captain's bars on his shoulders. 'The hell you say.' Some kind of scornful amusement mocked her accomplishment. 'And just what is it you fly? Cubs?'

'A B-17 Flying Fortress,' she retorted. A long silence followed, broken by the sound of ice cubes rattling as a drink was thrown back, then the glass lowered. 'Surprised?' Marty couldn't resist taunting him.

'I guess the Army doesn't give a damn who they stick into their planes,' he mused, uncaring.

His head was lowered; moonlight splashed across more of his face, revealing rugged, once handsome features that were lined and pitted. Silver wings, too, were on his uniform. The Army had few pilots over thirty, but this captain looked to be every bit of that and more. Despite his lazy, slouched posture, he seemed a coil of restless, brittle energy.

'What do you fly?' Marty asked.

'Nothing. Not any more.' Something akin to hatred was in his voice as it turned mocking and bitter. 'You see, I fooled the Army. I survived my fifty missions. When they extended it another ten, I survived that, too. They tried, but they couldn't kill me off. Now they gotta figure out what to do with me.'

'Did you lose your nerve, Captain?' Marty said with disgust.

'Maybe. I don't know.' He lapsed into silence and looked away, seaward.

'What *did* you fly?'

'Why, that great armada ship, the B-17 Flying Fortress.' The declaration was laced with a biting irony. 'They sent waves of them over Axis targets just to see how many of them would come back. We went again and again.'

'Where were you stationed? England?' Mary Lynn's husband was there . . . and Colin. Fate had thrown them together – fate and war. Wouldn't it be something if –

'North Africa in the beginning, flying Liberators, then England.'

'You wouldn't happen to know a B-17 pilot named Beau Palmer –' she began.

'No. Everybody I knew is dead,' he interrupted flatly and coldly. 'And I made it a point not to meet anybody else. It's better if you don't know the name of the pilot flying on your wing.'

His bitter self-pity irked Marty. 'I guess no one knows your name. If you'd died, no one would have missed you.'

'How true,' he agreed, unscathed by her attempt to

338

wound. 'Here comes your friend. I'm sure he's missed your cheerful company.'

'I'm sure you won't mind if I leave you to yours. You seem to love it so much.' She swept out of the lounge chair to rejoin Lieutenant Daniels emerging from the hotel with a pair of beer bottles in his hand.

When she joined him, he noticed the man in the shadows and asked, 'Who's he?'

'Some pilot' – the scorn was in her voice – 'who has lost his nerve.'

'I heard of a bomber pilot back from England who couldn't stand the sound of a car riding over the joints in the highway.' The lieutenant passed her a bottle of beer. 'The thumping reminded him of flak.'

Weary and nerve-torn, Cappy Hayward mounted the steps to the nurses' barracks. She'd flown for hours over cloud hills, guided solely by her instruments, not seeing the ground until she'd broken through the solid murk upon entering the traffic pattern for Bolling Field. To make matters worse, she had a nervous passenger aboard who constantly questioned her ability to find the field.

The strain of gritting her teeth and smiling thinly at his implied insults had knotted the muscles in her shoulders and neck. Not once had she said anything that smacked of insubordination, although she had been tempted on countless occasions to inform the oft-decorated colonel what he could do with the airplane and precisely where.

As Cappy entered the barracks, she was hailed by one of the nurses. 'Hayward.' She waited for Cappy to turn in acknowledgment. 'There's someone waiting for you in your room. She said she knew you. The two of you had trained together or something. I thought it would be all right if she waited for you there.'

'Thanks.' Puzzled and wondering if it could be Eden en route on some ferrying assignment, Cappy shook off some of her tiredness to walk quickly to her room.

As she opened the door, she spied the long-legged girl in the improvised WASP uniform with a mop of mussed, sandy curls in their typically shorn and carefree style. It was funny, but Marty Rogers was the last one of their group she had expected to see. Marty was sitting on her cot, her legs outstretched and her back propped on the pillows Cappy had stacked against the wall to give the room a homey touch. Smoke spiraled from the cigarette Marty held between her fingers.

'Surprised?' Marty mocked Cappy's slightly wide-eyed expression.

No demonstration of affection was expected. After a small hesitation, Cappy walked the rest of the way into the room and shut the door to shrug out of her battle jacket.

'Yes,' she admitted as she gave the leather jacket a toss and reached for her own pack of cigarettes. 'What brings you here? I thought you were basking in the Florida sunshine and flying all over those blue Gulf waters in a Fortress.'

'I was.'

The use of the past tense seemed significant. Cappy picked up the altering of pitch, the faint emphasis on the verb.

'Was?' she repeated in a prompting fashion.

'I've just been raked over the proverbial coals,' Marty replied on a scornful breath. 'They've pulled me out of the heavy bombers. I was lucky, though.' She shrugged. 'They damned near threw me out of the WASPs.'

'For what?'

'The Army pilot I was seeing happened to be married.' She swung her legs off the bed and turned to sit on the edge, her hands on the side of the cot.

'How'd they find out?'

'Scott was a fool. He wrote his wife a Dear Jane letter.' Her mouth curved wryly. 'She, of course, fired off a nasty note to the commander about this bitch who's stolen her husband.'

'That's tough.' Cappy was distantly sympathetic. 'So where to now?'

'I've been demoted to the ferrying division. Every cloud has a silver lining, though. I'm being sent to Long Beach, so I'll probably hook up with Mary Lynn and Eden. It'll be almost like old times.'

'Be sure to say hi for me, will you?' Cappy said, reaching for the ashtray that held the lipstick-stained butt of Marty's cigarette.

'I didn't come just to chat,' Marty stated, and met Cappy's questioning glance. 'I need a favor. You were always the one who knew everything. I figured you could help me.'

'With what?'

'You know a lot of people in town. Maybe you can give me the name of someone to contact to arrange an abortion. On top of everything else, I'm pregnant.'

After the first shock had receded, Cappy breathed out a troubled sigh and frowned. 'Are you sure that's what you want?'

'I want to fly. I've always wanted to fly,' Marty retorted grimly. 'What would I do with a kid? Hell, the father is already married. And even if he was free, I wouldn't want to marry him. So what's the alternative? If they find out I'm pregnant, I'm washed out.'

The olive-gray eyes remained steady, not a glimmer of doubt on their calm surface. Still, Cappy hesitated, not liking any of this, yet feeling a loyalty to her former baymate.

'How soon? How much time before you have to report to California?' she asked finally.

'Counting travel time, I've got three days.'

Cappy pulled in a breath and held it before letting it out slowly. 'That isn't much.' She cast another look at Marty. 'You are sure this is what you want?'

'I'm sure.'

Cappy nodded. 'Okay. There's an empty room down the hall. I'll arrange for you to stay here while I see what

341

I can do.' She paused. 'Just about anything is available in Washington, legal or not – moral or not.'

Being brought up in the Army included lessons in rumor. Cappy had learned well how to piece them together. Someone hinted this; another whispered that; this one suspected another thing; and that one heard something else. Things that weren't discussed and things that were – they were part of knowing what went on and pretending otherwise.

Between the confidences of a few discreet Army nurses and contacts in the ocean of Washington typists, Cappy got the name and address of a reputable abortionist – in her opinion, almost a contradiction in terms. Marty made her own contact.

When the time came to keep the appointment, Cappy couldn't let her go alone. Whether she liked it or not, she had become involved in this and she had to see it through to its conclusion. Marty didn't argue; with or without Cappy, she was going through with it.

Expecting the worst, Cappy was surprised when the address didn't take them into the slums which covered nearly half of the city, occupied mainly by Negroes. There, it was said, among the dreadful 'alley houses' where several families sometimes lived in a single room, gangs of seven- and eight-year-old boys roamed the streets armed with knives, and girls barely into their puberty were prostitutes on the corners.

The address was in an old neighborhood of the city, the back office atop a two-story building housing a pharmacy at the street level. Paint and plaster were peeling off the walls of the narrow, steep stairwell. Marty paused at the bottom of the steps and looked up.

'This is melodramatic as hell,' she muttered dryly and resolutely started up the stairs. Cappy followed, her lips pressed firmly together.

The frosted glass door on the right of the second-floor hallway was identified only by a number. Marty tried the knob and it turned under her hand. The air had a musty, closed-in smell, faintly tainted by an antiseptic odor. The small anteroom was devoid of furniture except for a standing ashtray by the inner door, but it was clean.

A soft scuffle of sound came from the adjoining room. The door was opened by a chocolate-dark Negro in a white starched jacket. There was a scrubbed look about him. His neatly trimmed hair was gray, and wire glasses sat smartly on his nose. Almost absently, Cappy noticed his shoes squeaked when he walked, a disconcerting sound.

'May I help you?' he said.

'I'm Miss Smith.' Marty calmly stepped forward.

'Of course.' The name mattered not – to either of them. He moved out of the doorway. 'Would you like to come in?'

'I'd like to go with her,' Cappy asserted, stepping to Marty's side.

The black gentleman hesitated, then politely inclined his head, granting permission. 'It isn't necessary, but you may observe if you wish.' His inflection betrayed an education, although a trace of southern accent remained.

The inner room was larger. At first, it appeared to be a storeroom for pharmaceutical supplies. However, behind the shelves and bins was a long table, standing beneath a bright ceiling light. The strong medicinal smells in the air were almost overpowering. A lighter-skinned Negro woman in a long white smock was standing by the table, of an age to be the man's wife or sister, her face unlined but her hair salty gray.

Modesty and dignity had little chance in this room. Outwardly, Marty appeared very casual, disrobing and climbing onto the table without a trace of awkwardness. Cappy couldn't tell what she was really feeling – remorse, fear, loneliness – and she did not want to know.

The black abortionist allowed Cappy to stand by the table and hold Marty's hand, more for her own moral support, since Marty didn't seem to need any. She kept her gaze fixed on Marty's face. She didn't want to know what those pink-palmed hands were doing between Marty's legs.

The minutes trickled by like slow-running grains of sand. She shut out the sound of half-muffled voices speaking in the shorthand of a close-working team. She felt hot.

When the white-smocked woman moved away from the table, Cappy glanced after her. Her gaze fell on the bloody placenta-covered embryo in the basin the woman carried, unrecognizable as anything human. She was shaken by the sight of it, and tried not to let it show.

The whole experience took on the hazy quality of a dream, something that really wasn't happening to her. When Marty came around, weakened more by the effects of the anesthesia than the operation, Cappy helped her out of the barren rooms and down the steep, narrow-walled staircase to the capital streets.

Back at the nurses' quarters, Marty lay down to rest and sleep off the drugs lingering in her system. Rid of her unwanted burden, she was almost back to her old, brassy self. 'You didn't really approve of all this, did you, Cappy?' she asked as she settled back onto the cot. 'I don't have any regrets. Why should you?'

Cappy left her without answering and went to sit in the large living room she shared with the nurses. She shouldn't have let it touch her, but it had gotten through the barriers. Somewhere there was someone to blame. Marty. The married officer who had impregnated her. The Army for its damned discriminatory system. Little unborn babies. At the disjointed connection, Cappy pressed her hands against her eyes.

Although oddly detached from her surroundings, Cappy vaguely knew others were around, moving, talking. Someone approached, invading that invisible sensory circle that enveloped her body. As she started to lower her hands, someone touched her shoulder. She looked around with a start, wanting to be alone and not welcoming company.

With a hitch of his trousers, Mitch folded his length onto the chair next to hers and leaned toward her. His look was warm, yet probing.

'Hi. Are you all right?'

Something close to anger or impatience flashed in the blue glitter of her eyes. She pushed to her feet before he could see more.

'I'm fine,' she insisted.

Mitch came slowly to his feet to stand next to her, studying her with closer interest and observing the unconscious toss of her head as she turned to look at him. Her temper was set against him, resisting him and wanting no part of him to intrude.

'What do you want? What are you doing here?' The words were a challenge.

But Mitch didn't respond to it. He had learned that that wasn't the way to handle her. 'Have you forgotten? We were to have dinner together tonight.'

Cappy dropped her gaze. 'I'm sorry. I did forget.' But there was more impatience than regret in her voice.

It stung him. 'Thanks,' he said, mocking her absence of artifice, then switched. As hard to fathom as she could be at times, this was not like her. 'What's wrong, Cap?' Before she could deny anything, he went on. 'Before I came out here, I called to make sure you were back from your flight. I was told you had switched with another pilot who was off duty. What's going on?'

'Nothing. A friend of mine – Marty Rogers, a girl I roomed with in Sweetwater – she had a couple days' leave and came by to visit.'

'In that case, I'll take you both out to dinner tonight,' Mitch offered.

'I don't think so.' She avoided his eyes. 'Marty's lying down. She wasn't feeling well.'

Something told Mitch he was close to the source of concern that preoccupied Cappy. He watched her, wondering what it was she held from him.

Someone swung into his side vision, drawing his glance. One look at the long, slim woman striding toward them and it clicked with a memory in his head. The name Marty Rogers hadn't meant anything to him until he saw the fair-haired woman with the lively face and those glittering gray-green eyes. No man could forget that earthy zest, that lusty sexuality that was refreshingly honest – and therefore somehow right.

'Hello. Major Ryan, this is a treat,' Marty declared in her throaty voice. 'Remember me? Marty Rogers from Sweetwater.'

'Of course.' Mitch clasped her hand and let his glance slide once again to Cappy. 'I had understood you weren't feeling well.'

There was a quick meeting of glances between the two young women, then Marty was declaring, hardly missing a beat, 'Whatever it was, I got rid of it. Now I need something to eat to get my strength back. Why don't we all have dinner together – and celebrate the occasion?'

'That's just what I suggested earlier.' He turned to Cappy, curious to see her reaction.

Her lips were red and full at the center, pressed firmly together in an expression of grim displeasure. Mitch was surprised to see a half-veiled dislike shimmering in the look she gave her friend. His own gaze narrowed, but when Cappy saw him watching her, she quickly wiped all expression from her face.

'If you feel up to it, we'll go,' she said to Marty, but something ran under the surface of her words, something pointed and hard.

'I never let little things bother me very much,' Marty answered. 'It's better than going through life like you do, always on guard against the slightest hurt and never living at all.'

Mitch was amused by the little flashing of claws between them, the little bitchiness. He glanced over at Cappy, and saw her consider the observation Marty had made, wondering at its accuracy.

'It'll take me a few minutes to get ready, then we can go,' Cappy said.

As she walked away from them, Cappy came close to hating Marty. It was one thing, she felt, to accept the abortion as the only recourse open to her, but it was

346

entirely another to be jubilant about the outcome. Cappy was disgusted by Marty's desire to celebrate. She couldn't understand that kind of callous indifference.

But Cappy was too caught up in the pullings and tuggings of her own ambivalent attitude to see the brittleness underlying Marty's ostensibly high spirits. The deed was done and though Marty was never one to look back with regret, she couldn't wipe away her sense of loss. Yet it was not so much grief Marty felt as failure. Marty had looked at herself and seen that she could never live up to her image of an ideal woman, the faithful wife, the adoring mother, and the happy homemaker. She had been born without the nesting instinct.

But she recognized it in others, just as she recognized all the moves of the mating ritual, the life coupling between male and female. During dinner, Marty saw the signs of it between Mitch and Cappy, the courting passes he made, the attempts to attract her interest, and the blind eye Cappy turned to all of them, the elusive way she kept slipping from him.

Something went wrong with the evening; Marty could feel it even while she laughed too loudly, drank too much, and flirted too often with the handsome major. In a way, she did it to rile Cappy – out of jealousy maybe, because she had what Marty didn't. But Cappy simply turned moody and quiet, withdrawing behind that self-sufficient pose of hers. And Mitch – Marty could almost feel sorry for him. He appeared to be losing ground with Cappy instead of making headway.

'Thanks for the evening, Major,' Marty said when he escorted the two of them back to the barracks. 'My train ticket's taking me out of here in the morning so I won't see you again before I leave. I'll say goodbye now and leave you alone with Cappy to . . . have your good nights.'

His brown eyes were faintly gleaming, thanking her for the moments he'd have with the silent brunette. The night air was briskly cool, but Marty didn't think he'd notice.

She'd known too many men not to recognize those urges, disciplined though they were for the time being. The major was a strong, handsome man, potently combining an easy charm with a shrewd intelligence. If she didn't owe Cappy something, she might have thrown up some competition for him.

'I'm glad you felt well enough to join us,' Mitch said graciously, then sent a puzzled glance at Cappy when she visibly stiffened.

'Old "button-lip" will never tell you, Major, but I think you should know the reason I was feeling "indisposed" earlier. I had an abortion,' Marty announced carelessly. 'A man and a woman shouldn't have secrets between them. And there's no need for you to wonder whether Cappy was lying to you earlier when she said I was sick and how I happened to have such a miraculous recovery.' There was a certain wryness, a self-mockery almost, in her voice. The confession was a way of repaying the debt she owed Cappy by eliminating any possible mistrust. 'Goodbye, Major.' With her good deed done, Marty left them and entered the barracks building.

At Marty's announcement, Mitch had gone rigid. When the door shut, his words exploded in a low rush.

'My God, you let her?' he said accusingly.

'I arranged it!' Cappy snapped, his fire striking her flint. Somehow she had known how he would react. 'She came to me. What was I supposed to do?'

'You could have refused,' Mitch replied stiffly.

'And have her wind up in the hands of some butcher?' she challenged in a taut, hurt voice. 'She was my friend. She didn't want the baby. What was I supposed to suggest? Using knitting needles or inhaling paint fumes?' Impatient, she looked away from him. 'What do men know about it? It isn't your life and it isn't your body. Most of the time, you don't even want to claim it's your responsibility. You take the Army's attitude – if the girl gets pregnant, tough. You know what would have happened if they had found out she was going to have a baby. They would have grounded her, or washed her out altogether because she wasn't married.'

'Does flying mean more than the life of an unborn baby?'

'To some it does,' Cappy flared.

His hands caught her shoulders and swung her around to face him squarely. 'To you?' His dark gaze burrowed into her.

Her glance fell, ever so slightly. 'No.' She couldn't do what Marty had done; that wouldn't have been her choice.

'I knew it.' The low, exultant words rushed out of him, vibrant with satisfaction.

The press of his hands brought her into his circling arms while his mouth came down to cover hers. The hot, fierce urgency of his kiss was consuming, firing her skin with its heat and pressuring a response that would match the fever of his needs.

When he drew back, his breath spilled in a moist, hot wave over her face and his restless, needing gaze went over every feature. 'I love you, Cap.' His voice vibrated in his throat. 'I've always loved you.' He stroked her hair with a trembling hand, smoothing the dark silk strands and touching its softness. 'I want to marry you, Cap. I want you to be my wife.'

The words ran coldly through her system, and a rejection of all he offered erased the inroads he had made on her will. Her hands pushed at his chest.

'No.' It was a choked refusal, too much pain lodging in her throat.

Mitch didn't believe her protestations after tasting her willingness and her answering passion. Instead, he read another reason into her denial and attempted to assuage it.

'I'm not saying we should get married right away,' he murmured, not letting her go, and continuing to let his hands roam while he held her. 'I know how you feel about the war and the future uncertainty. We'll wait until it's over to have the wedding. In the meantime, though, I want you to be wearing my ring. I –'

'No!' Her hands hit at his chest, surprising him with her violence, and his arms loosened around her. Cappy pushed free, twisting angrily out of his hold. 'I won't marry you – not now and certainly not later! I wouldn't marry you if you were the only man on earth!!'

Stunned, Mitch stared at her, his brows pulling together in a frown. 'What are you talking about? You don't mean that.'

'I do,' she insisted, breathing hard from the great pain in her chest. 'I won't ever marry you, Mitch.'

'Why?' Beneath the growl of his voice was an anguished demand.

'If I marry you, it means I marry the Army – and I'll die before I do that.' The words were wrenched from her, as tortured in their anger as his. 'I was an Army brat – never having a home or friends – and I swore I'd never be an Army wife. And I won't! If you want me . . . if you love me . . . you'll quit the Army.'

'There's a war –' Mitch began angrily.

'After the war!' she hurled back at him.

Silence pressed on them, the late winter chill finally touching them. His lips came together in a long, firm line as Mitch grimly eyed her. Cappy had known the answer to her ultimatum the minute she made it. Looking at him now, she didn't even need his words to confirm it.

'You can't ask a man to give up his career and think you'll be happy together.'

'You can't ask a woman to live a life she despises,' she countered in a rasping tone.

'Dammit, Cappy,' Mitch swore, his head turning away to hide the stinging in his eyes. 'I love you.'

'Not as much as you love the Army.'

'You've gone all right by the Army,' he flared. 'It's been good to you.'

'The Army has never given me anything. I've earned everything I've got.' The cool temperature turned her moist breath into puffs of smoky vapor, trailing exclamation marks that punctuated her words.

'You're wrong,' Mitch stated flatly. 'This job – this plum of flying assignments – you never earned it.'

'But . . . you told me that my father had nothing to do with it,' Cappy reminded him with a narrowed, suspicious look.

'He didn't. I did the string-pulling.' His strong, lean jaw didn't let the words out. He pushed them through his teeth, his lip curling back as Mitch roughly spoke them. 'I wanted you close at hand . . . where I could see you.'

'That was your mistake, Mitch,' she said. 'But I'll see if I can't correct it for you.'

CHAPTER TWENTY-FOUR

The southern California air shimmered with the silken distortions of a heat wave. Fresh from a flight in a fast and powerful P-47 pursuit, Mary Lynn was still trapped in the exhilarating spell of the hottest plane around. When she recognized Marty standing on the sun-warmed concrete of the flight apron, she thought it was a mirage.

A second later, she knew better, and broke into a running walk. 'I don't believe it! What are you doing here?' she cried in delight.

Between the hugs and laughter, the how-are-yous and I'm-fines, Marty gave her a rough synopsis of how she came to leave the four-engines, toning it down some and making it more of a lark and a misunderstanding so she wouldn't be placed in such a bad light. 'So I got my hands slapped and sent out here.'

'He was married?' That part troubled Mary Lynn, although she was loath to be critical of Marty.

'Hey, Scott and I were friends,' Marty insisted, deliberately implying her innocence. 'They made a big deal out of it.' By mutual accord, they left the flight line to seek the shady interior of the operations building. 'I saw Cappy while I was in DC,' Marty volunteered, but she left out any mention of the abortion.

'How was she?'

'Fine. She hasn't changed much.' Marty shrugged. 'She still walks around life rather than reaching out to embrace it. I guess that's why she flies – to soar above all of life's problems into an aesthetically pure sky.' Marty the astute.

'Don't we all,' Mary Lynn murmured.

'Not me.' Marty dropped a coin into the Coke machine and listened to the tumbling jangle as it tripped the lever and fell into the money box. 'You can bet I wouldn't let that major of hers walk around hungry if he were mine.'

Mary Lynn shied away from any speculation about Cappy's personal relationships. There was too big a hole in her own life. It had been too long since she'd had a man's company. Some nights, she felt the lonely ache for it, a need shared by thousands of other wives across the country whose husbands had gone to war – the simple yearning to feel a man's touch and once more to have the warmth of his body in the bed. With a faint shake of her head, she tried to dismiss such thoughts.

'Is Eden around?' Marty passed her a Coke bottle and turned back to the machine to get another for herself.

'No. She left a couple days ago to deliver a P-38 to Newark. It's anybody's guess when she'll be back. You don't always get orders to ferry another plane back. Usually it's some round-robin jaunt, dropping off planes in Farmington, Indiana, or Great Falls, or Dallas, and picking up new ones. If you're really unlucky,' Mary Lynn added, 'you catch a train back.'

'The glamorous life of a ferry pilot,' Marty remarked wryly, and she lifted the Coke bottle to her lips.

They drifted away from the machine, paying little attention to the other pilots and base personnel in the ready room. Some pored over tech manuals or cross-country maps, and others were simply winding down from the final leg of a return flight. The place was busy; it was a major

352

clearing house for one of the largest domestic ferrying divisions and soon to be home for the largest contingent of women pilots in the country.

'I won't be staying long this trip myself,' Marty said. A wry gleam was in her gray-green eyes as she met the questioning look Mary Lynn gave her. 'It's one of the Army's usual boners. They've got me – a multiengine-rated pilot with heavy bomber experience – and they're sending me to Palm Springs for pursuit training.'

'P-47 Thunderbolts and P-51 Mustangs are going out of here like crazy.' The demand for qualified pilots to fly the hot pursuits was a sufficient explanation for Mary Lynn. 'Wait until you fly one of them. There's only room for one pilot in the Thunderbolt – so your first flight is solo. But you'll love it.' She beamed with the fierce joy that came from sitting at the controls. 'In most of the planes we've flown, a hundred, a hundred ten miles an hour was a good speed. The P-47 *stalls* at a hundred and five.'

'Yeah, they say bomber pilots need a lot of guts, stamina, and leadership ability, and the fighter pilots are lone wolves – daredevils. I've heard that when they check a pilot out in a pursuit, they fail him if he can count to ten because he thinks too hard.' Smiling at her own joke, Marty glanced at a dark-haired woman walking by, dressed in gray-green slacks and a light gray shirt. She nudged Mary Lynn with her elbow and nodded in the direction of the female pilot in the unusual uniform. 'Who is she?'

'A WAF, part of Nancy Love's group before we were all brought under the umbrella of the Women Airforce Service Pilots.' The WAFs were an elite group of experienced female pilots, former aircraft instructors, racing pilots, or barnstormers, who were incorporated almost directly into the Air Transport Command as a separate ferrying squadron at the outset. 'They have their own uniforms.'

'I wonder when we're ever going to get ours,' Marty sighed. Mary Lynn tipped her head to the side and rubbed at the knotted muscles in her neck. Her glance skipped

353

past the nearest group of pilots, hangar-flying around a table, and fell haphazardly on a man lazing in a corner of the ready room. One leg was stretched across the width of a chair seat while his other foot hooked the side rung to act as a ballast as he rocked his own chair onto its back legs. He was a study of indolence, with his officer's cap sitting sideways on his head, the bill dipping over one eye.

Something about him – that lazy attitude or the rake of the hat on his head – for a split second reminded Mary Lynn of Beau. But the resemblance ended there. He looked every bit of thirty or older; his face was lined, and his skin was pitted and unnaturally scarred. That hint of a smile on his mouth seemed infected with a hard, cruel humor, and insinuating interest glittered in his dark eyes.

His gaze was boldly traveling the full length of her body and taking note of every curve along the way. She looked away, her heart striking quick, small beats. Amidst all the talking voices and walking footsteps, she heard the sound of the chair coming down on all four legs.

Soon, a drawling male voice said, 'What's a little thing like you doing here?' Mary Lynn didn't turn when Marty looked around, but she was aware of the slow-moving man drifting toward them. 'Don't tell me you're flying those big, bad planes out there.'

It was a deliberately condescending remark, designed to elicit a response. 'Are you talking to me?' Mary Lynn gave him a falsely blank look.

'No one else,' he said lazily.

Marty's gaze narrowed on him, conscious that Mary Lynn was the focus of his attention. She took note of the captain's bars on his uniform. She was almost certain she'd seen him somewhere before.

'Don't I know you?' Marty frowned.

His dark glance skimmed her once and dismissed her. 'No.' His interest centered again on Mary Lynn as he pushed the officer's cap to the back of his head. Thick, unruly hair, the color of Army coffee, strayed onto his forehead. 'What do you say, Little One?'

From the first, something had told Marty this man was trouble in capital letters, and the obvious play he was making for Mary Lynn merely confirmed it. Her dislike of the man was instinctive as Marty observed the stiff and agitated way Mary Lynn avoided the man's look. Marrying young, and to her childhood sweetheart, it wasn't likely Mary Lynn had come across many wolves like this one.

'You're a little off base, Captain,' Marty informed him.

'Walker. Captain Samuel Jamieson Walker.' He introduced himself with a mock bow to Mary Lynn. 'But you can just call me Walker.'

'She's married.' Marty bridled.

'Is that right?' He seemed amused by the discovery rather than put off by it. 'I promise I won't hold that against you over dinner tonight.'

'Dinner?' The word broke from Mary Lynn in surprise.

'I told you she wasn't interested, Captain,' Marty interposed in a cold and naturally husky voice.

'Does she always do your talking, Little One?' he mocked. 'Or don't you have a tongue? Now, that would be a pity.'

'Please.' Mary Lynn felt hot all over, an anger flashing at his continued impudence. 'I am married so I'm not interested.'

'A pretty little wife,' he marveled. Lifting her chin with the tip of his finger, he continued, 'Would you just look at all that goodness shining out of her?'

His eyes admired what his tongue mocked. But there was something bitter behind his taunting humor, and Mary Lynn jerked away from his touch, hurt and bewildered by his behavior. Marty was instantly at her side, aggressively shielding her.

'Why don't you pick on somebody your own size, Captain,' she challenged.

Those hard, laughing eyes skimmed Marty, testing, probing, measuring; then he was shrugging. 'It isn't as much fun,' he said, backing away while Marty glared at

355

him. She had the feeling he was just biding his time until he saw another opening.

'Come on. Let's get out of here,' she said under her breath to Mary Lynn and both of them headed out of the ready room.

Still dressed in his full military regalia, medals and ribbons pinned to his jacket breast, the AAF Commanding General 'Hap' Arnold sat behind his big wooden desk, pushed back in his large chair. The meeting with the House Committee on Military Affairs on Capitol Hill had not gone as smoothly as he had expected.

March was on its way out, but it was an irritated lion who was rumbling over the opposition he'd encountered from the congressional committee over the proposed bill to militarize the WASPs, as had been done with the WACs, and the WAVES the year before. The bill had been presented to Congress in February. In the past, anything the Commanding General had wanted for the war effort had been routinely approved.

'They didn't ask me a half-dozen questions about the WASPs,' the general snorted. 'Typical Congress, there were only two things they were concerned about – whether the women were paid and if they flew in combat situations. I explained again that they were not being used in war zones – that they were replacing men in domestic operations to free them for combat roles. That was all they needed to hear, they said. Then they started asking me questions about the shutdown of all the primary cadet flying schools we closed in January.'

In quick, sharp taps, Mitch Ryan hit his cigarette on the hard surface of the chair arm, tamping the tobacco and releasing some of his held-in anger at the subject matter under discussion. Women pilots were a sore topic with him, heart-sensitive as he was to anything that reminded him of Cappy.

Two weeks ago, one of the staff personnel from that department had called him aside and advised him that Cappy had put in a request for a transfer. It would have been a simple matter to block it, as he had maneuvered other things in the past. This time he hadn't stepped in, leaving it to be granted or turned down by someone else. With a certain fatalism, he felt whichever way the cards fell would be a sign, an indication of whether things could ever be worked out between them or not.

When Mitch had learned the request had gone through, he had gritted his teeth so no one would know how much it mattered. But it ground at him, turning him bitter and angry.

'We all knew there'd be some heat from those civilian pilots,' he replied in response to the general's previous statement. Roughly fourteen thousand men, instructors and trainees, had lost their jobs and their draft-deferred status. They were being called to active duty and assigned ground jobs.

'Yes. And those that qualify are being signed up as pilots. But I'll be damned if I'll lower the physical and intellectual standards of our pilots for them. It seems strange to me that now that these pilots have lost their safe, noncombat instructor's jobs, they are suddenly clamoring for the more dangerous assignments the WASPs have undertaken – like towing targets and testing planes coming out of the repair depots.' The general did not think much of these grousing Johnny-come-latelies, and it showed. 'Look at the morale problems we had with the male pilots over the B-26. They were half scared to fly the damned "Flying prostitute" until the women climbed into the cockpits and showed them how it was done. Hell, my own son's unit would never have qualified for an overseas assignment if a WASP hadn't willingly towed targets for the rough-terrain practice. The male pilots at Camp Irwin refused to do it.'

'Yes, sir. I know,' Mitch responded dutifully.

Rough-terrain maneuvers required armored vehicles, called half-tracks, to tear across open country at forty miles an hour while the gunners operating the fifty-caliber guns mounted on its back shot at an aerial target. With all the bumps, dips and gulleys it was invariably a wild ride, and the shooting was often equally wild until the gunners got the hang of it.

'Dammit, those girls are entitled to the same privileges and benefits the Army pilots receive,' General Arnold insisted impatiently. 'The committee says it's going to recommend passage, but we haven't heard the last of those pilots, I'm afraid.'

'I doubt that we have.' He rolled the burning tip of the cigarette around the inside rim of an ashtray, watching the paper-thin flakes of gray ash fall off.

'The whole complexion of the war is changing.' The chair creaked under the movement of his solid weight as General Arnold shifted to sit with shoulders squared. 'We're on the move. Those boys are off the Anzio beachhead and pounding their way to Rome. Our air raids have crippled their aircraft industry and we can start concentrating on the Germans' transportation and oil refineries. And the airfields in France. Britain is bulging with troops for Ike's Overlord operation. We not only have to soften the bastards up, but we've got to give air cover for our guys when they go in.'

'I've been wanting to talk to you about that, sir.' Mitch crushed out his cigarette and grimly faced his general. 'With the big push on . . . I want to be part of it. I want to be there when it happens, not . . . tucked away in some damned office. I want a transfer, sir.'

'The hell you do.' The challenging response was flattened by a kind of offhandedness. 'I doubt if you're alone in that.'

'You're going to need good pilots, qualified men to make these strikes. I've seen some of the estimates of losses for these planned raids on the oil refineries in Rumania, Hamburg, and the Ruhr,' Mitch argued.

'A soldier serves his country best where he's needed. And you are needed here. Transfer denied,' the general snapped impatiently. 'You surprise me, Mitch. I never expected you to stoop to such unprofessional heroics. You know damned well you've got a job to do here – a damned important one. I'll be the first to admit there isn't much glory in pushing papers around, but it has to be done.'

'Yes, sir.' Mitch grudgingly gave in, not liking it and not trying to hide it.

'I don't want to hear any more talk about transfers.' The general picked up a sheaf of papers on his desk and began glancing through them, muttering his displeasure under his breath. 'Grandstand play. Anybody'd think some gal singed your feelings.' He stopped to peer at Mitch. 'Haven't seen that Hayward girl with you in a while.'

'No, sir,' he admitted. 'It seems she doesn't like the Army.'

'It's probably just as well.' 'Hap' Arnold looked back at the papers. 'After today, I'm afraid it's going to be a fight to get her . . . and the rest of the women pilots . . . into the Army Air Force.'

Mary Lynn's orders instructed her to deliver the spanking new P-47 Thunderbolt to the Embarkation Center in Newark, but such flights in planes fresh off the assembly lines were seldom routine. There always seemed to be a few bugs in them somewhere and Mary Lynn found a problem in the flaps' hydraulic system which forced her to land in Tulsa.

While the Thunderbolt went to the hangar for repairs, Mary Lynn was given a new set of orders to deliver a P-39 Aircobra to Great Falls, Montana, a staging base for planes bound for Alaska, Russian lend-lease fighters. From Great Falls it was a PT-19 to Nevada, and a hop over the Sierra Mountains in a P-51 Mustang. In all, her two-day trip turned into four, ferrying four planes and covering approximately three thousand miles.

She had barely set foot inside the WASPs' barracks at Long Beach when Eden grabbed her. 'Come on. I've got something to show you.'

'What did you buy this time?' Mary Lynn assumed she had indulged in another one of her wild shopping sprees, almost a regular event since they'd been stationed in Los Angeles.

But Eden merely laughed and pushed Mary Lynn into her room, where she told her to sit on the cot. Then Eden darted to the door of her own room, an impishly gleeful light in her dark eyes. A tired smile lifted the corners of her mouth as Mary Lynn shook her head and leaned against the wall to wait for the expected fashion parade.

The door opened and Eden's voice began intoning, 'And here is Cappy Hayward.' Mary Lynn's heavy-lidded glance went to the doorway as Cappy came into view. Her eyes immediately widened in stunned surprise. 'You will notice she is wearing a belted jacket of wool serge and a matching skirt in fashion's latest color, Santiago blue. The outfit is completed with the deep blue color repeated in the tam she wears. The snowy white blouse provides a contrast to the suit, adorned with silver wings and a gold WASP insignia.'

'What are you doing here? And in our new uniform?' Mary Lynn released a bewildered breath at the sight of Cappy modeling the uniform suit, slowly turning with arms shifting and posing in mock stances.

'Miss van Valkenburg, you will see, is wearing' – Eden continued her mock recital as she swirled into the room, crowding the small floor space – 'slacks and the Eisenhower jacket, a sure choice for high fashion, in Santiago blue.'

The pseudo fashion show fell apart as Mary Lynn scooted off the cot. 'You look gorgeous, Cappy. When did you get here? Did you fly someone here?'

Eden jumped in with the explanation. 'She's been transferred here. Isn't that wonderful? She's been assigned to the Sixth Ferrying Group, too.'

'You're kidding.'

'It's true,' Cappy assured the disbelieving Mary Lynn. 'I'm going to be flying the C-47 Skytrains from the McDonnell Douglas factory to various bases around the country.'

'We're all going to be flying together again,' she marveled. 'Marty said she saw you in Washington so you know she's going to be joining us. She's in Palm Springs right now, finishing the last two weeks of the pursuit course.'

'Yes, I know.' Cappy nodded, but carefully said nothing more.

'I can't believe it.' Mary Lynn shook her head again. 'You're here . . . and our uniforms.'

'Wait until you see the flying suits,' Eden declared and dragged out her regulation jumpsuit, in that same deep blue color that was to become their trademark.

'Did I get mine, too?' Mary Lynn wondered belatedly.

'We picked it up for you,' Eden assured her, then cautioned, 'Don't get too excited though. In case you haven't noticed, we've been issued winter uniforms. Wool . . . in sunny, southern California.' The absurdity of it was obvious. 'Supposedly the summer uniforms are on their way.'

But winter uniforms were better than none at all. For Mary Lynn, just the thought of wearing an outfit measured to fit her small frame was a special bonus. All three of them piled into Mary Lynn's room while she tried on the Army issue of two jackets, a skirt, slacks and flight suits. She had saved one of her shoe ration stamps just for the new uniforms when they came.

Standing in front of the mirror, Mary Lynn studied her reflection, the cut of the deeply blue uniform on her petite frame and the set of the English-style tam on her raven hair. She reached up to touch the silver wings on her lapel, smaller than the regulation pilot wings, and traced the satin-finished silver lozenge in the center that had replaced the shield in the new regulation wings.

'I think I'm going to miss my old wings. They were special,' she said, not really needing to explain to Eden and Cappy. 'They're the ones we started with.'

'I know,' Cappy said with an agreeing look of regret. 'I heard the lozenge is supposed to represent the shield of the Amazons.'

'What does that make us?' Eden retorted. 'Mythical female warriors?'

'I suppose.' Cappy smiled faintly.

Mary Lynn swung away from the mirror. 'Why don't we go celebrate tonight?'

At the Officers' Club that evening they made an occasion of it, dining on the best steaks and ordering wine. No French brands were available so Eden decided they would sample a burgundy from one of the California wineries. Three unescorted females in the male-dominated club created a stir of interest and countless invitations to provide them with male company. But they kept the dinner strictly among the three of them.

'When I was in Great Falls –' Mary Lynn paused to sip cautiously at the after-dinner drink Eden had ordered for her. '– a WASP from the Romulus Base in Michigan was telling me why we aren't allowed to fly the ferry route from Great Falls to Fairbanks, Alaska, and only men can.'

'I always thought they were worried one of us might go down in those frozen wastes and maybe die from exposure.' A perplexed frown drew lines in Cappy's forehead as she eyed Mary Lynn, suddenly suspecting that wasn't the reason.

'So did I,' Mary Lynn agreed. 'But it seems some of the men have been stationed in Alaska for almost two years. They aren't afraid we might get killed flying there. They are worried about what might happen to us . . . on a base with all those men who haven't seen a woman in months.'

Eden laughed. 'It certainly doesn't speak very well of the men stationed there.'

'When I was flying out of Washington,' Cappy inserted, 'I landed at some bases that didn't have nurses' quarters and I stayed in the BOQ with men sleeping in the next bed and only a screen between us.' She shook her head in faint disgust. 'Half the time the Army doesn't make any sense.'

'I'll drink to that,' Eden agreed, and she lifted her glass.

After dinner, they took their celebration into the lounge side of the club. Few tables were empty. When they appeared, officers eager for their company scrambled to

362

pull out chairs. In a laughing eeny-meeny-miney-mo attitude, they picked a table. Once they were seated, the men fell all over themselves to crowd around it.

Except one, Mary Lynn realized, as she recognized that hardened captain sitting on the edge of the circle and watching the other officers with a detached amusement. Then his lazy, half-lidded glance swung to her.

'Celebrating?' The small slur in his voice led Mary Lynn to suspect the drink in his hand was not the first of the evening.

'Is that why you're here, Captain?' she returned instead.

'I'm always here – from the time they open to the time they close.' He looked at Mary Lynn. 'Whatever possessed your husband to let you out of his sight, Little One? If you were mine, I'd keep you under lock and key.'

Few were so boldly disrespectful of her marital status. Mary Lynn avoided more than fleeting contact with his glance, unsure whether she should be offended or flattered by the attention he gave her.

'That would be difficult, since he flies B-17s in the Eighth Air Force.' She took a cigarette from the pack on the table.

Before she could strike a match to light it, a flame was in front of her, the match held between Walker's fingers. It wavered slightly, and Mary Lynn steadied his hand with her own. The rough texture of a man's hand was a sensation she'd almost forgotten.

'Your husband's a pilot with the Eighth? Where?' He watched the release of smoke from her lips.

'In England.'

'Whereabouts? I was stationed over there, too. Maybe I know him.' He leaned back in his chair, a complacent smile tugging at the corners of his mouth, fully aware of the carrot he dangled.

'In the Cotswold area – somewhere near Gloucestershire, I think.' Beau had never been able to give her too much specific information as to the location or the censors

363

wouldn't pass the letter. Mary Lynn eyed Walker, hardly daring hope he might know Beau.

'Well, isn't that a coincidence,' he murmured.

'You were there?'

'For a while.' His half-smile became more pronounced, containing considerably less humor and warmth. 'But I fooled the Army and survived all those missions over Germany.'

That hard, embittered statement explained some things Mary Lynn hadn't understood. Those lines in his face and the cynicism in his eyes were products of that combat experience. It had given him those silver strands in his dark hair and made him old – and hard – beyond his years.

As she gazed at him, she wondered if Beau would come home to her like this. She felt a cold chill raise her flesh and absently rubbed a hand over her upper arm to rid herself of the sensation. She shook away the unpleasant thought and leaned forward, going for the long shot.

'Did you know him? My husband – Beau Palmer.' The cigarette was left to burn itself out in the ashtray as her earnest gaze watched him.

'The first time I saw you, you looked familiar to me.' Walker let his gaze wander over her face, lingering on each feature. 'I'll bet I've seen a picture of you. He probably has one, doesn't he?'

'Yes. It was taken on the beach. He has it in the cockpit.'

'That's it,' Walker said with a snap of his fingers. The music playing in the background changed tempo as the band, consisting of soldier-musicians from the base, began a slow tune. Taking her by the hand, he urged Mary Lynn to her feet. 'Let's dance.'

His hand at the small of her back guided Mary Lynn through the maze of tables to the dance floor. A thousand questions about Beau raced through her mind as she turned into Walker's arms.

'How long has it been since you've seen him? How did he look?' She paused at the amused expression on his face and realized she was starting to rattle like an excited child.

'I suppose I sound silly to you, Captain. But you don't know how happy it makes me to meet someone who's talked to Beau.'

'Let's drop the Captain and call me Walker,' he suggested while his arm curved around her lower back, molding her hip to thigh. 'And you don't know how happy this makes me.' That small smile on his mouth suggested many things, none of them related to her husband.

Mary Lynn had a moment of unease as he bent his head and carried the sensitive ends of her fingers to his lips. 'How was he?' She raised the subject of Beau again.

'Fine, as far as I know.' His knowing eyes watched the growing disturbance in her expression with a certain satisfaction. He continued his absent nibbling of her fingertips. 'That photograph didn't do you justice, Little One.'

Beyond a token shifting of feet, he was barely moving to the music. The smell of rum was strong on his breath. Mary Lynn blamed his behavior on the considerable quantity of alcohol he had consumed.

'About Beau –' she tried again.

'What about him?' Walker turned her hand palm upward and investigated the center with a nuzzling mouth.

The sensuous action prompted a little quiver of pleasure to run down her nerve ends. At the traitorous reaction, Mary Lynn strained to draw her hand down. Walker lifted his head at her show of resistance.

'Sorry.' But he didn't sound sorry. 'I got carried away. It's easy with a little thing like you in my arms.'

She chose to ignore his remarks. 'Tell me about Beau.'

His attention drifted from her in a bored fashion. 'What do you want to hear?'

'Anything. Everything.' It was difficult to be specific when any detail would suffice, any piece of Beau's life held importance, anything that would make where he was and what he was doing seem real to her. 'What's it like over there?' Mary Lynn meant England, the air base, the barracks – the place where he lived.

But Walker put another construction on the question

and his expression turned cold and forbidding. 'What's any war like?' he challenged harshly. 'It's about killing and dying. It's faceless enemies shooting at you, and bombs dropping on faceless victims. It's a living hell.'

Up close, she could see the graveled marks that scarred his face, recent wounds in a random pattern, like splintering glass or metal. She tried not to think how it might have happened, but a kind of terror clutched her throat. Her mind recoiled from the kind of war-horror Walker's words depicted in favor of the glory of a Hollywood war. She wanted to believe Beau was taking part in the latter.

'I'm sorry.' She felt so cold.

Then her skin was warmed by the moist heat of his rum-tainted breath along the side of her cheek. 'You are beautiful enough to make me forget all the ugliness.' His arm tightened around her while his mouth buried itself in the silken curls of her black hair.

Just for an instant Mary Lynn failed to protest, letting her flesh recall the feel of a man's body pressed against it – and letting his embrace melt that icy shaft of fear that Beau might never hold her like this again.

'You were saying about Beau.' She pushed firmly at his chest and lowered her head to draw a few inches away from him.

'Ah yes, Beau.' His low voice mocked her choice of subject. 'Let's see – what do I remember about him?' He lifted a shoulder in a careless shrug, then bent his head, angling toward her lips.

'Please,' Mary Lynn protested under her breath, and turned her head aside.

'Please what?' Walker challenged in faint amusement, not raising his head. It was only inches from her averted face.

'You shouldn't be making these advances to a married woman,' she said stiffly, a very prim tone in her soft, southern voice.

'I can't help thinking that if Beau had known I'd be seeing you he would have asked me to give you this.' As his mouth neared the corner of her lips, Mary Lynn turned, ever so slightly, to let him find them.

But it wasn't the shattering sweet recall of Beau's kiss that Mary Lynn experienced. The pressure of Walker's lips obliterated any memory of her husband's gentleness, imprinting his own rougher brand of masculinity that cared nothing about tenderness and the sweet sentiment of love. In confusion, Mary Lynn broke off the kiss, never guessing she could respond to one man's kiss when she loved another.

'It's been a long time, hasn't it?' Those lazy knowing eyes studied her.

'I don't know what you're talking about.' She lied rather than admit there were physical needs, longings to be touched that had no basis in emotions.

The song ended, but his hand kept her from turning completely away from him.

'Yes, you do,' Walker asserted. 'Your Beau is going through the same thing, only it's worse for him because of the need to reaffirm life before he goes to – maybe – meet death. For him, there's always that kind of woman around to satisfy his urge. Wives usually aren't that lucky.'

'Are you trying to tell me Beau has been unfaithful?' It seemed a cheap trick to play on her fears and jealousies.

'Do you honestly believe he's been celibate all this time you've been apart?' Walker jeered.

'It's none of your business what I believe.'

He was slow to respond as his cynical gaze thoughtfully studied her defiant expression. 'Maybe not,' he conceded. 'But I have my own beliefs. What's good for the gander should be good for the goose. Why should you go to sleep all tied up in knots when he doesn't?'

'Stop it.' She couldn't stand any more of his cruel insinuations about Beau's infidelity. She pulled her arm free of his hold and walked blindly toward the table.

Pausing, Walker watched her run away without a glimmer of remorse. Such a beautiful little creature with raven hair and eyes. She was running . . . straight into his arms, eventually. He knew.

CHAPTER TWENTY-FIVE

An ominous squall line of dark clouds loomed in the path of the racing, sleek P-51 Mustang. Eden pulled her gaze away from them to look at charts on her lap. At her last stop, they had warned her about the summer storm front along her route from Fort Myers to New Castle, but she had decided to fly as far as she could until the weather forced her to land. Her worry faded when she saw the Army base located near her present position. It wasn't the closest, but she could make it to Camp Davis, North Carolina, before the storm reached it.

In the swift-running Mustang, Eden made her approach to the swamp-surrounded field. She didn't look at that fire-scorched spot where Rachel's plane had crashed and burned. She landed the hot pursuit and taxied to the flight line. Pilots were streaming from the ready room to stare at the fighter plane all of them ached to fly. After cutting the engine, she pushed back the canopy and climbed out of the cockpit onto the wing.

A strong breeze ran ahead of the black storm clouds and swept thick strands of her titian hair across her face. She heard the male pilots' murmurs of shock that it had been a female at the controls of the powerhouse fighter, but she missed the stunned look on Bubba's face, the unbridled ache in his eyes at the sight of her, posed on the Mustang's wing.

Pilots from the tow-target squadron, male and female alike, crowded around Eden and the plane, asking endless questions. She didn't have a chance to speak to Bubba at all. The first fat raindrops sent everyone scurrying for cover before the storm broke. Eden retrieved her briefcase from the cockpit and ran between the drops to the operations office.

No improvement in the weather, she was told, was expected. Overcast skies and thundershowers were forecast for the next three days – through the weekend. She filed a RON, which meant Remain Over Night, one of the Army's endless acronyms, adding the code for weather as the cause. All movement of aircraft was considered top secret and the ferry pilots used a code to keep their home base informed where the plane was and why it was grounded.

After the first warning splatter of rain, it had stopped. The sky had turned prematurely dark and threatening. Eden ran across to the hangar area, scanning the ground crew working hurriedly to secure the aircraft on the flight line. Bubba was standing inside the towering doors, talking to one of the other mechanics. When he observed Eden's approach, he said something to the young corporal and the man left.

Conscious of the blood heating her veins, Eden stopped in front of Bubba, her brown eyes radiant at the familiar sight of his wonderful, broad-featured face. His hazel eyes smiled at her, crinkling at the corners.

'Long time, no see,' she murmured inadequately.

'Yeah.'

The place was too public, too open; too many eyes witnessed their meeting. Frustrated, Eden let it show.

'It looks like I'll be grounded for the weekend,' she told him. After looking around to see if anyone was close enough to listen, she lowered the pitch of her voice. 'Can you get a pass?'

'Hell, I'll kill to get it if I have to.' His extravagant assertion relieved some of the tension and brought a hint of a smile to both faces.

'I'll meet you in Wilmington at ten o'clock on Saturday. Where?' she asked.

'Greenfield Lake,' Bubba suggested.

'Okay.' Out of the corner of her eye, Eden was aware of two members of the ground crew coming their way. She backed away before they aroused too much interest and speculation. 'See you then.'

The rain-washed air was heavy with humidity. Low clouds carrying the threat of more moisture turned the sky a dark translucent oyster gray, pearlized and thick. Eden stood on the bank of Greenfield Lake, moss-draped cypress trees rising out of the water before her on their long, sinewy roots. Diamond beads of rainwater weighted the scarlet-pink azalea blooms and they drooped on the bushes, the spring profusion of blossoms waning with the advent of summer and spreading a red-pink carpet of petals on the wet ground.

Voices that had been a low murmur in the background suddenly broke into shrill, female laughter. Eden half turned to look their way. A trio of soldiers had obviously said something funny to two teenaged girls sauntering by them, hips waggling invitations while their red, red lips signaled encouragement over their shoulders. Finally, the girls stopped to let the soldiers catch up to them.

As she watched the byplay, Eden heard the whooshing run of bicycle tires over the water-laden ground. When she turned, Bubba was rolling his bike to a stop near her. Again, they were restrained by the potential onlookers, and the kiss they shared was achingly brief.

They started walking, side by side, bodies deliberately brushing while Bubba wheeled his bike alongside. They talked about nothing that mattered. The things they were saying to each other with their eyes were more important.

Eden released a heady sigh and looked around, expecting to see sunshine and a world bursting with the same life force she felt. Instead, clouds backed the dripping silver-green moss in the trees and a kind of stillness lay over everything. She looked at the two teen-aged girls flirting with the soldiers in the park.

'Those girls –' she began, nodding in their direction, and Bubba turned to look.

'You mean those V-girls?' he asked.

'V-girls?' She frowned at the strange term. 'What does that mean?'

'V for Victory,' he said, then made a motion with his head. 'Never mind.'

'Why do you call them that?' Eden persisted, all the more intrigued by Bubba's obvious discomfort with the subject.

'Forget I said it,' he insisted in his heavy drawl.

'Why?'

'Because it's an unseemly thing to discuss with a lady.'

Eden laughed at the thought that she needed to be protected from talk about something evidently wicked. 'What is a V-girl?' Her sidelong glance teased him. 'I'm not one of your southern belles who's liable to blush at indelicate talk.'

'You're Yankee-bold-as-brass, that's for sure,' Bubba agreed, but his look was lazy with deep affection. 'I guess the kindest thing to call 'em is camp followers. Wherever there's a bunch of soldiers, you're apt to find them.'

'Are you serious?' Eden took another look at the girls, trying to match what he was saying with the relative youth of these sixteen-and-seventeen-year-old girls.

'They're crazy over anything in uniforms. Maybe they're attracted to the glamor of it,' he suggested with a shrug. 'Take 'em to a dance . . . hell, buy 'em a Coke and you can have what you want from them. They're amateur whores . . . better than the professionals 'cause at least they aren't indifferent, but . . . the bad thing is . . . a soldier's more likely to catch something from them.'

'How . . . sad,' Eden concluded finally.

'Yeah.' In a change of mood and subject, Bubba began, 'Now I know my chariot isn't as fancy or fast as yours' – indicating the bicycle he pushed along to the side of them – 'but it's the only transportation we got. If you'd like to hop on these horns' – he patted the curved handlebars – 'I'll give you a ride to town.'

While Bubba held the bicycle steady, Eden climbed onto the precarious perch and gingerly rested her feet on the fender. Not feeling very secure, she gripped the handlebars

371

at a point slightly behind her and balanced her briefcase on her lap. She yelped a laughing alarm at Bubba's wobbly push-off.

'Hold on,' he warned.

'I am!'

He leaned forward, pumping the pedals hard with the added weight. 'You make a helluva nice-lookin' hood ornament,' he told her.

'Thanks.' Eden was dubious.

'Better hope it doesn't rain. This convertible doesn't have a top.'

It was a wild ride into the town situated on the Cape Fear River. Hanging on for dear life, Eden always seemed to be gasping halfway between a shriek and a laugh. When they reached the business streets and traffic buzzed around them, she demanded a halt, shaky-legged and out of breath from the madcap ride.

Bubba went back to walking his bike as they wandered down the sidewalk, past the window displays of merchandise in the various stores along the way. Eden glanced idly at them, only mildly interested until she saw a man's tweed sports jacket hanging in a window.

She caught Bubba's arm and directed his attention to the jacket. 'That would look great on you.'

'Do you think so?' He sounded interested, her comment appealing to his ego.

'Let's go inside,' she urged, her eyes bright on him.

After a scant second's hesitation, Bubba leaned the bike against the side of the building and walked with Eden into the store. A clerk brought out the same jacket in his size and let Bubba try it on.

The tailored wool tweed jacket gave breadth to his wide shoulders, erasing that lanky, country-boy look, and hinted at a muscularly trim physique. The camel-soft brown in the tweed highlighted the streaks of dark gold in his hair and deepened the brown. Bubba flexed his shoulders, testing the freedom of movement, while he studied his reflection in the mirror.

'What do you think?' he asked as Eden looked on with gleaming, satisfied eyes.

'We'll take it,' she told the sales clerk.

'Wait a minute. How much does it cost?' Bubba flipped over the sales tag tied to the sleeve button.

'It doesn't matter.' Price was not an object as far as Eden was concerned. 'It's my present . . . from me to you.' She opened her shoulder bag to pay for it.

'No.' It was a flat refusal. A second later, Bubba was shrugging out of the jacket and handing it to the clerk. 'I changed my mind. I don't like it.' He looked at Eden, an anger lurking beneath his expression. 'Come on. Let's go.'

This show of temper surprised Eden into silence. Bubba had always seemed so easygoing; nothing ever riled him. She didn't protest as he steered her out of the store and back onto the sidewalk.

'What's wrong?' She eyed him cautiously. 'Surely you didn't –'

'Forget it.' He cut harshly across her words, then paused, regret flashing across his expression as he lowered his head. 'Just forget it,' he said in a quieter tone.

Eden started to speak, then let her lips come together. Maybe it was better to let it alone for now, she decided. Bubba stood his bicycle up and they started walking down the street again.

After they'd gone a block, she asked, 'Where are we going?'

He seemed to hesitate, then looked at her directly. 'There's a hotel I know about, not far from here.' He paused, as if to await an objection from her, but she had none to make. 'It sits kinda outa the way. Best of all, I guess, it doesn't ask any questions.'

'Let's go there, then.' She slipped her hand into the grasp of his roughly callused, work-worn hand. Her touch seemed to tame him and bring the warm glint back to his eyes.

Twenty minutes later, Bubba unlocked the door to their hotel room and carried her briefcase and his small duffle bag inside. The room was small and furnished with only the necessary bed and dresser. The fringed area rug was threadbare, its pattern and colors fading. He laid their things on the bed, and turned, a trifle self-consciously, to face Eden.

'It isn't much.'

'It definitely isn't the Waldorf,' Eden agreed, a smile in her voice as she stepped forward to link her hands behind his neck. 'I missed you.'

His gaze became fixed on her lips while he seemed to hold himself on a tight rein. He rested his hands on the points of her hipbones, covered by slacks of Santiago blue. 'I missed you one helluva lot.'

Pent-up hungers were released as he took her lips, driving into them with a fevered need. She answered the pressure of crushing arms, her own winding around him in an ever-tightening circle. The strain was raw and wildly sweet. It was some moments before they broke apart under the weight of it, to catch their breath.

Eden moved away, turning her back to him while she took the blue tam from atop her red hair. She was disturbed by him, more deeply than she had been by any man. She was used to having control of things, but now she had none.

The tam was left to sit on the dresser while she unbuttoned her Eisenhower jacket. Wire hangers hung in the small closet in the room. She took one down and slipped her jacket onto it. When she turned, Eden caught Bubba watching her.

'If you want to look halfway decent on these ferry trips, you have to look after your clothes.' No maids came along to do it for her. 'You never know how long you'll be away . . . or how long you might have to wear your uniform before you can have it cleaned. There's only room in the cockpits of these pursuits for the briefcase. By the time you put your tech manuals, your orders, toothbrush and makeup in that, you're lucky if there's room for a clean blouse.'

She smiled at him, because it was really quite humorous. Her reputation as a clotheshorse was notorious. She laid her briefcase flat and unfastened the catches to open it and unpack.

374

'You'd be surprised at the tricks we've learned to stay looking neat,' Eden told him. 'We wash our underwear out at night and drape it over the radiator or the bedstead to dry. If you can't count on getting an iron, then you just rub the collar of your shirt clean and set it under the Bible so it will dry already pressed. The slacks we put between the mattress and the box springs. The next morning, they are creased to Army perfection.'

His chuckle widened her smile as Eden gathered up her cosmetics kit and carried it into the small bathroom. At least they had a private one and didn't have to share some community facility off the hallway.

'What's this?' Bubba's voice followed her. She came back into the room to find him standing by the bed, holding the .45-caliber pistol she carried in her briefcase. 'How come you're carrying a gun?'

'The planes we fly sometimes have sophisticated equipment aboard.' Eden took the loaded weapon from him and put it back in the briefcase with her manuals, charts, and orders. 'Gun sights, transmitters, and those IFF – If Friend or Foe – sensors. Some of them even have morphine in the medical packs.'

'But why the gun?' Bubba frowned. 'The Army doesn't expect you to shoot people, does it?'

'No,' she assured him with a faint laugh. 'But if we're forced down under "suspicious circumstances," the phrase they use, we're supposed to fire at a spot on the fuselage. Supposedly it will blow up the entire plane.'

He looked at her hard. 'That sounds dangerous.'

'And Camp Davis was a piece of cake, with artillery lobbing fifty-millimeter shells at a muslin sleeve towed behind a plane,' Eden reminded him ironically. She crossed to stand in front of him, then reached up and began unbuttoning his khaki shirt.

Halfway done with the task, she slipped her fingers inside to touch his warm, hard flesh. She felt the small tremor that shook him, and satisfaction ran hotly through her veins, smooth and fiery as aged Scotch whiskey – and just as intoxicating.

His long hands cupped her face, framing it. 'Do you love me, Eden?'

'Yes,' she whispered.

'No.' He shook his head, the strain of something else visible in the yearning of his look. 'Do you love me the way I am?'

'What nonsense is this?' Eden murmured. 'Are you talking about that jacket? Back there at the store –'

'I don't want you buying me things,' he said. 'I know you've got plenty of money, but I'll pay my own way. It isn't really that, though . . . it's just, I'm wondering if you're trying to change me. Eden, I'm a mechanic. I don't have any fancy houses or fancy cars or clothes.'

'Not now,' she said. 'How could you? The Army isn't exactly the place to get ahead.'

'What if I don't want to get ahead, Eden?' Bubba said. 'What if I like what I am? Can you be happy with that?'

She didn't like this talk. She didn't like the questions he was raising. She didn't want anything spoiling their precious time together.

'What does it matter?' she asked impatiently and pressed her body to his length. 'Does it change this?'

'No,' he admitted hoarsely and let his frustration be carried away by the roughening fire of a kiss.

A minute later, he was scooping her into his arms and depositing her on the bed. Wrinkled uniforms became the least of their concerns.

It was a balmy California afternoon, a fresh breeze was stirring, and the sky was high and blue. Mary Lynn didn't think a more perfect day could have been created. Even after the long flight she'd just completed, she felt revived and inwardly exuberant. Briefcase in hand, she moved away from the aircraft she'd just delivered to head for the operations building.

'Hey, Marty!' she called to the long-legged blonde in

her striking blue flying fatigues. This trip had been one of the rare occasions when their orders had taken them to the same destination, so they'd flown their planes tandem. 'Are you coming?'

Marty's hands were cupped to her mouth as she stood beside her plane with a mechanic. 'Gotta get my gear out of the plane.' Her megaphoned voice sounded even deeper and huskier. 'Go ahead without me. I'll be along.'

Mary Lynn waved an acknowledgment and crossed the wide flight line to the operations building. It seemed more crowded than usual, a lot more civilians milling around inside than she was accustomed to seeing. Most of them scowled at her with unconcealed dislike.

'What are you doing here?' one of them demanded, surprising Mary Lynn with the vehemence in his tone.

'I just flew a P-47 in –'

But he wasn't interested in her explanation. None of them were. 'Why don't you go home where you belong?' he challenged.

'No one needs you or the rest of your fancy-assed women. You aren't wanted here so why don't you clear out!'

'You got no business in the cockpit of an airplane!'

Unable to fight back against this barrage of verbal abuse, Mary Lynn tried to walk away from it, but the men crowded around her, not letting her by. Hostility swept from them in threatening waves, swamping her with the implied menace of their pressing bodies.

'Your organization is worthless. You're nothin' but a bunch of glamor gals.'

'Go home!'

Not knowing what to do, Mary Lynn looked at them in helpless confusion. She couldn't understand why they were attacking her.

An officer shouldered his way into their midst. 'Leave her alone,' a familiar voice snapped. In relief, Mary Lynn recognized Walker. 'Beat it. All of you,' he ordered, his low, hard voice commanding their attention and respect.

Reluctant and grumbling, they dispersed, moving slowly

away and leaving Mary Lynn standing there, shaken and confused by the experience.

'I don't understand. What did I do?' she asked.

'You didn't have to do anything.' With his usual disregard for the Army's uniform code, Walker's summer khaki shirt was unbuttoned at the throat, revealing a glimpse of the chain that held his dogtags. A cigarette dangled from a corner of his mouth while he squinted his eyes against the upward curl of smoke and stared at Mary Lynn. 'Don't let them get to you. They're just a bunch of former flight instructors, taking scheduled flight tests for Air Transport Command. I guess these guys didn't pass. Then you walked in and I suppose it was too much for their injured pride that a mere slip of a woman had made the grade and they didn't. You've got a job they want and can't qualify for.'

'I see.' She lowered her head, troubled by the venom that had been thrown at her so unjustifiably. 'That's why they said I didn't belong in those planes.'

'Hey.' His voice cajoled her while he touched a finger to the side of her mouth, trying to coax a smile from her. 'Not everyone feels like that. You can ride in the cockpit of my plane any time.'

His suggestive comment heated her skin. She turned away from the touch of his finger and made a move to leave, but his hand hooked her waist in a lightning reflex while he discarded the cigarette. She was stopped by the action, and turned of her own volition to face him. Indolent satisfaction darkened the gleam in his eyes as he traced her cheekbone and jaw with a caressing finger.

'Have dinner with me tonight,' he urged.

She lowered her glance, trying to elude his touch. 'No, thanks. You drink your dinner and I prefer to eat mine.'

With her head down, she walked quickly away from him, passing Marty just as she entered the building. Marty's glance flashed past her to strike at Walker. Ignoring her presence, he bent his head to light another cigarette, shaking out the match flame while he watched Mary Lynn walk away. Marty was rarely given to violent likes or dislikes, but she despised him.

'Why don't you keep your hands off her?' she snapped.

Without turning his head, Walker looked at her with amused scorn. 'What makes you think she wants to be protected from me?'

'What a ridiculous question.' Marty was angry. 'She's in love with her husband.'

The line of his mouth deepened its mocking slant. 'You . . . of all people . . . should know love has nothing to do with this.'

At a loss for a reply, Marty spun on her heel and marched out of the building after Mary Lynn. She caught up with her outside.

'Are you okay?' Marty peered at her.

'Of course.' Mary Lynn continued walking, head up and eyes to the front.

Marty matched the shorter stride of her friend. 'That guy is about as crude as you can get. Someone needs to teach him some manners and proper respect.'

'That's not quite true.' She defended him. 'Some pilots – men – were giving me a hard time because I was doing a job they felt should have been theirs. Captain Walker came along and sent them on their way.'

'Then *he* started bothering you.' Something about the man kept ringing more than alarm bells in her mind, but Marty couldn't place him. 'If I were you, I'd steer clear of him.'

'He knows Beau.' Mary Lynn mentioned it as if that gave him credibility.

'How?' Marty stopped, taken aback by the announcement.

Mary Lynn's dark eyes took on a lively, yet wistful quality. 'Captain Walker was a B-17 pilot in England with Beau. He knows all about him.'

'What's he doing here?' Marty didn't like the sound of any of this, and the graveled edge of her voice became rougher.

'Like Cappy, he's flying the C-47s to their embarkation

379

'points when they come off the assembly lines at Douglas.'

'Why should the Army have a B-17 pilot doing that?' she asked, skeptical of his story.

'Look at what they have you doing.' The lilt in her voice said it all as Mary Lynn resumed walking, prompting Marty into motion.

But a bell had rung loudly in Marty's head. 'I've got it!' The declaration was made under her breath as all her attention was turned inward. 'That's where I saw him before. I'd swear to it.'

'What are you talking about?' Mary Lynn paused before they reached the jeep parked outside operations, waiting to transport them to their quarters.

'I'd bet a month's pay he's the bomber pilot I bumped into in Miami Beach. The scars on his face. The voice. I'd almost swear to it.' In an aside to Mary Lynn, she added, 'He was a coward – trying to drink himself brave when I saw him. More important, he doesn't know Beau. He is lying to you, Mary Lynn. I asked.'

Tired and worn by a series of long flights, Cappy sat in the post canteen on her old home base outside of Washington, DC, and pushed the food around on her plate. Her appetite had fallen off – along with a lot of other things, like contentment – since she'd been transferred. When she'd been assigned to the same ferry command where Eden was stationed, she had thought everything would be fine. Close to three months had passed and everything wasn't fine.

A new set of orders was in the sealed envelope lying on the table beside her plate. She hadn't looked at them yet, not particularly caring what she would be flying or where. Since leaving Long Beach nearly four days before, she had logged a prodigious number of hours. Cappy felt she had earned this break – and these few rare moments with her family, specifically her mother, who sat across the table from her.

Her mother was doing nearly all the talking, recounting to Cappy her visit to Capitol Hill. The House Civil Service

Committee had been meeting in regard to the WASP program, which they had concluded was a waste of money and effort.

'General Arnold argued with them for more than an hour,' her mother reported. 'He was most insistent that women pilots were necessary to the war effort. Jacqueline Cochran was there, sitting beside him, but she didn't say anything. The committee was all for disbanding the entire organization. They could do it just by refusing to fund it, since it is a civilian program. It's all that business about those flight instructors who lost their high-paying civilian contracts to train pilots for the Army. The committee made General Arnold give them his assurance that the services of these men would be utilized immediately.' A small smile touched her mouth. 'They're afraid of getting drafted in the "walking" Army.'

Cappy wanted nothing to do with the Army in any form. She just wanted to fly planes – and the Army could go to hell as far as she was concerned. Her throat got tight and some wrenching pain pushed at her chest. A raw unnamed emotion seemed to strangle her.

'Did I mention I saw Mitch at the committee meeting?' her mother inquired.

Cappy's eyes were the deep color of her blue flying suit and they burned. 'No, you didn't.' Her voice seemed to come from some hollow well inside her. 'How is he?' So casually.

'Oh, he's still the same handsome devil,' her mother declared with a laugh. 'It's a shame you won't be able to see him while you're here.'

'I hardly have the time –' Cappy began stiffly.

'Mitch isn't here,' her mother hastened to explain, then lowered her voice. 'He's in England with General Arnold . . . for the Allied invasion of France.'

'It's happening?'

'Soon,' her mother replied, then looked around to be certain no one had overheard.

Mitch. She had trouble keeping the tears out of her

eyes. He was staff so it was unlikely he'd be exposed to any danger. It wasn't that causing the ache, the clawing frustration, the near anger. She had done the right thing, Cappy insisted to herself. It wouldn't have worked between them. She pressed her fingertips to the bridge of her nose, trying to fight back the tears.

'Cappy, is something wrong?'

A silent shake of her head first dismissed the question, then Cappy dragged in a breath and forced a smile to her lips. 'I'm just tired,' she said, then attempted a laugh that came out brittle and false. 'Did I tell you a cleaning woman in the lavatory mistook me for a lady plumber in my flight suit? I don't know what all this fuss is about in Congress. Ninety percent of the people don't even know we exist.'

CHAPTER TWENTY-SIX

'Our sons, pride of our nation . . .' As president Franklin Delano Roosevelt began his prayer, Mary Lynn sat close to the radio and bowed her head. She, Marty and Eden were with their fellow WASPs, massed in the common room of the barracks to hear the latest report on the massive Allied invasion of France's Normandy beaches. The President was now praying for those fighting men. 'Lead them straight and true. Give strength to their arms, stoutness to their hearts, steadfastness in their faith. They will need Thy blessings. Their road will be long and hard. For the enemy is strong. He may hurl back our forces. Success may not come with rushing speed, but we shall return again and again . . .'

Early on the morning of June 6, Walter Winchell had announced the news of the invasion to the West Coast. He told of American armies fighting on Utah Beach and bloody Omaha, while the British battled on Sword, Gold, and Juno. Tense, Marty leaned toward the radio. She'd heard the reports of paratroop divisions dropping behind German lines before the first Marines stormed onto the beaches. Her brother was bound to have been part of it. At this moment, he was over there fighting with the rest.

'. . .Give us faith in Thee; faith in our sons; faith in each other; faith in our united crusade . . .' FDR prayed.

When he finished, the room echoed with Amens, and a rush of talk followed the guardedly optimistic report. Amidst all the fears and prayers, there was a need to celebrate. Marty, Eden, and Mary Lynn headed for the Officers' Club. Everyone else seemed to have the same idea. The place was packed with officers eager to talk, predicting victory.

'My brother David is over there,' Marty announced proudly. 'He's a paratrooper, so he was in the initial assault.'

An unhurried latecomer to their table was Captain Sam Walker. As he slowly approached, Mary Lynn lifted her head against the steady pressure of his presence. A drink was in his hand; there was always a drink in his hand. She tapped an unlit cigarette on the table, packing the tobacco.

'A vile habit.' A match flared and his long fingers held it out to her. Her eyes briefly met his, then fell away as she bent her head toward the match, letting the tip of her cigarette touch the flame.

'So is drinking.' Mary Lynn straightened from him, blowing smoke into the air in a strained attempt at nonchalance. 'But I notice you do both to excess.'

'I have fallen into sinful and wicked ways.' He dragged a chair around to sit angled towards her. 'Maybe you should try to reform me?' In a gesture of suppressed agitation, she turned her glass in half-circles within its damp table-ring. Sam Walker picked up her every little nuance of movement and expression. 'Or maybe I should lead you the rest of the way astray?'

Marty leaned an arm on the table, her posture carrying more of a warning than a challenge. 'Walker, why don't you lay off her for once.'

'Mind your own business, Rogers.' Walker didn't bother to look at Mary Lynn's defender.

'Keeping wolves like you away from her is my business.'

With a finger, he hooked a loose curl behind Mary Lynn's ear and noticed the way her dark eyes nearly closed under his feather-light touch.

'Do you think you need protection from me, Little One?' he drawled.

'No.' A tension remained about her expression as she kept her gaze downcast.

Marty changed tactics from direct to indirect confrontation. 'Aren't you lucky Ike ordered the invasion of France? Now everyone will think you're drinking to celebrate that and never guess it's where you find your courage.'

Such talk didn't faze Walker; instead, he used it. 'Does it bother you that I drink, Little One?'

With a rare display of cynicism, Mary Lynn retorted, 'Would you stop if I said it did?'

'No.' His taunting smile was slow and even.

But Mary Lynn didn't react as Walker had expected she would. She pushed her chair away from the table. 'Please, I'm not in the mood for this.'

'Don't leave.' He caught her hand, holding her with the small pressure. But he knew better than to use force to keep her; instead he let his intent gaze make inroads into her will. 'It isn't good for a man to drink alone.'

'You shouldn't drink at all.' There was a reluctance in her voice. She wanted nothing from him, yet found herself responding to him against her will.

'Then keep me away from that evil rum and dance with me instead.' He changed his hold on her hand, slipping under her fingers to curve them atop his

A protesting sound came from Marty, but it seemed to goad Mary Lynn into action. That nervy restlessness could affect a person, push her into throwing aside caution. It was something he knew better than anyone there.

On the dance floor, he brought her inside his arms until her warm body was close to his. Her fragrance revived all his hungers. She was all things good and sweet – too good for him, but he wanted her all the same. And he'd have her, too. He knew that's where the wrong in himself lay. By taking her, he'd drag her down.

Her dark head came to his shoulder and her hand rested lightly on the muscled tip of it. Mary Lynn didn't lift her gaze higher than the silver captain's bars on his uniform. The sweet smell of her hair came to him.

'Do you think I'm a coward, Little One?' He asked gently.

'I try not to think about you.' She dodged his question.

'Do you succeed?' Walker tipped his head to the side, trying for a better view of her face.

'Most of the time.'

'At least you think of me once in a while. That's a beginning.' He smiled, but the look in his eyes was serious, completely sober despite the alcohol he'd already consumed. 'I think about you all the time.'

'In between the booze and the poker.'

'And the nightmares,' he added without thinking.

She looked at his face, striking him with the dark, earnest openness of her eyes. 'Why do you have nightmares?'

At that moment, he was careful not to shut his eyes, not to let in those images of fighter planes with black crosses painted on their wings tearing out of the sky, spewing rockets of death – or the sight of Flying Fortresses rearing out of formation as if clawing for life, with part of a wing or tail shot away, bleeding thick smoke from the wound – the crew of ten men inside, maybe friends and maybe strangers. More than anything, Walker shut out that sickening sense of helplessness when they went into their slow death spiral.

That bitterness came – that wretched, angry bitterness. 'Don't you know there's a war on?' There was cruelty in his voice.

Her head went down. 'Yes, I know,' she said softly.

The anger that welled in him took another course, deliberately seeking out sore spots and testing them to see if they were still tender – within himself and within her. 'Have you had a letter from your husband lately?'

She became stiff in his arms. 'Why? You don't know him.' Her glance rushed upwards to his face. 'Marty finally remembered where she had met you before. It was in Miami Beach. You told her that you didn't know him.'

'I did? Well, fancy that,' Walker murmured, untroubled. 'I must have made a mistake.'

'You deliberately lied to me, didn't you?' she said accusingly.

'You've had a long, lonely time of it, haven't you, Little One?' he murmured, ignoring her accusation. 'All that flying . . . and all that restless energy just has you taut as a drumskin. The ease of forgetfulness comes in the arms of a lover. That's what you need – someone to make love to you and untie those knots that have you all wound up inside.'

'Why did you lie to me?'

A rising energy made him impatient. 'You needed an excuse to be with me so I gave you one. We played a little game of pretend. You wanted to be able to say "He knows my husband" to explain why you spent so much time in my company. You use it as a reason to justify why we're dancing and why you're letting me hold you in my arms. The truth is it's what you want.'

Her feet ceased following the pattern of his steps as she halted in the middle of the dance floor. 'Marty was right about you. You're a liar and a coward. I must have been blind not to have seen it before.'

'You didn't want to see it,' Walker snapped. If it had been her intention to hurt him, she had done it well. For all his callous attitude, he had his pride.

'I love my husband,' she declared as if raising up a shield.

'Yeah? Well, he's not here and I am. That's the difference.'

Mary Lynn pulled out of his arms. 'You're a liar and a cheat and a coward.' Sensing how to hurt him, she struck deep to wound him and salvage some of her own self-respect in the process.

For a long minute he stood fast, then his mouth slanted

in a cruelly mocking line. 'Then what does that make you, Little One?'

It was a remark that struck low and hard. Mary Lynn whitened and swung away from him just as Eden danced right beside her, looking concerned. 'Are you all right, Mary Lynn?' she asked while her dance partner showed only mild interest.

'I . . . I have a headache. Tell Marty I'm leaving.' Mary Lynn left the dance floor, walking swiftly toward the exit with Walker following close behind.

Within seconds, Marty was pouncing on Walker, challenge glittering in her silvery-green eyes. 'Leave her alone, Walker.'

'What are you? Her keeper?'

'Yes. She's a decent kid, and I want to keep it that way,' she answered.

'Meaning what? That I'm not good enoough for her?' Walker taunted.

'You're a bastard, Walker,' she replied as if that explained it all. 'What did you say to her?'

Walker looked at her with hard, narrowed eyes. 'None of your damned business.' In a rank temper, he bulled his way to the bar.

A steady stream of reports came from the beaches of Normandy over the next few days, but most of the women pilots were in the skies. Marty hopscotched across the Southwest, gazed longingly at the B-17s in Las Vegas, and flew back to Long Beach on June 8. It never failed to amaze her how well the airfields on the Pacific Coast were camouflaged. Unless a pilot knew almost precisely where they were, she'd never see them.

Back at the WASP quarters after a three-day absence, she stuck her head inside Mary Lynn's doorway. 'Hi. I'm back.'

'How was your flight?' Mary Lynn set aside her letter-writing paraphernalia and swung off her cot to follow Marty down the hall to her own room.

387

'Not bad. I ran into some junk in southern Colorado, but I flew out of it before the weather got too rough.' She slung her briefcase onto the narrow bed and shuffled through the mail that had accumulated in her absence. She pulled out one envelope. 'Well, what do you know?' Marty said with surprise and curled a leg under her to sit on the cot. 'A telegram from my parents.' As she ran a finger under the flap, she looked at Mary Lynn. 'I haven't heard from them in weeks.' Marty took out the telegram to read it. 'No.' The soft word conveyed shock.

Mary Lynn started to speak, then saw Marty's whitened face and the glazed quality of her silvery-green eyes when she looked up from the telegram.

'My brother . . . David.' Confusion and disbelief swarmed through her roughly controlled voice. 'They've been notified . . .' Marty stared again at the telegram, as if needing to see it in writing. '. . . He was killed in action.'

The words, the finality of them, were silencing. Not David, not her brother – she kept thinking there must be some mistake. The shock seemed to suck all feeling out of her, draining her empty. He was her big brother, her idol and her rival; it was his feats she'd always tried to match or better. David couldn't die. He was supposed to come home the hero – with decorations on his chest. It wasn't right that he should be killed. It wasn't fair.

Mary Lynn gazed at the telegram, the kind mothers and wives dreaded to receive. A twisting fear weaved through her. This was the first time the lightning had struck so close. It wasn't a neighbor's son down the block, or a third cousin's husband. This was Marty's brother.

'Marty.' Mary Lynn took a step toward the silent, staring figure on the bed, wanting to comfort and thus be comforted.

'No.' Marty swung off the bed and faced the corner, turning her back on Mary Lynn and hugging her arms tightly around her middle. 'I . . .' Her husky voice was choked with grief. 'Mom and Dad . . . they'll need me. I'd better . . . make arrangements to go home this weekend.'

'I'll help,' she offered.

'I think . . . I'd rather do it myself.' She needed the activity to release the spiraling tightness. Marty couldn't stay still as the phrase kept hitting at her: 'killed in action.' David Allen Rogers III had always played such a big role in her life; his death left a gaping hole. 'Do you mind? I'd like to be alone.'

But Mary Lynn couldn't stand the thought of being alone.

She needed to be around laughing, loving, living people. She left the nearly empty barracks. Most of the WASPs were on flights somewhere, and the few present were catching up on laundry or sleep.

The hustle of the flight line pulled her. For a while she stood outside, listening to the ebb and flow of voices and airplane engines, life recirculating. Impatient for something more to fill the hollow ache inside, Mary Lynn entered the operations building.

The jocular voices and the back-slapping camaraderie going on didn't include her, as pilots milled about the ready room, playing cards or chatting idly, puffing on endless cigarettes. She wanted to be part of the living world, not an onlooker.

Mary Lynn couldn't put a name to the force that made her turn around so that she saw Walker when he came in. The dark stubble of a day's beard growth shadowed his angled cheeks, concealing the scars. Tired lines creased his eye corners, but the hard, glinting mockery remained in their dark surfaces. His officer's cap was raked to the back of his head, showing the heavy brown hair that grew with such unruly thickness. His leather battle jacket hung open and the tails of the white scarf draped around his neck were dangling loose.

Walker paused to draw a match across the abrasive strip of its match cover and cup the flame to his cigarette. Over the fire, he caught sight of the small, silent woman watching him from a corner of the room. Her dark eyes were on him, rousing him fully.

For an instant, she became the only living thing in the room for him. Slowly, he lifted his head, staring at her as he shook out the match. Steadily, she returned his gaze, not looking away or showing reluctance.

There was a message in that – one he wanted to explore . . . to be sure of its meaning.

He moved toward her, crossing the room at a sauntering pace. 'Hello, Little One.'

She spoke, without preamble, her voice soft as a whisper yet urgent. 'A telegram came for Marty. Her brother was killed in action.'

He'd gotten from her the opening he wanted. With no sense of guilt, Walker followed through, gathering her into his arms and holding her there for an easy run of minutes until her stiffness and frigidity softened and melted.

Bending his head, he rubbed his mouth against the silken fineness of her raven hair. In tentative movements, she shifted, slowly lifting her head to look at him and the nearness of his mouth.

Walker needed no more than that. His driving kiss tasted her needs without restraint. She let him glimpse the deep and passionate core of her feelings. Walker wasn't sure whether she had willingly given him this entry, but she had returned his kiss with a full and heated response.

His breath was running deep when he dragged his mouth from hers. 'Tonight –' He needed the promise inherent in that kiss. '– I'll pick you up at nineteen hundred hours.'

There was a moment when he sensed her conflict, but her answer ultimately came with no reservation. 'Yes.'

In the hallway outside the hotel room Mary Lynn waited, clutching her purse, while Walker inserted the key the clerk had given him and unlocked the door. He led the way inside, making a quick survey of the room before turning to draw her in and close the door.

The room was small, with space for little besides the bed and chest of drawers. Its use was starkly limited and it pretended to little else. Rigidly she avoided looking at the bed as she crossed to the window, but the view was restricted to a seedy back street of Los Angeles.

A paper sack rattled and bottles were set on the bureau. Without looking, she could discern Walker's movements. Mary Lynn stayed at the window, listening to the sounds of glasses being righted and caps screwed off bottles.

'What will you have – rum and Coke or Coke and rum?' The lazy inflection of his voice didn't have its customary note of spiteful mockery.

'Neither, thank you.' She managed the response, letting a smile take any sting out of her rejection.

'Sorry I couldn't get you any whiskey. I know that's what you usually drink – when you drink,' he acknowledged, and liquid splashed in a glass, bubbles fizzing in a soft hiss.

Out of the corner of her eye she saw him drape his jacket around the lone straight-backed chair in the room, then she turned to watch him loosen the knot of his tie. Walker was talking to her, but none of his words registered as he crossed to the bed, taking a swig of his rum and Coke, then setting it on the nightstand.

Once the tie hung loose around his neck, he unfastened the collar button of his shirt, then pulled the shirttails out of his trousers and unbuttoned it the rest of the way. Soon the shirt was thrown over the end of the bed and the undershirt was being pulled over Walker's head to join it. His dogtags jingled briefly against their securing chain.

When bare to the waist, he stood up to loosen his pants. Walker noticed Mary Lynn standing silently by the window. He paused, searching her still features. He tipped his head to the side. 'Is something wrong?'

She looked toward the door, a drift of self-consciousness running across her face. 'That desk clerk knew when we registered that we weren't man and wife, didn't he?'

'I doubt that he cared one way or the other as long as we paid for the room.' His shoulder lifted in a vague shrug. 'What does it matter anyway?'

'I suppose it doesn't.' Her glance fell. 'But the way he

looked at us ... it made this something ... sordid and cheap.'

And the situation wasn't improved by his behavior, Walker realized – undressing as if he were bedding a common whore. He silently cursed his thoughtlessness and went to her, gently turning her from the window to face him.

'You're wrong, Little One.' He urgently pressed his feelings on her. 'You're much too beautiful and fine to be sullied by any of this.' He heard the high-sounding words as he spoke them, so deeply sincere. Coming from him, they seemed out of character. He chuckled in his throat and stroked the hollow below her ear lobe. 'I sound so damned noble, don't I? But it's the truth.'

She gazed at him, a hint of regret in her velvet dark eyes. 'I'm not as good as you think I am, Walker.'

Slowly he accepted these words as true; otherwise she wouldn't be in this hotel room with him. At the moment, it didn't matter whether she was sinking to his level or he was rising to hers. In some decent part of his mind, he realized she'd never done this before.

Gently, he led her away from the window and held her face in his hands while he kissed it with slow, seeking ardor. As her stiffness and discomfort melted, he began to undress her, taking time to caress the areas he uncovered before moving on to the next. There were hungers to be satisfied, the taste of her skin beneath his tongue and the feel of her hard nipples under his thumb. Her hands were splayed across his chest and the heavy thud of his heart beat against them.

Long-held desires heated their flesh and quickened their breathing. When she was stripped of clothes and all the restraints of society's conventions, Walker swung her feet off the floor and carried her to the bed.

Here they were merely participants in the most basic of all acts – no more than a man and a woman discovering ways they fit together that gave them pleasure, glimpsing old glories made new and sensing some of the wonder so fleetingly possessed – and always the straining for more.

Part Four

We wanted wings,
Then we got those goldarned things
They just darned near killed us,
That's for sure.
They taught us how to fly
Now they send us home to cry
'Cause they don't want us anymore.
You can save those AT-sixes
To be cracked up in the ditches,
For the way the Army flies
Really clears them out of the skies.
We earned our wings,
Now they'll clip the goldarned things
How will they ever win the war?

CHAPTER TWENTY-SEVEN

The bedsheet was drawn tightly across her breasts and firmly tucked under her arms to keep it in place. Mary Lynn couldn't explain it, even to herself, this need to hide her body. Surely not from Walker – his invasion of her had been most complete . . . and satisfying. Was that it? Had she wanted it not to be as good as it had been with Beau?

The raw sweet pleasure was all gone and her feelings were getting twisted inside. The cigarette she was smoking lost its flavor and she turned on her side to crush it in the ashtray on the bedstand. When she rolled back, Mary Lynn was conscious of Walker, his head turned on the pillow to look at her. A ravel of smoke from his cigarette drifted in the air above them. The hard and knowing mockery in his eyes was difficult to meet.

'You're thinking about him, aren't you?' A faint harshness crept into the edges of his voice.

'Who?' Mary Lynn pretended obtuseness.

'Don't play games, Little One.' Some kind of anger made him sit up and swing around to the side of the bed, where he reached for the rum bottle and poured some into a glass. 'Your husband, of course.' He bolted down a swallow of liquor, then made a study of the glass. 'That nagging sense of shame and guilt won't last. It'll pass like everything else, until the next time, when the urge strikes again.'

'How do you know?' she demanded, angry that he had somehow gotten into her head as well as her body.

Walker turned to look across his shoulder. His mouth

crooked in a humorless line. 'Because I've been there, my love.' He reached backwards to stroke her cheek and cup it in a gentle fashion before turning away. 'I've been there.' The glass was tipped again to his mouth.

One lamp illuminated the room, throwing out shadows from its single pool. When Walker lifted an arm, the dim light cast a rippling sheen over the bare flesh stretched tautly across the muscles in his back. His body was marked with scattered dull-red scars. Flesh wounds, she supposed they were called. They weren't old ones, but recently incurred. It would take a long time before the reddened scars would fade to rose-brown and finally to white.

'Don't lose any sleep over it,' Walker advised her. 'He won't. Many other things may rob him of sleep, but not the comfort of a body's arms. He might feel a twinge of guilt once in a while – maybe when she does something that reminds him of you. Is that what I did?' His head turned, his glance sliding to her. 'Remind you of him?'

At times she could despise him for his brutal honesty; no subject was sacred; no topic was discreetly avoided. Worse, perhaps, he preyed on her doubts about Beau.

'You're not like him.'

'Aren't I?' he mused, but let it pass.

'You don't even know Beau.' Mary Lynn didn't know why she persisted in the subject, unless it was some kind of punishment. 'You're only guessing about the women.'

'He's a man, isn't he?' There was a rising heat in his voice, impatient and hard. 'What's any man want when he's thirsty? If he's far from home, he'll drink from the well that's close by. Maybe he'll miss the taste of the sweet water back home but he'll drink to satisfy the craving inside. That's just the way it is. Maybe that's why we're made of clay, because the impulses that drive us are dirt-common.'

'I never guessed you were a philosopher.' She was calmed by the things he said, but it seemed strange to hear him speaking in Beau's defense, offering justification for his infidelity. Or was he giving reasons for her own? Or his?

'It must be the war.' Walker stared into the glass as if it held the answer. 'At first, you try to understand the whys of it, but it's such insanity that none of it will tolerate a close scrutiny. So you either go on with blind faith in the people supposedly leading you or else you turn to the bottle and drink until it's all a blur and none of it matters.'

'What's it like?' It had done things to him, things she didn't understand. And she wondered if all the bomber pilots returning home would be like Sam Walker.

'Hell.' A long silence followed the one-word reply while Walker was caught up in his own thoughts. Then he roused himself to go on, in a flat, emotionless voice. 'It isn't like what they write about or what they show you on the screen. In the movies, you *see* the enemy, whether he's a yellow-skinned Jap or a strong-jawed Jerry. Man fighting man is an honorable thing; there's glory in it. But you aren't fighting men; you're fighting machines. There lies the horror of this war. The side with more and better machines is going to win.'

'It can't be that simple.'

'Why?' He turned to challenge her with certainty. 'Because we've got "right" on our side? Because we're better than they are? Or braver or stronger? It will be because we've got raw material and factories that can throw out tanks and airplanes almost as fast as their machines can shoot them down.'

Looking away, she resisted the things he was saying. 'Don't you think we have a cause . . . a reason to fight?'

'Yes.' A sigh took the anger from him and left the bitterness. 'Yes, we have to fight, but do we have to lose so much? When we come back from raids over German territory, our generals don't count our losses in lives. It's planes – how many machines did we lose?

'They order us up there – maybe twenty formations of

sixty bombers each. They fill the sky.' He was staring sightlessly into the room, the drink clenched tightly in his hand. 'Overhead, the fighters ride escort, but not for long. Before their fuel runs low, they'll turn around and we're left at the mercy of . . . they have no mercy. They're waiting for you, though. They know you're coming and they wait – with their fighters and their flak. But you keep flying. When those German Focke-Wulfs pounce on you, you keep flying. There's no breaking off course to engage the enemy. You've got a target to reach and a bombload to drop and you just pray that none of those rockets flaming from their fighter planes hits your Fortress.

'And all the while, the intercom is alive with warnings – shoutings of the crew calling in your ears . . . your own voice among them . . . telling each other of planes diving toward your ship. Explosions all around you, and the thud of bullets tearing through metal . . . and the sickening feel of the ship when you know she's been hit, but you can't tell how bad. You just try to keep her in the air and on course for the target – always on course. You can't fall out of formation. A crippled bomber is a sitting duck, and the fighters will be on it like a pack of wolves.'

Beads of sweat were breaking out on his forehead but Mary Lynn felt chilled by the terror in his images. 'They come at you with black crosses painted on their wings, shooting their cannon shells. You see other bombers take hits, engines flame out, tiny lances of fire licking close to fuel tanks, black smoke pouring from an engine. A Fortress wings over and you'll watch the pilot fight to bring her out of the dive and back to straight and level so the crew can bail out before she blows. Maybe you know them, maybe you don't, but you'll count parachutes and yell for that tenth one to come out.

'Not always, though. Sometimes, nobody bails out. They ride her down, and you know why. One of the crew's hurt, or a parachute is shot to rags, and the guys won't leave one of their own behind, so all the fools will die.' His teeth were bared now, the words pushed through them while a wetness shimmered in his eyes, all hot and bitter. 'Then you watch the German fighters zero in on the parachutes, and you see guys jerking frantically on the shroud lines trying to dodge the bullets streaming at them. Or the ones whose parachutes are on fire and they have a mile to think about the way they're going to die.

'And that's just the fighters,' he said savagely. 'With them, the guys had something to shoot at. But the flak is different. The German artillery's got your range and altitude. They sit on the ground and throw fire at us, peppering the sky with their explosions until the air turns gray-black. Mile after mile, the deeper into Germany you fly, the thicker it gets. More bombers drop out of formation, some blowing up in an intense ball of light and others too damaged to fly on. But the rest of you go on to the target.

'Once you get there and drop the eggs in your bomb bays, you turn for home. And you've gotta fly through that hell again. Chances of coming through it without a scratch are nil. Your plane will have taken a hit, maybe not a bad one. Or one of your crew will be hurt, maybe a scratch or maybe serious. You wait for the fighter protection to pick you up on your way home, and maybe there'll be a little smile when you see the English Channel 'cause you've beat the odds again.'

Walker half turned to look at her lying on the soft, soft bed. She wanted to cry when she saw his stark expression, but fear had her by the throat. She was frightened by his brutal view of the war.

'But that isn't the real hell, Little One. It isn't the air raids, the flight to the target and back. No. The hell is knowing you have to do it again and again. It isn't just once that you go there. It's over and over and over. And your chances of coming back alive dwindle every time until finally you know you're a dead man. So how can they kill you when you're already dead?'

'No.' The awful coldness that came with fear drove Mary Lynn from beneath the covers and against the warmth of his body as she wrapped herself around him, hugging to the living fire.

His words made death seem close, and she wanted to live. It was this instinct that made their urges so strong. Mating was an integral part of procreation – and procreation promised survival. People could live on in their children. Thus, it was not so strange that fear created an aroused sexuality, that before battle, man sought out woman or woman sought out man.

And if two people also found solace and a measure of human warmth in each other's arms, they were that much luckier.

Later, while Mary Lynn slept, Walker stared at the ceiling, one muscled arm flung over his head. He dragged on a smoke and nursed another shot of rum. The pint bottle was nearly empty. His glance wandered to her, her face framed by the dark background of her hair. He remembered the soft black of her eyes, so bottomless and compelling.

He wondered what it was a man searched for in a woman's eyes – what did he hope to see? He'd wanted her, he'd had her, but he still wasn't satisfied. What was wrong with him that he couldn't be happy with what he had? Maybe there was nothing beyond the pleasure of her body for the short time it lasted. Or could they make something that would last longer?

Bitterly, he took another swallow of rum. Many times over Germany, he'd breathed the acrid smell of brimstone. He'd lived in that hell and brought it home with him. It had blackened him and left him thirsty for the good things. But when you lived in hell, how could you expect to hear angels sing?

Again, he looked at her, with a wanting so deep inside him that he wanted to cry. He'd known the rough and wonderful excitement of her giving passions, and his envy of the love she held in reserve for her husband grew immense. It was not easy to take what he could have without wanting more.

400

Tears ran down her cheeks as Marty stood on the front porch of her parents' Michigan home and stared at the gold star on the service flag in the window. A gold star for the death of a soldier son. Oddly, its presence seemed to make David's death more real.

Beyond the windowpane a figure moved; Marty wiped at the wetness on her face and crossed to the front door. She entered the house as her father walked into the foyer. Grief had aged him, bowing his shoulders and draining the life from his stern features. It took him a minute to recognize her in her official summer dress uniform of tailored jacket and skirt in Santiago blue.

'Martha,' he said, somewhat uncertainly.

'I came as soon as I could, Dad.' She hugged him, seeking solace and finding a mechanical response in the arms that went around her. 'I'm sorry, Dad.'

'There's nothing you can do.' He sounded so blank, like someone lost who didn't care about being found. 'There's nothing anyone can do.'

Despite the brilliant June sunshine, a dark gloom prevailed inside the house. Marty felt it as she drew back from her father. There was a suffocating stillness in the air as though nothing lived here anymore.

A small noise came from the living room and Marty turned to see her mother, dressed all in black, framed in its archway. 'Did you tell her?' Althea Rogers said to her husband. 'They aren't even sending his body home to us. They buried it in France. So far away.'

Without once looking at Marty, she turned and walked back into the living room. Marty was left standing alone as her father followed after her tragically forlorn mother. She trailed behind him. When she entered the living room, her attention was claimed by a black-draped photograph of David sitting by itself on a table. Marty felt immediately that she was standing before a shrine.

Her parents sat close together on the couch near the photograph. Her father had a consoling arm around her

401

mother's shoulders while they gazed at the picture. Marty had the awkward feeling that she was intruding as she sat in the armchair across from them. Everywhere she looked there were mementos of David – a photo album, a scrapbook, his bronzed baby shoes.

'Did we tell you what happened?' Tears shimmered in her father's eyes.

'No,' she said softly, huskily.

'He was killed trying to save a buddy who was wounded. He was trying to pull him to safety when a sniper shot him. He was killed instantly.' That seemed to comfort her physician father.

'Some place called Mézières.' Her mother picked up the world atlas lying on the table, opened to a map of France. 'It's located here.' She pointed to one of a hundred dots on the Cotentin Peninsula, and Marty dutifully looked. 'He was such a good boy – so brave.'

'We can be very proud of him, Althea,' her father stated. 'He's been recommended for decoration by his company.'

Marty looked at them, surrounded by the mementos and the black-draped photograph of David, and realized how wrong she had been to think they would need her. She had never been able to compete with her brother when he was alive; she could never hope to win against him now that he was a dead hero.

It was a lonely bitter weekend, during which Marty did her grieving for her brother in private. She would ·miss him, too, but her parents never seemed to consider that. She was glad when she climbed back onto the train to head back to California.

When she arrived at the WASPs' barracks, she noticed Mary Lynn's room was locked. 'Anybody know when Mary Lynn's due back?' she asked the handful of WASPs lounging about the common room.

There was a general shrugging of shoulders until one of them suggested, 'You could ask Captain Walker. He might know.'

Motionless, Marty asked challengingly, 'Why should he know?'

'They spent the weekend together, so I thought she might have mentioned to him when she'll be back in.' The information was indifferently offered. 'He was over at the Officers' Club if you want to ask him.'

'What makes you think they spent the weekend together?' Marty demanded.

'Hey, all I know is that Walker picked her up on Friday and didn't bring her back until Sunday. And I figure during that time they were together. That's all I know.'

Trouble, she knew the man was trouble the first time she laid eyes on him. Marty stood there a minute longer, then went slamming out of the barracks and headed for the Officers' Club.

At Marty's approach, the corporal on duty came to attention and cocked his arm in a rigid salute, as Army protocol demanded, but Marty ignored it – and him – as she charged up the steps of the Officers' Club. The truculent set of her features and the hard flash in her olive-gray eyes were warnings for those in her way to move.

Inside the club, she paused long enough to scan the room and locate the man with the captain's bars on his uniform, sitting alone at a corner table. The evening was early yet, but he looked well ensconced. Marty made a straight line for his table.

Walker saw her coming, neither surprised nor concerned by her arrival. Taking another drink of Coke-diluted rum, he noted with indifference the killing temper that had her energies all coiled for an explosion.

A careless smile indented the corners of his mouth when she stopped by his chair, battle-ready in her 'Ike' jacket and the ruffled honey curls of her Earhart haircut. 'Hello, Martha Jane.' Without looking up, Walker greeted her with her hated given name.

She batted the glass he held so loosely out of his hand to the table. Spilling booze and Coke, it rolled with a crash to the floor. 'You bloody bastard!' She made no attempt to keep her voice down, or to conceal her rage. 'You rotten, stinking son of a bitch! How could you do this to her?'

Walker used a cocktail napkin to push the excess spillage to the far edge of the table, away from himself, and signaled for another drink to be brought. 'Want anything?' He finally lifted his head to look at her.

When he did, the fist that had been cocked on a hair trigger swung at his face, slamming against the side of his jaw and splitting the soft inner flesh of his mouth on his teeth. The blow stung him and coated his tongue with the taste of his own blood. She had penetrated his outward cool and aroused a heat in him. The chair was kicked over as he came to his feet to face his female attacker.

As he took one threatening step toward her, someone grabbed his arms from behind. 'Hey, Walker, cool down,' the voice chided. But he seemed to be the only one who noticed Marty didn't back down an inch. In their locked glances, there was an iron message.

He flexed his muscles to shrug off the restraining hold. 'What you don't know about Martha Jane here,' he said to the officer behind him, 'is that she'd fight dirtier than most men.'

A trickle of blood made a red stain on his lips, coming from the cut in his mouth. Walker wiped at it with his finger, glancing at the bloody smudge briefly, then looked again at Marty. Amidst the raw animosity, there was a glimmer of satisfaction on her face – not enough perhaps, but some.

Uneasy in this atmosphere so charged with hostility, the officer looked from one to the other and backed away. The risk of further physical violence seemed to have passed, although the officer noticed he still hadn't been thanked for coming to Marty's rescue.

The minute they were left alone, Marty started her denunciations again. 'You're worse than scum. You are –'

'Save it.' Walker cut across her words. 'I'm sure you can swear better than a sailor, but I'm not interested in hearing the names you care to call me. If that's all you want, you might as well leave.'

A waiter came to pick up the broken glass and mop up the drink on the floor. His presence stilled Marty's tongue more than Walker's reprimand. He righted his chair and sat back down at the table. Another drink was brought to him. But Marty couldn't leave it at this. She yanked out a chair and sat heavily on it.

'Why?' she demanded to know. 'Why did you do it? Why couldn't you leave her alone?'

'If it hadn't been me, it would have been somebody else.' His forearms rested on the table, both hands closed around the glass.

'No.' Marty didn't accept that weak explanation. 'You were too persistent. You kept after her and after her.' She glared at him, hating him. 'I'll bet you're feeling very proud of yourself. You're drinking to celebrate, aren't you?'

'Celebrate.' He seemed to ponder the word. 'I have very little to celebrate, Martha Jane.'

'Don't tell me you're sorry,' she retorted scornfully, not buying it.

'No, I have no regrets.' He knew what Mary Lynn saw in him – her husband, the way he might be when he came home from the war. But Walker kept that piece of conjecture to himself. It was never wise to examine things too closely, especially relationships. Sometimes it hurt to learn what was below the surface.

'You're nothing but a drunken, used-up pilot who used to fly the big ones,' Marty scoffed. 'The Army's kicked you so far downstairs that you're flying safe, little two-engine passenger ships. You're not a man; you're a coward.'

'I've got my skin – no thanks to the Army – and I mean to keep it.' Walker saw it as survival, rather than cowardice. 'You can be the hot pilot. I just want to live through the war.'

'That's a terrific attitude. I guess it's because of men like you that women pilots are doing most of the dangerous

405

work – the test flying, the target towing. When haven't the women gotten the shitty jobs?' Marty challenged.

'If you don't like it, get out.'

'I'm not a coward and a quitter like you,' she retorted stiffly. 'And a liar and a cheat and a rat – and all the other rotten things you are. I'll never understand' – an angry vehemence broke through – 'I'll never understand why someone like you is alive – and my brother is dead!'

'Look –' Walker lowered his gaze to his cigarette. 'I – I was sorry to hear about your brother.' The offhand offer of sympathy was a vague gesture.

'You shut up about him!' Her husky voice rumbled from deep in her chest, filled with grief. 'David was never afraid of anything in his whole life!'

Her hands were doubled into fists at her side, but Walker didn't say anything. He understood this resentment of the living, although it was seldom so openly admitted. Always, a vague sense of guilt clung to those who survived while their buddies fell.

Nearly finished, she pushed away from the table and stood up. 'Stay away from Mary Lynn while I'm gone, Walker. If you hurt her, I swear I'll get you for it.'

Walker smiled dryly. There was no going back to what had existed before. Always when he looked at Mary Lynn, there would be a sense of ownership. She had belonged to him – and would again. Each time their eyes would meet, a knowingness would be exchanged of the intimacy they had shared. It was a human weakness, this need to touch. And Walker had never claimed to be strong. He stared at his glass while Marty strode away.

Washington, DC, sweltered in the soaring summer temperatures while June officially ushered in the hot season. Major Mitch Ryan blotted the sweat beading on his upper lip. The air was close and stifling in the visitors' gallery of the House, and the heat made it difficult for him to concentrate on the endless debate being waged on the floor below.

His uniform clung damply to his skin and Mitch wished for the milder climate he'd so recently left in England. General Arnold, conferring with the Allied commanders as the combined armies battled inland, had yet to return. The air strategies that had come out of the Casablanca meeting more than a year before had proved successful. The bombing raids, by the US by day and the RAF by night prior to the invasion, had wreaked havoc with the enemy's transportation system, hampering the movement of Nazi reinforcements to Normandy, and their strikes on the aircraft plants had practically castrated the German Luftwaffe, rendering it impotent against the invading forces. The Allies had the superior air power.

So, while General Henry Harley Arnold remained in England, he had ordered Mitch back to the States to observe the House debate on the bill to militarize the WASPs. It seemed Mitch could not escape reminders of Cappy. In his job, it was too easy to keep tabs on her even if he hadn't seen her since they broke up – which was another reason he longed to be somewhere else.

The Washington *Post* had predicted a battle of the sexes over the legislation. Two days before, a Louisiana congressman, James Morrison, had fired the opening shot, critically referring to the WASPs as a glamorous and elite corps who wore stylish uniforms tailored by Neiman-Marcus and protesting the probable windshield-washing job the supposedly more qualified civilian male pilots were likely to get. From the outset, it was clear to Mitch the opposition to the bill was going to be as hot as the weather. He had his own problems being objective about the issue.

The second day, he had sat silently in the gallery while around him supporters of the civilian pilots' cause vocalized their objections to the WASP bill, constantly interrupting the member of the Rules Committee who was attempting to present the resolution and explain its provisions to the House. This turned into a forty-five-minute process. Once the rules had been adopted governing the debate and vote on the legislation, the House adjourned until the following morning, June 22, 1944, the first full day of summer.

Representative Charles Elston of Ohio, on the House Military Affairs Committee and a proponent of the bill, had the floor. '. . . Instructors are required to pass only the Class Two examination, which is the equivalent of the airline pilot test. On the other hand, a WASP must pass the combat examination . . .'

Mitch's attention drifted. All of the arguments for or against the bill were centered around the controversy regarding the civilian male pilots whose services were no longer required in the training of Army pilots. However, with the ground war in Europe beginning, the walking Army needed men. At issue was not whether the women were qualified pilots performing functions vital to the military, but whether they were taking jobs from men.

The thought triggered a flash of recall to the times he'd sat behind the pilot's seat while Cappy flew the plane – and he'd lean forward and kiss the curve of her neck, raising little shivers over her flesh. And the ache surfaced again, taunting and torturing him with images of her. Mitch wanted her – loved her no less than he did before – but the futility of it remained. She had allowed no room for compromise.

'What is it that these women are qualified to do that these CAA pilots cannot do?' Compton White, a congressman from Idaho, made this demand of the bill's sponsor, who had brought the matter to committee the past February.

John Costello, formerly a California lawyer, replied, 'The CAA pilots can qualify, probably for many of the same jobs, but what the Army needs now is fighting men.'

Mitch's glance sought out Costello's opponent in the House as he threw out the challenge, 'And the gentleman wants to take these men out of the flying corps and put them on the ground?'

'No.'

'That is the meat of the coconut, is it not?' White insisted.

408

To this, Representative Costello responded, 'No. If the men are qualified to fly planes, we want to put them in the Army flying planes. If they cannot qualify to fly planes we want to put them in as Army navigators and bombardiers. We want to use every man that is qualified.'

The heat, the debate, the prejudices of the gallery visitors, all combined to make Mitch impatient with the proceedings. White's reply was typical of other questioning comments that had gone before. So much of it was a repeat of arguments that had previously been expressed that Mitch's attention kept wandering.

Costello was speaking again. '. . .This should be done because these women, at present, are denied hospitalization; they are denied insurance benefits and things of that kind to which, as military personnel, they should be entitled. Because of the work they are doing, they should be receiving . . .'

Mitch glanced at his watch and wondered how much longer this would go on. While the debate droned on, he stepped out of the gallery to stretch his legs. When he returned, Karl Stefan was offering his opinion.

'No matter what this House feels about the women in our armed forces, Mr Chairman, I feel now that we are discussing them I cannot resist in some way championing their cause,' the Nebraska Representative said. 'My information is voluminous regarding the ability of these women in flying these monsters of the air through storms and clouds and making safe delivery after thousands of miles of flight. The knowledge of some of these women regarding the reading of maps and the handling of radio and their skill in emergencies are contained in many chapters of thrilling experiences of the Army Air Corps. It will be told more graphically when the war is over . . .'

They all spoke as if the end of the war were imminent, Mitch thought in disgust. The armies were only now entering Cherbourg to secure the Cotentin Peninsula, and in the Pacific, the Navy had engaged the Japanese fleet in the Philippine Sea near the Marianas.

The debate waged on until Representative Edward Izak brought the matter to a head, openly admitting his desire to kill the bill by striking the enacting clause from it. 'There are more than twenty-five hundred men sitting out on the beaches of California' – the state he represented – 'today, who have been instructing for four years, the finest aviators we have in this country. The Army says, "You cannot pass the examination so out you go, but we will uniform these women and let them take your places." Is that not a fine situation?'

That was the crux of it.

After nearly five hours of debate, Mitch was not surprised when the roll was called and 188 versus 169 representatives voted to kill House Resolution 4219 to commission women pilots in the Army Air Forces.

No doubt Cappy would be pleased to learn she would not be part of the Army.

On Monday, General Arnold was back in his Pentagon office, and meeting with his Director of Women pilots. Jacqueline Cochran interpreted the congressional defeat to mean Congress wanted no more women trained at the all-female Avenger Field base in Sweetwater, Texas. The general agreed. Telegrams were sent that morning to inform the class due to report June 30 that the training program was terminated. Those already in training would complete their courses, but no new classes would begin.

By the end of June 1944, twenty-three women pilots had been killed in crashes of their planes. Aircraft mechanical failures were the major cause, although a midair collision occurred when a tower controller negligently gave clearance to two pursuits to land. Some trainees at Avenger Field had been killed when their instructors were in the planes with them.

CHAPTER TWENTY-EIGHT

Jauntily swinging her briefcase and whistling a tuneless song, Marty ran up the steps to the barracks, and nearly bumped into Mary Lynn on her way out. They faced each other for tense, silent seconds while the July sun angled long afternoon rays at them, bathing them in its amber-tinged color.

During the two weeks since Marty had returned from Michigan, conflicting flight schedules had kept them apart – which was just as well because it gave Marty time to get over that first painful blast of anger and hurt at what she saw as Mary Lynn's fall from grace. She tried to put all the blame on Walker, certain that Mary Lynn simply couldn't see what a cad he was.

Irritation glittered in her silvery-green eyes as Marty noticed the raven-blue sheen on Mary Lynn's fresh-washed hair, silkily smoothed over its rat, then studied her face. Mascara blackened the heavy fringe of lashes around her dark eyes, her most striking feature, but the points of color on her round cheeks were not caused by rouge. Her glance dropped away from Marty's as she made a half-move to go around her.

'Going someplace?' Marty demanded, deliberately seeking to make Mary Lynn uncomfortable with her sins. 'With Walker, I presume.'

Mary Lynn attempted a stiff, but very quiet answer. 'I don't think it's any of your business where I'm going or with whom.'

'Is that right?' Hurt and angry, Marty hit her flash point. 'What about Beau? I suppose it isn't any of his business either! I thought you loved him!' She struck hard, trying to make Mary Lynn see sense and remember what she had.

411

'I do,' she insisted. Defensive and sensitive, she answered back with a protesting challenge. 'But I'm human, too. Don't you think I get lonely sometimes?'

'You've got us,' Marty retorted, meaning herself, Cappy, and Eden. In her opinion, that should have been sufficient company for a married woman.

'So do you,' Mary Lynn countered to refute the argument. 'Are you satisfied with our company alone?'

'It isn't the same.' She didn't want to know that Mary Lynn might have the same physical needs that she did – and if she did, it still didn't change anything. 'Nobody's going to get hurt by what I do. But you have a husband. How could you do this to him?'

Mary Lynn's only answers were selfish ones. She had needs and wants, the same as anyone else. Why was she denied the right to satisfy them? Why did she have to give up everything? But there was no real justification beyond the purely selfish reasons. So she walked by Marty without saying another word. She felt guilty about what she was doing, but she didn't know how to stop.

Marty watched her walk down the steps, knowing she hadn't accomplished anything. But she wasn't about to give up. More than ever before, Mary Lynn was going to need her. Turning, she started to enter the barracks, but Cappy was standing in the doorway, eyeing Marty with scorn.

'You've got a lot of nerve, Marty, throwing stones at her,' she said in low-voiced anger. 'Maybe you can tell me why sinners think they know so much more about morals than saints?'

Marty flushed darkly and pressed her way inside the barracks.

On an early August morning, the Douglas C-47 Skytrain made a sightseeing pass over Yellowstone National park in the northwestern. corner of Wyoming. Off the starboard wing, a clearing in the thick summer foliage revealed a log-walled lodge, a massive old giant of a structure that seemed in keeping with the mountain majesty around it. Not far from it, a blossoming fountain of steam and water shot into the air, a billowing spray of cloudy vapor and moisture.

'Did you see that?' Fran Davenport exclaimed excitedly from her copilot's seat, casting one glance at Cappy before turning back to the view. 'It was Old Faithful. What luck! Flying over it just as it erupted! We couldn't have timed that better if we had tried.'

Cappy smiled at Fran's contagious enthusiasm, the unabashed delight she took in things. This was the first time they'd been paired together as a flying team. The first leg wasn't over but Cappy could already tell Fran had the ability to turn a routine flight into a minor adventure.

'Do you plan your routes according to the points of interest along the way?' she asked in jest.

'When I can,' Fran Davenport admitted frankly while she continued to gaze out the cockpit window on the starboard side. Yellowstone Lake was a sapphire blue reflection of the late summer sky. 'Before I qualified for the WASPs and went to Texas for my training, I'd never been out of the state of Iowa in my life. Now I'm flying from one end of the country to the other. I may never get another chance to travel like this, and I'm going to see everything while I can.'

'I don't blame you.'

Climbing back to altitude, the twin-engined transport swung past Saddle Mountain and threaded between Windy Mountain and Sunlight peak, encountering only mild turbulence on the leeward side of the range. The thick forests of Yellowstone Park gave way to a barren stretch of rough Wyoming country.

'What's that?' Fran pointed out a collection of buildings grouped in the middle of nowhere. 'It looks like a town or a base of some sort, but my maps don't indicate anything here.'

Cappy tipped the plane so she could see over the wing. A large patch of green stood out in sharp contrast to the

413

surrounding arid land and the bleak-looking structures near it, fenced by a barbed-wire enclosure.

'It must be the Japanese internment camp at Heart Mountain,' she guessed.

'Really?' Fran strained for a better look. 'I thought they were in prisons of some sort. That doesn't look like one.'

'It's fenced and guarded,' Cappy reminded her. 'I doubt if it's the most hospitable place to live.' A stiffness was beginning to settle into her shoulders from being in the same position. She arched them in a flexing shrug. 'You take the controls for a while, Fran,' she suggested.

They had a long way to go to their destination, Wright Field in Dayton, Ohio. There was no need to make it a tiring trip when they could spell each other along the way. Fran took over as pilot and Cappy leaned back.

Late in the afternoon they landed at Wright Field and taxied to the flight line to deliver their craft. The base was the center of Air Material Command, in charge of monitoring research, engineering, testing, and procuring equipment for the Army Air Force. Experiments and tests of new engines, instruments, and aircraft designs were constantly being conducted at the field.

As they walked from their parked plane to the operations building, Fran had to run backwards to keep up with Cappy and still look at the unusual array of planes on the flight line. 'That's a Japanese Zero,' she exclaimed. 'And look! There's a Messerschmitt.'

A sudden, high-pitched whine came loudly across the field, an unearthly howl that halted both Cappy and Fran. They stared, trying to pinpoint the source of it, as the eerie scream continued to drift through the air.

'What is that?' Fran wondered, frowning at the weird sound.

'I don't know,' Cappy murmured.

'They're testing a prototype jet engine.' The female voice startled both of them and they swung around to look at the woman pilot in her Santiago-blue flight suit. She smiled easily. 'Hi. Where are you from?'

'The Ferry Command out of Long Beach.' Cappy answered automatically, intrigued by the revelation. 'A jet. It's powered by that new propulsion system that pushes the plane through the air with its exhaust, instead of pulling it with a propeller. I'd heard about those jet-rocket attacks on England and wondered what those German buzz-bombs sounded like. Now I know.'

'Have you seen it?' Fran asked.

'Don't I wish,' the WASP replied. 'I've had glimpses of it, but that's it. I sure would love to climb into the cockpit of a jet, though.'

'Do you fly out of here?'

'I'm one of their test pilots for new oxygen systems, gun sights and other experimental equipment, or new engine designs.'

'Sounds exciting,' Cappy observed while the three of them started toward the operations building.

'It is,' she agreed. 'This place is real futuristic. When they say the sky's the limit, they mean it. Some engineers here are talking about going to the moon.'

At operations, they split up, Cappy and Fran going one way to file their papers and the female test pilot going another. When they were finlshed, they passed up the food at the canteen in favor of dinner at the Officers' Club.

When they walked in, the first person Cappy saw was Mitch Ryan. The ground seemed to rock under her and her pulse made a crazy leap. for an unsteady moment, she didn't know what to do. Unbidden, her feet carried her to him.

'Hello, Mitch.' She stopped beside his chair, smiling hesitantly, unsure of her welcome. But Cappy knew she wanted to see him – to speak to him.

With a turn of his head he looked up, into the startling blueness of her eyes. For a small second, he betrayed himself, then quickly the shutters came down to block out the glow of pleasure. The pain was still cruelly fresh.

Just for an instant, Cappy experienced that sweeping rush of excitement his smile had so often evoked in the past. Then his warmth was pulled away from her, and it was gone, and his expression was set in rugged, forbidding lines.

'Hello, Cappy.' His voice was flat.

'I was surprised to see you here when I walked in.'

'I don't know why you were.' Mitch rolled the ash off his cigarette on the edge of the ashtray. 'This is an Army base. You won't find me anywhere else.' His dark eyes gleamed with challenge.

Cappy drew back, belatedly noticing the woman in a WAC uniform sitting at the table with him. 'Mitch and I are old friends,' she said to quell the speculating look from the curly-headed blonde.

'Yes, we were good friends.' Mitch put it in the past tense.

'If you'll excuse me, my friend's waiting,' Cappy said abruptly. The scene had become too awkward. She backed away, hating him for making her feel like an unwanted outsider.

Fran was waiting for her at a table. 'Is he an old friend of yours?' Her admiring gaze strayed to Mitch.

'Was.' Cappy used his past tense.

'Ah,' Fran guessed. 'An old flame, eh?'

Without confirming or denying it, Cappy sat down and picked up the menu, but her eyes darted to the table where Mitch was sitting. She watched as he bent close to the woman, saying something and smiling. Her teeth came together on the sudden surge of jealousy.

During dinner, Cappy tried to ignore the pair, but it was difficult as she became conscious of Mitch's attention centering more and more on the woman with the flaxen hair. The WAC officer was every bit Mitch's age, if not on the high side of thirty, she thought cattily.

The more she tried not to watch them together, the more compelling it became to look. She hated the twisting jealousy she felt as she observed the intimate way Mitch watched the words form on that vividly red pair of lips.

Minutes later they were getting up from their table to

416

dance. It was almost more than Cappy could stand to see them twined so closely together and that slow, caressing movement of Mitch's hand on the woman's back.

'You're really a lot of fun tonight,' Fran murmured dryly.

'Excuse me.' Abruptly, Cappy pushed away from the table and walked blindly to the powder room to escape the sight of the dancing couple, nuzzling and kissing on the floor.

Splashes of cold water cooled her hot face, the shock of it driving away the tears that had burned the back of her eyes. Cappy managed to rationalize her reaction, convincing herself it was to be expected, but she'd get over it. She remained in the quiet of the powder room until her nerves felt steadier.

As she ventured outside, she met Mitch coming out of the men's facilities. A smudge of vibrant red was near the corner of his mouth and all the hot feelings she'd struggled to suppress came running back to the surface.

'You didn't get all the lipstick wiped off, Mitch,' she informed him, and angrily watched his hand move instinctively to his mouth.

His fingers came away with some of the telltale red on their tips. 'So I didn't.' Untroubled, he wiped the rest of it away with his handerchief.

'You wanted me to see it, didn't you?' Her teeth were held tightly together as Cappy struggled with the pain she felt, the wish to somehow strike back.

His aloof bearing didn't alter as he made slow work of folding his handkerchief and returning it to his pocket. 'Have you seen the report your illustrious director released to the press the first of the month?'

'I've seen articles on it, yes,' she admitted warily.

'In it, she made the same mistake you did. She virtually issued an ultimatum to General Arnold, by stating that if her WASPs can't be commissioned, then serious thought should be given to ending the program.' At his statement Cappy tensed, and Mitch smiled in a slow, unkind humor.

'Congress is in no mood to militarize a bunch of women pilots. And General Arnold is a pragmatic man. He isn't about to whip a dead horse. I'd wager my oak leaves that you won't be in the air much longer. But you shouldn't mind. After all, the alternative would have meant becoming part of the Army. And I know how violently opposed you are to that.'

'I don't really blame you for wanting to get back at me for hurting you,' Cappy declared tautly. 'But I hate you for this, Mitch Ryan.'

His hands caught her, stopping her and holding her by the shoulders. For a long minute, he simply looked down at her, his jaw clenched and angry. With reluctance, his gaze traveled over her features in a memorizing pattern.

'Do you?' he ground out bitterly. 'You have no idea how badly I want to say, "Frankly, my dear, I don't give a damn!" . . . But the hell of it is – I still do!'

He released her with a roughness that indicated a wish that he could rid himself of her memory just as easily. Torn and troubled, Cappy looked at the broad set of his shoulders, which was all she saw of him as he strode away.

Amid all the smarting hurt, the jealousy and the resentment, she felt a stab of fear at the thought of losing her wings, or being taken out of the skies and out of the uniform she wore with such pride. If they were disbanded, where would she go?

The sight of a B-17 bomber on the Long Beach flight line was not that common. When Marty spied the big bird with its hundred-foot-plus wingspan, she gravitated to it, gripped by nostalgia at the hours she'd flown in similar Fortresses.

'The Big Friend,' she said as she trailed her hand along the fuselage, caressing the metal skin. Her glance flickered to the plexiglas nose and three-bladed propellers of the heavy bomber. 'Losing you over a man,' she murmured wryly. 'He wasn't worth it, I promise you that.'

A ground man bent low to peer under the plane's belly

at the trousered legs on the other side. 'Are you talking to me?'

Marty bent down, previously unaware anyone else was around. 'Yes,' she lied. 'Is it all right if I take a look inside?'

'Sure. It's all right with me. You can have a whole party in there if you want,' he said magnanimously. It wasn't the first time one of these women pilots had asked to crawl into the cockpit of a plane. He'd long ago decided it was some kind of compulsion to have been in as many as possible.

Not needing a second invitation, Marty walked to the belly hatch and tossed her gear in, then pulled herself up to swing inside the fuselage. Slowly she moved forward, taking her time to look around and rediscover.

As she approached the cockpit, Marty spied an Army captain sitting in the pilot's seat. With a welling disappointment she started to back up, but the man caught the sound of her footfall and turned. She locked eyes with Walker and a fine anger ran smoothly through her veins.

'This is the last place I expected to see you, Walker.' She came forward and maneuvered into the unoccupied right seat. She looked over the familiar instrument panel, remembering all those blindfolded checks during training when they had to point out the location of instruments without being able to see them.

'Well, if it isn't Martha Jane,' he mused dryly.

'Where'd you find the nerve to get back in one of these?' Marty asked tauntingly.

'It's been a while since I was in the cockpit of one of these.' Walker absently rubbed his hand along the yoke, remembering, while he glanced over the array of gauges and switches. 'I wanted to see how it would feel again.' Then he turned to her. 'What's your excuse?'

'The same,' she admitted, with a qualification. 'Except it doesn't scare me. If those engines started up, I'll bet you'd shake in your boots.'

'You still despise me, don't you?' His hard and knowing

eyes looked her up and down. 'You still think I led Mary Lynn astray, don't you?'

Facing the front, Marty gripped the yoke, her fingers flexing and tightening their hold on it, suggesting a seething anger. 'I'd rather not talk about her.'

'You're a hard woman, Martha Jane. A real bitch. Don't you know yet why she sees me?' The challenge in his voice sounded bitter. 'She's afraid her husband might come home all twisted up inside like me. You were right a long time ago when you said she loved him.'

'I'm sure you're an expert on the subject,' she retorted sarcastically, 'but I'm really not interested in hearing your opinions.'

'What does interest you?'

'Flying.'

'Only flying?'

'Sometimes I think men aren't worth the trouble they cause,' she muttered. 'I never have had much patience with cowards and cheats, either way.'

'You know it all, don't you, Martha Jane?' Walker scoffed. 'You think you're a hot pilot, don't you?'

'I know I am.'

'Yeah? Well, I think I want to find out just how hot you are.' He started to rise.

'Meaning what?' Marty demanded.

Half out of the pilot's seat, he paused, bent over in a crouch. 'Meaning – that we're going to take this Big Friend for a ride. I want to find out how much of you is hot pilot – and how much is hot air.' He pressed a hand on her shoulder, pushing her more deeply into the copilot's seat. 'Wait here while I get permission to take this lady. If you're not here when I get back, I'll know you chickened out.'

Part of her didn't expect to see him again after he disappeared into the operations building, but Marty made a preliminary check of the cockpit gauges. She had no pride. She'd fly with the devil if it meant a chance to pilot a Flying Fortress again.

Twenty minutes later, Walker was crossing the flight

line at a running jog, giving Marty a thumbs-up sign to indicate permission granted. With a leap of anticipation and soaring spirits, Marty grinned to herself and pulled out the pre-takeoff checklist to prepare for the engine start-ups. From the underneath fuselage, she heard the small thuds of movement when Walker hauled himself into the plane.

Upon entering the cockpit, he tapped her on the shoulder and motioned her to take the pilot's seat. 'You fly,' he said, quickly taking the seat she vacated. 'But for God's sake, stay off the radio. You know how they feel about mixed crews. They think my second is "Martin" Rogers.'

'Hell, even if I got on the mike, they wouldn't know,' Marty declared in her man-gruff voice, flipping on the electrical switch that activated the hydraulic pump which gave oil pressure to the number-one engine. 'How did you wangle this?' She pushed the button to start the first 1,200-horsepower Wright engine.

'There are ways, Martha Jane,' Walker answered above the rumbling cough of the engine before it caught and thundered into a steady growl, the huge propellers spinning into a blur of metal.

Soon, all four engines reverberated in a deafening roar. The immense power, and the excitement of it, vibrated through the throttles as Marty advanced them to begin the roll. While she waited for takeoff clearance at the end of the runway, she gave Walker a wry glance.

'You look a little pale, Walker,' she chided. 'If you're going to lose your stomach, wait until we're airborne.'

'You just worry about yourself,' he replied.

With the underhanded grip she'd been taught, Marty moved the throttles forward and the big bomber lumbered down the runway gathering speed. As the airspeed indicator approached the 110-mile-an-hour mark, she could feel the long wings grabbing for the air and the controls become more responsive to her touch. When she pulled back on the control wheel, the B-17 broke free from the ground, acquiring grace as it soared into the air. The hydraulics system hummed to fold the landing gear and tail wheel into the belly of the plane with a locking thud.

The exhilaration of flight pounded through her veins. She angled the Fortress for the high clouds and banked it toward the empty desert. Everything came back to her. It was just as if she'd never been away from the cockpit of the Boeing B-17. At twelve thousand feet above the low desert, she leveled the bomber out. The September skies around them were free of traffic.

'Now, we'll put her through her paces,' she said to Walker. 'We'll see if you've got the stomach for some real flying.'

For the next twenty minutes, Marty had the massive four-engine bomber performing a circus act of aerial acrobactics, putting it through spins and loops and chandelles with flawless precision – all for the sheer joy of it. It ceased to matter that Walker was sitting in the right seat.

His low voice intruded. 'Are you through showing off?'

'Are you still here?' she returned mockingly.

'Yes. And it's my turn,' he announced.

Grudgingly, she surrendered the controls to him. Seconds later, she was treated to an exhibition of flying skill such as she had never seen. Walker more than matched her level of excellence. A lesser pilot would have felt like a rank amateur in his shadow.

After they landed back at Long Beach, Marty lowered herself out of the belly hatch and turned to wait for Walker. As he joined her on the ground, she studied him with a keen respect, however reluctantly given.

'You're a helluva pilot,' she admitted, even though she loathed finding something to admire about him.

'So are you.' He returned the compliment in the same reserved tone. 'Funny, isn't it?'

'What?' Marty stiffened.

'We both love the same things – those big bombers and Mary Lynn – but we can't stand each other,' Walker stated.

'Yeah. That's true,' she admitted. She started to swing

away, then hesitated. 'That was some ride up there.'

'It was.'

Her hand lifted in a kind of acknowledging salute, which Walker returned. With her hands shoved into the side pockets of her blue uniform slacks, Marty walked away from the big plane and the Army captain standing in its shadow.

CHAPTER TWENTY-NINE

The mimeographed letters swept through the barracks like a shock wave on that first Tuesday in October. The first was from the Director of Women pilots. After Marty had opened the official-looking envelope from the Army Air Force Headquarters in Washington, she didn't get beyond the cold, impersonal first lines.

To all WASP: General Arnold has directed that the WASP Program be deactivated on 20 December 1944. Attached is a letter from him to each of you and it explains the circumstances . . .

There was more, but Marty didn't bother reading it. She bolted from her room, the letters half-crumpled in her hand, and charged down the hall, coming to Eden's door first. Without knocking she swept inside.

'Have you –' Marty didn't have to say any more.

The redhead's posture as she sat on the cot and the stunned look on her face were all the answer Marty needed. Slowly, Eden looked up. Her reaction bordered on outrage. 'How can they do this?'

Mary Lynn appeared in the door opening, the letters drooping from her hand and tears making a black shimmer of her eyes. 'You got yours, too,' she said.

'Yes.' Eden stared again at the typewritten words that signaled the beginning of the end.

'Surely there's something we can do,' Marty protested, goaded by the way they seemed to accept the decision as final. 'Are we just going to let them pat us on the head and send us home? "Be a good girl and run along – we don't need you anymore." That's what they're saying!'

'If it's the money, I'll fly for nothing,' Eden stated.

'Their minds are made up,' Mary Lynn interjected to end their windmill-tilting. 'You aren't going to change them. The letters were very clear.' She looked down to hide the thickening tears in her eyes. 'We really should be glad the war is being won. The middle of December, Beau might be coming home with some of the pilots they expect to release from combat duty.'

One of the prime reasons they had gone to Sweetwater over a year and a half before was the desire to contribute to the war effort. But a subtle change had taken place.

Now that seemed of secondary importance. More than anything, they wanted to fly.

'Hey, van Valkenburg.' A head was stuck inside her room long enough for the woman to relay the message. 'You've got a visitor at the gate.'

'Tell whoever it is to go away!' Eden snapped.

'Tell 'em yourself.' And she was gone.

'I might as well go,' she muttered, rising from her cot. As she turned to drop the letters atop the Army blanket, Eden wondered aloud, 'Do you suppose Cappy has heard?' She'd left the week before on a ferry assignment and hadn't returned to Long Beach yet.

'Cappy knows everything,' Marty responded. 'She probably knew what the Army planned to do with us long before these letters were written.'

'She would have said something to me.' Eden dismissed the notion as she grabbed up her uniform jacket and slipped it on.

She was not interested in seeing any visitors, especially at this particular time. Eden had many 'acceptable' acquaintances in southern California, who thought it was a 'kick' that one of their own actually flew planes for the war effort. She supposed it was one of them wanting her to attend some social event.

At a distance, Eden saw the man standing with his hands folded behind him. It was obvious from his dress that he wasn't a Californian, accustomed to warm, sunny weather virtually year round. In addition to a dark suit, he wore a vest and tie – none of the open-collared, ascot-scarfed look for him. Sunlight flashed a reflection off his glasses.

'Ham!' Eden cried in surprise and rushed to greet him. 'What are you doing here?' She grabbed his hands. Suddenly, she was glad he had come. She needed the support and comfort he always gave her. In a rare demonstration of sincere affection toward him, Eden let go of his hands to wrap her arms around him and hug him tight while she pressed her cheek against his. 'It's good to see you.'

For a second, conservative Hamilton Steele was too startled to respond, then his arms loosely embraced her. 'If I'd known I would receive such a warm welcome, I would have come sooner.' His attempt at levity made Eden wonder if she was embarrassing him.

She pulled back, her head hanging slightly. 'Your timing couldn't have been better – or worse, depending on how you look at it.' A short sigh ran from her. 'The notice came today that we're being disbanded . . . as of December twentieth.'

'That's it.' Hamilton kept his disappointment to himself. 'In the face of that bad news, you need some cheering up. I recommend dinner at the Brown Derby . . . with me, of course.'

'And lots of Scotch so I can drown my sorrows.' A smile tugged wryly at her mouth. 'Dear Ham, you always know what I need.'

At the famed Hollywood club, over drinks and dinner, he told her about the business trip that had brought him to the West Coast. Eden listened, admittedly inattentively, although she knew he was trying to distract her from the unpleasant news. Her gaze wandered around the club's plush interior, the walls festooned with celebrity caricatures, but Eden was unable to rise to its atmosphere of sparkling sophistication.

'Would you care to talk about it?' he invited gently.

A second's pause, then she shook her head. 'It wouldn't do anything but make me more angry and depressed.' She held her after-dinner drink of Cointreau by the top of the glass as she swirled the liqueur and watched its play of amber and brown.

'Maybe this will help,' he suggested mysteriously, and he reached in his pocket to take something from it and lay it on the table in front of her.

When his hand came away, Eden saw bright, burning lights reflected off thousands of diamond facets. The brilliant in the center of the ring was a large carat-and-a-half American-cut diamond, surrounded by baguette diamonds to create a star-shaped design.

'I picked that up in Tiffany's the other day,' Ham said in the most casual manner. 'I thought you might like it.'

'It's stunning,' Eden admitted. But the proposal the diamond ring implied made her response reserved. 'Ham, I –'

He lifted a silencing hand. 'Don't say anything yet,' he requested. 'It comes as no surprise, I'm sure, that I would like to marry you. I believe I have mentioned it innumerable times in the past. I thought on this occasion I should make my presentation to you before that . . . uh . . . mechanic whisks you away.'

'But –'

'Eden.' Hamilton reached across the table to take her hand. 'You know I can give you the kind of life you want. You would be happy with me . . . perhaps never deliriously so . . . but you would be happy. The way I see it, your mechanic and I are playing for very high stakes – you.' He paused to smile faintly. 'It's my opinion that you are too rich for his blood.'

'I wish you hadn't done this,' Eden protested mildly.

426

'I don't want you to give me an answer now.' He went on as calmly as if he were discussing a business deal. 'I want you to regard this as one of the options available to you when you decide what you're going to do with your future. After all, the Army isn't going to let you fly for them after December, so you'll have to find something to keep you occupied.'

'True.' She couldn't help smiling at his dry wit. He made a practical appeal rather than a passionate one, which, coming from him, would have seemed ludicrous.

'In any event, I wish you to keep the ring.' He folded it into the palm of her hand and closed her fingers tightly around it. 'It's yours . . . as an engagement ring or a dowry for your marriage to someone else . . . or merely a pretty bauble for your finger.'

Subdued, Eden looked at the sparkling brilliance of the ring. 'Sometimes, Ham, I think you're too good for me.'

The deactivation notice started the base commanders scrambling to find male pilots and train them to fill the roles the women were being forced to vacate. Qualified pursuit pilots were in particularly short supply while the number of planes to be delivered to embarkation points hadn't dwindled. The WASP squadron at Long Beach sent telegrams to President Roosevelt, General Arnold, and others, volunteering to fly for the annual salary of one dollar to alleviate the problem. But their offer was politely turned down.

It left a bitter aftertaste as far as Marty and the others were concerned. Their skills were still needed, but they were being dismissed just because they were women. The war wasn't even over. By the end of October 1944, France was liberated, MacArthur had returned to the Philippines, and Russia was in Norway; but they were getting cheated out of being there at the end, when victory came. After the war was over, everyone would have to go home, but they had to go now – before the job was finished.

When they finally accepted the inevitable, they started to look for jobs. With their training, flying time, and experience in a variety of aircraft, they were uniquely qualified. Most combat pilots had flown one basic type of aircraft, and sometimes logging most of their hours in one individual plane, knowing every groan and cough it made like an old friend, while Marty had flown everything from a B-17 and a Mustang to a red-lined Dauntless dive-bomber, hopping from one strange plane to another, never knowing its idiosyncrasies.

In southern California, Lockheed, Douglas, North American, and Consolidated-Vultee all had aircraft plants. Marty applied for a flying job at each of them, but she was turned down cold. They didn't need pilots. Others received similar answers. It was the same all across the country.

All four of them – Marty, Cappy, Eden, and Mary Lynn – were crowded into Cappy's room, straining to read the job opportunities listed in a newsletter put together by some WASPs stationed in Alabama. Marty was the first to pull away.

'Nobody is going to hire us – not to fly,' she declared. 'The airlines have invited us to come to work for them – as stewardesses. The Civil Aeronautics Administration needs control tower operators. Or we could work as aircraft accident analysts or Link training instructors.'

'It doesn't look very promising, does it,' Cappy murmured.

'Maybe you can trade that Air Medal they're going to award you in for a flying job,' Marty suggested caustically. 'It would be more useful.'

Supposedly the Air Medal was being given to her in recognition of the feat she performed when she ferried a P-51, two P-47s, and a C-47 Skytrain to their destinations over a five-day period, forty hours of flying, covering eight thousand miles. Although she had been singled out, Cappy regarded it as a gesture of recognition for all the women pilots. The medal was to be presented to her at Avenger Field in Sweetwater, she'd been told, in conjunction with

428

the graduation of the last class of trainees, 44-W-10 . . . a visible sign of praise, a last pat on the head.

'The only thing I see interesting in this newsletter is the list of aviation companies in Alaska,' Eden remarked, then jested dryly, 'At least it would give me an excuse to buy a bunch of furs.'

'I didn't know you needed an excuse,' Marty countered.

'Do you think you could live in Alaska?' Mary Lynn sounded skeptical.

Eden shrugged. 'I haven't decided if I could live in Texas yet,' she said. 'Which reminds me – did I mention that Bubba's in Texas on furlough? I've got a job interview for a flight instructor's position in San Antonio. Command is letting me have a plane and three days' leave. Regardless of how the job turns out, I figured Bubba and I could at least have a day sunning on Padre Island.'

South of San Antonio, the countryside turned flat, studded with mesquite and prickly pear, thick brush-covered scrubland, good for a rangy bunch of cattle and little else – in Eden's opinion. They'd driven for miles along dusty roads, through half-deserted little towns and lonely junctions.

'If you don't want to stop and meet my folks, it's okay,' Bubba was yelling over the noise of the wind blowing through the open car windows, letting in the choking dust and a blessed stir of air. 'We'll go straight on to Padre.'

'I'd like to meet them,' Eden insisted, and tried to hide the reluctance she was actually feeling. 'What's Refugio like? That is the name of your home town, isn't it?'

'Yep.' A smile edged his wide mouth as he took his gaze from the long, straight road to glance at her. 'It's a small place . . . not much different from some of these towns we've gone through. Pretty quiet most of the time. 'Course, Saturday night is the big night in town.'

The wind blew her hair across her face and she turned into the fast rush of air while she lifted it away and held it aside. With a heaviness of spirit, Eden stared down the road, not speaking.

429

'You never did say how that interview turned out,' Bubba prompted after a silence had run long.

'It didn't.' But that wasn't what was weighing her down. 'They thought by hiring a female instructor they might attract more women to learn to fly, but it seems female students have more faith in male instructors. So they'd already hired a man for the position, and simply neglected to notify me that it had been filled.'

'That's too bad.'

'Bubba.' She dragged her gaze from the empty road ahead of them and the equally empty landscape around them to look at him. 'Were you planning to come back here to Texas after the war?'

'It's my home.'

Again Eden stared absently out the window, searching for something that she couldn't find. Finally, she sighed in defeat. 'I think you'd better stop the car, Bubba. It's time we stopped kidding ourselves.'

After one look at her very sober expression, Bubba pulled the car off to the side of the road. The trailing dust cloud caught up with them and swirled around the car before settling on a cactus bush. For a long second, he looked at her, then he ran his hands up the steering wheel, pulling his feelings inside.

'Yeah, I reckon you're right,' he said finally while the narrowed pinpoints of his eyes examined the rough land beyond the windshield. 'You don't belong here . . . and I don't fit in your world.'

'I love you, Bubba.' Pain and frustration vibrated through her voice.

'You know I love you,' he said and pulled in a deep breath, releasing it on a laughing note. 'I guess the poets were wrong when they said love conquers all.' He reached for the ignition key to start the car motor again. 'I'll drive you back to San Antonio.'

Eden wanted to stop him – to have these last two days with him, but what would they bring? Only more heartaches and regret. So she said nothing as he reversed the car to turn around in the middle of the road and go back the way they came.

At the airport, he carried her bag to the plane and loaded it aboard. They stood awkwardly in front of each other. Eden had tears in her eyes.

'My daddy is probably going to have to buy an airline so I can get a job flying from him,' she joked weakly. 'If he does, you can be the maintenance chief.'

'Yeah, sure.' But they both knew it would never come to pass.

'I'll never forget you, Bubba.' Her voice started shaking. 'I wish –'

'No.'

His hands touched her and she went into his arms. They kissed fiercely, aching with all the tomorrows that would never be for them. Then Eden pulled away and climbed into her plane. Bubba stood on the ground and watched her take off for the last time.

The new gymnasium at Avenger Field was crowded with Army officers, families, and friends, there to witness the pomp and ceremony of the graduation exercises for the last class of WASPs. While the sixty-eight graduates marched into the gym, the Big Spring Bombardier School Band played the 'Air Corps Song.' Cappy thought they played better at the graduation of her class, but perhaps the tune had been stronger, more inspiring then. 'Off we go into the wild blue yonder, climbing high into the sun . . .' With the end near, the words had a poignancy they had not had previously.

The brass had turned out in force for this occasion. An array of generals was present, as well as the WASP Director, Jacqueline Cochran, and General H. H. Arnold himself. Mitch was here, too. Cappy had caught sight of him earlier when the Commanding General of the Army Air Force arrived. Somewhere in the audience, her parents were seated, on hand to see their daughter awarded the flying medal. Naturally, the Army had notified them of the

431

occasion, and Cappy had written her mother about it as well. She wasn't sure that her father would come but she'd seen both her parents at a distance before the ceremonies started.

Today was the third anniversary of Pearl Harbor. Cappy's thoughts wandered as General Yount of the Army Training Command addressed the throng. Avenger Field had changed since she had trained there. The construction was finished on all the runways; two new hangars had been built, and a swimming pool. A ground man told her they had electric runway lights, no more trucks racing out at dusk to set out the oil pots. But the painted rendition of Walt Disney's character, Fifinella, the WASP mascot, still sat atop the administration building and the Wishing Well was still there.

'. . . Well, now in 1944' – General Arnold was in the middle of the keynote address – 'more than two years since WASPs first started flying with the Air Forces, we can come to only one conclusion – the entire operation has been a success. It is on the record that women can fly as well as men. In training, in safety, in operations, your showing is comparable to the overall record of the AAF flying within the continental United States. That was what you were called upon to do – continental flying. If the need had developed for women to fly our aircraft overseas, I feel certain that the WASPs would have performed that job equally well.

'Certainly we haven't been able to build an airplane you can't handle. From AT-6s to B-29s, you have flown them around like veterans. One of the WASPs even flight-tested our new jet plane.'

At that announcement, Cappy wondered if it had been the girl they'd met on the flight line that day at Wright Field. She could still remember the scream of those jet engines.

'You have worked hard at your jobs,' the general said. 'Commendations from the generals to whose commands you have been assigned are constantly coming across my

432

desk. These commendations record how you have buckled down to the monotonous, the routine jobs which are not much desired by our hot-shot young men headed back to combat or just back from an overseas tour. In some of your jobs, I think they like you better than men . . .'

Cappy searched the crowd of faces for Mitch. There were so many things she hadn't seen – that she hadn't understood about herself the last time they'd met. She wanted the chance to tell him she'd been wrong – about the Army, about everything. She owed him that much.

The general had finished his speech and Jacqueline Cochran had taken the podium. After some opening remarks, she talked about the Air Medal and described how Cappy had earned it. When her name was called, Cappy came forward to receive the service medal. Distinguished, snowy-haired General 'Hap' Arnold pinned it over her breast, his round cheeks coloring slightly with embarrassment at the task.

After the ceremonies were over, the overflowing crowd spilled out the doors onto the base. Her mother waited to embrace her and proudly admire the medal she'd earned. Her father stood back, more silvered at the temples of his dark mane. Cappy noticed the shimmer in his eyes when she turned to him.

'You should be very proud,' he informed her with a military jut of his chin.

'I am.'

Lieutenant Colonel Robert Hayward tilted his head down and seemed to fumble awkwardly for the words he wanted to say, but they were difficult for him. 'Long ago . . . I used to wish for the day . . . a son of mine would . . . follow in the old man's footsteps, so to speak. But your mother and I weren't blessed with any sons. But today –' He lifted his head, and the tears glittering in his eyes were unmistakable. '– You made that wish come true. You, my daughter.'

Cappy hugged him. She knew he couldn't break that rigid discipline that frowned on emotional displays, so she did it for him. This day, she had gained his respect, a most precious thing. But Cappy also knew she had received it because the Army had acknowledged her worth, not because her father saw it. In these last couple of months since she had received the letter announcing the disbandment of the WASPs, she had mellowed and learned to accept the things she couldn't change and be grateful for the things she had, including her father's respect.

When she drew away, her father had managed to blink back the tears and display some military decorum again. 'When do you anticipate you'll be coming home after your mustering out?'

'I don't know.' But her glance went past him as Cappy spied Mitch standing near the generals. 'Excuse me, Dad. I'll only be a minute.'

So tall, so tan, lean, and muscular in his Army uniform, Mitch watched her approach with a blank expression. Her steps slowed as she drew near him, a thudding deep inside her.

'Hello, Mitch.'

'Congratulations.' He nodded at the Air Medal pinned to her jacket.

'Thank you.' Cappy hesitated only a moment, then asked with a false calm, 'Can we walk? I'd like to speak to you about something . . . privately, if it's all right.'

After a short glance at the generals to weigh how long they'd be, Mitch inclined his head in a nod of agreement and swung away to match her stride. As they made their way through the slowly dissipating crowd, she stole glances at his profile.

No one was around the Wishing Well. Cappy slowed her steps to stop beside the stone-walled reflecting pool. The fountain bubbled in the center and coins shimmered in the bottom. A plaque from General Arnold was mounted in the pool, inscribed: 'To the Best Women pilots in the World.' For no reason, she tossed a coin into the Wishing Well, without even making a wish. It made a plunking splash, sending out a small ripple.

'This brings back a lot of memories,' she said, then added wistfully, 'Soon that's all there will be.'

'Have you decided what you're going to do?' Mitch didn't sound interested, and when Cappy glanced at him, he didn't look interested either.

'I'm still looking for a flying job . . . without much luck.'

'I wouldn't feel too bad about it. Neither has Jacqueline Cochran. She's going aboard Northeast Airlines . . . as a director, in hopes of attracting more female passengers. And she's a flying ace with countless world records to her credit.'

'Like Earhart,' Cappy mused, but she didn't want to talk flying, at least not that aspect of it.

She sat down on the stone lip of the pool while Mitch remained standing. She let her fingers trail in the water. It seemed easier to talk if she didn't look at him.

'It isn't easy for anyone to swallow their pride and admit when they've made a mistake. I'm no different from anyone else in that respect,' Cappy said with a shrugging tilt of her head. 'When we were denied commissions in the Army, it took me a while to realize how much I had wanted it.'

Her gaze went to Mitch, needing to see his reaction to her words and discover whether they made any difference to him. His eyes were on her, watching, committing nothing.

'I don't want to turn in this uniform, Mitch.' Her voice was low and vibrant with the strength of her feelings. 'These girls are my sisters. I said I never had a home . . . family or friends. I was wrong. Home was every barracks I stayed in across this country for the last year and a half. The WASPs were my family and friends.' Cappy paused for a long second. 'I guess I'm trying to say that I had to be a part of it to understand. And I had to lose it to know it. I don't hate the Army any more, Mitch.'

'And?'

'That's all.' She looked again into the reflecting pool, a little ache starting inside.

'Is it supposed to make a difference to me?' Mitch asked.

She had hoped it would, but it obviously hadn't. With a quick move, she came to her feet, seeking to make her escape. Her head was up, held by that measure of pride that she wouldn't release.

'I wanted you to know, Mitch.' Cappy walked carefully around his question. 'Goodbye.'

His hand stopped her. 'Did you want it to make a difference to me, Cappy?' Mitch demanded. 'If you did, then dammit, say so!'

Her eyes were bluer than anything he'd ever seen, and her lips were trembling. She was the cool deeps and the fire, all the softness and the never-ending for a man.

'Yes. Yes, I did.' Her voice was a whisper, but a forceful one.

'I think I know where there's a place for you, if you want it,' Mitch said.

Her features were set in unbreakable lines, all the needing and wanting held inside while her gaze searched his face in near hope. 'Where?'

'Beside me,' he said.

'Mitch.' In his name was her answer.

Cappy came into his arms and her lips were hot and firm against his. It was all there. No one else would ever have as much from her as he did. She was proud and willful, her feelings and passions running as deep as his own. He'd heard the bitterness in her voice and seen the strain of hurt in her eyes. Now she was smiling, confident in herself and certain of him.

CHAPTER THIRTY

The slow, painful process of signing forms and turning in uniforms and flying gear was taking the bulk of Tuesday morning, the 19th day of December, the day before they were officially discharged. The four friends trooped to the various offices together, providing moral support for each other.

Marty rubbed a hand over the smooth leather of her fleece-lined flying jacket. 'I wish I could keep this.'

'Where would you wear it?' Eden wondered. For all its practicality, it was hardly the height of fashion. On her ring finger, the soon-to-be bride of Mr Hamilton Steele wore her diamond sparkler.

'Michigan winters are cold.' Marty shrugged vaguely.

'Then you've decided to go home,' Cappy surmised. Marty was the only one among them without any definite plans for the future, vacillating from one thing to another.

'I don't know. With David gone . . .' She still couldn't talk about her brother's death. 'I thought I might as well go back to Detroit. There's a bomber plant at Willow Run. If they won't let me fly them, maybe I can get a job building them.'

'Good luck.' But Eden was skeptical of her chances.

'Nobody's going to keep me grounded.' Her husky voice had a growl in it. 'I'll find a way to get back up in the air if it means ferrying war surplus airplanes from sale points to the homes of their new owners.'

'You know the kind of shape those planes are in,' Mary Lynn protested. 'They're all red-lined. How many have crashed just being ferried to the Army's sale depots? That's all you hear about.'

'So?' Marty countered. 'What do you think we flew at Camp Davis?'

With the roughly eighty WASPs stationed at Long Beach going through the discharge process, there was a lot of waiting in hallways and corridors. The four of them lounged along a corridor wall, part of a slow-moving line, supporting themselves with a shoulder against the wall, or sometimes their whole bodies slumped against it.

By day's end, they were divested of everything the Army had issued them – uniforms, parachutes, guns – but they

437

kept their wings, those silver, shining insignias that had set them free for a little while. What was left of the time was spent packing their personal belongings and saying goodbyes to gals they'd flown with, strangers now in civilian clothes.

As they walked out of the barracks that last time with their suitcases under their arms, the California sun was shining as if the day were no different from any other. An awkward silence reigned, a self-consciousness claiming them.

Eden glanced at the two suitcases she carried and joked weakly, 'Two suitcases instead of the two trunks I brought with me to Sweetwater. I've learned something, I guess.'

Faint smiles were offered in response to the attempted joke, but not even Marty commented on it. Loosely walking abreast, they headed for the gate house, feeling oddly out of place in their traveling suits and dresses instead of the familiar Santiago-blue uniforms they had worn so proudly. Their route took them past the flight line and the numerous war planes parked on the ramp.

'I heard they have sixty planes on line, headed for embarkation points to the war zones,' Cappy remarked as they all looked at the aircraft, wings gleaming in the sunlight. '– And no pilots to fly them.'

The irony of it was not lost on any of them. A man in an officer's cap with his flight jacket unzipped left the flight line to approach their foursome. Marty recognized Walker and glanced quickly at Mary Lynn to discover if she had seen him.

Marty saw regret and reluctance mixed in Mary Lynn's expression. In the last two weeks, assignments had kept the two of them apart, one leaving while the other was returning. Marty's opinion of their affair hadn't altered. Now that Mary Lynn was going home, Marty didn't want Walker trying to change her mind.

She intercepted him before he reached Mary Lynn. 'Let her go.' Today his dark eyes were sobered by something, although his mouth quirked.

'You can relax, Martha Jane. I'm not here to steal her,' Walker said in lazy assurance. 'I just want to tell her goodbye.'

'We'll wait for you at the gate.' Eden and Cappy walked on, but Marty lingered, standing off to one side, watchful and wary of this last meeting between the couple.

His officer's cap sat on the back of his head, pushing forward his coffee-colored hair. A gentleness was in his eyes, a longing and a regret, but he made no move to touch her, his hands thrust deeply into the pockets of his jacket as if to prevent such an occurrence.

'You're on your way home, I guess.' His gaze traveled over her lively dark beauty. She was everything perfect and graceful and strong – things a man dreamed of and never expected to find.

'Yes.' The soft drawl of her voice was musical and warm. 'I'll be there by Christmas. My suitcase is filled with presents for my parents.'

'They'll be happy about that,' he said.

'Beau said in his last letter that they'll probably send him home after the first of the year.'

His mouth twisted. The subtle message hadn't really been necessary. 'I've always known you'd be going back to him, Little One. You know –' He paused, turning his head to squint into the sun and hide the stinging in his eyes. '– All my life I've always taken what I wanted. Life can trap a man. Because now I find myself wanting to give . . . and I have nothing to offer.'

'I'm sorry,' she said, so softly.

His head shook it away; he didn't want her pity. 'Goodbye, Little One.' He looked at her with moist eyes. 'Tell that husband of yours to take care of you.'

'Goodbye.' Mary Lynn walked quickly from him.

For a long, long time, Walker watched her, then he turned to Marty and tipped his head back, his mouth crooking at an angle. 'Well?' he taunted.

'Maybe you aren't as rotten as I thought, Walker,' Marty suggested.

439

'It looks like I'll be out in a few months,' he said. 'I've heard there's a market for surplus cargo planes in South America. I thought I might see if I could make some money. 'Course I'd need some good pilots to fly them down there. What do you think?'

'Look me up.'

'I'll do that.'

They shook hands to seal the agreement, then Marty was hefting her suitcase and striding after the others to the gate house.

The moment had been prolonged but the time finally came when the four of them had to say their goodbyes. Clinging and crying, they forced smiles into their expressions.

'We'll keep in touch,' they promised, but they all knew they wouldn't.

A big piece of their lives had been cut from them, leaving a hole. Until they found something to fill it – husbands, family, or career, it would hurt too much to see each other again and remember all that they had lost.

So they went home.

When Marty climbed the steps to the front porch of her parents' Detroit home, she saw the service flag hanging in the window. The gold star was there, signifying the loss of the family's soldier son. She walked into the house and went straight to the cabinet where her father kept the liquor.

Eden's hands burrowed under the collar of her sable coat, its dark, dark luster a contrast to the rich red of her hair. Her high-heeled and fur-trimmed boots crunched into the packed snow on the edge of the flight line as she hurried to keep up with a fast-walking Hamilton Steele.

'What are we doing here?' None of her questions had been answered, but still she tried as her breath made little puffs of vapor.

Behind his smug look was a mysterious smile. Hamilton

stopped to open the side door to a hangar and hold it for her, indicating with a sweep of his hand that she should enter. Eden walked through.

'Merry Christmas.'

A renovated AT-6 Texan glistened with fresh paint in a soft shade of sky blue. Lettered on it were the words 'A Lady's Wings.' Eden stared at it, then looked at Hamilton.

'Mine?' she whispered. At his affirmative nod, she threw her arms around him and hugged him. 'You are going to spoil me,' she declared, then she walked over to inspect her plane.

The skies above Mobile were a-hum with training aircraft. The drone of their powerful engines filtered into the front room where Mary Lynn was stringing the last of the tinsel on the Christmas tree. Planes would always be a part of her life, whether she flew them or Beau did. His presents were under the tree, waiting for him with bright, beribboned expectancy – just as she was.

'I simply don't see why you can't cook the meals for our boarders.' Her mother made wide, vigorous swipes with the dust cloth across the side bureau, the loose flab under her arm shaking with the action. Her small-built body had gone to plumpness, giving her a squatty look in the plain housedress she wore. 'You might as well help while you're here.'

'Mama, if you want to start providing meals for your boarders, that's your business, but don't expect me to do the work for you.' Mary Lynn turned away from the decorated tree to confront her mother, respectful but firm in her refusal.

'You haven't got anything else to do except wait for your husband to come home.' The sullen glitter of her small, dark eyes was turned on Mary Lynn. 'You might as well be doing something that will bring some money into this house.'

'I'm not going to be here that long, Mama,' she replied. 'As soon as Beau comes back, we're going to find us a place of our own. Wherever the Army sends him, I'm going.'

A Christmas tree, all decorated with shiny balls, colorful garlands, and wispy clouds of angel hair, stood in a corner of the Georgetown home. Gaily wrapped presents were crowded around its cotton-covered stand, waiting to be opened. But Cappy was standing at the window, gazing up at the beckoning clouds in the sky.

She didn't see Mitch enter the room or hear his approach. She wasn't aware he was there until she felt the touch of his hands sliding onto her arms. She half turned with a start, then smiled as he bent to brush her lips with a light kiss. No more than that, since her parents would be joining them in the living room at any moment.

'A penny for your thoughts,' Mitch said.

'They aren't worth it,' she answered.

His fingers curled under her left hand to lift it, as if needing to see the diamond engagement ring on her finger to reassure himself it was still there. He carried her hand to his lips. His dark eyes were warm and ardent.

'Happy?'

'Yes,' Cappy said, and she knew she would be – once she got used to the idea that all windows look out to the sky.

EPILOGUE

November 3, 1977
House of Representatives, Washington, DC

Time had healed many breaches. In a row, they sat in the seats of the House visitors' gallery. Eden Steele, the socially prominent wife of the financier Hamilton Steele, sat with her mink cape folded across her lap, still a strikingly attractive woman in her late fifties. A wide streak of snow white ran through her silvered red hair. On her right was Cappy Ryan, the wife of Air Force Colonel Mitch Ryan, the metallic gray of her hair somehow flattering when combined with the blue clarity of her eyes, darkly outlined with thick lashes. The petite, white-haired woman sitting next to her was Mary Lynn Palmer, the wife of the former Trans World Airlines pilot, Captain Beau Palmer, now retired.

They all led full, busy lives, involved in many activities outside the home. But none of the three was too busy not to be here on this day to witness another battle on the House floor over a bill which would grant military status to the WASPs, an act of recognition.

Over the years, countless such bills had been introduced to Congress, rarely ever being reported out of committee. This time they had hopes. Senator Barry Goldwater of Arizona had championed the legislation in the Senate, and the upper house version had been passed the 19th of October. The senator had firsthand knowledge of the role the WASPs played during World War II, having flown

443

with them as a major general in the Air Force Reserve when he was based at New Castle, Delaware, as a pilot with the Air Transport Command.

Now the compromise version of the 'GI Bill Improvement Act' was to be voted on by the House. In the past, veterans had lobbied against any amendment giving military status and benefits to what they regarded as a civilian group of women pilots.

In the visitors' gallery, they waited tensely for the coming debate, for the battle on the House floor that they hoped would give them victory. They wanted to win. They had been 'Army.' Their discharge papers said as much: 'This is to certify that Eden van Valkenburg honorably served in active federal service in the Army of the United States.'

Outside, the sun was drifting lower in the early winter sky. Shifting, Eden thought she caught sight of a familiar, lanky figure on the House floor below and strained her eyes for a better look. William 'Bubba' Jackson was somewhere down there, she was sure. The representative from Texas was one of the ardent supporters of the amendment. With his silver-haired, down-home looks and country humor, he was a popular political figure in Washington. He'd married a pretty, freckle-faced Texas girl, who'd given him seven children. Eden had met his wife about six months before – the homespun type, exactly suited for Bubba. Congressman or not, he basically hadn't changed. During the committee hearings last May, she'd met him again for the first time in all these years. It had been outside, in the parking lot . . . and Bubba had grease all over his hands from tinkering with his car, which wouldn't start.

It was still there – the old magic – faded a little, as they were. But . . . Eden sighed. She and Ham had known many good years, and she had been happy with him. No, she had no regrets.

Congressman Olin E 'Tiger' Teague approached the table of the Speaker of the House. This Texas representative had long been a staunch opponent of any measure to militarize the WASPs and give their members veteran status. That afternoon, however, he requested a unanimous consent to pass HR 8701, as amended. According to parliamentary procedure, if there were no objections, it would be passed with no debate and no vote. No one objected. The ring of the gavel made it final.

It was over. The opposition had capitulated without a fight, robbing them of the glory of battle and victory.

Dazed by the anticlimax, they looked at one another, then stood to file quietly out of the gallery and down the stairs. The long, empty hallways of the Capitol were shadowed by the diminishing sunlight, and their footsteps echoed hollowly through the tall corridors.

'It was stolen from us again,' Cappy murmured.

'I don't know about you, but I need a cigarette.' Eden opened her Gucci handbag and took out a gold case.

'Did I tell you my youngest daughter, Lily Anne, is one of the women pilots taking part in the jet training program the Air Force just opened to females this past year?' Mary Lynn informed them in a musing tone. 'She's encountering the same prejudice and abuse that we did. Men still think the cockpit isn't any place for a woman.'

'During the war, we all found out there were a lot of jobs we could do that the men thought we couldn't,' Cappy said, then smiled, the corners of her mouth dimpling. 'And nothing has been the same since.

'Yes, probably much to the men's regret,' Mary Lynn agreed, a smile almost lightening her low spirits.

The quick, heavy stride of a man disturbed the quietness of the congressional halls. As the footsteps came nearer, Eden turned to look idly over her shoulder while she expelled a trail of smoke. A trim-looking man in a dark wool overcoat approached them on his way to the stairs leading to the visitors' gallery. A very handsome man with distinguished silver tufts threading the temples of his jet-dark hair, he had blue, blue eyes. The contrast of dark hair and blue eyes brought a flicker of recognition. At almost the same instant, Eden noticed the man look at her and hesitate, as if trying to place her.

He paused, frowning slightly. 'Excuse me, but' – he almost laughed the cliché-riddled words – 'I believe we've met. My name is Zachary Jordan.'

'Eden –'

'Of course.' He interrupted with an expansive regret that he hadn't remembered. 'Eden van Valkenburg.'

'Married name is Steele, now,' she volunteered.

'Mrs Steele.' Zachary Jordan made a continental show of bowing over her hand, as charming and gallant as he was handsome. 'It isn't likely you'll remember me. We met only briefly . . . at the chapel where the Army held the memorial service for Rachel.'

'I do remember,' Eden assured him, all the vague memories clicking into place. 'How are you?'

'Fine. I'm with the Israeli Embassy here in Washington now.' After the war, he had immigrated to Israel – then Palestine – as he and Rachel had planned so very long ago.

'I . . . I still remember Rachel's plane crash.' It was an image she couldn't shake from her mind.

'I believe she mentioned to you that her grandmother was in one of the Polish death camps,' Zach said.

'Yes,' Eden nodded, curious. 'She did say something once.'

'Rachel's grandmother was one of the survivors of Oświę :im – Auschwitz,' he added, supplying the American-known name. 'After the war, I managed to find her. She had an interesting story to tell about Rachel coming to her in a dream, all surrounded by flames and assuring her grandmother that she would never know the fires. Her grandmother thought it was very odd . . . because Rachel had always spoken very bad Yiddish. In the dream, she had understood every word. I have often wondered . . .' Zach let his voice trail away and shrugged expressively. 'We shall never know.'

'I suppose not.'

His glance traveled up the stairs in the direction of the

visitors' gallery beyond. 'You are here for the debate? I heard it was scheduled for today's session and I thought I would sit in on part of it. Has it begun?'

'It's over,' Eden informed him, and smiled when she realized there was no elation or triumph in her voice. 'The bill was enacted, unanimously.'

'Good.' But the startled tone indicated that he, too, felt something was missing. 'Rachel would have been glad about that.' He looked around, somewhat lost, as if there was no more reason to be there. 'Congratulations . . . to all of you.' He included Mary Lynn and Cappy.

'Thank you.'

'In that case, I must get back to the embassy. Goodbye.' Again, he took her hand and kissed it with a European flair. 'Perhaps we'll meet again someday.'

'I hope so.'

The click of his shoes tapped loudly down the corridor as he walked swiftly away. Outside, it was growing darker. In mutual and silent consent, they started toward the exit doors. Eden slipped on her fur cape against the November briskness awaiting them. As they emerged from the Capitol building, they paused at the top of the steps.

A man stepped from the shadow of a column. 'Little One. It is you,' he murmured.

The lazy voice jolted her with recognition as Mary Lynn stared at Walker, an old Walker whose body had finally aged to match his eyes. But the glitter was still in those eyes, despite the lines of dissipation that jowled his face. The scars had faded until they had all but disappeared.

'Walker.' Her voice was warm and sad all at the same time. The years hadn't treated him kindly. He looked like a broken-down pilot in his worn leather flight jacket and crumpled officer's cap. His dark hair was shot with gray and his chest had fallen down around his middle. 'What are you doing here?'

'I've been reading all the publicity about this bill they're trying to pass to make you a veteran like me.' He smiled crookedly. 'I heard it went through.'

'Yes.'

'I wish Marty had been here,' Walker said absently.

'We don't know where she is,' Mary Lynn said. 'We tried to find her a few years ago when we were organizing our first reunion, but her parents had died and she hadn't kept in touch with any of us so –'

'I'm sorry,' he said, frowning. 'I thought you knew.'

'Knew what?'

'After the war, Martha . . . Marty and I had a little partnership going – buying surplus transports and flying them down to Central and South America. We were talking about setting up an air cargo business. Then . . . she had a C-47 . . . she lost power shortly after takeoff. She didn't have enough altitude to make it back to the field. The only open patch of ground was a playground full of children. Witnesses said it looked like she deliberately plowed into the side of a hill. She was killed outright, but nobody else was hurt. Noble damned fool, if you ask me.'

Tears slipped down Cappy's cheeks, while Mary Lynn had trouble accepting that bold, wild Marty wasn't somewhere out there.

'That was the end of the good times for me. At least now I can put an American flag on her grave. She'd like that, I think,' Walker murmured. 'It looks like you're doing fine, Little One. I suppose you're a grandmother now.'

'Yes. And you, Walker? What about you?'

'Same as before. You strip away the pride and there's nothing.' He shifted uncomfortably. 'I just wanted the chance to see you one last time, Little One. Guess I'd better go now.'

'Goodbye, Walker.'

He lifted a hand and sauntered away, a lonely figure.

They stood on the Capitol steps, looking out at the gray dusk. 'The three of us is all that's left,' Mary Lynn said.

'I don't know how you feel,' Eden said in a tight choked voice. 'But the two years that we flew in those skies were the best years of my life.' Neither of the others disagreed.

448